Student Affairs:
A Profession's Heritage
Second Edition

EDITED BY

Audrey L. Rentz

AMERICAN COLLEGE PERSONNEL ASSOCIATION

Copyright © 1994 by
American College Personnel Association

University Press of America® Inc.
4720 Boston Way
Lanham, Maryland 20706

3 Henrietta Street
London WC2E 8LU England

All rights reserved
Printed in the United States of America
British Cataloging in Publication Information Available

Copublished by arrangement with the
American College Personnel Association

3062383 1

Library of Congress Cataloging-in-Publication Data

Student affairs, a profession's heritage /
Audrey L. Rentz, editor. — 2nd ed.
Includes bibliographical references.
1. Student affairs services—United States—History—
20th century—Sources.   I. Rentz, Audrey L.
LB2343.S79   1994   94–19521 CIP

ISBN 1–883485–05–3 (cloth : alk. paper)
ISBN 1–883485–06–1 (pbk. : alk. paper)

 The paper used in this publication meets the minimum requirements of
American National Standard for Information Sciences—Permanence
of Paper for Printed Library Materials, ANSI Z39.48–1984.

ACPA MEDIA BOARD 1992–1995

Dedication

This second edition is dedicated to Dr. Gerald L. Saddlemire, colleague and friend, whose years of service and guidance within the Department of College Student Personnel at Bowling Green State University (1969–1991) will always be honored and remembered fondly. He was not only the driving force in the development of the program at Bowling Green, but also its shepherd and nurturer during the years of its expansion. To literally hundreds of people, Jerry was teacher, advisor, mentor, colleague and "Sadds" as a result of his involvement in the graduate preparation of student affairs professionals. His personal dedication to professionalism and to practice guided by the values embodied in the Student Personnel Point of View were as much a part of his persona as his name. He is missed.

Audrey L. Rentz
August 15, 1993

Contents

vii

Foreword

This second and expanded edition of *Student Affairs: A Profession's Heritage* was undertaken to make the previously published collection of materials, spanning 57 years from 1919 to 1976, inclusive through 1990. This collection brings together selected pieces of literature contributing to the basic philosophy, ideals, and values that have and continue to shape the identity of our developing profession. As in the earlier edition, the decision to include materials was based on both an awareness of the history of student affairs and its context of American higher education. With these contexts in mind, articles and documents perceived to represent the basic elements that influenced the growth of the profession were collected, organized and are preserved in one volume. Materials included represent journal articles, various national committee, commission and task force reports.

Consistency in the selection of articles, regardless of authorship, was again maintained by choosing only those pieces of literature that describe the core values and ideas that have guided the development of student personnel to student affairs. Articles were not included that were devoted to issues or practices within particular specialty functions such as financial aid, even though many exemplary and definitive articles were available. However, in certain instances where specific articles alerted practitioners to significant issues that helped shape or alter practice, such as increasing legalism and its effects on the practice of discipline, these articles have been included.

When student affairs practitioners, preparation program faculty, graduate students and higher education scholars seek literature that describes the basic assumptions, concepts, and rationales associated with our developing profession and its practice, their ability to access desired materials is often hindered by out of print materials or by limited distribution. This edition and the earlier 1988 edition were initiated with the following purposes in mind:

1. To preserve and make available material reflecting the significant contributions made by early writers during the initial stages of the profession generally known as college student personnel.

2. To preserve and make available significant documents and statements issued by professional associations concerned with the development of the field of student affairs;
3. To present the selected literature in the style of a collection of readings that might be used by graduate students interested in understanding the evolution of student affairs and its practice;
4. To make readings available for the professional practitioner who is interested in learning about the contributions made by specific authors, committees or commissions to the growth of our field.
5. To identify early contributors and representative papers that help us understand the nature of our developing field and our role within it. some student affairs practitioners have entered the field without being introduced to our heritage or may have come to student affairs with educational backgrounds in other graduate specialties.

Another motivation for the first edition was the desire to rescue early manuscripts from oblivion such as Yoakum's article (1919). In this vision of the embryonic stage of student personnel, Yoakum applied his military personnel experience to higher education by calling for a systematic approach to the much needed records office being developed on many college campuses.

It is interesting to note that many of the ideas and views expressed by some of the early writers, such as Clothier (1931) and Bradshaw (1936) reappear in the 1937 American Council on Education committee report which represented a collaborative effort of scholars associated with student personnel work. Their description of the Student Personnel Point of View and the 1949 revision of their document illustrate the degree of agreement among preparation program faculty and practitioners as they considered the essential purpose and meaning of their new field. With the inclusion in this edition of the 1987 statement prepared by the NASPA sponsored task force commemorating the fiftieth anniversary of the Student Personnel Point of View, the thoughts of many of the early authors again serve as cornerstones of contemporary thinking about the mission and role of student affairs.

1

The Early Years

One measure of the maturity of the student affairs profession is the body of literature that describes its origin, its growth and the concepts central to its role in higher education. Until recently, the senior members of the profession had personally experienced and examined many of the documents at the time they were published or they were introduced to the early documents as a part of their advanced degree work. Since this is no longer possible, graduate students and younger practitioners must become familiar with the heritage of the profession by a systematic examination of representative articles as reproduced in this book. Our current identity, basic assumptions, roles and responsibilities can be traced to statements made in the early part of this century when the number of student affairs practitioners was finally large enough to encourage early authors to describe and justify personnel work.

In the late 19th century there had been several pioneer deans who were celebrated for their historical significance, but the literature describing their contributions to the field was not available until the early twentieth century.

In Part One: The Early Years, seven articles are included to illustrate both the early efforts to define and justify the field as well as to identify the individuals who had the courage and vision to publish articles describing the role of student personnel work in higher education.

One of the first persons to suggest the need for what was to become a student affairs department was C. S. Yoakum, who argued in 1919 that an important lesson learned in the War Department in World War I was the need to have a personnel bureau as part of (educational) institutions. He says that such a bureau needs to collect and codify accurate data on each student, collect and classify vocational information, present occupational information to the student, and establish cumulative student records. Yoakum, a major in

1

the Sanitary Corps USA when he wrote this article, also describes the specialized knowledge needed among the personnel staffing this bureau.

Robert C. Clothier, Chairman of the Committee on Personnel Principles and Functions, submitted a report in 1931 that responded to the charge from the Executive Committee of the American College Personnel Association to develop a statement of principles, functions and accrediting methods for student personnel work. It will be interesting to those now preparing standards for accreditation agencies to read this early comment about the accreditation process. The statement of principles and the list of functions were the basis for the A.C.E. *Student Personnel Point of View* (Commission statement) issued just six years later in 1937.

Esther Lloyd-Jones, in 1934, examines the definitions of student personnel work and concludes that a distinction must be made between student personnel work and student personnel administration. She argues for coordinating, organizing and administering as necessary duties in the student personnel field. Her commitment to the administrator role is reflected in the name given to the graduate department Student Personnel Administration at Teachers College, Columbia, one of the early graduate programs responsible for preparing student affairs professionals.

The length of the article by Cowley and Waller made it necessary to edit some portions of the manuscript while retaining the essential message. A call is made for the systematic study of student life by the behavioral scientist. This article is strengthened by including a number of examples of student behavior that, upon analysis, provide a better understanding of student life. Sociologists, social psychologists and cultural anthropologists were invited to examine the environmental pressures of the campus. Here is an early indication of the central role of the behavioral scientist in student personnel work.

In 1936 Bradshaw deals with the aims of educational personnel work at the college and university level. He summarizes the statements on core functions made by earlier authors and then presents his own convictions regarding trends and basic assumptions.

Any study of the widely used definitions of personnel work will depend heavily on Cowley's effort to clarify the nature of student personnel work. He distinguishes between "guidance" and "personnel work," a debate that still can be heard among professionals. Cowley's attempt to identify the nature of student personnel work leads him to call for representatives of all college personnel groups to come together for a definitive discussion of the nature of their common task.

Such a group did come together under the auspices of the American Council on Education and issued the widely acclaimed *Student Personnel*

Point of View in 1937. Chaired by E. G. Williamson, this committee of faculty and administrators developed a statement about the field that reflected a consensus of the philosophy, services, administrative relationships and a call for national leadership to undertake activities identified as essential to the future of student personnel work (e.g., position papers, research). It should be noted that this document was the first prepared by a cross section of educators who could speak authoritatively for the entire field.

Plan for a Personnel Bureau in Educational Institutions

C. S. Yoakum

Personnel problems connected with the formation of the United States Army brought into high relief certain difficulties that institutions dealing with the training and education of young men and women had vaguely felt. A few institutions had attempted to set into operation methods aimed at the solution of these questions. The systematic and persistent exploration of the difficulties and their solution were forced upon the War Department. Its rapid and unprecedented expansion gave clear definition to many unsettled personnel problems. It found the source of supply unanalyzed and its own needs but vaguely in mind. Large numbers of specialists were suddenly demanded. Experience quickly demonstrated that personal qualities were extremely important assets in war. It became necessary to specify in detail the personal, educational and technical requirements for each important task. To insure proper qualifications, specially devised tests proved necessary. The increased size of the army forced it to maintain complete and detailed systems of personnel records and to devise special "follow-up" methods.

Army experience can be duplicated in the experience of our educational institutions. We believe that the pressure of war has produced a clearer conception of the problems involved in training and placement. It has emphasized the advantages of carefully systematized procedure in discovering needed qualities of human nature, and the importance of freeing estimates of persons, as much as possible, from the errors of personal bias and incidental acquaintance. Vague memories of so-and-so's personality and qualifications broke down utterly as a means of building up an army.

This article proposes the general outline of a plan for a personnel bureau. The principal features of such a bureau can be put into operation in any educational institution, large or small. The plan considers the study of student personnel as fundamental in any institution that believes its function is connected in any way with the well-being of its patrons and with the

4

success of its graduates in their chosen professions. It also contains the implication that such an institution must keep fuller and more definite records of success and failure, of personalities and of the results of its training and teaching. The essential functions of such a bureau, or committee, are four. Modifications of the plan will emphasize one or the other of these functions, according to local conditions, the specific aims of the institution or the personnel of the bureau itself; subdivision of functions will increase with the growth of the bureau and the financial and moral encouragement given it.

The primary functions of the bureau are, to obtain accurate data on each student, to codify the requirements of different professions, to supervise the use of tests and to provide means whereby each student may become acquainted with his abilities and the requirements of the occupations in which he is interested. Properly to perform these functions as complete an inventory of the human material passing through the institution as is possible must be made in permanent form. Second, the files of this bureau must contain a similar inventory of the important vocations. Third, the bureau will provide the responsible agencies for bringing to the student seeking a life occupation all its systematic material on the opportunities and requirements necessary to attain a certain degree of success in those vocations open to him. Fourth, the bureau will proceed on the assumption that all of these problems can be investigated in a scientific manner and will initiate and encourage research in this field.

The essentials of the inventory of human material can be placed on a single card—the personal history card or qualification card. This qualification card will contain facts concerning the previous history of the individual. This previous history should contain items concerning his social and school life pertinent to the purpose of such an inventory. The card will also be a permanent record of his educational career. It is not necessary to summarize in detail the items involved in such a record. Ratings which will consist of elementary school grades, marks in college or technical school studies and the results of specially devised rating plans will also be recorded on this card. It is further expected that on the student's qualification card space be left for recording the results of intelligence tests and of other tests important in determining the qualifications of the individual. Recent determinations of the usefulness of such intelligence ratings and specialized tests make it probable that in the future no institution will be without such information concerning its student body.

The information desired as a part of the student's permanent record may be obtained in several well-known ways; though at present none of these is satisfactory. Extremely valuable estimates of the individual's qualifications and qualities of mind and person may nevertheless be obtained by careful interviewing when he reports for entrance to the college or other educational institution. Such estimates as the student himself gives at this interview can be supplemented and checked by carefully prepared letters of inquiry to persons who have known him in his previous school work and outside activities. Additional ratings and estimates on personal qualities and on special aptitudes should be obtained at least yearly from his instructors and fellow students. These estimates properly tabulated and combined with the objective ratings obtained from the tests give the foundation for tentative judgments of the student's ability and probable future career.

The second function of this bureau is the collection and classification of vocational information. This should include carefully obtained opinions on the qualities necessary for success in each of the vocations studied. Each vocation should be carefully studied from the point of view of the range of mental capacity that will stand a satisfactory chance for success. A card for a vocation should also indicate minimum and maximum educational qualifications so far as they can be returned. Such a record must also specify the need for any special ability if such is an essential. When properly completed the specifications for any vocation will also include a statement of the more essential qualities necessary for success in that vocation. It is not too much to believe that sometime in the future these may be given their proper weighting in a great many vocations. Bibliographies pertaining to special fields can also be made available to students through the bureau.

Again much careful investigation is necessary. This part of the work of the bureau must begin at the beginning. The utter lack of agreement on the qualities that produce success and satisfaction in life is easily demonstrated. Whether this failure to agree is a matter of permanent differences indicating many roads to success or satisfaction, or is rather one in which a limited number of qualities receive different weights under definitely describable conditions, is surely a problem worth experimentation. Minimal requirements of education and training can undoubtedly be specified and standardized.

The third important function of this personal bureau will be to bring to the student seeking a life vocation all material collected on vocations. By proper methods of cataloguing this material can be readily presented to the student. In this conference section of the bureau, problems concerning his college advancement may also be taken up with the student. It is, of course, here that the importance of the objective tests can most readily be seen. The collection and recording of the information as described above will be of extreme advantage to the dean, and to others whose duty it is to discuss with the student his place in the school work and his success in advanced studies.

Properly to develop the fourth function, it is important that a single responsible agency have charge of general intelligence tests and other forms of testing used. This agency should not be within any single school or department of the institution. The value of modern group and individual examinations of relative intelligence is now thoroughly established. The plan proposed aims to make these an integral part of the personnel inventory. The satisfactory development of their values rests on the scientific care and common-sense skill with which they are used. Their proper use is obviously in connection with the two inventories above described. So used they will undoubtedly prove invaluable aids in personnel interviews with students.

The importance of following up the use of tests is, of course, patent. The correlations desired are essential in estimating the significance of tests, the prophetic value of personal data and the weightings for vocational qualifications. Constant revision, retrial and experimentation are implied in this fourth function of the bureau.

The personnel of such a bureau should be carefully selected. During the first years of its operation and in preparing the final form of organization, its work should be supervised by a general committee. Immediate responsibility for the bureau should be in the hands of a smaller group of men who have shown themselves to be particularly interested in human qualities and their development. If properly managed, it will require part time from at least three men of professional rank. The chairman of this smaller group should be responsible for the general organization of the plan and its coordination with other university activities. The second member of the sub-committee should be a specialist who is thoroughly acquainted with business methods and vocational specifications. The third member should have special qualities fitting him for personal contact with the student and for the *unbiased* presentation of the requirements of different vocations. The direct management of the affairs of the bureau should be in the hands of a secretary, who should have at least the rank of an assistant professor. It is probable that practically full time will be required of this man, and in the current management of such a bureau he doubtless will be the important active member of it.

The proposed bureau does not present a scheme for vocational guidance. If an institution or a dean feels that it or he can properly carry the responsibility, the bureau provides the only safe procedure for obtaining guidance in passing out such advice. We believe rather that an institution owes it to its student body to provide systematically prepared information about life and its business. Further, if the study of human qualities is to be removed from the realm of palmistry and "get rich quick" schemes, system-atized research must provide the means. Persistent and organized research of this type must be done in permanent institutions that will provide continuous and accessible records. Several years of cooperative research among widely distributed institutions might even produce principles for vocational guidance.

College Personnel Principles and Functions

Robert C. Clothier

From the Executive Committee of the Association, the Committee on Personnel Principles and Functions has received instructions:
1. To prepare a statement of *principles* which the Association might propose as the basis of establishing personnel work in the colleges;
2. To prepare a *statement of functions* and techniques recommended;
3. To prepare a statement of the *methods of accrediting* various college personnel bureaus or departments.

Your Committee feels that the discharge of this commission is not something which can be accomplished overnight, if in fact it can be accomplished at all. The developing of a statement of principles, of functions and of accrediting methods must be an evolutionary process which must take into consideration the experience and point of view of many persons working in the field and of many institutions of differing size, nature, scope and purpose.

This report attempts to set forth a point of departure in this evolutionary process. We begin by presenting (a) certain definitions of terms. This introductory part is followed, in order, by (b) a statement of principles, (c) a statement of functions, (d) a statement relative to methods of accrediting, and (e) conclusion.

(A) Definition of Terms

It seems to us that the first step in this evolutionary process must be an attempt to define terms. There is urgent need for such definition. Even the term "personnel work" is interpreted in different ways. To some of us it is broad in its meaning, involving all those aspects of college work which affect the student as an individual. To others it denotes certain specific functions. The former concept is unsatisfactory to some persons because, in its general nature, it seems to lack specific meaning; the latter is equally unsatisfactory to others because it seems incomplete.

9

As a point of departure we recommend as a definition of personnel work the following:

> Personnel work in a college or university is the systematic bringing to bear on the individual student all those influences, of whatever nature, which will stimulate him and assist him, through his own efforts, to develop in body, mind and character to the limit of his individual capacity for growth, and helping him to apply his powers so developed most effectively to the work of the world.

One of the key words in this definition is the word "individual." The implication of this word involves the recognition of the entire principle of individual differences. Personnel work, consequently, accepts as one of its fundamental principles that students differ one from the other, not only in the mere physical characteristics of mind, emotion and character which affect so greatly their performance of different kinds of work and their reactions to different stimuli. By way of illustration, it recognizes that one student may perform with ease a task which another may perform only with the greatest difficulty; may respond with enthusiasm to a factor of environment which might leave another cold or even antagonistic; may possess a sense of right and wrong, of moral obligation, of courage, of determination which another may lack entirely. The individual's equipment in such terms as these must be known, understood and considered in planning his work and in directing him in its execution, if the college is to be fully successful in his education.

It is obvious that knowing and steering the student thus cannot be isolated in any one department. Personnel work cannot be departmentalized, except for certain specific functions which will be discussed later. Rather personnel work must be a leaven throughout the whole college and these influences, of which we speak in our definition, must be brought to bear on the student by all who come in contact with him—by professor, instructor, dean, registrar, adviser, coach, proctor, yes even janitor. It's not the official status that makes the good personnel man, it's the sincerity and intelligence of his interest in the student.

This statement of the nature and scope of personnel work naturally raises the question: What is the official status of personnel work in a college?

In other words personnel work in a college consists in promoting a point of view on the part of administrators and instructors which is favorable to the consideration of the student as an individual and in maintaining such services, outside the purely academic functions, as contribute to the individual student's success at college (e.g., personal and vocational guidance, health, mental hygiene, financial counseling and assistance, housing, placement).

Although personnel work is conducted in different ways in different institutions, it is generally directed through a department generally known as the Personnel Department. A definition might be expressed as follows:

The Personnel Department is that department of the administration or that group of persons in which initiative and responsibility for the personnel work of the college is vested.

This department may have different titles in different institutions, different powers, different responsibilities, according to the type of organization and nature of work in those institutions but its field and purpose is to promote throughout the college the sympathetic and thorough consideration of the student as an individual.

Except for such functions as exist as line functions within the Personnel Department (such as, for instance, personnel counselling, vocational guidance and placement), the Personnel Department usually functions without authority in promoting the personnel point of view throughout the organization, through developing a cooperative working relationship with administration, educational heads, members of faculties and others based on service rendered. The possession of administrative authority is regarded as a very questionable advantage as a personnel point of view cannot be legislated into existence; administrators and teachers will entertain it in their relations with students only if they believe in it and no amount of legislation can effect it otherwise.

The directing head of the Personnel Department, or where no formal personnel department exists, that officer or executive who by virtue of his position or his interest assumes responsibility for the personnel work in a college, is known as the Personnel Director, or other equivalent title. He reports directly to the president, or administrative head of the college, whom he represents in this work. Stated as a definition:

The Personnel Director is that official or executive, reporting directly to the administrative head of the college, who assumes initiative and responsibility for the development of the personnel program of the institution. As a staff officer he cooperates with other administrative and educational heads in promoting the interests of the individual student in all his college relationships both inside and outside the classroom. As a line officer he assumes direction of those personnel functions which administratively lie within the jurisdiction of the personnel department.

Our definition of personnel work includes the phrase "and helping him (the student) to apply his powers so developed most effectively to the work of the world." In short personnel work necessarily includes the functions of *vocational guidance* and *placement*. It seems appropriate, at this point, to set forth two additional definitions.

Vocational guidance is that service which the college renders to the individual student which serves to assist him in evaluating his own aptitudes and interests, to acquire knowledge about many fields of work and the requirements for success in those fields, and to decide wisely in which field of endeavor he will most likely find success and satisfaction.

And

Placement is that service which the college renders to the individual student which enables him to learn of opportunities in the field of his selection and to secure that position in which he will most likely find success and satisfaction.

(B) Principles

In these several definitions certain principles have been set forth. At the risk of repetition, we present here a general statement of principles:

1. Every student differs from every other student in aptitudes, inherited or acquired—those powers of hand and brain which are his tools of workmanship; in interests, those impulses and motives which stimulate or inhibit the exercise of those powers under different circumstances and at different kinds of work; in character traits—integrity, perseverance, etc. The college must know these qualifications so far as it is possible to do so and must utilize that knowledge in planning his college course, both within and without the curriculum, in stimulating him to pursue it, and in guiding him afterward to his vocational opportunity.

2. Every agency within the college should consider these differences between students—the administrative officials; the educational, personal and vocational counsellors; the members of the teaching staffs and others who come in contact with the students as individuals.

3. The Personnel Department, under the Personnel Director, is responsible for the development of this point of view throughout the organization. In promoting it, the Personnel Department will work through the administrative heads of schools and departments and through their associates and subordinates. The relationship is ordinarily an informal and personal one, without authority.

4. Each college should provide adequate facilities—in terms both of procedures and equipment—for the maintenance of harmonious and effective relationships among students, faculty members and administrative officials.

5. Each college should select its students with proper knowledge of their qualifications and with due regard to their fitness. This is a function in which the Personnel Department cannot fail to have an active interest.

6. Supplementing the teaching work of the members of the faculties, the college should make provision for the counselling of students on educational, personal and vocational matters. In each instance the counselling should be based upon a critical evaluation of the student's aptitudes and interests and of all other factors present in the situation. Good counselling provides for the student to reach his own decision in any uncertainty with the counsellor's assistance, rather than for him to accept the counsellor's decision.

7. The college should provide a plan for the continuing orientation of its students as they embark upon each new phase of their college life—from the secondary school senior entering the junior college to the college graduate embarking upon his life work.

8. The college must assume its share of responsibility for the physical health of the students, as their physical health is of paramount importance, not only for its own sake, but because of its effect upon their success in their college work. This function is usually exercised by a department of student health, consisting of one or more physicians according to the size and nature of the college.

9. The college must assume its share of responsibility for the mental health of its students for the same reasons as apply to their physical health, and must maintain a mental hygiene service as a part of, or parallel to, its physical health service.

10. The student's physical environment, including his living environment, has a real effect upon his morale and upon his success in his work. In still other ways it has its effect upon the student's personality development. It is the responsibility of the college to provide adequate housing facilities for its students.

11. The college should assist those students whose collegiate progress is threatened by financial anxieties to secure part-time employment; it should provide loan funds which can be made available, in emergency, to responsible students on a definite refund basis; it should provide scholarships to deserving and needy students.

12. The so-called extra-curricular activities should be recognized as potential agencies of character development and should be encouraged and directed by the college but without impairing the student's initiative, leadership, organizing ability and sense of responsibility. They should be integrated so far as possible with the work of the curriculum.

13. Adequate records are essential to good personnel work. The personnel records of a college should (so far as possible) be brought together in one

place so that personnel officers, deans, instructors—anyone interested in a student's progress—may find there a complete, cumulative record of his history, background, scholastic and extrascholastic activities, personal qualification, physical and mental ratings, interests, objectives, etc., in order that projected action may in each instance be taken with due regard to all the facts.

14. The college must recognize that research is an integral part of its personnel work and must make adequate provision, in staff and equipment, for it.

15. The college should make available to the student full information about the nature, opportunity and requirements of different vocations and should help him evaluate his own aptitudes and interests in the light of such information in an attempt to decide wisely what vocation to take up upon graduation. In each case the student should make the decision.

16. The college should establish contacts with as many employers as possible in fields of vocational activity in order to help its students, upon graduation, "to apply their powers most effectively to the work of the world." In each instance the student should "place" himself. The college should follow-up the students so assisted to make sure their powers *are* applied effectively, and aid those who are misplaced to find their proper places.

(C) *Functions*

A consideration of these principles emphasizes the point of view that in personnel work we are interested in the individual student's development, not in any one phase of his program such as scholarship, intellect, leadership, but from the aspect of his whole personality. We are concerned with all those methods and the procedures which bring influences to bear upon him "of whatever nature." And this brings us to the question of functions.

It is impossible for any agency, such as the National Association of Placement and Personnel Officers, to prepare a list of personnel functions with any expectation that such a list will satisfy conditions on all campuses. On one campus, certain functions will be found essential, on another unimportant. Where a restricted interpretation of personnel work is accepted, many of the functions which are listed in this section will appear irrelevant. Where personnel work is interpreted broadly in the sense of our original definition, it is apparent that all these functions should be considered.

Certain of these functions will fall under the administrative jurisdiction of the personnel department, over which the Personnel Director has a direct line of control. Others will fall under the administrative jurisdiction of other departments; these are the functions with which the Personnel Department has merely a staff relationship.

Whether the Personnel Department exercises a line or a staff influence over a given function depends upon the set-up in that particular college.

1. Selection of students. Debarment of applicants whose likelihood of success in college is negligible. Direction of others to those schools and courses in which they will most likely find success.

2. Selection of instructors. The personnel situation in a college is vitally affected by the type of instructors engaged. Those incapable of taking a sincere and intelligent interest in the individual student should be debarred.

3. Orientation of students. Adoption of procedures which serve to integrate the student with his new environment and offset those negative influences, arising from unfamiliarity with new personalities and procedures, which tend to retard a student in his work.

4. Educational guidance. Adoption of procedures which will serve to assist the student select those curricula and course of study which will best serve his cultural and vocational objectives.

5. Personal Counselling. Adoption of procedures which serve to assist the student solve those problems of a social or personal nature which, unsolved, tend to impede him in his work.

6. Scholastic motivation. Discovery and development of incentives, through personal conference or otherwise, which will stimulate the individual student to succeed best in his work.

7. Housing Service. Assuring the student a housing environment which will make for morale and effective work.

8. Financial assistance for needy students, in the form of part-time employment made available through an employment bureau or through loans or scholarships.

9. Supervision and direction of extra-curricular activities, including athletics and fraternities.

10. Supervision of student health, through control of environment and through individual examination and treatment where necessary.

11. Mental hygiene. Maintenance of staff of counsellors and psychiatrists equipped to help all students attain as favorable mental attitude toward their work as possible and to treat those who are badly adjusted or mentally ill.

12. Maintenance of adequate personnel records, furnishing full information about each student to instructors, advisers and others who have to do with him.

13. Research. A continuing study and investigation of factors in the personnel situation of the college.

14. Vocational guidance. Maintenance of an adequate informational and advisory service to assist individual students to learn about different occupations, and to analyze their own powers, and to choose wisely their life careers.

15. Placement. Maintenance of a service to assist graduating students find positions for which they are qualified and in which they will most likely find success.

It is not the Committee's claim that this list of functions is final, nor complete. These fifteen functions are set forth as a point of departure in the discussion and are subject to review.

(D) Methods of Accrediting

Your Committee approaches the problem of devising methods of accrediting colleges according to the effectiveness of their personnel work with grave doubts as to the desirability and practicability of doing so.

In the first place, we do not believe that any organization such as ours has yet arrived at a sufficiently clear and definite set of standards by which to measure the effectiveness of personnel work in a college.

In the second place, we are dealing with values it is hard to measure because the effectiveness of personnel work in a college depends not so much on *what* is done as on *how* it is done. By way of illustration, a college which has no plan for vocational guidance may be guiding its pupils very effectively through informal methods and another with a vocational guidance plan well worked out on paper may, through the personal inadequacy of its counsellors, fall far short of real success.

The devising of methods of accrediting colleges according to the effectiveness of their personnel work must similarly be a matter of gradual development, rather than of abrupt legislation. Without any thought of accrediting, however, it is logical that a college should constantly take stock of its own situation in order to know what phases of its personnel work are being well done and which are not being well done. As a point of departure in such a self-analysis, your Committee proposes the following questions which the administrative official of a college might ask himself and his associates.

1. Does the college make a conscious attempt to determine the qualifications of applicants for admission, to debar those whose previous record and personal analysis indicate a likelihood of failure, to direct others to those schools and courses in which they will most likely find success?

2. Does the college, in selecting instructors, consider their point of view on personnel matters and the sincerity of their interest in course content?

3. Does the college have a well-defined, carefully worked-out plan for the

orienting of its new students, for helping the student make a happy adjustment to each new phase of his college life?

4. Does the college have a well-defined, successfully-operating plan to guide its students wisely in organizing their college campaign and in selecting their curricula and courses of study?

5. Does the college have a well-defined, successfully-operating plan to guide and assist the student in solving social and personal problems?

6. Is the college as a whole inspired with the importance, not only of instructing the student, but of inspiring him to make the most of such instruction? Has it developed techniques of bringing definite incentives to bear on him?

7. Does the college provide for the adequate housing of its students?

8. Does the college cooperate effectively with the student in meeting his economic problems (a) by helping him obtain congenial and remunerative part-time employment, (b) by granting loans when necessary, (c) by granting scholarships to students of high potentiality?

9. Does the college regard extracurricular activities as supplementary agencies of education and character-development, and supervise them accordingly?

10. Does the college provide adequately for the physical health of the students through a medical department which studies each student as an individual and recommends specific treatment when necessary, either for prevention of disability or for cure; through continuous inspection of the student's environment from the sanitary point of view?

11. Does the college maintain a mental hygiene service through which students are kept in good mental health and those who are ill or seriously maladjusted are given restorative treatment?

12. Does the college maintain adequate personnel records in such a way that all significant information about an individual student is made available to administrators and teachers, enabling them to deal with him more understandingly and more effectively?

13. Does the college recognize the significance of research in personnel work and provide adequately for its maintenance?

14. Does the college maintain a cooperative relationship with employers on an extensive scale through which its graduating seniors are assisted in obtaining permanent positions in their chosen fields of work?

15. Is there a personnel department under an officer reporting directly to the administrative head of the college whose responsibility it is to promote the development of such personnel activities as these, either indirectly as a staff function or directly as a line function, into a *coordinated personnel program*?

(E) Conclusion

The heart of personnel work lies in the genuine and intelligent interest of instructors and others in the individual student. Its ends are well served if the instructor thinks of his subject as a means of teaching the student, poorly served if he thinks of the student as a means of teaching his subject. Its purposes are advanced if those services outside the classroom which remove obstacles and help him make the most of his college career are well-organized and operating effectively, retarded if they are not.

Sometimes personnel work is organized under a centralized control and this type of organization has certain advantages. More generally it is decentralized, each department and each individual assuming responsibility for his part of the work. When the work is decentralized in this way, provision should be made—as herein set forth—for the coordination of these independent but related functions through a Personnel Director, or other person or groups of persons, who can visualize the situation as a whole and contribute initiative and assistance where needed.

In closing we recommend that the Association regard this report as the point of departure in a continuing study of principles and functions, that our objectives may become clearer and clearer and our procedures more and more effective. There will be advantage in making haste slowly.

The Committee on Principles and Functions: Robert C. Clothier, *Chairman*, Mabelle B. Blake, Earl W. Anderson, N. M. McKnight, Grace E. Manson.

Personnel Administration

Esther Lloyd-Jones

Student Personnel work is in the stage where it is being talked about with sublime assurance by individuals who hold widely differing points of view as to what it really is; but a number of individuals possessed of wide theoretical background and sound experience have most helpfully defined and delimited the field. President Hopkins' classic definition of personnel work is, "Work having to do specifically with individuals." Dean Hawkes limited this broad definition to, "Work for the individual student which is being done outside the classroom." The definition of President Clothier and his Committee on Principles and Functions of the American College Personnel Association once more broadened the scope of personnel work at the same time that it made it more specific:

Personnel work in a college or university is the systematic bringing to bear on the individual student all those influences, of whatever nature, which will stimulate him and assist him, through his own efforts to develop in body, mind, and character to the limit of his individual capacity for growth, and helping him to apply his powers so developed most effectively to the work of the world.

The latest of these four definitions is that of Cowley, who, agreeing with Dean Hawkes, says that student-personnel administration is, "The administration of all university-student relationships aside from formal instruction."

There is by no means universal acceptance of any of these definitions. There does seem to be, however, fairly general agreement as to the functions that personnel work includes. These are: administration of admissions, including selection and pre-college guidance; orientation of students; educational guidance, including the use of such instruments as objective tests; personal counseling, whether classified as psychological, religious, ethical, vocational, or personal; administration of the social program; supervision and direction of extra-curricular activities, including athletics and fraternities; administration of housing; administration of financial aid and part-time employment; supervision of student health; provision for a mental-hygiene program; maintenance and administration of adequate personnel records; placement; and research.

It is important to describe more clearly what student-personnel administration is, what its relation is to general administration, and what its relation is to the various personnel services. In the first place, student-personnel administration and student-personnel work are not synonymous. Any of the "personnel services" included in student-personnel administration are "personnel work," but the co-ordination of student-personnel services into a total program and the supplementing of those existent personnel services by other necessary services is student-personnel administration. With this distinction in mind, President Hopkins' definition is seen to be one of personnel work; Dean Hawkes's, also, is a definition of personnel work. On the other hand, President Clothier's is an excellent definition of personnel administration, although he says it is one of personnel work. Cowley's definition is clearly one of personnel administration, and he so states it.

It is necessary for me in this connection to revise my own earlier definition of personnel work also: "Personnel administration"—not, as I formerly said, "personnel work"—"is the co-ordination and concentration of all the resources of the institution together with the information afforded by scientific investigations for the purpose of furthering the best interests of each individual in all of his aspects."[1]

Student-personnel administration is one of the three main divisions of educational administration. The others are instructional administration and operational administration. Student-personnel administration, unlike specific personnel service, is essentially a function of administration and resides originally and ultimately in the administrative head of an institution. It is generally delegated by the president or principal to a specialist in student-personnel administration, usually called by some such title as director of personnel, dean of mean or dean of women, adviser of boys or girls, and the like. It is split off from general administration when some such conditions as the following make it necessary: large numbers of students; pressure of total administration laid on the president or principal; lack of student training on the part of the president or principal to perform the functions of personnel administration, so that elements of the program of student-personnel work are being neglected; and appreciation on the part of the general administration of the desirability of a good deal of time and skilled effort being given to this aspect of education.

Those who have attempted definitions of personnel work or administration

---

1. Lloyd-Jones, Esther. *Student Personnel Work.* New York: Harper and Brothers, 1929. p. 207.

have had some difficulty in distinguishing the personnel field from that of education itself. Hopkins specifically says, "He does not assume that it does differ from education itself." Clothier might well have said that his definition was one of education itself. Hawkes and Cowley, however, try to separate it from the classroom. Student-personnel administration can no more be set apart from the intimate processes of education, either in or out of the classroom, than can general administration. Its sole reason for effort is to advance in every way possible the best development of everyone with whom education is concerned.

When one recognizes some distinction between personnel work and personnel administration, it becomes clear that the teacher as a personnel worker is indispensable in any adequate system of personnel administration. The director of student-personnel administration or dean will succeed only to the extent that he promotes among the teaching faculty the personnel point of view and utilizes every bit of skill and wisdom the teacher may possess a personnel worker in an ever evolving system of personnel administration.

There still exists, even in the minds of those professionally engaged in personnel work, considerable uncertainty as to what student-personnel administration is; consequently, there is still fogginess and confusion about the relationship between student-personnel administration and such personnel services as vocational guidance, psychological counseling, record-keeping, administration of extra-curricular activities, and placements. Some completely identify vocational guidance, placement, or research with student-personnel administration, fallaciously arguing that because student-personnel administration includes vocational guidance, vocational guidance is personnel administration.

The best philosophy of the administration of family life and that of student-personnel administration are identical. The finest kind of home life is not built through the exercise of despotism—not even of benevolent despotism on the part of some one member who is highly skilled; only through a truly creative group method in which each cooperates for the sake of the others' and his own happiness can individuals best develop. The greatest skill in achieving this type of relationship, in which all can thrive and be happy, consists in the ability to get spontaneous participation on the part of each member, as well as in the ability to supplement and co-ordinate individual efforts deftly and inconspicuously.

The stern, indomitable type of leadership found in typical matriarchies and patriarchies is recognized as inimical to the best development of personalities within the family group. While the dictator in government seems to be having his little moment again, dictators in the role of administrators of student personnel not only doom themselves and short tenure, but also greatly jeopardize the success of the work itself. A policy of "putting something over," of "making someone come to time," of "riding roughshod over the opposition," while temporarily intoxicating enough to make one feel the brilliant, irresistible leader, inevitably spells disaster to the professed purposes of personnel work and of sound education.

A home-maker does not do her duty completely when she fills the stomachs of her family three times a day with satisfying food. To the extent that she is intelligent and modern in her viewpoint, she utilizes eating for social values; she uses ceremony to achieve psychological satisfactions. The basic values guiding her everyday administration of the culinary side of household management are those having to do with health and physical development and social needs. The home-maker may use the specialized knowledge of dieticians, she may employ chefs in her kitchen, but, in general, the responsibility for administering the day-by-day program and having it carried out satisfactorily rests with her.

The director of student personnel in an educational institution may have a minimum of staff—perhaps only one cook, as he does in some small, poverty-stricken institutions—or he may have a splendid retinue of dieticians and cooking experts in charge of the cafeterias and dining rooms. To the extent that the experts utilize eating for education in health and social values, the personnel administrator is fortunate; residual responsibility, however, falls to his office. He is also responsible for co-ordinating this area for student life with all the other areas which personnel administration includes within its scope.

The housing of a family is not merely a matter of having a safe shelter from the elements. Even if a home-maker employs a staff of architects, interior decorators, and landscape gardeners, there is still much that someone must do to make functional living within that material setting happy and attractive. Similarly, although the director of student personnel may not have more than a consultative relationship to the architect in the planning of a dormitory, his his the voice that must insist that there is much that housing can contribute directly to aesthetic enjoyment, social education, recreation, health, and convenience; his is the responsibility for seeing that the housing of the students does contribute these values to a maximum degree. He may be able to work directly with capable, personally selected heads of dormitories; he may have to work with private householders who house the students in off-campus residences. In either case, this function of personnel administration is co-ordinated through his office with other personnel functions, and residual responsibilities fall directly upon him.

The health program is one that is included within the personnel-administration field. It, also, is one of the main responsibilities of the home-maker. The intelligent home manager realizes that health is to a very large extent a matter of hour-by-hour living. She realizes that it is of the greatest importance to build health that will withstand unavoidable strain and stress; accordingly, she guides the program of the family with this in mind. She believes in periodic health examinations for every member of the family. When need arises, she uses the best medical specialists available; but the really constructive work comes in putting into actual effect the recommendations arising from the examinations and from the advice of the medical experts. Parents, if they are wise, employ trained nurses and medical specialists in emergencies, but they also exercise common sense and ordinary skill in caring for routine scratches and minor injuries.

The director of student personnel recognizes the health program as on of the fundamental responsibilities of an educational institution. He will sacrifice other elements of a complete personnel program, if necessary, for the sake of the health aspect. Dean Smiley has set down the health factors which the average college student needs in order that he may most successfully develop through his college years as:

1. Healthful living conditions including:
    Good food at a reasonable price
    Comfortable and healthy classrooms and quarters
2. Balanced activities including:
    A wisely chosen schedule of studies
    Suitable physical exercise
    Suitable social and recreational activities
3. Efficient health service including:
    A thorough physical examination periodically
    A periodic inventory of health habits
    Convenient medical consultation service
    Communicable disease control measures
    Infirmary care and laboratory service
4. Effective health and character training including:
    Training in elements of biology and bacteriology
    Training in the elements of human anatomy and physiology
    Training in personal hygiene and the elements of community hygiene
    Training in the elements of religion, ethics, and mental hygiene.[2]

From this outline it is apparent that a complete health program as viewed by a college health officer must be a co-operative enterprise. The school or

2. Smiley, Dean F. "Provision for the Health of Students," *Provision for the Individual in College Education*, W. S. Gray, editor. Chicago: University of Chicago Press, 1932. pp. 177–88.

college medical staff may have the vision and ability to achieve an integrated health program; to the extent that it can, and does, the director of student personnel can feel less direct responsibility for this aspect of the personnel program. His responsibility in this case would consist of co-operating at every point with the health officers, and in co-ordinating the total health program with the other aspects of a complete personnel program.

An intelligent family gives serious consideration to the vocational plans and adjustment of its members. Parents attempt to give the kind of character training that will make their children stable and productive members of economic groups; they attempt to build strong bodies and nerves to serve their children as participants in a working society; or they attempt to guide their interests and provide training that will enable them to be self-supporting in spite of some physical handicap; parents attempt to provide opportunities for education that will fit their children as well as may be for some profession or occupation. They use their own experience and that of friends in attempting to help their children decide the general vocational trend which they should adopt. In addition to all this, however, they will gratefully use the scientific information of a specialist in vocational guidance who can make a careful objective inventory of their children's abilities and disabilities and interests, provide sound and extensive information about vocations in our complex economic society, and give definite information about opportunities for employment.

Similarly, in a school or college, the director of personnel who can have within the institution an expert in vocational guidance and an expert in placement must gratefully utilize the valuable services which these experts can provide for the students. The task of "assisting the individual to choose an occupation, prepare for it, enter upon and progress in it" is one requiring expert knowledge and skills. It is also a task requiring a high degree of cooperation with the director of the health program, the director of the curriculum, and with many outside agencies. The relationship of the director of personnel, then, to the vocational-guidance program is that of co-ordinator, supplementer. He will integrate the valuable services of the director of vocational guidance, and the director of the appointment bureau with the total plan of personnel administration. In the event that the director of vocational guidance, the health officer, and the director of religion, each may conceive as one of his primary duties that of training students in the elements of ethics and mental hygiene, the director of student personnel will attempt to co-ordinate their efforts and make the total impact on the student as effective as the enthusiasm of these specialists makes possible.

In similar fashion, one could point out the relationship of the director of student personnel to other parts of the total personnel program and as the mental-hygiene program of the institution. Specialists and psychiatrists, if available, are exceedingly valuable, but mental hygiene actually comes about to a large extent through day-by-day living in an environment that is favorable to it.

One of the most important functions of personnel administration is that of co-ordinating information about each individual. The physician will collect much information about the student's health history, and will, for each year of his college life, summarize his health and physical status. The academic adviser will discover and record year after year facts of considerable importance about his academic interests, his successes and failures. There may be considerable overlapping between the facts gathered by the physical and the academic advisers. Other personnel workers, similarly, will possess specialized information about the student. The duty of the administrator of student personnel, however, is to take the contributions of each one who has information and insight concerning the young person, verify this information, supplement it, co-ordinate it, and record it cumulatively, and make it function as an important guide for his education.

The growth of personnel services in educational institutions since 1920 has been amazing; personnel experts of all sorts have been employed in rapidly increasing numbers. The relationship of all these specialists among themselves, and between them and the person responsible for the administration of personnel work, has been extremely indefinite and unsatisfactory in most instances. On the one hand, each personnel expert has felt a compulsion to encompass the whole field: psychiatrists, for instance, starting with their more immediate professional duties, soon see the necessity of relating their information to all other phases of personnel work; directors of vocational guidance soon see the value of directing aspects of the total personnel program other than the vocational guidance function; it is obvious that the health offices encompass a broad field. On the other hand, deans or directors of student-personnel administration have felt to some extent a sense of guilt if they were not equally skilled in all the personnel functions, if they were not competent medical officers as well as vocational-guidance experts, psychoanalysts, statisticians, dietitians, architects, and administrators.

We hope it is clear from this analysis that the specialist in any aspect of personnel work may have a distinct professional field within which he may render inestimable value, just as the pediatrist, while advising with regard to and directing the upbringing of a child, performs an expert service of inestimable value to the parents in their total plan for the welfare of the family. On the other hand, we have also tried to point out that the administrator of personnel work has a distinct function in co-ordinating the efforts of these specialists, supplementing them in every way possible, and in making the total impact of the complete personnel program as beneficial to each individual student as it can be.

We cannot assume, unfortunately, that all personnel directors, any more than all home managers, are going to be burdened within the next few years with an oversupply of expert help. Just as mothers are going to have to get along without interior decorators and cooks, so directors of student-personnel administration are going to have to do their own directing of extra-curricular activities, and much of their own counseling. The home manager will have to be adjustable enough, intelligent enough, and well enough trained to be able to keep her home attractive and livable, even to the extent of doing her own scrubbing; she must keep her family well fed, even to the extent of preparing the vegetables and washing the dishes afterwards. The director of student-personnel administration, likewise, must be adaptable enough, intelligent enough, and well enough trained to be able to supplement the services of those few experts in personnel work who may be available. It will be well for everyone entering the field of student-personnel administration, in addition to having thorough preparation in the field of education and administration, to know something about organizing a testing program, about administering a social program, and about the principles of counseling, of making a case study, of vocational guidance, of statistics, and of record keeping.

A Study of Student Life

W. H. Cowley and Willard Waller

Obviously, it is not necessary to point out the importance of student life in the educational process. Sociologists do not need to be reminded that the sanctions and compulsions of college life influence every student on every campus. How vigorously the undergraduate may apply himself to his academic work, what friends of both sexes he may choose, what clothes he may wear, where and what he may eat—all these, and much besides, are largely determined for him by the social heritages of the groups and subgroups of which he is a part.

The sociologist, of course, has no interest in taking sides in any verbalistic evaluation of so-called "college atmosphere." He may well concern himself in his choice of research projects, however, with the judgments of these leading educators who have for many years watched students in their communal life together and who have been moved to strong favorable or critical utterances. Over a million undergraduates are today being subjected to the environmental pressures of student life. What these pressures are, whence they come, and how they operate should be thoroughly assessed. These influences present a rich and challenging field for sociological and anthropological study. It is the purpose of this paper not only to report what has been undertaken thus far, but also to petition the aid of other sociologists and anthropologists in the enterprise.

For pragmatic purposes the investigation has been called a study of student traditions. More correctly it might be labeled "a sociological study of student life."

The investigation seeks to examine the whole range of socially inherited behavior among college students. The phrase "student tradition" is employed only because much of the material for appraisal must of necessity be secured from undergraduate participant observers. We seek, in brief, to review and analyze the cultural complexes and processes of American student life.

Clearly the influences which shape college life are much the same as those which play upon all other groups. In the first place, the college generation is

27

but four years long in contrast with the much longer span of adult groups. Traditions age rapidly in the student world because of this telescoping of social processes, and thus the campus furnishes an experimental laboratory comparable to that of the biologist with his white rats, guinea pigs, and drosophila flies.

In the second place, the ancestors of each generation do not die and pass out of the picture. On the contrary, they are very much alive and vocal and must be reckoned with in the persons of alumni who return at frequent intervals to beat their tom-toms "lest the old traditions fail."

In the third place, the college community is a smaller and better defined unit than most groups available to the social scientist. The compact small college and even the more heterogeneous large university present a laboratory for sociological and anthropological investigation much more easily available for study than Middletown, the slums of the great cities, or the taxi dance halls of Chicago.

In order to achieve their objectives the investigators must bring together a great mass of descriptive material about college life. For this they must depend upon students who are at once participants and observers. To discover such students it is first necessary to enlist the cooperation of college teachers of sociology because they understand the problem. Thus far thirty-five sociologists in as many colleges have associated themselves with the undertaking, and the reports from their students are now being tabulated.

When all collectible data have been gathered and classified, they may be analyzed from several points of view. It is the responsibility of the investigators to discover well-defined patterns of human behavior, to refine and universalize them, and to formulate and publicize concepts in the interest of obtaining a better understanding of student life.

To begin with, the history of the college culture complex and of traditional patterns of student behavior may, without too much difficulty, be traced. Communities of students have for centuries been an important part of western European culture and have changed their forms and functions as that culture has evolved. There are, however, in the college world numerous examples of survivals of cultural lag. Town and gown riots are still with us, although it seems likely that they will never reach such violence as the fourteenth century riot at Oxford when 63 students were killed by the townsmen. Initiations, hazing, hell weeks, and the like obviously reach down from the past into the present day college. . . . The tearing down of goal posts after football victories and the wiggles of snake dancers have also a manifest relationship to the victory dances of warlike tribes.

These illustrations perhaps serve to indicate the abundance of material for the genetic study of student group life. This material must be unscrambled and unraveled in a hunt for specific origins. The presence of a given culture trait in the traditions of any student body indicates that it was either invented by the members of that group or borrowed from another group. It is possible, therefore, to approach student life as Wissler and Koreber have approached the culture of the American Indian, namely, in terms of invention and diffusion. The examples of these mechanisms at work in the American college strike one on every hand. When Harvard and Yale engaged in their first intercollegiate athletic contest (a crew race on Lake Winnipiseogee in 1852), other colleges soon followed their example. When Rutgers and Princeton played the first contest of intercollegiate football in the United States, the game spread rapidly and is now recognized as more of a national sport than baseball. In dramatics, in debating, in student publications, and in fact all down the line of extra-curricular activities invention and diffusion are continuously shaping and reshaping campus life. These not only thread through the much publicized sectors of student affairs, but also through the more intimate life of students.

Another example comes from women's colleges. Years ago someone at Vassar had the happy notion that commencement ceremonies would be made considerably more pretentious if the best looking girls in the sophomore class would parade carrying a daisy chain. This ceremony has become so well publicized that Vassar is better known to the layman because of its daisy chain than because of its School of Euthenics. In time other institutions took over the pageantry for themselves.

Because of the mentioned brevity of the college generations traditional practices change rapidly, and the investigators are discovering some difficulty in fitting together as complete a mosaic of the genetic factors involved in student traditions as they should like.

We are also interested in the process of social control, that is to say, the whole set of interactions by means of which behavior norms are established and enforced. A large number of patterns from the past shape the behavior of college students. One student generation transmits them to the next, and they are unreflectively accepted and obeyed. This is control through indoctrination. Indoctrination is supplemented by other varieties of regulation: informal gossip; initiation practices and other mores of assimilation; ceremonies, which usually have definite and ascertainable functions; the coercions and selective mechanisms of activity groups such as fraternities, athletic teams, campus publications, and other extra-curricular activities. . . .

All of these varieties of social control, as well as several others, might be exemplified. Consider the Princeton honor system. At that university no proctors have been present at examinations since 1893, and cheating is all but non-existent because the student body governs its own behavior in examinations through its highly developed standard of honor. This is a clear-cut example of control through indoctrination.

Traditions operate not only in this area but in every other conceivable direction. Faculty and student relationships are in a large measure determined by custom. Even though a student may honestly desire to know his professors outside of class, at many institutions he may achieve a faculty friendship only at the risk of being labeled a "chiseler," a "sponger," or an "apple polisher."

Turning to the selection practices of student social groups many dramatic situations can easily be spotted, more especially among fraternities. A noted social psychological atomist has stated his belief that the fraternity does not mold personality but obtains its unanimity largely by selection. Incidents have come to light which clearly indicate that it both selects and molds. For example, a few years ago a brilliant Freshman matriculated at an eastern college, and because of his credentials one of the better fraternities immediately rushed him. It did not elect him, however, because of two personal characteristics which led the rushing committee to believe that he would turn out to be a flighty and, therefore, undesirable member. In the first place, he wore his curly hair much too long, and, in the second place, he shook hands with his right elbow so far in the air that they thought him an affected fop. Another less prominent group pledged him, and many were the regrets of the first fraternity when he turned out to be a track star and the valedictorian of his class. The second fraternity had been annoyed by these same superficial traits but rapidly brought him into line, making possible his subsequent success. One fraternity had exerted control by not electing him. The other had expressed its control by molding him to its model.

All social organizations, of course, have admissions barriers of one sort or another. The analysis of these selective patterns reveals how the control culture of the college intermeshes with that of American society. The social hierarchy of the campus parallels that of the world outside. The old-line fraternities, in general, almost universally discriminate against Jews and many of them against Catholics. A large number will not consider an individual who does not come from a monied family, and the preparatory school from which a student comes has much to do with the fraternities which seek him out.

Speaking of preparatory schools, Corliss Lamont in 1924 demonstrated that the large majority of campus positions at Harvard were held by the graduates of a few eastern preparatory schools: Groton, Exeter, Andover, and the Hill School. No matter what abilities an undergraduate might have, his chances of success in the campus life of Harvard, Lamont found, depended in large measure upon the school from which he had come.

A little historical perspective with regard to the relation of the class system on the campus to the class system of the world outside serves to develop tolerance. Class distinctions on the campus were once a great deal more in evidence than they are today. Students at Harvard College in Colonial days were seated in class according to the social positions of their fathers. An amusing story is told of the son of a shoemaker who innocently listed his father's occupation as "the bench." This the aristocratic president interpreted to mean that the student's father held a judgeship, and he seated the shoemaker's son at the head of the class.

The methods of the big business are also pushing their way into student affairs. Within the past few years two large public relations organizations have undertaken to help fraternities choose their new members. They have devised an elaborate system of follow-up letters to the alumni asking for their recommendation of recent high-school graduates who might be rushed. They not only write and mail the letters but receive the answers, tabulate them, and in some cases even investigate the nominees. It is now possible for a rushing chairman whose fraternity subscribes to one of these services to do little more than insert a pledge button in the lapel of the Freshman who has been so carefully and thoroughly looked over by these experts.

These illustrations are only the most spectacular of a wide variety which demonstrate how adult culture complexes shape undergraduate life. That these influences work both ways is, of course, obvious, but as yet no comprehensive attempt has been made to canvas and plot them with any degree of completeness. To arrive at an understanding of these mechanisms becomes a natural and important objective of the present study.

This brief overview of social controls is perhaps sufficient to indicate its importance. We may turn, therefore, to the consideration of the social utility of the many varieties of student institutions. What, in general, one may query, are the functions of extra-curricular activities? On the one hand, many alumni and students, as everybody knows, think them much more valuable educationally than course work. On the other hand, an appreciable percentage of most faculties agree with Woodrow Wilson that these side shows have ruined the business of the big tent. Without taking sides in this now-and-then heated controversy, the investigators must sort out fact from verbiage and attempt to discover the functions of the wide assortment of campus activities.

In all this endeavor they must first of all go back several decades to the beginnings of extra-curricular life as we know it today. The fact must not be overlooked that non-academic organizations on the college campus arose to meet a very definite need. The college of the middle nineteenth century . . . possessed a solicity and compactness the like of which cannot be discovered even in the most self-contained small college of the 1930's. In those days every student took the same course as every other student, and an entering freshman class went together as a group through every class meeting from matriculation to graduation. Because the elective system had not yet appeared, the universally accepted classical curriculum gave undergraduates a common meeting ground and a common range of conversation. But the adoption of the elective system scuttled all this. The new method brought divergence of courses of study and intellectual and conversational isolation. The growth in numbers of student accelerated the disintegration.

At this point extra-curricular activities began to appear and to grow with great rapidity. The old and desirable solidarity had vanished, and gregarious youth sought a substitute, a ground on which to meet, to understand one another's conversation, and to feel a sense of oneness. Extra-curricular activities—especially athletics—furnished the necessary common denominator. All . . . could . . . (students) talk about the flying wedge, the new crew stroke, and yesterday's editorial about the importance of attending tonight's football rally.

If this is a sound analysis of the major reason for the rise of extra-curricular activities, it must be continuously borne in mind in appraising student affairs. Other factors have, of course, contributed to the widespread opinion that the campus has seemed to swallow up the classroom. Our fundamental point, however, is unchanged: the functions of all student organizations must be canvassed and evaluated in terms of fulfillment of human purposes.

A different type of functional approach is that which leads into the analysis of configurations of student culture. A number of anthropologists have put us greatly in their debt by insisting that cultural facts must not be wrested from their setting, but they must be studied in their total interrelatedness. Thus a given cultural fact externally the same may have one meaning in one culture and a totally different meaning in another. Ruth Benedict in her provocative discussion of "Configurations of Culture in North America" appearing in the *American Anthropologist* for January, 1933, has brilliantly analyzed the effect of these total configurations. Her point of view may be readily applied to the study of student life. What undergraduates mean to imply when they speak of the traditions of their campus is not that the details of their traditions are distinctive but that the configurations are different. Partly this is an optical illusion which results from the fact that they are participants in one group and view the behavior of other groups as outsiders, but unquestionably these are distinguishable patterns from campus to campus.

Among women's colleges the configurational pattern of the finishing school contrasts strikingly with that of the feminist school. Finishing schools emphasize social ease, familiarity with the amenities, and probably give their graduates some advantages over their sisters in competition for eligible mates and for social prestige in general. On the other hand, in the feminist school the revolt against male domination gives tone to their cultural complex and is aptly illustrated by the girls at one leading women's college who pride themselves upon not washing their necks and upon dressing in slovenly skirts, sweaters, and smocks.

Other configurations might be cited. Professional schools commonly take their accent from the occupational groups to which their students look forward. Where most students live in dormitories the student form of life differs from that in the so-called "trolley-car colleges." A common configuration is that of the small denominational college best exemplified by an Ohio institution which for the first time in its history permitted a dance to be held this year upon its campus.

The ramifications of these designs must be scrutinized in terms both of structure and of function. The study of configurations of student culture requires a combination of quantificative and case study methods. Institutions must be reviewed by size and complexity since the cultural processes of the large urban institution differ markedly from those of the small rural college. They must be similarly considered by age, by the socio-economic status of their clienteles, and by religious and political affiliations. Likewise coeducational institutions must be contrasted with men's and women's colleges, professional institutions compared with one another, and public and private institutions surveyed for their distinctive characteristics. Besides these there are other variables to be reckoned with. Student life differs from place to place depending upon the combinations and permutations of at least a half-score of factors. All need isolation and interpretation.

In view of all these considerations it perhaps becomes clear that educators must come more definitely to recognize that to the average undergraduate student life constitutes the real life of the college. From his first day as a Freshman to the last ceremony of commencement he is being fashioned by pressures which he understands little, but which he knows to be vital. Cardinal Newman even went so far as to adjudge the educational values of student give-and-take as above those of the classroom. Whether or not one agrees with him, there is no gainsaying the obvious fact that educators must actively and intelligently seek to understand and to capitalize the educational potentialities of college life.

It is no less clear, however, that such a study as this must constantly raise more questions than it can answer. We have seen that some features of college life are spread by diffusion, but to what extent can fundamental attitudes be diffused? Student tradition on American campuses is fundamentally conservative, and we explain this by saying that the college is an expression of American life. The universities of Europe, however, are centers of revolutionary sentiment. Why do these differences exist? To what extent is student tradition an independent variable in the life of the larger society? To what extent can faculties control and manipulate student tradition? The answer to these and similar questions is: We do not know.

If we are ever to have the answers, the sociologist must play a major role in framing them. He alone of all the academic family has the equipment that the undertaking requires: a set of conceptual tools with which to make social and cultural processes intelligible. Aside from the practical value of the findings in the educational programs of the college, the problem constitutes an unusually attractive field for sociological research. The material is highly accessible: the students are right at hand; the forces being studied shape and reshape themselves daily before the investigators' very eyes; the necessary documents can be secured for the asking; and the sociologist may carry on his studies without leaving his teaching job. The interested and even enthusiastic response of three dozen sociologists over the country for co-operative assistance in the present exploration has been most gratifying. Perhaps this paper will bring the participation of still a larger number.

The Scope and Aim of a Personal Program

Francis F. Bradshaw

Since the scope of a program of any sort must be determined by its aim, or aims, I shall deal first and foremost with the aims of educational personnel work at the college and university level. These aims grow out of the general aims of American educational tradition, in accord with which the college is responsible for furnishing service to its students over and above classroom instruction. Arm-chair thinkers day-dream of a release from this responsibility in order that the faculty members may receive the total income of the institution for salaries and supplies and give in return scholarly lectures and occasional advice relative to their field of study. However, the student gets sick, has no money, goes slack because of vocational anxieties, encounters poor study conditions, becomes dissipated by unwholesome recreations, rebels against misunderstood university regulations, registers for the wrong level of French instruction, is harassed by debt, finds the moral and religious universe of his childhood too rudely shattered, or is home-sick or love-sick; and any of these may entirely negate the best of instruction. The American college has been sufficiently practical-minded to realize that instruction itself demands allied services to the student. The student cannot be sent to college without bringing his body, emotional status, and moral make-up with him. Nor can his mind function without regard to the status of other aspects of his development. The practical wisdom of the American tradition seems incontrovertible. All theory of release from it seems to the writer to be 100 percent wishful thinking on the part of the faculty. And this conclusion is based not on the interests of parents, students, alumni, and trustees, but solely upon consideration of the teaching effectiveness of the institution— the interest of the faculty itself.

Until approximately 1900 the policy described above expressed itself mainly in two directions; namely, on the one hand many faculty meetings, faculty committee meetings, and faculty-student interviews devoted to the problems listed above; and, on the other hand, the gradual absorption of college presidents in such problems. Then, as the colleges grew in size and

35

the faculty became increasingly unwilling to spend time on such matters not directly germane to their teaching and research, there have arisen additional administrative provisions, viz., academic deans, registrars, deans of men and women, student advisers, student associations (religious and secular), guidance bureaus, infirmaries and health officers, psychological consultants, psychiatric experts, etc.

In the beginning such administrative duties as dealt mainly with students were primarily regulatory and disciplinary. Gradually they became conceived of as prophylactic and morale building. In addition, they have come to be considered definitely and directly educational as dealing with the total needs of the total student personality. Finally, they have come to be thought of as mediating between general curricula or regulations on the one hand and the limitless individualities of motives, needs, and abilities on the other hand. In all this development, however, there has been no element of the program that could not *theoretically* justify itself in terms of service to the teaching faculty through release of the teaching staff from duties they were least interested in performing, and through delivering the student to the classroom in the optimum condition for profiting by instruction.

The foregoing running start from history is taken in order to afford for our discussion of aims and scope a standard for validating such aims. This standard would probably be acceptable to all if we define student personal service as all the instructional service to students which demonstrably increases the effectiveness of instruction. When the personal service introduces a placement test in French which reduces student mortality 25 per cent, such increased effectiveness is immediately obvious. More adequate admissions programs or sanitary inspection of student residences may have less obvious but equally real value to the instructional objectives of the institution.

There is one point in this historical summary that has been omitted—namely, the introduction of the term "personnel." Probably this term was not used in college circles until after 1917. The term has been used in many senses since that date. H. D. Kitson published in 1917 a monograph supplement of the *Psychological Review*, entitled "The Scientific Study of the College Student." The application of social case work methods, psychological techniques, and more refined statistical methods of handling data on large groups began to demand a new term for a new administrative point of view.

L. B. Hopkins, in a study of "Personnel Procedure in Education" (October, 1926, EDUCATIONAL RECORD), listed the functions of personnel work as including: Selective process, Freshman Week, psychological tests, placement tests, faculty advisers, other organized student interviews, health service, mental hygiene service, vocational information, employment and placement, discipline, curriculum improvement, selection of instructors, improvement of teaching methods, objective examinations, research concerning teaching, research concerning the individual, coordination of personnel services in the college and the whole institution, and coordination of outside agencies affecting students.

The general aim embracing the functions listed above Hopkins presented as follows:

The concept I have had before me has been that it means work having to do specifically with the individual. In education one might question how this differs from the concept of education itself. I do not assume that it does differ. However, other factors constantly force themselves on the minds of those responsible for administration. In industry, it would be fair to say that management must concern itself with raw materials and output, with buildings and equipment, and with innumerable other items. So also in education, the administration is beset with many serious problems and certain of these problems become so acute at times that there is danger that they may be met and solved without sufficient time for their ultimate effect upon the individual student. One of the functions, therefore, of personnel administration in education is to bring to bear upon any educational problem the point of view which concerns itself primarily with the individual. Thus, in this particular as in all others, personnel work should remain consistent with the theory and purpose of education by tending constantly to emphasize the problem that underlies all other problems of education; namely, how the institution may best serve the individual.

Esther Lloyd-Jones, in 1929, in her book, "Student Personnel Work at Northwestern," elaborated the position that educational personnel was a major division of university work equal in importance and unity to teaching and finance.

R. C. Clothier, as Chairman of a Committee on Policy and Procedures and Standards of the American College Personnel Association, included in his report in 1931 the following principles of educational personnel work:

1. Every student differs from every other student in aptitudes, inherited or acquired. . . . The college must know these qualifications so far as it is possible to do so and must utilize that knowledge in planning his college course, both within and without the curriculum. . . .

2. Every agency within the college should consider these differences between students. . . .

3. The Personnel Department, under the Personnel Director, is responsible for the development of this point of view throughout the organization. . . .

4. Each college should provide adequate facilities—in terms both of procedures and equipment—for the maintenance of harmonious and effective relationships among students, faculty members, and administrative officials. . . .

M. E. Townsend, in 1932, studying "The Administration of Student Personnel Services in Teaching Training Institutions of the United States," describes the function of personnel as follows:

Personnel is a new term. On the other hand, the province of personnel is as old as the establishment of society itself. As the name itself indicates, personnel is concerned with those inquiries about and those relationships toward persons—as persons—carried on primarily for the purpose of insuring human effectiveness in productive work. It is, of course, interested in the skills, informations, and techniques already mentioned, but essentially with a view to establishing proper physical, mental, emotional, social, and ethical readiness within the human being who is to do the work, to the end that these factors may serve the worker in a positive, constructive manner in the pursuit of the activity. The personality pattern of the individual at work is its legitimate field.

President Townsend calls attention to the fact that the term "personnel" is so recent that with one unimportant exception it does not appear in the *Readers Guide* until the volume of 1919–1921. He says further:

. . . Just what forces combined to change the emphasis is industry and in all fields of vocation from the task to be done to the doer of the task, is not very difficult to discern. Until the first decade of the twentieth century psychology—one of the basic instruments of investigation in this field—was practically unprepared for the task. The rise of the testing movement, largely experimental and academic at first, provided practical means at hand for the further refinement of the techniques of research in the field of personality. And upon the accumulation of authentic and usable information about personality itself all of personnel as a scientific procedure depends. That one stands at present in possession of anything like a fully competent body of predictive or diagnostic procedures in this field is far from the truth. But important beginnings have undoubtedly been made . . . The interview, the case history, tests, measures of relationship between significant personal conditioners, the survey, the controlled experiment are familiar procedures, whether the personnel researcher is inquiring within the fields of the skilled trades, engineering, medicine, civil service, or teaching. The fact that personal factors affecting accomplishment are relatively more easily discernible, and bear a more direct relationship to output, in terms of goods produced or goods sold, has probably resulted in more investigation being carried forward within the general field of commerce and industry than within those fields of service where results are more intangible, and more complicated by delay of fruition, or by the operation of extraneous factors, as is the case with the professions.

Although "personnel" did not appear in the *Readers Guide* before 1919, W. H. Cowley, of Ohio State University, was able in 1932 to issue a volume entitled "The Personnel Bibliographical Index." To prepare the Index it was necessary to read 4,902 books, articles, monographs, and pamphlets, of which 2,183 are annotated and indexed in the resulting volume.

Dr. Cowley, who had just previously devoted considerable time to the development of techniques for making surveys of personnel work in universities, bases his volume upon five assumptions concerning the aims and scope. In abbreviated form these assumptions are as follows:

1. Student personnel administration is not analogous to industrial personnel administration. The accepted function of industry, perhaps incorrectly, is the production and the sale of goods and services. Individuals are contributors merely. In education, however, the individual takes the center of the stage. His training and development are the *raison d'etre* of the college. All units of the college staff make their contribution toward the common end. The Personnel Division is one of these units, performing its specialized services toward the education of the student.

2. Personnel administration is one of four main divisions of university administration. As educators become interested in and cognizant of the development of management techniques in industry, they are recognizing that college or university administration may be classified functionally in at least four divisions: operational (or business) administration, instructional administration, research administration, and personnel administration.

3. Recognizing student personnel administration as a major functional division of university administration, we may define it as the administration of all university-student relationships *aside from formal instruction*. . . . These include counseling of various types, medical attention, supervision of extracurricular activities, administration of admissions, of intelligence-testing programs, of housing, and so forth. Moreover, these functions group themselves together as thoroughly different from formal instruction, and as a group they are generally thought of as personnel services.

4. Ideally, every instructor is essentially a personnel officer, but he must depend upon specialists to perform certain personnel services for which he is untrained. In the best of possible colleges every instructor would be individually interested in the students under his direction, but he cannot treat

them when they are ill, nor counsel them concerning complex vocational problems, nor administer loans and scholarships, nor direct intelligence-testing problems, nor undertake responsibility for a number of other personnel services.

5. Student personnel administration divides itself logically into individualized services, administrative services, personnel research, and cooperative research services.

(a) Individualized personnel services include educational counseling, vocational counseling, personal adjustment counseling (namely, social counseling, psychological counseling, and religious counseling), discipline, placement both part-time and permanent, health counseling, and loans and scholarships. In all of these relationships the individual student has the center of the stage. The contact between the personnel officer and the student is always a face-to-face and one-to-one contact. It is seldom a group relationship. One may properly, therefore group these functions together and label them individualized personnel services.

(b) Administrative personnel services include admissions, freshman orientation, intelligence-testing programs, supervision of extra-curricular activities, housing, personnel record-keeping, and supervision of social life. It may frequently happen, of course, that these administrative personnel services may also be individualized personnel services, but in general they are administered for groups of students rather than for individuals. They are, therefore, set apart from the individualized services because of their distinctive and more or less impersonal emphasis.

(c) Personnel research takes in all types of investigations of individualized and administrative personnel problems. The effective administration of both individualized personnel services and administrative personnel services requires continuous research in problems as diverse as they are numerous. No ideal personnel program can be conducted without research. The function is so important that it must be recognized as a major classification of personnel administration.

(d) Cooperative research services are those research services performed for departments of instruction. Although by definition a clear-cut distinction is made between instructional administration and personnel administration, it frequently happens, and very likely must continue to happen, that the personnel organization conducts research for instructional departments in problems of two general types:

1. The measurement of students for sectioning on the basis of ability, for honors courses, for the discovery of gifted students, for the prediction of scholarship, and for similar instructional purposes.

2. The development of techniques for probation courses, remedial instruction, how-to-study course, orientation courses, and the like.

Not only has this item of "personnel" appeared in *Readers Guides,* indexes and research summaries, but it also has an important section of the Manual of Accrediting Procedures of the North Central Association (1934). The Accrediting Committee proposes to examine the adequacy of what it calls "Student Personnel Service," under which heading it does not include "Admission and Orientation of Students," but does include "Student Records," "Counseling Procedures," "Extra-curricular Activities," "Loans, Scholarships and Grants-of-Aid," "Health Service," "Housing and Boarding of Students," "Placement Service," "Student Discipline," and "Administrative Arrangements Whereby the Various Types of Student Personnel Service Are Effectively Coordinated." Under this better heading the admission and registration of students is included in the group of functions to be effectively correlated.

I have called attention to these various statements just quoted in order to avoid settling down on any one point of view in regard to a movement still in its formative stages. I am willing, however, to record some convictions as to valuable trends within the movement. I am confident the following are clear gains and worthy of development at any institution:

1. The emphasis on the essentiality of certain services to students.

2. The grouping of these together to form a single general function calling for special staff with special qualifications, training, etc.

3. The realization of the existence of ultimate individual differences in student needs and aptitudes, and their radical importance for instruction and adjustment.

4. The adoption of scientific techniques in the study of individual problems and institutional processes.

5. The realization of the unity of student personality and the necessity of dealing with each student at each contact as a total person—and end in himself, and never a mere abstraction or a means to an end.

6. The necessity for continuous research and revision in the work of an educational institution instead of periodic and explosive re-planning, followed by periods of static and routine administration of unchanging plans.

Furthermore, I believe that this movement is thoroughly appropriate to the present nature of American civilization which is trying in all its institutions of government and business, as well as education, to substitute science for guess work, humanistic values for unrestricted institutionalism, and continuous development for cataclysmic alternations of repression and revolution. It is part and parcel of the unique effort to create a better relationship between individuals and institutions that is central in the American way of life.

The Nature of Student Personnel Work
W. H. Cowley

I. Introduction

This article represents an effort to clarify the nature of student personnel
work. During the past forty years, and more particularly during the past two
decades, a new group of educational officers have made their appearance
upon American college campuses. Generally referred to as student personnel
workers, they include among their number deans of men, deans of women,
deans of freshman, directors of admission, social directors, directors of
student health services, student counselors, vocational counselors, psychological clinicians, directors of placement bureaus, directors of dormitories,
and a variety of others.

These personnel workers have been appointed to perform a wide range of
activities which have come to be regarded as educationally significant and
indeed indispensable. Devoting their attention to the student as an individual rather than as a mind merely, they enhance and supplement the formal
instructional programs of the college. They are interested in his emotional
and social development, in his health, in his selection of courses as they
relate to his personal objectives, in his place of residence, in his extra-
curricular activities, in his financial needs, and in any number of other
considerations which bear upon his education broadly considered.

The literature of student personnel services and their administration has
been abundant in recent years. Most of what has been written, however, has
been segmental rather than comprehensive. Few attempts have been made to
view these services in the broad, to see the work of one personnel officer in
relation to the work of his fellows, or to appraise the concepts common to
them all. An essential unity underlies all the many types of personnel service
fostered in the colleges, but this unity has seldom been stressed. Very
properly personnel officers as individuals and as specialized groups have been
absorbed in pioneering efforts to cultivate their own sectors of the terrain.

They have had little leisure to discuss common objectives and common problems.

The pioneering days of the student personnel movement are rapidly passing, however, and the time seems to be ripe for a systematic discussion of what personnel people do, what they stand for, and how their activities fit into the educational programs of colleges and universities. In this article the writer seeks to do two things: first, to point out the inadequacy of several widely used definitions of personnel work; and second, to indicate and develop another which is implicit in the publications of several writers in the field and in recent developments at a number of universities.

II. The Prevailing Confusion

Speaking before a meeting of personnel[1] officers at Purdue University in October, 1929, President L. B. Hopkins of Wabash College expressed concern because "the word 'personnel' means one thing to some people and another thing to others" and particularly because "so many of our associates on the faculties of colleges and universities have no real understanding of what we are thinking or trying to do in . . . personnel work."[2]

If Mr. Hopkins were still writing and speaking about student personnel problems, he would more than likely express even greater concern today. The confusion and lack of understanding in 1936 are considerably greater than in 1929. The terms *personnel work, personnel administration, personnel services, personnel research,* and *personnel point of view* continue to be bandied about so variously and carelessly that faculty members cannot possibly be expected to know what personnel workers are about. Indeed, plenty of evidence exists to suggest that personnel people do not themselves know. At least, few personnel workers agree among themselves; and until they do, faculties and administrators will continue to be perplexed and apathetic if not unfriendly and even antagonistic.

Two years after Mr. Hopkins' Purdue address a committee of the American College Personnel Association, headed by Robert C. Clothier, who was soon to become the president of Rutgers University, called attention to the "urgent need for . . . definition." In their report they said in part:

1. Every time the word *personnel* is used in this discussion the qualifying word *student* is understood. It is perhaps unnecessary to observe that educational institutions have personnel problems relating to faculty members and to employees which are important but different from student personnel problems.

2. Hopkins, L. B., "Personnel Procedures in Education," *College Personnel Procedures,* Proceedings of Purdue-Wabash Conf. of College Personnel Officers, October, 1929. Bulletin No. 21 of Eng. Extension Depart. at Purdue, p. 43.

Even the term "personnel work" is interpreted in different ways. To some of us it is broad in its meaning, involving all those aspects of college work which affect the student as an individual. To others it denotes certain specific functions. The former concept is unsatisfactory to some persons because, in its general nature, it seems to lack specific meaning; the latter is equally unsatisfactory to others because it seems incomplete.[3]

The Clothier committee set about defining the personnel field in an attempt to end the confusion to which they and Hopkins referred. That their discussions were unsatisfactory to some personnel people at least is demonstrated by the plea of A. B. Crawford, written several months after the appearance of the Clothier report.

Referring to personnel work as a "murky subject," Crawford suggested "that college personnel officers more broadly establish their position, purposes, and procedure" and "that as a body they prepare a statement of . . . the total scope and purpose of personnel work." He wrote in part as follows:

College personnel work has necessarily developed rapidly but unevenly. Pressure for immediate action has led to makeshift procedures, with resulting confusion and loss of perspective. . . . In this comparatively new field great advances have already been made, but rather by the process of scurrying forward from one immediate objective to the next than in pursuit of comprehensive or farsighted ends. The time therefore seems to have come for an estimate of the situation as a whole, for comparative study of its component parts and for trying to visualize their interrelations more clearly.[4]

Despite the Clothier and Crawford attempts at clarification, no generally accepted interpretation of the nature of personnel work has yet been stated. Instead the appearance of new books and articles have served to compound the confusion rather than to eliminate it. Bad as this may be for personnel people in their relationships with one another, much worse is its effect upon their programs. As Mr. Hopkins has pointed out, few faculty members and administrators understand what personnel workers are trying to do. Yet the need of such understanding cannot be too urgently stressed. If personnel

3. "College Personnel Principles and Functions." *The Personnel Journal*, Vol. X (June, 1931), p. 10. President Clothier's name is used because he served as chairman of the committee of the American College Personnel Association which made the report submitted in this article. The other members of the committee were Earl W. Anderson, Mabelle B. Blake, Grace Manson, and N. M. McKnight.

4. Crawford, A. B., "Educational Personnel Work." *The Personnel Journal*, Vol. X, No. 6 (April 1932), pp. 405–6.

services are to contribute to higher education as effectively as they properly should, the personnel point of view must pervade the thinking and influence the activities of all members of college and university staffs. This will never happen, however, until personnel people arrive at an understanding among themselves as to what they are trying to accomplish. To achieve such a common understanding requires a definition of the field which is logical, lucid, and generally acceptable.

III. Clarity of Definition the BAsis of Understanding

In his book *How We Think*[5] John Dewey has devoted considerable space to an appraisal of the nature of understanding. He points out that "to understand is to grasp meanings"[6] and that "the process of arriving at . . . units of meaning (and of stating them when reached) is definition."[7] In brief, understanding follows from clarity of definition. If, therefore, personnel people are to understand one another and in turn be understood by their faculty and administrative associates, they must obviously give careful thought to defining their field of endeavor.

To date a good definition is no simple matter Without going into an involved discussion of types of definitions and their characteristics it may be pointed out that a definition is "a declaration of intention to use a word or phrase as a substitute for another word or phrase."[8] For example, in Euclidean geometry it would be cumbersome to use the phrase "lines that do not intersect in a plane" every time such lines are encountered. The shorter expression "parallel lines" has therefore been substituted; and whenever one want to say "lines that do not intersect in a plane," he can say instead "parallel lines."

Anyone can, of course, manufacture as many definitions as he pleases. It is perfectly possible, for example, for an individual to define a chair as a thingamabob. He can go through life so designating every chair he encounters. No one can logically prove that a chair is not a thingamabob. The most that anyone can do is to indicate that such a definition has no utility, that people do not understand what he means. The only test of a definition, the logicians agree, is its utility, and utility is determined by practice. If people readily and regularly substitute one term for another, then the definition thus stated can be said to be useful.

5. Revised edition, D. C. Heath and Company, 1933.
6. *Ibid.*, p. 137.
7. *Ibid.*, p. 160.
8. Eaton, Ralph M., *General Logic*. New York: Chas. Scribner's Sons, 1931, p. 295.

To summarize: a definition is a substitution of a word or a phrase for another word or phrase, and that definition is useful which is generally acceptable. This statement may now be applied to several current definitions of personnel work.

IV. Definitions That Are Too Inclusive

The Hopkins-Clothier Definition: Perhaps the most widely accepted definition of personnel work is that which avers that personnel work and education as synonymous. This definition has been stated by L. B. Hopkins and by the committee of the American College Personnel Association of which R. C. Clothier was chairman and to which reference has already been made.[9] As the most frequently quoted definition of the field, it should properly be appraised first.

In 1926, after a careful inspection of personnel practices in fourteen colleges and universities, Hopkins defined personnel work as "work having to do specifically with the individual."[10] He then observed that "one might question how this differs from the concept of education itself. I don't assume that it does differ." Clothier in 1931 presented a similar formulation in these words: personnel work is "the systematic bringing to bear on the individual student of all those influences, of whatever nature, which will stimulate him and assist him through his own efforts, to develop in body, mind, and character to the limit of his individual capacity for growth, and help him to apply his powers of developing more effectively to the world."[11] In 1935 he repeated this definition substantially and wrote that "very largely we might define education itself in such terms. If so, personnel work and education are the same thing—which, broadly speaking, is perfectly true."[12]

To say that "personnel work and education are the same thing" is just another way of saying that personnel work is education and that education is personnel work. On the face of it, this is not a useful definition of the personnel field. As indicated, a definition has utility only when one term of the statement can be substituted for the other term with general agreement among interested individuals. But can the term *personnel work* be consistently substituted for the term *education*? Obviously not. Learning the scientific

---

9. *Op. cit.*

10. Hopkins, L. B., "Personnel Procedure In Education," Supplement to *The Educational Record*. No. 3, American Council on Education, Washington, D.C. (October, 1926), p. 50.

11. *Op. cit.*

12. Clothier, R. C., in the Foreword to *Individualizing Education*, by J. E. Walters. New York: John Wiley & Sons, Inc., 1935, pp. vii.

method is admittedly education, but who is there who would say that learning the scientific method is personnel work? Similarly learning the principles of economics is education, but it certainly is not personnel work. Hence, although the Hopkins-Clothier statement (the two are so much alike that they can be considered as one) constitutes a definition, it has no utility as a definition of the personnel field.

The Scott Definition: A second unacceptable definition is that of Walter Dill Scott which reads: "Personnel work is the systematic consideration of the individual, for the sake of the individual, and by specialists in that field."[13] If anything, this is even more inclusive than the definitions of Clothier and Hopkins. They label all education personnel work, but Scott outdoes them. He brings into the personnel field dozens of varieties of experts from the pediatrician who directs the individual's weaning during his first months to the attorney who draws up his will upon his death bed. All these specialists patently consider the individual systematically "for the sake of the individual," but they would be surprised to discover that they are personnel workers. And, of course, they are not. To define personnel work so broadly is to render the term meaningless.

Personnel Work Is the Individualization of Education: Faced with this critique President Scott would very likely suggest that his words have been taken too literally and that his definition is not meant to be so broad as it reads. In all probability he would point out that what he really means by personnel work is the individualization of education. Hopkins[14] and Clothier[15] would more than likely make similar statements. All have generally been so interpreted. Walters, for example, has just published a book on personnel work and has called it *Individualizing Education.*[16] Strang in her book, *The Role of the Teacher in Personnel Work*[17] recognizes that the terms *personnel work* and the *individualizing of education* are frequently used interchangeably. Caliver[18] and numerous others have implied that they are one and the same concept. To these writers personnel work is the individualizing or personalizing of the educational process.

---

13. Scott, Walter D., in the Foreword to *Student Personnel Work at Northwestern University* by Esther McD. Lloyd-Jones, Ph.D. New York: Harper & Brothers, 1929, p. v.

14. Hopkins, L. B., *The Educational Record*. American Council on Education. Vol. 7, No. 3 (July, 1926), p. 174.

15. Clothier, Robert C., "College Personnel Principles and Functions." *The Personnel Journal*, Vol. X, No. 1 (June 1931), p. 17.

16. *Op. cit.*

17. Strang, Ruth, *The Role of the Teacher in Personnel Work*. New York: Teachers College, Columbia University, 1935, p. 11, pp. 14–15.

18. Caliver, Ambrose. *A Personnel Study of Negro College Students*. Columbia Contributions to Education, Teachers College Series.

But this third definition is also too-inclusive and therefore undesirable. If every device to individualize education is personnel work, then most of the techniques to improve instruction developed during recent years must be so designated. These include the Harvard system of tutors, the preceptorial conferences at Princeton, the honors courses at Swarthmore and a hundred other institutions, the project and unit plans adopted by a number of academic departments in several colleges, the innumerable programs established the country over for gifted students, the grouping of classes according to ability, and such total programs as that of Bennington and Sarah Lawrence which stress individual instruction through the whole curriculum. Merely to list these curricular and instructional methods of personalizing education is enough to demonstrate they are beyond the scope of personnel work. According to the definition under discussion the Harvard, Princeton, Swarthmore, Bennington, and many other faculties, whether they know it or not, are personnel workers. Personnel work is individualizing education, therefore perforce, anyone who individualizes education is a personnel worker.

The flaw in such a concept is the same as that in the first definition discussed. A definition to be acceptable must delimit the field being defined. If it cannot be delimited, then nothing distinctive exists to define. Ergo, if there is nothing distinctive about personnel work, the term should be abandoned.

To abandon the concept is, of course, out of the question. It has an important place in education and must be protected from some of its friends who seem to want to smother it with generosity. Unfortunately the impression has grown that personnel workers want to encompass all education. The result has been that frequently they have met with antagonism and more frequently with deadlier indifference. Such faculty attitudes have been inevitable, and because of them personnel programs have in general marked time or actually lost ground.

This unhappy situation is not likely to change for the better until personnel people agree among themselves upon boundaries within which to operate. It cannot be reiterated too often that exact thinking requires exact limiting expression. The natural sciences, and the professions which have grown from them, have advanced so much more rapidly than the social sciences, and the professions dependent upon them, chiefly because of the exactness of their concepts. Social scientists—personnel workers among them—must strive for a similar precision.[19]

19. A pertinent discussion of this point with particular reference to education may be found in R. O. Billett's volume, *Provision for Individual Differences, Marking, and Promotion*, U.S. Dept. of Interior, Office of Education, Bulletin, 1932, No. 17, Monog. No. 3, pp. 234–36.

V. Definitions That Are Too Restrictive

Side by side with these all-inclusive definitions may be placed a number of too-restrictive definitions most of which are implicit in the literature rather than clearly stated. One must look for them in such passages as the following from a recent article by Cowdery:

A psychiatrist on the staff of a large eastern university—himself carrying on high-grade personnel work—was recently asked in conversation what is his relation to the Personnel Director of his institution. His reply was that there is no occasion for relations to or with the "personnel organization and its director." Pressed for an explanation of this reply, the psychiatrist pointed out that with them the personnel office carries on one primary activity—placement in jobs and followup of graduates.[20]

The psychiatrist referred to in this report obviously considers personnel work to be placement and graduate followup—nothing more. A number of other people similarly define the personnel field. For example, a bulletin appeared in 1931 entitled "Twenty-five Years of Personnel and Placement Work at the Carnegie Institute of Technology." Its thirty-one pages are devoted entirely to the placement activities of the Carnegie Bureau of Recommendations, and although in the introduction a word is said about vocational and educational guidance, one is given the impression that essentially personnel work at Carnegie means only placement.[21] The same definition is in vogue at a number of other institutions.

A second narrow interpretation confines the scope of personnel activities to personnel research. This definition goes back to the years immediately following the war when the word *personnel* came into educational terminology for the first time. In those early days personnel work meant personnel research almost exclusively. Yoakum, for example, while still an army psychologist, proposed a plan, in the spring of 1919, for a college personnel bureau. He wrote:

The primary functions of the bureau are to obtain accurate data on each student, to codify the requirements of different professions; to supervise the use of tests and to provide means whereby each student may become acquainted with his abilities and the requirements of the occupations in which he is interested. . . . The bureau will

20. Cowdery, Karl M., "The Guidance of Youth in the College." *Occupations*, Vol. 12 (Dec., 1933), p. 14.

21. This impression is borne out by the editorial campaign during 1934–35 of the student newspaper, *The Carnegie Tartan*, for the establishment of what the editors called a student personnel advisory service.

proceed on the assumption that all of these problems can be investigated in a scientific manner and will initiate and encourage research in this field.[22]

The Yoakum bureau was, obviously, essentially a research organization confining itself largely to vocational problems. A number of personnel departments were established after the Yoakum pattern or after others much like it. Some of these still continue to operate within the confines of their original commissions; others have extended their investigations to other types of student problems; and still others have added counseling and other activities to their research work.

To many people, however, personnel work is still considered to be nothing more than personnel research. In 1927 Howard R. Taylor of the University of Oregon wrote that "the task of a university personnel organization is . . . a threefold one." He proposed that these tasks are:

(a) To evaluate the information already available concerning each student so that the collection and recording of non-essential or inaccurate information may be dispensed with.

(b) To develop additional and better measures of such factors as are needed to give a fairly complete picture of each student as he differs from others. In this way he can be understood and advised wisely and accurately.

(c) To coordinate and translate these data so that they can be readily interpreted and widely used.[23]

Four years later Professor Lorin A. Thompson, Jr., of Ohio Wesleyan University, speaking before the National Association of Deans and Advisers of Men, similarly restricted personnel work to research. He said in part:

The personnel officer in any college, whether large or small, as I conceive it, should be a man who is technically trained in methods of research and methods of handling and dealing with all forms of collected data. His chief purpose should be that of studying the policies of the institution, collecting information and data, preparing reports and advising both faculty and administration concerning policies dealing with all phases of student life. In a very strict sense he should be an expert whose chief interest is in personnel research, rather than in the field of individual guidance.[24]

22. Yoakum, C. S. (Major, Sanitary Corps, U.S.A.). *School and Society,* Vol. IX, No. 228 (May 10, 1919), p. 559.

23. Taylor, Howard R. *School and Society,* Vol. XXVI, No. 673 (Nov. 19, 1927), p. 654.

24. Thompson, Lorin A., Jr., "Relationship of the Dean of Men to the Personnel Officer in the Small College." *Secretarial Notes for the 13th Annual Conf. of the Nat'l Assn. of Deans and Advisers of Men.* April, 1931, p. 39.

Without making a national canvass it is impossible to determine how many personnel people accept this limited notion of personnel work. Their numbers are very likely small, but that even a few define the personnel field in this narrow fashion is a fact to be reckoned with.

A third point of view restricts personnel work to counseling. Boucher, for example, devotes a chapter of his book *The Chicago College Plan*[25] to "Student Guidance and Personnel Work." In this chapter he discusses nothing but student counseling: Freshman Week counseling, educational counseling after Freshman Week, and vocational counseling. As this chapter stands the reader must conclude that Boucher confines guidance and personnel work (he does not indicate if and how these two terms are different) to counseling in the three areas which he has discussed.

Jones considers personnel work in much the same light. He writes that many colleges have organized personnel departments for the special purpose of assisting the individual student in his adjustment and in preventing failures. . . . Personnel directors arrange personal conferences with students who are in trouble of any kind, assist in improving study habits, and give very useful help of all kinds."[26] This is a broader statement than Boucher's, but it still confines personnel work to counseling. It is broader only in that Jones includes more types of counseling, i.e., "trouble of any kind" and "help of all kinds."

Several other narrow definitions might be cited, but the limitations of these three examples apply to all similar definitions. What, briefly, is wrong with statements of this sort? For some people it is sufficient to observe categorically that they are too restrictive. Others, however, will require demonstration that they actually are too restrictive.

The logical error involved in these narrow definitions is the fallacy of illicit simple conversion.[27] One cannot argue that because all Ohioans are Americans that all Americans are Ohioans. If anyone (taking the first of those three narrow statements) defines personnel work as placement; he implies that it is false to say that some personnel work is not placement. This affirmatively stated means that all personnel work is placement. Perhaps a few individuals will make such an affirmation, but certainly no more than a few. Most personnel people will shy away from using *personnel work* and *placement* synonymously.

One may reasonably say that some personnel work is placement since the

25. Boucher, Chauncey Samuel, Ph.D., *The Chicago College Plan*. Chicago: The Univ. of Chicago Press, 1935, p. 151.

26. Jones, Arthur J., *Principles of Guidance*. New York: McGraw-Hill Book Co., Inc., 1930, p. 270.

27. Eaton, *opus cit.*, p. 201.

converse of such a statement reads that placement is a part of personnel work. Similarly one may acceptably observe that research is a part of personnel work and that counseling is a part of personnel work. It is fallacious, however, to say either that research is personnel work or that counseling is personnel work. To make such statements involves confusing the part with the whole.

VI. "Guidance" and "Personnel Work" Not Synonymous Terms

Frequently the word *guidance* is used synonymously with the phrase *personnel work*. Strang writes, for example, in the opening pages of her book *The Role of the Teacher in Personnel Work*[28] that "in this book *guidance* and *personnel work* will be used interchangeably"; Doermann in his book, *The Orientation of College Freshmen*,[29] footnotes *personnel service* with the observation that he uses the term "as designating the guidance organization"; and McConn[30] typifies a large number of people who use such expressions as "the personnel or guidance movement" indicating that they consider guidance and personnel work to be the same thing.

Exactly what these authors mean by guidance it is difficult to discover. They seem not to be aware that the guidance people on the lower educational levels (who coined the word in its technical sense) are divided into three camps which define *guidance* dissimilarly. Brewer of Harvard and Kitson of Columbia, as the most vocal representatives of two of these groups, have been wrangling in the journals for several years. Koos and Kefauver represent the third position which stand somewhere between those of Kitson and Brewer. If college personnel people are to use the word, they ought properly to indicate in which sense they employ it. Their positions cannot otherwise be intelligently understood.

Consider first the Brewer definition. By guidance Brewer means a complete philosophy of education. He writes that "a true education . . . means guidance"[31] and that guidance is "the heart of education."[32] His "general statement of whole process of guidance" includes the following agencies or media:

28. Strang, *op. cit.*
29. Doermann, Henry J., *The Orientation of College Freshmen*. Baltimore: Williams & Wilkins Co., 1926, p. 113.
30. "Fifty-seven Varieties of Guidance." *Bulletin of the American Association of Collegiate Registrars*, Vol. 3, No. 4 (April, 1928), p. 359.
31. Brewer, John M., *Education is Guidance*. New York: The Macmillan Co., 1932, pp. 2–3.
32. *Ibid.*, p. 23.

1. An organized, rich life of normal, interesting, and important *activities*, making up the juvenile community.

2. *Classes* and study groups for the discussion of the problems involved in these activities, for such information and technical knowledge as may be needed to develop an appropriate skill in them, and for the wise motivation and integration of all the activities of life.

3. *Counseling* in these activities, with fostering and friendly supervision, to develop wisdom in specific activities and to develop skill in planning, balancing, and integrating them.[33]

Brewer takes the position that these guidance media "should gradually supplant most of the present subjects of instruction"[34] to the end that guidance be recognized as the "chief function of school and college."[35] Succinctly expressed Brewer proposes that education and guidance are exactly the same thing—or ideally should be.

Such a conception of guidance is sufficient demonstration that personnel work and guidance (as Brewer defines it) are not synonymous. Brewer has defined guidance in exactly the same way that Hopkins and Clothier have defined personnel work, but their statements have been proved too inclusive. It follows, therefore, that Brewer's interpretation is also too broad to make guidance an acceptable definition of personnel work. Brewer, incidentally, recognizes the difference between the two terms and never uses them synonymously.[36]

Kitson's interpretation of the scope of guidance is as narrow as Brewer's is broad. In taking Brewer to task for his all-inclusive use of the word he writes that "the term 'guidance' appears to be about to swallow up all education and all types of life activity."[37] He therefore "proposes that the term 'general guidance' be abandoned—that the word 'guidance' be reserved to designate only vocational guidance, its point of origin."[38]

It should be made clear that Kitson does not take the position that the activities which Brewer and others lump under the term *guidance* is such a catch-all that it should be abandoned except when associated with the word

33. *Op. cit.*, p. 111. Brewer includes a fourth factor in this general statement, but this is not reproduced here because it concerns the administration of guidance and is therefore not germane to this discussion of definitions.

34. *Op. cit.*, p. vii.

35. *Op. cit.*, p. 112.

36. *Op. cit.*, p. 23.

37. Kitson, Harry D., "Getting Rid of a Piece of Educational Rubbish.' *Teachers College Record*, Vol. xxxvi, No. 1 (October, 1934), p. 30.

38. *Ibid.*, p. 33.

vocational in the term *vocational guidance*. It is not within the scope of this article to discuss the merits of Kitson's proposal. All that is important here is to demonstrate that the term *guidance* (i.e., vocational guidance), as he uses it, has no utility as a definition of personnel work. Certainly few will agree that personnel work includes only vocational guidance. Thus the Kitson interpretation of the scope of guidance must be ruled out as a statement of the nature of personnel work. It falls clearly under the classification of too-restrictive definitions.

Koos and Kefauver accept neither the Brewer nor the Kitson idea of the nature of guidance. They suggest "a concept which is neither restricted to vocational guidance at one extreme nor extended to make guidance synonymous with all education at the other."[39] They criticize the Brewer position in these words:

Guidance is not the whole of education. The term should not even be regarded, as some seem to regard it, as a beneficient synonym for education. It represents one aspect only of the process of education, notwithstanding this is a momentous one. The scope of guidance cannot be understood to comprehend in any large measure the other processes of features of the school, such as teaching, supervision, curriculum-making, vocational training, or the extracurriculum. At the same time, as the illustrations given have indicated, there are vital points of contact that permit the guidance program to enhance the service of these features, or *vice versa*. The type of expansion of the concept that would include these other features of the school is sheer inflation.[40]

They criticize the Kitson position in these words:

Guidance in relation to vocation is only one portion of the whole program, although a most important one. The word "educational" is understood to comprehend preparation for vocation and to admit additional relationships, no less important than the vocational.[41]

Guidance according to these authors includes three general functions: "(1) informing students concerning educational and vocational opportunities, (2) securing information concerning the student, (3) guiding the individual student."[42] Functions one and two are designated as preparatory to function

39. *Op. cit.*, p. v.
40. Koos, Leonard V., and Kefauver, Grayson N., *Guidance in Secondary Schools*. New York: Macmillan, 1932, p. 19.
41. *Ibid.*, p. 15.
42. *Ibid.*, p. v.

three,[43] under which fourteen counseling problems are listed. All of these are educational and vocational, and thus one may conclude that by guidance Koos and Kefauver mean educational[44] and vocational guidance. These are of course important personnel functions, but few personnel workers have restricted the personnel field to these two activities. The Koos and Kefauver concept of guidance is therefore no more acceptable as a definition of personnel work than those of Brewer and Kitson.

It would be interesting, if space were available, to review the positions of Myers, Proctor, and several other guidance authorities. All are related, in the broad, to one of the three guidance definitions discussed. It can be concluded, therefore, that no definition which has as yet been stated makes guidance and personnel work synonymous.

VII. A Definition Implicit in the Literature and in Recent Practise

Up to this point in the discussion the writer has sought to do four things: (1) to indicate the confusion in the personnel field, (2) to suggest that the disorder will continue until a common understanding has been reached through a generally acceptable definition, (3) to demonstrate the most current definitions are either too inclusive or too restrictive, and (4) to point out that guidance and personnel work are not the same. The remaining pages are devoted to an attempt to develop what seems to the writer to be a more adequate definition of the personnel field. This definition, it will be indicated, is implied in the writings of a number of personnel people. It is also implicit in the organizational plans which have recently been adopted by several universities.

At the outset one must recognize the justice of Esther Lloyd-Jones' criticism[45] of the synonymous use of such terms as *personnel work, personnel services,* and *personnel administration.* She points out, and correctly, that although many individuals employ these terms interchangeably they do not mean the same thing. Before attempting to distinguish between them, however, it should be observed that they have something to do with the relationships between colleges and students. If the nature of these relation-

43. *Ibid.*, p. 403.

44. In the early pages of their book Koos and Kefauver include recreational, health, and civic-social-moral guidance; but they pay little attention to them from that point on. It seems fair to say, therefore, that *guidance* to these writers means educational and vocational guidance.

45. Lloyd-Jones, Esther, "Personnel Administration." *The Journal of Higher Education,* Vol. V (March, 1934), p. 142.

ships can be determined, then the nature of personnel work can, perhaps, also be determined.

In general three different kinds of college-student relationships are recognizable: those that have to do with business arrangements, those that have to do with instruction, and those that have to do with extra-instructional activities. Under business relationships come the payment of fees, the renting of equipment and apparatus, the purchase of supplies, and a large number of other routine operations that have to do with *matèriel*. Under instructional relationships come all varieties of contacts having to do with the formal courses of the curriculum whether these be with individual students or with groups, library and laboratory work, and the determination by examination of the results of instruction.

Under extra-instructional relationship come a range of activities including among other admissions, student orientation to college life and work, housing, health, the securing of part-time employment and financial aid, social and extra-curricular programs, and many types of counseling upon such diverse problems as the course to be taken during a particular term, the way to develop one's social intelligence, and what to do about homesickness or lovesickness.

In the nineteenth century college faculty members engaged in all three of these types of relationships with students, but in recent years the increased size of colleges and universities and the development of more comprehensive and complex programs have made a functional division of responsibilities inevitable. Especially since the Cooke study[46] of business practices in 1910 faculty members have relinquished to business offices practically all business relationships with students. Similarly faculty members have more and more tended to give all their energies to instruction and research rather than to extra-instructional relationships with students. This has been true because in most institutions promotions and increases in salary have come to be determined chiefly by scholarly production.

To assume responsibility, therefore, for extra-instructional relationships with students a new group of officers have within the past few decades been appointed upon practically every campus in the country. These individuals have been, and are, called by all sorts of names, but in recent years they have come generally to be known as student personnel workers. The term is a genetic designation for all individuals whose relationships with students are neither routine business relationships nor instructional relationships.

With these three distinct types of institutional-student relationships in

46. Cooke, Morris Llewellyn, *Academic and Industrial Efficiency*. A Report to the Carnegie Foundation for the Advancement of Teaching. Bulletin No. 5. New York: 1910.

mind it is possible to discuss the nature of student personnel work. Obviously personnel work is what personnel workers do, the activities for which they assume responsibility. These activities, as indicated, are distinct from business and instructional activities. An acceptable definition of personnel work must, therefore, state its separateness from business and instructional activities.

Business activities must be ruled out because business relationships with students are, and must be, essentially impersonal. The fact that a college or a university is an educational and only incidentally a business organization should dominate the thinking of every member of the business staff, but business managers and their assistants have their necessary and specialized work to do which cannot include giving attention to the personal development of individual students.

At several points the business and personnel divisions meet. Both organizations are interested in housing, food services, loans, scholarships, and in one or two other activities. The business staff is concerned, however, only with the financial aspects of these undertakings. The personnel staff assumes—or should assume—responsibility for their direction as educational enterprises, keeping of course within the frame-work made necessary by financial considerations. Business departments exist to facilitate the educational work of the institution, but they are not educational units. They serve best by concentrating upon the purposes for which they have been established.

Instructional activities must also be ruled out because faculty people everywhere recognize a distinction between their teaching and their extra-instructional relationships with students. At few institutions have faculty members relinquished all out-of-class responsibilities to personnel officers, but the tendency everywhere is to assign extra-instructional activities to members of the staff who teach part time or do not teach at all. This tendency has been strengthened by the growing conviction that not all professors are temperamentally equipped to deal with students outside the curriculum.

The tendency has further been strengthened by the development of techniques which require special training or unusual aptitude and experience. No matter how much a faculty member may be interested in his students as individuals he is only occasionally prepared to develop, administer, and interpret intelligence tests, personality inventories, and other instruments which have become essential to effective counseling. Moreover, few professors are willing to add to their teaching and research loads such duties as the administration of dormitories, loans and scholarships, placement, discipline, social programs, extra-curricular activities, and other divisions of student life. More often than not it is even difficult to secure the service of professors on policymaking committees for these activities; and, by and large, most faculty members have been willing to see their administration assigned to personnel workers.

If this analysis of the separateness of business, instructional, and personnel activities is correct, what then is the nature of personnel work? The writer proposes the following definition:

Personnel work constitutes all activities undertaken or sponsored by an educational institution, aside from curricular instruction, in which the student's personal development is the primary consideration.

This definition distinguishes personnel from routine business activities by the phrase "in which the student's personal development is the primary consideration." It also distinguishes personnel from instructional activities by the phrase "aside from curricular instruction."

Is this an acceptable definition of personnel work? That remains to be seen. The writer presents it for the critical appraisal of those who may be interested. It can be pointed out, however, that the definition is clearly implied in the discussions of several other, if not most, personnel writers.

In the first place consider the Koos and Kefauver discussion of guidance. As indicated they use the term *guidance* to designate the counseling function of personnel work which they separate clearly from instruction. Explicitly they write, for example, that "*teaching cannot often be guidance and guidance does not comprehend methods of teaching.*"[47] They also rule out both the supervision of instruction and curriculum problems from the field of guidance. They write that the "*supervision of instruction is concerned with the improvement of teaching and is not guidance.*"[48] In other words instruction and counseling are distinct functions which is much the same as saying that instruction and personnel work are distinct.

Turning to higher education as examination of the itemizations[48] of Jones,[49] Lloyd-Jones,[50] Townsend,[51] Strang,[52] to name but four writers upon personnel problems in colleges and universities, will demonstrate that all of these authors exclude all business and instructional relationships from their

47. *Op. cit.*, p. 18. Italics theirs.

48. Because of spatial limitations these cannot be reproduced. The reader is referred directly to the cited statements of the writers.

49. Jones, Lonzo, *A Project in Student Personnel Service Designed to Facilitate Each Student's Achievement at the Level of His Ability.* Pub. by Univ. of Iowa, Vol. V, No. 1, of Iowa Studies, November 1, 1928.

50. *Op. cit.*, p. 141.

51. Townsend, M. E., *"Administrative Phases of a Student Personnel Program."* Educ. Adm. & Supervision (December, 1935), pp. 641–56.

52. Strang, Ruth, *Personal Development and Guidance in College and Secondary School.* New York: Harper & Brothers, 1934.

list of personnel functions. No one of them, in the opinion of the writer, submits a full compilation; but completeness is not now important. What *is* important is their implicit recognition that personnel work and business and instructional activities are different. The definitions of these writers do not make the clear-cut distinctions proposed in this article, but their lists of personnel activities manifestly do.

It is interesting to compare the functions enumerated by Jones, Lloyd-Jones, Townsend, Strang, and still others with those of Hopkins and Clothier. In 1926 Hopkins[53] proposed twenty personnel functions. Six of these had to do with instruction: placement tests, curriculum, selection of instructors, methods of instruction, objective tests, and research concerning teaching. Five years later Clothier,[54] in making his tabulation, dropped five of these six keeping only the selection of instructors as a personnel function. Clothier's other fourteen items are all clearly personnel activities having no direct relationship to instruction.

Clothier must have checked over the Hopkins table of activities since he referred to his monograph in his article and since the table is its very core. One may assume, then, that he purposely eliminated these five items. And why? Because, it is submitted, he had become aware of the growing opinion that personnel work and instruction are separate. He did not, however, go the whole way, still considering the selection of instructors a personnel activity.

But is it a personnel activity? In a few institutions personnel officers have something to say about the choice and promotion of members of the faculty, but at no institution of which the writer knows have they any real administrative voice in the matter. The selection of faculty members properly belongs in the hands of instructional administrators. Neither by definition nor practice does it belong in the bailiwick of personnel administrators. Personnel people can be influential at this point only by developing attitudes among deans and department heads which are favorable to the choice of instructors who, to quote Clothier, take "a sincere and intelligent interest in the individual student." More will be said on this point in connection with the discussion of the personnel point of view.

VIII. Supplementary Definitions

Before discussing the personnel point of view, however, three other terms should be discussed—*personnel services, personnel research,* and *personnel*

---

53. *Op. cit.*, p. 7.
54. *Op. cit.*, pp. 14–15.

administration. Two of these may be disposed of promptly. It is proposed that the term *personnel services* is exactly synonymous with the term *personnel work.* It is proposed that *personnel research* is a type of personnel work, i.e., investigation of problems arising in personnel work. By this definition much of the research being done in personnel bureaus is not personnel research at all. It is really instructional research which personnel people have undertaken because no other agency exists to do it. The sooner instructional administrators see the need of initiating and directing their own research programs the better for higher education. Properly every institution should be continuously and thoroughly studying its curriculums and methods of instruction using the best research techniques available. Such research, however, is not personnel research even though it is erroneously so designated in a number of places.

The third term, *personnel administration,* requires discussion although it may be briefly defined. The word *administration* has different meanings in government, business, and education. In education it means the supervision or direction of an activity or group of activities. Personnel administration may therefore be defined as the supervision or direction of personnel work.

Lloyd-Jones has suggested that "student-personnel administration is one of the three main divisions of educational administration:[55]—the other two being instructional and business administration. The writer has elsewhere[56] made a similar observation. In very few institutions, however, has the importance of personnel administration yet been recognized. Business and instructional divisions have been distinct entities for many decades, but the personnel division in most institutions has not yet achieved a comparable status. Many personnel units have been established on innumerable campuses, but usually they operate independently and without coordination. Personnel work will not attain its potential stature until all agencies which work in the personnel field are correlated and placed under the direction of a major administrative officer.

The present plan of decentralized functioning should be supplemented by centralized policy making and general supervision. Steps in this direction have already been taken at several institutions: Chicago, Duke, Oregon, and Northwestern. At all of these institutions all extra-instructional relationships with students are coordinated under the direction of a major administrative officer. At Chicago he has the title of Dean of Students, at Duke, Vice-

---

55. *Op. cit.,* p. 142.

56. *The Personnel Bibliographic Index.* Columbus, Ohio: The Ohio State University, 1932, p. 3. Four instead of three administrative divisions are here listed, the additional one being the administration of research. To this a fifth should perhaps be added, the administration of public services and public relationships. Neither of these two divisions, however, is concerned directly with student affairs.

president in Charge of Student Welfare, at Oregon, Dean of Personnel Administration, and at Northwestern, Personnel Director. The responsibility of these officers is to see that all functional personnel people work together harmoniously and that extra-instructional relationships with students are developed. It is also their responsibility to coordinate the work of the entire personnel staff of their institutions with the instructional work under the direction of academic deans and heads of departments. Each is the officer to whom the president turns in student personnel matters. Because of the success of this method of organization, it is likely to become more common within the next few years.

Much more than this needs to be said about personnel administration; but since the space is not now available, the discussion may proceed to the definition of a fifth term, i.e., the *personnel point of view*. Many writers use this term, but either they use it as the equivalent of one of the other expressions or their meanings are vague. The writer proposes the following as a desirable definition:

The personnel point of view is a philosophy of education which puts emphasis upon the individual student and his all-round development as a person rather than upon his intellectual training alone and which promotes the establishment in educational institutions of curricular programs, methods of instruction, and extra-instructional media to achieve such emphasis.

This definition has two parts, and each should be examined separately. The first part has to do with *a kind of emphasis*, the second with the media through which the emphasis is expressed. An understanding of the difference between these parts is essential.

The emphasis "upon the individual student and his all-round development as a person rather than upon his intellectual training alone" is not, it should be made clear, the private concern of personnel workers. As a matter of fact personnel people are merely subscribing to the point of view of a long line of philosophers dating at least from Socrates and leading to John Dewey and his adherents. The personnel movement will improve its progress and its status by recognizing that its roots are deeply imbedded in the thinking of some of the world's major social philosophers. The psychology of individual differences from which many personnel activities have directly grown is but a verification by science of an age-old philosophical insight.

Turning to the second part of the definition, it must be similarly emphasized that promoting the establishment of media to achieve the student's all-round development is again not the peculiar responsibility or objective of personnel workers. Many other individuals and groups are striving toward this same end, and personnel people are but co-workers with them. Unfortunately no organization has as yet been established in higher education which undertakes to accomplish objectives similar to those of the Progressive Education Association and other groups in elementary and secondary education. Every year, however, more administrators and faculty members are stressing the need for a more intelligent interest in individual students. The programs at Harvard, Princeton, Swarthmore, Bennington, and several other institutions are monuments to their insight and enterprise. Personnel people, in general, have had little if any part in developing them.

In many colleges and universities, however, personnel workers are the chief proponents of the concept of all-round development. Most faculty members are so completely engrossed in their own subjects that they perceive only a single facet of the student's mind and personality. In such institutions personnel people must carry the torch. By education and persuasion they must seek to stimulate faculties to modernize and humanize their curriculum, their methods of instruction, and their attitudes toward personnel work. At all times, however, they must remember that the philosophy which they call the personnel point of view is a common heritage of several groups of progressive educators who know it by many other names. Personnel workers prejudice and sometimes defeat their purposes when they give the impression, as they too frequently do, that they want to run the entire educational show.

Is this proposed definition of the personnel point of view[57] implied in the literature? The answer seems to the writer to be in the affirmative. Only one reference needs to be cited in support of this opinion. If the reader will substitute the words *the personnel point of view* for the words *personnel work* quoted from Clothier on page 7 of this article, he will have a definition of the personnel point of view which concurs with that which the writer has submitted above. The labeling of this statement as a definition of personnel work is not consistent with Clothier's enumeration of personnel functions, but it makes a most acceptable definition of the personnel point of view.

IX. This an Incomplete Discussion

A short review of the personnel field, such as this, must necessarily leave much ground untouched. A great deal more, for example, should be said about personnel administration; and several pages should properly be devoted to a discussion of the relationships of academic deans, department heads,

---

57. A number of principles stem from the personnel point of view which the writer hopes to discuss at another time.

and ordinary faculty members both to personnel administration and the personnel point of view. A complete list of personnel services should also be developed. These and other developments of the proposed definitions must be left to another time.

Two considerations, however, need brief attention to avoid misunderstanding. In the first place the distinctions proposed between business, instructional, and personnel administration do not mean that the student needs to be compartmentalized. A division of labor is both unavoidable and desirable, but at every institution some one individual must seek to know the whole student. Properly that individual should be his educational counselor, who is often a faculty member serving part time as a personnel officer. To him should come data from all sources so that he may counsel the student intelligently. In a later article on personnel coordination the writer hopes to develop this idea. Enough now to indicate its importance.

In the second place, the proposed separateness of instructional and personnel activities does not mean that personnel work should be undertaken only by a special staff of personnel workers completely distinct from the instructional staff. A number of technical services such as the management of health programs and the making of thorough personality analyses of students must be done by experts, but faculty members almost universally participate in practically every variety of personnel work. This arrangement is inevitable and desirable; but when members of the instructional staff are doing personnel work, they are working (or should be working) under the direction of a personnel administrator and not under their department heads or academic deans. Institutional morale as well as economy require that many faculty members act both as instructors and personnel workers, but this necessary dual service should not confuse the difference between personnel work and formal instruction. These interrelationships the writer hopes to discuss at greater length in the article he plans on the coordination of personnel activities.

X. The Need of Agreement

In conclusion the writer should like to observe that the point of view presented in this article seems to him to be but a summarization of the thinking of a number of individuals. Personnel people in rather widely separated areas are recognizing the natural affinity of their work. In 1934 seven personal organizations[58] came together to organize the American Council of Guidance and Personnel Associations. Kitson reported the organization meeting, in part, as follows:

At the Cleveland meeting (February, 1934), the centripetal force of our idea became so strong that we exclaimed: "Why, we are kinfolk!" And at an enthusiastic luncheon we instructed our several presidents to appoint delegates who should meet and organize a national association through which we might jointly work for the realization of our ideals.[59]

A conviction of kinship among personnel people is undoubtedly developing with some rapidity. It is particularly obvious among personnel workers in colleges and universities. The time is perhaps ripe, therefore, for representatives of all college personnel groups to come together for a definitive discussion of the nature of their common task. Nationally and on every campus personnel officers should be working together in a coordinated effort to spread the personnel point of view and to develop programs commensurate with the extra-instructional needs of college students. Such coordination requires an understanding of the unity of their several fields of activity under the basic team *personnel work.* Until a generally acceptable definition is achieved, coordination will very likely not be realized. More than that, faculty members and administrative officers will continue to be perplexed and therefore uncooperative.

58. American College Personnel Association, National Vocational Guidance Association, National Association of Deans of Women, Collegiate Bureaus of Occupations, Personnel Research Federation, Institute of Women's Professional Relations, and Southern Woman's Educational Alliance.
59. Kitson, Harry D., "Our Common Cause." *Occupations,* Vol. 13, No. 8 (May, 1935), p. 709.

The Student Personnel Point of View

American Council on Education

Foreword

In January 1925 the Division of Anthropology of the National Research Council sponsored a meeting in Washington, D.C., of representatives of fourteen institutions of higher education to discuss the problems of vocational guidance in college. Out of this conference developed the Intercollegiate Council of Personnel Methods which undertook to investigate ways and means of making available to educational institutions knowledge concerning students as individuals. In 1926 this group requested the American Council on Education to sponsor a study of personnel practices in colleges and universities. As a result of this request the Council established the Committee on Personnel Methods with H. E. Hawkes as chairman.

The initial undertaking of the Committee on Personnel Methods was a survey by L. B. Hopkins to determine what a number of institutions were then doing to assist the students to develop as individuals. The publication of the Hopkins report in *The Educational Record* of October 1926 focused national attention upon the importance of this area and upon the need for further research. During the next several years, the Committee on Personnel Methods, working through a number of subcommittees, inaugurated studies on certain aspects of the total student personnel problem. As a result of these studies, certain tools were prepared including the cumulative record cards, personality rating scales, and comparable achievement tests, which have influenced the improvement of student personnel services.

The American Council on Education in 1936 received the report of the Committee on Review of the Testing Movement[1] which recommended the establishment of a Committee on Measurement and Guidance to coordinate activities of the Council in the preparation of measurement materials. As a

---

1. *The Testing Movement*, American Council on Education Studies, Series I, Vol. I, No. 1, (February 1937).

result of this recommendation, the Council discharged the Committee on Personnel Methods and assigned its measurement functions to the new committee. The Council, however, recognized the need for further investigation of certain fundamental problems related to the clarification of so-called personnel work, the intelligent use of available tools, and the development of additional techniques and processes. Consequently, the Executive Committee authorized the calling of a conference to discuss the possible contribution of the Council in this area.

The following individuals met in Washington, D.C., on April 16 and 17, 1937, and unanimously adopted the following report. The group voted to refer the report to the Committee on Problems and Plans in Education of the American Council on Education.

Thyrsa Amos	D. H. Gardner
F. F. Bradshaw	H. E. Hawkes
D. S. Bridgman	L. B. Hopkins
A. J. Brumbaugh	F. J. Kelley
W. H. Cowley	Edwin A. Lee
A. B. Crawford	Esther Lloyd-Jones
Edward C. Elliott	D. G. Paterson
Burton P. Fowler	C. Gilbert Wrenn

C. S. Marsh
D. J. Shank
G. F. Zook

The Committee on Problems and Plans in Education at its meeting on May 6, 1937, approved the report of the conference and recommended to the Executive Committee of the Council that a Committee on Student Personnel Work be established with instructions to propose a program of action in line with the general statement of the conference. The Executive Committee authorized the organization of the new committee at its last meeting.

George F. Zook
President

June 1937

Philosophy

One of the basic purposes of higher education is the preservation, transmission, and enrichment of the important elements of culture—the product of scholarship, research, creative imagination, and human experience. It is the task of colleges and universities so to vitalize this and other educational purposes as to assist the student in developing to the limits of his potentialities and in making his contribution to the betterment of society.

This philosophy imposes upon educational institutions the obligation to consider the student as a whole—his intellectual capacity and achievement his emotional make-up, his physical condition, his social relationships, his vocational aptitudes and skills, his moral and religious values, his economic resources, his aesthetic appreciations. It puts emphasis, in brief, upon the development of the student as a person rather than upon his intellectual training alone.

A long and honorable history stands behind this point of view. Until the last three decades of the nineteenth century interest in the whole student dominated the thinking of the great majority of the leaders and faculty members of American colleges. The impact of a number of social forces upon American society following the Civil War, however, directed the interest of most of the strong personalities of our colleges and universities away from the needs of the individual student to an emphasis, through scientific research, upon the extension of the boundaries of knowledge. The pressures upon faculty members to contribute to this growth of knowledge shifted the direction of their thinking to a preoccupation with subject matter and to a neglect of the student as an individual. As a result of this change of emphasis, administrations recognized the need of appointing a new type of educational officer to take over the more intimate responsibilities which faculty members had originally included among their duties. At the same time a number of new educational functions arose as the result of the growing complexity of modern life, the development of scientific techniques, the expansion of the size of student bodies, and the extension of the range of educational objectives.

These officers were appointed first to relieve administrators and faculties of problems of discipline; but their responsibilities grew with considerable rapidity to include a large number of other duties: educational counseling, vocational counseling, the administration of loans and scholarship funds, part-time employment, graduate placement, student health, extra-curricular activities, social programs, and a number of others. The officers undertaking responsibility for these educational functions are known by many names, but during the past two decades they have come, as a group, to be called personnel officers.

A number of terms are in general use in colleges and universities related to the philosophy of education which we have outlined. Illustrative of these terms are "guidance," "counseling," "advisory," and "personnel." Of these, we believe the term "personnel"—prefaced by "student"—to be the least objectionable. Rather than attempt a specific definition of "student personnel" as it is combined with such nouns as "work," "service," "administration," "research," etc., we offer the term, "the student personnel point of view" as indicative of the total philosophy embodied in the foregoing discussion. The functions which implement this point of view—indicated in the next section—may be designated as "student personnel services." Similarly, the performance of these functions may be designated "student personnel work."

This background and discussion of terminology we believe to be important. Personnel work is not new. Personnel officers have been appointed throughout the colleges and universities of the country to undertake a number of educational responsibilities which were once entirely assumed by teaching members of faculty. They have also, because of the expansion of educational functions, developed a number of student personnel services which have but recently been stressed. The philosophy behind their work, however, is as old as education itself.

I. Student Personnel Services

This philosophy implies that in addition to instruction and business management adapted to the needs of the individual student, an effective educational program includes—in one form or another—the following services adapted to the specific aims and objectives of each college and university:

1. Interpreting institutional objectives and opportunities to prospective students and their parents and to workers in secondary education.

2. Selecting and admitting students, in cooperation with secondary schools.

3. Orienting the student to his educational environment.

4. Providing a diagnostic service to help the student discover his abilities, aptitudes, and objectives.

5. Assisting the student throughout his college residence to determine upon his course of instruction in light of his past achievements, vocational and personal interests, and diagnostic findings.

6. Enlisting the active cooperation of the family of the student in the interest of his educational accomplishment.

7. Assisting the student to reach his maximum effectiveness through clarification of his purposes, improvement of study methods, speech habits, personal appearance, manners, etc., and through progression in religious,

emotional, social development, and other non-academic personal and group relationships.

8. Assisting the student to clarify his occupational aims and his educational plans in relation to them.

9. Determining the physical and mental health status of the student, providing appropriate remedial health measures, supervising the health of students, and controlling environmental health factors.

10. Providing and supervising and adequate housing program for students.

11. Providing and supervision an adequate food service for students.

12. Supervising, evaluating, and developing the extra-curricular activities of students.

13. Supervising, evaluating, and developing the social life and interests of students.

14. Supervising, evaluating, and developing the religious life and interests of students.

15. Assembling and making available information to be used in improvement of instruction and in making the curriculum more flexible.

16. Coordinating the financial aid and part-time employment of students, and assisting the student who needs it to obtain such help.

17. Keeping a cumulative record of information about the student and making it available to the proper persons.

18. Administering student discipline to the end that the individual will be strengthened, and the welfare of the group preserved.

19. Maintaining student group morale by evaluating, understanding, and developing student mores.

20. Assisting the student to find appropriate employment when he leaves the institution.

21. Articulating college and vocational experience.

22. Keeping the student continuously and adequately informed of the educational opportunities and services available to him.

23. Carrying on studies designed to evaluate and improve these functions and services.

Coordination

The effective organization and functioning of student personnel work requires that the educational administrators at all times (1) regard student personnel work as a major concern, involving the cooperative effort of all members of the teaching and administrative staff and the student body; and (2) interpret student personnel work as dealing with the individual student's total characteristics and experiences rather than with separate and distinct aspects of his personality or performance.

It should be noted that effective personnel work may be formally organized or may exist without direction or organization, and that frequently the informal type evidences a personnel point of view in an institution. In either case the personnel point of view is most likely to permeate an entire staff when it is the result of an indigenous development in the institution. Imposition of personnel theories and practices from above or from outside is likely to result in pseudo-personnel work, with probable antagonism developing therefrom. However, it is obvious that coordination of student personnel work is urgently needed. We suggest several varieties of such needed coordination.

I. Coordination within Individual Institutions

The student personnel functions set forth earlier in this report should be coordinated within each educational institution. Existing conditions emphasize the need for such coordination. All personnel workers within an institution should cooperate with one another in order to avoid duplications of effort and in order to develop student personnel work evenly. The plan of coordination and its administration will, of course, vary with institutions of different types.

II. Coordination between Instruction and Student Personnel Work

Instruction is most effective when the instructor regards his classes both as separate individuals and as members of a group. Such instruction aims to achieve in every student a maximum performance in terms of that student's potentialities and the conditions under which he works. Ideally each instructor should possess all the information necessary for such individualization. Actually such ideal conditions do not exist. Therefore a program of coordination becomes necessary which provides for the instructor appropriate information whenever such information relates to the effective instruction.

An instructor may perform functions in the realms both of instruction and student personnel work. Furthermore, instruction itself involves far more than the giving of information on the part of the teacher and its acceptance by the student. Instructors should be encouraged to contribute regularly to student personnel records such anecdotal information concerning students as is significant from the personnel point of view. Instructors should be encouraged to call to the attention of personnel workers any students in their courses who could profit by personnel services.

Certain problems involving research are common to instruction and student personnel work. Any investigation which has for its purpose the improvement of instruction is at the same time a research which improves personnel procedures. Similarly, the results of any studies, the aim of which is to improve personnel procedures, should be disseminated throughout the instructional staff. In both cases wherever possible such projects should be carried on as cooperative ventures.

III. Coordination between the Business Administration and Student Personnel Work

In all financial or business matters having to do with student activities or student problems, either in terms of individuals or groups of individuals, coordination and correlation must exist between business administration and student personnel work. Examples of such matters are:

Student loans
Dormitories
Dining halls
Scholarships
Student organizations
Athletic management
Deferred payments of fees
Student participation in business management of institution.

IV. Coordination of Personnel Work between Institutions of Secondary and Higher Education

There is a pressing need for further coordination between secondary schools and institutions of higher education. Since a special need exists for coordination between student personnel work in colleges and in secondary schools, copies of the data sent to the admissions department should be available to other college personnel officers. This would be a desirable place to begin coordination. The selection of students, where conditions will permit, should be based upon total personnel records as well as grades in courses. Examples of items in such a record are:

Ability in critical thinking
Ability to cooperate

Physical and mental health

Aesthetic appreciation

Test records such as aptitude tests, reading ability, etc.

Vocational objective

Summarized predictions of college performance.

Coordination should also result in more effective interchange of information, problems, and techniques between the personnel units of colleges and secondary schools. Competent individuals should be available whenever secondary schools desire a presentation, either to students or faculty, of college opportunities and requirements.

Problems of research which require coordination between secondary schools and colleges reside in such areas as:

a. Transfer from high school to college with particular reference to the last year in high school and the first year in college.

b. The basis upon which high schools guide toward college.

c. The basis upon which colleges select entrants.

d. Freshman failures.

e. Variations in the total requirements of different types of colleges; for example, engineering, dentistry, liberal arts, teacher training, etc.

f. Existing types of coordination between secondary schools and colleges; for example, high school visitors, examination systems, coordinating committees, experimental investigations, etc.

V. Coordination among National Personnel Associations

During the past two decades a number of associations of various types of student personnel workers have come into existence. These associations perform valuable services in furthering personnel work and in bringing workers in the field into closer professional and personnel contact. We believe that the point of view for which all personnel people stand and the services which they render would be greatly enhanced were closer coordination developed between these associations. Hereinafter we propose that the American Council on Education establish or sponsor a committee on student personnel work in colleges and universities. We recommend that this committee, as one of its functions, undertake to bring about closer relationships between these associations.

VI. Coordination of Student Personnel Work with After-College Adjustment

Effective student personnel work should include as its culminating activity adequate provision for induction of students into after-college life.

The satisfactory adjustment of graduates to occupation life constitutes one important basis for evaluation of an institution's educational effectiveness, since it stimulates a continual re-examination of educational procedures and the effect of those procedures upon the men and women who make up the student body of the college. Moreover, coordination between college and occupational life rests essentially upon more complete information covering the various types of work into which college graduates go.

This conference also wishes to emphasize the necessity for conceiving of after-college adjustment as comprehending the total living of college graduates, including not only their occupational success but their active concern with the social, recreational, and cultural interests of the community. Such concern implies their willingness to assume those individual and social responsibilities which are essential to the common good.

Future Development

Student personnel work is developing with some rapidity throughout the country. Annually a large number of institutions undertake for the first time additional student personnel functions or they further develop services already established. At the same time new methods of organizing student personnel services are coming into prominence; the literature of the field is expanding voluminously; and problems in need of careful investigation become more numerous every year.

Because of these and other considerations a need for national leadership in student personnel work is becoming continuously more obvious. If the expansion and development that the colleges and universities of the country are experiencing in the student personnel field is to be as desirable and effective as it should be, some national agency needs to be available to assist administrators, faculty members, and student personnel officers in their developmental efforts. No such national agency now exists, and a careful canvassing of the student personnel associations which have grown up brings us to the unanimous conclusion that no one of them is able to become that national agency.

We, therefore, propose that the American Council on Education establish or sponsor a committee on student personnel work in American colleges and universities. This committee should, in our judgment, undertake the following activities:

I. National Survey of Student Personnel Work

This survey should be conducted throughout the country after the pattern of the one undertaken by L. B. Hopkins for the American Council on

Education in 1926. Such a study would require the services of but one individual who would visit five or six institutions in each of half a dozen institutional categories. The undertaking would result in an overview rather than a detailed study, and its publication would satisfy the growing demand for current authoritative information about the student personnel field. It would be built around a check list of the functions we have listed. The Hopkins survey had such great influence that we believe an up-to-date and analogous study published in concise form would be of immediate interest and value to administrators and faculty members throughout the country.

II. Interpretation of the Problems of College Students

A short volume with some such title as "The College Student and His Problems" should be written and published. The purpose of this volume would be to inform administrators, faculty members, and the general public of the complex human problems that are involved in education. Stressing scholarship and intellectual development, educators frequently take for granted or actually overlook the philosophy which we have hereinbefore called the student personnel point of view. The preparation and publication of the volume which we propose would, we believe, do much to bring this philosophy to the attention of all individuals concerned with higher education. It would, moreover, bring this philosophy to their attention in terms of the actual experiences of students rather than through an abstract discussion.

III. Handbooks on Student Personnel Functions

A series of handbooks on particular student personnel functions should be written and published. The survey proposed above would provide a panoramic picture of the entire field. The handbooks that we are suggesting would furnish detailed information about specific personnel functions. Data for these handbooks would come from two general sources: first, from the information gathered by the surveyor on the detailed operation of specific personnel functions in the institutions he visits and, second, from the literature. Each handbook would stress the best practices developed in the handling of each function. The work of writing each handbook should be under the direction of a committee of three. This committee should include an active worker in the special field under discussion and a representative of the appropriate national personnel organization.

IV. Research

Obviously, student personnel services will never develop as they should unless extensive and careful research is undertaken. We, therefore, urge that the facilitation and direction of research be considered an essential responsibility of the committee. In this field we envisage the committee as important in two directions: first, in encouraging other agencies to undertake investigations, and, second, in carrying on several investigations on its own. We list below projects of both types.

Research by Other Agencies

We propose that the Committee on Measurement and Guidance of the American Council on Education be requested to consider the desirability of the following four investigations:

1. *Aptitude testing.* The investigation of aptitudes on a national scale comparable to the work undertaken by the Cooperative Test Service but in the field of differential vocational as well as educational aptitudes.

2. *Social development.* The development of instruments for measuring social adjustment and social maturity.

3. *Diagnostic techniques.* The study of the field of usefulness of existing diagnostic instruments and the development of new instruments.

4. *Scholastic aptitude test scale.* Bringing together on a comparable scale the norms of various widely used scholastic aptitude tests.

We also propose that the National Occupational Conference be requested to consider the desirability of carrying forward the following work:

1. *Occupational information.* Gathering and publishing occupational information for college students with particular emphasis upon periodic census data and trends.

2. *Traits needed in occupations.* Working with the Committee on Measurement and Guidance in the study of human traits significant for various occupations, particularly those which college students enter.

Research by the Committee on Student Personnel Work

A number of research projects need to be undertaken in the immediate future, responsibility for which no existing agencies seem able to assume. We, therefore, propose that the committee secure support for the following four studies:

1. *Student out-of-class life.* College students spend the majority of their time outside the classrooms and laboratories. We have, however, no significant data as to the activities in which they engage. In order to understand the educational importance of their activities we propose that on a score of campuses throughout the country data be collected. Incidentally, this research would be relatively inexpensive since on every campus individuals may be found to do the work without compensation.

2. *Faculty-student out-of-class relationships.* Much is said frequently of the place that faculty members have in student personnel work. We have, however, few facts and we propose that data should be gathered from a number of institutions following much the same technique as proposed in study "I" above.

3. *Financial aid to students.* Large sums of money are available in many institutions for scholarships and loans. In addition the National Youth Administration has been spending many millions during the past three years to help students to stay in college. The problem of who should be helped and how much is growing more important every year. We propose that this problem in its wide ramifications might well be studied. Perhaps funds for much of this work could be secured from the National Youth Administration.

4. *Follow-up study of college students.* Every year over a hundred thousand students graduate from our colleges. What happens to them and what effect their college work has had upon their vocational and personal adjustments we can only guess. We, therefore, propose that the committee develop a method for making follow-up studies and that this method be made available to interested institutions.

V. Advisory Service to Colleges and Universities

An advisory service to colleges and universities interested in the improvement of student personnel work should be developed. While the proposed survey is being undertaken and while the suggested handbooks are being written, the committee will inevitably have addressed to it a number of inquires about problems within its field of interest. These inquiries cannot be answered authoritatively until these two ventures are finished, but meanwhile the committee should assume responsibility for directing such correspondents to the individuals best qualified to assist them. When the survey is finished, and the handbooks available, however, we propose that the committee actively promote the best student personnel practices which its work has brought to light.

II

Reaffirmation After World War II

Educators turned their attention to their professional roles in the late forties as hostilities ceased and educational institutions were called upon to help the armed forces veterans return to civilian life. At the same time, the traditional aged high school graduates were seeking college admission in greater numbers than ever before.

From this changed setting, attention was again given to the need to identify the parameters of the student personnel field. One of the first authors to continue the examination of the field was E. H. Hopkins in his article, "The Essentials of a Student Personnel Program." Hopkins, one of the early Vice Presidents for Student Affairs, included the list of services to be provided as well as basic and fundamental assumptions. He acknowledged the importance of the American Council on Education pamphlet published in 1937. His greatest concerns in this new post World War II era were getting more faculty participation in implementing the student personnel point of view, and secondly, obtaining more research-supported facts about students and the programs that serve them.

In 1949 Williamson edited the book *Trends in Student Personnel Work*. He invited Kate Mueller to address problems in counseling women. She argues that since the student personnel point of view calls for development of students as a whole, it should mean both men and women. She examines life patterns, differing social pressures, frustrations of women, and even considers the question of a special curriculum for women. Her insights and conclusions provide a background for the issues that surround sexual equality among staff, students and faculty on campus today.

A speech delivered by W. W. Blaesser at the National Educational Conference in 1948 and published in 1949 as one of the collection of papers, *Higher Education in American Society*, provides another view of the field that links the American Council on Education 1937 statement with the decade of change and concludes with a look to the future. This article is a synthesis of definitions of student personnel work, a review of the essential aspects of a student personnel program, and an indication of how student personnel work in the future might be related to the objectives of higher education as set forth in the President's Commission on Higher Education. This work by Blaesser is an impressive and comprehensive outline of the current status of the profession and an accurate indication of how student personnel work in the future must be related to various processes and functions of higher education. It is apparent that Blaesser brought much from this document to the American Council on Education 1949 report, *The Student Personnel Point of View*, where he was one of the committee members responsible for this document.

The American Council on Education continued its support for student personnel work by authorizing Williamson to convene a committee of twelve to reexamine the purposes of higher education as they affect the student personnel worker. They focused on goals that were obviously related to the upheaval of World War II and the post war social climate. This 1949 A.C.E. document builds on the 1937 A.C.E. document by expanding the statement of professional goals and objectives. The section on student needs and services includes a first time awareness of new types of students—married, veteran, and international. The committee concluded their work by calling for careful attention to the manner of administration of student personnel work—campus interrelationships, and program evaluation. For many newly appointed student affairs staffs, this statement provided the rationale for and a definition of their work on the campus.

The final paper to be selected from that productive year was the American College Personnel Association Presidential Address (1949) delivered by C. Gilbert Wrenn. After giving assurances of personnel work's legitimacy, he proceeds to identify certain faults that stand in the way of an even higher level of performance. He tells us why it is unnecessary to be either belligerent or apologetic about the significance of our work, and improper for us to fail to make a distinctive contribution as specialists in human behavior and human need. He warns about other psychological problems in the life of the personnel worker. Wrenn uses his counseling orientation to suggest ways to handle the factors that cause tensions in our lives. It may be reassuring to know the fatigue and burnout that concerns student personnel professionals today has been a continuing problem—a perplexing one, but not one that has destroyed our effectiveness. Wrenn's message is current.

W. H. Cowley, a higher education historian, had a particular interest in the history of student life. In 1957 he forecasts the campus as a likely setting for agitation and destruction if social conditions galvanize the increasing numbers of students to demonstrate. Deans of Students should prepare for this possibility by research on the historical continuum of student life. He also gives considerable attention to the relationships among 7,500 student personnel workers. He sees their communication and mutual support systems in complete disarray and calls for a linking together of all the national associations whose members are engaged in student personnel work in colleges and universities. He accurately forecasts the movement that later resulted in the formation of The Council of Student Personnel Associations (COSPA), an organization that was to help unify the fast growing profession from the early 60s through the early 70s.

The Essentials of a Student Personnel Program

E. H. Hopkins

. . . let me state very briefly the outline of this paper. . . . *First*, I shall merely list those essential and specialized student personnel services, which in one form or another, must be provided as an integral and inseparable part of any program of higher education. *Second*, I shall list a group of basic and fundamental principles and assumptions, which are just as essential as the student personnel services themselves. *Third*, I shall make a plea for "optimum" instead of "minimum" essentials in student personnel work, and education generally. *Fourth*, there is a degree of urgency about all of this which we as educators, and citizens, have not fully appreciated, or if we have, we have done little about it. And last, I wish to single out for special consideration and discussion two of the eleven essential principles which I shall propose.

Essential Student-Personnel Services

For the sake of brevity, I shall merely list eleven specialized student personnel services, which I consider to be essential to a sound program of higher education. Each of these could be discussed at length, but let us merely assume that each of these services should be organized, coordinated, and integrated into the total educational program, in a sound and effective manner. With this assumption, I shall eliminate further discussion with respect to the "hows" and "whys" of these eleven essential services. They are as follows:

1. A program of *pre-college counseling, selection, and applicant-centered admissions.*

2. An organized program for diagnosis and counseling of students. This includes both *intensive clinical* counseling and the normal day-to-day educational and personal counseling provided by the faculty and other less professionally trained counselors.

3. An effective *orientation* program, spread throughout the entire first year.

4. *Remedial assistance in various areas* for those students who need it.

5. Definite provision for the supervision, coordination, and integration of the "*co-curricular*" program on the campus.

6. A *student health service*, providing professional services in areas of both physical and mental health.

7. An adequate program of *supervision of living arrangements*, including the food service program. This program must be provided in such a manner as to contribute to the maximum extent possible to the social-educational objectives of the institution, as they relate to the individual student.

8. A well-organized program for administering *financial aids, student employments, post-graduate placements, and job follow-ups*.

9. Special facilities for developing and evaluating the *religious life and interests* of students on the campus.

10. There must be devised and maintained an adequate system of permanent *cumulative personnel records*, which include pertinent information relative to *all* aspects of student life and student accomplishment.

11. At the present, and for the next few years, a special service providing for the coordination of Veteran's affairs is an essential part of the total program.

Basic Principles and Assumptions

There are certain basic principles and assumptions which are just as essential as are the student personnel services. . . .

1. First, of course, is the student personnel point of view. . . . It must be considered as the fundamental and basic principle underlying the total program. It is well defined and described in the American Council on Education pamphlet, entitled *The Student Personnel Point of View*, published in 1937. In essentially the same form and in 1938, it was adopted as the first chapter of the charter of this association. It is just as up-to-date in 1948 as when it was adopted in 1938.

2. The second principle. . . is the necessity for thorough-going and effective coordination not only between and among the services and principles themselves, but between the services and the instructional program. This coordination must prevail both horizontally and vertically, not only within the institution, but with the pre-college program and with post-college adjustments. A program of student personnel services, of and by itself, just does not exist.

3. Education and the processes of education are strictly individual proc-

esses. The individual student must be considered as a total unique personality. Consequently, education must be flexible to the needs of individual students. This principle of considering the individual student as an individual is absolutely essential to a sound program of education which is based upon the student personnel point of view. Furthermore, there is nothing in this principle which is in conflict with the social objectives of education; there is no dichotomy between education for the needs of the individual and education for the improvement of society.

4. Educational programs, policies, and procedures cannot be established at least in a healthy manner by administrative edict or by fiat. These are matters demanding the combined wits and wisdoms of the entire faculty—with the additional help of the students. In addition, such a democratic policy is psychologically necessary for the success of the program.

5. Another essential principle, at least as it applies in coeducational institutions, has reference to what I consider to be a psychological fallacy apparent in some institutions where separate and parallel organizational structures prevail, one for women students and one for men students. I, of course, have reference to the traditional "Dean of Men" and "Dean of Women" organizations. Therefore, I consider it a sound principle to assume that the problems of men and women students on the campus are of the same order, and that the principles and methods for solving them are the same.

6. The college campus, both in action and in spirit, must be made an efficient *laboratory for training in democratic living.*

7. While I have no intention, here and now, of listing all of the principles or assumptions basic to education generally, there is another educational or psychological principle which I regard as being . . . closely akin to the objectives of student personnel services . . . I have reference to the concept of "deferring the selection of a major." The actual process of "selecting a major" is an individual student process, and a mental process. Therefore, there can be *no* institutional edict which says categorically to the student that faculty member may not select a major field of study until "such and such a time." On the other hand, there should be a policy which prevents students from being forced into such decisions too early in their college careers. Along with this principle goes a strong endorsement of the principles and objectives of general education, *but not to the exclusion of training for jobs.*

8. As a principle, student discipline, in the broad as well as the narrow sense, must be judiciously administered and in such a manner that the individual student will be strengthened and the welfare of the group preserved.

9. As mentioned before, a student personnel program does not exist, per

se, in spite of the tendency of most members of the faculty to think so, and to act accordingly. Consequently, when we refer to the essentials of "the student personnel program," we must necessarily refer to "higher education generally." We simply cannot talk about student personnel work, in educational institutions, without talking about *education* itself. Student personnel services *are* education. We must assume that both the objective and the methods of student personnel work, and of education generally, are *absolutely* inseparable, if not identical. The plain truth *is* that student personnel work *still* is considered by far too many faculty members, deans, and presidents simply as a fifth wheel. And they are not referring to the "steering wheel." Consequently, it is imperative that you bring the *entire* faculty, administration, student body, and alumni into active and constructive participation in the practical implementation of the program.

10. In discussing the principle of "faculty participation" and other sound principles of organization, I should like to take issue with one of the currently accepted university organizational patterns which organizes the President's office into four divisions: Namely, the academic, the student personnel, the business management, and public relations. This *is* the current trend in the larger institutions. I am aware that on many campuses it has been a *struggle* for status, particularly for the Dean of Students, or Director of Student Affairs. I am indeed happy that on many of these same campuses, the Dean of Students now has a parallel position with the Dean of FAculty. That is appropriate. However, I do not concur with an institutional organization which permits the student personnel program on the one hand, and the academic program on the other, to be so separated that they are brought together *only* by the President.

11. There must be a principle, a policy, in fact a plan for continuous appraisal and evaluation of the program and a *willingness* to adjust and readjust it to fit changing conditions. Closely related to this principle, in fact a part of it, is the compelling need for curricular and student personnel research at all levels of the higher education ladder, but most important at the post-graduate level, i.e., a follow-up of our graduates, and for that matter of all others who leave our schools before graduation, in order to find out what are the results of our particular brand of education. Just how effectively are we doing what we propose to be doing? This point, also, I shall discuss later.

Too Much Emphasis on "Minimum Essentials"

In the first place, I am reminded of the Office of Education publication, published, I believe, in the middle thirties, entitled *Minimum Essentials of a*

Guidance Program; for our purposes, it must just as well have read, "Minimum Essentials of a Student Personnel Program." I fear that too many of us, and our deans, our presidents, and our governing boards, think too frequently in terms of *minimum* essentials, when thinking of the student personnel program in our respective institutions. Why should we put ourselves so clearly on the defensive? Why should we show such lack of confidence, such half-heartedness, such weakness of moral courage, when we try to sell the student personnel point of view, and the kind of program which will put that point of view to work? That point of view, with which we are all familiar and to which we all subscribe, is of little consequence until and unless we put it to work in rather concrete and practical situations. Indirectly, we have been apologizing for what we have to offer, by asking merely for *minimum* essentials. Perhaps we have not called them that, and in some cases probably we have not even been aware ourselves that we were seeking merely minimum essentials.

If we really *want* to make education effective . . . let us start defining the *optimum essentials* of education, and gear these essentials and their practical implementation to the *immediate* problems facing education today. Let us direct our thinking, and therefore our *actions*, toward the *maximum potentials* from *optimum conditions*, rather than toward the *limited potentials* from minimum conditions. Without this kind of forward thinking, without this courage to face reality—and I mean facing reality in 1948, not in the distant future—we might just as well toss whatever strength we have into the military machine and wait for the consequences.

Urgency for More Effective Higher Education

In asking for optimum conditions we must stress the *urgency* of our purpose, and we must also get across the idea that we have no "vested interests," no selfish motives, no axes to grind, but that these conditions are essential, and essential now, if we are to do the kind of job we *must do—for our own survival.*

The situation is both critical and urgent and further complicated by emotions of fear, distrust, prejudice, selfishness, indifference, and general "uneasiness."

This "uneasiness" and its consequent fearful speculation are very real, and undoubtedly represent a significant "cross-roads" in civilization as we know it. The first question is "Can we survive?" and the second, "How can we adapt ourselves to the new age if we do survive?" In either case, the "cross-roads" unquestionably is here. But let us concentrate on the first question;

there is no time in this discussion to concentrate on the second. What consequences are likely, if we become a world frightened by our own disorganized efforts to cope with it? If fear is an individual's greatest enemy, as the psychologists say it is, it is a far greater enemy of a nation—or for a world—because in an individual, therapy is more easily and more effectively administered. We must meet this world-wide fear with *understanding* and with *education*. How else can we bring about changes in the attitudes and motivations of individuals, except through education? But do we have the "stuff" in ourselves and in our ranks to provide the leadership needed in these critical times? I am confident that we do have, but it is absolutely essential, and essential now, that organized education in this country come decisively to grips with the worldwide crisis of mankind. We cannot afford to let this crisis just "take its course."

The second urgent and compelling reason for a fresh view and a revitalized program of higher education based upon the student personnel point of view is the fact that too often our graduates simply do not measure up to our expectations, to their own capacities, or to the demands of the society of which they become a part. While there is continuously mounting evidence which clearly indicates this weakness in higher education today, for the sake of brevity I shall use but a few references. Perhaps the overall problem in this connection is nowhere better summarized than in the Editor's Foreword to Robert Pace's report of the Minnesota study, completed just prior to the war, entitled *They Went to College*. This foreword, as faculty would expect, is based upon the findings of the study, in which Pace reported on the differences between college graduates and non-graduates, at the University of Minnesota. I quote:

We need desperately to know why there appears to be little or no difference between graduates and nongraduates, between high-ranking students and low-ranking students, after they have been a decade away from the campus. Why most of them appear to want security and contentment instead of taking a vigorous delight in 'looking upon the bright face of danger' and welcoming blood-stirring change. Why, if we have taught them—far above their fellows—to think critically, they are in after-college years so obviously uncritical and inconsistent in their thinking. Why, if we have taught them to read good books, most of them read only 'slick' magazines of huge circulation, newspapers, a few books of a standard below that of the freshman English class. Why, in a democracy, the most highly educated people we have fail so miserably to engage in community and political activities.

Much more could be said with respect to the *need* for an effective student personnel program, one which is thoroughly meshed into the total educational program and which would be capable of producing products of which we could be proud. Just take a look at our attrition rate, throughout the country, where from fifty to sixty-five per cent drop out before embarking upon the third year of college. Just take a look, without even a pretense at scientific evaluation, at the appropriateness and effectiveness of the training which from year to year is being given those who do drop out along the way. Just find out, in your own institutions, what percentage of *your* students do not know what occupational objectives they wish to follow, or for what occupational pattern they are best fitted. Just find out, *in your own institutions*, the extent to which individual students *are* following intelligent and *planned* college careers.

While this picture is a rather discouraging one, representing a combination of a critical, serious, and urgent national and international situation, and what appears to be an inefficient and ineffective educational system, I do feel that there *are* ways out.

Although I do not recall the specific reference, I recall reading not long ago in another article by President Hutchins in which he made some such statement as this:

> As a means to a peaceful world, education is either everything, or else it is nothing; if it really is everything, then it should be encouraged, implemented, financed, and made to work; if on the other hand, it is nothing, there should be no more time nor money wasted on it.

I think we agree on the fundamental importance of education; I think we agree that it is everything, so far as progress is concerned. We agree on the wisdom of the student personnel point of view in education, but apparently we have had little agreement on what constitutes the most fruitful means of putting this point of view and education to work.

Two Positive Approaches

In the light of this setting: first a war-torn, tattered, and unstable world; second, a rather unenviable record of civic and social participation and contribution on the part of the average college graduate, as compared with non-college graduates; and, third, a heterogeneous and conglomerate mass of student personnel and educational practices being used and misused throughout our respective institutions; I should like to focus more attention on two of the eleven essential principles which I mentioned at the beginning of this paper: *first, the principle of getting more active faculty participation in the implementation of the student personnel point of view, and secondly, the need for many more facts, i.e., curricular and student personnel research.*

Regarding the first: if we are going to have an effective educational program, based truly upon the student personnel point of view, that point of view must be known, believed, accepted, and *practiced* by the teaching faculty, by the administration, and by those responsible for the specialized services within the institution. This is essential—but "How?" This is where you come in—in fact, it is *your* first essential. We must first create an organization, a faculty, in fact, an institution, which by its composite and coordinated efforts, by its sound educational policies which will have been put into action, will do for the masses what a few counselors and a few instructors have been trying desperately to do for too few students. Certainly, I do not mean that you will eliminate the need for individual counseling by specially trained and qualified workers . . . but we will get far greater results with the masses of our students, if we provide on a wholesale and preventive basis, what we have been attempting to provide on a retail and therapeutic basis. It is comparable with the effects of a public health program. You need relatively fewer physicians in a community having an intelligent and carefully administered public health program than in communities where no such program exists.

This would be merely empty "mouthing" if I did not believe that we *can* go a long way, in a relatively short time, toward the development of this kind of a program. You are the people who must carry the torch; you must become crusaders, and maintain that zeal and enthusiasm, along with a necessary amount of patience and diplomacy, until the process begins to "take." More than ever before, you must devise better means of informing your faculties, and doing it repeatedly, of the significance of the student personnel point of view. In weekly or periodic staff bulletins, report and review individual cases, report and review the kind of facts which Pace reported in the study of the 951 graduates and non-graduates of the University of Minnesota. If possible, find out these facts from your own institution and your own students. Also, report continuously and repeatedly what other institutions are doing, significant, urgent, and compelling statistics on such matters as student failures, student drop-outs, the criteria for success and the reason for failure on post-graduation jobs, and the failure of college graduates to assume more than a minimum of civic responsibility.

Why not prevail upon your President, your Dean of Faculty, or your Budget Committee for enough money—and it would take a surprisingly small amount—to purchase sufficient copies of the *Report of the President's Commission on Higher Education* so that each department in your college would have copies of the complete report, and insist that it be rotated among the members of the respective departments until all had read it. The reading of that report should be an absolute requirement of every person who justifies his name on a college faculty payroll. Also, for a very small budgetary consideration (75¢ per year per person), your institution can subscribe to *Higher Education*, the semi-monthly publication of the Higher Education Division of the U.S. Office of Education; I recommend it as a good investment by the institution for every single member of your faculty.

How many of you take time, or make time, to visit *regularly* with members of your instructional staff to discuss with them common policies and procedures, institutional objectives and your *joint* responsibilities for achieving them, to encourage or solicit constructive criticism from them, to demonstrate through a discussion and consideration of *their* teaching and research interests that you understand and appreciate *their* important role in the overall educational program of the institution?

This year on our campus we inaugurated a series of monthly faculty meetings, for *all* members of our faculty; such meetings are devoted exclusively to lectures, discussions, and panels covering matters of current educational and faculty personnel policies. Although our faculty probably is as busy and overworked as the average faculty, I am happy to say that these meetings have been unusually well-attended and unusually successful. As a result we have set aside $10,000 for next year, to bring to the campus outstanding authorities, consultants, and visiting lecturers on matters of current educational interest to the faculty.

Another example of the degree of genuine interest in, and willingness to participate in and contribute to, a dynamic program of educational improvement on our own college campus, was demonstrated a few weeks ago when I called for volunteer memberships on a large number of subcommittees of the Educational Policies Committee. It was understood that these subcommittees were to delve *deeply* into such matters as "improvement of instruction and the relating of instruction to contemporary issues," "integrated courses," "instruction in community, national, and international affairs," "student counseling," "Graduation requirements," "a deferred-major plan," "the integration of student activities into the educative processes," "terminal education," "how to teach worker education," and a number of others. With faculty members already "committed to death," you would be astonished to know that we had approximately one hundred and fifty faculty volunteers who indicated both an interest in, and a willingness to serve on, such committees. Those committees are going to stir up a lot of grass-roots thinking on the Washington State College campus within the next few months, and the next year. Our faculty has just completed working out its own plan for faculty evaluation. This means appraisal of faculty performance and effectiveness in areas of instruction, research and publications, and in over-all benefit to the institution and to the community. They have now asked that the faculty be evaluated by the students and by the alumni. They *are* deeply interested in self-improvement and in the improvement of instruction and education generally. Our faculty voted, as a result of their own deliberations, not merely to adopt a deferred-major plan, but to place the administrative responsibility for the entire lower division in the hands of the Dean of Students and his student personnel staff. This plan has been in operation for two years. They are sold on it, and are improving it.

In connection with institutional committees, may I suggest also that you, as student personnel workers, have an important and urgent role to play in the determination and implementation of educational policies within your respective institutions. Therefore, you should see to it somehow that you and other selected members of your student personnel staff are placed on such committees as the curriculum committee, educational policies committee, admission policies committee, and other important committees charged with policy determination functions. Also, on your important policy committees, place some of the best students on your campus. If you have not already tried this, I think you may be both amazed and pleased with the nature of the contribution which they can and will make.

The second postulate on which I wish to focus more attention has to do with the dire need for *curricular and student personnel research* to guide us in our policy determinations. How on earth can we expect to develop new curricula, new programs of study, proper combinations of general and specialized courses, integrated courses which we know are effective, adequate vocational and other counseling services, student activity programs which are supposed to train for democratic living, sound admission policies, sound re-instatement policies, and sound and defensible graduation requirements, when we do not even know what the effects and the results of our present curricula, instructions, and services are?

We set up admission policies without knowing what really makes for success in college. For example, we are still clinging to high-school gradua-tion and certain patterns of high-school subjects, when we have known for years that there is no scientific basis for believing that high-school subject-matter patterns are related to academic success in college.

In addition, we should know far more about the students who come to our campuses for educational training. Before we admit them, we should know something of their aptitudes, interests, personality characteristics, as well as their scholastic achievements. We have no right to admit them, and then later to tell them that we are sorry, but we just do not have what they need. Usually we do not even tell them that; they struggle along for a year or two, and then discover for themselves that not only are they swimming upstream, but up the wrong stream. We need to know what the individual need of our prospective students are, and in addition we need to know the overall pattern of individual, social, and employment needs of the regions which we serve, if we are to fulfill our missions efficiently and to the best of our abilities.

In my opinion, the effectiveness of any educational institution, and therefore the effectiveness of its governing board, of its President, and of those others responsible for educational policies and practices within the institution, should be measured by the quality of the product which the institution produces. This, of course, assumes that the qualities and qualifications of the product would have to be measured, and measured consistently and continuously. It means, in all institutions, that such studies as the one reported by Pace at Minnesota should be made, and the data should be kept current. "But," you say, "this would cost money." I can only say that it would cost far less than what is now being spent providing teaching faculties, services, housing, and over provisions for the students who are "swimming up the wrong streams," not to mention the loss of time, money, prestige, and "face" of each student in that category. Consequently, if we really are interested in developing an educational program based upon the student personnel point of view, let us find out a little more about the individual needs of those students who come to us for training, the social and employment needs of the regions which we serve, and the effects and results of the training which we are now providing for our students. *This research is essential*, and you are the people who are best qualified and who are in the most strategic positions to carry it on. You are the persons to see to it that the findings of such research become the common property of your administration and your faculty.

Summary

1. The *essentials of a student personnel program* consist of:
   a. The student personnel point of view as applied to all educational processes;
   b. A group of at least eleven specialized student personnel services, requiring specially trained counselors and technicians;
   c. Certain basic and fundamental principles and assumptions which apply to all phases of the program. Eleven such principles and assumptions have been specifically mentioned.
2. We must strive harder than we have ever striven before for "optimum"

conditions and the wherewithal to carry out an effective educational program.

3. We must devise countless practical and spirited means of transforming the student personnel point of view into institutional and *faculty action* patterns—not only as a long range objective, but as an immediate one.

4. Through scientific research we must *get at the facts* which are basic to an intelligent and effective program. *We must know wherein we are ineffective or weak.*

5. There is a degree of urgency which we can ill afford to ignore. In short, all that I have been trying to say is that it is high time that we come down from the ivory towers, that we face the urgency before us, that we follow the courage of our convictions, and develop an educational program which will bring about the full realization and meaning of *democracy in action.* This means an educational program which will turn out emotionally mature men and women *capable, willing,* and *desirous* of acting intelligently in a world where men depend upon men, and in a civilization which depends upon understandings among men. In the words of the President's Commission on Higher Education, "the responsibility for the development of these personal qualities (in our students) can no longer be left, as heretofore, to some courses, or a few departments, or some scattered extra-curricular organizations; *it must become a part of every phase of college life.*"

Problems in Counseling Women

Kate Hevner Mueller

The college years always represent a period of accelerated progress and a telescoping of previous rates of growth. The half-decade of adolescence has its own characteristic misdirections, frustrations, and disillusionments, to say nothing of irresponsibilities and impertinences. Youth in the process of establishing independence of family. He is working out his relationships with the opposite sex. He is deciding on and preparing for his career. And with more or less conscious effort he is fusing his varied assortment of values into a usable system and his conglomeration of personality traits into a smoothly functioning whole.

These findings are equally characteristic of both sexes, but there is a differential impact of the college campus on men and women. Counselors who are responsible for putting their students in rapport with their environment, both present and future, need to be aware of what is happening in the world so that they can pick up their cues the more expertly.

Sex Differences

In considering the special problems encountered in counseling women, our first question is, How do women differ from men? Although there is no lack of differences if we select at random any one man and any one woman, it is more difficult to divine strong and important differences that are significant for the sexes as a whole (2, chapters 14 and 15). Physical differences in size and shape are obvious, but the more important differences of endurance and vitality are questionable. It is difficult to find reliable differences in amount and variability in intelligence; in achievement, however, there are very consistent differences, with girls excelling in verbal ability, in memory, and in certain curriculum areas corresponding to their interests.

Various tests bring out certain differences or similarities in personality

94

which are probably more related to the nature and technique of the testing procedure than to the two sexes. Men are said to give highest values to things economic, political, and theoretical; women to the aesthetic, social, and religious. The feminine are more interested in domestic affairs, aesthetic objects, sedentary and indoor occupations, and ministrative occupations, particularly with the young, helpless, and distressed. The masculine have more self-assertion, aggressiveness, hardihood, fearlessness, and roughness of manners, language, and sentiments. The feminine are more compassionate and sympathetic, timid, fastidious, aesthetically sensitive, probably more emotional, and the severer moralists.

The more important investigators (19) emphasize the role of cultural factors in establishing these differences, and show that the masculinity-femininity index is related to the amount of education, to occupation, and to the domestic milieu (e.g. deprivation of one parent and number and sex of siblings). In summary, it is difficult to discern any fundamental differences in the abilities of men and women (even though masculinity and femininity can be more accurately defined than formerly) because the issue is always confused by differences in opportunity. *Women are closest to the pattern for men in abilities, farther apart in interests, and farthest apart in opportunity.*

Men and Women in Society

Life Patterns

Since it is the social expectancy which is so very different for men and for women, it will be necessary to analyze at some length the roles of men and of women in society, and to describe and differentiate their life patterns.

The role expected of man is much more clear-cut and well defined than the role—or better, the various roles—expected of woman. Woman must be prepared to alternate between at least two roles, her business or professional or citizenship career, and her life as a homemaker. Her life pattern will include several well-defined periods, when the time and emphasis will shift from inside to outside the home. A typical adult life pattern for the upper middle class woman might include first a business or professional period; then a family period of perhaps ten or fifteen or even twenty years, during which she may or may not be able to keep up her professional contacts or build the bridges into the world of civic and economic responsibility; and finally a period relatively free from family duties and from financial strain during which some of her best creative or organizational activities may occur.

These life patterns of modern women of the upper middle class have changed quite definitely from those of even fifty years ago. The family period—child bearing and rearing—has been shortened very perceptibly with our lowered birth rate and the cutting off of the third and fourth children (14). Women live longer and enjoy better health, and their housekeeping routines—cleaning, cooking, canning, sewing—have been shortened and lightened. These changes become effective especially in the third period, making it possible and even necessary for a woman to find some worthwhile activity outside the home during the years of her later maturity.

Technological advances and urbanization in the past century have brought about larger changes in the life patterns of women than in those for men; therefore women more than men feel the conflict between these advancing forces and the slower moving mores and ideologies.

Advances in the field of clothing, grooming, and personal services have greatly enhanced woman's attractiveness. Such heroines of fiction and fact as Amber, Scarlett O'Hara, Anna Karenina, and Lillian Russell created problems for themselves because they were beautiful. Beauty was an unusual trait in their day, making them stand out from the masses of lesser, unhistorical women who had no beauty and therefore no problems of interest to the tellers of tales. In 1847 the average woman of forty was dowdy and provincial in her dress. She had no permanent wave and no silk stockings, and she had a large family whose constant needs kept her close at home. Today the woman of forty is slim, fashionably dressed, and well groomed, as attractive as the heroines of fiction, and she therefore encounters some of their problems. As she moves about in her car, she meets a large circle of men who also show the effects of technological improvements. Unfortunately, she also meets the same old mores—the Christian ethic, the Victorian code—all very little changed from the time of her grandmother. Obviously she needs help.

Differing Social Pressures

Neither men nor women can be conceived of merely as human beings free and self-determined according to their inner needs and stresses. Man is a social being as well as a human being, and his personality is a social as well as a psychological construct, growing out of the many roles he plays and the status he enjoys. We could not, of course, claim that this social milieu is more important for women than for men, or more effective, or even more oppressive, or more unfavorable. We could be persuaded to believe, however, that it does give to men a greater amount of freedom in several respects.

1. *Sex behavior and social standards.* A woman is not quite as free an agent,

not equally in control of the situation, in regard to choosing a mate. She is forced into the more passive role, which gives her a feeling of greater helplessness, a feeling on which she may or may not be able to capitalize. If a woman is unsuccessful in the art of attracting the attention of men, she has no opportunity to use many of the other skills and knowledge with which she may be richly endowed (7, p. 560). Men in the more active role can always do something about such a situation and avoid the ensuing frustration. Women, forced into more devious methods of approach, suffer more readily from maladjustments.

Most of us are well aware that "the present state of our love and sex mores is chaotic, inconsistent and transitory" (7, p. 563). "The most accurate picture of current attitudes would be in terms of ambivalence and conflict" (17). One writer reports that there is nothing really strong enough and firm enough to warrant the term *conflict*. There is, especially on the college campus, just an ooze, with everybody worming around in it. Most of us have likewise noted the decline in the efficacy of religious sanctions and the effect of the increasing availability of contraceptives. There is also to be observed in these troubled and complex times an increasing need for personal intimacy, for escape in terms of "whatever happens at least we have each other"—even though this solution represents merely an exchange of one set of compulsions for another, and often prove, no matter how satisfying and consoling, no real substitute for these other needs (17).

As other arguments for sex behavior become less cogent, sex and morals educators are forced to rely increasingly on the idea that exclusiveness beautifies and ennobles intimacy. The very intensification of these uplifted expectations of monogamous bliss call for substitute satisfactions (6, p. 722). Our culture continues to emphasize "youth and beauty" as the only love stimulants, although we might do better to develop a higher valuation of woman's personality, intellect, and health.

What can women be sure of in our culture? Acquisitiveness, competitiveness, emphasis on feminine sexual attractiveness, socio-political irresponsibility; and the cult of success (9, p. 321). On these values she must build her own, her husband's, and her daughter's social position, buttressing them with whatever attitudes, prejudices, and sentiments she can lay her hands on.

In summary, social pressures and technological advances are creating new problems for women; social expectations are misleading her; and the techniques for building new values and teaching them to her are inadequate.

2. *Economic limitations.* Women are, to say the least, less free than men in regard to their professional or business or civic careers. The economic limitations for women, following Folsom's analysis, are these: (a) she receives lower pay for the same work; (b) positions requiring greater skill and authority

are closed to her in favor of men; (c) her geographic location and socio-economic status are dependent on her husband; and (d) housekeeping (her fundamental occupation) offers no regular pay and gives no prestige.

The fact that women are paid less for the same work than men, especially in the professions and white collar jobs, is too obvious to argue. Except for a few areas where equality prevails, professional women earn about a thousand dollars less annually than men in a parallel position. Some women feel that this gives them an advantage in the hiring market, without which they could not compete even as well as they do. There is also some justification for the differential—not, as many would like to think, because woman has less financial responsibility and does not need the money (15, p. 41), but because she is a less permanent worker. She may leave her work to have a child, or her husband may move his household to another part of the country.

The more important economic limitation is the prejudice which the woman professional or business or civic worker finds barring her advancement to better paid positions with more authority and responsibility. Sometimes the limiting policy is stated quite openly and frankly. More often it is concealed under the guise of sentiment and chivalry.

How deeply this prejudice is imbedded in our thinking appears in Allport's explanation for the superiority of women in interpreting attitudes. He says a woman learns the skill because ". . . her success depends upon the attitudes of people toward her. It is important for her to know, for example, whether her male associates in business have an antagonistic, jocular, patronizing, or fairminded point of view regarding her presence in their profession" (1, p. 517). What man labors under this added handicap in his business or professional dealings?

The whole ideology of the "success story," and the emphasis given to the more glamorous careers by the smart women's magazines has a vicious effect on the morale of young women workers. "In our present culture she must have a source of prestige in the form of a career if she is to be well thought of. She must work, and the more her work is a career preceded by specialized education and yielding great monetary rewards, the greater will be her prestige" (5, p. 118).

This confusion in motivations, this unrealistic attitude is the more damaging because the career ideology has already declined with men. "No longer are boys brought up on the Alger and Henty books, which suggests that any boy can become President and that only the right attitude is necessary to insure a steady rise from office boy to general manager" (7, p. 617). Women must learn that vocational life is unpredictable and subject to many forces outside our personal control. Sociologists have given us more careful analyses of these factors in our culture, and neither women nor their counselors can afford to ignore them.

Another discouraging factor in the status of the professional woman is the defection among her own kind, the lack of solidarity within her own ranks. Every contented housewife, every pretty little secretary or schoolteacher who works a few years before marriage, even if they can be aroused to an awareness of the situation, are on the man's side of the argument. Women, especially young college women, need a longer perspective as well as a more objective analysis of their status in society and their personal and emotional needs. It has been suggested that the emancipation of women is really a part of the long emergence from feudal society, in which men were driven from the home at an earlier stage by the growth of capitalism but in which women have lagged behind (3, p. 15).

Women on the Campus

How can this complex societal background which we have sketched be related to the problems of women on the campus?

First, let us remember that on the college campus woman's environment is most nearly the equal of man's. She takes the same courses, and in the intellectual realm her successes are welcomed and encouraged by her teachers. She is a vital part of the social life, and conditions favorable to her participation in extracurricular activities are usually arranged for her. Her college situation is therefore peculiarly misleading to her, which means that her counselors must take special pains to devise and apply the necessary correction or prediction formulas so that her later disillusionment will be, nor a bitter one, but as good humored as it can possibly be made.

Both her formal academic training and her informal training through day-to-day campus life introduce the college woman to a pattern of living which will show a cruel discrepancy with actual life experience. The concentration of the upper middle class and especially the age structure on the campus are both abnormal. There is a parasitic existence in a sort of socio-political vacuum (9, p. 326). All the adolescent enthusiasms and irresponsibilities are reinforced in daily contact and are at the same time unrestrained by the social controls that result from closer contact with older ages, family life, business, and civic obligations. Added to this is the present confusion in the minds of both men and women because of the tempo and the radical nature of current economic, psychological, political, and social changes.

Vocational Problems

The *central* problem for the young college woman of today is the difficulty of choosing and preparing for the ambiguous life pattern described above, especially of fitting the role of homemaker into all the other roles she wants to play in her life. She is uncertain as to whether she will even have the opportunity to play the role of homemaker; whether her husband's economic status will be high or low; whether the family period in her life pattern will be a long one, keeping her closely at home, or a short one with plenty of leisure in which to experiment. Fortunately for her present peace of mind the later and perhaps more devastating conflicts do not immediately unfold themselves before her. She cannot yet imagine that the heavy costs in time, energy, and money of freeing her personality from the soporific of homemaking may be more than she can ever afford to pay, or that she may have to fight for the privilege of using her talents to build a better social and economic world.

The old problem of *career or marriage* has become, at least in the minds of the girls, the new problem of *career and marriage*. It is no longer an either-or dilemma; it is merely a question of assigning the proper emphasis to achieve the nicest balance between the two interests. The marriage rates for college graduates no longer lag so much behind the rates for other women of comparable age and status, and college girls now frankly admit, 99 percent of them, that they would prefer to marry if they can. At the same time they crave the independence that goes with earning power, and they dread the thought of inactivity after the exhilaration of campus life.

This does not make vocational and educational counseling easy. Freshman women and other women students will exhibit a strong resistance to preparation for any role except the professional or business career. This is partly because the role of earner is the only one a woman can be sure of, the only one she feels is within her control, and partly because her mother has convinced her that homemaking skills and knowledge can be "just picked up somehow." She will probably resist also the exclusively women's vocations in which she has the best chances for advancement and material success, because they have no prestige value, or because she knows, without Mr. Popenoe's warning, about the certain "occupational segregation" (18) that will lower her chances of finding her future husband through her business contacts.

The process of working through with a freshman girl the problems involved in choosing a vocation and preparing for any one of the various life patterns which she may try to arrange for herself involves continuous and specialized effort: not only her academic program but also her extracurricular activities and her group living can be organized to make invaluable contributions to this phase of her development.

Personal Problems

Fortunately the freshman will talk quite frankly and has a good deal of insight into her problem of career and life pattern. She is equally harassed—but no so able either to formulate her problem or to ask for help—in her daily routine of keeping herself socially afloat in the campus marriage market. The counselor who works with women will soon learn to shift the fulcrum and achieve a better balance between personal and vocational needs. For this reason, with women it is more difficult to divide the functions of educational and personal counseling between two sets of counselors in two different departments. The best means of entry into the uncertain area of personal problems is often through the well-traveled paths of vocational problems.

Personal counseling becomes largely sex and social behavior counseling, because "for most persons, the dominant motive of college attendance is the desire to rise to a higher social class. Behind this we see the ideology of American life, the projection of parents' ambitions upon children" (20, p. 727). The college freshman never heard of Mr. Popenoe's mating gradient, "the widespread (and praiseworthy) tendency of women to marry above their own level and of men to want to marry below," but she has, nevertheless, exactly the same idea in mind. "In the absence of help from the curriculum, she has had to get her education on marriage from the other great educational agencies of the present day" (18, p. 739): the movies, the women's magazines, the radio, the advertisements. She has strange ideas and strong feelings, very little organization, and some surprising resistances.

In this area the counselor, in order to be successful, needs to understand the social milieu of the campus, the hierarchy of the various groups and organizations, and the social complex of "rating and dating." He should know the functions and techniques of courtship as described by the sociologists (20), as well as from the more naive points of view of the students and their parents. How much of college dating is a "sort of dalliance relationship, largely dominated by the quest of a thrill, and regarded as an amusement and a release of organic tensions"? Under what conditions and for how long will a date bureau flourish and who will reap the advantages and suffer the disadvantages and suffer the disadvantages? When shall he use Moreno's technique (16) for analyzing a group of of persons in terms of attractions and repulsions among individuals?

Women students will spend a substantial portion of their time discussing among themselves these personal and romantic problems. The counselor who can introduce perspective and objectivity into these discussions needs a strategic position from which to work as well as special knowledge and perfected techniques. College freshmen can learn much from the discussion of such questions as these: How many persons of the opposite sex have you known well enough to pass judgment on whether they would be a fit marriage parent? How does the progress of your campus love affair differ from the typical charts? How many ways can you use to enhance your attractiveness for a man other than the use of your body? They will be glad to know about the research studies which show that college men and women have an average of approximately 2.2 campus love affairs, of which about 70 percent are broken off (10, 11). They will give openminded attention to the advice: "Young women should take into account the age differential in marriage and cultivate the acquaintance of men a few years older than themselves" (18).

A Special Curriculum for Women?

There are many who feel that a special curriculum or a core curriculum for women, or the establishment of a women's college within each university, is the next important step in the solving of women's problems. But these earnest well-wishers fail to pay enough attention to two major factors: (1) the wide range in abilities, interests, and cultural backgrounds of women students, which makes any one curriculum or even a core curriculum as ridiculous as one curriculum would be for men; and (2) the tremendous and admirable energy and dynamic force in the modern woman, which, in combination with technological advances, gives her the leisure and the verve to play two roles—which, in fact, probably makes it necessary for her to play two, or any additional number of roles it pleases her to undertake (13).

The determining factors in a curriculum for women are: (1) The educational requirements of the field of study itself, which are given most weight in the academic world and without which the field cannot be mastered. (2) The requirements of society, for higher education is inevitably concerned with the critical problems of the day and all hands, including women's, are needed for the job of solving them. The special skills and interests and point of view of women are essential and should be used to best advantage equally with men's. (3) The special needs which grow out of the life patterns of women, whether their home life and family relationships are absorbing and continuous or of incidental interest, or intensive but concentrated in a certain period of years.

The range of women's interests is as large as men's, although there is no overlapping throughout the whole of these ranges. Therefore, women's needs are best met through a broad framework, not merely the elective system, but a whole range of college and university programs, liberal, general, pre-professional, and applied arts and sciences. The emphasis in any one institution should be keyed to the demands of its student body and the proportions of various kinds of students of all ages, sexes, and classes which are to be found in it. Women should then have the best possible advice in choosing their courses, but so also should men. Some women should be advised to take courses in homemaking, and some men should be urged to take courses in family relationships. Volunteer community service should be an extracurricular activity for both men and women.

The inclusion of nutrition, applied economics, and child care as a core curriculum for women has been advocated for practical reasons: the inade-quate preparation for meeting life's daily problems without these emphases; on a scientific basis, namely, women's different biological structure and function; and more recently on a psychoanalytic claim that woman finds satisfaction only in filling her role as wife and mother and that conflict follows any attempt to change it into a career or intellectual life. These arguments distort the problem by making it seem the woman's only; they ignore the possibility that the husbands (that is society, "the man's world") may be equally at fault. Besides, there is no evidence that any certain courses or curriculums would be effective in correcting this or any other of our educational faults.

Extracurricular Activities

Sex differences in interests and values are apparent in the extracurricular activities which women plan for themselves and in their attitudes toward these activities. They are more self-conscious about them and plan them with much more thoughtfulness and in a more democratic spirit. Fewer women see these activities as a means to climbing the campus success ladder which leads to future employment advantages. More of them seek the opportunity for both personal development and campus service. This situa-tion does not obtain because of any innate highmindedness of women; again it is the obvious result of circumstances and social pressures.

Both historically and currently the "double standard" has made it neces-sary to regulate campus life for women more than for men. Because of society's insistence on getting the girls into their residences early at night and on regulating the hours when their halls and their parties should be open to men, supervision becomes a vital part of women's campus life.

Supervisors, whether they are called chaperones or housemothers or wardens or deans or counselors or personnel workers, have always been aware that these social regulations (in contrast to the business or academic regulations) can be effective only with full student participation in making and supporting them. Therefore, the fundamental assignment of any counselor who works with women is the building of morale high enough to contain this particular problem.

High morale and effective student governments are especially characteristic of the women's colleges. Long traditions of responsibility and success and high selection of student bodies have furnished the undergirding; and there is a continuous process of buttressing, including careful curriculum adjustments, more attention to the teaching process, a more elaborate religious program, and the use of counselors experienced in women's problems. The honor system in examinations and even in social regulations is a commonplace in women's colleges, and is practically 100 percent successful, a phenomenon which men find it difficult to believe, because it is almost if not quite impossible to achieve on the coeducational campus.

Other Personnel Functions

In similar fashion it is obvious that any single function of campus personnel services—housing and group living, discipline, finances, government, leadership, and social programs—is different in certain aspects for men and women. Woman has much more to lose than man under disciplinary action, because social position and prestige are so much more important in her life. The bad manners or behavior deviations of a man will be dwarfed and overshadowed by his business successes, but a woman's little inadequacies are sometimes the only things by which she can be remembered.

Woman's social prestige often suffers when she engages in certain types of part-time campus employment. She cannot so easily rationalize her work as employment experience. She is also a poorer risk for loans because of her lower salaries, shorter working period, and restricted opportunity for work. Because she must at all costs maintain her respectability, her standard of living must be higher, which means higher living costs.

Conformity and acceptability in dress and grooming have become almost a fetish on the college campus and are more difficult to achieve for women than for men. No single item in the maintaining of appearance is as easy for women as for men. Choosing, designing, fitting, cleaning, and repairing of clothing and caring for and camouflaging the skin, figure, and hair make tremendous inroads on the time and energy of women students.

Home ties are stronger for women students, and parental attitudes and prejudices are harder to shake off (17). Parents are at the same time more in evidence, and more deeply embarrassing when off-standard in manners or behavior.

More women than men read the current popular magazines with their misleading ideologies and their dishonest advertisements. More women than men attend the movies and listen to the radio to absorb their romantic infantilism. Women will, therefore, offer more resistance to the objective and realistic point of view so necessary to the solution of the current problems of the social order.

The leadership which women must develop is different from the leadership qualities appropriate for men. To be sure, they must learn the techniques of the men in order to be able to deal with them, but in so far as a woman's own leadership may be exercised among other women, it must be based on different personal qualities and different interests to meet the different social forces. A woman's leadership, or perhaps we should call it a certain kind of "followship," for dealing with men must also be of a special kind. She can never assume that men will have acquired her point of view, and she must learn to teach it to them with patience and good humor while she indulges them by pretending to learn their patterns of ideas and behavior, which she already knows. "We will ask these men to meet with us," offered one college adviser in a moment of crisis, "and ask them what they think about the situation, which will probably be the best way for us to tell them what we think."

The naiveté of women in dealing with the techniques of "leadership" exercised by men is, of course, very patent both on the campus and in the economic and political arenas. Here especially it would be important for the college woman to acquaint herself with the history of women's groups and their accomplishments so that the gains already made can be evaluated and the losses appreciated.

Another function in which the personnel division sometimes plays a part is the interpreting of the college to its constituency. More than this, the institution sometimes feels an obligation to introduce a better perspective, or to disseminate information necessary and important for a progressive social or economic program. Without knowledge of and insight into women's problems, which under present conditions men have no adequate means of acquiring, mistakes will be made and opportunities for leadership in women's work will be missed when women are not given a voice in administrative councils. Few men understand the nature and hierarchy of women's clubs and professional organizations or can differentiate among those which are progressive and realistic and those which are anachronistic and reactionary.

In this respect the leaderships shown by some of the women's colleges is in sharp contrast to the failures of the coeducational schools in serving, not the interests, but the best interests of women.

Conclusion

According to the popular press the frustrations of women seem to be, if not increasing, at least claiming more attention in recent decades. At least we have no books entitled *Modern Man, The Lost Sex* (12), *Men After Forty* (4), or *Men After College* (8). Up to this time the correctives are being applied in terms of a more elaborate understanding of woman's emotional and physiological nature in addition to manipulations of her education. It might seem more feasible to attempt manipulation of the social forces in her situation, since they are now in a fair way to being understood. If women have more frustrations than men, it might be logical to explain them in terms of the factors in which women are most different from men, namely, in their social expectancies and their life patterns.

Because of these still greatly different life patterns, women students must be helped toward greater insight into the psychological and social forces which lie behind them. An important factor in building these insights is the knowledge of the history of women and the perspective gained by differentiating her nature and her problems from those of men and projecting them against the background of society as a whole. Are men interested in this field, the history and status of women? Will men develop it and introduce its study into the curriculums of both men and women? Is not the denial of its importance by men one of the techniques by which they cheat women of the opportunity to solve their problems and eliminate their frustrations? Does not the failure to include women as active and competent (that is, equal) participants in planning and administering the curriculum and personnel work insulate the men from their most useful source of information in this area?

The student personnel point of view in education declares that it is the task of the colleges to assist the student in developing to the limits of his potentialities and in making his contribution to the betterment of society. It puts emphasis, in brief, upon the development of the student as a person rather than on his intellectual training alone. It seeks to train the student *as a whole.* Or is it merely the man as a whole? Or is it perhaps the student, man or woman, as a psychological but not a social whole?

References

1. Allport, G. *Personality: A Psychological Interpretation.* New York: Holt, 1937.
2. Anastasi, Anne. *Differential Psychology.* New York: Macmillan, 1937.
3. Bruton, Margaret P. "Present-Day Thinking on the Woman Question," *Annals of the American Academy of Political and Social Science,* 251:10–16 (May 1947).
4. Elliot, Grace. *Women After Forty.* New York: Holt, 1940.
5. Farnham, M. F. "Battles Won and Lost," *Annals of the American Academy of Political and Social Science,* 251:113–19 (May 1947).
6. Folsom, Joseph K. "Changing Values in Sex and Family Relations," *American Sociological Review,* 2:717–26 (October 1937).
7. Folsom, Joseph K. *The Family and Democratic Society.* New York: John Wiley and Sons, 1943.
8. Foster, R. G., and P. P. Wilson. *Women After College.* New York: Columbia University Press, 1942.
9. Hartshorne, Edward Y. "Undergraduate Society and the College Culture," *American Sociological Review,* 8:321–32 (June 1943).
10. Kirkpatrick, Clifford, and Theodore Caplow. "Courtship in a Group of Minnesota Students," *American Journal of Sociology,* 51:114–25 (September 1945).
11. Kirkpatrick, Clifford, and Theodore Caplow. "Emotional Trends in the Courtship Experience of College Students," *American Sociological Review,* 10:619–26 (October 1945).
12. Lundberg, F., and M. F. Farnham. *Modern Woman: The Lost Sex.* New York: Harper, 1947.
13. McBride, K. E. "What Is Women's Education?" *Annals of the American Academy of Political and Social Science,* 251:143–52 (May 1947).
14. Metropolitan Life Insurance Company. *Statistical Bulletin,* Vol. 25, No. 8, August 1944, and Vol. 27, No. 7, July 1946.
15. Miller, Frieda S. "Women in the Labor Force," *Annals of the American Academy of Political and Social Science,* 251:35–43 (May 1947).
16. Moreno, J. L. *Who Shall Survive?* New York: Nervous and Mental Disease Publishing Co., 1934.
17. Newcomb, T. "Recent Changes in Attitudes toward Sex and Marriage," *American Sociological Review,* 2:659–67 (October 1937).
18. Popenoe, Paul. "Mate Selection," *American Sociological Review,* 2:735–43 (October 1937).
19. Terman, L. M., and Catherine C. Miles. *Sex and Personality.* New York: McGraw-Hill, 1936.
20. Waller, Willard. "The Rating and Dating Complex," *American Sociological Review,* 2:727–34 (October 1937).

The Student Personnel Point of View

American Council on Education

E. G. Williamson, Chairman   Helen G. Fisk
Willard W. Blaesser   Forrest H. Kirkpatrick
Helen D. Bragdon   Esther Lloyd-Jones
William S. Carlson   T. R. McConnell
W. H. Cowley   Thornton W. Merriam
D. D. Feder   Donald J. Shank

I. Philosophy and Objectives

The central purpose of higher education is the preservation, transmittal, and enrichment of culture by means of instruction, scholarly work, and scientific research. During the past few decades experience has pointed up the desirability of broadening this purpose to embrace additional emphases and objectives. Among these new goals, three stand out:

1. Education for a fuller realization of democracy in every phase of living;
2. Education directly and explicitly for international understanding and cooperation;
3. Education for the application of creative imagination and trained intelligence to the solution of social problems and to the administration of publications.[1]

Although these added goals aim essentially at societal growth, they affect positively the education and development of each individual student. The development of students as whole persons interacting in social situations is the central concern of student personnel work and of other agencies of education. This emphasis in contemporary education is the essential part of the student personnel point of view.

The student personnel point of view encompasses the student as a whole.

---

1. Adapted from *Higher Education for American Democracy: The Report of the President's Commission on Higher Education, Establishing the Goals* (Washington: Government Printing Office, 19475 New York: Harper & Bros., 1948).

The concept of education is broadened to include attention to the student's well rounded development—physically, socially, emotionally and spiritually, as well as intellectually. The student is thought of as a responsible participant in his own development and not as a passive recipient of an imprinted economic, political, or religious doctrine, or vocational skill. As a responsible participant in the societal processes of our American democracy, his full and balanced maturity is viewed as a major end goal of education as well, a necessary means to the fullest development of his fellow-citizens. From the personnel point of view any lesser goal falls short of the desired objective of democratic educational processes, and is a real drain and strain upon the self-realization of other developing individuals in our society.

The realization of this objective—the full maturing of each student— cannot be attained without interest in and integrated efforts toward the development of each and every facet of his personality and potentialities. His deepening understanding of his world is not sacrificed to his emotional maturing. His physical well-being does not become a limited end in itself. His maturing sense of values, social and spiritual, is not sacrificed to his understanding of the world of man and nature. His need for developing a sound philosophy of life to serve as the norm for his actions now and in adult life is not neglected in the college's emphasis on his need for intellectual and professional competence. Rather are all known aspects of the personality of each student viewed by the educator and personnel worker as an integrated whole—as a human personality living, working, and growing in a democratic society of other human personalities.

A long and honorable history stands behind this point of view. From the Middle Ages until the beginning of the nineteenth century, European higher education and its American offshoots gave as much attention to the social, moral, and religious development of students as to their intellectual growth. But the rise of the modern research centered German university early in the nineteenth century led to the abandonment of this personal concern for students and centered on an intellectualistic concern. Influenced by German models, American educators steered American higher education toward intellectualism.

Prosecution of scientific research and the stimulation of the intellectual development of students became the dominant emphases in American higher education. The earlier concern of Colonial educators for the spiritual, social, and personal development of students was shunted aside for more than a half century in most universities and in some colleges. At the turn of the present century certain great social forces matured and converged to shift attention back to the student's broad development in all aspects of his personality.

The student personnel movement developed during the early twentieth century in part as a protest against German-born intellectualism and also as the result of the findings of the psychology of individual differences during the second decade of the present century. Its evolution was stimulated by the huge growth of American colleges and universities following the First World War. With hordes invading institutions of higher education, colleges sought means to maintain some personal and individual relationship with students.

Present-Day Objectives

The student personnel movement constitutes one of the most important efforts of American educators to treat the college and university students as individuals, rather than as entries in an impersonal roster. The movement, at the same time, expresses awareness of the significance of student group life in its manifold expressions from student residence to student mores, from problems of admission to problems of job placement. It has developed as the division of college and university administration concerned with students individually and students as groups. In a real sense this part of modern higher education is an individualized application of the research and clinical findings of modern psychology, sociology, cultural anthropology, and education to the task of aiding students to develop fully in the college environment.

The specific aspects of the student personnel program stemming from the above point of view will be discussed in a later section. In addition, however, certain fundamental issues in education are affected by the application of the personnel point of view.

The optimum development of the individual necessitates the recognition by teachers and administrators, as well as by professional personnel workers, of individual differences in backgrounds, abilities, interests, and goals. In the light of such individual variations each institution should define its educational purposes and then select its students in terms of these purposes. This concept of development demands flexibility in methods of teaching and in the shaping of content to fit the individual differences found in students. It also requires integration of various aspects of the curriculum.

The individual's full and balanced development involves the acquisition of the pattern of knowledge, skills, and attitudes consistent with his abilities, aptitudes, and interests. The range of acquisition is a broad one. Through his interest experiences he should acquire an appreciation of cultural values, the ability to adapt to changing social conditions, motivation to seek and to create desirable social changes, emotional control to direct his activities, moral and ethical values for himself and for his community, standards and habits of personal physical well-being, and the ability to choose a vocation which makes maximum use of his talents and enables him to make appropriate contributions to his society.

But such broad-gauge development of the individual should in no sense be considered as a sufficient and complete goal in itself. It is axiomatic today that no man lives in a social vacuum. Rather individual development is conditioned by the kind of society in which a person lives, and by the quality of interpersonal and group relationships which operate around him. He is constantly affecting society; and society is constantly shaping him. These relationships constitute the cultural patterns with which higher education must be concerned in its efforts to stimulate and guide the development of each of its students.

The cultural patterns of America have been, and will continue to be, deeply affected by the emergence of the United States as a world power. With the nation's new status in world affairs, the preservation of basic freedoms and responsibilities at home becomes increasingly important. Our way of life depends upon a renewed faith in, and extensive use of, democratic methods, upon the development of more citizens able to assume responsibilities in matters of social concern, and upon the active participation of millions of men and women in the enterprise of social improvement.

Such a social philosophy as that outlined above thrust upon the college an urgent responsibility for providing experiences which develop in its students a firm and enlightened belief in democracy, a matured understanding of its problems and methods, and a deep sense of responsibility for individual and collective action to achieve its goals. Both classroom and out-of-class activities of the college should be related to these ends, and students' organizations should be incorporated in the institution's total educational program. In both the curricular and the cocurricular program of the college the dynamic forces of society should be skillfully organized for the use of their learning values in furthering the development of students.

As educators, our attention should be focused upon the social forces of the institution itself, which also provide learning experiences for the student. For example, the relationships among the various groups on the campus affect such social development. If faculty and students and faculty and administration work closely together in achieving common objectives, curricular and cocurricular, the learning of socially desirable processes is thereby enhanced.

The college or university which accepts these broad responsibilities for aiding in the optimum development of the individual in his relations to society will need to evaluate carefully and periodically its curricular offerings, its method of instruction, and all other resources for assisting the individual to reach his personal goals. Among its important resources, it also will need to provide and strengthen the type of services as outlined in the next section, encompassed within the field of student personnel work.

II. Student Needs and Personnel Services

During their college years, students have opportunities for intensive class-room learning supplemented by many of the major elements of community living. Students live, work, make friends, have fun, make financial ends meet—all within the community of scholars. Since colleges seek to assist students to achieve optimum development of powers and usefulness, a comprehensive and explicit plan and program embracing many personnel services are necessary for this undertaking. The essential parts of such a plan and program are outlined in the following sections.

The student personnel point of view holds that the major responsibility for a student's growth in personal and social wisdom rests with the student himself. Necessarily, however, his development is conditioned by many factors. It is influenced by the background, the abilities, attitudes, and expectancies that he brings with him to college, by his college classroom experiences, and by his reactions to these experiences. A student's growth in personal and social wisdom will also be conditioned by the extent to which the following conditions are attained:

The student achieves orientation to his college environment. Individuals are freer to learn, are under less strain, suffer less confusion, and have more consistent and favorable self-concepts if they feel at home and oriented in relation to their environment. The personnel worker attempts to help students feel at home in their college environment through:

1. Interpreting institutional objectives and opportunities to prospective students, to their parents, and to high school faculties;
2. Selecting students who seem, after study, to be able to achieve in relation to the college offerings and requirements;
3. Orienting students to the many phases of their college lives through a carefully designed program that involves such methods and experiences as personnel records, tests, group instruction, counseling, and group life.

The student succeeds in his studies. The college or university has a primary responsibility in selecting for admission students who have the basic qualities of intelligence and aptitudes necessary for success in a given institution. However, many otherwise able students fail, or do not achieve up to maximum capacity, because they lack proficiency or personal motivation for the tasks set by the college, because of deficiency in reading or study skills, because they do not budget their time properly, have emotional conflicts resulting from family or other pressures, have generally immature attitudes, are not wisely counselled in relation to curricular choices, or because of a number of other factors. In order that each student may develop effective work habits and thereby achieve at his optimum potential, the college or university should provide services through which the student may acquire the skills and techniques for efficient utilization of his ability. In addition to the contribution of counseling in removing blockages from his path toward good achievement, the student may also need remedial reading and speech services, training in effective study habits, remediation of physical conditions, counseling concerning his personal motivations, and similar related services.

He finds satisfactory living facilities. Comfortable and congenial living arrangements contribute to the peace of mind and efficiency of the student. If effectively organized and supervised, the facilities that provide for food and shelter can also contribute to his social development and to his adjustments to group opportunities and restraints.

The student achieves a sense of belonging to the college. To a large extent the social adjustment of an individual consists of finding a role in relation to others which will make him feel valued, will contribute to his feeling of self-worth, and will contribute to a feeling of kinship with an increasing number of persons. The student personnel program will help him achieve these goals through:

1. Stimulating the development of many small groups;
2. Fostering the development of a program of student-initiated activities;
3. Encouraging the development of a diversified social program;
4. Developing opportunities for participation in college-community cooperative activities;
5. Fostering teacher-student intellectual and social relationships outside of the classroom.

The student learns balanced use of his physical capacities. It is not enough to conceive of a health service as an agency only for the treatment of illness in order to keep the student operating in the classroom at regular maximum efficiency. To be broadly effective, the health program should also aggressively promote a program of health education designed to equip each student with self-understanding and self-acceptance at his optimum personal level of physical competence. The adjustment of the individuals to his physical potentialities as well as to his irremediable limitations is a basic element in his full development of personality.

The student progressively understands himself. This is the process of self-discovery and rediscovery which, progressively over a period of time, must unfold for the student in terms of his individual readiness for it. Through a rich program of experiences and skillful counseling, the student may acquire an understanding of himself, his abilities, interests, motivations, and limitations. With such understanding the student becomes ready to make long-range life plans; he acquires the understandings and skills necessary to cope with life problems; he learns to face and solve his own personal problems; he grows personally and, in the process, make constructive social contribution. To aid in this development, the college or university provides:

1. Adequate services for testing and appraisal;
2. Skilled counselors trained in the art of stimulating and self-understanding without directing decisions;
3. Useful records available for study so that the student may inform himself of his present status and be apprised of whatever growth and development he has thus far achieved;
4. Other services which will help the student acquire such specialized knowledge as the individual should have concerning himself in order to make reasoned and reasonable choices and decisions.

The student understands and uses his emotions. As mainspring of action, emotions either may lead to disorganized and random behavior or to concerted, directed, worth-while accomplishment. Directed emotions may enrich and strengthen action which is otherwise sterile and terminal. A human being is a creature of emotions as well as intellect. Effective personal counseling will help the student to understand and use his emotional powers for maximum, directed action. Without such understanding and self-direction the student may soon find himself not only ineffective, but also socially inept and unacceptable. The counseling service, psychiatric services, and organized group activities are among the parts of the student personnel services which may assist the student in this area of achievement.

The student develops lively and significant interests. Many aspects of personality directly related to attractiveness, alertness, and forcefulness are conditioned by the number and depth of interests in an individual is able to cultivate. The effective college will recognize this by:

1. Helping the student to discover his basic interests; and,
2. Fostering a program of recreational and discussional activities that is diversified.

The student achieves understanding and control of his financial resources. Learning how to live within his income, how to increase that income, how to find financial aids that are available are part of an understanding of the student's economic life. Such an understanding of money-values must be achieved in balanced relationships to physical energy, curricular, and social demands.

Counseling students on financial matters and administering financial aids in such a way as to help the most worthy and most needy are important parts of the student personnel program.

The student progresses toward appropriate vocational goals. Some students enroll in college without a definite plan of preparation for a career. Others will modify their plans as they acquire new interests or gain clearer understanding of their own capacities and of requirements for certain occupations in relation to the needs of society. But many men and women who come to college do so without any plans or understanding of themselves in relation to the world of work. The college has a responsibility to see that these students have access to accurate, usable information about opportunities, requirements, and training for various occupations appropriate to their possible levels of vocational preparation. Vocational counseling given on a basis on insight, information, and vision can help students to relate their future work to their life goals. When conducted with social imagination, such counseling can help to develop these leaders who will pioneer in new professions and in the extension of needed services for the country's welfare.

The student develops individuality and responsibility. Progressive emancipation from the restrictions of childhood is a major challenge to every adolescent. Reveling in his new found freedoms, for which he may not yet be prepared by adequate self-discipline, the college student may find himself in conflict with accepted social patterns and standards. Other students, whose domination by their families may extend to the college campus, may voice their rebellion in actions offensive to their fellow-students or embarrassing to the college family to which they now belong. In such situations, preventive therapy may be accomplished by enlisting parental cooperation in counseling in such personal problems when they are discovered and diagnosed. When the need for social discipline does arise, the college should approach in the problem as a special phase of counseling in the development of self-responsibility for behavior rather than in a spirit of punishment of misbehavior.

The student discovers ethical and spiritual meaning in life. For many students the introduction to scientific understandings and meanings in the classroom may necessitate a drastic reorientation of religious ideology or a new level of objectivity. The time-honored teachings of organized religion may lose their effectiveness both as explanatory and guiding principles. The resultant disturbance may have deep and far-reaching ramifications into personal as well as family, and even broader, social conflicts. In his new search for values which are worthy of personal allegiance in a time of social conflict, the student needs mature guidance. The religious counselor and the religious-activities program with a broad social reference may assist the student in developing an understanding of proper concepts of behavior, ethical standards, and spiritual values consistent with his broadened horizons resulting from newly acquired scientific and technical knowledge.

The student learns to live with others. The maintenance of individual integrity within a framework of cooperative living and working with others in a spirit of mutual service is the highest expression of democracy. By intelligent followership as well as by permissive leadership the student prepares himself for his social obligations beyond the college. By means of special-interest groups, student government, dormitory and house councils, and other guided group activities, the student personnel program can provide opportunities for developing in the student his capacities for both leadership and followership. The counseling service will also use such activities as may be appropriate for individual therapy and development as the needs may be revealed through suitable diagnostic procedures.

The student progresses toward satisfying and socially acceptable sexual adjustments. During the years when young people are in college, they are normally deeply, although perhaps covertly, concerned with finding congenial marriage partners. This concern may produce anxieties which evaluate in behavior that may be either acceptable or unacceptable to society, and satisfying or unsatisfying to the individuals. Since marriage adjustment is basic to family stability, and since the family is our most important social institution, colleges should help students to effect satisfying, socially acceptable, and ethically sound sexual adjustments by (1) encouraging the development of a rich and diversified social and recreational program, (2) providing counseling on relationship and marriage problems.

The student prepares for satisfying constructive postcollege activity. For most students the activities of postcollege years will be a combination of the practice of a profession, progression in an occupation, marriage and family life, and service as a community and world citizen.

Personnel services of the college appropriate to these attainments may include job placement, information about jobs, internships, graduate training programs, or opportunities for volunteer service. Some colleges include also some periodic follow-up contacts to determine the success of their graduates.

Elements of a Student Personnel Program

The achievement of the foregoing objectives requires the cooperative and integrated functioning of classroom and extraclass activities with the growth and development of the student as the focal point of all that is implied in the educational process. To be sure, not every student will need or make use of all the student personnel services just as, by the same token, not every student studies courses in every academic department. But the college should make optimum provision for the development of the individual and his place in society through its provisions for:

1. The process of admissions, not as a credit-counting service, but rather as a first step in the counseling procedure designed to interpret the institution to the student, his family, and his high school teachers in terms of its requirements for success, its services, and its ability to satisfy his educational and personal needs.

2. The keeping of personnel records and their use in the improved understanding of, and service to, the individual student as he has contact not only with the classroom, but also in all phases of his college or university life.

3. The service to the student of trained, sympathetic counselors to assist him in thinking through his education, vocational, and personal adjustment problems. Such a service should be so designed as to be in effect a cohesive agency drawing together all the institution's resources in the process of facilitating the student's efforts to achieve the objectives of higher education. This service will have access, either through direct association or as a supplementary service, to psychological testing and other special diagnostic services as may be necessary to achieve better and more objective appraisal and understanding of the individual. Resources for adequate vocational information as may be needed by the student in the process of his orientation should be closely correlated with the counseling program. Special attention should be given to the educational importance of supplementing the efforts of counseling specialists by the use of carefully selected, specially trained faculty members serving as advisers and counselors.

4. Physical and mental health services whose orientation is not only the treatment of illness, but also, and even primarily, an educational program of preventive medicine and personal-hygiene counseling.

5. Remedial services in the areas of speech, reading, and study habits, recognizing that the presence of defects in these areas may seriously impede the functioning of many able students and also restrict the contributions which may be made by otherwise adequate personalities.

6. Supervision and integration of housing and food services to the end that they shall not only provide for the physical comforts of students, but also shall contribute positively to education in group living and social graces.

7. A program of activities designed to induct the student into his new life and environment as a member of the college or university family.

8. The encouragement and supervision of significant group activities arising from the natural interest of students.

9. A program of recreational activities designed to promote lifetime interests and skills appropriate to the individual student.

10. The treatment of discipline as an educational function designed to modify personal behavior patterns and to substitute socially acceptable attitudes for those which have precipitated unacceptable behavior.

11. Financial aid to worthy students, not as a dole, but as an educational experience in personal budgeting and responsibility.

12. Opportunities for self-help through part-time and summer employment, geared as nearly as possible to the defined vocational objectives of the student.

13. Assistance to the student in finding appropriate employment after leaving college and subsequently assisting alumni in further professional development.

14. The proper induction, orientation, and counseling of students from abroad.

15. The enrichment of college and postcollege life through a well-integrated program of religious activities, including interfaith programs and individual religious counseling.

16. Counseling for married students and for those contemplating marriage to prepare them for broadening family and social responsibilities.

17. A continuing program of evaluation of student personnel services and of the educational program to insure the achievement by students of the objectives for which this program is designed.

III. The Administration of Student Personnel Work

The administrative pattern of student personnel work in any one college or university will necessarily be adapted to the local resources and personnel. Although no definitive and evaluative studies of different types of administrative organization are available, yet in the last decade of student personnel work, the following generalizations have evolved.

Interrelation of Campus Resources

Everyone on a campus, from the students to the president, participates in some phase of the student personnel program. But certain personnel functions are usually the direct responsibility of designated staff members.

Interested teachers devote time to counseling and the guidance of student organizations. Dormitory directors organize recreational and hobby activities. Such specialists as counselors, medical officers, psychiatrists, and psychometrists assist students in various ways. Many other examples of the range and types of personnel workers will be identified by the interested observer.

The nature of student personnel work is such that certain aspects of most activities may involve the interrelationship of a number of individuals in varying ways. For example, the operation of an effective orientation program for new students draws on many different persons. The teacher-counselor, the admissions officer, the doctor, other students, the administrative heads of the institution, the housing officer, recreational leaders, and others must contribute to an effective orientation program. Such interrelation of resources makes coordination necessary.

Administrative Structure

Experience indicates that specialized functions performed by trained personnel staff members should be organized with the customary definiteness found in instructional departments and colleges. For example, functions related to counseling need to be organized in a department, bureau, or center manned by the staff performing such functions. In similar manner, the functions of admissions, supervision of extracurricular activities, and many others of those discussed in the previous section need to be assigned to designated persons and departments.

This is not to say, however, that each personnel function needs to be organized in a separate bureau or assigned to a different individual or that each bureau or individual has a monopolistic control over its special functions. In smaller institutions, where the volume of work and the number of available staff members are limited, the form of organization can be simpler. But the principle of definiteness of assigned responsibility for each personnel function should be clearly established, even though only one member of a staff may be available to perform the function. In larger institutions, the volume of work permits, and sometimes compels, more formal organization and greater degrees of specialization.

As volume of services and size of staff increase, the necessity for centralization of administrative responsibility of an over-all nature becomes more readily apparent. The experience of the past decade indicates the desirability of assigning the responsibility for personnel work to an administrator. This generalization follows the pattern clearly established historically of designating instructional responsibility in the dean of a faculty or in the president in a small institution. When volume of work and other factors warrant it, a personnel administrator should be free from responsibility for any one personnel function or service in order that he may be able to deal effectively with over-all program development and coordination on a college-wide basis. As in the case of the instructional program of a college, the major personnel administrator, working with and through a staff council of personnel workers, should be held responsible for such administrative functions as budget-making and distribution; recruitment of staff; appointment and induction of staff members; stimulation of professional growth of personnel staff members; planning the continuous development of cooperation and coordination among the personnel specialists and between personnel work and the instructional program of the institution; and evaluation of the effectiveness of the total program.

The advocacy of a single administrative head for personnel work does not imply the assignment to such a person of complete and arbitrary authority. Instructional administrators have developed modifications of this centralization of authority in the form of program and policy committees composed of deans and faculty members and students. Indeed, the president of a college leans heavily upon his council of deans for aid in administration. In turn, each dean shares his administrative responsibilities with an executive committee of his faculty. In similar manner personnel administrators must enlist the help of specialists and of members of the instructional staff in determining policies and in planning personnel programs. Policy committees and coordinating councils should assist in administration and in continuous development of more effective services to education.

Decentralization of functions, as opposed to centralization in one person or one department, actually may increase the direct effectiveness of these services to students, provided that coordination produces the exchange of information and leads to the avoidance of conflict of services. Each institution must develop its own coordinating mechanisms for bringing together these decentralized services into a balanced, institution-wide program. Coordinating councils, informal meetings, exchange of memorandums, the maintenance of friendly working relationships—these and many other administrative devices need to be developed and maintained at a high level of effectiveness.

Process in Program Administration

Preoccupation with problems of administrative structure should not lead to neglect of process. Personnel literature to date is full of discussions of structure, of line and staff relationships, the points at which various responsibilities should rest, assignments of responsibility to various points of the structure, the ways in which parts should fit together, how they may be expected to work in relation to each other, and related topics.

Equal attention should be given to process. In a simple line and staff structure, for example, communication involves sharing information through organizational lines—down from the top in a relay pattern and sometimes up from the bottom along the established lines. Personnel administrators recognize that even two-way communication, however efficiently carried out, is not adequate for personnel work, and further experience is needed with respect to alternative forms of communication and administrative relationships. For example, personnel workers of all types need to meet regularly for discussions of common problems and for planning of interrelated programs of services. Experience indicates that not only information, but also feelings, always important in cooperative undertakings and other types of human relations, can best be transmitted in such face-to-face situations, and in well-planned and executed staff discussions of common problems and cooperative enterprises. Similarly, group planning of programs and discussions of issues and problems may produce better results than are obtained through the efforts of any single staff member. Furthermore, although each group will almost always create a leader role and ask someone to take this role, full participation of all members is best achieved when the role is passed from person to person within the group in terms of the differing competencies and experiences of the members in relation to the varying needs of the total program.

Participation in Institutional Administration

Personnel workers at all levels of specialization and administrative responsibility should be given appropriate opportunity and responsibility for participating in planning and policy-making for all phases of the institution's instructional and public-relations programs.

Students' Participation in Administration

Students can make significant contributions to the development and maintenance of effective personnel programs through contributing evaluations of the quality of the services, new ideas for changes in the services, and fresh impetus to staff members who may become immersed in techniques and the technicalities of the professional side of personnel work.

In addition to the use of advisory student councils and committees for reviewing programs and policies, personnel administrators and specialists should avail themselves frequently of opportunities for informal consultation with many individual students.

A Balanced Staff

Personnel specialists as well as personnel administrators should be chosen for their personal and professional competence to discharge their responsibilities. Personnel specialists and administrators, both men and women, should be available in all of the personnel departments. That is, competent men counselors should be available for those students who prefer to consult a man. In like manner, competent women counselors should be available for those men and women who prefer to consult a woman about scholastic or personal adjustments. Both men and women administrators should be members of top policymaking councils.

Special attention needs to be given to the maintenance of balance in another respect, namely, narrow specialization in one type of technique, adjustment problem, or school of thought. Each personnel staff should be maintained in a balanced manner with respect to desirably varied professional points of view and professional backgrounds of specialists.

Criteria for Evaluating Program

The principal responsibility of all personnel workers lies in the area of progressive program development. Essentially this means that each worker must devote a large part of his time to the formulation of new plans and to the continuous evaluation and improvement of current programs. The test of effectiveness of any personnel service lies in the differences it makes in the development of individual students, and every worker must develop his own workaday yardsticks for evaluation. The following suggest themselves as possible criteria for a continuing day-by-day appraisal of the program. No single criterion, alone and independent of others, would probably have much validity, but, taken together, they may provide an effective working relationship among staff members with respect to their program responsibilities.

These criteria are:

1. Students' expression of satisfaction and dissatisfaction with services received. These expressions may be informally collected or may be gathered systematically. Obviously such expressions need to be critically evaluated in terms of the total situation.
2. Expression of satisfaction and dissatisfaction with the programs by members of the teaching staff. Again, such expressions need to be evaluated.
3. The extent of students' uses of the personnel services. Again, this criterion must be applied with full cognizance of the limitations of financial resources and other institutional factors balanced against the needs of the personnel departments.
4. The continuance of improvement in the professional training and professional status of members of the personnel staff through additional formal training, experiences, committee assignments, and other local, regional, and national recognition.
5. The quality of the interpersonal relationships and cooperation between personnel workers and members of the instructional and noninstructional staffs, and among personnel specialists themselves.

Institutional Mores and Policies

The effectiveness of a student personnel program is determined not solely by either its technical quality or its administrative and financial structure, but even more by its institutional setting. In an institution where conditions are favorable to the maintenance of friendly, informal working relationships between teachers and students, and where the institutional leaders explicitly support such relationships, effective counseling may be developed far more readily and effectively than would be the case in institutions burdened with an anti-faculty attitude established among student leaders.

Personnel workers of all types, particularly those involved in groupwork functions, need to give continuous attention to the development of positive relationships in their work with student leaders. But, essentially, the institutional leader, the president, must set the standard of such mores. He can accomplish this by making clear his own basic attitudes toward students, teachers, and personnel workers, and the interrelated contributions of each group to the total institutional program of assistance to each student in his efforts to achieve full and broad development.

The Future of Student Personnel Work in Higher Education

W. W. Blaesser

Our title, "The Future of Student Personnel Work with Higher Education," may sound rather ambitious for a symposium entitled "Counseling, Guidance and Placement." Possibly the theme of this conference, "Improving the Effectiveness of Higher Education," prompted it. We prefer to use the term "student personnel work" because it encompasses more accurately those educational services which need greater emphasis today. We shall discuss the meaning of student personnel work shortly, but let us first briefly outline the full paper. First, we wish to discuss the student personnel point of view, the meaning of student personnel work, and the need for a much broader application of this point of view and meaning to educational practices today. Secondly, we shall review what we consider to be the essential aspects of a student personnel program, as well as the major assumptions underlying the total program. We shall treat very briefly the history of student personnel work, its status today, and lastly we shall comment upon those aspects of the program which we consider most in need of emphasis in the future.

The philosophy underlying student personnel work was clearly stated by the American Council on Education in 1937 as follows:

One of the basic purposes of higher education is the preservation, transmission, and enrichment of the important elements of culture—the product of scholarship, research, creative imagination, and human experience. It is the task of colleges and universities so to vitalize this and other educational purposes as to assist the student in developing to the limits of his potentialities and in making his contribution to the betterment of society.

This philosophy imposes upon education institutions the obligation to consider the student as a whole—his intellectual capacity and achievement, his emotional

Author's Note: E. H. Hopkins, State College of Washington, was co-author of this paper.

makeup, his physical condition, his social relationships, his vocational aptitudes and skills, his aesthetic appreciations, his moral and religious values, his economic resources. It puts emphasis, in brief, upon the development of the student as a person rather than upon his intellectual training alone.[1]

This philosophy has had a profound influence upon recent trends in higher education. We choose to use it as a point of departure, a point of view in defining more specifically what we have in mind when we refer to student personnel work.

Obviously, any institution of higher education must offer a sound and adequate program for the intellectual development of its students or its very existence is not justified. But that is not enough. We suggest a broad definition. In our opinion, student personnel work consists of all those processes and functions undertaken by an educational institution which place emphasis on:

1. the individual student and his intellectual, social, emotional and physical development;
2. the building of curricula, methods of instruction and extra-classroom programs to achieve the preceding objective;
3. democratic procedures in working with students in order to help bring about their greatest possible self-realization;
4. the *performance* of student personnel functions rather than on specifically designated individuals to perform them.

If we analyze this definition, we find that it has several implications.

It has reference to the *application* of the student personnel point of view, the *application* of a democratic method, and the *application* of a consistent purpose in education. It puts emphasis upon work actually done by the various members of the staff, and not merely upon a point of view which may be accepted enthusiastically because it sounds good, but which may not reach a stage of practical use by the members of the faculty and staff who have immediate contacts with the students.

It should help to eliminate the controversy between "student personnel work" on the one hand, and "instruction" on the other. It assumes that student personnel work can and should be done by *all* members of the academic, instructional, and administrative staffs, differing only in extent and in the respective roles of the staff members involved. It implies the concept of "every teacher a personnel worker." It does not imply that *all* teaching (good, bad, or indifferent) is personnel work. The researcher, and

---

1. *The Student Personnel Point of View*, American Council on Education, Series 1, Vol. 1, No. 3, 1937.

even the good teacher, normally would be spending far less of his time in actually performing student personnel work than would the clinical counselor, the dean of students, or the faculty counselor. Thus, student personnel work is carried on *throughout* the institution, differing from staff member to staff member, but only in terms of role, degree, and types of specialization.

The definition does not assume that a hard and fast line can be drawn between student personnel work on the one hand and instruction on the other. It does assume, however, that each of these functions can be defined and that each may exist alone or that each may overlap in any single instance. In other words, some teaching and particularly good teaching, might well be student personnel work. Certain types of student personnel work would also be teaching. This concept may be illustrated by showing at one end of a graphic continuum the strictly teaching functions, and at the other end, the strictly student personnel functions, but in the middle a "gray" area of service which could and should be referred to as both teaching *and* student personnel work. An example of this dual purpose function would be an instructor teaching a course in "Vocational Guidance," or a course in "Mental Hygiene." These are the obvious examples of the dual functions, where a distinctive line between student personnel work and teaching cannot be drawn—but by definition they clearly overlap. This overlapping is good, it is healthy, it is an objective for which to strive.

We are not proposing anything new. We are merely emphasizing a broader concept of student personnel work than is currently prevalent. We think that this broader view is urgently needed if student personnel work is going to contribute its maximum to higher education. There are some critics who believe that student personnel work is solely a field of specialization engaged in by those who are *professionally* trained—that the regular faculty member or the "untrained" administrator must not venture into the sacred bounds of the student personnel specialist. There is nothing in our proposed definition which excludes the professionally trained clinical counselor, the professionally trained full-time student personnel administrator, or any other professionally trained and competent personnel technician. All are sorely needed, and with higher standards of professional competence than we now have generally. The wide variety of student problems and the various ways by which the student can get individual help from his teachers, his counselors, his deans, and others who are in strategic positions to help him, necessitate a recognition of these various roles within the field of student personnel work. *All* these roles are equally necessary and are equally important. When they are all truly coordinated into a single-purpose program, then we believe we will be *well on our way* to an effective program of student personnel services, and therefore a *more effective program of higher education.*

Six major assumptions underlie the foregoing concept of student personnel work:

1. That individuals will inevitably have problems in adjusting to a complex society.
2. That personality must be considered as a whole.
3. That there must be emphasis on prevention.
4. That personality and environment are interrelated.
5. That the individual has the capacity to take the major responsibility for his learning and for the solution of his problems.
6. That a common purpose must be defined and must operate in an interdependent democratic society.

The first fundamental assumption is that individuals inevitably will have problems in adjusting to a complex society. Many problems confront the college student making the necessary social, physical, and emotional adjustments. Some students, without being "problem cases" in themselves, need assistance in meeting the stress and strain of these adjustments. Problems differ from individual to individual and each student must be recognized as having unique problems and characteristics. It is n this area that the *specialized* personnel services make their major contribution. It follows that personal problems should be turned into constructive learning experiences.

Second, in considering the wholeness of personality as a basic factor in sound personnel work, we must assume that the intellectual person, without his emotional, physical, and social reactions, is a logical abstraction rather than a reality. The natural but regrettable tendency is to consider each individual in terms of parts. With the integrated personality as a goal, we must of necessity eliminate any distinction between the primary objectives that have been separately designated in the past to personnel workers on the one hand and faculty members on the other. The student must be helped to understand that the educative process is a vital part of "real life," of living now.

In considering the third assumption, the necessity for the emphasis on prevention, it is assumed that the development of the whole student can best be achieved by preventing the more serious problems. More failures can be avoided by appropriate admissions and distribution policies than by adjustive measures employed after the student has become educationally and personally demoralized. These adjustive measures are of course important because their services are essential as a means of further prevention. Unless institutions of higher learning are prepared to exercise adequate adjustive measures to alleviate problems that have their roots in earlier development, such institutions are to a large extent responsible for the continuance and even the further aggravation of social and emotional maladjustments.

The fourth assumption calls attention to the interaction of the personality and the environment. A student's highly individual responses to his college experiences, and their cumulative effect, will have influence throughout his lifetime. The individual functions always in a social medium; consequently, the educational program must take into account the social pressures, mores, and accepted cultural patterns of the college community. Furthermore, the college environment cannot be assumed to be identical for all individuals.

Because of our conviction that the integrity of each person must be respected, our next assumption, that the individual has the capacity to take the major responsibility for his learning and for the solution of his problems, is of outstanding importance. People have a right to assume responsibility for their own action and development. We believe strongly that each individual has the inner drives and the capacity for self-development—that all learning basically is self-education. It is imperative that students have the opportunity to direct their lives in constructive ways. Good personnel work strengthens the decision-making abilities of students and aids in this self-growth process. Students can develop to their fullest and function effectively only in a democratic environment in which they have roles to play. In such an environment they should be encouraged to participate with the faculty and administration in making policies and setting up educational programs.

The sixth assumption is a rhetorical one. The need for common educational purposes for both personnel workers and instructional staff is being emphasized throughout this paper. Such an institutional atmosphere is imperative.

We need now to indicate the services and functions which are essential to a sound program of student personnel work. The American Council on Education published a list of twenty-three student personnel functions in 1937, and since that time a number of revisions and regroupings have been made.[2] We have regrouped them as follows:

1. Interpretation of institutional objectives to prospective students and to workers in secondary education.
2. Selection and admission of students.
3. Orientation of the new student to his college environment.
4. Provision of diagnostic and counseling services.
5. Remedial assistance in speech, reading, and other subjects as needed.
6. Supervision, coordination, and integration of the "co-curricular" program on the campus.

2. Wrenn and Kamm, "A Procedure for Evaluating a Student Personnel Program," in *School and Society*, Vol. 67, April 3, 1948; E. H. Hopkins, "The essentials of a Student Personnel Program," in *College and University*, July, 1948.

7. Provision of physical and mental health services.
8. Supervision of living arrangements, including the food service program.
9. Administration of financial aids, student employments, post-graduate placements, and job follow-ups.
10. Development and evaluation of the religious life and interests of students.
11. Development and use of permanent cumulative personnel records.
12. Application of a knowledge of student needs to the curriculum and to the instructional functions of the institution.
13. Use of both preventive and counseling procedures in carrying out discipline work.
14. Systematic evaluation of student personnel services.
15. On-the-job training, development, and stimulation of all persons performing student personnel functions.

While this paper is concerned mainly with needed emphases in student personnel work, we should like now to comment very briefly about its heritage. The minutes of the early faculty meetings at the University of Wisconsin are excellent source material, but we will have to limit ourselves to a few generalizations.

We know that Professor Sterling was not the least bit concerned about the *definitions* of student personnel work when he welcomed the first University of Wisconsin students about one hundred years ago. Nevertheless, in the tradition of American collegiate education at that time, he thought of education as involving a concern for *all* aspects of the student's life. James F. A. Pyre's book, *Wisconsin*, informs us that on the afternoon of Chancellor Lathrop's inauguration in 1849, the Board of Regents reported to the legislature the urgent need for dormitories if the University was to begin "its proper work."[3] The only new buildings constructed between 1849 and 1855 were dormitories, and one of these, South Hall, contained quarters also for members of the faculty and their families. This made it easy for the faculty to watch over the students, checking on student conduct, study habits, sleeping habits, etc. In fact, the minutes of the University of Wisconsin faculty meetings of those early years abound with references to faculty concern for the manners, morals, and character of the student as well as his intellectual growth. Misdemeanors were solemnly reported in the minutest detail at these faculty meetings; there was serious consideration of the action that should be taken for the welfare of both the student and the institution.

Wisconsin was not unique in this regard. Cowley's research into the

3. James F. A. Pyre, *Wisconsin* (New York, 1920).

history of higher education has revealed that these "Alma Maternal ministra-
tions to students had characterized the universities of the Middle Ages and
had been the most notable element in American higher education up to the
time of the Civil War."[4]

Personnel activities in American institutions of higher learning, according
to Cowley, fell into disrepute because of secularization, specialization, and
especially as a result of the influence of the intellectualistic impersonalism
imported by American scholars trained in Germany. He places the heyday of
the intellectualists between 1870 and 1920 and relates that during this period
personnel work was considered to be a necessary evil. Reactions, however,
came from (1) the humanitarians who tried to promote mental hygiene,
vocational counseling, and other individual services for college students, (2)
from far-seeing administrators like President Gilman of Johns Hopkins who
created the country's first system of faculty advisers, or like President
Harper of Chicago who emphasized *residential housing*, (3) from the applied
psychologists who began to identify individual differences in intellectual
capacities and personal characteristics, and (4) from the students themselves
who began to build an extensive extracurriculum.[5]

The personnel movement made considerable headway after World War I
as psychologists, interested in the measurement of intelligence, turned their
attention from the Army to colleges and universities and to industry. Also,
during this period, the professional aspects of student personnel work were
stressed heavily by the applied psychologists, interested administrators, and
the professional organizations in the field. Research efforts brought forth
improved tests, inventories and other devices to measure interest, aptitude,
and personality characteristics. Findings were applied to the development of
a systematic approach to educational, vocational, and personal counseling,
in which diagnostic procedures played an important part.

There were also numerous attempts during the thirties to identify relationships among the many student personnel services and functions. This effort
was devoted largely to keeping each function from obstructing the other.
This made possible the development of neat organization charts with box-
tight compartments—but with relatively unsatisfactory results.[6]

Services and functions did expand rapidly during this period. This led to

4. W. H. Cowley, "The Past and Future of Student Personnel Work," *Proceedings, University
of Minnesota Personnel Institute*, November, 1947.

5. W. H. Cowley, "The History and Philosophy of Student Personnel Work," in *Proceedings,
American College Personnel Association*, February, 1940.

6. Esther Lloyd-Jones, "Personnel Work Today," in the *Journal of Higher Education*, 13:81–86
(February, 1942).

considerable talk about centralization, although a somewhat counter trend toward coordination of decentralized services was in evidence.

In the years immediately preceding Pearl Harbor, there was a definite attempt on the part of student personnel work to discover its role in relation to the objectives of higher education. Several new colleges began to develop a more unified plan of education by appointing faculty members who were good teachers and good scholars and who in addition had ability, interest, and successful experience in working with students.

Student personnel work became almost entirely military personnel work after Pearl Harbor. Most of the specialized personnel workers donned uniforms and helped to develop the vast testing, interviewing, and classification programs of the Army and Navy. Others did urgent research on tools, techniques, and training devices. Some went into industrial and government personnel work. A few remained on college campuses to help administer wartime training programs and to keep alive a minimal personnel program for the greatly reduced numbers of civilian students.

A challenging book by Carl Rogers reached the colleges early in the war, in time to start a ground swell of controversy about the counseling procedures which he advocated.[7] His book attacked the diagnostic tools and techniques of the clinical counselor and argued for a counseling approach which relied upon the counselee's capacity for self-growth rather than upon the counselor's diagnostic skill. Although the full implications of Rogers' approach for student personnel work are only now being recognized, special note is made in this section to record its origin during the war years.

The Veterans Administration Guidance Centers appeared on many campuses at the end of the war. These centers have affected the development of student personnel programs on numerous campuses, but their full significance cannot yet be determined.

Today, we have a situation representing the composite influences of all these forces. Especially pertinent were the developments during and since the war.

The complexity of the present situation at best is baffling to all of us. We are faced with a changing, groping, unstable world. We have a heterogeneous mass of educational practices being used and misused throughout our respective institutions. The rapid postwar expansion of all our educational services, the vast increases in student enrollments caused principally by the influx of veterans, the personnel problems arising from these increased enrollments—in teaching, housing, feeding, and counseling—have all tended to complicate further the picture of "student personnel work today." In addition to these,

7. Carl R. Rogers, *Counseling and Psychotherapy* (New York, 1942).

we have a shortage of qualified student personnel workers, teachers, and administrators. As a consequence, the standards for all this work have necessarily fallen, and at a time when quality is needed more than ever. Student personnel services, as well as other educational functions, have been greatly multiplied on most of our campuses, and frequently without adequate regard to sound administrative and coordinating structure. Inadequate faculties, heavy teaching loads, research demands, and other institutional responsibilities are preventing even the good teachers from doing the kind of job they would like to do and are capable of doing.

Out of all this, however, some promising trends can be identified. There is an increasing tendency to assign to one person the coordinating and administrative responsibility for the student personnel program. There is an increasing emphasis on the need for the improvement of standards and "quality" of work performed. More attention is being given to personal-adjustment counseling. Finally, but very important, is the prevalence of institutions' evaluations of their own programs. Many college faculties, in the past three years, have taken an inward look at their institutions, their curricula, their objectives, and the relation of all these to the crucial problems ahead. This is significant. Improvements should follow.

This leads us to the important question, "What about the future of student personnel work?" The formula for the future is no different now from what it might have been at any point in our historical past. It calls for an analysis of our problem, including a study of the past and an unbiased appraisal of the present, a critical determination of accepted, pertinent, and constructive educational objectives, followed by a concrete and realistic plan of action. This formula is relatively simple and is applicable to virtually all problems. It involves also the responsibility for following through with constructive programs of action. However, the current societal situation is different from any other even remotely comparable situation in history, and therefore may call for a program of action heretofore considered inappropriate or unnecessary. "Urgency" is now the driving force behind any analysis and program of action. The tremendous complexity and the "interwoveness" of our social, economic, political, military, and security problems have never before been so strategically related, and the responsibility of higher education in these areas is a matter of real concern.

While our instruments for dealing with these problems need far greater refinement than yet has been achieved, we do have more scientific "know how" in dealing with social problems than we have had previously. We not only have more refined research and statistical techniques, but recent fruits of scientific research have given us a broadened understanding of the learning processes and an appreciation of the significance of individual and trait differences. Also, we have revised our concepts of mental discipline theories. We have developed new emphasis on motivation and purpose in learning. We have reached a better understanding of the importance of "learning by doing" (hence the college campus as a laboratory in democratic living), and we have a new emphasis upon "teaching for generalized meanings and abilities" rather than knowledge for knowledge's sake. These are examples of only some of the current findings which have a significance to the over-all problem of determining the most appropriate programs of student personnel services and, in fact, the most appropriate programs of higher education generally.

A consideration of the future of student personnel work leads directly into the last process included in the simple formula already indicated. We need a vigorous "action" program, based upon the findings of scientific research and upon a concerted effort to apply the revised definition or concept of student personnel work at the various levels and in the various roles of educational work.

One of the best attempts to do just this is represented by the procedure followed, the appraisals made, and the "proposals for action" set forth by The President's Commission on Higher Education. This report is a truly significant document. One part of the report contains a critically determined list of constructive and attainable objectives of higher education for the future. The commission's method of stating objectives, i.e., in terms of individual student outcomes desired, is itself a result of research in the problems and nature of learning and of human behavior. These outcomes demand further attention, since we are concerned with "mapping out" a program for future action. They illustrate clearly the implications of our broader definition of student personnel work. They are paraphrased from Volume I of the commission's report as follows:

1. Development for the regulation of one's personal and civic life of a code of behavior based on ethical principles consistent with democratic ideals.

2. Participation actively as an informed and responsible citizen in solving the social, economic, and political problems of one's community, state, and nation.

3. Recognition of the interdependence of the different people of the world and one's personal responsibility for fostering international understanding and peace.

4. Understanding the common phenomena in one's physical environment, application of habits of scientific thought to both personal and civic problems, and appreciation of the implications of scientific discoveries for human welfare.

5. Understanding the ideas of others and the ability to express one's own ideas effectively.

6. Attainment of a satisfactory emotional and social adjustment.

7. Ability and willingness to maintain and improve one's own health and to cooperate actively and intelligently in solving community health problems.

8. Understanding and enjoyment of literature, art, music, and other cultural activities as expressions of personal and social experience, and participation to some extent in some form of creative activity.

9. Acquisition of the knowledge and attitudes basic to satisfying family life.

10. Choice of a socially useful and personally satisfying vocation that will permit one to use to the full his particular interests and abilities.

11. Acquisition and use of the skills and habits involved in critical and constructive thinking.

With these realistic objectives in mind, let us indicate how student personnel work in the future might be related to these various processes and functions in higher education.

1. *Student Personnel Work and Instruction.* More consideration should be given to the instructor as a personnel worker. In our brief treatment of the history of student personnel work, we indicated that in the early American college the instructors usually maintained an informal and personal relationship with their students. This relationship was not usually restricted to instructional or subject-matter problems but extended to all sorts of extracurricular and personal problems as well. We might decry the paternalistic emphasis of these early professors but not their basic interest in the total education of their students.

We have already indicated that during the period between the two world wars the pendulum swung too far in the opposite direction. Student personnel work and instruction became further and further apart. An impression was developing that teachers were to teach and personnel workers were to do the counseling; that teachers had neither the time, the inclination, nor the training to perform this function. We urge that the pendulum should swing back to some extent, at least to the point where teachers will continue to play an important role in the over-all program of student personnel work on the campus. We have already indicated that this point of view is not a new one. As a matter of fact, Williamson in 1938 presented the following list of student personnel functions which may be performed by the teacher:

(1) Creating and maintaining in the classroom an atmosphere psychologically conducive to the development of optimum motivation, health emotional balance and socialized attitudes.

(2) Maintaining friendly and personalized relationships with each student.

(3) Cultivating in each student an intense desire to learn what can be learned and to achieve satisfaction as well as success in life adjustments.

(4) Maintaining constantly a student point-of-view as opposed to the textbook emphasis.

(5) Modifying teaching and subject-matter in terms of the needs and readiness to learn of each pupil; i.e., individualizing instruction and making it appropriate to the capacities and needs of each student.

(6) Observing and recording significant and relevant data about those intangible but important factors we call motivation, attitudes, and social skills.[8]

The emphasis needed, now and in the immediate future, is one which assumes that all members of the instructional staff should consider as one of their most important responsibilities for the job of relating instruction and counseling directly to such educational objectives as were proposed by the President's Commission.

One more needed emphasis in this general area is a new role for the graduate schools throughout the country, since they produce practically all of our college and university teachers. Approximately two thirds of all persons with Ph.D. degrees are engaged in, and probably will continue to engage in, college or university teaching or other phases of educational work. Would it not then appear appropriate to include, as an integral part of the graduate training program, some definite preparation for the important job of teaching? Beyond this, there should be effective programs for the improvement of instruction at all levels on every campus.

2. *Student Personnel Work and Academic Administration.* By the same analogy a certain portion of almost every administrator's work could and should be referred to as "student personnel work." This is true whether he is the business manager, the registrar, the manager of dormitories, or the president of the college or university. It is just as important for these officers to perform their jobs in harmony with the student personnel point of view, by democratic methods, and with the basic purposes of the institution in mind, as it is for the instructor or for the dean of students.

In relation to academic administration, a dean of a college—liberal arts or professional—should be encouraged to perform many of the duties of a student personnel worker. He should devote much of his energy to the implementation of the student personnel point of view and toward the use of democratic methods both in relation to his staff and in the relation of his

8. E. G. Williamson, "The Teacher as a Personnel Worker," in *Proceedings of the 1938 Annual Meeting,* Association of Texas Colleges, *Bulletin,* July 15, 1938.

staff to their students. Finally, he should consider the paramount purpose of his academic program that of developing to the fullest extent the individual capacities, interests, and abilities of the students enrolled in his college. Such a person, in such a position, could contribute as much to the over-all program of student personnel work on his campus as any other person on the staff, including the dean of students. On the other hand, such a dean might actually be engaged in a type of academic administration and research which could not, by any stretch of the imagination, be included within the scope of the definition of student personnel work referred to earlier.

The same could and should be said for other administrators on the campus, particularly those engaged in the business and financial aspects of educational administration. Unless current and sound educational objectives are con-stantly in the minds of the persons administering these programs, the tail is very likely to wag the dog. Here, then, lies the second and urgently needed emphasis in higher education today.

3. *Student Personnel Work and Public Relations.* If higher education is to do the job which all of us feel that it must do, it is precariously in need of far greater understanding and financial support than it now has. It is our contention that if a college or university first defined its objectives in some such terms as those just outlined, if its faculty dedicated itself to the task implied by those objectives and definitions, and if the public relations program conveyed this message adequately and forcibly, adequate support would be forthcoming. If it is to get this support it must do a better job of public relations, which like teaching and counseling involves an educational point of view. Our publics want to know, and are entitled to know, what we are doing in an *educational sense*, not just to know that "we need money."

In this connection, it is significant to quote from the September 16, 1948, issue of the *Educator's Washington Dispatch* in which the following question was asked:

What would an industrialist do if he were faced, like many a school executive is today, with lack of trained personnel, antiquated plant, outworn equipment, and lack of funds?

This *Dispatch* query went to a top United States manufacturer, who was quick to answer:

He'd put on the biggest selling campaign faculty ever saw. And he'd have a moral right to, because he has the best product in the world to sell. If the manufacturer were in the unhappy position of that schoolman, he'd tell every parent, every citizen, every taxpayer about his problem. If he did that he'd get the resources he needed. No community will starve its schools. But it has to know what the school system faces. And it has to be assured that the money raised will be spent soundly. Give business men these facts, and they will go to the limit supporting the schools.

This then is the third needed emphasis today, namely, the consideration of broad educational objectives and the essentials of student personnel work in the public-relations programs of our respective institutions. It should pay great dividends.

4. *Student Personnel Work and the Students.* If the broader definition of student personnel work and the President's Commission's objectives of higher education should bring about corresponding institutional patterns on the college campus, there would spring up dozens of "democratic laboratories" in nearly every phase of student activity and student life, including the instructional classrooms. Rogers and other client-centered counselors have brought forth some very significant clinical and research data regarding a person's capacity for growth and self-realization under proper psychological conditions. They report that many of the same principles seem to apply to groups—in group therapy, in staff relationships, in classroom teaching. The broad implications of their approach merit serious consideration and experimentation in many phases of the student personnel program. It must be kept constantly in mind that it is the student for whom our institutions exist. If the results of all our efforts are not reflected in the development of desirable educational outcomes in our students, we might just as well "turn in our suits."

5. *Student Personnel Work and Institutional Research.* Another emphasis which is sorely needed to guide the kind of program we have outlined is a vigorous, critical, but constructive plan for student personnel and institutional research. This program should be designed to find out what the real needs of our students are, what the needs of society are, and how effectively or ineffectively we are now meeting these needs. We need this kind of information not only to guide policy determinations, but to convince ourselves, our faculties, our administrations, our governing boards, and our publics what is really important.

We can't develop adequately new curricula, new programs of study, proper combinations of general and specialized courses, truly integrated courses, vocational and other counseling services, student activity programs which will train for democratic living, sound admission policies, sound reinstatement policies, and sound and defensible graduation requirements until we know about the effects and the results of our present curricula, instruction, and services.

6. *Top-Level Coordination Needed.* We believe that each institution must provide the organizational mechanics, and the necessary leadership at the appropriate levels, if it is to expect noteworthy results. In our opinion, this calls not only for a faculty and institutional organization which provides for a definite coordination through appropriate consultation among staff members, but also for a carefully planned line and staff organization designed to accomplish these objectives. In addition to carefully planned faculty and staff organization, with optimum use of student-faculty advisory committees on all aspects of educational policy, there is a need, especially in the larger colleges and universities, for a "top-level" educational *staff* officer, whose chief responsibilities would be to provide this coordination and this educational leadership, the kind of leadership that the president would provide—if he were twins, or in some cases, triplets. Since few presidents have the time actually to pull together all these important educational functions, at least in a day-to-day and practical manner, we suggest a top-level *staff* administrator, especially for the larger institutions. The importance of these duties should be properly emphasized by the title of educational or academic vice-president, an administrator who could devote his full energies to this broad-gauge program.

Let us summarize briefly: First, we attempted to clarify the meaning and philosophy of student personnel work, with an increased emphasis upon its broader applications and implications throughout educational institutions. Secondly, we stressed that such a program, if sound, must be predicted upon certain basic and fundamental assumptions. These were identified. Thirdly, and to further clarify the scope of a sound program of student personnel work, the essential elements comprising such a program were enumerated. Fourthly, to interpret more intelligently the role of student personnel work in education today, and in the future, a minimal historical sketch was included, as well as a brief overview of its present status. Lastly, six aspects of the student personnel program were chosen for more detailed consideration, in an attempt to emphasize those functional aspects of student personnel work most urgently in need of emphasis now, in order that higher education will be able to provide the type of leadership which is so imperative today.

"The Fault, Dear Brutus—"

C. Gilbert Wrenn

A logical interpretation of this quotation would lead to the conclusion that I believe that personnel workers are in the position of "underlings." There are times, of course, when each of us is quite sure that he is an underling, subordinate to far too many people, but it is not my belief that the profession is now in a position subordinate to that of other educational specialties. I think we have grown out of our swaddling clothes, that personnel work is a distinct personality in the family of professions. Personnel work never was an unwanted child for it was born of a need, a need well recognized by both students and administrators. It is true that some of our relatives, our academic aunts, uncles, cousins and the like, have raised their eyebrows at us, but we are now a member of the family, whether always approved or not, and we are here to stay. I am, however, suggesting that certain faults in the performance of personnel work lie within us as individuals and that we might examine these and learn a bit thereby.

Compensations for Lack of Assurance

Our very lack of assurance . . . is one of our grestest faults. We are too young to be a science and not old enough to be a tradition. We are on the way toward accumulating a science of practice, and certainly psychology upon which we depend can be considered a young science, but upon the whole we cannot stand out in an academic gathering with the assurance of the natural scientist, nor yet with the complacency of our older academic relatives, such as literature, history or the languages. In many a social gathering I have seen this lack of self-assurance upon the part of the college personnel worker. It is often evident in one of the two familiar patterns in which defense behavior is expressed. When we are defensive against questions that we cannot answer, accusations about which we think there may be some truth, or in the presence of such ignorance of our work as to give us

139

doubt that it is as important as we thought it was, we are apt to respond with either belligerent behavior, on the one hand, or apologetic behavior on the other. Both, as all psychologists know, are expressions of the same sense of inadequacy.

A belligerent pattern is frequently expressed in overselling of personnel work. This is done by claiming more for student personnel work than it can legitimately perform or by claiming outcomes for personnel services for which no proof can be offered. This pattern of behavior is common for the younger members of the profession who have not yet learned the limitations of the work in which they are engaged. Nor have they learned that such over-salesmanship is resented by professional colleagues with whom personnel people must work cooperatively. "It is better to remain silent and appear a fool, than to speak and remove all doubt." One does not have to be too boastful about one's self or one's vocation to assure the other person that either the person or the vocation is significant. This same belligerency is sometimes revealed in an over-sensitiveness to criticism of one's vocation or of one's own part in personnel work. It is again well known that the over-sensitive person is merely revealing his basic insecurity. One of our problems in this area is that we are not well enough assured of the really valid and stable contributions of our vocation so that we can readily take criticism of the many aspects of our work that justify criticism.

The opposing attitude, that of apologetic response to criticisms or discussions of our professional field, is perhaps even more reprehensible than the belligerent attitude, for, in so being apologetic, we are betraying both ourselves and our profession. We have nothing to apologize for in spite of the fact that we are doing many things poorly. We should make known that we are engaging in a work so complex that we shall never perform as well as we should like to do. We must admit failures and weaknesses and at the same time be proud of certain achievements and basic concepts that will stand up under the most rigorous examination. I well remember Dean Harold Benjamin some years ago speaking of the fact that until teachers held their heads up and stuck their chins out and said "I am a teacher and proud of it" that the teaching profession would never get the respect from the public that it deserves. With this I heartily concur. We must start that, it seems, by attaching importance not to the quality of what we are doing, but to the *significance* of the job to be done. Furthermore, as I have said, there is much more to be proud of than we have sometimes admitted.

One can honestly say to young people that society . . . has done too good a job of making them aware of their liabilities and weaknesses. Perhaps we, as a young profession, are in the same category. There is no reason for us in personal conversations with colleagues or in professional meetings to be other than realistic about the work that we are doing. This realism consists, in part, of admitting our weaknesses, but, also, in stating our strengths. We have many more strengths, as a matter of fact, than some of the academic disciplines that have prestige because of long life. Age does not necessarily bring wisdom. . . . I propose that we accept ourselves as a young profession with much to learn, but at the same time that we consider it unnecessary to be either belligerent or apologetic about the significance of our work. Let it speak for itself—with some assistance from us! And, most of all, let us accept gracefully criticisms of our personal part in the performance of personnel work without puffing up our dignity . . . or exhibiting more obvious signs that our feelings have been hurt.

A second psychological problem of personnel workers is the strain upon the individual of constant contact with human beings. No one but teachers and individuals in similar human relations occupations appreciate the drain made upon nervous energy by the daily routine. For many people, those in the academic field have a soft life. We know differently. The only trouble is that we know it in such terms that it frequently cannot be understood by anyone outside of our own field. I am . . . drawing attention to the effect of this constant contact with people and their troubles, decisions that must be made in terms of human reaction rather than objective fact, the necessity for constantly shifting in terms of the various personalities whom we meet from time to time throughout the day, the necessity for attempting to see beneath the surface and to infer attitudes and conflicts from exterior behavior and verbalization. These, and other conditions of our work, cause us to suffer a kind of nervous fatigue unlike that experienced in most other fields.

This fatigue leads to a peculiar danger of personnel workers, the adoption of a kind of surface defense to protect us from the results of fatigue. This mask frequently results in a blunting of our sensitivity to intimate human reactions. Administrators are more often accused of this than are counselors or teachers. The solution rests within ourselves and our own program of personal mental hygiene. It rests with our own program of conserving our energies so that the more important things can be handled adequately. The most important thing is the reaction and the growth of each individual human being with whom we deal.

One of the solutions in this connection is for us to become less concerned with paper work and less concerned with personal prestige than we are with the significance of the behavior of the persons with whom we deal as professional workers. It is not easy to ignore a crowded desk and a crowded schedule, to appear at ease and wholly absorbed in the self-revelations of a given individual, whether a student or colleague. It is not easy, but it is *essential* if we are to fulfill our highest obligation as personnel workers.

If we are crowded at our office by people who wish to see us and if we, at the same time, must get out certain correspondence or perform other essential tasks, then perhaps we should perform these other tasks away from the office, so that our office time will not be jammed with affairs not connected with personal relationships. If we are truly to act as counselors, whatever our personnel title, then we must give every indication that our primary concern is with the individual who is consulting with us. And in order to do a good job of dealing with that person's needs, we must give our undivided attention to observation of what might be called the clinical signs of behavior. To allow ourselves to be licked by the human fatigue factor, to become insensitive to the nuances of human behavior, is to lose our distinctiveness as specialists in human behavior and human need.

Self-Glorification

There is a third danger. . . . This is the temptation to become smug and superior in our attitudes toward others. Because the other person comes to us for help and because we try honestly to help him, we are apt to feel pretty good about ourselves, a little like Jehovah and his children. The client is grateful and we have seen him, but we should not take particular satisfaction from that reaction. Being bluntly realistic, it is our chosen task to help people and there is no particular merit in our doing so. All of us like love and admiration from others, although sometimes we ask for it a little too obviously. When the student or the client gives us gratitude and affection, deserved or not, we are apt to glorify ourselves a bit, although we would not admit it to anyone but ourselves!

One way to keep one's self from this particular psychological temptation is to constantly remind one's self of the social obligations and social aims of personnel work. Our job is to help individuals become more effective and integrated members of their current society. The fact that they are grateful for our helping them in this regard is of little moment. The real point is that it is our job. If we are completely honest we will admit that what we do for others is seldom done as well as we should like or well enough for us to feel complacent about it. Another thing to consider is that much of the value to the student comes from his own reactions to himself rather than from anything that we have done. I am increasingly convinced that we have placed too much stress on techniques and not enough upon the interaction of the two personalities in the counseling situation. The interaction of these two people may bring a considerable degree of the benefit to the counselee without regard to what either one may have consciously done or of the particular techniques employed by the counselor. The student *may* have benefitted in this way—we do not know that he did. In fact, so little is know of *how* counseling benefits others, that all of us who counsel would do well to take little credit for ourselves.

Discouragement

Now to look at a fourth psychological problem. . . . This is the opposing danger of self-disparagement over the enormous complexity of the human problems faced by any personnel worker. Here I am speaking not only of counselors . . . but of personnel workers who counsel with colleagues or who are responsible for colleagues in their own institution. Because we have the title "personnel" attached to us, it is assumed that we are interested in people and their welfare, and, for this reason, many problems come our way which are not necessarily those of a student-counselor type. If our interest in people is a thoughtful interest, we are frequently discouraged at the enormity of the need, on the one hand, and the smallness of our possible contribution, on the other. Of course, we frequently expect too much of ourselves. We frequently forget that growth in any essential characteristic takes time and that no one or two interviews are going to change a person's life unless we can assume that certain dramatic cases that have been publicized in literature are common occurrences. We frequently become emotionally involved in the client's problems and identify ourselves closely with him. In this we lose one of the great advantages of a professional counselor, his ability to remain objective and neutral in spite of the client's perturbation.

We must constantly tell ourselves that the goals of counseling are limited and that we cannot remake a person's life. We merely assist him in one connection. We furthermore must know that what we are trying to achieve is a process of re-education of the individual, that is, helping him to re-educate himself. This is not done quickly. It takes time to translate a change of attitude into a change of behavior. If we are realistic about ourselves and our job we will not assume that we are going to make great changes in a person's life, and we will, therefore, not be discouraged over a lack of achievement. The counselor is but a tool or a catalyst in the life pattern of the individual with whom he is dealing at the moment. Many other factors are present; he is but one. He can neither take credit nor blame for all that happens.

Perhaps one of our peculiar liabilities arises out of this limitation. This is the liability of never actually feeling mastery over situations. The intricacies of human nature are so great, the bulk of what we do *not* know is so large, the rapid growth of new knowledge so perplexing, that we never seem to feel that we are doing a complete and thorough job in any of our human relations responsibilities. One of the perplexing things for those of us who have been in the field for some time is that the thing which we once thought right is now considered wrong, or is, perhaps, *proved* wrong. This, of course, is not unique to our field of endeavor. It is true in medicine and many other areas, but it seems to hit us with peculiar force. I think this matter of never feeling complete mastery over a situation or never feeling that we are right without equivocation is one of the penalties of dealing with intricate human behavior. We must simply live with this particular liability. We will probably never dispense with it.

Strain of Indecision

Another of our peculiar problems is that of being so frequently undecided as to the best course of action. Psychological counseling and any of the professional personnel functions that deal with human decisions are particularly subject to this strain of indecision and for a specific reason. Our problem is always that of "how far shall we go in transmitting to the other party our convictions with regard to his best course of action?—how far shall we attempt to load the dice in terms of a particular alternative by the way in which we discuss the alternatives or by our very tone of voice?—how far shall we simply keep quiet and allow the individual to work through completely on his own?" These are the questions that trouble us and bring about, it seems to me, an unusual amount of strain upon the part of those who are conscientiously trying to work with individuals in terms of facilitating the process of growth within the individual himself. We may know what is best for the student or best for our colleague, but our knowing it will never solve the problem for him. The real situation is solved only when the individual concerned finds for himself a resolution of conflict, a best way out, a changed attitude.

The Temptation of Authority

In speaking tonight of the personnel worker, I am stressing the point that he or she is, without question, the most important element in the personnel program. Henry Murray has spoken of "psychology's forgotten instrument—the psychologist." Rapaport[1] lists four factors essential to the understanding

1. Rapaport, David. "The Status of Diagnostic Testing." *Journal of Consulting Psychology.* XII (1948), 4–7.

of diagnostic information: the basic personality theory that is held, test rationale, familiarity with previous research, and the self-knowledge of the counselor. He writes that "the richest source book of psychological understanding is carried by the individual within himself," that through a process of self-examination and heightened self-awareness as an instrument in the psychological process, we can develop a greater sensitivity to the meaning of information about human behavior. All of this is just as true about the personnel administrator. About one-half of the membership of ACPA is classified as personnel administrators, and certainly they have no more important function than the consideration of the personnel worker, his qualifications, his welfare and his progress. If the personnel administrator gets too much engrossed in programs and forms, in public relations and budgets, he misses his chance to make his greatest contribution to the personnel work of his institution—the development, encouragement and support of the personnel workers subordinate to him.

Administrators, as such, have rather distinctive psychological problems. In the first place, many administrators such as Deans of Men, Deans of Women, or Deans of Students, actually have authority over the lives of students, and the temptation is to use that authority in ways that will facilitate a given situation but which may not necessarily be best for the student concerned.

Part of this arises from the administrator's tendency to look at the outcomes of programs rather than at the outcomes in the lives of individual students. Part of it may come from the fact that he is frustrated at times in dealing with his colleagues or with his superiors in the academic organization, and this frustration leads to arbitrariness with students or with subordinates, the only people with whom he can be arbitrary. Our most dangerous time in dealing with individuals who are in any sense subordinate to us is just following some frustrating experience upon our own part. The phenomenon of projection is too well known to demand emphasis here, but it is not too readily recognized by the person exhibiting the mechanism.

The administrator may be engrossed in a complex program, but he cannot forget that impersonal manipulation of staff personnel, no matter how immediately helpful to program development, will only result in lowered morale for these and *every other* staff member who hears about it. The tolerance of leader domination of group activity seems to increase with the size of the group . . . but even here the efficiency of result may decrease in spite of tolerance. The power factor, the authority complex, the advancement of program at whatever cost to staff security, is the worst and riskiest kind of personnel administration.

There is an excellent argument for an emphasis upon a clear-cut line-and-staff organization of the student personnel functions and staff of an institution. The administrator in higher education must remember . . . that he is dealing with individuals on a staff who are . . . his colleagues. In policy making and in the initiation of new ideas, they must work *with* him and not *for* him. I have written elsewhere ". . . the student personnel program should operate under policies established by an agency representing the administration, faculty and students," and "Student personnel procedures do not function well under an administrative *fiat* arrangement."[2]

Misinterpreting the Administrator's Relationship to his Staff

Another problem of administrators is their frequent failure to recognize that in dealing with the staff they are *not* dealing with students but are, at the same time, responsible for people who have common human need for counsel and encouragement. The prestige factor is an important one in a decision to assume administrative responsibilities as is the realization that certain things could be done with the program if the individual had more control. When this move is made, however, the thing which is frequently not realized is that one must change within himself when he changes from teaching or counseling to administration. Now he is engaging in a process of *adult* education and counseling. He is responsible for staff intellectual and emotional growth, their independence, their morale. Williamson[3] states that "developing counselors" is one of the three major objectives of a program of supervision of counseling services. He writes, "The counselor, himself, is as often as much in need of counseling as the client is, and any administrator that forgets that is not a good administrator." ". . . in administration we almost refuse to do for the doctor what the doctor does for his patients."

Perhaps it is hard to be both an administrator and a counselor. Dean Clifford Houston, in writing to me of the work of his Committee on Professional Standards, makes the following observation: "One does not draw conclusions from so few cases, but it is becoming very obvious that the personal and professional qualifications of a good counselor are not *always* identical with those of a good Dean of Students. Leadership and persuasiveness are very important characteristics for the latter. On the other hand, the careful research type of psychologist might find it difficult to become a real influence with the interfraternity council."

If the personnel administrator states that he is concerned with the morale

2. Wrenn, C. Gilbert. "The Administration of Counseling and Other Student Personnel Services." *The Harvard Educational Review*, May, 1949.

3. Williamson, E. G. "Supervision of Counseling Services." *Journal of Consulting Psychology*, VIII (1948), 297–311.

of the *students* in his institution, he must first be concerned with the morale of the *staff members* who deal with those students. His primary responsibility is to his staff and through them to his students. This is not an easy thing to accept, particularly if one likes to deal with students. One is apt to relegate staff to a position of subordinate responsibility, but this the administrator cannot and must not do. He must depend upon these staff people for their interpretation of student needs. Yes, the administrator has difficult enough problems in terms of developing his program and keeping his various bosses satisfied, but that is nothing to the problem he has in dealing adequately with his staff.

I have said nothing here of the difficulty faced by the personnel administrator by virtue of student reaction to his title, whatever it may be. This is serious enough in the case of the "Dean," for this word carries with it a connotation of authority and officialdom that the personnel administrator would like very much to avoid.

This might sound as though I were overly aware of psychological problems in the life of the personnel worker. Perhaps what I have been doing is reflecting the problems in my own life at various stages in my development, and I may have had more difficulties than the average person. There seems to be some basis, however, for believing that these problems and temptations of the personnel worker are common to many. What, then, can be done about them? Is there anything that could be suggested that would help point the way for a personnel worker to become more effective in dealing with these intimate psychological factors in his life?

One might use a basic approach and examine the factors that *cause* tensions in our lives. This has been ably done by Lewin in several of his brilliant essays collected under the title *Resolving Social Conflicts*.[4]

If it is not presumptuous, let me suggest some simple rules of mental hygiene that may be appropriate to each of us as personnel workers. These suggestions are for me even more than for you.

The first thing to suggest is that we attempt to have fun from our associations with people. I feel that sometimes we take people, and their relationships to us, too seriously. We become involved in what they think of us, or become involved in their troubles, and much of the actual joy of human companionship is lost. Perhaps we could adopt a principle that we might *learn* more from others and *instruct* them less frequently. This would put us in a different relationship to many people, particularly our clients and our associates. None of us should have entered the field of personnel work

4. Lewin, Kurt. *Resolving Social Conflicts*. Harper and Brothers, 1948. (See especially pp. 89–90.)

unless we had enjoyed constant personal contact with people. This enjoyment may have been evident in the beginning, but now some of us have become so engrossed with programs, public relations, publications, and promotions that the joy we once had from simple human contacts has been greatly diminished. When this has happened, we become less effective in all of our personal relationships. People enjoy less being around us, since we enjoy less being around them. Any uniqueness we may have had as far as understanding and sensitive personality is concerned, has been merged in the common pattern of personal ambition and drive.

A second point is that we should recognize our fatigue points and deliberately avoid any extensive contact with people once that point has been reached. We certainly are not effective after we have reached this fatigue point. It is at this time that our voices become sharp, our attention wanders, our patience with the slow progress of others falters, and our effectiveness drops to the vanishing point. This fatigue point will be different with each individual. Furthermore, we must learn to recognize the symptoms of that approaching state of tension. Perhaps only a brief respite is necessary to reduce the fatigue and tension. For some this respite is in a candy bar. Others read something light, and still others will look out the window. Someone else may stretch for a few seconds or take a deep breath. All of these have a combined effect of releasing our physical tensions and at the same time bringing new associations into our intellectual existence.

A third suggestion is that we stop setting up impossible goals for ourselves in terms of the amount to be accomplished each day. If we plan on *less* than we actually expect to do each day, the unexpected things that always arise will fill in the chinks of our time without strain. We almost *always*, on the contrary, plan on more than we can do and then feel frustrated and unhappy because the impossible has not been accomplished.

A fourth possibility is a habit of blocking out a small amount of professional reading each day and thereby reducing the feeling of frustration that we develop because we are not making professional progress. Most of us know that we have several hours reading ahead of us each day and seldom get more than a fraction of it done. Our journals pile up. The books that we have to review become older month by month.

The fifth point that I should like to suggest is that we deliberately practice small courtesies in our relations with other people. In the first place, it is easier on others and will pay large dividends in social effectiveness. In the second place, by practicing these small social courtesies, we are actually demonstrating that we believe in the integrity of each human personality with whom we deal. This point is not easy to express, but I am trying to say that if we practice courtesy and consideration for the welfare and dignity of the other person in small affairs, then it will be easier for us to measure up to our ideals in major human relationships.

Finally, I would like to suggest that we should remember that ultimate values persist regardless of what happens to our personal lives. Things that we believe in, that have permanent significance, do not change no matter how much the world about us seems to deteriorate. We may be personally in a minor position and we may suffer in comparison with others. We may have little in the way of goods or money. Prices may go up, and our state legislators may rob the schools to pay bonuses to veterans and pensions to the elderly. The United Nations may lose its prestige and we may have grave fears about our policy with regard to the atomic bomb. But in the face of all these, certain basic values do not change. Human rights and dignities, the integrity of each human personality, the warmth of love and friendship, the beauty of the earth, the eternal significance of the spiritual,—these things endure. The physical and the political world about us may cause suffering of body and mind, but the things of the human spirit do not die and it is with these eternals of human life that we must be concerned if we are to live up to our high calling as specialists in human relationships and as trustees of human values.

Student Personnel Services in Retrospect and Prospect[1]

W. H. Cowley

During the past century, American college students have been extraordinarily well behaved in comparison with former times. Until the Civil War, riots and rebellions broke out in most colleges every few years. Some of them led to bloodshed, some even to killing. The pattern went back to the town-and-gown riots of the Middle Ages, the most famous being the Oxford outbreak which began on St. Scholastica's Day, 1355. More than 50 students and townsmen died in that encounter. It lasted almost a week, and because of it the City of Oxford annually paid fines and obeisance to the University of Oxford for the next 470 years. To this day, Cambridge University continues to be prepared for the consequences of such outbreaks, the only duty of its High Steward being "to attend the hanging of any undergraduate."

Nothing in the history of American student life compares with European antecedents, but, during the early years of the 19th century, Princeton students blew up Nassau Hall three times with dynamite, Yale students stabbed to death at least one New Haven fireman in their annual spring "hose riots," and a student blinded the left eye of the famous historian, William H. Prescott, by hitting it with a piece of stale bread in one of Harvard's numerous food riots. Describing these uprisings as they occurred at Harvard, its tercentennial historian, Samuel Eliot Morison, has written that

. . . the half century from 1807 to 1857 is studded with explosions in lecturehalls, bonfires in the Yard, smashing tutors' windows, breaking up chapel exercises, and rebellions. There was even a traditional Rebellion Tree opposite the south entry of Hollis, where they started. . . . Josiah Quincy, who lived in Wadsworth House when

1. Adapted from an address before the National Association of Student Personnel Administrators, Stanford, Calif., June 21, 1956.

he was President, complained after his resignation that he could not sleep in Boston—it was so quiet compared with the Yard![2]

In the high-spirited South even fewer restraints prevailed, as witness the following summary statement of conditions there:

In North Carolina they [students] rode horses through the dormitory and "shot up" the place generally. At a great drinking bout, attended by students and faculty, that signalized the celebration of Washington's birthday in 1804, a young instructor, according to a student's letter, achieved a feat of getting drunk twice. Shooting, blocking stagecoaches, and singing ribald songs in front of churches are reported from the University of Virginia. Students here went even further and on occasion assaulted and whipped members of the faculty. In the course of the riot of 1842 Professor Davis was shot and killed by an exuberant undergraduate. A similar outrage was the murder of President Jeremiah Chamberlin of Oakland College in Mississippi. During the political excitement attendant upon the discussion of the Compromise of 1850 a drunken student, enraged over a fancied injury, stabbed him to death.[3]

Compared with the lawlessness of pre-Civil War college students, today's panty raids seem so mild that the historian of college life is tempted to dismiss them as inconsequential. Deans of students, however, cannot be so complacent and must deal with them wisely if they occur and prevent them if they can. In both enterprises the historical continuum provides the richest available case records as well as foreshadowings of potential dangers and of possible ameliorations.

Panty raids may even constitute a blessing in disguise for deans of students, because, if they will view them as events on the historical continuum of student riots and rebellions, they can learn what—about a hundred years ago—stopped the gory atrocities of earlier periods, what remedial techniques of the past have relevance today, and what to expect in the future.

At least six factors seem to have been involved in reducing the number and intensity of student outbreaks. Administrators initiated three of them, and three emerged from the changing times. The three administrative devices were: changing the college calendar so that vacations would come at time of the year during which students had been prone to hell raising (including the Christmas season which did not become a vacation period until about 1850), abandoning dormitories (a solution which led fraternities

2. S. E. Morison, "The History and Tradition of Harvard College," *Harvard Crimson*, 1934, pp. 20–21.

3. G. P. Schmidt, "The Old Time College President," (New York: Columbia University Press, 1930), p. 86.

to change from literary societies meetings once a week to housing units and social clubs), and helping students to organize for self-government.

Meanwhile, three powerful social developments in American life at large forced the colleges to change spectacularly: coeducation, organized athletics, and the establishment of curriculums for the training of kinds of students that universities never before had served—engineers, dentists, farmers, intending scientists, and a growing variety of others, including those planning to become businessmen. Among these three societal influences upon the colleges, the third seems to be the most important because those preparing for careers as individualistic workers in medicine, law, and in the professions generally do not have to explain to potential employers their student behavior as do those going to work for large organizations. Upon investigation, deans of students will probably find that those planning to work for large industrial and governmental units constitute their best resources for maintaining law and order.

In any event, panty raids present deans of students with the challenge of research. Should another serious depression strike, the deans might not be dealing with coed panties but, instead, with the banners of political agitators from both the left and the right. We had a taste of such agitation during the 30's, and another long depression would probably make those years seem placid. Because, today, college campuses bring together such a large proportion of the youth of the nation, groups of agitators would descend upon them; and students, believing their prospects to be blighted, would flock to their banners and do their destructive bidding.

This is a possibility for which deans of students ought to be preparing. How? The only answer is research, research on the historical continuum of student life—that is, investigating the present in the light of the past with a view to preparing for the constantly arriving future.

The same formula can be used in meeting the issues raised by the U.S. Supreme Court decisions concerning racial segregation, in studying fraternity and sorority trends, in administering admissions and financial aid programs, and, indeed, in every sector of student life. The history of each sector has shaped its present characteristics, and both the past and the present can be assessed to glimpse and to prepare for the future.

Another question could well be what can be done to promote a better spirit of co-operation among the various kinds of workers who perform student personnel services in colleges and universities. Specifically, what can be done to lessen the antagonism between deans of students as a group and deans of women as a group, to make registrars and directors of health services better co-ordinated members of the student personnel team, to bring the psychological testers more effectively into camp, to educate the growing number of clinical counselors to the points of view of deans of students, and vice versa?

Three kinds of people engage in student personnel services professionally: the humanitarians, the administrators, and the scientists, more especially psychologists. The humanitarians came upon the American scene first and continue to be recruited in fairly large numbers. Next came the first wave of administrators, but a second wave has been more important. Then came the psychologists—first the tests-and-measurement psychologists and next their clinical brothers. These three kinds of personnel people seem to have little in common; hence; the so-called student personnel movement is not a movement at all, but, instead, a collection of independent wheels turning at different rates and often in different directions.

Consider first the humanitarians. Most deans of women, many deans of men, but only a few deans of students belong to their numbers. They are the people who have come into the field primarily because they want to help others. As students or as faculty members, they were appalled by the impersonalism of research-minded professors and the resulting failure of colleges and universities to give students the individual, extra-instructional help so many of them need. They have become personnel workers because essentially they want to do good in the world especially among college students.

The humanitarians have made and continue to make precious contributions to student personnel work; but they incline as a group, recalling William James' classification, to be tender-minded rather than tough-minded. Frequently, therefore, they tend to be sentimentalists in the Deweyan definition of sentimentalism: they often advocate building Utopias without knowing much about architecture and construction engineering. Student personnel services, like all enterprises, need humanitarians—but not too many of them.

The first wave of student personnel administrators came largely from the rank of the humanitarians, and some of them became distorted sentimentalists—that is, individuals who still believe in Utopia and will use any means to bring it into being—and, thus, dangerous people. However, the second wave of administrators includes few simon-pure humanitarians. By and large, those who have come into the field during the past 25 years to administer the huge co-ordinated programs that have developed have been appointed primarily because of their administrative ability rather than because of any compelling interest in students. They are primarily executives in charge of large and important operations.

They come from a wide range of backgrounds: people from almost every subject-matter department, some from industry, and some from other administrative units of colleges and universities. They are the top dogs of the enterprise. They deal with presidents and academic deans; they wangle budgets; they direct the work of staffs that steadily increase in size; but generally they are too busy to talk with students other than presidents of student organizations or those in serious trouble with the administration.

Other limitations seem to include, first, inadequate knowledge of the backgrounds and trends of American higher education in the broad; second, relative ignorance of the preoccupations and points of view of the specialists who work under their direction; and third, an inclination to solve problems by rule of thumb rather than by the slower but more effective method of careful study.

Even though psychologists often take credit for initiating the student personnel movement, they arrived on the scene late. They did not appear until just after World War I; but with their tests, their correlations, and their counseling techniques they rapidly took the center of the stage. Tough-minded in sharp contrast to their tender-minded humanitarians and zealously evangelical for their cause in comparison with the relatively placid administrators, they have jostled both of their groups of associates into frequent antagonism. Yet, they have brought much of incalculable value into student personnel work; and, because of the solid facts they have gathered, they have probably had more to do than any other group with giving the program status with administrators, faculty members, students, and the general public. Every time anyone uses a student's I.Q. or intelligence percentile rating, he salutes the work of the psychologists. Every time an institution modifies its admissions program in the light of studies of the criteria involved, it acknowledges its debt to psychologically initiated concepts. Every time a college or university improves its counseling program, it endorses conclusions reached by psychological investigators.

Beyond doubt, psychologists needed to be engrossed until recently in measuring the capacities of individuals and in amplifying counseling conceptions and procedures. These scientific sectors of the personnel field had to be plowed and cultivated first and must be kept productive. The time appears to have come, however, when more attention should be given to issues involving group psychology—in brief, to the social psychology and sociology of student life.

At least 7,500 persons devote all of their working time to student personnel activities, an average of four in each of the 1,900 colleges and universities of the country. Probably this is too conservative an estimate, and in any case it must be supplemented by the large number who do part-time counseling. These workers come from a wide variety of backgrounds and have many kinds of training and a miscellany of points of view with no recognizable common core of knowledge of, interest in, or commitment to student personnel work. Only a minority are organized into a number of non-co-operating and, what is worse, non-communicating national associations.

Perhaps, at this stage of the student personnel movement such topsy-turviness is inevitable. One day, however, some will conclude that something should be done to pull the sprawl together. Toward that end I have some suggestions.

I begin with two negative proposals. First, it would be folly to try to organize a national association seeking the membership of all personnel people in secondary schools, colleges, and universities. An attempt to do this has been made, and it failed. The interests and loyalties of those in higher education differ so markedly from those in secondary education that all such efforts must inevitably fizzle. Second, it would be similarly profitless to propose to existing organizations—such as the National Association of Deans of Women and the American Association of Collegiate Registrars and Admissions Officers—that they should go out of business. They would be understandably deaf to the suggestion. They have important functions to perform and will continue to perform them. Yet, somehow, all student personnel people should be helped to understand their common interests and their common destiny. The question is how.

My proposal is that this association, in co-operation with any or all of the other 15 in existence which care to join, undertake the establishment of an agency to serve all higher educational personnel workers. For a modest fee the agency could put upon the desk of every subscriber every week a communication something like the Kiplinger Letter. Its essential function would be to keep student personnel people in touch with the major activities and thought of their field. Some of the letters would include only succinct news items; some would report one or two conspicuously important events; some would give brief abstracts of leading articles and addresses; some would be entirely devoted to epitomes of outstanding books; and some would review all important research completed.

How would an agency be organized? Who would edit the weekly letter? What group would make the agency's policies? How much would its services cost? These, clearly, are basic questions; but they and others like them have workable answers which would soon emerge should the desire for these services be widespread enough and strong enough.

The agency would not be a panacea, of course, but it would constitute a significant beginning toward meeting the three needs—helping all groups of personnel workers in higher education better to understand one another, supplying them with information about the historical and current frontiers of their own terrains and of the enterprise in general, and promoting needed research in presently neglected areas.

III

A Period of Activism and Professional Reflection

College and university campuses, characterized by a period of growth, pride and relative tranquility during the 1950's, are significantly and permanently affected by the dramatic events of the 1960's. Frequently referred to as the "age of student activism," "the downfall of in loco parentis" and "the years of civil disobedience," the authors of this decade produce a body of professional literature that echoes respected elderstatespersons and at the same time heralds a new philosophical and theoretical orientation to student personnel work.

Three major themes influence this period: 1) an identity crisis grips individual professionals and the field as a whole resulting in a period of reflection and reconceptualization that alters our roles and daily practice; 2) student activism serves as a seed that produces more effective relationships between students, institutions and administrators; and 3) the embryonic stirrings of a new movement, later to be called "student development," begin to be heard.

It is a period of turmoil and violence that includes a presidential assassination, the murder of a Black civil rights leader and the killing of a presidential candidate. Many major cities witness their ethnic neighborhoods burning, their stores looted and their people rioting out of a sense of frustration and anger. Depersonalization again becomes a characteristic of the college student experience particularly at many large research universities: Berkeley, Columbia, Stanford, University of Michigan and New York University, to name a few. "Do not fold, staple or mutilate" is the dominant student cry against the increasing use of technology on campuses, overcrowded lecture halls and decreasing student faculty interactions. Student reaction against the rampant popularity of rationalism, their desire for an emphasis on person centered values and a deemphasis on the authority of "the Establishment" were central issues of the activists of the 1960's.

157

The equality of Black students' access to higher education is tested over and over again. Affirmative action plans and quota systems are developed as part of this decade's temporary resolution to the struggles of its minority students.

This decade is also a time of retrenchment, reallocation, and redefinition. The emergence of a "steady state" economy, in which federal and state governments allocate fewer dollars to higher education, marks the second half of this decade. A few institutions, experiencing severe budget reductions attach highest priority to academic matters and conclude that their student personnel divisions may be expendable. Within a few short years, many of these institutions reinstate student personnel professionals and the field's future, perceived by many as cloudy or even non-existent, regains a new footing. Professionals look toward a more tranquil time, a more student-centered time, and a more stable time; the 1970's.

An early call for bridge building is inferred as Shaffer (1961) recognizes that the academic community has been split by traditional organizational lines into separate segments of specialization and influence. Effective education, he contends, will not be realized unless an integration of the goals and efforts of faculty, student personnel workers and students can be achieved. Cooperative relationships must be forged by student personnel if the significant problems confronting higher education are to be resolved.

Crookston and Blaesser (1962) collaborate on an application of Lewin's force-field analysis to the issues facing student personnel. A campus can be viewed as constantly shifting between states of equilibrium and disequilibrium, depending on the strength of constraining and restraining forces. The only constant, claim the authors, is change. Our new role is to plan systematically for change, not merely to react to it. Crookston and Blaesser are planting the seeds of a reconceptualization of the practitioner role as one of campus change agent.

Hardee's ACPA Presidential Address (1963) calls for a renewal of the image of student personnel work in the arena of higher education. Based on the assumption that our efforts are integrated with the aims and activities of faculty, Hardee sets forth 12 propositions designed to bring about a greater degree of ACPA members' participation in professional and governmental groups. One recommendation is for ACPA members to contribute to the efforts of the Committee of Academic Affairs of the American Council on Education and the Interassociation Coordinating Committee, later to be known as COSPA. Hardee's challenge is for ACPA to develop a strong and influential voice at national, regional and state levels to help shape major legislation affecting students, student personnel workers and their campuses.

"Reflections of a Troublesome But Hopeful Rip Van Winkle" by Cowley

(1964) is a significant piece of literature because in it Cowley admonishes the field for its failure to resolve issues that he himself faced 26 years earlier as a neophyte professional. Believing that student personnel work's purpose and functions reside within the extra-instructional arena of the academy, he views teaching and research as core functions of higher education and the domain of faculty. Cowley's assessment of the maturity and status of our specialty field, through the application of the centric triad, concludes that student personnel work has yet to achieve adulthood status.

Another author who perceives the need for bridge building to span the traditional void between student personnel professionals and faculty is Trueblood. In 1965 he proposes that the student personnel practitioner of the future be an educator rather than a procedural technician. The focus of this new practitioner role is to be on the total campus environment rather than the current and narrower perspective of the college student.

With the field struggling in the midst of its own identity crisis, Kirk (1965) draws upon her expertise as a counselor to address the critical issues confronting student personnel practitioners. For a professional to have an identity, one of the requirements is that ". . . we must be recognized and perceived by others . . ." (p. 198), as having a unique purpose. This ACPA Presidential Address, using Ericksonian ideas, reminds us that our field is developing much as an adolescent does. Kirk suggests steps that need to be implemented if the developing field is to survive and overcome its present identity crisis. Included are: a reexamination of our basic set of values, the creation of innovative methods, and most importantly, the process of introspection. Introspection could assist ACPA members in identifying those beliefs that will ultimately form the core belief system of the field for the future.

The mission and role of student personnel are discussed by Berdie during another ACPA Presidential Address. He views student personnel as "different but not apart from other persons and functions in higher education" (p. 240), "an integral part of the whole educational process . . ." (p.240). The student personnel worker ". . . is the behavioral scientist whose subject matter is the student and whose socio-psychological-sphere is the college" (p. 240). Higher education's purposes and methods are seen as paralleling the purposes and methods of student personnel work.

Mueller identifies three dilemmas student personnel workers face that separate them from their faculty and administrative colleagues. In the areas of goals, roles and the relationship between students and the institutional bureaucracy, she suggests a new theory and role for the personnel division. Students need to be taught how to function in the campus society and need to learn those democratic and participative skills they will need to apply in the larger society after graduation.

A return to humanism is the message of Williamson (1967) as he speaks of the persistent and unresolved issues confronting student personnel. The issues, posed as questions, may continue to perplex the field for years to come. Williamson describes a series of paradoxes that professionals must not only recognize but address. He encourages us to add research as one of the components of our mission.

Greenleaf's 1968 ACPA Presidential Address also focuses on the identity crisis that continues to engulf the profession. She asks "Will there be any student personnel workers in the years ahead?" (p. 226). Seeing a need for the profession to define its role and the contributions professionals can make in institutions of higher education, Greenleaf focuses on how other campus constituencies view us: students, faculty, administrators, parents and the general public. She concludes, on a note of optimism, that our professional functions, defined earlier by Leonard, will not vanish, but the strategies we implement and the roles we play may change.

The disappearance of the traditional Protestant work-ethic by the year 2000 and a new role for student personnel professionals are predicted by Tripp (1968) in "Student Personnel Workers: Student Development Experts of the Future." An increasing recognition of "life as a continuous process of change" and a new respect for "humanness" (p. 280) will characterize the next thirty-two years. The future student personnel workers will be defined as a "scholar in student development," one who applies strategies associated with the role of change agent.

The 1968 article by Penney, frequently considered controversial, is unusual in the criticism directed toward student personnel for its failure to achieve professional status. Penney is convinced that the goal of professional status is beyond our reach. He identifies those issues that he believes will continue to prevent student personnel practitioners from gaining professional recognition on college and university campuses. Penney attributes an increasing specialization in functional areas, a preoccupation with housekeeping responsibilities and a paucity of quality professional literature to the field's current lack of professional status.

Student Personnel Problems Requiring a Campus-Wide Approach

Robert H. Shaffer

The traditional organizational structure of colleges and universities has led to an artificial separation of duties for administrative purposes. This structure fhas led to a classification of many problems into academic, student personnel or business. In turn, this classification has militated against the marshalling of resources, wherever they might be in the campus community, to meet many pressing problems which cut across the artificial lines.

Effective education on the campus depends upon the degree to which the total environment or community provides a consistent, forceful stimulus in the direction of intellectual growth. Various duties within the educational enterprise may be assigned to specific offices. Assignment of responsibility to such offices does not make them solely responsible, however, nor does it free them of responsibility in other areas which might be delegated to other divisions of the college or university.

A significant challenge to educational administrators particularly in the years ahead is to exercise initiative and ingenuity in utilizing the total resources of their institution for the achievement of its objectives. This will require aggressive efforts to overcome the traditional tendency to divide the campus community into discrete line agencies each independent, in its opinion, of responsibility and authority for meeting problems classified as falling under another office.

Student personnel work has particularly suffered from this tendency. Some practitioners have carved little empires for themselves, possibly from feelings of insecurity. In other situations the "academic" or "business" personnel have been so relieved at divesting themselves from various student problems that they have heaved a sigh of relief at the creation of student personnel offices and have promptly disclaimed responsibility for such in the future.

There are a number of significant problems facing higher education which have some personnel implications but which require a unified, cooperative approach by all segments of the campus community. Among them would be at least the following:

1. *Securing a coherence among the many cultures and forces operative on the campus.* Such a coherence must arise from the integration of the goals and efforts of students and faculty alike. All elements of the college community contribute to student growth. Whether this growth is in the desired direction is a question of great concern to all educators. What the student learns in his out-of-class life, for example, determines to a great extent the attitudes, the aspirations, and the motivation he brings to the classroom and the level of achievement he attains there.

For this reason, not only student personnel workers are interested in this environmental influence. All staff members of the college are. It is not enough for the instructor to say, "You keep the residence halls quiet so my students can study and I'll educate them!" Frustrated and exasperated hall personnel can only reply, "If you would work them harder, they wouldn't feel they could play around all night and still make acceptable grades!"

The relation of student conduct to general scholastic achievement is almost exactly the same as the relation of good English usage and achievement in the English class. Some professors say to their colleagues in English, "For heaven's sake! Can't you do a better job of teaching these jokers to write?" The frustrated and exasperated English instructor can only reply, "If you would demand a higher quality of English in your written work, we could and would be able to do a better job."

The "yellow slip" plan used in a number of colleges is a good example of integrating efforts from a number of sources to motivate the student. At Indiana University the English Department provides gummed slips which the instructor in any class may paste to any piece of written work and check one of three comments:

The English in This Paper
Is Not Acceptable

___ It appears to be the result of carelessness. In the future I will expect you to write with more care.

___ The English in this paper is so poor that I have lowered your grade. It would pay you to write with more care.

___ You should take this paper to the Writing Clinic for assistance with your problems in writing. Report to the English Office for an appointment at the Clinic. Do this within the next week; then return this paper to me.

The Writing Clinic is available to any student having trouble with English. Information about it may be obtained at the English Office.

Closer agreement on the goals and objectives by all segments of a college and the aggressive realignment of all forces within the campus community is essential to a vital and effective academic effort. While the student personnel worker is interested in this effort, he must to be successful direct his interest and work towards organizing, uniting and cooperating with all other elements in the university.

2. *Facilitating the conscious and effective interpretation of the concepts of a college, a college education and a college educated person.*

The best interest of any enterprise demands that all associated with it clearly understand its objectives both over-all and of its component parts. Students particularly need to understand what the college feels to be a good education, what it feels to be marks of its greatness and success, and what it expects of its graduates.

Just as a definite relationship exists between communication and employee productivity in a business enterprise, so in the educational enterprise, is there a definite relationship between the effectiveness of the communication of the spirit and meaning of the college and the productivity of its students.

Many students have goals other than those felt by the college to be of primary importance. Such students are satisfied with the relative satisfaction of these goals and usually feel little disturbance if they do not live up to the expectancies of the college. This is particularly true when the expectancies of the college are vaguely stated and communicated. Because they feel satisfied when their own goals are met to a minimum degree, they sincerely do not understand or are not greatly disturbed by anguished cries of faculty members and educational critics that our colleges are not doing an adequate job.

It is important that every institution examine carefully what it is doing to interpret more effectively to its students its nature, goals and expectancies. Included in such an examination should be analysis of literature sent to prospective students, orientation procedures, the approach and content of the opening days of classes, the public relations and alumni programs, the campus extra-curricular program and, particularly, the dominant forces in the student culture.

The importance of this latter aspect of the campus, the student culture, has been emphasized by the reports on the studies at Vassar.

"The student body as an entity may be thought to possess characteristic qualities of personality, ways of interacting socially, types of values and beliefs, and the like, which are passed on from one "generation" of students to another and which like any culture provide a basic context in which individual learning takes place. We contend, in fact, that this culture is the prime educational force at work in the College, for, as we shall see, assimilation into the student society is the foremost concern of most students. Suffice it to say now that in our opinion the scholastic and academic aims and processes of the College are in large measure transmitted to incoming students or mediated for them by the predominant students culture."[1]

Thus, any consideration of securing a more coherent campus environment and interpreting the meaning and significance of this environment to students must take into account the values, the status figures, and forces prevalent in the campus culture.

3. *Assisting each student in understanding the relevance of higher education to his life and problems.*

The writings of the last few years on the relationship, or probably more accurately, the lack of relationship between the formation of certain values and a college education document the need for attention to this function. If colleges are to have serious, motivated and thinking students on their campuses, they must help their students see their college experience as more than a passage of time, the accumulation of credit hours, or merely training to earn a better living.

Nevitt Sanford, also reporting on the Vassar research, concluded that students "perceive the curriculum as more or less irrelevant and look to each other for the instruction that really matters."[2] His observation had particular reference to sex roles in society but are applicable equally to other societal issues. Whether or not his observations and those of such writers as Jacob, Eddy, and others are completely accurate, the function of helping the student find real meaning in his college experience is an important and necessary one. The personnel program should provide agencies or stimulate forces which will organize resources in the college community to perform this function.

4. *Re-orienting the orientation program.*

Traditionally, orientation programs have tended to emphasize physical and social orientation to the possible exclusion of orientation to the academic and cultural environment. Student personnel workers have given the new freshman tests, told him about the health service, introduced him to the campus, mixed him with students of the opposite sex, taught him the school song and yells, introduced him to the campus leaders and athletes, organized

1. Freedman, Mervin B., "The Passage Through College," *The Journal of Social Issues*, 12:4, 1956, p. 14.

2. Stanford, Nevitt, "Changing Sex Roles, Socialization, and Education," *Human Development Bulletin on the Ninth Annual Symposium*, Committees on Human Development, University of Chicago, 1958, p. 66.

him into groups, and then, at the end of so-called orientation week, dumped him into class with a sigh of relief.

Critical analysis of the content of many of our orientation weeks really reveals them to be dis-orientation weeks when judged by the extent to which the student was introduced to the fact that college is a challenging, disturbing, perhaps even a shocking experience, and one which will demand more from him in the way of self-discipline and motivation than he has been called upon to exercise previously.

It is necessary that student personnel workers review their approach to orientation to make certain the major emphasis is made unmistakably clear amid all the procedural and social exercises. Orientation is a function of the whole institution, not just that of the personnel worker.

5. *Emphasizing that the student must assume responsibility for his education, exercise self-discipline in his behavior and provide self-direction in his personal and intellectual growth.*

Symptoms of the failure of higher education in this regard range all the way from panty raids to cheating on one continuum, usually the dean's, and from choosing easy courses to doing just enough to get by on another continuum, usually the faculty's.

Sound personnel practice is based upon the principle that every contact with a student should lead to his increased independence and ability to handle his problems on his own in the future. Yet many colleges and universities in their relations with students, parents and the public attempt to assume a degree of responsibility which robs society of an important lesson it must learn if higher education is to be truly higher education. That lesson is the fact that a college student must grow up and assume certain responsibilities for himself.

The concept of *in loco parentis* should not lead colleges to assume more authority than the parents themselves would exercise if the students were at home during the comparable four years. Colleges properly have all sorts of personnel workers and aids to help the student achieve this independence and self-discipline but it is important for the whole collegiate community to make certain of the direction of such work. Certainly, student personnel agencies should strive to avoid being what one professor describes them; namely, a "haven for the incompetent."

Faculty members need to review their thinking in this area with care. Many will endorse without reservation the ideas expressed above. Yet in another context they will demand that personnel workers eliminate such time-wasting activities as queen contests, fraternities, automobiles, social affairs, and campus marriages.

Involved in the question is the achievement of a balance between the authority exercised by the institution in all its areas and the freedom granted to students. Vice President Haskew of the University of Texas has described the situation well when he characterized present practice in higher education as one of:

"such alternation between the practice of authority and the practice of freedom that the student is left with nothing more than rudderless motive power . . . Some schools deal with this issue on the basis of self-defense, I fear, championing enough freedom to keep students reasonably happy and practicing enough authority to keep teachers from resigning . . .

"On three points the protagonists of freedom, the protagonists of authority, and perhaps all the rest of us are agreed. One is that we are not satisfied with the results to date of society's efforts to resolve this issue. The second is that the synthesis to be worked out must include elements of both freedom and authority. The third is that a synthesis for schools is integral with a synthesis for the family and for the community."[3]

6. *Developing the optimum use of housing facilities for educational purposes.*

American higher education has passed from the dormitory era, when halls were thought of as a place for the students to sleep and eat while they were being educated in the classroom, to the residence hall era when programming in the halls was emphasized for social and cultural ends. The next phase will surely be the integration of the living-unit program into closer relationship with the academic and intellectual life of the institution. Artificial distinctions between business, personnel and academic interests must be eliminated in favor of a careful analysis of the most effective organization and operation of the halls and other types of housing from the point of view of the entire institution and its institutional objectives.

Residence hall libraries, seminar and classrooms, writing clinics, budgeted aid for educational and cultural programs and faculty relations, and many other innovations must all be considered. These developments are not new on the educational scene. What is new in present-day thinking is the point that provision of funds and expenditure of energy must be directed with the thought of utilizing them where they will accomplish the most from the point of view of education, not from artificial distinctions or past custom. Attention particularly must be directed to experiences of other institutions to see what adaptations might be made or what programs might be adopted even if similar funds or facilities are not immediately available. Too many

3. Haskew, Laurence D., "The Fields Are White Unto Harvest," *Teachers College Record*, 57:6, March, 1956, p. 349.

educational administrators have dismissed promising developments without consideration because their particular institutions did not have the special funds or grants others might have.

7. *Striving for the development in each student of a strong feeling of identification with his college.*

This feeling is not necessarily related to agreement with the stated objectives of the college or even with its efforts to have the highest possible academic standards. Rather, it is a feeling of belonging to and possessing a part of the institution.

American higher education seems to be doing this very well as a whole. In *What College Students Think*,[4] Goldsen and her colleagues report the strongly personal feeling most students in all the eleven universities studied had towards their individual institutions. They did not see them as impersonal entities with just an educational function. Instead most students at each institution saw it as having its own personality over and above the individual students in it.

Such a feeling of identification provides a base for efforts to integrate students and their cultures into the efforts of the total institution. It does not preclude strong criticism of phases of the college, nor should it, but it does furnish a positive basis evaluating differences among and between student groups, eliminating misunderstandings and integrating effort towards common objectives.

Failure to develop further and to use this asset in the years immediately ahead will constitute sheer administrative and professional incompetence.

8. *Assisting institutions in the development of effective positive public relations programs defined in the best and broadest sense of the term.*

Every institution created by a society has the obligation to interpret its work and functions to that society. It is almost a tragedy for higher education that intellectuals as a group have built up such a feeling of disdain if not antagonism toward the concept of public relations for higher education. An important contribution of student personnel work is to work with administrative officers and students in developing a program to explain and interpret the rational way of life, its importance to free society, its essential elements, and the support society must give its institutions if they are to progress in effectiveness and significance.

If the colleges and universities of the country do an effective job with the students currently enrolled, both in giving them something of real value and in helping them understand what it is they have, there should be no real

4. Goldsen, Rose *et al, What College Students Think,* Princeton, N.J., D. Van Nostrand Co., 1960.

difficulty in explaining the needs and problems of higher education to the various publics involved.

Related to all of the preceding points but particularly the latter, is the importance of the image the students of any institution have of themselves and their institution. In all colleges and universities there are greater resources for a higher quality education than most educators and students recognize. In their student bodies there are probably greater talents, abilities and personalities than commonly recognized. Basic to a release of their latent educational potentialities is the destruction of the image of college students as irresponsible youngsters and the widely held idea that a quality education can be secured in only a small number of colleges and universities across the country.

A systematic approach to this problem area will up-grade higher education very greatly but will require the cooperative efforts of all segments of the educational world. Student personnel workers are in a strategic position to assist in the advancement of such a program because of their relationship with students, parents, high schools and student activities. This is not to imply that a superficial image-building campaign is in order. An effective program can be developed on the highest professional and ethical planes.

In summary, there are a number of pressing problems facing higher education in which the student personnel aspect seems to be particularly important. However, these problems will not be solved by student personnel workers alone because they involve all aspects of campus life. Student personnel administrators specifically and higher education administrators in general must take the lead in overcoming narrow organizational lines to mobilize all resources available in the educational community to meet these problems.

An Approach to Planned Change in a College Setting

Burns B. Crookston and Willard W. Blaesser

Death, taxes, and change are among the inevitable elements of life today. In contrast with the first two, change has the potential of improvement, depending upon our value system, as it relates to a particular situation. Change, whether "good" or "bad," has been given increased and more systematic attention during recent years, particularly in the organizational settings of business and industry. There is pressure upon managers as part of their major organizational responsibility to diagnose changes in process, to predict the nature and extent of change in the years ahead, to identify changes which seem more urgent, and deliberately to plan and help execute certain changes. Training departments are asked to develop in-service training programs which will help lower, middle, and top management to work more effectively toward improvements in the total organization. Managers are frequently sent to training laboratories, institutes and courses which include emphasis on skills of analyzing and carrying out change potentialities in organizational settings.

Colleges and universities appear to be giving less attention to systematic approaches to change within their institutional settings. Many have utilized management surveys to outline recommendations for changes in structure and function. Usually these are accomplished by outside consulting firms which are not available for continuing service and training functions. Faculty committees often study various phases of the college program, usually curricula, and develop plans for improvement. However, the concept of deliberate and continued planning for change as the responsibility of administration, teaching faculty, and student personnel staff does not seem to be recognized as a responsibility of higher education today.

Yet, the idea that considerable change will occur in higher education during the sixties has wide acceptance. Yeast-like rises predicted for both costs and enrollments portend enforced, if not planned, change. Clearly, student personnel programs will be among those affected. In fact recent literature contains frequent references to the need for student personnel administrators and counselors to prepare for working with a far greater number of students per staff member. Additional pressures identified include: proliferation of student personnel functions which increase communication, human relations, and efficiency problems; demand for more intensive "pursuit of excellence"; decreasing time of teaching faculty for advising students; depersonalization caused by the "mass" approach; and the need for more and better evaluation and research with less time and money. The elements of planned change outlined in this article, while directed toward a student personnel program, may also prove useful if applied to other aspects of the college program.

Changes in college student personnel programs are typically brought about in diverse ways—through administrative fiat, staff turnover, financial ups and downs, recommendations from faculty and student committees, marshaling of data from local, regional and national research, or pressure groups from students, faculty, administration, alumni and surrounding community. Planned change involves carrying out a decision to effect improvements in a given setting by means of a systematic methodology. In student programs, as in other phases of higher education, it seems that little attention is given to planned change. However, it is possible that more planned change is taking place than appears in the literature.

In any event it is likely that most student personnel workers would agree that more could be done about the nature and direction of "change" in the college student personnel program.

Force-Field Analysis

One useful scheme for thinking about change has been proposed by Kurt Lewin [4]. He described it as a level or phase of behavior within an institutional setting, not as a static "habit" or "custom," but as a dynamic balance of the institution. An example would be a production level of work teams in a factory. This level tends to fluctuate, but, by and large, the pattern persists at a given level over a period of time. The reason, according to Lewin, is that the forces which tend to raise the level of production are equal to the forces that tend to depress it [4].

Examples of forces which might raise the level of production are (a) pressure by supervision on the work team to produce more; (b) desire of some team members to "look good" and therefore get ahead individually; (c) the desire of team members to earn more under the plant incentive plan; and so on. Lewin called these *driving forces.*

Forces tending to lower the level of production might be: (m) a work group standard that a team member should do no more than a certain amount of work; (n) team resistance to accepting training programs which would increase productivity; (o) feelings by the workers that their product is not important; and so on. These are *restraining forces.* When these sets of forces balance each other a certain level of production is established which Lewin called quasi-stationary equilibrium. This equilibrium may be diagrammed as follows:

Force-Field Diagram

Restraining forces	(m)	(n)	(o)	. . . (etc.)
	↓	↓	↓	↓
Present level of production		Quasi-stationary Equilibrium		
	↑	↑	↑	↑
Driving forces	(a)	(b)	(c)	. . . (etc.)

Change takes place when an imbalance occurs between the sum of the driving forces and the sum of the restraining forces. Such an imbalance "unfreezes" the pattern and the level changes until the opposing forces are again brought into equilibrium. An imbalance may occur through a change in the *magnitude* of any force, a change in the *direction* of a force, and/or an *addition* of a new force.

Suppose that members of the work team join a new union which is challenging the over-all wage structure of the company. This may heighten dissatisfaction with current policy and increase workers' suspicion toward management motives, including supervisors. The results may increase restraining force (n); the equilibrium is unfrozen and the level of production moves down unless increasing driving forces also take place. In the present illustration as the production level falls, supervisors increase their pressure toward greater production and driving force (a) tends to increase. Thus, the increased counterforce brings the system into balance again somewhere near the previous level. These are changes in *magnitude* and may create problems. An increase in magnitude of opposing forces may heighten tension and make the situation less amenable to rational control.

A war situation demanding greater productivity may convert restraining force (o) from a feeling that the product is not important to a feeling that the product is important and that one should work harder to assist in the war effort. The level of production will rise as the direction of force (o) is reversed to help elevate production until a state of equilibrium is reached at a higher level.

Suppose a new driving force is added when a supervisor wins the trust and respect of the working team. The new force motivates the working team to make the well-liked supervisor look good. This force may operate to offset a generally unfavorable attitude toward management. Or the work team, by setting their own standards of production as a result of a different supervising approach, may significantly reduce restraining force (m) [2].

Force-Field Analysis in a Student Personnel Program

The force-field model has been used by researchers and practitioners in various organizational settings during the past dozen years. Can this conceptual approach be utilized in helping with planned change in a college setting? One aspect of a student personnel program may serve as an affirmative illustration:

Suppose one of the goals of the student personnel program is to stimulate and assist student leaders more closely to identify the student activities program with the intellectual objectives of the university. The force-field situation is described in the accompanying diagram.

These sets of forces are in quasi-stationary equilibrium. It is recalled that change takes place when an imbalance occurs between the sum of the driving forces and the sum of the restraining forces.

Suppose a student-faculty committee appointed to develop a new honors program attacks student activities as anti-intellectual and a waste of time. Their report is circulated among faculty and printed in the student newspaper. The committee action increases driving forces (a) and (b), thus tending to move the situation toward intellectually oriented programs. But the attack on student activities as being inadequate is responded to strongly and defensively by the student leaders, thus increasing restraining force (n). The result would be the force field system coming into balance again, somewhere near the previous level.

These opposing changes in magnitude, as in the factory example, may increase tension and stress, thus making the entire situation less stable and predictable.

Suppose a series of exploratory seminars is arranged for the student leaders with several articulate and highly respected faculty members discussing the nature of a university. This may convert restraining force (m) from a feeling that the present student activities program is adequate to a feeling that it is

Table 1
Force-Field Diagram of Degree of Identification of
Student Activities with Institutional Intellectual Objectives

Restraining forces	(m)	(n)	(o)	(p)	(. . . etc.)
	Feeling of student leaders that present student activities program is adequate	Counter dependence: against idea because faculty and administration are for it	Student feeling that intellectual activities should be confined to the classroom	Faculty disinterest in spending time with students outside the classroom	
	↓	↓	↓	↓	↓
Present situation			Quasi-stationary equilibrium		
	↑	↑	↑	↑	↑
Driving forces	(a)	(b)	(c)	(d)	. . . (etc.)
	Efforts of faculty advisers, personnel deans, residence hall, union, and other personnel staff members	General faculty and administration concern that student activities are busy-work and anti-intellectual	Group of student "intellectuals" have requested such a program	Community reaction against student emphasis on social life and "college escapades"	

inadequate. Thus, a restraining force becomes converted to a driving force. Hence, concern for the role of student activities becomes more closely identified with the objectives of the university and raises the student activity program to a new level. In addition, faculty satisfaction with participating in the seminars may result in reducing restraining force (p).

Finally, suppose a new driving force is added. As a result of an in-service training program student personnel staff members acquire new skills and insights in working with student leaders. This new force may result in strengthening driving force (a) and reducing restraining force (n).

In brief, the three major strategies for achieving change in a given situation are: (a) increasing the driving forces, (b) decreasing the restraining forces or (c) a combination of the two. The strategy of increasing the driving forces, as pointed out earlier, creates higher tension. It is therefore better to initiate a change effort with the second or third strategy listed as these are more stable, more predictable, and less threatening [5, 8].

The examples utilized suggest that change takes the form of unfreezing—upward or downward movement—refreezing. In planned change, forces must be arranged or refrozen to prevent backsliding. Change in any human situation is often followed by a backward reaction toward the "old ways" after the pressures toward change are relaxed. For example, following a survey, a college puts into effect recommended changes under pressure of the board of trustees. As vigilance relaxes, old patterns creep in. Whenever change is effected it is important that the "refreezing" at a new level will be stable. Not only must the forces "for" change be analyzed, but the new restraining and/or driving forces which will exist after the change must be anticipated as clearly as possible.

In planning for change it is important to identify all relevant driving and restraining forces impinging upon the given situation. Of equal importance is the taking into account the many neutral, uncommitted, or unknown forces. Changes in one force field situation are likely to affect others directly or indirectly related to it. For example, a change in student activities toward more intellectually oriented programs might result not only in other student activities being discarded but might also mean involving many more faculty in student activities than anticipated. Some of the faculty involved might as a result of their experiences with students in these settings experiment with new approaches in their classroom teaching. Moreover, the identification of these uncommitted forces might make possible their utilization as driving rather than restraining forces. For example, in the foregoing illustration the student newspaper may be uncommitted. Whether the newspaper becomes a driving or restraining force might be crucial as attempts are made to unfreeze and refreeze the situation.

A Case Illustration

The following case example of a force-field situation on a state university campus is a further illustration of the use of such a model as a way of analyzing and effecting change. One of the goals of the University student personnel program has been to help the fraternity system become more closely identified with the University and its educational objectives. The force-field situation as it appeared in 1954–1955 is diagrammed in Table 2.

Among the more important driving forces were (a) pressure on fraternities by the fraternity dean and the administration to produce more meaningful

Table 2
Force-Field Diagram of Degree of Fraternity Identification
with the Educational Objectives of the University

(m)	(n)	(o)	(p)	. . . (etc.)
Suspicion and distrust of university motives based on fact and fiction of past dealings with the administration	Feeling of fraternity members that the present situation is adequate, due in part to lack of understanding and concern with university educational objectives	Traditional counter-dependency: desire to be free from university "control"	Tendency to become defensive and withdraw further when criticized	
↓	↓	↓	↓	↓

Quasi-stationary equilibrium

↑	↑	↑	↑	↑
(a)	(b)	(c)	(d)	. . . (etc.)
Pressure on fraternities by dean and administration to produce better chapter programs	Some fraternity leaders recognize need for closer fraternity identification with the university	Need for new fraternity housing means closer ties since only land available is owned by university	Some faculty and town people attack fraternities as anti-intellectual and advocate their abolishment	

chapter programs and to become more closely identified and cooperative with the University; (b) some fraternity leaders recognized the need for a closer fraternity identification with university objectives and were attempting to get the fraternities to change in this direction; (c) the need for new fraternity houses meant developing closer ties with the University, since the only land available for such houses was owned by the University; and (d) some faculty members and townspeople were attacking fraternities as anti-intellectual and were advocating their abolishment.

Major restraining forces were (m) fraternity suspicion and distrust of

University motives based on factual and fictional reports of past dealings with the administration; (n) the feeling among fraternity members that the present fraternity situation is adequate, coupled with an unwillingness to evaluate current programs and face their problems; (o) the traditional counter-dependency of fraternity members: their need to be aggressively resistant to parental and other authority symbols, which is reflected in their desire to be free from University "control"; and (p) the tendency of fraternities to become defensive when criticized, thus withdrawing further from the University orbit.

An initial strategy directed toward heightening fraternity identification with University educational objectives was to reduce restraining force (m), fraternity suspicion and distrust of University motives. This could be initiated by reducing driving force (a), thus lessening pressure on fraternities by the administration. The appointment of a new fraternity Dean, who was skilled in human relations and experienced in working with fraternities, implemented the reduction of driving force (a). Thus within a year restraining force (m) was considerably reduced, making it possible for driving force (b) and restraining force (n) to become the next leverage point. Having developed new fraternity confidence and trust in the administration, it became possible to add a new driving force, consisting of a series of workshops and conferences with individual fraternities, fraternity leaders, and the interfraternity council. These were directed toward evaluating individual fraternity programs heightening understanding of fraternity and university objectives, and planning programs of improvement. Hence driving force (b) was augmented by increasing the number of fraternity leaders and members who recognized a need for a closer fraternity identification with the University. The result was the reduction of restraining force (n), from the feeling of satisfaction to dissatisfaction with the present fraternity situation on the part of many members. Restraining force (n) therefore became converted in part to a driving force.

Meanwhile an additional new force was introduced by the creation of an alumni interfraternity council, whose major objective included facilitating mutual understanding between the University and alumni groups and working toward the acquirement of University land for the construction of fraternity houses, thus increasing driving force (c). Shortly thereafter, however, the University administration made public its priority list for the long-range building program on campus. The "campus of 1970" projection did not include provision for fraternity houses. These announcements brought about a resurgence of fraternity suspicion and distrust of the University administration, which increased restraining force (m). Hence the quasistationary equilibrium was pushed down somewhere near its original level. In

1957 a survey of fraternity housing needs by the alumni interfraternity council was reported to the board of regents. The result was the passage of a resolution by the board of regents, recognizing the urgent need for fraternity housing and favoring fraternity housing on campus when land became available. This increase of driving force (c) tended to reduce restraining force (m) and raise the quasi-stationary equilibrium level. More recently a fraternity study committee, consisting of faculty members, fraternity members, other students, administrators, and regents was appointed by the president. Outcomes of the study would be to define University and community goals and expectations for fraternities, to anticipate potential developments and needed changes, and to plan accordingly. It is hoped that the fraternities themselves will become deeply involved with the project. The appointment of the study committee as a new driving force may reduce driving force (d) and convert restraining force (p) from defensiveness and withdrawal to honest self-criticism and willingness to collaborate towards improved programs.

In five years the level of fraternity identification with the educational objectives of the University has heightened somewhat. There have been ups and downs, and there are likely to be additional set-backs in the future. An understanding of the forces at work in the situation will help in the minimizing of restraining forces, and by bringing the right forces into play at the right time it is hoped that the level of equilibrium will continue to rise as more meaningful programs are developed.

Force-field analysis can be utilized in other college areas where the need for planned change is indicated; for example, to facilitate communication among expanding departments as enrollments mount; to establish more effective articulation with high schools directed toward stimulation of gifted students; to help departments find and take the time for continuing research and evaluation; to get teachers and counselors to collaborate toward the total education of the student; or more simply, to help personnel workers and instructors relate more effectively and productively with each other.

Additional Guideposts

The problems which have been summarized exist in most if not all colleges and universities. Usually there is motivation to bring about improvements—to effect "planned change." It is difficult, however, to come to grips with the complex human and organizational forces within a college setting. A force-field analysis, one systematic method of diagramming situations in which organizational change is desired, has been described. Regardless of what approach is used, it is clear that the rate of change will be strongly accelerated in the years ahead. Controlled or planned change will come about only by means of some type of systematic methodology. Force-field analysis is the core of an approach which colleges and universities may find useful.

Administrators, instructors, or personnel workers desiring to collaborate in effecting planned change will have in mind further guideposts or principles as they develop their approach. Some of these can be briefly noted.

The processes of change within an institution can be constructive only if conditions permit reassessment of goals and the means to their achievement. If a college is to function in relation to the changing needs of faculty, students, and community, it must provide for an objective evaluation. A responsibility of each staff member is to help build the climate within which he and his associates can think and act upon facts in a manner different from the usual norms. Such a climate would encourage both academic and student personnel departments to make periodic self-studies which may lead toward change as results are analyzed and acted upon.

A most powerful barrier to organizational change is the resistance which persons can express when a projected change seems threatening to roles in which they have invested considerable security. The process of change is facilitated by the following conditions suggested by Coffey and Golden [3]:

a. When leadership is moving as far as possible in the direction of participative action and group members have optimal freedom to participate in decision-making.

b. When norms have become established which make changing (innovating, inventing, experimenting) an expected aspect of institutional development.

c. When change can be brought about without threatening the individual's membership in a group.

d. When the group concerned with a change of trying to change has a strong sense of belongingness, is attractive to its members and when it is concerned with satisfying members' needs.

e. When group members actively participate in the leadership functions, help formulate goals, plan the steps toward goal realization, have the freedom to "try out" new roles, and to participate in the assessment of these functions of leadership.

A change within a given group must be supported by the organizational structure or the group will become a target of mistrust by other groups in the organization. Therefore, communication must flow from one authority level to another, and proposals for change must be legitimatized within the organizational authority structure.

Changes in one part of an organization produces strain in other related parts which can be reduced to toleration only by eliminating the change or by bringing about adjustments in related parts. As in the earlier illustration, if the student activity program is changed toward more intellectually oriented activities, then greater demands upon faculty time and energy would result. Either the faculty would adjust to these increasing demands or the new program would fail.

A change attempt is most likely to be successfully introduced through an experimental approach [7]. This approach includes the continuous cycle of diagnosing a problem situation in the organization, planning action steps, taking these steps, and studying their results [6]. In this way, the process of planned change becomes an integrative force in an institution's developmental program.

References

1. Cartwright, D. Achieving change in people: some applications of group dynamics theory. *Hum. Relat.*, 1951, *4*, 381–392.
2. Coch, L., & French, J. R. P., Jr. Overcoming resistance to change. *Hum. Relat.*, 1948, *1*, 512–532.
3. Coffey, H. S., & Golden, W. P., Jr. Psychology of change within an institution. *Fifty-sixth yearbook*, National Society for the Study of Education. Chicago: University of Chicago Press, 1957.
4. Lewin, K. Frontiers in group dynamics. *Hum. Relat.*, 1947, *1*, 5–42.
5. Lewin, K. Group decision and social change, Swanson, G. E., Newcomb, T.N., & Hartley, E. L. (Eds.), *Readings in social psychology* (2nd Ed.). New York: Henry Holt, 1952.
6. Lippitt, R., Watson, Jeanne, & Wesley, B. *The dynamics of planned change*. New York: Harcourt, Brace, 1958.
7. Miles, M. B., & Passow, A. H. Training in the skills needed for inservice training programs. *Fifty-sixty yearbook*, National Society for the Study of Education. Chicago: University of Chicago Press, 1957.
8. National Training Laboratories in Group Development. *Reports of summer laboratory sessions*, twelfth, 1958: thirteenth, 1959. Washington, D.C.: National Education Association.

Perception and Perfection

Melvene Draheim Hardee

Directives and Directions

Presidential addresses show a singular affinity. If you were to examine them, you would find interlocking themes, recurrent ideas, as well as implied—if not outright—parting directives. In a very real sense, an outgoing president structures the life and times of the incoming officer.

Through the Lenses

By way of initial charting for these remarks, I shall cite my perceptions of ACPA at several levels—national, regional, state, local and global. Thereafter I shall make editorial comment about our professional image, commenting upon perfections which influence perceptions.

At the outset, may I describe the lenses by which I perceive? Throughout, I am defining *the place of student personnel work in higher education*. First, I am speaking of higher education as a field of specialty—a discipline worthy of scholarly study in its own right. Currently there are some 93 graduate institutions which offer coursework in higher education—courses in the history of higher education, in organization and administration, in student personnel work, in curriculum and teaching, practicum and internship—these preparing candidates for positions of president, dean, controller, student personnel administrator or counselor, development officer, teacher, or researcher in junior or senior colleges and in universities and professional schools. This view of higher education (as a discipline worthy of scholarly study) is dramatized by the rapid growth not only of courses but also of full-blown departments of higher education. The inclusion of the major in student personnel work as a contributing area can be seen in the graduate programs of higher education.

Second, I regard student personnel work as an integral part of the

180

educational enterprise in the 2,100 collegiate institutions of the country. My concept is one of a *comprehensive* program with the efforts of student personnel workers integrated as closely as possible with the instructional program and the curricular process. Those engaged in the total educational endeavor—including student personnel workers—must understand and there-after articulate—(1) what they want students to learn, (2) what personal qualities they expect the college experience to include and, (3) as Ordway Tead affirms . . .

What kinds of adults with what kinds of competences they would like to be able to point to with pride in their graduates. . . .[1]

I believe that student personnel work must take its rightful place among the forces—instructional, administrative, managerial, noninstructional—that combine on a campus to effect this educational product of singular quality.

The National Scene

My visits to Washington in the past twelve months have been four—all of them "side saddle" trips for other main missions. It does not take long, in visiting thirty or more offices and agencies, to discover that the most powerful voice in Washington with respect to American higher education is that of the American Council on Education, composed of 1,000 member *institutions* and 175 member *organizations.* Currently our organization, ACPA, has a separate membership in the American Council, but it also holds another one-sixth membership by virtue of its Division I status in American Personnel and Guidance Association which is a constituent member of ACE.

You will recall that our association has enjoyed several decades of good working relationships with ACE, as can be seen in the impressive list of student personnel publications which began with *The Student Personnel Point of View* and continued with more recent releases. *They Come for the Best of Reasons* and *Spotlight on the College Student.*

At the bidding of our own Executive Council, I conferred last May in Washington with Dr. Logan Wilson, President of American Council on Education, inquiring about the way in which ACPA could figure in the work of the newly re-organized American Council. Dr. Wilson was quick to affirm that the work of our association was related to that of the newly designated

1. Ordway Tead, *The Climate of Learning,* Harper and Brothers, New York 1958, p. 30.

Commission on Academic Affairs. He suggested we begin negotiations with the about-to-be-appointed chairman of this Commission, Mr. Lawrence Dennis.

As a result, conferences have taken place during the year both in Washington and Chicago. Mr. Dennis' participation in our program this week is testimony of the fact that negotiations have been mutually profitable, and thus, I share the first perception.

Perception 1: I have abiding confidence in the ability of ACPA to contribute meaningfully, through designated representatives, to the important work of the Commission on Academic Affairs of the American Council on Education. This meaningful participation, however, is dependent upon other perceptions to follow—a baker's dozen of them, twelve-plus-one, separate but inter-related.

Now, to keep the muscle of its ambition from atrophy, ACPA must be at the cutting edge of competence with respect to study of the profession of student personnel work, to the centrality of its philosophy and practice with respect to the whole of higher education. Both *intensive study* and *extensive participation* of members would seem to be two inseparable requisites.

Perception 2: The twelve commissions, activated in Summer 1961 for the designing of the Boston program appear to offer a convenient vehicle for continuing study of our profession. Some 250 persons have been attracted to the commission activity prior to Boston. For this convention the commissions have designated sixty-eight programs, utilizing 372 participants. The product of these permanent commissions would be reflected in convention programs in the future, in issues of the *Journal of College Student Personnel* and in the *ACPA Monograph Series*, the latter recognized as two communications media of growing excellence.

At your places, you will find a veritable blizzard of paper. From time to time, I shall refer to one or another item in this Easter gift packet. The first reference is to a copy of *Higher Education as a National Resource.* This booklet, made available to you through the offices of Mr. Charles Dobbins, Chairman of the Commission on Federal Relations of the American Council, bears the date of January, 1963, and urges the federal government to take early and definite action. This same information has been reprinted in the *Congressional Record* of Tuesday, January 19, 1963. In Section 1, p. 5, you will note the proposal for student housing. In Section III, pp. 8–10, there will be found consideration of student loans, student grant assistance and international student exchanges. In Section IV, pp. 10–11, you will note the proposal, anticipated a year ago in our Chicago conference, relating to extension of guidance institutes to include college student personnel workers. Finally, on p. 12, of the brochure, it is stated that:

The American Council on Education is convinced that it speaks not only for organized higher education but also for a much broader American consensus when it asserts that the opportunity for quality education beyond the high school should be widened and deepened through Federal action.[2]

I am concerned with this statement. If ACE speaks for organized higher education, then it purportedly speaks with knowledge of what we in ACPA think, but how *does* our organization think with respect to student housing, student loans, grants and international exchanges, as well as in the matter of extending NDEA institutes to college personnel workers? Are the opinions of this association transmitted with clarity and force to key personnel who in turn speak with clarity and force into legislative ears?

There is, among the twelve study commissions of American College Personnel Association, one designated as Commission V, Student Financial Aids. This commission has drafted goals for working with recently appointed financial aids officers—surveying their functions and assisting in their professional upgrading. However, by affirmation of its chairman, Rexford Moon, Commission V plans *not* to enter into discussions which will attempt to influence legislation in this area.

Therefore, of the moment, ACPA must look *outside itself* for both initiating and implementing legislative goals in the area of financial aids. There are two possibilities visible—(1) through the parent organization, American Personnel and Guidance Association and (2) through the efforts of a newly-organized Joint Commission on Financial Aids under the sponsorship of the Inter Association Coordinating Committee.

Permit me to backtrack, as best I can, to recall the record of legislative activity affecting higher education in the past few months. On the tables you will find copies of the bill which has been under study by the House Committee on Education and Labor. (These publications have been contributed through the kind cooperation of Dr. John Russel, Chief of Faculty and Student Services, Division of Higher Education of the U.S. Office of Education.) Note, please, Title I covering college student loans and the college student work program. I have been asked by a number of you to reply to the question: *Has ACPA been heard with respect to particulars of this bill?*

Now, if you will re-cast your persisting question to read: *Can ACPA be heard with respect to the particularities of Title I, I shall respond with a perception.*

Perception 3: As of this moment of time, I should adjudge the IACC Joint Commission on Student Financial Aids as the best medium by which ACPA can figure in Federal legislative action affecting student financial aids. I see the possibility of an uninterrupted conveyor-belt operation, with the ideas of

ACPA being moved (1) to the IACC Joint Commission on Financial Aids and thereafter (2) to the ACE Commission on Legislative Affairs, the U.S. Office of Education, the House and Senate Committees on Education or other.

For those of you who resist Perception 3 and the two to follow, possibly on the grounds that lobbying is unbecoming to student personnel workers, I would urge that you acquaint yourself with the fine differences between *lobbying* and *leading*. Decisions affecting each of us will be made regardless of our activity or inactivity. It would seem to be the better part of wisdom for us to give constructive assistance to those who will make the decisions ultimately.

There are other legislative concerns—student housing, international student exchanges, and extensions of NDEA institutes to include college personnel workers. On the last-named, I would speculate as follows:

Perception 4: Assuming the IACC Joint Commission on Financial Aids provides a voice in federal legislation that *is* heard, we would do well to lend support to another established IACC sub-committee which can, in conveyor-belt escalation, tkae our ideas on NDEA institutes for college personnel workers to appropriate Washington receptors. I refer to the IACC Committee on Preparation and Education of Student Personnel Workers which has, with vigor and purpose, begun to explore its relationship to offices and agencies in Washington.

Perception 5: There is likely an intermediate or enabling step needed which is that of naming an ACPA Committee on Omnibus Legislation which I suggested last May without any knowledge of an "omnibus bill" in education in the offing. Such a proposed committee, with strong regional ramparts which I shall discuss shortly, would determine association posture on particular issues in order that our designated IACC representatives be informed spokesmen for the Association.

Last June, I selected from the Directory of Higher Education some seventy associations which centered their work on higher education. Believing the way could be paved for conference, I directed a letter to the executive officer of each association inquiring whether our two organizations could work together along these five lines: (1) in reciprocal programming through seminars, work conferences joint committees, consultations, and similar; (2) in exchange of personnel in convention or conference programs; (3) in exchange of journals or other professional materials; (4) in joint research activities; and (5) in effecting legislation at national, regional, state and local levels.

What has come of this overture? By mimeographing 100 copies of our Boston program early to send to key personnel, and by follow-up in conference or letter, we have at this conference representatives from many educational associations, both as observers and participants, who have hitherto not met with us. The exchange of materials of mutual interest before the convention has been spirited. All this amounts to an observation long overdue.

Perception 6: ACPA resides in a professional-educational world with many centers of power. Our Association must find its place—and with some haste—among the alphabetically souped-up groups of recognized associations in higher education. Personnel from these groups must be encouraged to continue their communication with us. In addition, ACPA must send official observers to conventions like this of other associations. Convening in the next few weeks are national meetings of the American Association of Collegiate Registrars and Admissions Officers, the American College Health Association, and the National Association of Foreign Student Advisers, to name but three deserving of our cooperation.

Other Than Washington Operations

May we turn our attention now to the cruising of regional, state, local and global areas? I am convinced if we build only on a Washington base, we will demonstrate a singular myopia.

Among the letters I alluded to earlier were three directed to the trio of regional compacts: (1) the Southern Regional Education Board (SREB); the New England Board of Higher Education (NEBHE); and the Western Interstate Commission on Higher Education (WICHE). I call attention to the reprint at your place. WITHIN OUR REACH, which summarizes the Report on the Commission on Goals for Higher Education in the South. (This brochure was sent to us through the kindness of the Southern Regional Education Board in Atlanta.) On p. 2, column 2, item 4, please note the Committee's citation of student counseling, actually a reference to comprehensive student personnel programs. That this is no counterfeit nod is seen in the continuing assistance provided by the Southern Regional Education Board to the Southern College Personnel Association—assistance in the form of three summer work conferences dealing with student personnel programs, in-service education, the contemporary college student, and a fourth workshop on institutional research productive of data on student characteristics.

You of the West know of WICHE's sponsorship of institutes on college student characteristics and the assessment of the campus climate. NEBHE, operating in the area in which we are meeting, is moving to sponsor institutes on admissions, the profile of the college student, and the organization and administration of housing programs.

Perception 7: There are about us benevolents in the guise of regional Dutch uncles. ACPA should familiarize itself with the work of the regional compacts in higher education, for there is much to be shared in ideas for research and programming, facilities, publications and grants which can effect change in the climate of learning on campus.

Attendant upon this move is the need to take inventory of numbers and activities of the regional college personnel associations. The pink Quick-Check sent to ACPA members in the recent mass mail-out brought replies indicating (1) that many knew of no regional or state associations where, in actuality, they existed. (2) More regrettable is the indication that regional personnel groups seem to be peculiarly incommunicado.

Perception 8: Regional *encapsulation* weakens a profession. There is a common market of ideas in our profession that stretches country-wide. A mutual upsurge of strength would surely be felt if—at this convention—there were called a meeting of the representatives of the various regional college student personnel associations, the gains being these: (1) *coordination* of ACPA's program with that of the regions—but not superimposition of program; (2) communication of regional groups by newsletter or other media; (3) identification of competent officer and committee personnel for ACPA and (4) research and/or legislative activity-in-combination among the regional groups and ACPA.

Perception 9: ACPA's friendly handclasp must, on occasion, form a fist for our Association has not spoken out firmly on the adequacy of regional—or national—accreditation criteria. Before ill-conceived criteria are applied to the detriment of good programs and the plaudit of poor ones, our association must investigate and act!

Other grassroots and tidelands areas to which ACPA must look are the 50 individual states and the 2,100 individual college campuses. There are rapid triggerings of statewide studies of higher education in New York, Michigan, California, and Louisiana. In the past 15 months, we in Florida have been confronted with facts from three major studies authorized by the State Board of Control and spelling out the future of higher education—and of student personnel work—in our warm peninsula. I am gratified to find in the most recent report a fact-packed chapter on college student characteristics.[3]

Perception 10: This association must effect a means for the study of

3. *The Setting for Higher Education in Florida* edited by Charles M. Grigg and Charles N. Millican, Role and Scope Study Project, University System of Florida, Board of Control, Tallahassee, Florida, 1963.

statewide surveys of higher education, for they not only prescribe minimal to model programs in student personnel for existing institutions but also for colleges and universities now only on the drawing boards. Likewise, ACPA must find a means for collecting and disseminating data derived from self-studies and similar appraisals of both the private and public institutions to obtain barometic readings on the status of student personnel work in respect to the total educational endeavor.

Perception 11: ACPA, somewhat like the fabled Rip Van Winkle, is awakening from a deep sleep in the hills, aroused but recently to its responsibilities relating to the international dimensions of the institution. This association must seek to work increasingly with the Programs and Services unit, Cultural Affairs Section, U.S. Department of State; with the U.S. Office of Education; with the Institute for International Education and other agencies whose global program demands more than we have hitherto given. ACPA must concern itself increasingly with what in student personnel work is readily exportable—that is, with what is packaged to carry abroad by scores of our colleagues in overseas assignments, long term and short. What does the basic philosophy and current practice in *American* college student personnel work presage for faculty and staff in Nigeria, India, Afghanistan, Ecuador? What kind of *image* goes overseas in our professional name—beneficent, benign, impressive, or superficial?

And thus, the time has come to face *the image* we portray to those who observe us. That there are some distortions in this collection of perceptions will be obvious. In Washington, we appear to some to be riding *piggy-back* with student personnel work in higher education balancing on the shoulders of counseling and guidance which stretches K through G—kindergarten through graduate school.

Then, it is thought that personnel work is chiefly regulatory—that, in fact, student personnel workers are, in the words of one thoughtful colleague, "wild life managers" who relieve members of the reaching faculty of onerous out-of-class activities. A member of the budget commission in my own state adjudges student personnel work to be the supervision of student recreation—of fun and games which detract from the real educational mission.

Finally, we have been viewed in the literature as parent surrogates, substitutes for mother and father, in *loco parentis,* and—say the wags—mostly in *loco!*

In my judgment, the length and breadth, width and depth of student personnel work has not been sufficiently well enunciated for at least a decade and a half during which time a whole new generation of college presidents, development officers, controllers, members of governing boards, and teaching personnel have assumed their posts on campuses of the land. These coworkers lack a carefully delineated picture of us.

But, I prefer NOT to speak of *building* an image but rather of *restoring* one. Madison Avenue, of certainty, has no claim on restoration. This is a delicate, old-world craft that we, as professionals, can effect if we but flex our memories and exercise our faculties.

There needs to be recalled to life the image of student personnel work NOT as a gilded dynasty; NOT as an island in splendid isolation cut off from the mainland of activity; NOT as a string of service stations stretching over academic acres; and NOT as a student welfare state. Rather, the likeness should be one reflecting our earned place in the mainstream of purposeful education which, in an era of automation, effects a precision product, well-tooled in competence, insight, and morality. Ours is a proud profession with a durable heritage. *This organization represents that profession well.*

Our task—one to test our skill and patience—is that of stripping or peeling off the accumulated film of years masking the touch of true genius beneath. If the image of student personnel work in higher education *is* to be renewed, it will come about in the multiple ways enumerated: (1) active participation in policy formation in the committee-rooms of American Council on Education; (2) active participation in legislation affecting student financial aids, student housing, institutes for preparation of student personnel workers and other; (3) collaboration with the multiple associations whose work, like ours, is higher education directed, (4) cooperation, at appropriate levels, with the regional compacts and the regional accrediting associations; (5) planning in combination with regional, state, and local college personnel associations; (6) analysis of state-wide studies of higher education as well as local campus studies, and (7) a grasp of the international dimensions of our work in acknowledgment of the fact that the *local* and the *global* are closer than we think. The weight and extent of all this endeavor to restore an image leads to a twelfth perception.

Perception 12: It is my considered judgment after these years of service in the executive eschelons that no president of this association nor any executive group scattered about the country can do all of this. To try would be to emulate what industry terms "moonlighting"—that is, extending the working day beyond sundown or the working week to encompass both Saturday and Sunday. Too many of us in leadership roles in education are "moonlit"—more of shadow than real substance in our fulfillment of the expectations of our rapidly growing constituencies. The Self Study Committee suggests a means—the naming of an Executive Secretary within the existing APGA framework, which idea has already been under discussion with APGA headquarters staff.

Perfection—and Conclusion

We have been talking of the renewal of the image of student personnel work in higher education. Last week, the truth was again apparent to me. In the basic class in student personnel work on our campus, twenty students, ages varying from twenty to fifty, presented in a two-platoon system their end-of-course project—a model student personnel program for our newest state institution, the Florida Atlantic University at Boca Raton, for reasons of class anonymity designated as The College of the Clouds.

To the best of knowledge, only oen of these twenty students had ever been a college student personnel worker. The other nineteen were department heads or teachers of such subjects as music, public health, business administration, nursing, mathematics or psychology. They were retired from the military service or they were homemakers recalled to academic life.

The performance of these students in roles assumed by them—deans of students, deans of men or women, directors of admissions, counseling, placement, health, financial aids—is indelibly etched on my mind, for they reflected *their* image of *our* profession in *their* decorum. These students in their dual performances last week declared the goal of student personnel work was one shared with all forces on the campus aiming to

. . . assist the student in effecting an understanding of himself and his studies in relation to the culture, creation, and the Creator.

Reflections of a Troublesome But Hopeful Rip Van Winkle

W. H. Cowley

Washington Irving's Rip Van Winkle, you'll recall, took a swig from the keg of a stranger before the American Revolution and woke up twenty years later burdened with years and bewildered by the wonders of the new age in which he found himself. I liken myself to that fabled Dutchman because in 1938 I too took a swig from an intoxicating keg and left the ravines of personnel work which I entered as a neophyte forty years ago this coming September.

Washington Irving portrayed Rip Van Winkle as troubled by the fantastic changes that had occurred during his long absence but I'm not a bit troubled. On the contrary, I'm delighted with the enormous growth of student services as epitomized by such facts as these: the numbers of men and women engaged in these services has multiplied at least 25 times; the institutional budgets for your programs have grown from a few thousand dollars to more than a million in a number of universities and have increased proportionately in most small colleges; and the membership of this Association has grown from 91 in 1934 to 3,200 last year.

These and other advances "pleasure" everyone who has been or is now engaged in your area of higher educational activity; but, it seems to me, the debit side of the ledger very considerably outbalances the credit side. For example, this Association and the three dozen or so others devoted to student affairs in colleges and universities are currently struggling with the same crucial problems that afflicted them 25 years ago. Here and there a bit of headway has been made, but in the main the confused and vexatious situation of the past continues to prevail.

For example, Bill Craig's presidential address of two years ago listed and discussed much the same congeries of problems over which the Association perspired during my day; and an article in the June, 1963 issue of your journal

190

once again goes over the same ground that I traversed in a still relevant article of 1936[1] and which a score of other writers have explored meanwhile.

I became aware of a very recent development about which I had not previously heard. Its tremendous importance and potential led me to the decision that I should throw off the mantle of self-chartered prosecuting attorney and instead become an advocate for the alluring plans now maturing in the just organized group known as Council of Student Personnel Associations in Higher Education or, for short, COSPA.

Suffice it here to say that it is the latest and by all odds the most promising of the many efforts made to develop cooperation among the national associations concerned with the extra-instructional student affairs of American colleges and universities. Ed Williamson has called it "the most auspicious development in the student affairs field that has occurred during the past 30 years." I agree heartily with his judgment, and in this paper I want to do my bit to help convert its high promise into buoyant reality.

Toward that end I began with a postulate, namely, that the activities or functions of colleges and universities fall into three categories: first, teaching and research which constitute their *core* functions; second, the extra-instructional services performed to facilitate education, denominated in my paper *complementary* functions; and third, the maintenance and promotional activities which institutions undertake in order to continue in operation and to prosper which I labelled *continuity* functions. The members of this Association all give their attention to activities in the second of these functional categories. That is to say, they perform complementary functions.

Some members of this Association—counselors in particular—believe, I know, that their activities should be considered core functions; but may I make a distinction that will perhaps help them to agree with designating them complementary, namely, the distinction between formal and informal teaching. As a one-time counselor I yield to no one in the value I put upon it; but the fact remains that many students learn more from counseling than they do from some of their formal courses.

What functions do you and your fellow workers in related associations perform? You do many different kinds of things, but all of them have one distinctive characteristic, namely, they occur outside the formal curriculum. Some of you, of course, teach courses; but those who do wear two hats—one donned occasionally as a faculty member, the other worn most of the time as a student service officer. Mark well the designation *student service officer* because in operational fact all of you do work that directly serves students and indirectly the institutions in which you live.

---

1. "The Nature of Student Personnel Work," *The Educational Record*, April, 1936, pp. 198–226.

These activities appear to me, as remarked earlier, to be complementary to the core teaching and research functions of colleges and universities; but regardless of whether you like or dislike the term complementary functions, the fact stands out clearly that the distinguishing characteristic of all the members of all the groups in your field is this: you serve students in various non-curricular ways. In short, you are student service officers.

I submit three reasons why you should not only accept this fact but also, welcome and, indeed, broadcast it. First, if the terms guidance and personnel have been obstacles to consummating the urgently needed cooperation among your associations and among their members on college and university campuses, then it seems essential that a generally, acceptable name be found. Second, since not a few administrators and universities grant credit toward degrees from learning acquired through classroom instruction and do not grant credit for learning resulting from counseling. In short, regardless of the enormous importance of counseling and other student services, faculty members and administrators consider them to be supplementary to curricular teaching and hence complementary functions of colleges and universities.

It will be recalled that counselors and their student-service associates perform functions historically handled by faculty members. In addition, colleges and universities today serve their students in numerous new ways. For example, not until about the time of the Civil War did chaplains appear on college campuses, presidents and faculty members being the preachers and religious advisers of students. Not until about the same time did any American college give direct attention to guarding the health of their students, but today rare are the instutitons which do not have at least a part-time chaplain and a part-time physician.

The kinds and numbers of the extra-instructional officers on American college campuses multiplied slowly and unobtrusively during the last half of the nineteenth century, and either before or immediately after the First World War their growth and self-awareness led several groups of them to organize associations for mutual assistance.

1. The deans of women who first began to meet annually in 1903.
2. The directors of student unions, seven of whom met at Ohio State University for the first time in 1914.
3. The teacher placement people who met informally soon after the establishment of the first appointments office at Harvard in 1898 and formally organized in 1924.
4. Several deans of men who similarly conferred as individuals created the National Association of Deans of Men in 1917.
5. College physicians whose roots go back to 1861 and who organized the American College Health Association in 1920.

You'll observe that these groups appeared upon the scene before or soon after the introduction of two new terms, namely, *guidance* and *personnel*.

As most of you know, the so-called "guidance movement" began in secondary education in Boston about 1905. Some of you also know that for a quarter of a century a vigorous debate went on concerning the meaning of the term, one group led by Harry Kitson emphatically insisting that its meaning should be limited to the *vocational* advisement of students. Kitson and his fellow thinkers lost the debate. Thus they substituted the term *counseling*.

Soon after the Boston Vocational Bureau put the word *guidance* into circulation, Ernest Martin Hopkins, who later became president of Dartmouth College, helped establish the word *personnel* in English by introducing it at the Hawthorne plant of the Western Electric Company. He had just been appointed to help improve employer-employee relations there, and against considerable opposition he suggested that his unit be called the personnel department.

I've been unable to discover how rapidly American industrial organizations adopted the word, but everybody knows that the U.S. army employed a phalanx of psychologists to test and assign First World war draftees and that they became known as personnel officers. The head of the psychology department of Northwestern University, Walter Dill Scott, headed the group with the rank of colonel; and one of his associates, Major Clarence S. Yoakum, appears to have been the first individual to bring the term over into higher education.

When in 1927, I became director of the Board of Vocational Guidance and Placement at the University of Chicago, three clusters of student service people had become well established in American colleges and universities: first, the special service officers such as chaplains, deans of men and women, directors of health services and student unions, etc.; second, counselors sometimes referred to as guidance people; and third, psychologists primarily concerned with testing.

Like many of you, I believe that APGA has been a boon and that the bridge it has built between school and college people needs to be widened and lengthened. I also believe that the present energies of this association (ACPA) and of other higher educational groups should at this juncture be primarily devoted to promoting cooperation among the organizations whose interests center in post-high school institutions. Toward this end COSPA has already taken the initial steps, and because of its impressive prospects I shall make bold a bit later to submit some suggestions to it through you. I heartily wish that I had had a part in its launching; but since I didn't, perhaps I can help it and faculty members look upon you with something less than enthusiasm and even on occasion call you by such epithets as obnoxious upstarts and wearisome do-gooders, you need an appellation that will win you friends among your institutional colleagues. Third, the concept of service chiselled in your name will continuously help to illuminate and to enrich your day-to-day activities.

This brings the discussion back to COSPA which has for its prime purpose the enrichment of the day-to-day activities of the approximately 25 thousand men and women who work with students outside the confines of the curriculum. They hope to initiate a number of programs which will do for all groups what no one of them can do for itself. These include, I've been told, publications, upgrading seminars, a central placement office, and a united front in dealing with organized groups of presidents and with governmental agencies.

I can perhaps be useful to both ACPA and COSPA by reviewing a concept which I believe, will help in mapping the road ahead.

• The concept goes by the name of "the centric triad." It has evolved from the efforts that my students and I have made over the years to describe the components of crafts, professions, and other foci of human interest as they advance to and achieve maturity. Consider the application of the triad, for example, to medicine. In preliterate societies families looked out for the well-being of their members. Then primitive specialists in the persons of medicine men appeared, and gradually in more advanced societies these specialists began to study the causes and cures of diseases and to pass on their findings to disciples. Later—much later—some of these specialists dropped the daily practice of medicine and devoted all their time to teaching and research. Others in turn took on the task of educating people at large about how to keep well.

Today all three of these kinds of medical people flourish and interact. One group centers its attention upon the practice of medicine and are, in the terminology that my students and I use, practicentrists. The word derives from the Greek noun *praxis*, meaning practice, and the adjective *centric* which means centered in. Those who teach esoteric medical knowledge and who undertake research to expand it we call logocentrists from *logos*, one of the Greek words for knowledge combined with *centric*. The third group, the democentrists (from *demos*, as in *democracy*, meaning people in general), inform the general public about medical progress and problems. They include not only physicians and surgeons but also those who teach courses in physical and health education and laymen who write about medicine.

By means of the centric triad the maturity and status in social esteem of any field of human activity from bricklaying to nuclear physics can, I believe, be gauged.

At the outset probably most of you will agree that the great majority of student service people are practicentrists, that is, specialists in various kinds of functions ranging from counseling students to administering overall programs. Some of you will probably also agree that you have had insufficient training for your work and that therefore you somewhat resemble the rule-of-thumb medicos who have been denounced by well-trained members of the medical profession since Hippocrates' day. This, may I observe, isn't your fault. Rather, you are handicapped in your activities because as yet few logocentrists have emerged in your field to create a solid body of knowledge upon which you can draw.

In support of this generalization about the scarcity of logocentrists among you, I submit a series of observations. First, over the country only three or four professors have been appointed to date who give all their attention to student services in *higher* education. Many scores of courses typically including the phase "Guidance and Personnel" in their titles have been offered for several decades; but I've been able to discover, as I say, only three or four professorships focused upon college and university problems. The paucity of such professorial specialists chiefly accounts, as I see it, for the relative dearth of fundamental knowledge in your field and also for the limited training of so many of its practicentrists.

Second, among the 30 writers who contributed chapters to Nevitt Sanford's volume of two years ago, *The American College*, which everyone I've talked with acclaims as the most important logocentric book yet published in your bailiwick, only one—I repeat, *only one*—belongs to this or any interrelated association.

Third, the letters that I've recently written to deans of students and others who work with students asking them about the number, size, and affiliations of the groups championing student participation in social and political demonstrations and other direct-action activities have given me practically no help at all. My requests for the names of others to whom I might write for such information have also been largely fruitless, my respondents almost all replying that if they needed such data they would write or telephone colleagues in other institutions, Ed Williamson in particular. None of them referred me to a definitive source, and this situation also strikes me as a justification of my conclusion that your craft lacks and badly needs a corps of logocentrists to help carry it beyond its present trial-and-error stage.

I'd also like to importune COSPA to take steps to facilitate the emergence in your ranks of gifted democentrists. You urgently need a group of gifted speakers and writers to elucidate your activities to your academic colleagues—both faculty members and administrators—and, further, to clarify for trustees, alumni, and the general public the characteristics of present-day students and the raging ferment of student life. My reading may be limited, but I've come across very few such elucidations and clarifications bearing the names of members of student service associations. Those I have encountered have chiefly, instead, been produced by psychologists, sociologists.

• By means of this quite incomplete exposition of the centric triad I've sought to sketch some of the problems with which I imagine COSPA will be dealing, and now I'd like briefly to discuss ACPA per se. I doubt that any of you—including such old hands as Esther Lloyd-Jones and Ed Williamson—know that in 1931 I collaborated in converting the National Association of Placement and Personnel Officers into the ACPA and, in fact, proposed its new name. I recall this ancient history only to record my long if also sporadic concern for its wellbeing, a concern which accounts for my being here today. I'd like, in short, to be helpful to the Association which I helped launch; and toward that end I'll rapidly sketch some pertinent background and then make a suggestion about the future.

The National Association of Placement and Personnel Officers became ACPA because a handful of its members saw the need of a national organization to interrelate all segments of student services and affairs. The most evangelical members of the group included F, F. Bradshaw, A. B. Crawford, J. E. Walters, and me. Francis Bradshaw, Dean of Students at the University of North Carolina, believed that his fellow deans and also the deans of women could be induced to join such an association or at least to integrate with it. On my part, like Crawford a psychologist, I contemplated an influx of measurement people, of more placement officers, and of the educational and personal counselors then being appointed in fairly large numbers—at least these looked like reasonable prospects from my new post at Ohio State where my work criss-crossed with that of everyone engaged there in extrainstructional work with students.

I can't recall all the efforts we made to convert our hopes into actuality, but at all events we failed. Thus the groups we hoped to entice into our visionary consortium continued to go their independent and generally uncooperative ways and, to boo, the placement people, whose organization we had commandeered, broke away from us and established a number of structures of their own. These circumstances sidetracked our conception of ACPA and converted it into an organization largely made up of people interested in counseling and psychological testing, of individuals who performed functions for which no specialty society had yet been established, and of earnest souls who still wanted to help create an all-encompassing confederation of associations whose nucleus would be the ACPA.

Since the war, as everyone knows, you have grown helter-skelter; but most of your leaders with whom I have been in correspondence seem to be uncertain about what ACPA ought to be and what it should seek to become. I gather from other sources that an undetermined proportion of your membership also ponders the Association's place in the sun, and these ambiguities pose two questions: first, how large a proportion of your membership is puzzled about your activities and direction? Second, if the aggregate is sizable, what should be done about the situation?

I suggest that answers to these questions should promptly be sought and that your new officers immediately upon taking over their duties petition one of the foundations for a grant to investigate not only your own situation but also, in conjunction with COSPA, the whole sweep of the student service undertaking with a view to making an inventory of it and determining the most practicable methods of capitalizing its potentials. Now as never before, you are ripe for such a full-dress self-study, and I earnestly urge that it be undertaken as soon as possible.

• Throughout this paper, I have been annoyingly critical, and you may well reject my avuncular nagging. Before you do, however, may I tell you that as one who during recent years has been engaged in the task of mapping all sectors of the higher educational terrain I believe to the depths of me that the activities you perform—although I consider them complementary to the core functions of teaching and research—have incalculable significance in maintaining and improving the health of student life, of colleges and universities, and moreover of the nation. Thus this troublesome but hopeful Rip Van Winkle prays that you'll tirelessly exploit the opportunity created by the establishment of COSPA and that you'll make your compartment of higher education as vital, impressive, and influential as it should and can be.

The College Student Personnel Leader of the Future is an Educator

Dennis L. Trueblood

The development of functions in our society into an identifiable career area or professional identity area would be within itself an interesting study. The evolvement of the student personnel function has been one in which there has been on-going conflict between those who perceive themselves as procedural technicians, service station attendants so-to-speak, and those who perceive the student personnel leader as an educator whose special interest is the college student and the environment which affects him both as a whole person and as a scholar-student.

The definition of function has been further beclouded by the failure of college faculty and student personnel staff to properly understand that there need be no basic conflict between an interest in the "whole" student and the scholar-student. Certainly what happens in any facet of a person's life affects other aspects of that "whole" person including frequently his ability to perform as a scholar-student. The human factor being that which it is, there is little question that there are student personnel staff who perceive themselves in direct conflict with the faculty and his concern with the scholar-student in the classroom; and therefore program and otherwise behave with an improper understanding that, historically, society has assigned to the institution of higher education the function of preparing the intellects of its young. On the other hand, there are those faculty who fail to recognize that the student's out-of-class behavior is obviously going to influence his ability to perform as a scholar-student. Furthermore, with the increasing pressure to publish or research, the faculty member may be tempted in the future, at least in the next two decades and in the larger institution, to be even less concerned about good teaching which includes an understanding that the student is a "whole" person.

The void which appears to be developing in the higher education scene because of the pressure for publication, research, increasing larger classes, and the ever widening base of knowledge seem to force more and more faculty to be less concerned with teaching and more concerned with academic discipline matters, and the attention to the student as a "whole" person must be filled by the college student personnel leader who perceives himself as an educator. This role for the student personnel leader is a multiple one involving reinforcement of classroom activity, programming for other learning needs of the "whole" student, and behaving in his relationships with students, with the primary attitude of an educator-teacher. The challenge is a great one, but nevertheless one which must be accepted if the student is to gain the utmost from the college attending experience.

The implications are many to the development of the college student personnel leader:

1. He must be selected as a person with the intellectual capacity to comprehend the educator-student personnel leader role.

2. He must develop his skills and knowledge to be able to become the administrative leader with the information about student behavior, environmental factors which affect student behavior, the context of higher education, and the necessary channels to keep communication about matters affecting the student with students, administrative staff, and faculty.

3. He must have the necessary commitment to a way of life which includes an understanding of and a willingness to implement those basic values which are important to a humanitarian way of life. In many ways the student personnel leader and his staff play the role of "ethical counselors" as described by Chief Justice Earl Warren,[1] "I can conceive also of lay scholars who, having mastered the ethical thought of the study of the modern world and its problems, could helpfully suggest courses of action and alternatives which might prove helpful to the modern business man, politician, academic executives and other professionals who wish to discern the right." Or to place in the context of student personnel, to quote E. G. Williamson,[2] "I firmly believe that, in order to be a practical counselor, one must think out his value orientation and commitments to the big philosophic questions about human beings and the culture they have developed."

4. He must be committed to accept the personal implications of the effective college student personnel leader's unique function in the

1. Warren, Earl (Chief Justice of the Supreme Court), "Address before Louis Marshall Award Dinner of the Jewish Theological Seminary of America," New York, New York, November 11, 1962 (mimeographed).

2. Williamson, E. G., "The Societal Responsibilities of Counselors," *IGPA Newsletter*, Winter 1963.

university community. The student personnel leader of the future must not be apologetic for not being a member of the "teaching faculty" nor in any sense feel insecure in his contribution to the learning of the scholar-student.

5. He must be committed to the inherent importance of the professional position that he is willing to aggressively recruit to the career young people with the intellectual interests, mental ability, personal values, and motivation to work to develop and succeed as a college student personnel leader.

The implications to the American College Personnel Association of the evolving role of the student personnel leader as an educator seem many. Primarily and most important we must again recognize that ACPA has been and must continue to be an organization which must set the standards for research on students and the professional functions of student personnel staff and for the intellectual development of the student personnel staff. Our every effort in the future should reflect this emphasis.

The recent meetings of IACC, (Inter-Association Coordinating Committee), now COSPA (Council of Student Personnel Associations in Higher Education), showed a continuing concern with cooperation among the various student personnel associations. The content of the pre-COSPA meeting was high level showing that there is ability to attack the difficult problems which face the student personnel leader as an educator—it was in three areas: (1) the implications of equal educational opportunity to all youth, especially the Negro, (2) the implications of the year round calendar for programs of higher education, (3) the implications of academic freedom and student rights. The business meeting of COSPA showed a continuing developing base for cooperation among student personnel associations in higher education—the Joint Commissions on Financial Aids and on Professional Development are continuing, Lillian Johnson of NAWDC has succeeded to the chairmanship of COSPA, and two annual meetings were set with an all COSPA meeting just following the annual ACE meeting (usually October) and the Executive Committee to meet at the time of the annual AHE meeting (usually March or April).

This is my last message to you as ACPA president. Let me again share with you my enthusiasm for the development within ACPA and student personnel in the past two years. The evolvement of COSPA seems to be the long range base for real significant progress for the student personnel field—the progress may not be as rapid as all would want but if we in ACPA can be patient there is excellent potential development in COSPA. The resolution of ACPA-APGA relations has been healthy. For ACPA there is a bright future within APGA if we can and will continue to see the unique opportunity that the "bridge" function of ACPA for APGA to the higher education scene contributes to all of education. It is a difficult role and one where tensions are undoubtedly bound to occur, but challenging, and I would hope that all 3,400 of ACPA'ers will continue to work hard to implement this role.

Identity Crisis—1965

Barbara A. Kirk

It is a great pleasure for me to be together with so many of you today. For us to meet in Minneapolis, the home of the University of Minnesota, has especial significance. The college student personnel field, and student personnel work, are deeply rooted in the philosophy, the research, the practice, and the training that emerged, beginning several decades ago, on this campus. Its influence has been widely felt, wherever universities and colleges have been concerned with their students as individuals who have ongoing personal lives, even while they engage in the struggle to learn. I am sure that if I should ask any of you here today to rise who has studied or worked at the University of Minnesota, or studied or worked with someone trained at the University of Minnesota, we would have a very considerable shuffling of chairs, including those at these head tables, notably that of our President-Elect.

I trust you are in a mood to forgive personal references, because I feel some coming on! I, too, have my student personnel roots in Minnesota's soil. When I came many years ago to the University to work in the Institute of Child Welfare with Florence Goodenough and John Anderson, I found myself migrating in every spare moment to the then very young and novel Student Counseling Bureau. I have never ceased to be grateful to Ed Williamson, extraordinarily busy as he then was (and still for that matter is) for giving me the opportunity to learn to counsel students, and taking the time and great pains to read and review every single case record I produced that year.

It is of the growth and development, and present status, of our profession that I want to talk with you today. I suppose I should at the outset disabuse you of the expectation that today's title refers in any direct way to the events that have taken place on my campus this year! As a matter of fact, however, they are illustrative of some of the problems of our era, and its changing times, in which many young adults, and some not so young adults, are unsure at many times of who and what they are.

202

A *New Yorker* "Talk of the Town" item recounts attendance at a lecture of Dr. Leonard J. Duhl's at the New York Academy of Medicine last July:

"The lecture was billed as being addressed 'to the laity,' but, like most psychiatrists, Dr. Duhl, who is chief of the Planning Staff of the National Institute of Mental Health, in Bethesda, Maryland, began by diagnosing the problem in professional terms: 'The most prevalent disease of our time [is] urban man's loss of self-identity.' *Unlike* most psychiatrists, however, he quickly switched to a more personal vocabulary, and in a chat with us after the lecture he explained what he meant.

" 'In the past, when people grew up in closely knit communities, there was seldom any problem about making independent value choices. The community had its own ways of coping with the world, its own stable system of values, which it passed along to the child. In relation to these, one's self-image was clear. But these reinforcing factors have broken down, just as the individual is being handed a tremendously increased fund of information through radio, television, and travel—other people's, if not his own. So, instead of four or five variables, let's say, he's suddenly faced with thousands. And no one has trained him to make the choices. It's like sending an astronaut into space without preparing him for a weightless environment.' . . . the loss of self-identity is the most prevalent disease of our time."

With changing times, the nuclear age and the insecurities it brings, so even our diseases vary! Cultural complexity, lack of structure and stability cause us to respond in different ways. And, indeed, for several years psychiatrists and psychologists, notably Rollo May, have been reporting what purports to be considerably more than a semantic shift in diagnosis: considerably fewer neurotic and hysteric manifestations are observed, many more character disorders and identity difficulties, essentially problems of growing up and maturing.

Because so many young people are suffering from diffusion and uncertainty, Harvard and other universities to follow came to the adaptive policy of permitting students to take a leave of absence when and as required to "find themselves" before forfeiting the precious opportunity for education. Indeed, we are all cognizant of the hordes of students arriving at our campuses with no clear idea of their reason for being there, who they are or what they wish to become, and lacking, in varying degrees, the "readiness" for college, as I choose to call it.

And even as the growing complexity of our culture and its resulting uncertainties and anxieties is having its impact upon the identity formulation of the individual, so I submit it is equally true for our profession of student personnel work whose identity crisis in 1965 no less is a product of rapid and major social and sociological change, change in economic, industrial and occupational structure, change in ideologies, rapid growth in technology and knowledge.

This growth and change may or may not have the value of "progress" attached to it at this time, depending upon your own personal views, but change it all is, I suspect you will admit, and fast, and in the direction of complexity rather than simplicity. Thus it is movement rather than status quo which we as a profession are attempting to meet, and it is little wonder that we are searching and questioning, rather than being firm from our antecedent "closely knit families and communities."

What has happened to the community in which the student personnel profession has grown—higher education, the university and college campus? With the well publicized "population explosion" following the World War II, coming to a peak for higher education in the sixties, very few university or college campuses have been able to hold the line and retain their smallness, or on the other hand accommodate fully their rapid expansion. State universities especially are bound to provide education to the children of citizens of their state; private institutions have attempted to do their share. New institutions also come into being, new campuses, new junior colleges. It is not only the population explosion which has caused the crowding of our institutions of higher learning; it is also the space age's concept of how to get along in this world—get an "education," whatever that may be, but specifically obtain a "degree." Several decades ago, four per cent of our population went to college. Currently it is 40 per cent or more. A national survey sample of parents of high school pupils a year or two ago tells us that over 80 percent of parents expect their children to attend a college or university.

The "stable system of values" of higher education has indeed been subject to change. There has been insufficient faculty of high calibre to go around. Faculty student ratios decrease. Classes become larger. Faculty loads become heavier, permitting less faculty time or opportunity for contact and exchange with students. Student housing becomes crowded and inadequate. Because uncertainty exists regarding the definition of who is qualified for a college education and for a particular institution, admission requirements frequently become more stringent. Grading practices may not be revised as the calibre of student capacity increases. With the ever-greater need for more and more specialized education there is the need to maintain grades for admission to graduate school, and, indeed, for very many pressured students there is the desperate struggle for academic survival itself in the increasingly competitive atmosphere. There is also, in this generation of students, a keen interest in the social and political forces in the broader community.

So our young profession is groping. The symptomalogies are evident.

There is incomplete agreement about whether we are a profession at all, or several professions.

How do we prepare those greatly needed recruits for student personnel work? Some of us believe that a broad base in social and behavioral sciences is our best approach, some believe that the focus should be on the field of higher education as a discipline, some in a more specific practical address to student personnel administration, others in an emphasis upon counseling, adapting secondary counselor education or counseling psychology preparation to the generality of student personnel.

Let us take a specific example, that of financial aids administration. Rapid expansion of provision of federal funds for financing students' education has caused a lag in adaptation of the counseling approach to the individual student's confusion about financing himself through college. Nor has the student personnel point of view been incorporated in many instances where business and financial concerns have been predominant.

We are also unresolved as to role. To what extent are we policy makers or policy executers? Am I an educator or an administrator? Whom do I represent? Do I stand in *loco parentis?* If I am a parent, what kind of parent am I? Am I a parent or someone else? If someone else, who?

Beside uncertainty as to role, there is uncertainty as to functioning. How do I function? Am I consultant to the institution or part of its administration, or separate? To what extent do I work with groups or with individuals? What methods, approaches, techniques can I use which will be most fruitful?

What do we mean by identity? Erikson[1] says, "the conscious feeling of having a personal identity is based on two simultaneous observations: the immediate perception of one's *selfsameness* and *continuity in time*; and the simultaneous perception of the fact that others recognize one's sameness and continuity to the ego's synthesizing methods and that these methods are effective in safeguarding the sameness and continuity of one's meaning for others" (p. 23).—that is, his social role. This description of individual identity seems, as we examine it, to apply to a profession: our *awareness* of a consistent, continuous inner organization, which is recognized and perceived by others.

Attending to the ways in which identity is formed for the individual should have meaning for us also. Self-esteem is a basic attribute upon which such development depends. Without adequate and appropriate self-esteem, confirmed at the end of each major crisis, grows to be a conviction that one is learning effective steps toward a tangible future, that one is developing a defined personality within a social reality which one understands" (p. 89).

1. Erikson, Erik H. Identity and the Life Cycle. *Psychological Issues,* 1959, Vol. 1, No.

"Ego identity develops out of a gradual integration of all identifications," in our case role models, and values, if you will.

• For our purposes, a strategic point in development in the "relation of the final adolescent version of the ego identity to economic opportunities, realizable ideals, and available techniques" (p. 41). "In general, it is primarily the inability to settle on an occupational identity which disturbs young people." "The young individual is forced into choices and decisions which will, with increasing immediacy, lead to a more final self-definition, to irreversible role pattern and, thus, to commitments." While identity *formation* is a lifelong development, identity *crisis* occurs at the end of adolescence.

We who work in the field of vocational counseling deal with this stage as our most common undertaking. Choices and decisions must be made before there is the readiness to make them. The ways which we have learned to help the individual to accelerate his development, to resolve his crisis, to come to know who and what he is, have relevancy and form an analogy, it seems to me, for the resolution of our profession's identity crisis.

First of all, an adolescent needs to embark upon his undertaking with the desire to move ahead, the motivation to progress, attain maturity. Having, or acquiring this, he needs to have or acquire the belief, faith, confidence—self-esteem, if you will—in its attainment. Enough desire needs to be present to get him started, going; it will augment itself as he moves forward.

We encourage him to explore, to investigate, to sample experiences, to try things out, but not to experience in the behavioral sense alone. He needs to *think* about what he experiences, to wonder, consider how it may fit him and his needs—how he feels about it, how right it seems, how it relates to him. And so by broadening his context, extending his operational and experimental behavior, espousing and rejecting, he comes gradually to establish for himself stable values, the image of the admired performer with whom he wishes to identify, and thus evolves his knowledge of who and what he is.

How can our student personnel profession move toward its identity? For, as President Johnson said in his State of the Union address in January, "Progress must be the servant, not the master, of man," and we must have command over the complexities that change has brought about, and surely we want to, and believe that we can.

• We can explore. We can try new methods, we can innovate, we can be attentive to what others are doing, are studying, are trying. We can *look at* and *think about* what we and others are doing, what their studies mean to us, investigate, find out what is effective and why. As T. R. McConnell at our ACPA luncheon in San Francisco last year so well put it, in winding up his address: "Student personnel work will become less and less the practice of a mystery and more and more the practice of a profession as its methods take root in relevant basic research and sound clinical evidence."

• We can examine our values. In writing recently of the growing shortage of college teachers, John W. Gardner, President of the Carnegie Foundation, refers to what he calls the current "crisis in values" that has infected a generation of young scholars with "the crassest opportunism in grantsmanship, job hopping and wheeling-dealing." Traditionally, student personnel workers are thought to be other-oriented, devoted to student welfare and student growth and development. Are we free from infection and likely to remain so? Surely we can determine our common ideals, our beliefs, and our positions and so arrive at those "stable values" that give us identity and purpose.

Let us consider the image of the "admired performer" with whom we wish to identify. Here comes into play the standards which we set, and adhere to, that degree below excellence for which we will settle. There are many facets to the performance of our profession as a profession. What standards do we set and how can we raise them for professional preparation, for the calibre of person we recruit and employ, for the kind and quality of performance within the profession? At present surely we can utilize to the full all that we have which is high quality and work ever more actively towards improvement and advancement. We can also recognize and accept our current limitations and, as is true in any good profession, work within our competences and not in disregard of their borders.

• I should like to suggest just one more of the ways of overcoming our identity crisis. This is to look inward, seeking that which is internally consistent. We have many special functions, many different aspects of working with the student among us. What is the central core? We can synthesize, taking the best from one another, conceptualizing our similarities in objectives and approach. Furthermore, we can supplement and complement one another in practice, finding identity in the common effort to which we contribute our specialty. This means sharing, team work, pulling together rather than apart. Partly this comes from attitude, partly from communication. Clearly we can increase communication within our profession, and without: to have identity you remember, it must be recognized and perceived by others. Our "others" include chiefly our academic administration, our faculty and our students.

We are busy putting our puzzle together. You may remember the story of the young child who was trying valiantly to fit together the many tiny fragments which together would make a picture of the world. But he was too small, too frustrated, too unsuccessful. And so he turned to his elders, and his father said, "Have you forgotten that the other side of your puzzle is a picture of a man? Turn it over, put it together, and when you turn it back you will have your world put together."

• Consideration of the ways in which we may achieve identity is not to be taken by any means as saying that we are *not* moving forward. Let us remind ourselves of Gesell's psycho-biological concept of "equilibrium and disequilibrium." You remember, a child moves from an integrative to a disintegrative phase to an integrative. While he is in a state of disequilibrium, he is growing, changing, moving. *Then,* temporarily, he is sunny, easy, at peace with himself and the world—until again he is in a state of disequilibrium—difficult and incomprehensible, while change and growth takes place. That this occurs in adults, too, as they experience change or movement, was attested to by Freud. Just as there is symptomatology of our identity crisis, so are there many evidences of vigorous and constructive efforts on our parts to attain our identity. Here, today, we should speak of the American College Personnel Association, our organization which serves as an instrument of the profession, and works in close co-operation with other organizations of student personnel workers in higher education. The viability of our organization is a sign of our energy. Our organization has grown by a thousand members this year. It is past, it seems to me, its earlier and then necessary preoccupation with its own organizational structure. Now its attention is turning to substantive areas of ideas, research, programs, activity. It is getting on with a number of the infinite fascinating concerns which surround us and what we do. Remain for our Divisional Meeting and you will have abundant evidence as you review the year that was. Throughout this week's program, also, will be highlights of what we have been doing, not to mention what has been done to us! The American College Personnel Association has the prospect of being the unifying force through which we may become the profession we want to be.

A personal word, in concluding. As you know, I am a counselor. Counselors have a number of organizations where they talk with each other, rewardingly, about what they do. I joined the American College Personnel Association in order to have the unique opportunity to get to know the majority of student personnel workers and what *they* do. I hoped to broaden my perspective, to be able to help students better by understanding better the others on my campus team, what they offer the student and how. I hope all of you, as I am, are richer for the association with our membership. It cannot help but be so, it seems to me, with the people who make up our organization.

I want particularly to thank you for the honor and privilege of being your President. The expansion of my horizons could not have been so effectively accomplished in any other way. The learning has been immense. I want to express, also, my appreciation to all of you who have had the interest and taken the trouble to communicate with me, and in so constructive a fashion; my appreciation of the devoted services to the association of those, so many of you, who have been active in it; and most especially of the officers, and committee and commission chairmen. It is a wonderful, experience to have close working relationships with so fine, congenial, and helpful a group of people. It has been a real pleasure to be associated with our President-Elect, in whom we are very fortunate, and under whom we should have a most productive year. Thank you very much.

Student Personnel Work: Definition and Redefinition
ACPA Presidential Address

Ralph F. Berdie

The years I have been associated with ACPA have contributed to my knowledge and awareness of student personnel work and higher education, but more than that, these years have shown how important it is, and how difficult, to recognize the important questions that face us. What is student personnel work? What is its place in higher education? What are its purposes and how do we achieve them? What are and should be our relationships with students, instructors, and administrators? What is our scientific heritage? How do we use our professional associations to attain our educational goals? Almost every report I see from an ACPA committee or commission, almost every letter I receive from a member, almost every article and book I read, implies or directly asks some of these questions.

A person's sensitivity to questions such as these depends in part on the intellectual curiosity of his associates, and certainly I must acknowledge the influence others have had on me and attribute to them the credit but certainly none of the blame for what I say today. First, Ed Williamson, through his constant search in higher education, has provided all student personnel workers with a continuing dissatisfaction about the little we know and much of our urgency to explore is due to him. Donald G. Paterson and E. K. Strong provided me, as they provided to many of you, with a need to be hardheaded. Many of our questions were faced earlier by W. S. Miller and T. R. McConnell and the latter has had at least two opportunities to present his questions to you directly. Barbara Kirk and Leona Tyler are two of the wiser women in our generation and they bring many old questions into new focus. The people with whom I have worked directly at the University of Minnesota, although they do an excellent job of providing answers, are even better at discovering questions and among these I should name Martin Snoke, Lavern Snoxell, Don Zander, Theda Hagenah, Vivian Hewer, Forrest

Vance, Ted Volsky, Dave Campbell, Bill Layton, Jack Merwin, and many others. What I say today comes out of the atmosphere which these friends have provided and the questions I raise are theirs as well as yours.

Let us attempt to define and redefine. Let us approach the question, "What is student personnel work?" and examine its purposes. Let us look at the avenues through which we achieve our purposes and review our methods.

Each student personnel worker has arrived at his own tentative definition of student personnel work. Some define it in terms of its purposes, some in terms of its relationships with other activities, and some in terms of the persons engaged in the activity. My own definition is oriented more toward the activity itself and certainly it reflects a background of psychology and research. Student personnel work is the application in higher education of knowledge and principles derived from the social and behavioral sciences, particularly from psychology, educational psychology, and sociology. Accepting this definition, student personnel work is different but not apart from other persons and functions in higher education. Neither is it the exclusive responsibility of any one or several groups of persons in colleges and universities. The student personnel worker is the behavioral scientist whose subject matter is the student and whose socio-psychological-sphere is the college. Student personnel work is effected by any person in the college applying knowledge and skills derived from the behavioral and social sciences to further the education of students.

Purposes

If this definition reveals the values and biases of the speaker, his list of purposes of student personnel work is nothing but the reflection of his own value system. A primary purpose of student personnel work is to humanize higher education, to help students respond to others and to themselves as human beings and to help them formulate principles for themselves as to how people should relate to one another, and to aid them to behave accordingly. This is a purpose implicit in higher education, particularly in liberal education, but the student personnel worker carries it a step further. The traditional assumption is that as a person has increasing experience with the story of man's development, as he gains appreciation of the arts and humanities, and as he learns more of man and his world, this knowledge will have a humanizing impact. The student personnel worker accepts this assumption but contends that this is not sufficient. More is needed.

When we help fraternity members to respond to prospective pledges on the basis of interest, merit, and personality, and not on the basis of race or religion, we are humanizing their education. We are doing this when we help students express their charity and compassion in social service programs, or when through our counseling, they learn that parents are people, too.

Another purpose of student personnel work is to individualize higher education. We recognize the presence and significance of individual differences and hope to structure the education of each individual accordingly. Many educational patterns are required if the needs of most students are to be met and the student personnel worker is concerned not only with helping each student discover what his needs are and make appropriate choices but also with helping the college develop the alternatives and resources from which students can make wise choices. We are doing this when we discuss with students their abilities and interests and attitudes, and help them select from the many available resources. We are doing this when we encourage the development of new educational programs.

Student personnel work also has as a purpose to bring into balance the world of the student, that of the university, and the enveloping "real" world that encompasses all. Students come from families, high schools, and communities that share many of the values of the University but that also are unaware of or perhaps rejecting other values. From the college, the student moves into a world of work, family, and community that again in many ways is different from his alma mater. While in college, the stresses and demands of the curriculum and college life are balanced against those of social problems, religious conflicts, racial discrimination, civil rights, and a society out of joint. The purpose of the student personnel worker is to facilitate movement into and out of the institution and to keep the student an effective member of the college and at the same time a real member of the community.

Another broad purpose of the student personnel worker is to implant, nurture, and extend students' drives, interests, and motives, so that college and community resources will be used maximally by students to achieve their educational purposes, both in and after college. Institutional atmospheres are developed and individual student attitudes fostered, and I might even say *manipulated* to arouse and maintain intellectual curiosities and to develop habits of searching and learning that will last long after college. We do these things when we arrange seminars for entering students, when we bring visiting scholars into dormitories, when we have special camps for talented students, and when we admit students into the mysteries of institutional decisionmaking.

Finally, a purpose of the student personnel worker is to increase the immediate satisfaction and enjoyments experienced by students so that higher education is perceived as a pleasantly productive experience. Learning, and the hard work required to learn, should be seen by students as providing satisfactions outweighing almost all others, and the extent to which this goal is achieved provides one means for us to appraise our success. Perhaps we best do this by exhibiting to students the satisfactions to be derived from our own intellectual pursuits.

Avenues

Through what avenues does student personnel work function? Sometimes we tend to regard ourselves as mainly concerned with face-to-face contacts with students, either individually or in groups. Certainly, one of our most effective and frequently used avenues in education is our relationship with students and the primacy we assign to our counseling function attests to that.

However, our relationships with many other individuals and groups provide us with additional avenues. For example, the work done by student personnel workers with college and university administrators does much to establish the atmosphere within which our objectives can be attained—the relationship between the student personnel worker and the president, the dean, the assistant and associate deans, the admissions officers. Another important avenue is provided by the faculty and the curriculum, and here I refer to the people who actually teach classes and to the teaching they do, their actual classroom and classroom-related activities. The curriculum and the instructional program of a college, along with the people who are primarily responsible for it, provide a means for the attainment of our goals.

As college student personnel workers with our origins in psychology and the behavioral sciences, we are imbued with the fact of psychological individual differences. We are so aware of the variability among persons that we tend to forget a fact that Strong (1943) repeatedly emphasized. Persons are more similar than they are different, and the similarities among persons are larger than and as equally significant as the differences between persons. The classroom teacher and the college instructor are mainly concerned with the commonalities of their students. Students share certain abilities, competencies, and needs, and the college professor sees as his main purpose satisfying these common personal and social needs. We student personnel workers, in our concern that individual differences be recognized, sometimes overlook the importance of common objectives, group programs, and mass instruction. Perhaps our respect for our teaching colleagues, and their respect for us, can be increased through mutual recognition of the significance of both these similarities and differences among students.

Increasingly, college student personnel workers' are finding opportunities to work effectively with high school counselors and principals. The problems of high school and college relationships often are viewed in terms of curricular continuity, but equally important are the attitudes of students as they move from high school to college, and the problems they bring with them, along with the habits for solving these problems. ACPA's involvement in the National Council on School-College Relations is evidence of this concern.

Increasing also is the student personnel worker's involvement with other persons in the community, particularly those in local, state, and federal government, and private industry and foundations. NDEA Institutes, graduate fellowships, research grants, funded conferences, all result from these relationships.

Methods

The definition, purposes, and avenues of student personnel work all are dependent on the methods we employ. If any one tool is basic in our kit, it is counseling. Counseling is a means of establishing and maintaining an individualized and personalized relationship with students, and in colleges, the primary purpose of counseling is an educational one. That is, the relationship with which we are concerned has as its purpose the development of the student as an educated person.

My own view of counseling presents it as a discussion between a counselor and a student where the topic of the discussion consists of the characteristics and behaviors of the student within the framework of his social setting and with the purpose of helping the student understand and realize the implications of the ways in which the student differs from and resembles other persons. Counseling can be a part of the classroom teaching process, but it must be a part of almost all, if not all, student personnel work. It is a kind of teaching, a kind of therapy, and perhaps, according to Schofield (1964), a kind of friendship.

Advising is a method of student personnel work somewhat related to counseling. The immediate purpose of advising is to help a student make a decision, and the advantage of advising is that it provides a vicarious experience to the student which can save him both time and effort and at the same time increase his knowledge concerning the probable outcomes of various alternatives. Advising is one of the means adopted by society so that each individual does not himself have to recapitulate the painful history of mankind. Advising, or providing to students, opinions, previous experiences of one's self or others, or explanations of probability, is a basic educational function of the student personnel worker.

The student personnel worker also uses many of the teaching methods used by the classroom instructor. Although usually he employs a different terminology in a different setting, he may at times refer students to publications, advocate library research, suggest laboratory and research approaches, organize and present information and skills to be learned, and even examine the student's mastery of what is expected. He must rely as much as the classroom instructor on the little that is known about the psychology of learning as it pertains to the development of the college student.

Persuasion is another procedure important in the personnel worker's repertoire. The student personnel worker, like most persons in education, is concerned that the student incorporate into his behavior and personality those conformities that constitute civilization. Persuasion is defined as demonstrating or proving that something is true, credible, essential, commendable, worthy of belief, adoption, practice; bringing about by argument, the doing, practicing, or believing of a desired action or condition (*Webster's Unabridged Dictionary.*). Surely, much of education consists of persuasion, and the student personnel worker uses persuasion to aid students to become honest, truthful, reasonable, compassionate, and tolerant. In a sense, persuasion consists of counseling, advising, and teaching, but perhaps there is a difference insofar as the persuasion process requires that both the persuader and his subject be well aware of the objectives or behavior change the persuader has in mind.

A fifth essential method of the student personnel worker can be encompassed under the term "research." By this I do not mean only experimental designs, laboratory research, or statistical analysis, but the constant study of problems and search for new answers. The research about which I am speaking is an attitude as well as a behavior. The research perception or orientation of the student personnel worker is one of his most important tools. It is what allows him to listen to a student and while listening, consider the reasons why he is not able to better help the student. It is the perception that shows him the gaps in his knowledge and urges him to explore new avenues, develop new procedures, and perhaps as important as any of these, examine the impact he has on the student and the institution. The recent publication by Volsky, Magoon, Norman, and Hoyt (1965) provides an excellent example of how student personnel workers ask themselves the question, "What are we doing when we counsel students?", and then determine if they really are doing this. They found, as many of you know, that they were not doing what they thought they were doing, but in fact they were doing other things that were equally, if not more, important.

I also include among the methods of the student personnel work, adminis-tration. Apparently, people regard administration in many ways. Recently I had an opportunity to discuss the administrative aspects of a position with a couple of candidates being considered for employment and they told me they did not like administration. They meant they did not like spending hours on maintaining and reviewing budgets, preparing reports, and supervising and reprimanding employees. All of this is essential in the management function of administration but the student personnel worker's concern with adminis-tration is primarily in terms of organization, staffing, programming, policy determination, and relationships within and outside of his institution that facilitate all this. All the responsibilities involved in program development and operation are included in administration and like other methods dis-cussed here, administration encompasses counseling, persuasion, advising, teaching, and research.

Implications

From what I have said, it should be obvious that student personnel work in higher education is of a piece with higher education and is not a separate function, part, or segment of the college pattern. It is an integral part of the whole educational process and everything encompassed in student personnel work is found in some other aspect of higher education; nothing is unique. Obviously, the purposes of the student personnel worker are the purposes of higher education. The avenues of student personnel work are those of higher education. The methods of student personnel work are not unique to it. The student personnel worker is a behavioral scientist employed in higher education to help achieve the goals and purposes of higher education through means of whatever knowledge and skills his background provides.

We have heard speakers at these sessions in the past more effectively discuss relationships between student personnel work and higher education. In Buffalo and again in San Francisco, Dr. McConnell showed us what student personnel work looked like to at least some other people in higher education. He asked the question really of *why* we were outside the college door. President Craig (1962) asked a similar question several years ago and essentially raised the question as to whether student personnel workers in higher education really belonged in a professional organization of guidance workers.

Following the questions and reasoning presented by these persons, and the introduction I have made, let me raise the following questions. Is there and should there be a profession of student personnel work? Or should we who

are concerned with the objectives, purposes, and methods of student personnel work cease considering ourselves as student personnel workers and
begin to regard ourselves as educators with particular competencies in
the behavioral sciences, working with college and university students and
institutional programs to further the ends of higher education? Should we
cease attempting to train persons for a profession that may not exist and
make sure that we are training persons to work in higher education with
broad backgrounds and skills that can be employed to meet institutional and
student demands? Should we resist attempts to standardize professional
preparation programs, to define curricula, and even to accredit training
programs? Should we say that we want instead good psychologists, sociologists, anthropologists, and political scientists, who know a lot about higher
education and a lot about students and who are willing to place themselves
in situations where they can apply their knowledge and learn more through
such application?

Let me restate Bixler's comment directed to the Association for Counselor
Education and Supervision (1963)—

If those now active in the counseling and guidance movement refrain from
standardizing training at this point and instead frankly experiment on a wide range
of approaches to the problem of directing youth to goals, then they will retain their
leadership in this area.

His warning, given only three years ago, is still most relevant.

Currently, I am reviewing texts in guidance, including my own, to select
one to use in a course I will teach this summer. Do you realize how little the
authors of these texts refer to research, how little verified information they
cite? Do you appreciate the extent to which such texts assemble and discuss
opinions instead of research, the extent to which authors pontificate and
how little they demonstrate? In guidance and student personnel work perhaps
we have too few principles and too little systematic knowledge to constitute a
discipline, and perhaps we are committing a fraud by introducing specialized
student personnel work courses and seminars into the curriculum. Should
courses and seminars be devoted to more disciplined knowledge, and should
students learn how to improvise to handle dormitory riots and union
programs through practicums and internships?

If we attempt to alter the current trend toward professionalization in
student personnel work, what are the implications of this for our relationship
with the American Personnel and Guidance Association? Currently, APGA
increasingly defines itself as a professional organization concerned with the
development of professional programs in government, schools, and commu-

nity agencies. In a sense, the high school counselor faces the same dilemma we do in student personnel work in higher education and the wise counselor is concerned with the relationship between himself and the rest of elementary and secondary education. How will he solve his dilemma? Both our colleagues in secondary education and we in higher education have much to gain through our associations with APGA and we must do all in our power to see that it is a strong organization.

Perhaps, however, our future lies as closely to other associations in higher education—the American Council on Education, the Higher Education Association, the Council of Student Personnel Associations and its affiliated organizations, the American Association of University Professors, the United States National Student Association. Perhaps we have as much in common with organizations such as these as we have with the various professional associations explicitly defined in terms of guidance and counseling.

I am not proposing here that we have the answers. They will not be found within the next year or few years. Constantly, we will be faced with these problems, and I am concerned that we always remember our primary commitment to higher education and that as student personnel workers, we are educators who share with our colleagues in higher education responsibility for the transition of the student into a citizen.

References

Bixler, R. H. The changing world of the counselor II. Training for the unknown. *Counsel. Educ. Supv.*, 1963, 2, 170.

Craig, W. G. The student personnel profession: an instrument of national goals. *J. Coll. Stu. Personnel*, 1962, 3, 162–168.

Schofield, W. *Psychotherapy: The purchase of friendship.* Englewood Cliffs, N.J.: Prentice-Hall, 1964.

Strong, E. K., Jr. *The vocational interests of men and women.* Stanford: Stanford University Press, 1943.

Volsky, T., Magoon, T. M., Norman, W. T., & Hoyt, D. P. *The outcomes of counseling and psychotherapy.* Minneapolis: University of Minnesota Press, 1965.

Three Dilemmas of the Student Personnel Profession and Their Resolution

Kate Hevner Mueller

On whatever campus he may find himself, any personnel worker will face three dilemmas which other faculty and administration workers are able to escape. The first of these grows out of the contrast between the goals that his profession embraces and the functions that higher education assigns to him. The second dilemma stems from the inadequacy of the personnel worker's methods for achieving either his own objectives or those that the faculty and administrative officers expect of him. The third dilemma involves the paradox of developing student individuality in the increasingly bureaucratic structure of the campus.

I. Professional vs. Assigned Goals

In 1937 the goals embodied in *The Student Personnel Point of View* were expressed as follows:

One of the basic purposes of higher education is the preservation, transmission, and enrichment of the important elements of culture—the product of scholarship, research, creative imagination, and human experience. It is the task of colleges and universities so to vitalize this and other educational purposes as to assist the student in developing to the limits of his potentialities and in making his contribution to the betterment of society.[1]

In 1961 Nevitt Sanford and others stated more explicit goals in modern psychological terms:

1. American Council on Education. *The Student Personnel Point of View: A Report of a Conference.* (Series 1, No. 3) Washington, D.C.: the Council, 1937.

Education means openness to change. It means that we help the student shed the conventional wisdom and enable him to make rational choices by the use of information, insight, and sensitivity. It means, first of all, that we generate the willingness to change. We communicate excitement about the worlds of knowledge and of the arts, so that our students will want to expose themselves to unaccustomed experiences . . . For the student, too, education is self-revelation. He must be able to expose himself to the teacher and to other students so that he may be helped better to realize his own potential.[2]

Sanford also mentions such traits as freedom in the expression of impulse, independence of pressures toward conformity, sense of social responsibility, and sensitivity to ethical issues. Reports from research at Berkeley and elsewhere show that these same traits are also those that distinguish the creative from the non-creative personality, the freshman from the senior.[3]

Since the original 1937 statement, however, it has been pointed out that this "personnel point of view" is an imprecise basis for theory and there has been an emphasis on the importance of social interaction in development and on the larger society as the milieu in which personal development must take place. The personnel profession seems to have accepted these criticisms with little or no dissent.

The first dilemma appears when the personnel officer finds himself actually on the job. He knows that his job is to offer services to all students— including the foreign student, the financially needy student, and the entering student; but all too soon the personnel officer learns he is also responsible for the *control* of the student, the supervision of the student's activities so that they will provide satisfactory developmental experience for him, and the provision of a residential life that fosters the kind of socialization process which the student *needs* but does not *want*. The studies of Pepinsky and Correll have exposed this dilemma with great clarity:

Personnel people, as agents delegated by the institution to perform institutional functions, must administer and control in order to do their jobs efficiently—indeed, in order to survive in the institution. They must, on the other hand, be benign and ever attuned to the needs of individual students in order to meet the demands of their own self images, as well as those of the students, the institution, and society alike. How to resolve this dilemma?[4]

2. Sanford, Nevitt, editor. *College and Character.* New York: John Wiley & Sons, 1964, p. 277.

3. *Ibid.*, p. 286.

4. Correll, Paul T. "Student Personnel Workers on the Spot." *Journal of Counseling Psychology* 9:232–37; Fall 1962.

See also: Correll, Paul and Pepinsky, Harold. "The Overt and Covert Control of Students." *American Psychologist* 17:409; July 1961. (Summary statement only.)

"Control" and "supervision" are key words in this dilemma. Control may be elaborate and ingenious, understated and casual, or kindly but firm; supervision may be comprehensive or superficial and welcome or resented. Each campus has a spirit and method of its own. Student rebellion against either control or supervision has been demonstrated in every decade of educational history, and the present *seeming* increase in student antagonism may actually represent a decrease in view of the smaller proportion of the student body which becomes actually involved in campus demonstrations and the disproportionate attention given by newspapers to this aspect of college life.

Qualitatively, however, there is a difference between the student rebellions of 100, 50, or 25 years ago and today's rebellions. Today there is a larger proportion of youth in the total population and a much larger proportion of these young people attend colleges.

Education is now the chief business of the college student, his occupation. The college student is as mobile, as affluent, and as independent as most citizens; and he is encouraged to be as well organized as any other citizen in our democratic society. He has observed the easy, dramatic, and effective civil disobedience methods. From the faculty, the only voices he has heard are those that use the magic word *freedom*.

The profession of personnel work is not without its own methods of attack on these dilemmas. The primary approach for the professional is always research, and in this case more research is needed on students' precollege expectancies and postcollege behavior. More research should be done on the attitudes of parents, alumni, and the general public who might be educated to other expectancies and to more sympathetic support for whatever degree of supervision the administration expects. Research is also needed on social control and communications but especially on the process by which administration in higher education can promote an environment for individual development.

In addition to research, two kinds of action are needed to solve the first dilemma: First the study of group counseling, of communication, and of social control must share the emphasis on individual counseling in the training of future personnel officers. Counseling concepts and techniques as rigidly defined in their purest form will prove of limited use to the campus personnel officer whose assignment is control and whose goal is maximum self-development in the campus milieu.

The second needed action is more difficult but more important: The old-

---

Snoxell, L. F. "Counseling Reluctant and Recalcitrant Students." *Journal of College Student Personnel* 2:16–20; December 1960.

fashioned concept of supervision and control and its exclusive assignment to the personnel division must be recognized for the impossibility that it is, and this responsibility must not only be modified but distributed more equably among other administrative officers and faculty.

II. The Authority Behind Personnel Practices

The second dilemma stems from the inadequacy of present personnel methods for achieving either the stated goals of the profession or those usually assigned to it. In other campus disciplines the student is treated as a client, not as a customer. He cannot present himself to the health service and say, "I have decided that it would be a good idea to have my appendix taken out this semester." He accepts the physician's right to guide him in such a matter. Likewise, the student accepts the authority of the professor to say, "If you do not learn these rules of French grammar, you will not be understood," but what authority can the counselor invoke to convince the student that it is to his best interest to conform to certain standards and practice certain behavior patterns?

In today's society, authority, the basis of all professionalization, is largely based on scientific proof, on a model found in nature itself. Science is the darling of the public; and research, the rock upon which it rests, is conceived in terms of experimentation, laboratory work, apparatus, basic elements, and logical structures. We are a science-oriented society. We believe that progress is made in terms of scientific endeavor, and we demand proof for any course of action and a soundly supported hypothesis for any adventurous departure.

The student, as any other citizen, feels therefore that it is his right to demand proof from the personnel worker that the education in living he teaches and the process of maturing he promotes are exactly the right ones to achieve the goal that the personnel worker envisions, namely, full realization of all individual potentiality and the fullest development of individuality and creativeness. However, it is clear to the personnel worker and, unfortunately, to the student as well that he cannot produce proven methods for reaching his goals in the same way that the classroom teacher can invoke the authority of this discipline. Psychology, sociology, philosophy, economics, and anthropology have taught the counselor a great deal; but they have not given him proven methods and results.

There is hope that the residence hall director may eventually be able to say as a professional: "We have searched the literature, made experiments, surveyed the field, and analyzed the problems. We now know that our present method is the best possible way to manage group living." But he would also have to add in all honesty, ". . . on this particular campus, in order to meet the stated goals of this institution and the needs of its students, within the prices charged, and in the present world situation."[5]

Personnel has always hoped that its basic sciences—psychology and sociology—would give the data and hypotheses about attitudes and behavior, communication, and human development which would be useful for interpreting the post-adolescent youth and the nature of the campus society. But this hope has now grown dim because unlike the natural and physical sciences, the social sciences have no model in nature to serve as a criterion for the ultimate truth.

What reasons are behind the student's refusal to accept extraclassroom learning with the same deference to authority that he generally assumes toward the teaching of the faculty?

The first reason, a psychological one, is that the student is at an age when freedom from authority means most to him. He is breaking away from the restraints of family authority and family living. He feels the responsibility that goes with taking a large share of the family income for education. The departure from the old neighborhood to another where he must make his own way as an independent person is the most significant milestone he has yet encountered in life. He has long anticipated this freedom and will resist any inroads into it. Naturally, many students abuse this new freedom. Indeed, for many students it is only through this abuse of time, effort, and feeling that self-discipline will be acquired.

The second reason, a sociopsychological one, is that there is a clash between the student's growing awareness of self-potential and the many frustrations and complexities of modern life. The student is asked to assimilate too much in too little time. He is confronted simultaneously with new ideas, new personalities, and new opportunities but also with stiff competition, unaccustomed rebuffs, and disappointments in himself and others. Half of this clash is his own fault because of his own prejudices, bad habits, and ignorance. He recognizes some of these deficiencies, although not always accurately or fully. This lack of recognition is a healthy trait at this stage of his life. He must maintain a balance between self-confidence and humility to allow for the growth of a self-identity that can adapt to both success and vicissitude. The other half of the clash comes from the pressures of new knowledge which challenge old habits of thought and pressures from the total society, especially from its characteristic bureaucracies which require adaptation and conformity.

5. Useem, Ruth Hill. "Professionalizing an Academic Occupation: The Case of Student Personnel Work." *Journal of the National Association of Women Deans and Counselors* 27:94–101; Winter 1964.

Conformity in and of itself is not unacceptable to youth. The student practices it willingly each day of his life. Some of it is of his own choosing—as dress, manners, and entertainment. Some of it is forced upon him—as payment of tuition in designated amounts at set times and following the requirements of classroom learning. Conformity offends him when it interferes with his natural desires and habits in regard to pleasure. Conformity also offends him when it touches his pride, his ideals, his faith in justice and other virtues, and his dignity as a human being with individual rights and privileges.

In seeking the answers for this second dilemma of authority and professional autonomy for personnel's special kind of teaching, much useful research has already been done on campus subcultures, their goals, and their characteristics.

It would help a great deal if some scholar would gather all this research together; discard the insignificant locally limited pieces once and for all; place it in historical perspective so that some of it would be eliminated and some enhanced; classify the materials in large-small, selective-nonselective, and other categories; translate the diverse philosophical, psychological, and sociological concepts into one unified vocabulary; separate the hypotheses from the empirical evidence and the management factors from the learning elements; and organize the whole around some feasible theories. We could then identify the researchable problems and the significant questions; carry on more useful research; and probably arrive at some operating principles that our clients, the students, could more readily embrace.

Reasonableness is the best basis for authority in most phases of management of group living and student activities. This would mean having insight into and sympathy with student needs and behavior and having regular revisions to meet changing fashions in manners, dress, and recreation.

III. The Individual Student and the Campus Bureaucracy

The third dilemma arises for the personnel worker because in recent decades higher education has inevitably been caught up in the bureaucratic trend characteristic of many other aspects of modern life. So long as the student may be dealt with in an individual, face-to-face relationship, the training and skills of the dean or counselor are adequate and his work can be joyful, challenging, and rewarding. Students are intelligent, ambitious, often troubled, sometimes reluctant, but, on the whole, eager and responsive.

But the personnel worker is no longer able to deal in a face-to-face, primary relationship and not always in the individual-to-group, or secondary, relationship—except on the smaller campus or with the relatively few student officers or in the groups which he serves as adviser. Rather, he must deal with the student in a tertiary relationship as a part of a complicated bureaucratic structure, a man-to-organization confrontation and process which is a new relationship still to be learned by both student and counselor.[6]

As preparation for dealing with the organization world—that tertiary, man-to-management relationship inescapable in our society—America's youth has had no specific formal education and a great deal of informal miseducation via observing the current adult folkways. In the family the child learns how to deal with human beings as individuals—how to please, cajole, defy, manipulate, and so forth. But between the ages of 18 and 22, the student has his first significant experience in one of the many large organizations with which he will find himself dealing all the rest of his life. It is a new and difficult experience for which he is totally unprepared.

The bureaucratic structure that stands between the counselor and the student is obnoxious but inevitable. It may be elaborate or simple, efficient, or wasteful, but every campus has *some* of it. The president cannot deal with the student directly in teaching him his culture, in developing his potential, or in offering him the services of his everyday life. Between the student and the president then stands the personnel division, that bureaucracy of people and function designed to mediate the extraclassroom activities and opportunities that develop student potential and foster individuality.

As the student meets the bureaucracy of any large campus, the very mechanisms designed to expedite, equalize, and protect his interests will irritate him. For example, if he wishes to schedule a social event, he must register two weeks in advance in triplicate; to charter a bus for an off-campus game, he must guarantee the number of riders, take out insurance, and finance in advance. The closer he comes to the hierarchy which pyramids human beings for their interlocking operations, the more disillusioned he may become.

The faults of the bureaucracy itself—the ineptitude or downright viciousness of the adults within it and its lumbering impertinence—aggravate the clash of the individual with campus organization. On the campus the student begins his lifelong experience with disappointing agencies and personalities in society. In this postadolescent period, the youth's own individuality is of prime importance to him. This trait is psychologically acceptable to his elders although it is not his most admired or most ingratiating trait. Can we teach him that there are useful methods and a "due process" for dealing with

6. Coleman, James S. "Research in Autonomy and Responsibility in Adolescents." *Journal of the National Association of Women Deans and Counselors* 28:2–9; Fall 1964.

bureaucracies and that it would be rewarding for him to study and practice them for their value to him in later life?

It is exactly at this point that the student's lack of training in such methods is critical for his self-esteem. He sees only two possible actions: either to submit and let the bureaucratic structure take its toll of his ego strength or to rebel and suffer the role of outlaw to the "good" society. But he *could* learn how to brace for significant inroads on his freedoms and shrug off the insignificant ones, how to count the cost of resistance and organize in accordance with what he can afford, how to circumvent impossibilities, or how to follow necessary routines with the least expenditure of his emotional energy.

No other bureaucratic structure seems so obnoxious as that which touches group living and student activities. Even within the personnel division some specialties escape. But in housing, student government, activities, fraternity relationships, and discipline, the personnel worker is definitely the front man on the firing line.

The student finds it much more natural and easy to embrace the classroom bureaucracy because he views it as the eventual entrée into his chosen profession. He can, for the most part, tolerate the conformity that his curriculum requires because of the authority of the discipline itself. The student is also reconciled to the unfeeling bureaucracy of the business office, to fee payments, to meal tickets, to library rules, to parking fines, and to half a hundred other routine restrictions. He accepts them as extraneous to his learning, as not pretending to be other than they are: pure management processes developed to the highest possible degree of efficiency for the structure and its workers.

IV. A New Theory and Role for the Personnel Division

The three dilemmas of the student personnel worker call for a new perspective on student personnel goals, functions, and methods. Suppose that we begin with the third all-embracing dilemma and realize that the student needs to learn how to meet this tertiary relationship, how to deal with organized society and all its institutions, including its bureaucratic ones. Why not emphasize that we are student personnel *administrators*, demonstrate that we are good ones, and teach the students how good administration works and what it can mean to them now and in the future. We can streamline our efficiency procedures for the benefit of the student rather than for our own benefit.

Each teacher, each personnel worker, and each student has his part to play in the total campus structure. To be a whole person, to achieve full personal and intellectual maturity within a modern, industrialized, democratic society, is one of the student's major developmental tasks. It is not easy to achieve this in a world made up of hundreds of organized and bureaucratic structures. Actually, the campus is a wholesome and benevolent organization, the best possible place to learn how to deal with other, perhaps vicious and difficult ones.

Certainly, by teaching students how to deal with organizations in general and campus hierarchy in particular, it is the personnel worker who has the most to gain: He should show the student that he is himself a part of and a full member of the campus bureaucracy and that there are accepted functions and roles which go with this status.

Could not the student government become an important part of the campus administrative and bureaucratic structure on its own under the sponsorship of the personnel division?

The student then will understand that he has no rights of "citizenship" or vote in somebody else's organizational structure but that he does have the right to the expression of his opinion, to a voice which can be heard in the making of any policy which may concern him—along with all the other voices to be heard by those campus officers to whom authority for general policy and action is delegated by the trustees. Granted, to be effective the "voice" may sometimes require "action." But riots, demonstrations, and civil disobedience techniques are not the appropriate means of communication between the individual and the university administration.

Students, parents, and counselors are now well aware of the "due process" that any offender can claim in the implementation of policy in his own individual case. Likewise, a "due process" must be observed in the opposite direction: When the student finds it necessary to deal with the bureaucracy, there are channels for the proper approach, protocol, and authority—all of which call for careful observance and must be set up as the first responsibility of the student body and the personnel division.

The student should understand his own carefully prescribed part in the process by which campus policy is made and implemented if he is to accept the authority behind the counselor. The student would learn that although the larger society has become oriented to research and scientific proof in the accepting of authority and in the bestowing of prestige, there are several other bases on which to accept authority and to bestow prestige and that there are several other kinds of authority practiced and acceptable in the organizations of modern society. Law has been developed out of precedent, which is in turn the product of reasoned evaluation of both sides of any problem. Precedent serves for a while in a dynamic society until it is eventually changed. Policies often are also based on consensus after careful consideration for individual and group differences, responsibilities, and rights. Reasonableness will also serve as the basis for authority and can be arrived at satisfactorily after proper study. These are the democratic traditions. Law and policy must be clearly stated and closely followed; deviations will call for vigorous protest.

This new perspective then helps solve the dilemma of authority by invoking new sources. Some experiments are available, and there are many useful precedents in the traditions and history of higher education. Consensus, reasonableness, and due process are all appropriate and available to be carried on always by dialogue, never by negotiation. This will not be easy, for society itself offers students only the wrong examples.

Among other things, students need to learn that much patience is required in any man-to-organization relationship, that delegation of some rights and responsibilities makes life simpler, that one chooses his conformities as carefully as his freedoms, and that tolerance for ambiguity is the quality that distinguishes the sophisticated from the naive.

The student learns all of these by many methods: by direct communication, by formal study in orientation, and, most especially, by experience and by observing such campus models as junior and senior students, counselors, and faculty members. Of special importance for students would be the working out of a code of behavior which would help an individual student solve his own moral problems. Students need to learn that in a power-and-status-conscious society, there are many forces at work that might undermine the intelligent approach to problems and the maintaining of general behavior standards and outlook.

In the various campus departments there should be codes of behavior for the student to observe at first hand, not fragmented or invisible codes, such as those for athletics, for hiring and firing the faculty, and for freedom of speech, but a code for the total university as a leading institution in our society.

The entering freshman's orientation to his new status and responsibilities should also be thorough and formal, his behavior code adequately taught. The organization of his affairs to his own best advantage and by the best management principles will be a joint project but certainly a major project for the student personnel administrator. This is the new and appropriate "assignment" of function to replace the former "control" and "supervision"; but only as a bona fide assignment from highest authority with the concern and cooperation of all campus adults can it succeed.

Some Unsolved Problems in Student Personnel Work

E. G. Williamson

I turn now to one of the fundamentals of my resurging harmonic theme: Students are human beings. At least they are human beings in their potentialities of becoming motivated and humane persons. Some of them have not yet achieved eligibility, but one always lives in hope.

And one fundamental theme needs constant restatement. I recall Professor John Anderson's *obiter dictum* that a "good" doctoral thesis is one that raises more questions than it answers. Thus, as educators, we must constantly reformulate both our purposes in seeking to motivate and educate all students to their full potentialities, as well as seeking to reforge the means to that objective.

Our efforts to aid more students achieve higher learning discloses increasingly and definitively what we do not know, as well as what we have already learned. I happen to believe in the theory of education as essentially a matter of mapping out one's areas of ignorance, in the hope that one can reduce those areas. My concept of education is essentially *knowing as endless learning*. And this kind of education is not restricted to "inert knowledge," as Whitehead described much of classroom exercises. Rather is education a style of living characterized as progressive search in learning of the not-yet-known.

And in the spirit of learning as living and living as learning, I suggest that the unity, or the essence of our profession as student personnel workers is not so much its current *corpus* of technique (often mere *ad hocism*) or even its foundation *technology* of program development and maintenance. For me, the essence of our professional mission, as deans of students, is rather a restless and eternal quest for answers, often provisional, to the "great" queries about what has traditionally come to be defined as our own sphere of concern—our mission: The facilitation of humane maturity.

To be sure, we professional educators, usually denoted as deans, are reconciled to the fact that most of the time our efforts to achieve humane maturity produces *paradoxes* rather than *definitive answers* of a simplistic type: such as either-or, yes or no, true or false. We have come to empathize with our colleagues in cognate disciplines who must labor with paradoxes and uncompleted and provisional "conclusions" in their search of understanding and unknowns of human existence.

With these efforts at mood-setting and thematic backgrounding, let me etch some unfinished questions—problems which may worry us well into the next century. From this "old guard" I gladly and cheerfully bequeath these unanswered queries (perhaps unanswerable?) to the new generation of deans!

1. Is student personnel work a profession in its own status, or is it "popularity" with students? Or are the professor's assent and students' acceptance the ultimate criteria of the relevance of our profession to the higher learning?

It is about time we began to emerge in our own right as a relevant part of higher learning, not as an adjunct or even as a repair station for something gone wrong. You know, we began that way, "something went wrong," that is a squeaky axle, and we specialized in repairing and regreasing squeaky axles ever since. One is entitled to ask the question whether or not we have anything unique, or whether or not we are merely a little more relevant in the hierarchy of the academic environment just a bit above the janitors and the groundsmen.

2. Within the accelerating urbanized and impersonalized American culture, what can and should we deans do to avoid losing the student in complex organization, processes and massed numbers?

This is a horrible nightmare when you think of all the forces that make for impersonalization of our urban culture. Shall we give up, and deal only with the few, particularly the discipline cases, who are the squeaky axle, or shall we innovate and invent new ways of personalization in the midst of large numbers?

The essence of student personnel work has from its very beginning centered the emphasis upon individualization. As my mentor used to say, "It is the individualization of mass education." And little did he anticipate what mass education would mean today.

3. Why do we persist in assuming that individualization is necessary or desirable in education? As one dean said to me one time, why not just give up and just process students, one every 10 minutes? That was before the computer made it one every nine minutes. Should we rather be reconciled to the possibility that alienation of some individuals is inevitable in our education and society?

4. Is personalization of the educational experience—Kindergarten

through College—necessary? In what ways, if any, does personalization facilitate human development, via education? Is the personalized relationship an outmoded concept of the 19th century and no longer relevant or appropriate in these days of mass congestions of humans in urban centers of population?

5. What can we do to live with the paradox of "authority" within the "democratic" educational experience and with benign concern for the individual student's development according to external criteria of the good life? Are we justified in "imposing" *external criteria* of excellence upon the "free" individual within our form of democracy?

Some day you may want to read a very interesting book on this topic by Levine, in which he uses the phrase "imposed posture" which seems to be contradictory to the concept of freedom and certainly is contradictory to the concept of self-chosen criteria of the good life so prevalent in adolescents today.

6. What, if anything, can we deans do with the paradox (often conflict?) of formal classroom learning (memorization) of fact, concept, theory in contrast with the informal development of motives, internalized criteria of the good life? How can we become, and how can we aid our students to become socialized persons through the interpenetration of each other—in sharp contrast with the established American doctrine of autonomy of the individual?

7. Are there conflict and mutual exclusion between the intellectual mission of American education and the post-Freudian assertion that man is also irrational and impulse-dominated? Hutchins is fond of referring to a university as a sort of intellectual monastery where one cerebrates, but does not viscerate. Have we exhausted the possibility of mediating between these two paradoxical and conflicting models of man, as a rational animal and as an irrational animal? How can we reconcile these conflicting points of view to achieve our mission of humanizing the maturity of the individual student?

8. What do we do with the paradox of privation (often the resultant of excessive autonomy of self) and the requirements (opportunities) of membership in groups within school, community and society?

9. How can we survive the paradox of uniform, or even unitary, ideology in contrast with the proclaimed virtues of cultural pluralism, producing as it does diversity and often fragmentation of our campuses and, indeed, our society? Which is relevant and appropriate within our democracy—or are both possible and desirable or necessary? What degree of ambiguity or divergence of individual or subgroup efforts and activity is possible and desirable to maintain some measure of unity within our student culture? Too much fragmentation obviously destroys unity. Too little produces standardiza-

tion. What is our role, as personnel deans and student personnel workers to aid in seeking some centripetal force to stabilize the forces of disruption, disunity, and autonomy of individuals?

10. Should we continue to serve as agents to aid each individual to seek and serve his own ends and purposes and thus abandon the search for unity or some degree of commonality within our campuses? Has the half century of efforts to organize and maintain "services" for students experiencing "problems" proved to facilitate maturity of student clientele, or have we merely patched them up? Are we now searching for new and hopefully more effective student personnel services beyond those inherited from our professional founding fathers and mothers who never faced a Berkeley of this proportion and diversity?

My own prediction is that in the years ahead we need to innovate new services for a new kind of clientele and new kind of society. We are going to find alternatives to the old services instead of merely reshuffling them. And one of the reasons is that we are in the midst of a revolution in morality, and have been for the past three decades. And it may be to the end of the century before we find some stabilized way of helping individuals adopt satisfying moral commitments with regard to sex, drug addiction, honesty, and LSD.

We need to invent new forms of services. One of the ones that I am advocating now is that we go back to school and learn how to help students organize revolutions. Every time I say that, my fellow deans shudder because they grew up in the tradition of trying to maintain a mid-city operation, a Pandora's box, a calm campus. And I say that the decades ahead will demonstrate that conflict is natural and is of the very essence of the higher learning.

11. What have we personnel workers accomplished in our efforts to reduce scholastic failure, human misery, and withdrawal from college? Do we have any professional obligation to seek to innovate new and more effective services to reduce or alleviate these forms of "waste" in manpower utilization in our urbanized and technological society? Or should we conclude that such "wastes" are inevitable in Western civilization, and indeed within education itself? Many of our faculty colleagues have reached that conclusion, that those who are doomed to failure are doomed to failure, and there is not very much you can do about it, so spend your time on those who are going to become professors.

12. Has our assigned mission within education continued to be efforts to "control" students through "lid-sitting" and punishment? To my way of thinking, controversy is at the very heart of 20th century education, "lid-sitting" is an operation of the 1920's, doomed to failure, and our efforts to

maintain orderliness and calm and decorum are middle class virtues that need to be re-examined.

13. Should personnel deans seek to insulate the campus from the disruptive forces of the surrounding community? I glory in the fact that students have really sought to do what John Dewey sought to do, but never succeeded completely, and that is to bring the disorder and disruption of the 20th century on to the campus and to apply reasoned inquiry in the search for innovations of those new kinds of services which will aid students to deal with unsolved problems. I glory in the fact that the bearded ones are among us. I agree with their objective to bring the 20th century into the campus.

14. In addition to our services supportive of the educational mission of the follege (financial aid, counseling about choice of curricula, remediation of study skills, and the like, which are all relevant personnel services, just as relevant today as when they were invented) what can personnel workers do to create a campus and residence climate and mores, indeed even an environmental stress of standards conducive to significant learning outside of the classroom? The whole extra-curriculum is ours. The faculty does not care about it, and does not believe that it really contributes much except distraction to what they consider to be the main mission of the institution, namely, intellectualism. Hundreds and hundreds of opportunities to saturate the extracurriculum with learning that is worthy—not worthy of credit, heaven forbid, but worthy of esteem and respect.

What a topsy-turvy world this is. Only Alice in Wonderland would have understood it. Professors are entitled to due process before dismissal and students are now claiming the same inalienable right. But a college president was dismissed ungraciously without due process, and so allegedly was a dean of women at Stanford. When will deans of students come next in line for La Guillotine? Have you thought about that? Do you have due process? No. No, you don't even have rights. You only have obligations.

We are several decades retarded in our efforts to apply rationality and reasonableness to university problems of control, restraint, and academic freedom both for students and faculty, and now for presidents—hopefully soon for deans of students. Our profession's traditional posture, nationally, of non-involvement in controversy has done much to produce our image as campus agents of resistance to contemporary, current, unsolved problems of our urban culture. But professional problems continue to arise from these unsolved societal problems of our decade. What will we do to seek solutions or at least resolutions?

Without in any way diverting our *expertise* in programs of necessary services to students in need of assistance, we must add to our mission as a profession, research on these and other unsolved questions and problems.

And in a prevailing spirit of experimentation and innovation, I suggest that we deans and all of our staffs turn ourselves into researchers and thinkers concerning these unsolved problems of the higher learning, conceived as the releasing and cultivation of motivations of striving to become one's full potentiality of humane being. This is our categorical imperative as deans and student personnel workers in the higher learning.

How Others See Us

Elizabeth A. Greenleaf

Each year, members of the American College Personnel Association assemble at a national meeting and each person comes with his own anticipation of the event. For some this is an opportunity "to get away from it all"; for others it is a fulfillment of a professional responsibility to keep in touch with major concerns in specialized areas. Although it may be a vacation time for some, many still have their minds on the Dow Chemical interviewers due on campus, the student body elections, the problem of budgets and the need to hire staff while in Detroit, or on the officers of the Black Power organization whom you couldn't see until next week.

A study made two years ago to determine the effectiveness of conventions indicated that our members come to convention to share ideas with one another, to become aware of current practices on other campuses, and to hear papers presented on the major research and innovative practices of colleagues and leaders in our professions (Hoyt & Tripp, 1967). These opportunities will be available this year in more than sixty programs planned by ACPA commissions and the 1968 program committee.

The tradition of these national conventions has been for the president of ACPA to present a luncheon address. These addresses have centered around the presidents' speciality areas or have dealt with major student concerns of the day.

As I have visited various college campuses, and read the current litera-ture—including our *Journal* and *The Chronicle of Higher Education*—as one actively engaged in preparing young men and women for entering positions in the student personnel field, as one actively involved as a student personnel administrator and educator, as the problems of accreditation for the prepara-tion of student personnel educators have been considered, one question comes to mind: *What is the future of student personnel administration?*

There is much concern today for what one sees and hears. Few if any persons with experience in student personnel administration or counseling have been promoted to top level student personnel positions on any major

235

college campus during the past two years. During the past few years, there as been a major reorganization of student personnel services on campus after campus. When this takes place, most often a major problem is how to reassign the Dean of Women. She is left either as Director of Women's Education (and one questions how women's education today differs from men's) or she is given an undefined job as a general administrator. Rarely are women in our profession given a real functional responsibility. The concern is strong enough that many in our profession are asking whether women should be encouraged to earn advanced degrees or strive for top level positions.

On campus after campus the chief student personnel administrator has become the "whipping post" for students, faculty, and other administrators. The dean is seen as responsible in some way for the Student Power movement, for the image of the university as seen by the public. Outstanding senior members of our profession are leaving administrative responsibilities and going into teaching positions in Higher Education or in a Counseling department, where the emphasis is placed on the preparation of student personnel educators.

As I myself view the eight-hour teaching load of a faculty member and as I consider the possibility of having time to do one task well, I am faced with the question, "For what are we preparing the young men and women who will enter our field? What will be their role on the college campus in the 1970's?" I remember a question raised by one of our own members at a recent accreditation meeting: "Will there be any student personnel workers in the years ahead?"

It appears to me that at this time, Spring, 1968, if there is any one thing we need to do as a professional group, it is to define our role in the contributions we are to make in the institutions of higher education which we represent. Are we seen as student personnel educators, or as babysitters, managers, operators on our college campuses? Are we administrators with real responsibility for determining and interpreting policy, for making decisions and budgets, or are we to carry out the orders of the students, the faculty, and the general public? *How do others see us?*

I'll begin by defining the *us* as student personnel educators, as those on the campus of an institution on higher education who traditionally, and in many cases *still* have job descriptions which indicate that their responsibilities include the setting of an environment in which the community can meet its academic objectives, the counseling of young adults to the end that each person becomes more self-directive and can secure the widest possible benefits from the college experiences, and teaching in the out-of-class curriculum; a curriculum to better prepare the young adults as a citizen with skills in human relations.

Titles such as Director of Residence Halls, Director of Financial Aids, Dean of Men, Dean of Women, and Vice President for Student Affairs, may be new, but their functions long have been performed within the American college campus. Leonard (1956, pp. 106–114) best describes these early functions and beginnings:

One of the strengths of the American Higher Education system has been the freedom to develop institutions that expressed the specific educational aspirations of many groups of people. This freedom gave our educational structure an unparalleled vitality and flexibility, but it also made necessary the assumption by the institutions of learning of certain responsibilities that are not carried by similar institutions in other countries.

One such responsibility has been overseeing the general welfare of students which was first assumed by Colonial academies and colleges brought about in part by the compelling urge of the colonists to have their children learn the principles of their particular religion that led to the establishment of the early academies and colleges and to the housing, boarding, and disciplining of students in accordance with their sharply defined standards of conduct.

Thus from the early days, governments and institutions assumed the responsibility "not only for the intellectual development of the youths but also for the aspects of their lives that in the Old World had been carried by families. As a result, in most of the Colonial academies and colleges the students were housed or boarded. Their recreation, manners, morals, religious life, and general welfare, in addition to their studies were closely supervised. Personnel services were a constituent part of the program and the [reason] for the founding of the institution . . . The colleges sought to extend supervision to include every hour of the day and every activity of students. The rule governing student conduct were numerous and detailed. Punishments for even minor infractions were severe.

The first personnel officers in an American college were the colony overseers at Harvard and the members of the Boards of Trustees in other colleges. Later presidents and members of the faculties shared the responsibilities and were assisted by tutors, ushers, stewards, and student monitors. They acted "in loco parentis" and were required to patrol the dormitories frequently and report all absences and misdemeanors to the boards of trustees, which determined the punishments.

During the early 19th century colleges gradually began to recognize that the positive approach to behavior was preferred. Students were even "permitted" to assist the administration in meeting the current problems of the college, financial aid in the forms of scholarship became available and there was a clear concern for health and general welfare of students.

Are these historical responsibilities still seen as the major function of student personnel educators, or are the students responsible for their environment? Is counseling performed only by a clinically trained counselor in a central counseling office? Is there any education outside of the classroom? How do others accept these as our functions and responsibilities? When I say others, consider four groups: the students; the faculty; other administrators; and the parents and citizens of the community responsible for our institutions.

The Students

Much space is given in current publications and news releases to the strength and importance of Student Power. As defined at the August, 1967 meeting of the National Student Association, it is a "movement designed to gain for students their full rights as citizens, their rights to democratically control their non-academic lives, and their right to participate to the fullest in the administrative and educational decisionmaking process of the college or university." In all the years that I have attended meetings of this association I have heard much talk among the activity advisers as to how we could secure the involvement of students in responsible student government, be it the Union Board, the Residence Hall Council, Judicial Boards, or the many committees on our campuses. Are we seen as opposed to Student Power?

I'm reminded of a panel I heard a few years ago at a Southern College Personnel Association meeting. A panel of students were asked to describe what they considered to be their relationship with the Dean's office and the students' role in influencing their college or university. These were officers of campus organizations on various types of college campuses—a student body president at a small Catholic men's college, an AWS president on a large residential college campus, a Panhellenic president from a liberal arts college, etc. The students were most perceptive in describing the actual situations on their campus. A student body president said that the average student never saw the dean except when he welcomed the freshmen or as he dealt with students who had seriously violated rules or regulations. This student felt that they as students had a responsibility for activities, but that it was not real involvement. Another student felt that they really made the rules on their campus which affected them, and that they as students had a great deal of influence.

Are we, as student personnel educators, seen as really available to students, and do we have responsible, well prepared, intellectually sharp staff available to students? What students do you really know on your campus? With whom do students see you eating in the student commons or at a fraternity or sorority house? Do they see you talking to the "Green Bagger," the man with the long hair and earrings; the couple not married but living together in the off-campus apartment, the person or persons challenging the right of the university to be responsible for students' out-of-class activities? Do students see you at a meeting with those who advocate "Black Power," and can you really understand what our Black students are saying? Are you seen as spending your time only with the "elected" officers, with the Dow Chemical violators, or do you sometimes see "Mr. Average College Student?"

Students are saying, "Trust us, take us as adults; we are capable of and willing to be responsible for our own way of living." Are we trusting them, taking them as adults, giving them responsibilities for their way of living, and then, as educators, are we holding them responsible for their participation?

Those of us who are becoming gray, who are over 30, are often seen by the average young adult as the authoritarian they left at home. They want no help until the time they need it. I'm reminded of a young man who won the presidential election in a residential community on our campus. With 800 of a possible 1100 votes cast, he had won by 25 votes and had won on an anti-staff campaign. Students were to have no "interference" or assistance from the dean of students' staff in that community. As director of residence hall activities, I received a call from this independent student leader about nine o'clock one evening. Without proper scheduling of either space or event, an elaborate installation program had been planned and many campus leaders were in attendance for the ceremony. The inter-residence hall judicial board had issued an injunction against his installation because of election campaign violations. Would I tell the board that he was to be installed? How tempted would one be to remind him that he had won on an anti-staff campaign, that he had followed no university regulations in scheduling his event, and that now it was up to him! No, as an educator, he was showed the functioning of student government, assisted to understand what an injunction was, and then student government was held responsible for evaluation of his actions.

How can we be seen as responsible for helping students find a balance where they can have real involvement and concern for their in- and out-of-class life? This should mean self-direction brought about on the part of students, with a realization of what real responsibility they can take in terms of time, and in terms of legal and financial responsibilities. Do students see us as helping, or are they hiring us? Do they view us as persons with a joint concern for the total environment of our college campuses?

Do students see us as concerned about world affairs, concerned with the scientific wonders of today's world, concerned with the political issues of the day? Do they see us at campus lectures, do we carry on conversations with them about anything academic or about concerns of today's world? Are we seen as encouraging a learning in the free University discussions and lectures held outside the classroom, held in our residence halls, in our sorority and fraternity houses, and in our student union buildings?

Are we still seen as serving "in loco parentis," or are we, as indicated in *Goldberg versus the Regents of the University of California,* responsible for the regulation of "conduct and behavior of the students which tends to impede, obstruct or threaten the achievements of [the college's] educational goals." Are we seen as providing an environment in which free inquiry and learning can take place?

Do students see us as available and helpful, or have enrollments increased so rapidly that today we are only managers? Have we given students their due respect? Are we so busy sitting in meetings that we are no more help to students than the faculty member who puts first and foremost his research and writing? Have we taken our strongest personnel into administrative posts and failed to reward financially those who will work regularly with students? How many campuses are developing student personnel preparation programs in order to have staff in residence halls, and thus are placing persons to work directly with students who are no different than the teaching assistants we have complained about in the classrooms? Are we giving students real responsibilities and respect for their capabilities, and are we as educators holding them responsible for their actions?

The Faculty

How does the faculty view us? How many times can you walk into a faculty gathering and have someone say, "Well, are the students all under control today," "Guess you'll have all the students out of classes next week to work on homecoming floats," or "I wouldn't have your job for anything!"?

Each year as a part of the practicum seminar for second year student personnel interns some time is spent with representatives of our Indiana University faculty council. I'm reminded of two recent incidents. A distinguished senior member of our faculty, a member of the University's Faculty Council and the Student Affairs Committee, a Faculty Associate in one of our residence halls, made the statement to our future colleagues that "the dean of students' staff is an arm of the faculty council." He pointed out that on our campus, as is true on many others, the responsibility for student affairs belongs to the faculty and that they have delegated this to the dean of students. At about the same time another distinguished member of our faculty was asked by a young member of our residence hall staff how the faculty viewed the role of the residence hall staff. Without hestitation, the faculty member replied, "Oh, most of them don't even know you exist."

Are we seen only as an arm of the faculty, or are we partners with the faculty in helping to meet the needs of our educational community? As we have become more and more specialized in our jobs, as we have added many new staff members, are we seen by faculty as making a contribution to the campus, or are we seen as taking away from the budget money that might go for more adequate teaching staffs? Having grown up in a faculty home, I'm conscious of my father's colleagues asking, "Who are all those new counselors over in the dean's office? What are they supposed to do? They had better not begin to advise my students!"

It appears certain that no members of ACPA would question the fact that the first objective of our institutions is an academic one. Many student personnel educators may accept the fact that they are an arm of the faculty, but there must be an acceptance of student personnel staff as professional persons with knowledge and skills to help meet the needs of students. If we have educated, professionally prepared, experienced personnel and are specialists in working with students, how are faculty who are specialists in academic disciplines seen as prepared to move in and make decisions on policies affecting student life? How adequate is our data seen when we are called on to present to faculty committees information to serve as basis for their decisions? Are we really seen a having done our research and shared this adequately with one another? In a meeting before a faculty-student committee discussing visitation in our residence halls, I was asked for evidence from other campuses on the effects visitation had on the educational environments. Have we the answers?

How do we interpret our role to the faculty? How do we prove that we are more than policemen and disciplinarians? Do we go to faculty meetings and are we seen sitting only with members of our own division, do we go only with our colleagues to the faculty room for lunch, do we take the opportunity to attend faculty functions? Not just the dean, but is the dean seen as making it possible for assistants to have the opportunity and take advantage of faculty contacts?

Are we seen taking the leadership in suggesting ways in which faculty may become more involved with students? Have members of the dean of students' staff been included when residential colleges or special scheduling of classes by residential areas have been considered, or has the dean's office been informed that a hall was being taken for an academic program? What are we doing to work with the commuter student to the end that he has faculty contacts? When we hear students complaining because they cannot secure academic advising, when we hear that a faculty member is failing to meet his classes, are we seen as responsible for pointing out these problems? Do we have free access and do we take the opportunity to suggest corrections needed in the teaching field as the faculty through AAUP have indicated to us how we should handle discipline? Have we as a professional personnel organization effectively reacted to the AAUP *Statement on Rights and Freedoms of Students?* Why are we not, like librarians, seen as eligible for membership in AAUP? Are we not seen as having a teaching role?

Administrators

Thirdly, what is our relationship with fellow administrators? As one considers responsibilities fundamentally a part of administration, one would expect student personnel administrators to have a major role for determining policy, interpreting policy, enforcing policy, decisionmaking, selection and supervision of staff, and budget making.

Does the President, the Dean of Faculties, the Board of Control of your institution consult student personnel educators on your campus on matters concerning students? Does the student personnel staff keep them well informed on problems which may affect the campus? Can the student personnel educator tell them about the demonstration to take place, or what type of reaction might be expected from various groups of the campus community when a new policy is announced? How often do the student personnel divisions recommend possible actions to the board of control or to the administrative committee on campus?

How realistic are the student personnel educators in defending their budgets? There are many concerns today as to whether money is effectively used to meet the objectives of the institution. The student personnel budget easily can be seen as going a long way in paying for a great number of new teaching faculty.

In terms of the relationship of our role to students and faculty, is it our role to co-operate with the Dean of Faculty to shape the direction of the educational experiences of students? How can student personnel educators serve as catalysts to bring all forces of the campus together to the end that there is a joint direction given to educational experiences?

How do the President and the Board of Trustees view student clashes with the Dean? Is it best to just reorganize and get the problem out of his hair? How does the president view the basic philosophy of the student personnel services on your campus? Are student personnel educators seen as so idealistic and so dedicated to their work that they are unable to view situations realistically in terms of today's world? We must not be defensive as societal changes bring about many changes in our responsibilities.

How does the budget officer look at the request from the dean of students office for travel to meetings of ACPA, APGA, ICPA, IPGA, NAWDC, IAWDC, NASPA, Midwest NASPA, ACUHO, ACU, NASFSA, Financial Aids Officers, AAHE, ACE, etc.? Do we today have any professional organization to give us direction as we work with the college presidents? A major concern for all of us should be what is happening during a one week period which may end this afternoon. Within a week NASPA, NAWDC, and ACPA will each separately have passed resolutions on *The Statement of Rights and Freedoms of Students,* and we will have jointly or individually acted upon other areas of mutual concerns. How can we be seen as working together for a common goal?

A last question as we look at how other administrators view us: How do our own staff view us? Do we give real responsibility to staff who work with us and who come into contact day by day with the students, and at the same time do they keep us informed on student feelings and student needs? Many of us need to take an honest look at our student personnel structure, responsibilities of various members of the staff, and to be certain that we are dealing with one another in a respected way.

Parents and the General Public

We are often responsible for the first contacts with parents and students as they come to visit campus. Members of the student personnel division are most often the ones to prepare the orientation materials which go to parents and send out the rules and regulations which parents often *do* read. Have you taken a real good look lately at the types of materials which go into the homes of your students? On our campus it took a conference on the Negro in Higher Education before most of us were aware that we had no pictures of Negro students in any of our student orientation materials. Are we seen as realistic in extending expectations to parents for what we can do or are we seen as placing certain educational responsibilities squarely on the shoulders of their daughters and sons?

How does the student personnel educator interpret the college to the taxpayers of the community who see more and more property going off the tax lists? What are your institution and your student personnel services doing to bring about new experiences for students in realistic community projects? As we move towards the day when the students on our campus will have a right to vote, will we be taking a lead in the involvement of students in political affairs of the wide community? Do we as student personnel educators have any concern for the way the draft law is currently operating? If so, have we done anything about it?

I expect that all that has been done in this presentation is to raise questions, but that is what I intended to do. I have no more of the answers than each of you has. More important, each of us on our own campus must evaluate how others see us in relation to the goals and the objectives of our colleges. Each of us must evaluate ourselves as real educators. If our role is to set an environment in which the academic process can take place, is to provide counseling to the end that each student sets effective goals for himself, is to serve as an educator in out-of-class education, are we seen doing this effectively on each of our campuses?

Is there a future for student personnel educators? My answer is Yes! The functions are there to be performed, but the way these functions are to be performed are changing and must change. It depends on how others see us as effective in carrying out these functions that we may become real educators taking a leadership in the world of today's students. We must take a lead in bringing together faculty, students and other administrators to the end that each contributes to the education of the leaders to the future.

References

Hoyt, D. P., & Tripp, P. A. Members' evaluation of ACPA programs and services, *Journal of College Student Personnel*, 1967, 8, 40–45.
Leonard, E. A. *Origins of personnel services in American higher education.* Minneapolis: University of Minnesota Press, 1956.
Received April 4, 1968

Student Personnel Workers: Student Development Experts of the Future

Philip A. Tripp

If our objects is to predict trends in student personnel work for the next 30 years, we must hypothesize what our country will be like 30 years from now. The forecast of 300 million people in the United States in the year 2000 indicates that space will be an acute problem. Most people will live in megalopoli; society will be more complex and will depend on sophisticated problem-solving skills. Power in all its forms will be available to all competent to use it; physical energy will be harnessed to perform most work. A cup of sand, we already know, contains enough energy to run a city for a day.

By the year 2000 psychological and social knowledge will be vastly expanded. We will have detailed knowledge of how to foster, prevent, and manipulate learning through teaching. We will be able to transform life itself. All the world will be immediately accessible to many people, and increased leisure will make men increasingly mobile. Probably the most striking change will be the disappearance of the Protestant work ethic as a basic paradigm for organizing Western society.

There will be a new perception of what it means to be a human being, and that perception will be invested with a new respect for humanness and for the individual worth of human beings. Because we are beginning to see their value and necessity, we will see openness and greater honesty in interpersonal relations. We have been sensitized since World War II to the social hypocrisy in our society. Student personnel work has been accused of some of this hypocrisy and, in efforts to answer the charges, has made some real progress in the recent past. The twenty-first century may see a new era characterized by greater sensitivity and deeper qualities of love between and among people generally.

We have lived in our own times, and perhaps even throughout our country's entire history, in an adversary society. Adversary relations will shift to more wholesome ends in the future. There will be increasing awareness of the need to compete for everyone's benefit instead of exclusively for individual benefits. This is what is meant by deeper qualities of love among men. We, as a people, will develop greater sensitivity and a national set of values with deeper roots in moral and ethical concerns.

We will develop a more profound understanding of life as a continuous process of change. This will replace the search for a Holy Grail of knowledge that is, by implication, static, permanent, and unchanging. The promise of leisure is that it will give men time to fulfill themselves in all realms of their beings, both cognitive and affective.

All of these predicted changes have either direct or indirect implications for student personnel work and higher education in general. Students will require more individualized attention, and instructional patterns will become increasingly tutorial. Education will continue to be highly cognitive, but more attention will be paid to developing emotional and affective capacities. There will be more concern for selfawareness and development of warm and fulfilling interpersonal relations as significant objectives in the educational experience. Although education will continue to become more technical, curriculums will be highly individualized, and there will be no concern for credit hours or quality points or the kind of formalized mechanics now used in an attempt to quantify what is essentially a qualitative experience. Much of the future will fall to a new generation of *student development experts*. They will be responsible not only for integrating the intellectual experiences of the individual but also for assisting students in their study and treatment of moral and ethical problems. They will consult in the development of life styles and on the affective and aspirational aspects of student development.

To accomplish these educational goals, a new type of institution will be required. There is much evidence already that the multiversity is something of a dinosaur, an anachronism that must be replaced by a more viable social organization. The multiversity is the logical conclusion of our old conception of what education is about. There is an obvious need for a new mode of operation with more concern for primary groups and individualized instruction. Since many of the functions that the university-educated man now performs, such as engineering and middle management, may well be performed by machines, the university will turn to a different kind of task, i.e., making man more personally effective and a more fulfilled human being.

It is difficult to conceptualize the new forms of preparation for student personnel work. The old mission is obsolescent, and the new mission is not quite in sharp focus yet. As a result we have many dislocations, many disruptions, and a sense of anxiety about what seems sensible to do to bring about some stability, some order, where it no longer exists. It is to be hoped that all of the solutions of problems created by the "new mission" will not be administrative solutions, but rather that social phenomena of the kind that I discussed earlier would be brought to bear in rethinking these problems. The future role of the student development person must be an increasingly professional role in the sense that he will be a qualified scholar in student development. He must have clear-cut status in the academic community, and this mission must be supported or at least accepted by all quarters of that community.

Rather than merely transmitting the stable, enduring facts from the past, we will learn to live in a world of change. Our mission is basically phenomenological. We are presumably prepared to deal with the idiosyncratic materials of the individual student's life. We are presumably competent to take process and to turn it to educational ends in a way that traditionally prepared scholars are not. This has not been their mission, and we have not specified it as our mission in these terms. But that is what we are talking about when we talk of ourselves as agents of change and when we talk of ourselves as instruments for promoting the effective use of the facts of change in achieving educational ends. We must prove ourselves in the coming decades.

Student personnel work is in a primitive stage of development. Many of our forebears and many of our colleagues have been motivated by a "good Samaritan" instinct. We have been applied persons who tend to regress to immediate needs and to settle for practical solutions to problems, without any philosophical anxieties, because we think we are doing what situations require. This is no longer adequate. In fact, it is a passé conception of what it means to work to help young people grow up and to grow up ourselves. In the future, the student personnel worker will be much more knowledgeable than his present-day counterpart. He may even be more sophisticated than his traditionally trained disciplinary brethren, inasmuch as he knows that process has as great a force in life as content. If he is skillful in the use of process in promoting educational ends, he can substantially change the face of higher education.

In preparing professionals to be effective, as higher education evolves into a new form, we must prevent being caught in the old paradigms. It is easy to be captured in these because they are forced on us by history, custom, and tradition. We have a style of academic life now that is pretty ridig and formal. The first thing that must be done is to look at those rigidities and formalities with a very, very critical eye. We must begin to raise suitable questions about the techniques of teaching and learning in colleges and universities, in terms of a new mission of education. We have evidence of the beginnings of a new approach in group sensitivity training and dynamics programs. We have yet to deal with the area of teaching people generally to understand their feelings. Our society has been disposed against people admitting they have any feelings. Here is a zone where we must be pioneers and the precursors and the showers of the way.

In the development of an environment that is conducive to the kind of growth in students that we might strive for, the use of technological advances within the university must be carefully examined if we are to prevent machines from being disadvantageous to our mission. The reliance of student personnel workers on technical hardware can be a form of professional regression. These devices, improperly used, identify us as adversaries of the students. Our machines seemingly become our swords against them. A student saying, "Please do not fold, bend, staple, or mutilate me," is, in fact, saying to us, "You are trying to dehumanize me and I resist you." We should be gald for that affirmation and use technology only insofar as it clearly serves developmental purposes.

Student personnel workers have an unprecedented opportunity to point the way as higher education undergoes a major transformation in the next 30 years. If they become qualified student development experts, they may be major partners in the reformation of this social institution. They can help make it better able to treat matters of love, knowledge, and wisdom and thereby to foster the growth of persons.

Student Personnel Work:
A Profession Stillborn

James F. Penney

In half a century, student personnel work has not achieved professional recognition on campuses. As evidence, basic literature is cited both quantitatively and qualitatively. Preoccupation with housekeeping functions remains a major reason for the field's low esteem. The personnel point of view provides an inadequate base for professional organization. Fragmentation into a growing number of specialties characterizes current developments. The early dreams of a profession of student personnel work cannot be realized.

Few occupational entities have devoted as much energy to self-examination and attempts at self definition as has the amorphous body calling itself student personnel work. The specialty is roughly half a century old—surely time enough to achieve whatever degree of recognition and maturity the academic community is likely to allow. It is certainly time enough for it to establish itself as a profession among professions, if it is ever to do so. In that same half-century or less, a score or more new specialties have been born, matured, and become professionally established in the world of academe.

Student personnel work has not achieved professional recognition in the community of professionals operating on campuses. While it has sought to establish a position among the dominant power centers—faculty, administration, students—a realistic assessment of campuses in the 1960's can lead only to the conclusion that the effort has failed. Student personnel workers, their philosophy, and their goals are not among the major influences today in colleges and universities.

Basic Literature: Quantity

An attempt to identify causative factors may begin with an examination of the literature in the field. Analysis suggests several characteristics, each of which contributes to the conclusion that the occupation is not truly a

249

profession and is not moving toward becoming one. Striking is the observation that there is a paucity of basic literature in the field. Though disconcerting to practitioners inundated by a plethora of journals, research reports, convention proceedings, position formulations, and policy statements, the observation remains supportable.

Where, for instance, are to be found basic writings that trace in their conceptualizations the development of a field of endeavor? Where are the rival statements of thesis, antithesis, and synthesis that have provided the crucial methodology through which knowledge has developed in the West? Where are the fundamental descriptions of the occupation and its practitioners that can serve to identify for it a place in the sun?

The student personnel specialty has produced surprisingly little of this sort of writing that endures. What are the basic textbooks in the field? Arbuckle (1953), Lloyd-Jones and Smith (1938), Mueller (1961), Williamson (1961), and Wrenn (1951) constitute the core. Included as historically significant might be the pamphlets in the american Council on Education Series on Personnel Work in Colleges and Universities, produced sequentially between 1939 and 1953. While each dealt with a specific topic, it is not unreasonable to consider the series as an entity that provided basic textual material representing the activities, rationales, and objectives of the field in an important period of its development. Altogether, the list is not quantitatively imposing as to represent a half-century of effort.

In contrast, problem-centered writings abound: Journals, abstracting services, and monographs multiply *ad infinitum*. Quantity, however, may be misleading. The fact of its timeliness implies that a journal article, research report, or monograph is likely to be of short-term value. Further, it has probably been developed upon already available principles and accepted concepts instead of having focused upon the production of original formulations. In this context, the problem-centered literature of a field, appearing in periodical publications, may not be a valid index of the field's strength, endurance, or professional status. Student personnel work has not historically produced, and is not currently producing, a body of permanent, fundamental literature by means of which the specialty can be identified, evaluated, and its progressive development calculated.

Basic Literature: Quality

A qualitative assessment of the literature in student personnel work leads to other observations. The contents of the seminal books fall generally into three groupings. In the first is a large quantity of material taken over

wholesale from the social sciences, chiefly psychology. Included is information on counseling, vocational development, group processes, the subculture
of the campus, human development, and learning. The implication is that
these materials have direct relevance to the activities of the student personnel
worker. The inclusion of a major emphasis on counseling, for example,
suggests that he is a psychological counselor. But is he also to be a test
administrator-interpreter? A group dynamics leader-trainer? A manager of
residences and food services? A manipulator of environments to enhance
their contribution to learning? The student personnel worker, by implication, must be a multi-specialist. Can one individual be adequately prepared
to do all the things that student personnel workers are supposedly competent
to do? In an age of specialization and expertise, it seems unlikely. Perhaps,
then, he should be considered not a specialist, but a generalist.

The value of the generalist and the point of view he can bring to
administrative and managerial tasks is an important concept in the era of the
specialist. Is there a place for the generalist in student personnel work? Can
the student personnel worker, "broadly educated," expect to be accepted as
competent when he performs tasks that overlap with the operations of
more "specialty-educated" colleagues? The hope has historically been that
generalist preparation plus good will and the "personnel point of view" will
enable the student personnel worker to perform student-related tasks in ways
that "experts" could or would not do. Three results may be discerned currently:

1. The student personnel worker has not been accepted by academicians
as competent in some areas where recent developments have produced highly
trained specialists with whom the student personnel worker competes. This
is especially true in counseling, where the specialty of counseling psychology
has developed; other areas where parallel trends are visible are housing
administration, union programming and management, foreign student advisement, and financial aid administration.

2. Student personnel workers tend to be relegated to subordinate and
peripheral positions as middle- and lower-level administrators who are seen
by academicians as essentially uninvolved in the real-life issues of campuses
in the 1960's.

3. When given the option, students, having learned to value expertise,
will turn to "fully qualified" specialists rather than to generalists whose role
and qualifications are less clearly identified.

Personnel Work as Housekeeping

A second category of textual material is concerned with administrative,
organizational, and coordinating matters that may appropriately be called

housekeeping activities. To so designate them is not to deny their urgency, but to suggest that they are hardly matters about which a learned, academically based discipline or profession will be fundamentally concerned. Indeed, the student personnel specialty's longtime preoccupation with such how-to-do-it issues as admissions, orientation, housing, financial aid, student activities, and campus discipline has been a factor that has encouraged campus colleagues to denigrate the student personnel worker and to reject his aspiration to equality in a world dominated by teaching and research.

The fact that current thinking continues to focus on housekeeping and technique-centered matters is evidenced by the subject matter of the monographs in the Student Personnel Series of the American College Personnel Association. Eight booklets have appeared since 1960; included are considerations of financial aid, housing, health services, discipline, testing, and group activities. While in most cases the contents represent careful thinking about some functions of student personnel work, it is quite possible to read the entire series without recognizing that the field under consideration is one that should, by its nature, be at the center of campus life and activity. Discussion of the matters with which students are centrally concerned in the 1960's is conspicuously absent in these publications. One wonders how the publication series of a major student personnel group could appear so irrelevant and prosaic in a decade of monumental change.

The Personnel Point of View

A third portion of the texts in the field is devoted to elaborations of the personnel point of view. The authors are unified in urging that not only workers in the specialty but all members of the academic community embrace what is essentially a value orientation. The personnel point of view may be characterized by three postulates: (a) Every student should be recognized as unique; (b) Every individual should be regarded as a total person; (c) The current needs and interests of individual students are the most significant factors to be considered in developing a program of campus life. Concern with particular values, of course, is not uncommon among professions. Medicine, law, and the natural sciences—all, in their devotion to objectivity, are committed to humanly derived values. But in contrast to the established professions, student personnel work has developed primarily as an enterprise defined by a point of view rather than by its content or the services it provides. Indeed, as Shoben (1967) pointed out, most of the services that represent personnel functions are not distinctive to student personnel work, but fall also within the province of other professions and occupations. The things that make such activities part of a student personnel program are the outlook, the assumptions, and the general philosophy of those who participate in them. The concept of a single professional entity, student personnel work, is therefore abortive.

Emergence of the Council of Student Personnel Associations (COSPA)* in the 1960's indicates that in reality there are several readily identifiable specialties (together with organizations representing them). All of them may be seen as falling more or less within the province of student personnel work, while at the same time each provides a service reasonably distinct from the others. Are there, then, enough common interest, activities, and objectives to provide a base for any sort of shared professional identification?

Parker (1966) proposed that it should be possible to identify a student personnel worker as one whose occupational tasks enable him to find membership in one of the COSPA organizations. His approach rests on the assumption that counseling is the one common aspect of all student personnel jobs. It follows that each student personnel worker should be educated primarily as a counselor who includes in his preparation some peripheral study of other aspects of personnel work. Parker's rationale includes the observation that there are five critical skill areas possessed by the counselor that are basic to virtually all student personnel functions. They are: (a) the counselor's sensitivity to others, enabling him to develop effective working relationships; (b) the counselor's skill in objectively analyzing the strengths and weaknesses of individuals; (c) the counselor's skill at interviewing; (d) the counselor's awareness of the nature and extent of individual differences in those with whom he works; (e) the counselor's ability to identify learning difficulties and his expertise in knowing how learning takes place.

No one is likely to disagree that these would be distinct assets for student personnel workers to possess. This is not to say, however, that they are *uniquely* valuable to student personnel workers. On the contrary; they would be invaluable to *anyone* who deals directly and professionally with human relationships. To conclude that education in counseling should be the basic preparation for student personnel work, therefore, is to say very little. The question is whether such preparation is enough to identify a professional

---

*The Council of Student Personnel Associations includes the following organizational members: american College Personnel Association, Association of College Unions, American Association of Collegiate Registrars and Admissions Officers, Association of College and University Housing Officers, Association of College Admissions Counselors, Association for Coordination of University Religious Advisors, College Placement Council, Conference of Jesuit Student Personnel Administrators, National Association of Student Personnel Administrators, National Association of Women Deans and Counselors, National Association of Foreign Student Advisors.

group, or to serve as the foundation for membership in professional organizations. Obviously, it is not.

Organizational Fragmentation

The COSPA phenomenon represents a proliferation of so-called professional organizations. Several of these organizations are of quite recent origin: More than half the COSPA groups have been organized since approximately 1960. Examination of the literature, activities, and job titles represented suggest that several of the organizations have quite specific and unique interests that are shared only peripherally—if at all—by the others. For other members who attempt to be more general in their interests and global in their constituencies (i.e., ACPA and NAWDC), the literature suggests a major concern with unresolved matters of identity, purpose, and role. Such observations lead reasonably to the conclusion that the field of student personnel work is in the process of becoming increasingly fragmented and diversified as time goes on and new specializations develop. The longer this process continues, the less likely it will be that common interests, activities, and a universal core of training can be possible or relevant for all.

Conclusions

The issues raised here lead to a fundamental conclusion. No longer viable is the hypothesis under which the early writers of the 1930's and 1940's operated—namely, that there was an identifiable point of view and an occupational entity that might be recognized as the student personnel work profession. The field is now composed of a number of relatively separate and distinct specialties linked largely by organizational contiguity (i.e., they all involve working with students out of classrooms) and, to a lesser extent, by the sharing of a common philosophical view of their tasks. The long-sought "profession" of student personnel work has not been, is not, and will not be recognized or accepted as a vital aspect of the academic world.

References

Arbuckle, D. S. *Student personnel services in higher education.* New York: McGraw-Hill, 1953.

Lloyd-Jones, E. M., & Smith, M. R. *A student personnel program for higher education.* New York: McGraw-Hill, 1938.

Mueller, K. H. *Student personnel work in higher education.* Boston: Houghton Mifflin, 1961.

Parker, C. A. The place of counseling in the preparation of student personnel workers. *Personnel and Guidance Journal,* 1966, 45, 254–261.

Shoben, E. J. Psychology and student personnel work. *Journal of College Student Personnel,* 1967, 8, 239–245.

Williamson, E. G. *Student personnel services in colleges and universities.* New York: McGraw-Hill, 1961.

Wrenn, C. G. *Student personnel work in college.* New York: Ronald Press, 1951.

IV

The Emergence of Student Development

Student activism, confrontational politics, individualism, sit-ins, and civil rights protests characterized the decade of the 1960's. These major societal issues continued to exert influence on college and university campuses, and particularly college student personnel, during the early 1970's. The literature of this ten-year period is rich with a number of critical issues: the struggles the field experienced regarding its own sense of mission and purpose; the effects of an economic crisis or "steady state"; a new perspective on practice grounded in the application of developmental stage theories; an emphasis on change, and an enthusiasm for the roles student development educators could play as integral partners in the academy. Noteworthy are the descriptions of the evolving field, increasingly called student development or student affairs, and the many authors who offered futuristic visions and whose thinking helped guide the field through its own transitional period of development. A new vocabulary appears in professional journals. Professionals now read about vectors of development, institutional impacts or educational outcomes, encounter techniques, facilitation, tort liability and milieu management. Emerging models of practice and new organizational structures are proposed utilizing a developmental approach to student learning and growth. The focus of the 1960's seems always to be on change . . . different concepts, new roles, different interpretations, new partnerships, and a new sense of identity, not only for the individual professional, but for the field as well. Student personnel experienced a rebirth characterized by an enhanced mission, broader goals, new titles and strategies and widening spheres of influence in the academy.

The 1970s' roles for student affairs professionals incorporated the concepts of consultation, instruction and milieu management. Collaborative relationships with faculty and students were forged and the environment was recognized for its significant influence on behavior. The goal of the evolving practitioner, the student development specialist/educator, became the creation of a positive learning environment and the provision of forces of challenge and support to move students toward higher levels of cognitive and affective development. The seeds of a major paradigmatic shift, to be described almost twenty years later, were planted during this decade.

College and university educators turned their attention toward questions of curriculum relevance and human values, while placing a new emphasis on the process of learning in addition to the goal of acquiring knowledge. The importance of skills and competencies associated with problem-solving, both in and out of the classroom and particularly in the areas of career development and life planning, received recognition.

"The task of relating with students on a meaningful level is one of the most pressing issues facing higher education" (Ivey & Morrill, 1970, p. 226). These authors address the need for a more effective means of interaction with students, one based on the concept of encounter rather than confrontation. Ivey and Morrill (1970) also propose the use of the term student development specialist to describe the increasing complexity of the role student affairs professionals must play combining the roles of "psychologist, administrator, human relations specialist, and educator" (p.229). Problem solving skills should be taught while stressing the generalizability of these skills to several other service areas within student affairs.

Viewing the junior college movement at a critical crossroads in its development, O'Banion, Thurston and Gulden (1970) offer their perspective on an emerging model for the profession of student personnel based on the assumption that the "student development point of view is a behavioral orientation in which educators attempt to create a climate of learning . . ." (p. 9). They call for participative administration and a decentralized structural organization. ". . . the importance of student personnel work in the junior college is supported by their conclusion that "the 'student personnel point of view' and the 'junior college point of view' are one and the same" (p. 13).

Hurst & Ivey (1971) identify fundamental issues of concern to students and conclude that a "complete radicalization of our present point of view" (p.) is needed to ensure the future viability of our field. Students' feelings of insignificance, impotence and their lack of confidence in authority figures with "an unimpressive record in nontechnical areas of human existence" (p.) are cited as major themes undergirding student concerns. A new term, "proactive posture" appears as a future alternative to the reactive mode that many in student affairs believe characterized professional practice in the past.

In what may well be the first article to compare the traditional student personnel perspective and the emerging approach called student development, Crookston (1972) begins by reminding us of the contributions of earlier works by Cowley (1936) and EstherLloyd-Jones (1954). The demise of *in loco parentis* is credited as a major factor in practitioners' movement away from student services and the related goal of controlling student behavior. Suggesting that an inherently bureaucratic model is contradevelopmental, Crookston proposes an organizational model incorporating the concepts of encounter, egalitarianism, and collaboration with an emphasis on competence.

Addressing the serious problems of confronting the field, Dewey (1972) lays much of the blame at the doorstep of existing graduate preparation programs. She identifies curriculum and course selection as two issues recurring in the literature between 1927 and 1970. She recommends that preparation programs begin to offer courses in substantive areas heretofore lacking: organizational theory, dynamics of institutional and societal change, futuristics and a strong research component. In contrast to many earlier authors, Dewey does not envision the demise of the student affairs function, but rather presents us with the challenge of who will perform its functions.

One of the most influential pieces of literature from this decade is the monograph by Brown, "Student Development in Tomorrow's Higher Education: A Return to the Academy" (1972). The significance of this document lies not so much in Brown's assessment of the current state of the field as his summary of student development research findings, focused on students and environments, and his identification of major key student development concepts. Brown concludes with a discussion of needed future roles for the student affairs professional (diagnostician, consultant, programmer . . .) and presents a series of recommendations for higher education and student affairs to encourage the acceptance and implementation of student development. Central to Brown's view are the required cooperative efforts and relationships with faculty as partners in the academy.

Recognizing that the field of student personnel, grounded in the student personnel point of view, is in the midst of a significant transition, Chandler (1973) proposes an organizational model for student affairs as a vehicle to implement student development concepts and programs. Overall supervisory responsibilities can be grouped into three major areas: managerial, student development and judicial control.

Representative of the emerging body of literature describing the student development perspective or movement is Parker's classic "Student Development: What Does It Mean?" (1974). His description of developmental stage theory and its application to the undergraduate experience directs our attention to the potential benefits to be derived from the interconnectedness of student affairs personnel with other areas of the educational community.

Harvey (1974) reflects one educator's view of the changes that lie ahead for student personnel. Predicted trends include an increasing use of the term "avuncularity" to describe the nature of the relationship between students and student personnel professionals, the merging of student personnel with educational administration and the need for the role of environmental administrator to "orchestrate institutional resources for the total benefit of students" (p.). Concluding that student personnel services are increasingly defined by functions rather than offices, Harvey suggests five alternative paradigms for student personnel functions.

The Commission of Professional Development of the Council of Student Personnel Associations (COSPA) published a statement that applied student development concepts to graduate preparation programs and suggested a model for a competency-based curriculum. Three roles are prescribed for the future student development specialist: administrator, consultant and instructor. Tomorrow's practitioners and today's preparation program faculty are encouraged to be sensitive to viewing learning as a continuous process that includes self-assessment, goal setting, allocation of resources and the implementation of behavioral change strategies.

Addressing the 1974 NAWDAC conference, Rahtigan's thesis is "one of evolution rather than a portrayal of reconceptualization" (p.). Reacting to the unfavorable attitude of many to student services, he suggests that the traditional concept of service may no longer be viable. Instead, the application of theory and the use of behavioral strategies will allow professionals to engage in classroom instruction and to broaden the traditional concept of service to include remedial, preventive and developmental approaches.

Another of Crookston's contributions is "Milieu Management" (1975). In these pages a new role for the chief/principal student affairs (officer), that of milieu management is proposed. The basic competencies needed to foster student development on a campus include instruction, consultation and milieu management. Definitions are provided, a conceptual framework described and strategies suggested.

Phase Two of the Tomorrow's Higher Education Project, originally initiated by the American College Personnel Association in 1968, is the development of an operational model for student development. In "A Student Development Model for Student Affairs in Tomorrow's Higher Education" the new philosophy is defined, functions and staff competencies are identified and suggestions for the implementation of the three part model are proposed.

Retrenchment and a proposed focus on mastering "micromanagerial tasks" (p.243) should not dictate the future student personnel workers' role or function. Instead, Nash, Saurman and Sousa (1976) suggest that it is time for an enlargement of our function to include instructional reform. They describe a resurgence of humanistic learning theory in higher education and discuss new roles student development educators can play serving as humanistic teachers assisting faculty. Several pitfalls of this new co-equal status with faculty are identified.

Probably the most frequently cited Crookston article is "Student Personnel—All Hail and Farewell!" (1976). He believes that important distinctions must be made among the terms now used interchangeably to describe our role and functions. Three terms are examined: student personnel work, student affairs and student development. According to Crookston, the latter term should connote the field's new philosophy as well as operational concepts. He calls for all future nomenclature to be grounded in an understanding of student development. Professional associations, journals and graduate courses should be renamed and revised. We are encouraged to consider student personnel work as deceased in the same way we have come to view *in loco parentis*.

Reasons for an increasing interest in legal issues among student affairs professionals is reflected in the 1979 article by Hammond. A respected authority in the area of law and higher education, he alerts us to our new vulnerability due to a number of recent court decisions concerning personal and institutional tort liability. The student-institutional relationship, now described as contractual by the courts, is examined from both a private and public institution perspective. Negligence is a key issue that will guide practice for years to come.

A point of view essay by Bloland (1979) raises the question of the requirement of professional preparation for chief student affairs officers. Identifying four propositions, with tongue in cheek, he proceeds to discuss the implications of each. Included is the conclusion that student personnel/ student development and administration probably need to be considered as two distinct career tracks in higher education. As we seek to involve all aspects of the academy in intentional student development, we must be able to convince others that our goal is a goal of higher education and our expertise is not available from any other campus source.

Confrontation, Communication, and Encounter: A Conceptual Framework for Student Development

Allen E. Ivey and Weston H. Morrill

Recently, a student leader on a college campus stood up in a demonstration against a university regulation and said, "To H—— with the administration. We'll force them to give in." This type of feeling and approach is not uncommon on university campuses today. Students are *demanding* to be heard, and their demands are placing administrators in a bind such that even if they wanted to, they could neither hear nor communicate with these students.

The task of relating with students on a meaningful level is one of the most pressing issues facing higher education today. Few administrators and faculty reach students in any depth. Clearly, there is a need for new approaches. This paper discusses a conceptual framework for more meaningful interactions on a university campus. Further, a new developmental model is suggested for the student personnel worker and for the university. The university has too long been a static institution which has had difficulty involving students in the process of their own education.

The master teacher learned long ago that his most productive teaching resulted from an active interchange and involvement with his students such that both he and his students grew. This meant that the teacher was both a teacher and a learner and that the learner was both a learner and a teacher. The dialogue resulted in growth for both the student and the teacher. The willingness for the one to grow and change produced growth and change in the other. This process of education has important implications for administrative personnel in higher education. It is now recognized that the classroom is no longer the only vehicle of education. The total university environment with various personnel and management experiences is an important part of the educational process.

A crucial goal for higher education in this time of change is that of helping individuals and groups on campus (e.g. faculty, administrators, student leaders, activists, dormitory residents) start talking with one another in such a way that a process of growth for all is possible. Administrative planning should aim to create a climate of mutual understanding and respect. In the past college administrators and student personnel faculty have tended to be content with smoothing the troubled campus waters and intervening between conflicting groups. In the future, we must be more concerned with promotion of meaningful interaction among many viewpoints on the college campus.

College students are in a stage of development which is typified by efforts to establish independence and develop a personal set of values which they can consider to be their own, rather than values which have been imposed on them by parents, by society, and by authority. Universities need to provide a climate which allows students to examine issues critically and develop values based on a thoughtful and meaningful investigation of the issues rather than permit situations in which students assert their self-direction and independence by opposition.

As the master teacher found that his teaching was most effective when both he and his students were actively involved in a process of seeking answers, that both learned in the process, and that both were involved together in seeking these answers, universities need to provide the kind of climate which will allow students, faculty, and administration to concern themselves about issues in such a way that all parties involved are free to learn, to grow, to change, and to develop.

Confrontation, Communication, and Encounter

Confrontation was demonstrated in a press conference in Washington (October 25, 1967) when National Student Association President Edward Schwartz denounced the use of force in dealing with student demonstrations. He said, "If college administrators continue to rely on their unrestrained, even brutal, use of police force to disburse these demonstrations, we are heading for the most serious crisis higher education has faced in this century." This represents the ultimate in *confrontation* by both parties—attempting forceful imposition of a point of view upon an opposing individual or group. Confrontation is defined as the meeting or confronting of viewpoints with relatively little regard to the ideas of the other party. Confrontation too often occurs between administrative officials and students in regard to rules and regulations. Neither group makes an effort to see what the other is really saying.

Another approach, perhaps representative of the "modern" student personnel point of view, is that of *communication*. Recent movements in counseling, psycho-therapy, and student personnel labeled as client or student-centered approaches perhaps best typify the communication model. Under a communication model, the college administrator would meet with student leaders and student activists. He would attempt to understand and demonstrate to the students that he understands their point of view. As is implied in the term student-centered, the focus is on the student and the message that *he* is attempting to articulate.

Communication is an effort to "smooth the waters" and provide points of contact and understanding between different groups. An effort is made to communicate to student groups that administrators in the university understand their point of view and understand their feelings and concerns. Emphasis is usually placed on positive aspects of the relationship between or among groups. Communication is often concerned with just talking to "see if something can develop." In the typical communication model, student personnel tries to understand the other person or group and start a dialogue which aims for "understanding." This theory implies that content is not relevant. Values and personal commitments are too often missing: there is nothing to communicate about . . . we simply aim for an exchange of views.

When the confronting activist student meets the confronting student personnel staff members, an automatic tension point is established and an inevitable power struggle will follow with neither party growing. If confronting students are met with "understanding" student personnel "communicators," student personnel staff may find itself laughed at or ignored at best. A third, and possibly all too frequent occurence, is a student personnel staff which alternates between communication and confrontation approaches and ends up with respect and trust of neither students nor faculty and administration nor themselves.

Encounter is suggested as the basic model for student personnel and for higher education. Encounter as used in this paper is perhaps best typified by the methods of the master teacher in which both parties bring their points of view, their knowledge, their frame of reference, and their feelings to bear on issues of common concern. To better understand and better cope with the issues and problems involved, the teacher and the student jointly attempt to seek solutions, to broaden their own understanding, to change their perspectives or set, and to view problems from a different perspective. Encounter could be defined as "confrontation with communication" in that each party constantly confronts the other, but at the same time makes a constant attempt to "break his own set" and see the viewpoints of the other. Encounter concepts imply that the administrator or personnel worker would not hesitate to speak for what he feels is correct, but would never retreat into his viewpoint to the point that communication is denied. Neither party attempts to forcefully impose his viewpoints on the other. Further, constant self examination of values and awareness of possible changes in one's set and one's point of view is required.

The college administrator takes a value stand, but at the same time attempts to involve himself with the students in the process of seeking solutions to problems and concerns. He attempts to see other alternatives or viewpoints. Key in the concept of encounter is awareness of one's own "set" and willingness to examine the tenets on which that set of values, opinions, and ideas is held. It could be stated that the values, opinions, and ideas are basically predicated on emotional loadings underlying intellectual concepts. Thus, in any meaningful encounter, the student personnel worker must not only look at other views, but also understand his own fully. The personnel person who takes encounter as his model will sometimes find himself "stirring things up" and providing new points of tension between groups or individuals. On the other hand, encounter concepts will serve as the best vehicles for developing *real* communication and positive action.

Encounter Concepts for Student Development

Instead of traditional methods of confrontation and more recent communication efforts represented by the "student personnel point of view," student personnel workers must move increasingly to the use of encounter concepts. Administration must become more concerned with developmental aspects of college youth and not be willing to limit their interests to "keeping the lid on" or helping students plan programs to solve campus problems.

Student personnel is becoming increasingly involved in the question of the meaning of higher education to the individual person. The future role of student personnel should be that of maximizing the student's ability to learn and, at the same time, working with the college and university to enable it to change and meet the needs of today's youth in a changing world. The totality of these concepts imply that a completely new definition of student personnel is now necessary. *Student development specialist* is suggested as the title for a new professional who may need to be a combination of psychologist, administrator, human relations specialist, and educator.

Basic to the encounter and developmental framework is the need for a major change in administrative emphasis. Focus should be on the *process* of planning and the organization which goes into the development of an activity or resolution of an issue. As such, the task becomes one of helping the students learn to ask important questions instead of the traditional one of helping them find *the* right answer. In the past the tendency has been for student personnel to assume that they can solve all problems. As such, student personnel has maintained a problem orientation to students and has ignored the process of problem solving. It is suggested that this basic process, which can be more easily generalized to settings other than the activity in questions, is the "content" of the new profession of student development. Goodman (1964), Friedenberg (1959), and Holt (1964) all approach this issue when they imply that "learning how to learn" is far more important than the learning itself.

As an example, residence halls offer a vital and unique setting for implementation of encounter and developmental concepts. The typical residence hall program is too frequently centered on problems which students may face in the residence hall. An examination of the orientation for head residents or student counselors generally reveals an emphasis of *what* one should do in each anticipated problem situation. There is little emphasis on the process of problem solving in which the person encounters all aspects of himself and others. Residence halls should focus on the processes of human interaction in small and large groups. Viewed from this perspective, residence halls actually do become "laboratories" for student development. The old concept of university residence halls also mentioned laboratories, but the implication was that the laboratory was a production unit; somehow the residence hall was to produce the "well-rounded student." The encounter concept implies a process orientation which suggests that the residence hall may better aim its interests toward helping the student face the important questions of responsible group living.

Student development workers should become more involved with faculty consultation and in improving the educational climate of the institution. Korn's (1966) use of television at Stanford to help faculty view their teaching is but one example where student personnel can make a change in educational planning. The principle of faculty consultation is not to tell faculty members to refer their problem students to student personnel, but rather to help the faculty themselves work with the students. Faculty members are not necessarily open, socially skilled individuals. A program of consultation could provide much to help them learn to use the untapped talents they possess. It should be possible, for example, to interest faculty in students through calling the faculty in as "consultants" and requesting them to help student personnel study student development. Danskin at Kansas State (1966) asked faculty to join him in studying a small group of students over an extended period of time. In addition to new insights about students, he found that faculty can be introduced to how interesting students can really be and this experience tends to generalize to the classroom.

It should be possible to run an experimental sensitivity training course in which a student development counselor and a supervising master teacher from the education department meet weekly with returning practice teachers to discuss feelings and attitudes toward student teaching instead of the traditional methods emphasis. It should be possible to establish a "Friday Afternoon Controversy" on a weekly basis with a different faculty member each week interacting with the same group of students. A psychologist could be present to help interpret the students to the faculty and the faculty to the students. More traditional programs could include "T-groups," pre-marital groups, and vocational groups. In as many programs as possible, we would hope to influence not only the participating students, but also the faculty member participating with the student development counselor.

Traditional counseling concepts would not be dismissed within such a concept. Individual counseling, information programs, and group therapy all are relevant to the developmental concepts. These programs have, in the past, been too oriented to problem solving, rehabilitation, and remediation. Counselling must become more developmental in nature. Students should not be counselled to solve problems, but should be counselled in such a way that they learn the techniques involved in problem solving. Vocational counselling, then, should center on how a person makes occupation decisions. Therapy with the disturbed student should center on how the student relates with himself and others and how he faces key developmental tasks of human growth.

Financial aids should be focused on how to plan finances rather than on solving specific problems; placement should be centered on how a person obtains a job rather than on the end result of finding a job. Placement offices, in addition, might wish to emphasize a career approach more developmental in nature in which the student is helped to see his life as consisting of many jobs and locations instead of one final choice. The recent trend to alumni placement seems to be one example of this type of approach. Student health services might move from their medical repair model to a preventive and developmental health point of view. In short, encounter and development concepts seem to have relevance throughout the many areas of student personnel.

Summary

Today's university is typically established within a confrontation or problem-solving model. Relatively little attention has been given to the process by which problems are solved. It is suggested that the challenge which activist students present is in reality a basic questioning of the method of higher education. Unfortunately, these students have clouded over the basic issues as they too have used a confrontation, problem-solving approach.

As an alternative approach to confrontation, the "student personnel point of view" will often be found. Here we find student personnel workers attempting to communicate with students. Unfortunately, too often there is nothing to communicate about as the student personnel worker is simply interested in the communication process itself. This method of dealing with campus problems too often results in student personnel workers finding themselves irrelevant and ignored.

It is suggested that a deeper concept of *encounter* be considered as an alternative approach. Encounter, the process of "confrontation with communication," implies that the process of solving problems may be as important or more important than the solution achieved. Student personnel workers may be better defined as student development faculty who are concerned with bringing more process and encounter into the total university community.

References

Danskin, David, Personal Communication, 1966.

Friedenberg, Edgar Z. *The Vanishing Adolescent.* Boston: Beacon Press, 1959.

Goodman, Paul, *Compulsory Mis-Education.* New York: Horizon Press, 1964.

Holt, John C. *How Children Fail.* New York: Pitman, 1964.

Korn, Harold A. "Counseling and Teaching: An Integrated View." *The Journal of College Student Personnel 7*: 137–140.

Student Personnel Work: An Emerging Model

Terry O'Banion, Alice Thurston, and James Gulden

"If we don't change our direction, we are likely to end up whre we are heading."
— Chinese Proverb

The junior college is at a critical crossroads in its history. Can it make meaningful its commitment to the inner city? Can it respond to the manpower needs of business and industry? Can it participate in higher education as a respected partner with the university? Can it rehabilitate where so many others have failed? And, in all these valiant efforts, can the junior college provide the climate and the encouragement for individual students to feel more keenly, experience more deeply, live more fully—to encounter a fuller range oftheir human potential? Can the junior college be many things to many people?

The junior college—claiming to be dynamic, innovative, and responsive— has risked its future on an affirmative response to these questions. Yet, like other facets of higher education, the junior college has tended to cling to an outmoded educational model appropriate to a society coping with economic scarcity rather than abundance. Inthis model, which is paternalistic at best and autocratic at worst, the educational process has been *educare*, "to put into"; students have been the passive recipients of education as a product.

With the rapid changes in society, however, the old educational model is becoming obsolete. MartinTarcher says, "The times call for new social goals, new values and assumptions, new institutional arrangements that will allow us to complete our unfinished war against scarcity and move beyond production to the development of human potentialities."[1] Nevitt Sanford writes, "The time has come for us to control our zeal for imparting knowledge and skills, and to concentrate ou efforts on developing the individual student. . . . By education for individual development, I mean a program consciously undertaken to promote an identity based on such qualities as flexibility, creativity, openness to experience, and responsibility."[2]

Thus, the dimensions of a new model begin to emerge: education becomes *educere*, "to lead out of," so that education is not a pouring into, but

269

the means of providing a learning climate in which the greatest possible development of potential and fulfillment can take place.

In response to this emerging model, the junior college is struggling toward educational innovation and change. Its doors are opening wider yet—to the handicapped, the factory worker, the high school dropout, and the impoverished ghetto youth with serious learning disabilities. If the junior college is to be truly the people's college, it must provide its increasingly diverse student population with meaningful learning experiences. Lock-step scheduling, instruction primarily by the lecture method, ill-defined and poorly evaluated instructional objectives, and ineffective student personnel programs are being gradually abandoned in favor of new goals and new approaches.

Junior college educators are breaking down outmoded interdisciplinary boundaries, utilizing the new technology of the systems approach, retooling grading practices, and setting specific educational objectives toward which students can move at their own pace. The focus is shifting from instruction to learning. What is known about behavioral change is gradually being put to use.

Any hope of achieving even a modicum of success in fulfilling these goals depends, to a very great extent, on the student personnel program. Jane Matson points out, "Student personnel workers must assume appropriate responsibility in this monumental effort. This may require almost complete re-designing of the structure or framework and even the content or practices of student personnel work."[3]

In the last years of the decade of the 1960's, student personnel workers were examining with great seriousness the status of the student personnel profession. Student personnel work has developed for half a century as a series of services in reaction to forces within the college community rather than as an action program for shaping forces. The wave of student discontent and open disruptions has forced an examination of educational practices, and student personnel work, along with most other factions of higher education, has found itself woefully inadequate to respond to the needs and demands of students. Existing models of student personnel work—regulatory, servicing, and therapeutic—are inappropriate to needs of students in a changing society.

One of the historical models for the student personnel worker is that of *regulator* or *repressor*. The student personnel profession came into being largely because the president needed help in regulating student behavior. In the early 1900's, student personnel workers were given the titles of "monitor" and "warden."

In this model, the student personnel regulator works on colonial campuses as a mercenary of the president at war with students. He is the president's *no-man*. He tends to behave in ways that regulate, repress, reject, reproof, reprimand, rebuff, rebuke, reserve, reduce, and even remove human potential. In this system, all the negative aspects of *in loco parentis* are practiced as staff members attempt to maintain a strict supervision over the affairs of students.

This model has been more prevalent on residential campuses and, therefore, on four-year college and university campuses; but junior colleges have been much too eager to copy the style. Perhaps the continued existence ofthis model contributes to much of the student distress evident at such places as Berkeley, Harvard, and Columbia. Under such repression students have had to develop their own bill of rights in the historical tradition of all repressed minorities.

Perhaps the most prevalent model of the student personnel worker is that of *maintenance* or *service man*. In this model, the student personnel program is a series of services scattered around the campus: financial aid, registration, admissions, student activities, academic advising, etc. The student personnel worker provides services for students who seek them. In 1964 the Carnegie Corporation contributed $100,000 to the American Association of Junior Colleges for an evaluation of this maintenance model. Thirty-six different student personnel functions or services were isolated for study; the findings were disillusioning to those who had committed themselves to student personnel programs in junior colleges. T.R. McConnell, chairman of the national advisory committee for the study, stated, "The conclusion of these studies may be put bluntly: when measured against criteria of scope and effectiveness, student personnel programs in community junior colleges are woefully inadequate."[4]

A third model of the student personnel worker is that of *therapist*. In this model the student personnel worker behaves as if he were a psychotherapist or a counseling psychologist. His contribution to the educational program is to provide therapy for a few selected students who have intense personal problems. He is often disdainful of other student personnel functions such as academic advising and student activities.

In this model counselors become isolated in their counseling cubicles which have become identified in the perceptions of students as places to go only when you have serious problems. If the dean of students is also a practitioner of "early Rogers," he becomes confused regarding his responsibility for educational leadership. The program is likely to remain safely constricted in the therapeutic confines of the counseling center.

In recent years several states have endeavored to develop statements of models as guidelines for junior college student personnel programs. Perhaps the most thorough state report has been that of California, entitled *Guidelines for Student Personnel Services in the Junior College.*[5] While the basic philosophy expressed in the California guidelines represents an emerging model of student personnel work, the functions, or implementation of philosophy, are those of the Carnegie study and, therefore, reflect the model of service. Other state studies in New York, North Carolina, and Maryland also reflect an orientation that perceives student personnel work as a series of services designed to meet student needs. Out of the Maryland guidelines, however, came a statement that has significance: "Many of the old, cherished ideas that guided student personnel workers are being questioned, remodeled, or cast aside as no longer 'relevant' to this day."[6] The Maryland guidelines begin tentatively to identify some of the dimensions of the new model needed for student personnel workers.

An Emerging Model

As the student personnel profession enters the decade of the 70's there is a clear call for a new model for the profession—a new model for the role of the student personnel worker. The call is for a new kind of person, a person who is hardheaded enough to survive the battles that rage in academe and yet a person, warmhearted and deeply committed to the full development of human potential.

As old concepts of human nature and of education are uprooted, it is a precarious venture to attempt to articulate new directions when they are so dimly perceived. Educational Don Quixotes are likely to fabricate models out of their own dreams and frustrations. The authors openly admit that the fragments of an emerging model presented here represent their own hopes of what might be, but hopes that are buttressed by a growing number of educators, student personnel workers, instructor, and administrators who believe in and who have begun to provide opportunities for the full development of human potential. *The emerging model described, then, is only a tentative statement. It needs testing out in practice. It needs rounding out with the concepts of others.*

While student development has historically been defined as development of the whole student, educational practice has focused with few exceptions on development of intellectual capacities and skills that have been narrowly defined. At the present time, however, a growing number of educators, supported by the humanistic psychologists and a developing humanistic ethic, are beginning to define "student development" in some creative and exciting ways. Fundamental to the new definition is a belief that man is a growing organism, capable of moving toward self-fulfillment and responsible social development, and whose potential for both has been only partially realized.

In the new model of student development there are implications of climate and outcome. A student development point of view is a behavioral orientation in which educators attempt to create a climate of learning in which students have:

1. Freedom to choose their own directions for learning
2. Responsibility for those choices
3. Interpersonal interaction with the learning facilitator that includes:
   a. Challenge, encounter, stimulation, confrontation, excitement
   b. Warmth, caring, understanding, acceptance, support
   c. Appreciation of individual difference.

Through such a facilitative atmosphere the outcomes of student development would be increased in:

1. Intellectual understanding
2. Skill competencies
3. Socially responsible behavior
4. Flexibility and creativity
5. Awareness of self and others
6. Acceptance of self and others
7. Courage to explore and experiment
8. Openness to experience
9. Efficient and effective ability to learn
10. Ability to respond positively to change
11. A useful value system
12. A satisfying life style.

This student development model, only briefly described, requires a new kind of person for its implementation. Terms that have in the recent past attempted to describe the student personnel worker in this emerging model are "the counselor as catalyst" and "the counselor as change agent." More recently, model builders have talked about the student personel worker as student development specialist.

A term that may reflect more accurately some of the special dimensions of the emerging model is that of the human development facilitator. "Facilitate" is an encountering verb which means to free, to make way for, to open the door to. The human development facilitator does not limit his encounter to students; rather he is interested in facilitating the development of all groups in the educational community (faculty, secretaries, administrators, custodians and other service workers, and board members). In the community college his concern extends into the community.

One way of describing the model that needs to be developed is to present an idealized prototype of the student personnel worker as a person. While it is helpful to have a model as a goal, it is to be understood that individuals exist in a process of becoming in whichthey reflect only certain degrees of attainment of these characteristics. The kind of person who isneeded has been described by Maslow as self-actualizing, by Horney as self-realizing, by Privette as transcendent-functioning, and by Rogers as fully-functioning. Other humanistic psychologists such as Combs, Jourard, Perls, Moustakas, and Landsman have described such healthy personalities as open to experience, democratic, accepting, understanding, caring, supporting, approving, loving, nonjudgmental.

They tend to agree with the artist in Tennessee Williams' play *Night of the Iguana* who said, "Nothing human is disguiting." They tolerate ambiguity; their decisions come from within rather than from without; they have a zest for life, for experiencing, for touching, tasting, feeling, knowing. They risk involvement; they reach out for experiences; they are not afraid to encounter others or themselves. They believe that man is basically good and, given the right conditions, will move in positive directions. They believe that every student is a gifted person, that every student has untapped potentialities, that every human being can live a much fuller life than he is currently experiencing. They are not only intersted in students, in helping those who are unhealthy to become more healthy, and in helping those who are already healthy to achieve yet even greater health. They understand the secret the fox told the Little Prince: "It is only with the heart that one can see rightly; what is essential is invisible to the eye."

The model student personnel worker, however, must not only be committed to positive human development; he must also possess the skills and the expertise that will enable him to implement programs for the realization of human potential. He must be able to communicate with other administrators in the college, and he must be able to keep the functions and services under his responsibility operating efficiently. In the new model, present services and functions would not be disregarded. These are needed because they serve students in important ways. The emphasis however, would change. *The program would be focused on positive changes in student behavior rather than on efficient functioning of services.*

In order to develop and implement a humanistic program in his institution, the student personnel worker must understand the social system in which all members of the academic community live and work as well as the ecological relationships of those members in the academic setting. He must understand the nature and complexity of bureaucracy and how it affects student development. He must understand and appreciate the diversity of student subcul-

tures, and learn to use those subcultures in the development of an institutional climate that allows for full growth and development in the collegiate
community. He must learn to conduct relevant research on student behavior
to evaluate the success of the student personnel program and to communicate
to his colleagues what the program is accomplishing.

To provide focus for the program, the chief student personnel administrator would ask, "What kinds of programs can we build that will allow greater
numbers of students to explore the dimensions and potentialities of their
humanity?" Or he might ask, "Can we create an environment for the student
in which he can search out his identity, grapple with the problems of
commitment, and become attracted to and involved with the health-engen-
dering aspects of life?"

Within what kind of an organizational structure can student personnel
workers develop a program which facilitates the release of human potential?
How do they function to implement philosophy and goals?

The most appropriate organizational structure would be decentralized,
with responsibility and authority shared through the college. A climate of
"participative administration," set by the president, should permeate the
institution. Gibb describes this concept as follows:

It seems to me that joint, interdependent, and shared planning is the
central concept of the kind of participative, consultative leadership that we
are considering. . . . Our assumption is that the blocks to innovation and
creativity are fear, poor communication, imposition of motivations, and the
dependency-rebellion syndrome of forces. People are innovative and creative.
The administration of innovation involves freeing the creativity that is
always present. The administrative problem of innovation is to remove fear
and increase trust, to remove coercive, persuasional, and manipulative efforts
to pump motivation, and to remove the tight controls on behavior that
tend to channel creative efforts into circumvention, counterstrategy, and
organizational survival rather than into innovative and creative problem
solving.[7]

A chief student personnel administrator deeply committed to the facilitation of human development will offer his own staff participative leadership.
However, if he attempts to create a democratic staff island amid a network of
rigid bureaucratic controls, he does so at considerable psychic cost, both to
himself and to his staff, and with a corresponding loss of creativity. The
autocratic president is the antithesis of the democratic dean of students—
when they attempt to work in the same institution, neither they nor the
institution can function effectively. The problem is just as acute when an
autocratic dean of students is employed or inherited by a democratic president. Unfortunately, many "new model" presidents have become disillu-

sioned with student personnel workbecause they have known only "old model" deans of students.

In line with the concept of "participative administration," the dean of students should function as a full member of the administrative team. President Samuel Braden of Illinois State University calls his administrative team "the president's see." As a member of this group, the chief student personnel administrator functions not only as a student personnel dean, but as an officialof the college working with other administrative officers, and hopefully with representatives both of faculty and students, to solve problems confronting the entire college.

The administrative officers responsible for student personnel services and for instruction should be on the same administrative level, and should work closely together. Joseph Cosand says:

As president of a comprehensive junior college, I believe strongly that the student personnel program on the campus must be given the same status as the instructional program. For that reason, I feel that the administrative structure should have a dean of student personnel services and a dean of instruction at the same level in the organizational chart, both of whom would be responsible to the president of the college.[8]

The chief administrator of a student personnel program works democratically with his staff to develop plans which will assist in implementing the goals of the college. As an administrator, he delegates and defines staff responsibilities, and coordinates the work of the staff, helping each staff member to see how his work relates to the total institution. He conducts planned, in-service programs for professional and personal development. The larger his staff, the greater the proportion of his time is spent in integration, communication, and coordination, rather than in performing direct services to students. He is necessarily both task-oriented and people-oriented.

Most student personnel programs are clustered in a single building, often next to the central administration offices or in the student union. Thus, student personnel staff members often become isolated from the rest of the college. There is little interaction with the faculty. Students are seen only in the safety and security of the counselor's office. To obviate the problems of such isolation, several recent writers have suggested the deployment of student personnel workers to divisions. Blocker and Richardson[9] advocate that counselors be assigned to instructional divisions and report directly to the chairman of the division to which they are assigned. Because of the conflict of multipurposes, divided loyalties, and professional backgrounds, this proposal may not work out in practice. Harvey[10] proposes that counselors be assigned to instructional divisions, but that they continue to report to the dean of students.

If the human development facilitator is to be effective in accomplishing his purposes, he must work closely with faculty and students *where they are.* Student personnel staff members can extend the impact of the student personnel program by serving as liaison persons with instructional divisions in terms of their interests or backgrounds. They should attend divisional meetings, participate in projects and workshops, and assume responsibility for informing the other student personnel staff members regarding developments within the divisions. The student personnel worker should become acquainted with each faculty member in his area to insure continuing communication and liaison with the student personnel program. It would strengthen relationships if the student personnel worker were assigned to advise students enrolled in the division, and had responsibility for acting as a resource for the faculty advisors of the division. He should also encourage the development of student activities that reflect the special interests of students in the division.

When the student personnel program is extended into each instructional unit of the college, and when such activities are carefully coordinated by an effective student personnel administrator, students and faculty alike become more aware of the significant impact that student personnel can have on their development. When the president of the college coordinates the student personnel program with other programs in the college, when he provides equal status for student personnel workers by appointing them to faculty committees and granting them faculty rank and tenure where these exist, he sets the tone for a college climate in which lines of demarcation can disappear and teams of devoted and excited professionals can work closely together with and for students.

Role and Function

Student personnel staff members should offer student development courses not usually available in instructional programs. Such a course is not a psychology course in which the knowledge of facts and principles concerning psychology form the subject matter. It is not a traditional orientation course in which the student is introduced to the rules and regulations of the college and given "tips" on how to study. Nor is it an introduction to vocational development in which the student sifts through occupational information and writes a paper on a career. This is not the old adjustment course of the 1950's designed to help the student make a satisfactory adjustment to college and society.

Such a course is a course in introspection: the experience of the student is the subject matter. The student is provided with an opportunity to examine his values, attitudes, beliefs, and abilities, and an opportunity to examine how these and other factors affect the quality of his relationships with others. In addition, the student would examine the social milieu—the challenges and problems of society—as it relates to his development. Finally, such a course would provide each student with an opportunity to broaden and deepen a developing philosophy of life. Such a course would be taught in basic encounter groups by well-prepared human development facilitators. In many cases, sensitive instructors can work with student personnel staff to develop and teach such a course.

The student personnel worker should also move directly into contact with the community beyond the campus if his impact is going to be significant. He must arrange community laboratory experiences if he is to encourage the development of a growing student social consciousness. Working with faculty members in appropriate divisions, the student personnel worker should seek opportunities for students to participate in recreational and educational programs for the socio-economically disadvantaged, tutor the undereducated, campaign in elections, contribute time to community beautification pro-grams, and explore and question the structure of community government.

Getting Students Involved

Another role of the new student personnel worker is to participate actively in getting students involved in the life of the college. New alternatives for student involvement should be explored: special task forces, ad hoc groups, town meetings. If the traditional committee system is to be used, then students should be on all the committees of the college. This should extend far beyond the old worn-out student government association in which students play sandbox government and spend their time quarreling over student activity fee allocations.

Students should be on the curriculum committee of the college; they should be on the administrative council that makes all major decisions; they should have representation on the board of trustees; they should be constantly involved in teacher evaluation; they should have responsibility for helping to relate the college to the community; and they should participate in the planning of new buildings. Students will also need educating in "academic and bureaucratic dynamics" so they can function effectively as contributing members of committees. Student personnel workers in cooperation with interested faculty members can provide these experiences for students.

The student personnel worker should also consider the means of getting students involved in the education of other students. In this way, he can discover new and creative learning experiences for students, and then relate them to faculty and student personnel staff. Students with special skills should be selected to assist in courses requiring their expertise. Work-study programs should be designed to utilize students in instruction, curriculum development, and student services rather than as menials.

Guarding Against Oppressive Regulations

Another important role for the student personnel worker in the junior college is to be a guardian against the oppressive regulations that tend to develop without question in most institutions. Junior colleges notoriously and often unconsciously borrow repressive rules and regulations from the catalogs of four-year colleges and universities. It is the role of the student personnel worker to question at every turn the traditional rules and regulations. Hopefully he can convince the college that every rule and regulation needs to be examined carefully for its basic rationale and its applicability to the community college and the community college student.

The junior college needs to examine carefully whether or not it needs academic calendars, probation and suspension regulations, F grades, social probation, dress codes, regulations regarding work load, and final examination periods. These traditional educational trappings may hinder the development of human potential more than they help. The student personnel worker must help ferret out the sometimes repressive philosophy that has become associated with such rules and regulations as he assists in the development of a total institutional climate conducive to the development of human potential. He must function with a sound rationale, however, so as not to appear a standard-wrecker to faculty members.

Involving the Instructors

If instructors are freed by the new technology from the role of transmitting knowledge to a role of assisting students in integrating and applying knowledge, the student personnel worker will relate to instructors in important ways. With his background of preparation in psychology, human relations, and learning theory, the student personnel worker can assist instructors in a team effort to help students examine the personal meaning their education has for them. Student personnel workers can conduct group discussions and organize experiences for students to apply what they have learned. They can also help students evaluate their progress and make decisions about further learning.

Cooperative work-study programs should be planned so that the students' work for pay is also a planned learning experience. Student activities programs should be developed to provide leisure-time learning experiences as a basis for later leisure activity. The focus of the financial aids office should be to supply students' financial needs in ways which contribute to their personal and social development. High priority should be given to health counseling and to preventive and compensatory health programs for students with special health problems.

These are only a few of the dimensions of an emerging role for the junior college student personnel worker. A number of years will be required for the role to be developed, tested, and finally evaluated for effectiveness. In the meantime, student personnel workers will continue to develop particular aspects of this role for practice on their own campuses.

An "Open Door" to Student Personnel Work

New models of student personnel work should have good opportunities for imaginative development in the junior college. The climate there for acceptance of student personnel work is quite positive. In no other post-high school educational institution is student personnel work considered as important as in the junior college, where it is recognized and proclaimed as a function that is equal to instruction, curriculum, library services, and the management of the college. Fordyce has said:

I am convinced that student personnel work can and must come to full fruition in the comprehensive junior college. No other educational institution can afford the broad expanse of educational opportunities that provide a setting in which students' choices can be so fully implemented. By the same token, student have generally reached a level of maturity in a time of life when most important decisions can and must be made. Opportunities and necessities then combine to make the junior college the ideal setting for the most effective student personnel programs.[11]

Noting one of the important roles of the student personnel program in the junior college, Medsker has said, "One can predict that if a junior college does not properly distribute students among programs, the whole idea of the junior college will fail and a new structure for education beyond the high school will emerge."[12] The executive director of the American Association of Junior Colleges has described the role of student personnel work as "a senior partner in the junior college."[13]

The basic rationale that supports the importance of student personnel work in the junior college is that the "student personnel point of view" and the "junior college point of view" are one and the same. From *The Student Personnel Point of View*, first published by the American Council on Education in 1937, the following terms are indicative of student personnel philosophy: students as individuals, optimum development of the individual, preservation of basic freedoms, renewed faith in an extensive use of democraticmethods, development of mature citizens. "The individual's full and balanced development involves the acquisition of a pattern of knowledge, skills, and attitudes consistent with his abilities, aptitudes, and interests."

A Shared Philosophy

Any one of these descriptions could have come from the list of purposes and objectives of almost any junior college. From the purposes of one junior college comes the following declaration that is repeated many times in junior college catalogs throughout the nation:

The educational offerings of Santa Fe Junior College are based upon the belief that development of the individual for a useful and productive life in a democratic society is the chief obligation of the public educational system. This philosophy implies a deep and abiding faith in the worth and dignity of the individual as the most important component of a democracy. This faith and this recognition of need for responsibility suggests that the college must find appropriate programs and effective educational techniques to help each student discover his abilities and interests and develop them to the fullest extent, consonant with his own goals and capabilities and the needs of the society.[14]

The philosophy that is common to the junior college and to student personnel work is based on a foundation of democratic, humanitarian principles. It is the upward extension of the American ideal of equal opportunity. Without doubt, student personnel work and the junior college rank among the most important of American educational inventions. As such, they reflect the basic pattern of American democracy with its concern for individual opportunity.

An important historical parallel also exists between the two movements. According to some, the junior college movement began with the founding of the first public junior college in Joliet, Illinois, in 1902. Nunn, in the first complete history of student personnel work in American higher education, suggests that student personnel work as an organized movement began about 1900.[15] Regardless of the exact date or origin, both movements had their major beginnings in the early twentieth century, and both reached a mutually high point of recognition and development in the present decade. The junior college has now become the community college. The student personnel point of view has now become the student development point of view. There exists today a claim of one upon the other—a bond of mutual purpose. Both movements are young, both have critics, and both have high aspirations for meeting and fulfilling the needs of students.

Just because philosophical and historical congruence between student personnel work and the junior college exist does not necessarily mean that creative programs will flourish. At the present time junior college student personnel work is in a state of confusion. If junior college student personnel workers do not develop a clear sense of direction, they are likely, as the Chinese proverb warns, to end up where they are heading. It is hoped that the emerging model presented here will provide some sense of direction for those who are committed to the fuller development of human potential.

References

1. Tarcher, Martin. "Leadership: Organization and Structure" *In Search of Leaders*. (ed.) Smith, G. K. Washington, D.C.: American Association of Higher Education, 1967.
2. Sanford, Nevitt. *Where Colleges Fail*. San Francisco: Jossey-Bass Co., 1967.
3. Matson, Jane E. "Trends in Junior College Student Personnel Work." *GT-70 Student Personnel Workshop*. (ed.) Harvey, James. William Rainey Harper College, 1968.
4. McConnell, T. R. "Foreward." *Junior College Student Personnel Programs: Appraisal and Development: A Report to Carnegie Corporation*, November 1965.
5. Matson, Jane E. *Guidelines for Student Personnel Services in the Junior College*. California State Department of Education, Sacramento, 1967.
6. Ravekes, John E. *Functions of Student Personnel Programs in Maryland Community Colleges*. Maryland Association of Junior Colleges, April 1969.
7. Gibb, Jack R. "Dynamics of Leadership" *In Search of Leaders*. (ed.) Smith, G. K. Washington, D.C.: American Association of Higher Education, 1967.
8. Cosand, Joseph P. Quoted in O'Banion, Terry. "Student Personnel Work: A Senior Partner in the Junior College." May 1966, mimeographed.
9. Blocker, Clyde E., and Richardson, Richard C., Jr. "Teaching and Guidance Go Together." *Junior College Journal*. 39:3, November 1968.
10. Harvey, James. "The Counseling Approach at Harpers College," *Junior College Journal*. 38:2, October 967.
11. Fordyce, Joseph W. Quoted in O'Banion, Terry. "Student Personnel Work: A Senior Partner in the Junior College." May 1966, mimeographed.
12. Medsker, Leland L. "The Crucial Role of Student Personnel Services in the

Junior College." Paper presented at the American Personnel and Guidance Association Convention, Denver, Colorado, March 28, 1961.

13. Gleazer, Edmund J., Jr. "Student Personnel Work: A Senior Partner in the Junior College." Paper presented at the First Annual Junior College Student Personnel Workshop. Dallas, Texas, April 1967.

14. Sante Fe Junior college. *Bulletin of Santa Fe Junior College.* Gainesville, Florida, Catalog Issue 1966–67.

15. Nunn, Norman. *Student Personnel Work in American Higher Education.* Unpublished dissertation, Florida State University, August 1964.

Toward a Radicalization of Student Personnel

James C. Hurst and Allen E. Ivey

The university and society are today facing radical attempts to seek either the abolishment of institutions or a complete change of the philosophical basis on which these institutions have been founded. McLuhan (1964) and Skinner (1953) clearly foretell the possibilities of radical changes in society by the year 2000. Futuristics, the science of futures, is becoming an essential adjunct to the planning process for the university and society in general.

In contrast to this dynamic situation which demands complete renewal and reconceptualization, student personnel, once again, appears to be *responding* to the crisis. The traditional role of student personnel has been reactive rather than proactive. Even some of the current student personnel efforts which emphasize prevention in place of remediation are still responding to crisis situations with little thought for determining what should or can be existent in the university community.

If student personnel is to be fully relevant to the evolving mission of the university, it must devote more of its energies toward planning for the future. Such planning may eventually call for a complete radicalization of the foundations on which student personnel has rested for the past 50 years. For example, it is suggested that student personnel should devote more of its energies to diagnosis of the *nature* of crisis, which is in itself only a symptom of deeper student discontent. Diagnosis of student discontent, in turn, must be followed by imaginative programs designed to make students more fully mature participants in the educational process.

This article is an attempt to diagnose basic issues of concern to students and to suggest new alternative programs for the future of student personnel based on the needs suggested by this diagnosis. If the presented diagnosis is valid, it would appear that a viable future for student personnel may require a complete radicalization of our present point of view.

The Diagnosis of Students' Major Concerns

The report of the Commission on Current and Developing Issues of COSPA (Straub & Vermilye, 1968) identified six prime issues relating to

284

students which are relevant to the university's functioning. Important among these issues was the suggestion that the university reconsider its mission to include the three functions of social critic, implementer of social change, and the provision of *associates* for students as they develop critical facilities through the process of disciplined reflection. The remaining issues centered on implementation of this primary concern: the question of how the university can effect this aim through policy action.

It is our contention that careful diagnosis of student concerns is essential before action is prescribed. Students have forced issues on university faculties and administrations for a variety of reasons, but several themes are being voiced consistently by activist students throughout the country. First among these is the student's feeling that he is insignificant in the scheme of things; that he feels like an object rather than a person. The university communicates this message of insignificance to students implicitly through large classes, restricted contact with faculty and administration, lockstep degree programs, and rigid policies that fail to take into account the uniqueness of the individual. An evergrowing group of students has now become sophisticated enough to recognize these implicit messages and are in the process of making them explicit through actively seeking to modify the very practices and policies responsible for communicating insignificance and impersonality.

The second theme is a result of the first, for when the modifications are attempted, students find themselves *impotent!* Frustration is experienced with the institution's unwillingness to listen or, after listening, with the unwillingness to share responsibility for the governance of student life. Students have become sufficiently sophisticated to recognize their impotence for what it is and become even more dissatisfied with the university. Students are communicating their absolute unwillingness to remain in an impotent role and have set about finding ways to manipulate their environment, change their circumstances, and control their own destinies. They shout in ways that the institution cannot ignore, *"I am a man!"* The parallels between student unrest and the Black Power movement are indeed noteworthy.

A third theme is that students are unwilling to submit to an authority with an unimpressive record in nontechnical areas of human existence. Students suggest that they could play a teaching role in addition to a learning role in the university and in society in some technical and nontechnical areas if only they were allowed. Related to this theme is the perceived irrelevance of much of the educational process today. A perceived preoccupation with words when there is such a critical demand for deeds reduces respect for formal education. Students for the most part have looked in vain for action-oriented coursework dealing with the issues of civil rights, Vietnam, overpopulation, drugs, environmental pollution, poverty, and their roles in society.

The result of this upheaval in the educational establishment is reports such as that of the COSPA Commission. The identification of the relevant issues is, however, only a first step if student personnel services are to play a meaningful role in shaping the direction of higher education. Many of the revolutionary demands being made are such that a viable creative student personnel services organization is in the enviable position of being the best qualified and organized to help effect the desired modifications. If this role is to be assumed, however, immediate steps must be taken to modify present attitudes and practices and adapt and adopt procedures for filling it.

Directions for a Viable Future

If student personnel is to meet the demands of a complex and changing university scene, radical new approaches need to be considered. Following are some possible future directions for a new student personnel point of view—that of Human Development.

1. Student personnel workers will be most effective as colleagues of students sharing in a learning experience. At times, he will give students advice; at other times he will learn from students. Primarily, however, student personnel, in order to survive the wave of activism, must join hands and participate *with* students in reforming higher education. In a time when students ask for participation in determining the direction of the university, student personnel should not abdicate their own responsibility for educational reform.

2. Facilitators instead of controllers of counselors

The student personnel worker will become a facilitator or consultant to the college campus. He will be an expert in applied educational psychology and will teach students how to be helping agents (Carkhuff & Truax, 1965; Ivey, Miller, Morrill, Normington, & Haase, in press), how to run groups (Whalen, 1967), and how to be more effective "people." He will work with faculty to help them improve and change the structure of the curriculum and their teaching habits, (Korn, 1966). Eventually, he will teach faculty how to relate to students on more than an intellectual basis. Equally important, he will show faculty how to use affective learning to advance cognitive goals. We will work toward the day when a professor can run a personal growth group on a weekend with his class, then use the students the following week to help him restructure his course. In such activities as this the student personnel worker will constantly serve as adviser and consultant to administration, students, and faculty, helping them to maximize their own growth potential, (e.g., Brown & Gaynor, 1967; Garfield, 1966; Raths, Harmin, & Simon, 1966).

3. Training in student personnel

Training in student personnel will move increasingly to applied educational psychology and to experiential learning such as human interaction training and microteaching in human relations skills (Ivey, 1967). Students will be increasingly given the opportunity to participate in developing their own unique curricula through the identification of behavioral deficits and selection of behavior change goals. Student personnel trainers will begin to see their students as junior colleagues who can give as well as learn in this process of development.

4. Teaching human relations skills instead of administering

A major emphasis on teaching skills of effective human relations will be found within student personnel. Instead of counseling students, the student personnel worker will be teaching college students how to be helpers to each other, how to listen, and how to understand. Techniques such as teaching via television in human relations (Higgins, Ivey, & Uhlemann, 1969), T-groups (Berzon, Reisel, & Davis, 1968; Rogers, undated; Schutz, 1967), programmed texts (Berlin, 1965; Smith & Smith, 1966), and computers will be just some of the vehicles used by student personnel workers to teach students and faculty how to experience life more fully together. Some traditional therapists and counselors will still be needed, but the new emphasis on teaching people directly the skills of effective behavior will greatly reduce this need.

5. Recognition of physical activities as a province of student personnel

Relaxation training, Yoga, Zen meditation, psychoanalytic bodily exercises, and related techniques will take their place in student personnel as supplementary activities (Gunther, 1967; Jacobson, 1938; Kamiya, 1968; Lowen, 1958; Oetting, 1964). The importance of body-mind relationships is being recognized, and student personnel would help implement this recognition.

6. Systems analysis and cybernetics will be applied to the university setting in relation to the community

The concepts of systems analysis will demonstrate to the university the interrelationship of knowledge and the importance of all parts working together in harmony (Buckley, 1968; Cole & Oetting, 1968; Miles, 1965; Miller, 1965). Along with this trend will come awareness of the artificiality of boundaries between the university and the community and the nation. As such, people will move in and out of a university more frequently and easily. As degrees and grades will have been deemphasized, students and faculty alike will concentrate on developing new and improved skills and on eliminating behavioral and intellectual deficits. Competitiveness will for the most part disappear and be replaced by new models of cooperative behavior.

7. A new model for the university

Personnel workers will help the university to become completely restructured so that degrees will be deemphasized and perhaps eventually abolished. Instead the university will offer a set of development tasks which have been planned or specifically programmed to lead to specific behavioral skills (Oetting, 1967). A student in consultation decides what skills he wishes to obtain from the university and proceeds through programmed steps to achieve these skills through a contract with the university.

One important possible emphasis for all students will be on the structure of knowledge. Behavioralism, gestalt psychology, psychoanalysis, humanistic and existential psychology, and other theoretical models will be recognized by the field as just that—"models" of human experience. Similarly other fields will increasingly realize that model-building is a useful art, but that different models offer different pictures of "truth." A major goal of education in the future in sciences, social sciences, and humanities will be to help students to develop their own unique models. Distinction between academic fields will become increasingly blurred.

8. Student personnel and counseling as professions known to us now will disappear

Although the profession will be important in developing the procedures to implement these ideas, once the system is started it will be self-perpetuating, and a professor of chemistry or a student in English literature will also have sufficient skills (in concert with others, of course) to redesign and update the total educational system, thus finally helping us realize our true objective: the elimination of the field as it now exists. In its place will be an office of campus consultants for ongoing training and the continual modification of the evolved campus community in the direction of Human Development.

The best of student activists have a critical message for student personnel to hear. The time for insignificance, impotence, and docile submission to authority is past. The time for interaction as colleagues in teaching, training, planning, facilitating and radically modifying is here. If student personnel is to survive, its traditional reactive stance must be replaced with a proactive posture for Human Development of all people implemented through the university environment.

References

Berlin, J. I. *Management improvement program.* Atlanta, Ga.: Human Development Institute, 1965.

Berzon, B., Reisel, J., & Davis, D. P. *Peer: Planned experiences for effective relating, an audio tape program for self-directed small groups.* LaJolla, Calif.: Western Behavioral Sciences Institute, 1968.

Brown, G., & Gaynor, D. Athletic action as creativity. *Journal of Creative Behavior,* 1967, 11 (2), 155–162.

Buckley, W. *Modern systems research for the scientist: A sourcebook.* Chicago: Aldine, 1968.

Carkhuff, R. R., & Truax, C. B. Lay mental health counseling: The effects of lay group counseling. *Journal of Consulting Psychology,* 1965, 29, 426–431.

Cole, C. W., & Oetting, E. R. *Measures of stress and concept evaluation: The experimental modification of factor structure.* Technical Report No. 2, Colorado State University, Contract RD-2464-P, U.S. Department of Health, Education, and Welfare, January 1968.

Garfield, O. Human relations in the classroom. Paper presented at the Annual Conference of the American Personnel and Guidance Association, Washington, D.C., April 1966.

Gunther, B. *Sensory awakening and relaxation.* Big Sur, Calif.: Esalen Publications, 1967.

Higgins, W., Ivey, A. E., & Uhlemann, M. *Media therapy: Programming human relations skills.* Amherst: University of Massachusetts School of Education, 1969.

Ivey, A. E. Confrontation, communication, and encounter: A conceptual framework for student development. Unpublished manuscript, Colorado State University, 1967.

Ivey, A. E., Miller, C. D., Morrill, W. H., Normington, C. J., & Hasse, R. F. Micro-counseling and attending behavior: An approach to pre-practicum counselor training. *Journal of Counseling Psychology* (separate monograph), in press.

Jacobson, E. *Progressive relaxation.* Chicago: University of Chicago Press, 1938.

Kamiya, J. Conscious control of brain waves. *Psychology Today,* 1968, I, 57–60.

Korn, H. A. Counseling and teaching: An integrated view. *Journal of College Student Personnel,* 1966, 7, 137–140.

Lowen, A. *Physical dynamics of character structure.* New York: Grune & Stratton, 1958.

McLuhan, M. *Understanding media.* New York: McGraw Hill, 1964.

Miles, M. B. Planned change and organizational health: Figure and ground. In R. O. Carlson, A. Gallaher, Jr., M. B. Miles, R. J. Pellegrin, and E. M. Rogers (Eds.), *Change process in the public schools.* Eugene, Ore.: Center for the Advanced Study of Educational Administration, 1965. Pp. 11–34.

Miller, J. G. Living systems: Basic concepts. *Behavioral Science,* 1965, 10, 193–411.

Oetting, E. R. Hypnosis and concentration in study. *American Journal of Clinical Hypnosis,* 1964, 7, 148–151.

Oetting, E. R. A developmental definition of counseling psychology. *Journal of Counseling Psychology,* 1967, 14, 382–385.

Raths, L., Harmin, M., & Simon, S. M. *Values and teaching.* Columbus, Ohio: Charles E. Merrill, 1966.

Rogers, C. R. *The process of the basic encounter group.* LaJolla, Calif.: Western Behavioral Sciences Institute, undated.

Schutz, W. C. *Joy: Expanding human awareness.* New York: Grove Press, 1967.

Skinner, B. F. *Science and human behavior.* New York: Macmillan, 1953.

Smith, J. M., & Smith D.E.P. *Child management: A program for parents.* Ann Arbor: Ann Arbor Publishers, 1966.

Straub, J. S., & Vermilye, D. W. Current and developing issues in student life. *Journal of College Student Personnel,* 1968, 9, 363–370.

Whalen, C. K. *The effects of a model and instructions on group verbal behaviors.* Ann Arbor, Mich.: University Microfilms, 1967.

An Organizational Model for Student Development

Burns B. Crookston

As they view introspectively as well as retrospectively the turbulent, often traumatic past decade of dramatic, accelerating change, student personnel administrators must face up to the practical realities and consequences of such changes. Deans of students, deans of men and women, trained in the nuances and skills of applying in *loco parentis*, are now consequently, with its demise, looking for new ways and means to function effectively in a new ball game in which the rules appear to be made up as one goes along. Many are becoming intrigued, if not enamored with the rhetoric of student development. Discussions and writings extolling the virtues of a "new" developmental approach began as a small trickle early in the sixties. Now, there is widespread support for the idea. Draft statements articulating student developmental philosophy have been under preparation by COSPA and other student personnel associations.

This paper is directed toward the problem of building an organization to fulfill the goals of student development. While accepting student development as a theoretical concept aborning, certain assumptions concerning student development are discussed as applied to problems of organization. Arguments are presented that assert bureaucracy as a system of organization does not support the goals of student development. An organizational model for student development is presented together with operational suggestions.

Contrasts in Student Personnel and Student Development

An examination of assumptions around student development as a concept compared to the old student personnel point of view indicates some critical differences that warrant discussion. Although for approximately twenty years, culminating at the end of World War II, most authorities in the field

291

accepted Cowley's view that student personnel work consisted of all non-instructional activities in which the all around development of the student was of primary concern,[1] for the past two decades increasing support has developed for the view that it was erroneous to speak in terms of a dichotomy between student personnel work and instruction. Student personnel was to include not only those processes and functions that emphasize intellectual, social, emotional, cultural, and physical development of the individual, but also those which help build curricula, improve methods of instruction, and develop leadership programs. In sum, it was held student personnel work complemented as well as supplemented the instructional program in the total development of the individual.[2]

The principal differences between the student development idea and the old student personnel philosophy rest in (1) doing away with the term "student personnel," which has always been a descriptive anomaly, and (2) asserting that student development is not merely complementary or supplementary to the instructional program, *it is a central teaching function of the college.* Thus, while Lloyd-Jones wrote in the mid-fifties that the student personnel worker should no longer be viewed as a technician or specialist but as an educator collaborating with the teacher in the development of the student as a whole person in a democratic society,[3] the student developmental view makes no such educator-teacher distinction. According to student developmental theory the entire academic community is a learning environment in which teaching can take place, whether it produces academic credit or not; hence, the teacher in multiple development teaches in multiple situations, including the classroom.[4]

Student Personnel Orientation. As indicated by Figure 1, there are contrasting behavioral orientations descriptive of the student developmental and student personnel approaches. Under the student personnel approach staff behaviors tended to be passive. Staff would wait, usually in their offices, and

Figure 1

Contrasting Behavioral Orientations Descriptive of Student Personnel and Student Developmental Methodologies

Student Personnel	Student Developmental
Authoritarian	Egalitarian
Reactive	Proactive
Passive	Encountering
Remedial	Developmental
Corrective	Preventive
Controlling	Confrontive
Cooperative	Collaborative
Status oriented	Competency oriented

as a problem developed, react, applying counseling, mental health, or advising skills as appropriate to correct or ameliorate the situation.

In the general area of student activities, advising student personnel workers took a service approach, providing the means by which the students could do their thing. The style was to be helpful but only rarely to get involved. In the areas of student behavior and welfare, student personnel administrators exercised traditional in loco parentis control prerogatives. Rules and expectations were established. When students broke the rules staff reacted by punishing, imposing sanctions or conditions, or by utilizing paternalistic counseling or various rehabilitation efforts.

Staff generally stayed clear of issues, rarely took a stand and were timorous to test whether they had, or were entitled to faculty prerogatives of academic freedom. After all, as Shoben exhorted, student personnel workers had long since allowed themselves to be sucked into the administrative establishment.[5] The battle for academic freedom of administrators is only now in a state of preliminary skirmish.[6]

Student Developmental Orientation. In contrast, perhaps in response to the student revolt of the sixties, perhaps in recognition of the inadequacies of the old student personnel approach, there developed a movement at a few institutions, which has since spread rapidly, of moving toward a proactive, developmental, preventive, collaborative model. Counseling psychologists were discovering that seeing students on a one-to-one basis in their office was not the locus of the action. Adapting earlier community mental health approaches, they developed a new style of training and acting as mental health and student development educators.[7] They moved out onto the campus, into the residence halls, off campus, into the drug scene, actively seeking out, encountering, confronting or otherwise influencing students toward more effective solutions of their developmental and maturational problems.[8]

The move toward a developmental approach was accelerated by the demise of in loco parentis. Deans of men and women and others trained to function and apply their knowledge and skills under the protective umbrella of control over students with power to impose sanctions discovered that with the loss of control, upon which they built their relationships with students, they were unable to function with confidence and effectiveness. A number have not been able to make the adjustment of functioning from a status-based relationship with students to a relationship based on competency and collaboration. The result has been a methodological and staff skill retraining problem of first magnitude for many persons in the field.

Of course the inference should not be drawn here that the student personnel methods described above are all to be abandoned in the student developmental approach. Some—like the status behaviors and control functions—should be abandoned, while obviously remedial and mental health functions should continue. The difference is the latter become secondary in thrust to proaction, collaboration, and other student developmental technologies. Success in developmental approaches should result in less need for remediation.

Bureaucracy is Contradevelopmental

The dramatic changes during the past decade in the conceptual development of learning outside the classroom that culminated in the redefinition of student personnel work into the student developmental model have not been accompanied by organizational schemes to achieve the new goals set forth by modifying the system. Most writers and practitioners in the field still appear to be assuming that these changes can be accommodated to the existing bureaucratic organization of the institution.

Admittedly it may be a bit early. New concepts need a period of incubation and testing before any radical organizational modification. Having worked in no other system than a bureaucracy, most staff cannot conceive of another model that could possibly work. Consequently, the logic persists: all that is needed is to make modifications *within* existing bureaucratic line-staff structures. Is it not merely a question of being more effective and efficient, perhaps reorganizing here and there, perhaps setting up another department or subdivision, perhaps firing a department head or hiring new people? The trouble is these old organizational bromides no longer work.

Bennis and Slater identify four principal conditions that are making bureaucracy obsolete as an effective twentieth century organization: rapid and unexpected change, growth in size of organizations, increased diversity, and change in managerial behavior.[10] During the past twenty-five years many of the larger industries have exhibited a rather dramatic shift in philosophy. A growing awareness and sensitivity has developed: the old push button idea of man must be replaced with the concept that man has needs, aspirations, and problems that transcend the mechanistic view of him as part of a production machine. The self actualization formulations of Abraham Maslow and the concerns for human values expressed by behavioral scientists such as Douglas McGregor, Rensis Likert and Chris Argyris have profoundly influenced the thinking of the leaders of many industrial organizations. Consequently business and industry have moved much further toward humanizing their organizations than have the universities. In many leading companies concepts of power have shifted from the autocratic model based on coercion and threat to one based on rational processes and collaboration.

The old student personnel approach was nicely suited for the bureaucratic model that has been utilized by higher education for more than a century. The passive, reactive, correctional, control modes of student personnel staff behavior described in Figure 1 (above) were congruent with a bureaucratic reward system which emphasized conformity, control, stability, punctuality, predictability, evolutionary change, and behaviors that strengthen the institutionalization of the bureaucracy. Bureaucracy is based on a power and status hierarchy and fosters the notion of a career line to the top through promotions and good work. Thus, with the possible expection of counseling, a successful "career" in student personnel meant getting promoted to the top of the organization.

Bureaucracy generally demands a relatively high degree of conformity in its membership. Uniform standards are common and seen as desirable in the hierarchy. A junior staff member, for instance, is assigned a small office and a small desk. A bigger and better office, dictating equipment, travel budgets, and other emoluments of status come with promotions or with seniority in the system. Such preoccupation with acquiring status symbols works against goal achievement.

Rewards inherent to student developmental theory go counter to the rewards built into a bureaucratic system. Student development emphasizes creativity, flexibility and innovativeness, egalitarian rather than authoritarian concepts; it emphasizes planned, often rapid, if not revolutionary change rather than evolutionary. It builds its organization on the basis of symbiosis between individual and group need satisfaction and goal achievement and organizational goal attainment. It rewards taking reasoned positions, commitment, risk taking and action in support of legitimate issues in contrast to what appears generally to be an unwillingness in student personnel administrators to risk being on the "wrong" side of an issue in the face of administrative censure or other coercive power within the academic bureaucracy. This tendency is also illustrated by the high degree of faculty and student abstention from participation in political processes noted by Wise in his study of small colleges. [11]

The contemporary university is a striking example of how bureaucratization is preventing the flexibility and adaptibility needed to respond to needs of students and of society. Developing means and skills to bring about modifications in the system through planned, systematic change in higher education must head the priority list for the seventies.

The Student Developmental Model

What kind of system, then, should be invented that will be futuristic enough in concept and function to serve the interests of a changing institution within a rapidly shifting world scene? Let us begin with reiterating the behaviors we have already identified as descriptive of the developmental methodology: egalitarian, proactive, encountering, preventive, confrontive, collaborative, and competent. An organization that would foster and reward the expression of these qualities should include the following:

A. *Shared power and decision making.*

Evidence suggests that the most effective decisions are those made by those at, or close to the source of relevant data needed for the decision. Decision making authority for most operational matters should therefore be distributed to those closest to the data sources. Influence should stem from competence and knowledge rather than "the vagaries of personal whims or prerogatives of power."[12] In a modern organization no human being is so omniscient as to possess the knowledge and technical competence needed to make all decisions The selection of administrators and managers should be based on their human management capabilities rather than technical competence. In the old days the man chosen to run a railroad supposedly knew more about it than anyone else. Societal and technological change and organizational complexity are modifying this image to one who knows how to mobolize human resources and deal effectively with human problems of work, interaction, communication, decision making, and actualization.

Paradoxically studies have shown both the military and industry have developed more democratic ways of functioning than has the university. Bennis and Slater think it is because increasingly they have come to rely on science for the furtherance of their objectives, the reason being that *science methodology is based on and geared for change.*

The new professionals in and outside higher education are therefore more likely to identify initially with the adaptive values of science-democracy than with establishment bureaucracy. Witness the drive toward change manifested by many young college professionals before they yield to the bureaucratic status and power pressures of the establishment. The rise of faculty power during the past fifty years has been motivated in part at least toward achieving and protecing scientific-egalitarian values. There is evidence that individual support of organizational goals accompanies an opportunity to participate in their establishment.[14] Thus "we-ness" becomes the feeling of members who share in decisions and who consequently become identified with the organization, rather than the "they-ness" that expresses an attitude of non-identification with a centrally controlled organization where decisions flow from the top.

A developmental system should require full representation and participation in all major policy decisions, including selection of principal leaders. In a university this means that trustees would represent the public interest in decisions that are made but that they no longer should have the sole power to make such decisions. The academic community government, including representation and participation from all segments—administration, faculty, student and public—should make major policy decisions.

B. *Flexibility.*

To keep ahead, or at least abreast of the demands of accelerating change, the developmental organization must have built-in ability to adapt and adjust quickly and painlessly to meet changing situational demands or data modifications. For the moment a combination management by objectives-action research-systems model of functioning (action$_1$—data collection$_1$—analysis$_1$—new goal and priority setting$_2$—reorganizing for action$_2$—action$_2$—data collection$_2$, etc.) appears suited for such flexibility. This model requires continuous reorganization as needed to place people and resources in ways to carry out the objectives most effectively. It is in marked contrast to the bureaucratic model which assigns priorities in such a manner as to disturb the existing structures as little as possible.

Such a flexible, free-wheeling system admittedly has greatest appeal to competent professionals secure in their relationships and confident of being able to meet their personal needs in temporary systems. Individuals dependent on the security offered by an authoritarian bureaucracy would be threatened, if not immobilized by such shifting organizational and group boundaries, role expectations, and interpersonal relationships. They would need help in developing the necessary confidence and skills.

C. *On open communications system.*

It is essential that the developmental organization permit maximum communication between and among individuals and groups as well as with other elements of the academic community. An open system is possible only if a high degree of acceptance and trust exists among group members and among groups within the system.[15] Free flow of data leads to realistic goal setting and sound decision making based on adequate information. In contrast is the restricted communication resulting from fear and distrust often typified in bureaucratic organizations where the "news is managed," games are played and strategies employed. An open communications system is, of course, difficult, if not impossible to achieve in a bureaucracy where the power and control over communication channels emanate from the top.

A prominent feature of an open system is that it not only permits, but encourages reorganization of the system as needed to achieve most efficiently the goals set forth. With a high degree of confidence and trust, there is little need to build in any substantial organizational controls, rules and regulations that restrict individual behavior. Rules are made because group members do not trust others. If trust exists few rules are needed—which, of course, fosters the flexibility required (B above) to make a developmental system work.

D. *Term leadership.*

Student development should be based on the belief that there is no such thing as a career leadership position. No one should assume that once he achieves a position of top leadership that he is to remain on indefinitely. Enough competence within the organization should allow for rotation through leadership positions. Rotation may be greatly facilitated by the presence of organization development specialists within the system to train leaders, administrators and managers to function effectively during their tenure.[16]

Thus term leadership functions like the other elements of the organization that shift, modify, adapt to changing goals, needs and priorities. Leadership by this definition sheds the aura of status and power and becomes viewed as another set of competencies needed for effective organizational functioning and should be rewarded on that basis, not in terms of span of power or responsibility. Consequently, pay differential between a leader and members of a team should not be significant. Salary should be based on competence, professional preparation and merit. Professional people committed to egalitarian principles should have a built-in expectation that those who are inclined towards administrative and leadership positions through abilities, interests and capacities should expect to assume their share of responsibility for taking leadership where needed. There should be no assumption that higher pay is a necessary consequence.

In those positions embracing sensitive public relations areas there might be some justification for "hazard pay," but even here, since one expects to remain in the position only for a specified period before moving into another area, or back into an original area of interest, there should not be that much of an argument for "hazard pay."

E. *Individual and organizational symbiosis: the developmental contract**

An organization member is more likely to experience personal and professional growth if he shares in the development of organizational goals, and consequently becomes committed to their achievement, while at the same time is able to work toward the attainment of personal and professional goals that coalesce with those of the organization through the process of the

*The author is indebted to Alley C. Ivey for a number of ideas considered in this section.

developmental contract. Putting it another way, each individual within the organization shares in the development of a plan that will allow him to grow and develop as a person and professional while at the same time maximizing the use of his talents and energy in furthering the goals of the organization. Thus the relationship of the individual to the organization is symbiotic: living together in a mutually beneficial way—a "developmental contract" between the individual and his organization.

How does the developmental contract work? It can be summarized in the following steps:

1. *Organizational goal and priority setting.* On an annual basis (or more frequently if needed and manageable) the organization proceeds to reassess its goals and set action priorities on the basis of evaluation of current efforts and new data emanating from within and without the system. The procedure:

a. *Initial goal setting.* Each individual and each subgroup within the organization evaluates what has been accomplished, looks at intervening events and other data, including future projections, and sets objectives for a quarter or semester or an entire year. Immediate and long-term targets can be modified as needed. Within this context, for example, it will not be enough to plan and execute a student-faculty conference to modify student attitudes unless an evaluation is built in and the attitude change ascertained.

b. *Organizational goals and priorities decision.* The behavioral objectives of each individual and group within the organization are collated centrally by a "goals and priorities" team. The collated data are fed into a decision making process, the outcome of which is to establish goals and priorities for the next time period together with any modifications in the long range goals. The decision, which is determined through a process of involving the entire community, should take into account any externally imposed priorities or conditions, recent events, evaluation of current programs, and future projections.

c. *Organization modifications to best achieve goals and priorities.* Modifications in the organization are made as needed for most efficient and effective goal achievement. The elimination of some activities, addition of new tasks or projects along with the continuation of certain high priority functions with or without modification would be likely consequences.

d. *Individual goal reassessment.* Once the goal and priority setting exercise is completed and the decision on organizational modifications is made then each individual reassesses his own goals in the light of these modifications and puts forth a proposition that would best achieve his own objectives as well as best utilize his talents to help meet the goals and priorities of the organization.

e. *Negotiation with individuals.* Once the entire picture can be presented according to individual and organizational goals, an attempt is made to match the total institutional expectations with the objectives of each individual. Appropriate negotiations at several levels make as congruent as possible individual behavioral objectives with organizational goals and expectations. Upon completion of negotiations there is a written develolpmental "contract" articulated between each staff member and his unit head and with each head and his organizational head according to each person's goals, how they are related to the organizational goals, how they are to be accomplished and within what time frame, and how they are to be evaluated and measured as products. This contract is used as a measure for merit salary increases and a basis for organizational goal and priority modifications during the next period of developmental contract negotiations.

2. *Organizing for the task.* A hallmark of a developmental organization is its flexibility and adaptability. Unlike the bureaucracy which adapts goals and priorities to its existing structure with as little discomforture to the system as possible, the developmental organization modifies its organization as needed to best achieve the goals and priorities. Putting it simply, in the developmental organization you put the people and the resources where the priorities are. This means the likely utilization of work teams, task forces, and other common goals and interest groups that are constructed to do a job, evaluate it, dissolve, or reconstitute in modified form depending on the settling of new goals and priorities. Leadership focuses on coordination and management of the human resources and providing communication linkage within and without the system.

3. *Allocation of resources.* These are allocated centrally or by the goals and priorities group in accordance with developmental contracts agreed upon. No individual or subunit can assume that the receipt of a fund allocation means automatically receipt of a like or increased amount for the next period of negotiation. In this way vested interests over control of funds cannot be established, nor "squatters's rights" on equipment or facilities obtained, but must be based on priorities on a continuous basis.

How would it work? One possibility is to start with a "seed money" approach. Each individual is given an allocation to spend as he sees fit, the sole stipulation being that he must make an accounting for the manner in which all his funds are spent. The individual may wish to pool his resources with another person to buy equipment or to develop a special project. Under such circumstances travel is likely to become of lesser importance, particularly if travel has been viewed as a status symbol. As master of their own funds staff might well reorder their priorities and use the money in other ways.

It is important that resources be allocated in accordance with goals and priorities. It makes no sense to continue to fund or maintain programs that have little or no value and are not evaluated as significantly contributing to the overall goals of the organization. To do so is to fall into the bureaucratic trap of justifying work to keep people on the payroll.

In summary, the developmental contract idea has the singular advantage of systematically establishing for each individual, as well as the total organization symbiotic objectives for a specific time period. There is a built in system for a regularly evaluating and rewarding performance on the basis of merit and not on the basis of bureaucratic criteria.

References

1. Crowley, William H. "The Nature of Student Personnel Work," *Educational Record* (April 1936), pp. 3–31.
2. For a review of the early literature on philosophical development see Blaesser, Willard W. and Crookston, Burns B. Student Personnel Work—College and University. *Encyclopedia of Educational Research*, Third Edition, 1960, pp. 1414–1427.
3. Lloyd-Jones, Esther. Changing Concepts of Student Personnel Work. In Esther Lloyd-Jones and Margaret R. Smith (eds) *Student Personnel Work as Deeper Teaching*. New York: Harper & Bros., 1954.
4. Crookston, Burns B. "A Developmental View of Academic Advising as Teaching." *Journal of College Student Personnel* 13:1 (January, 1972), pp. 12–17.
5. Shoben, Edward Joseph, Jr. "The New Student: Implications for Personnel Work." CAPS CAPSULE 2:1 (Fall 1968), pp. 1–7.
6. For example, see statement of desirable conditions and standards for maximum effectiveness of the college administrator, adopted by NASPA Executive Council, *NASPA Journal* 9:1 (July 1971), pp. 3–5.
7. Oetting, E. R. "A Developmental Definition of Counseling Psychology." *Journal of Counseling Psychology* 14, (1967), pp. 382–385.
8. For a discussion of the concept see Ivey, Allen E. and Morrill, Weston M. "Confrontation, Communication, and Encounter: A Conceptual Framework for Student Development." *NASPA Journal* 7:4 (April 1970), pp. 226–243. For application see Crookston, Burns B. "Coping with Campus Disruption." *Student Development Staff Papers* 1–2, Colorado State University, 1969. For background theory see Morrill, Weston, Ivey, Allen E. and Oetting, E. R. The College Counseling Center—A Center for Student Development. In Heston and Frick, *Counseling for the Liberal Arts College*. Antioch, Ohio: Antioch Press, 1968, pp. 141–157.
9. Bennis, Warren. "Organic Populism." *Psychology Today* (February 1970), p. 48.
10. Bennis, Warren and Slater, Philip E. *The Temporary Society*. New York: Harper and Row, 1968.

11. Wise, Max W. *The Politics of the Private College*. New Haven, Conn.: The Hazen Foundation, 1968.
12. Bennis and Slater, *op. cit.*
13. *Ibid.*, p. 6.
14. See the early studies on human motivation by Allport, F. H., *Social Psychology*. Boston: Houghton Mifflin. 1924. Also see Gordon, Thomas. *Group Centered Leadership*. New York: Houghton Mifflin, 1955. For application see Crookston, Burns B. and Blaesser, Willard W. Planned change in the college setting. *Personnel and Guidance Journal* 49:7 March 1962), pp. 610–616.
15. Gibb, Jack R. "Climate for trust formation." In L. P. Bradford, J. R. Gibb and K. D. Benne (eds), *T-Group Theory and Laboratory Method*. New York: Wiley, 1964.
16. For a discussion on organization development theory and practice see Beekhard, Richard, *Organization Development: Strategies and Models*. Reading, Mass.: Addison-Wesley, 1969; also see Bennis, W. G., *Organization Development: Its Nature, Origins, and Prospects*. Reading, Mass.: Addison-Wesley, 1969; additionally, Buchanan, Paul C. "The Concept of Organization Development, or Self-Renewal, as a Form of Planned Change," in Watson, Goodwin (ed.), *Concepts for Social Change*. Washington: NTL IABS-NEA, 1967.
17. Mager, Robert F. *Preparing Instructional Objectives*. Palo Alto: Fearon Publishers, 1962.

The Student Personnel Worker of 1980

Mary Evelyn Dewey

To plan appropriate professional preparation for the field of student personnel work for the future realistically, we must place the topic in its larger setting, namely, the life situation of the field of work. We must also have some knowledge of what has gone before, in order to know what has or has not been successful. Some attempt must be made to project into the future, both on the basis of what we can learn from the first two elements and on what we are told portends for society in the post-industrial world to come. Obviously, time does not permit a full and comprehensive development of the task so defined; however, one may, using such an outline, attempt a condensed coverage, a précis, that will seek to identify major issues, questions, and suggestions for further discussion and/or exploration. Actually, this discussion can be condensed in a telegram based on the three factors and, of course, appropriately spiced with interrobangs:

1. THE FIELD IS IN SERIOUS TROUBLE.
2. THE FIELD HAS ALWAYS BEEN IN TROUBLE—AND DOES NOT SEEM TO HAVE LEARNED MUCH ABOUT RESOLVING ITS PROBLEMS.
3. UNLESS THE FIELD TAKES SOME ACTION, THE STUDENT PERSONNEL WORKER OF THE EIGHTIES MAY WELL BE EXTINCT.

That, in essence, is the message this writer would send, and I would address it to all professional preparation programs, to practitioners, and to all our various national associations. I very much fear, however, that in that form it would promptly be placed in the circular file as being nothing new, and life would proceed as usual. Therefore, the message must be fleshed out a bit for emphasis, underlining, and highlighting. Most important, new focuses to the argument must be introduced, lest the message be received as merely another alarm call—the 1971 version of Chicken Little.

Hence to Point 1: THE FIELD IS IN SERIOUS TROUBLE. There is no doubt that the identity crisis of student personnel work appears to grow only more acute with each passing month. The trickle of works in earlier decades now more resembles an avalanche, the boulders of which typically signal the same basic problems: the field has no clear definition of function acceptable to the educational field at large; there exists no clear status or reward system; there is little recognition or acceptance of the field by the students it presumably serves, or by faculty and administrative colleagues. The Hodgkinson data reported in the July 1970 *NASPA Journal*[1] tell the story—and it is a painful one—of a national study confirming what our critics have said for years: we have not made it in the central arena of the institution. This, coupled with the acute financial distress facing higher education (indeed, this emerged as the central theme of the AAHE conference in Chicago in March), causes increased apprehension in student personnel circles, as indeed it should, and we see in the field an ill-defined but increasing malaise characterized by defensiveness, anxiety, and frustration. The frustration that develops under these circumstances leads to cries for unionization, demands for recognition and for tenure or other forms of job security, and calls for control over working conditions. There is a hope that unionization will provide the strength necessary to force the field's will on the academic community and that organization will establish the field as a bona fide profession. New attempts at role definition appear periodically, as do new constructs for services, and new pleas for activism, relevance, and effectiveness emerge as deans are urged to "stand up and be counted," to get on all those policy-making committees, to do a better job of publicizing their activities and accomplishments on their individual camupuses, to obtain and retain faculty status (if you can't beat 'em, join 'em), to work for faculty status for members of their staffs (apparently whether or not they may qualify), to contribute to research knowledge, and so forth. Old arguments are resurrected and restated: e.g., counseling is or is not the major function of the field; there is or is not a body of knowledge that may be defined as a discipline known as student personnel work; there is or is not a role for the generalist; the field is or is not going to establish itself as a profession. All in all, a serious reader of the literature is given the impression of vaulting idealism alternating with discouraged despair, interspersed with horrifying periods of becalmed inertia and startling complacence. If any pattern is to be discerned in this, it is a circular one. As the arguments repeat, the suggested solutions recur, while the issues remain constant.

Why is this? Doth the lady protest too much? Surely if good work is done, it will be recognized. Surely if the work is truly educational in nature, someone will notice and will give due credit where credit is due. Surely if the professional expertise warrants it, the top professional title will go to a "professionally trained" person, rather than a faculty member from an unrelated but respected academic discipline. . . . surely, but apparently not so.

Can so many effective personnel workers be wrong in this matter? Can they, honestly believing in their efforts, knowing their function is vital, sensing intuitively (if in no demonstrable way) that they are close to the matter, be so mistaken? There is evidence that such might be the case, despite the paradoxical fact that in all the years of development of this field, there has been a constant and abiding faith (now well supported by research) that student personnel work's realm of operation is situated closer to the truth of educational growth and development than is standard classroom learning.

How are we then to resolve this dilemma, this frustrated defensiveness, this apparent inability to break through to the matter successfully, with confidence and with appropriate recognition??

Let us move to Point 2: THE FIELD HAS ALWAYS BEEN IN TROUBLE AND DOES NOT SEEM TO HAVE LEARNED MUCH ABOUT RE-SOLVING ITS PROBLEMS. The argument over the decades has singled out many villains: the recalcitrant faculty, safe in their academic security and self-respect; the overbearing administrator who hands out policies to be enforced by personnel lackeys who are presumably incompetent to contribute to the formulation of those policies; practitioners endowed with goodwill but short on effectiveness; the "anti-intellectualism" of the applied fields; overidentification with the custodial-control role; lack of sound theory in which to ground the field; et cetera, et cetera, et cetera. It is likely that all of these elements contribute to the problem, but it is also apparent that they do not totally encompass it. Without denying the necessity of working toward the solution of the many problems extant or without claiming that there is one approach to a grand solution, I would direct attention to what seems to me to be a more culpable villain. In the many analyses of issues, there is too little *pertinent* discussion of the role and responsibility of professional preparation programs in this state of affairs. An intensive examination of the literature indicates two major themes, which in my view are questionable and therefore stand as unresolved issues: curriculum and selection of students.[2]

First point, *curriculum.* Examination of typical programs reveals just that— "typical" programs, involving human relations skills, some counseling, some overview of practice, some internship experience (M.A. level). One sees an awesome similarity of approach; one sees a recurring sameness in the periodic attempts to develop guidelines for professional preparation; one sees "new" formulations developed that always seem to be based on surveys of existing practice; and one wonders if it is too simplistic to suggest that this approach tends to perpetuate the problem rather than solve it. Within these programs one does *not* typically see much emphasis on organizational theory, dynamics of institutional and societal change, American studies, sociology of student life and culture, futuristics, heavy research components, or the like—indeed, one does not even see a great deal of the field of higher education as a major social institution and as a discipline in its own right in the typical curriculum. The focus is too much on the specificity of student services and much too little on the institution as a whole, an organism, a system—of which student personnel work is but a part, albeit, one hopes, a vital one. We have not educated professionals to see the institution whole. Worse than that, we have not done a good job of educating people to see the field itself in its entirety, but have tended to look at counseling as the be-all and end-all. We have not done a good job of listening to some of our best friends and most severe critics—as, for example, Wrenn saying in 1948:

I'd also relegate "counseling" to its appropriate position as one of a *number* of the personnel functions and not have it substituted in people's thinking for the entire personnel program.[3]

Or Barry and Wolf saying in 1959:

By our overuse of the word counselor, we have identified ourselves with a single phase of our activities.[4]

Too often graduate programs launch into the field neophyte professionals who have been led to believe that their function will not only be central to the educational process, but that in all probability it will be the most significant—a concept supported by aspiration, stated goals, and supportive counseling tools than by clear methodologies for achievement. Too often the neophyte's program has perhaps unintentionally shielded him from the realities of the situation by not including in his professional preparation certain elements which would, at the very least, provide him a more comprehensive and realistic knowledge base from which to operate.

Second point, *selection.* Just as there has been too little challenge of the typical curriculum, there has been an ongoing simultaneous belief that the real problem in professional preparation was *selection.* If we could but develop the right instruments to assess personalities, we could admit that ideal type to our graduate programs. *That* would be the answer. And we *knew* over the years what we were looking for. The pattern recurs and recurs: we wanted as primary factors in candidates for admission sincerity, warmth, loyalty, enthusiasm, ability to relate to others, interest in people—in short, counsel-or-types as they are known. (Some lists advocated a sense of humor as desirable—perhaps to enjoy the irony of the situation?)

Is it not paradoxical that this field which above all others has proclaimed a belief in uniqueness has made its graduate programs so similar? Is it not paradoxical that this field, with its time-honored adherence to belief in individual differences, over the years has sought to identify *the* ideal personality type to work with all those different, unique, individual students? Critics of the field have pleaded for more research on the part of its practitioners, yet we have not made serious efforts to recruit individuals who will do this naturally and by inclination. We recognize specific needs within the field, but we do not widely promote varying plans for recruiting and developing people who have the needed skills. We recognize the need for the comprehensivist mind applied to higher education, but we do not know how to develop it or how to recruit it in its raw state. We have continually sought the mellow and the smooth rather than the abrasive, the critical, the onesided, the questioning—we have sought the cooperative, the loyal, the enthusiastic (in its narrow sense) and have avoided the individualist, all the while proclaiming to be the champion of individualism. We have assumed that warmth of personality correlates with good research ability, with mental acuity, with individuality of approach, with interest in change and innovation. We have sought and honored good intentions over realistic achievement—and none of us can doubt that the resulting holier-than-thou syndrome has done extensive damage to the field's aspiration for recognition as a profession, not to mention its effectiveness in working with students.

Thus we have a field in serious trouble, and the trouble has been of long standing. I have attempted to argue that professional preparation programs have contributed heavily to this condition by being too limited in design, too repetitive, too reluctant to question themselves, too unimaginative, too committed to fitting the field into psychology instead of vice versa. I submit that professional preparation programs must bear much of the onus for the harvest we are reaping and that the effective practitioners of artistry and skill may be successful in spite of and not because of their professional preparation. We know, for example, from the very provocative study by Blackburn[5] in 1969 that—

both preparation and experience contribute to perceptions of student personnel work in unique ways. Preparation in student personnel work contributes emphasis upon the individual, counseling, educational reform, models for behavioral learning, and the use of behavioral science techniques to create an environment for learning. Experience in student personnel work contributes an emphasis upon research, needs of students, interpretation of the nature of education and experiences to achieve personal developmental tasks (133).

After ten or more years of experience, the chief student personnel officers with academic preparation and the chief student personnel officers without specific training tend to view the purposes of student personnel programs more similarly. Those with academic preparation, after ten or more years of experience, place less emphasis upon counseling and the individual student. Those chief student personnel officers without specific preparation, after ten or more years of experience, embrace many of the philosophic foundations on which counseling is based (136).

The implications of this are fascinating and bear further discussion and investigation.

At any rate, as we move to Point 3: UNLESS THE FIELD TAKES SOME ACTION, THE STUDENT PERSONNEL WORKER OF THE EIGHTIES MAY WELL BE EXTINCT. Obviously, it is my argument that it is the major responsibility of professional preparation programs to effect necessary change if they are to help avoid extinguishing the field. Some of the suggestions naturally grow out of what has gone before, some will grow out of what we have seen predicted as coming in the future. To look briefly at the first category:

Professional preparation programs must begin to supply our effective and experienced practitioners with the variety of individuals they need to meet the complexities of today's campuses—individuals to fill a variety of roles— research, communications, residence personnel of the highest order, group specialists, comprehensivists. Programs must recruit for diversity, for interdisciplinary orientations, for individuality as well as for persons whose strength lies in the counseling methodologies and interest. And, dare I say it, in a time when so-called "elitism" is in disfavor, for intellectual excellence. We need some unique types, some powerful brainpower, some doers instead of maintainers, some questioners, some thinkers—perhaps some people who do not like to work with people, but who are fascinated by institutional processes, decisionmaking patterns, research questions, etc. Programs need to distinguish between the pros and the pseudo-pros of the future. Let me explain: currently, it seems to me, we have a clear distinction in the field between the real "pros" (the "all-rounders" by virtue of their ability, leadership, and experience—those people "in spite of" and those people from other fields who came in because of their commitment) and the "pseudo-pros." My point is that we must start the *real* pros in our professional preparation programs, for there will be no positions for pseudo-pros in the future. Financial stringency may be the initial reason, but one hopes the better reason will be that the professionalization of the field will not allow it.

Professional preparation programs must be reconstructed to offer preparation heretofore lacking in substantive areas. Flexibility, individuality, a genuine "exploitation of the institutional resources" available, crossing disciplinary lines, creating new degree structures, new approaches to the study of that ill-defined "personnel function" in higher education—all these will be necessary.

The curriculum will reflect and respond to and contribute to what educational processes will exist in the future. Personnel professionals will perhaps operate on the modular pattern that is being forecast, in specialty teams on short-term bases, in a variety of situations. We are told that linear thinking will not be the mode of the future—nor will it define the future. Just as undergraduate curriculums of the future will be modular, restructuring itself, redesigning itself, reapplying itself in new formulations—an exciting prospect, wild in its possibilities and demanding the very finest professionals. May I conclude by reiterating my third point about the extinction of the field: I did not say the personnel *function* would be extinct. In my view, that is not in question. The question lies in *who will perform it*. Professional preparation programs in higher education have no small responsibility here: If they (professional preparation programs) choose McLuhan's description of the average person's approach to the future—that is, happily driving forward looking into the rearview mirror, it will be all over in the year 2000.

References

1. Hodgkinson, Harold L. "How Deans of Students Are Seen by Others—and Why?" *NASPA Journal* 8: 49–54; July 1970.
2. Bibliography available from the author.
3. Wrenn, C. Gilbert. "The Greatest Tragedy in College Personnel Work." *Educational and Psychological Measurement* 8: 413; Autumn 1948.
4. Barry, Ruth, and Wolf, Beverly. "Guidance-Personnel Work: The Near Look and the Far Vision." *NAWDC Journal* 12: 175; June 1959.
5. Blackburn, J. L. *Perceived Officers as a Function of Academic Preparation and Experience.* Doctor's thesis. Tallahassee: Florida State University, 1969. 194 pp. (Available from University Microfilms, Inc., Ann Arbor, Mich.)

Student Development in Tomorrow's Higher Education—A Return to the Academy

Robert D. Brown

Foreword

We are pleased to witness the publication of this monograph, particularly because it represents the culmination of the initial phase of a project to which we are all personally dedicated: the American College Personnel Association's (ACPA) Tomorrow's Higher Education Project. Since 1968 when ACPA President Donald Hoyt appointed a group to develop a strategy for examining the future of college student personnel work, ACPA has taken deliberate notice of the currents of change operating in higher education. Tomorrow's Higher Education (THE) Project, is ACPA's planned response to the prospects of great change in our profession.

The essence of THE Project is an attempt to reconceptualize college student personnel work in a way that will serve to provide a measure of creative input from our profession toward the shaping of the higher education of the future. By reconceptualization we mean the systematic reconstruction of our fundamental conceptions as to the specific roles, functions, methods, and procedures that will characterize our future professional practice. Ultimately, we hope to implement a number of model student personnel programs in which the products of our reconceptualization will be practically tested in a variety of environmental contexts.

Robert Brown was commissioned to write this monograph by an ACPA Task Force that included Paul Bloland, Russell Brown, W. Harold Grant, Donald Hoyt, Jane Matson, Albert Miles, and Philip Tripp.

The Task Force intended that the monograph provide a focus for the dialogue which will be a necessary part of the subsequent model-building and implementation phases of THE Project. To this end, the success of the monograph will not be measured in the degree of assent that it attracts, but in the nature and quality of the reaction and discussion that it evokes.

We recognize that the ambitious scope of THE Project dictates that its successful completion will require the cooperation and resources of many persons and organizations within and beyond the total higher education community. We are hopeful, however, that the noble objectives of the project will be realized, and that interest in the ultimate improvement of the educational experiences of college students will transcend any professional differences that the project might reveal.

William R. Butler
President, ACPA

G. Robert Ross
President-elect, ACPA

Donald E. Kubit
Coordinator, THE Project
Task Force

Chapter 1
Hold Up the Mirror

Have you ever been in a fun house hall of mirrors? Do you remember the ambivalence you felt when you saw yourself reflected in the maze of images that were at once grotesque, funny, and sad? It was probably easier to laugh at someone else's foreshortened reflection or giraffe-like elongated image than at yourself. One could speculate as to the kind of psychic damage that would accrue if a person spent a long time in such a maze. Would he forget what he really looked like and who he really was? Or even worse, suppose all the mirrors of the world cast back similar weird images forcing everyone to live his entire life without ever knowing what he really looked like. This Kafkaesque world has existed in higher education for some time.

American society has expected higher education to play many different roles—a finishing school, a trainer for the military, a guardian of culture, a research arm of the nation, a force for democracy, and at times even a mother, father, and stepbrother to its students. Sometimes it has been slow to respond to the needs of society and the roles thrust upon it, and at other times it has reacted impulsively. In fact, higher education has changed its face many times, although it has never gained a reputation for being flexible. With each new epoch it has added new roles but seldom shedding the old ones, thus making it difficult to retain a clear perspective as to what its real intents and purposes are.

During the past decade, the debate over the basic purposes of higher education has intensified, even though many of the same issues have been discussed for centuries. Today, however, a broader public is examining them and asking these questions. Should the university reflect society or attempt to change it? Should the university be politically neutral or should it be a strong force for social action? Is higher education a right or a privilege? Should the curriculum be more practical or more theoretical? In the past, these issues were debated almost exclusively by philosophers or pedagogues, but today they are also the concern of legislators and parents. What is disturbing about these dialogues is not that they have been heard before or that they are being discussed by an increasingly diverse group, but that there is little discussion or debate about what is to happen to students as a result of their exposure to higher education. Students are expected to *know* what they did not know before and, in many instances, are expected to be able *to do* what they were unable to do before. But, what are they expected *to be*?

Colleges have demonstrated that they are adequate proving grounds for scholars and are proud of their success in training people for careers. Annual reports enumerate the number of successful lawyers, doctors, scholarship winners, congressmen, and other distinguished personages who are among the ranks of the alumni. The amount of success that colleges have had in developing "humane" beings, however, is clouded. Maslow's (1962) self-actualizing man, Heath's (1964) reasonable adventurer, and Sanford's' (1966) goal of individual development serve as pleasant rhetoric for college bulletin goal statements and as inspirational literature for small clusters of faculty members, but do they mean anything apart from goal statements? Do they have an impact on how a college plans for the future? Recently, there have been just enough reported instances of new programs for student development or reaffirmations of student development goals to keep the hearts of the young optimists beating. Maturer voices wait with skepticism, however, for evidence of widespread behavioral change among administrators and educators before they will attest to the fact that a new day has dawned.

Student Development as a Goal

One major assumption underlying the entire discussion here is that total student development has been and must remain one of the primary goals of higher education. For the present it is sufficient to define student development in terms of what college catalogs and goal statements often describe as the "whole student" or the "liberally educated" person. Most college goal statements include intentions to promote in students independence of thought along with critical thinking, to make students better citizens as well as to make them more knowledgeable about their culture heritage, and to help students understand themselves and relate better to others, as well as to prepare them for a profession. In simpler terms, higher education *has sought to make its students better persons*. This goal needs critical scrutiny. There have been many changes suggested for higher education and some have been implemented, but how many are congruent with the enhancement of student development.

Since the end of World War II, student personnel workers have identified themselves as the professional group on campus most concerned about the development of the total student (Williamson, 1949). This assumption, too, needs to be questioned. The college experience was viewed by the student personnel staff to be a total one with the out-of-class activities and experiences being an essential part of that total. Some student personnel workers have seen themselves as true educators, albeit ones without rank, tenure, or status. This concern for the "whole" student implied a needed emphasis and concern about personality and character development, e.g., social skills, good citizenship, and altruism. Specialties developed, such as the union manager, the student activities supervisor, the counselor, and the residence hall adviser. There are really two assumptions here that need to be questioned. First, is the student personnel worker the only person on campus concerned about student development? The answer is obvious, but it seldom results in asking the next question. Can student development really be fostered effectively without the support and influence of the academic dimensions of college life? These questions deserve some examination.

Purpose

The plethora of publications about the dilemma of higher education is matched only by the continual self-flagellation of college student personnel workers at conventions and in professional journals. Both sources declare that a crisis exists and propound the need for change. The purposes of this monograph are to: (a) look at the predictions and proposals being made for higher education in terms of their implications for student development, (b) examine student development research and key concepts to see if they suggest alternatives for the future of higher education, which merit more attention than they are currently being given, and (c) make recommendations for those planning the future of higher education and student personnel programs.

Do the myriad prognostications for the future of higher education mesh with student development goals? What changes will they demand in how administrators, faculty, and student personnel workers think and behave, if colleges and universities are to have a positive impact on students in other ways than acquisition of skills and knowledge? What considerations are the futurists omitting? The results of these explorations should provoke some thought and reactions among all those concerned about student development, whether they are deans of faculties or deans of students, faculty members or residence hall directors, academic advisers or counselors.

The current plight of higher education and college student personnel work will be examined in this chapter, concluding with a brief rationale of the need for a statement about student development during the college years. This background picture of the present should help explain the worry and concern many have regarding the importance of student development in the future of higher education. Chapter 2 summarizes the many recommendations being made for higher education and the predictions about what the future holds, as well as their particular implications for student life and student development. The reader is asked to consider the implications these new directions have for student development. In a number of instances support of student development goals suggests needed supplementary or even alternate directions. Chapter 3 asks whether or not student development has ever been and is now a viable goal for colleges. A summary of the research literature serves to highlight what we do know about student development and presents some key concepts and their implications.

The reader who is very familiar with the recent literature about higher education might want to glance at Chapter 2 chiefly for the discussion of the implications future directions in higher education have for student development. On the other hand, the reader who is knowledgeable about student development research may wish to examine Chapter 3 as he thinks about the few basic concepts of student development that exist and the future research needs that are described.

Chapter 4 looks at some possible future roles for student personnel workers. A behavioral scientist role, which involves the student personnel person more directly in the academic arena, is suggested as one of the needed directions for at least a significant segment of the college student personnel profession. The monograph concludes with Chapter 5 recommending changes for higher education in general and college student personnel workers specifically.

The Current Picture

Where Is Higher Education Today? Since the advent of McLuhan's world tribalism via television, the word crisis has been with us daily. Higher education was having its share of crises long before McLuhan or television. Clark Kerr (1971) was probably most apt when he suggested that higher education is in a period of "Climateric II," the first climateric occurring during the years 1820 to 1870 when the curriculum changed from the classical to the liberal-professional and the Morrill Act made public land grant institutions a thriving reality. This view is more optimistic, if not more realistic than the catastrophic consequences that crisis implies. Uncertainty abounds, conflict is omnipresent, and confusion is unsettling, but at the same time the potential for change and growth has never been much greater.

Jacques Barzun has referred to today's colleges and universities as baroque, while other critics have found them homogeneous, meaningless, and irrelevant. Robert Hutchins facetiously referred once to the central heating plant as the unifying part of the university; Clark Kerr thought that today it would have to be the parking lot. Tomorrow's pundit may suggest the TV transmitter tower. If one believed their worst critics, colleges and universities are not unlike library book shelves that offer their readers the same fare year after year. Some variations occur as new books are added or dusty books are rearranged, but the shelves themselves have no heart and are incapable of asking what impact they should or could have on the reader. When higher education was the interest of the few, it could accept criticism from the intelligentsia with a shrug of its shoulders and literally go on about its way. Today, the universities' public is broader, its critics closer to home, and sometimes its defenders more thin-skinned.

Regardless of how strong a case is marshalled for the responsiveness and flexibility of American higher education, and despite the fact that it may have changed more quickly and dramatically than many other bureaucratic institutions, it is apparent the critics are not satisfied. Many Americans have lost faith in higher education. Public indignation has been expressed in many ways—the most significant being the drastic cutbacks in funding that have taken place nationwide. This loss of confidence threatens freedom within the university as well as the budget. Many states have passed laws intended to curtail protest on their campuses and, in more than one instance, have come close to blackmailing their state institutions when appropriations were being considered.

This climateric period is likely to last at least a decade according to the seers. Optimists have felt that the crest of dissension and unrest has already passed. Recent evidence, however, suggests that even though the most recent academic year, 1970–71, was less tumultuous than the previous year, the impression that it was dramatically quieter was due more to the diminishing interest of the mass media than to reality. No Kent State's or Jackson State's occurred, but the level of protest was almost as high as 1968–69—the previous high water mark (Bayer & Astin, 1971). While violence is subsiding and protest marches are less frequent, tensions and conflict are not. Prognosticators are almost universal in their expectations of continued tension and unrest.

Through this gloom appears no miraculous rainbow or silver lining, but there are definite signs that higher education intends to respond. The host of studies and proposals coming forth from groups such as the Carnegie Commission suggest that higher education is not just tightening its belt but that it is taking a serious look at new directions. The Newman Report (1971) has prompted much discussion and a current Health, Education, and Welfare (HEW) Task Force promises to make specific suggestions for changing the face of higher education. The renewed interest in undergraduate education, the recent focus of student movements on educational reform, and the experimental college ventures clearly suggest that American higher education has the potential, if not the will, for self-renewal. With new programs and a new variety of students, higher education is going to be challenged in more fundamental ways than it has ever been. As these predicted and proposed changes are examined in more detail in the next chapter, it is important to ask whether or not the response of higher education is sufficient and in the right direction.

Where is Student Personnel Work Today?

If higher education is in Climacteric II, student personnel work must be suffering through its own Climateric I. It has been having an identity crisis for some time. It came through the most trying periods of student unrest unscathed but also without any laurels. Student personnel staff have ascended to institutional positions equivalent to vice-presidencies, but few are consulted for advice regarding the total institution. In the eyes of many faculty, student personnel workers are second-class citizens, and students see them as not being much different from other members of the establishment, although perhaps more paternalistic. Institutional presidencies remain in the hands of academicians turned administrators.

The recent interest in the use of paraprofessionals in student personnel positions is an omen that can be interpreted as either good or evil. One interpretation might be that this is a fine movement that adds to the diversity of backgrounds of student personnel staffs, provides the professional campus staff with more time for substantive concerns, and is generally indicative of the growth of the profession. However, another viewpoint interprets this movement as providing clear evidence that student personnel work is not a profession and that almost anyone with certain personal qualifications can perform well with minimal on-the-job training.

Not too many years ago the then president of the American College Personnel Association (Berdie, 1966), asked whether or not there needed to be a redefinition of student personnel work and even wondered if there needed to be a professional entity known as "student personnel work." More recently other spokesmen have declared the profession stillborn (Penny, 1968) and compared it to the perennial bridesmaid. (In days when advocacy of zero population growth is popular, these fates may be virtuous, but still quite frustrating.) Such painful soul-searching is hardly the sign of a complete healthy, confident profession.

Some of the traditional functions of student personnel work, such as discipline and out-of-class control, are being given less attention as the *in loco parentis* role of universities wanes and students gain more voice in the governance of their lives. Students are the leading advocates of the need for a campus ombudsman as student personnel workers have often found themselves ineffective and powerless to change or influence administrative policies. Those who once served as go-betweens are now being bypassed.

However, just as there are some hopeful signs when the total higher education scene is examined, student personnel work may be undergoing progressive change also. Most promising omens include the increasing summons from within the profession for student personnel workers to view themselves as behavioral scientists and the growing volume of research and thought on what influences and promotes student development.

The Need for a Statement About Student Development

Reports, books, and periodicals issuing warnings, making suggestions, and summarizing the current status of higher education in America are coming off the presses as fast as news bulletins from a ticker tape machine. Major national associations and commissions are making pronouncements about where higher education could be or should be going in the future. Change is in the air like the hot sultry stillness before a tornado. Administrators on each college campus are looking closely for guidelines and seeking help as they face a troubled public and restricted budgets. The changes made now will affect the course of higher education for at least a decade and, ultimately, its impact on students. Now is the opportune time, maybe even the last, for those concerned about the priority given to student development to react constructively and creatively.

The emphasis of a number of the reports, such as *Less Time, More*

Options, (Carnegie Commission, 1971a) is on time and money. If the recommendations are followed, students will spend less time in college, and degrees will be awarded at more frequent intervals. The implications such recommendations have for cost effectiveness is given much attention, but discussion of what students are to learn and become during the reduced time is limited. This is not to deny the value of fiscal concerns, nor even to place them second, but rather to suggest that questions about what happens to students be given equal attention. Few student protests have been lodged against how long it takes them to get a degree or how close their community college is to their hometown. No, students have instead been critical of the very educational experience they have in college.

Much has been written recently about open admissions and easy access to college. Expectations have been that simply opening the college doors wider will solve all racial problems and the ills of poverty. The motives cannot be questioned, but the effectiveness of programs planned to implement them can be. Several critics have raised the pertinent question, "Open admissions to what?" Students can be admitted and still be bored or still fail. These outcomes create more problems.

Other recent reports (Newman, 1971) have been viewed as attacks on higher education even as they pose thought-provoking questions and suggestions. These, in turn, have been criticized for being either too radical or too conservative, depending on the critic's orientation. With the exclusion of the Hazen Foundation Report (*The Student in Higher Education*, 1968) few reports on higher education have looked closely enough at student outcomes and the impact of their recommendations on student development.

During a period of financial restrictions and loss of trust, it is especially important that institutional goals be continuously reformulated and accomplishments reassessed. These are the times when fiscal and political pressure are heavily weighted as they enter the decision-making funnel. This is when it is important that ultimate goals remain clear, and hopefully administrators will live with the words of their own ultimate objectives on their lips, like a Jesus prayer refrain that could be chanted during all their waking moments.

For these reasons it is essential to alert the decision-makers to the impact their future judgments will have on students, to ask those in the student development movement who have ideas about facilitating student growth to step forward with program proposals, and to ask both groups to respond to the challenge of providing a more humane educational experience for students of the future.

Don Quixote was brought crushingly back to reality when he saw his real self reflected in a shield of mirrors. Now is the time for college administrators and college student personnel workers to hold up to each other mirrors that reflect not only what is, but what could be. Hopefully, the result will not be fatal, as it was for the "knight of the woeful countenance." This monograph attempts to hold up one mirror with the intention of opening up an honest dialogue between the academy and student personnel.

Chapter 2
Where Higher Education Might Be Going Tomorrow

Man has been trying to predict the future ever since one of his remote predecessors stepped out of a cave and saw what he thought was a distant rain cloud. Sine that time he has been constantly trying to have an impact on that future, advancing from rain-dancing to cloud-seeding. Today, fortune-telling is not left to passing gypsies or to prophets coming forth from the desert. Nearly anyone who can write and who thinks he has diagnosed a trend is likely to start prognosticating. Studying graphs has replaced scrutiny of a bird's entrails, and prediction equations have replaced palm-reading. The computer prints out fortune cookie messages faster than the oven can bake the dough. And, most often, the warnings are ominous.

Predictions, Proposals, and Predicaments

It might be possible to sort out the prediction from the proposals being made for higher education in the future, but this will not be done in many systematic way for several reasons. First of all, predictions have a way of becoming wish-fulfilling prophesies, especially if they are made by a person or group having some control over the outcome. If a group of college presidents predict that less money will be spent on graduate programs in the future, they obviously have the power individually, if not collectively, to influence the eventuality of that prediction. Proposals, suggestions, and recommendations have their own way of becoming reality. This is especially true if they are made by authoritative sources, such as the federal government or major foundations. In some instances, recognized experts are making predictions that are identical or quite correlative to recommendations being put forward by others.

These considerations make it rather meaningless to sort out predictions from proposals. Whether a statement is made as a predictions or a proposal probably has little relationship to its eventual fruition in reality. If one is concerned about outcomes, he must respond with equal passion to predictions, suggestions, recommendations, and proposals.

The predictions made in the following sections are not those of this author, but rather represent a consensus of more recent pronouncements made in the higher education arena. No doubt, however, personal biases affected the selection and compilation of the list. As the projections for the future are discussed, some of the possible implications for both higher education and student development will be illustrated.

The reader who has kept pace with the recent major publications in higher education will find that some sections of this chapter are chiefly a review. The potential impact the new directions hold for student life, however, warrant considerably more attention than they have been given. The interwoven discussions of the implications of the changes in society and student life, the nature and number of students, the variety of college options, the undergraduate programs, and the governance and financing of higher education is intended to serve as a catalyst for further thought.

Society and Student Life

One's view of history and providence will influence what kind of predictions one would make about what our society and our students will be like during the next decade. Will there be continued student dissent? Will society's moral values continue to change? A cyclical view would suggest a quiet era to follow the recent period of unrest with the general mood of the public being repressive. Student dissent would be limited and liberalism would be retarded if not regressed. Those who view history somewhat as a spiral would forecast a continued openness and increased pluralism to prevail through intermittent periods of repression. Others would predict an almost revolutionary straight line ascent (or descent) with only temporary plateaus. Current forecasts seem to fall into each of the historical perspectives, but it appears that the most predominant theme is one which forecasts continual change, constant ferment, and uneasy confusion. New movements will come, gain a head of steam, but will not vanish.

Max Lerner (1971) sees revolution, not death, in the air. This revolution is based on consensus rather than violence. France's Jean-Francois Revel sees America as the most likely ground for great social transformations to take place (1971). Changes that will take place are those supported initially by 40 percent to 45 percent of the populace and then by 50 percent to 55 percent; increased support of a relatively small percentage of people can lead to major social transformations. Although an apparent contradiction in terms, many predict that the future promises an "evolutionary revolution."

Listing all the possible and predicted changes in society and student life would fill pages, but examination of some of the major threads is a necessary preface to exploring equally profound expectations for higher education.

Society. The very fact of change itself, as well as the nature of the changes, can have a profound effect on higher education and student development. Perhaps it is best simply to predict change and let it go at that. Certainly Toffler (1970) is correct when he chronicles the rapidity of technological and sociological change in recent years. Regardless of whether or not one attributes change to specific events or to an evolutionary process, the proximity of events or the flow of the process has accelerated to the point that the stream of life is like a rock-strewn rapids and just as treacherous. For anyone over 30, the events of World War II seem almost as close, if not closer in time than the nostalgic events and personages chronicled on TV specials, such as the gyrations of Elvis Presley in 1957 and the clean-shaven Beatles of 1965. Such electronic reminiscences appear anachronistic in less than a decade.

The fate of future man rides the crest of whatever the current and popular doomsday prophet portrends. In recent years it has been Huxley's *Brave New World*, Orwell's totalitarianism, or Skinner's *Walden II*. Man's destiny may be fatally affected by the hydrogen bomb, overpopulation, or an imbalance in the ecological system of the planet. Outside of destruction of man, we may now have the ultimate doomsdayism concern, Toffler's "Future Shock." Man of the near future will face a trauma potentially as powerful as that of a person finding himself in a completely different culture. Changes will occur so fast that he will have little or no time to adjust without severe stress. The generation gap may occur in 5-year differentials rather than 15 or 20.

Besides change itself, any one looking ahead has to consider the problems that man has now, as well as the projected ones. Those that come readily to mind include possible exhaustion of food and fuel supplies, pollution of the air we breathe, overpopulation of the planet, and the prospect of making the land over into a cement graveyard. Poverty, decline of liberty, artificiality of work and culture, absence of a sense of community, personal feelings of powerlessness, and a loss of self are all possible plights of future man. If this isn't gloomy enough, man can always smoke, drink, or "drug" himself to death. Of course, a nuclear holocaust is an omnipresent mushroom cloud. Perhaps the one sign of hope in all this is that society seems to be making efforts to cope with these problems, both as individuals and jointly as citizens. When politicians and TV commercials speak out against pollution, for example, the direction of concern seems appropriate, even if specific program solutions are few and far between.

One of the more positive possibilities for the future has been the break-down of the myth that technological progress is inevitable and inevitably good. There are a few signs, such as the forestalling of the construction of the SST plane and the moratorium on the Alaskan oil pipeline which suggest that society is not always going to write blank checks for technological advances. It is doubtful that this tide can be held back long, but if a measure of caution is followed by accountability, another growing movement, the death of this planet seems less likely.

There also appears to be a growing concern, not only about keeping technology in tow, but an increasing interest in finding ways to truly put it to use in an effort to help men better manage their own lives. Research and theoretical knowledge might be programmed for the development of tools and techniques that will help man live a fuller life and not just make it easier for him to fry an egg or drive his car. A new emphasis on improving the quality of life and relationships would represent a significant shift in priorities.

The growing acceptance of the principle that each person has the right to develop himself to his fullest potential has implications for both man and education. A recent court case ("rights for the Retarded," *Time*, 1971) established what may be a precedent when it ruled that even children classified as "uneducable and untrainable" are entitled to public education as it is applicable to their potential. While this is addressed onto one end of the intellectual spectrum, it may well reflect a direction our society is going in its attitude toward and response to the needs of all of its citizens.

The importance of religion in the life of the individual in the future remains problematical. Trends have a tendency to peak and even reverse themselves. Pope John XXII was followed by the more conservative Pope Paul VI. Drug freaks are now joined by Jesus freaks. Paradoxically, our technologically advanced society harbors witchcraft movements and astrology advocates. However, if there is an underlying drift, it is in the direction of greater religious pluralism within our society.

Certainly the women's liberation movement, changes in attitudes toward marriage, and supposed changes in morality will all have an impact on the life styles of the future. Our ability to cope with racial problems and the plight of the poor will most certainly directly affect the amount of tension existing in the country. Economic changes that affect leisure time, the job market, and inflation will certainly play a major role in determining what the future will be like. Any one of these trends could be and have been pursued by others in detailing what the future holds. All that can be noted here is that some of the most basic dimensions of our society, e.g., family life, promise to be examined critically, especially by the young, and changed in very fundamental ways.

Student Life. Major changes in student life are certainly going to reflect those taking place in society at large. Most of us have read the statistics that reflect a continually receding median age, although this is subject to change through population control. Further, we have noted that the 18-year-old vote will make the voice of youth more important, if not more serious and intent. Among the predicted trends, perhaps the most important for higher education are:

1. *Fewer, in fact, perhaps no parietal rules governing student behavior.* Accordinging to many, the days of in loco parentis are numbered.

2. *A greater voice for students, in the governance of the university.* Some of this will be the result of actual participation on university committees and councils. Perhaps an even more powerful voice will be their role as consumers. The increased importance of tuition, government loans and perhaps eventually scholarships, and a greater variety of collegiate opportunities, may all serve to make students determiners of curriculum offerings simply by their opting for particular colleges and programs.

3. *A decrease in general unrest, although tensions are expected to prevail.* The new issues are likely to be those closest to the student's everyday life, such as parietal rules and educational reform. There will be continued interest in current issues and politics. Increased support may come from young new faculty members.

4. *The continuance of the counter culture.* But there is likely to be increased tension between extreme student groups, i.e., the vocational-collegiate subcultures and the nonconformists; those who see college as primarily a means of occupational and social mobility and those who see college as a means of gaining self-insight and self-expression. Hopefully students will back away from continued confrontation and violence, but survival of the counter culture depends on youth addressing itself to the fears and needs of middle America. Many Americans over 30 have the same basic concerns about their life styles as do critical youth, but it is less open and less visible. If a concerted effort is made to foster a dialogue, this may portend the beginning of a "more compassionate and comprehensive movement that would extend far beyond youth and universities" (Keniston, 1971).

5. *The remaining of the perennial problems of youth.* The college freshman of today may be physically and psychologically more mature than his or her counterpart of 20 or even 10 years ago, but many of the same developmental problems and processes remain. The conflicts associated with separation from parents, establishment of a sense of identity, the development of a self as a social and sexual being, and ultimately choosing a vocation and life style, will still require resolution. Even though some of these questions may be faced earlier in a student's developmental history, it is doubtful that they will be resolved or, at least, not followed by other problems. For example,

communal living presents a whole new host of potential developmental problems.

6. *The promise of more individualism among students.* If Charles Reich (1970) and other are right, many students will be more concerned about developing as persons rather than fulfilling a need for status or a need to have a clear occupational choice. "Doing your own thing" will be a more pervasive code for student life. Pluralism in society will be matched by pluralism of life styles among students.

7. *The coming of a whole new crop of students whose interests in post-secondary education will be quite specific and generally vocational.* The increased college enrollments during the next decade will be proportionately greater among technical and community colleges than among four-year institutions. These students have concerns and interests that are not identical with those pursuing the traditional liberal arts curriculum.

Implications. If higher education is going to respond adequately to the challenges that changes in society and student life represent, then it must respond differently than it has in the past. There are implications that should affect what is taught, how it is taught, and who teaches. In the past, when knowledge or job skills in a particular profession changed, for example, colleges have typically updated their present course offerings and added new courses. New content was squeezed into old containers and old content was passed down the line to freshmen courses on the secondary schools. These are temporary measures at best, and do not serve over the long haul; colleges must start taking the long view.

It is not overstating the case to say that we should concern ourselves with predicting what students will need to *survive* in the future. The key to this survival does not lie in anticipating the knowledge or the specific skills or values they should possess. The solution is much simpler. It involves giving attention to some rather basic skills now considered as by-products of content courses. One of the more fundamental skills, for example, is the ability to learn and solve problems. But how many real problems are students asked to solve in their sociology, psychology, political science, or even in many of their science courses? Problem-solving is left for graduates or for seniors, while freshmen suffer through vocabulary-like drill classes. The great percentage of students go through their college experience without being asked to tackle a problem of any consequence that has not been solved by others years ago—they are simply asked to remember who solved it and when. Yet, their college experience is expected to prepare them for resolving professional and personal problems. If college football coaches followed such a formula to prepare for Saturday's game, they would soon be forced to retire to the classroom.

Similar changes are necessary if students are expected to be prepared to live in a world in which values and attitudes are constantly subjected to challenge. It is questionable just how much impact current classroom experiences have on student values. This is sad. Though most would agree that professors should not proselytize, it is unfortunate that they cannot influence how students think about and decide on what values to hold. The student of tomorrow will need to examine his values during his college years and posit a reformulation of them to his own satisfaction, but he will also need to be capable of and open to doing so at repeated junctures during his life. This means he needs to understand his own values, to critically analyze his values when faced with conflicting views, to have an awareness of the forces affecting his value system, and to be able to act as well as react. Collegiate curriculums currently give the student a chance to examine the values of others and those of past societies and cultures. Seldom if ever is he asked to confront his own values system. Somehow this is expected to take place independently of formal course work. For example, ethics professors, too seldom, stimulate students to examine their own behavior in ethical terms.

To endure, in an uncertain future with shifting values and one that may mean changing jobs and even professions at critical times in one's life, requires a personal makeup that includes a rather clear self-concept and a positive attitude toward oneself and one's potential for future development. The student of the future will have to develop the capacity to be able to create a new self at the same time that he has the passion to defend his current values. These characteristics are critical. Where in the curriculum are provisions made for this type of development? Are they to be continually entrusted to the out-of-class activities or ignored?

The signs of the changes expected in student life are already upon us, though it remains to be seen whether or not the trends are reversible. Parietal rules are diminishing, students are more involved in the governance of the university, and pluralistic student subcultures have been with us for some time. Expected changes represent, perhaps, changes in degree rather than in kind. The direction of these changes suggests a lessening need for student personnel workers, especially for those whose role has involved mostly good-guy policeman or paternalistic parental surrogate duties. College student personnel workers have typically responded to student's out-of-class needs, but in the future even this role may be limited. If student independence in deciding questions about their own living arrangements and organizing their own activities continues to increase, a sizable number of the student personnel cadre may be unemployed unless role definitions are revised.

Nature and Number of Students

Although it is generally agreed that higher education will not face the population explosion it has in recent decades (when enrollment figures doubled every 14 years), more people will be involved in postsecondary educational experiences, and, more importantly, the variety of kinds of people will be expanded. One recent Carnegie Commission report predicts that there will be a period of steady enrollment increase during the current decade, followed by no increase between 1980–1990 and a one-third boost during the 1990–2000 decade (Carnegie Commission, 1971b). This growth will be a differentiated one with community colleges, technical colleges, and two-year programs gaining substantially more than the four-year universities. Most prophets suggest that the current average of about 50 percent of secondary school graduates matriculating at universities will continue for major universities, but that another 25 percent will be involved in some other form of post-secondary education.

More important than numbers is the variety of students expected to pursue some form of higher education. Blacks are still underrepresented in the college population; but, their numbers will increase. The gulf between the national population percentages for other minorities and their representation in the college population will also be reduced. A significant trend is the predicted expansion of adult enrollments. Some of this will be evidenced in adult education programs, and other continuing education programs, but adults are also expected to be on campus in regular collegiate programs. Even though there is expected to be a continuing oversupply of PhD's (which by the way was not predicted by most seers of a decade ago), the MA, rather than the BA degree, is likely to become the new symbol of educational eliteness.

Open admissions policies, much debated, but in operation in some fashion at land grant colleges and junior colleges for some time, are going to add to the diversity of student bodies. Intended to provide equal opportunity for minority groups, full implementation will bring as many or more majority students on campus. There is fear in some quarters that open admissions will lead to a lowering of standards within current programs and will, in fact, result in a redefinition of what constitutes higher education.

Some predict less attrition, though there may be more transferring from college to college as new options become available and more accessible. The more optimistic foresee a reduction in the number of involuntary students, those in college because of the draft or because it is expected of them. However, major changes will have to occur in society's expectation that education serve as the step ladder for social mobility, if the involuntary student is going to fade away.

There is much debate about the merits of differential higher educational systems. Should some institutions be comprehensive while others focus on special groups or programs? There has even been some discussion of establishing upper division colleges. This debate will continue with resolution made at each state level. However, it is unlikely that comprehensive universities will ever be eliminated as one of the available options. This means that all institutions will eventually be faced with students who in the past would not have knocked at their doors.

Implications. Arguments are still being waged, but the prospect of universal higher education waits in the wings while proponents of open access and/or equal opportunity debate. Universal secondary education had its critics, but those who favored it held that a certain level of education for the populace was not only an ideal, but a necessity in a democracy. Universal secondary education is essentially with us, even though the attendance percentages vary for some selected portions of the population.

It is not necessary to justify universal post-secondary education or lifelong education on the grounds that it is necessary for democracy. A case can be made that socioeconomic equality demands at least equal opportunity to further education, but even this concern does not warrant such a provision for the entire population. A better case, one congruent with the direction our democracy seems to be taking us, ties post-secondary and lifelong education to the goal of individual self-fulfillment. Rather than starting with the viewpoint that everyone has the right to try to get a college education, one starts with the belief that everyone has the right to develop himself to his fullest potential. This has to be the starting point—the philosophical basis—from which it is possible to talk about equal opportunity, open admissions, easy access, and the other pertinent admissions and access questions. It is the starting point too, because it forces one to think about ends and means, programs and policies.

One of the most serious questions facing the higher education establishment is how best to educate those who some are calling the "new student" (Cross, 1971b). These are students who will be going to college (mostly to community colleges) with records of past failure. In the minds of many, there remains the notion that somewhere there is an untapped reservoir of geniuses who have not yet thought of college. It is questionable whether this pool is very large. Bright students from all walks of life are now getting into college. The new students are going to be those from the lower one-third on scholastic measures and from the lower one-third of the socioeconomic scale.

They will differ in some significant ways from the minority population who have tended to be pictured as bright, but not ready for college.

The higher education establishment has not asked itself straightforwardly whether or not a liberal education (one that aims for personal, social, and cultural development, as well as career preparation) is something that should benefit and, in fact, should be available to all students. Arguments pro and con have focused primarily on the relative merits of certain courses that are labeled vocational-technical or liberal arts. These labels are truly misnomers. Surely, vocational-technical courses can be taught in a way that promotes personal and cultural growth, while the so-called liberal arts curriculum is not necessarily "liberalizing," but is often "vocational."

Not enough attention has been given to the question of whether or not a liberalizing education is of some value to the student with lower Scholastic Aptitude Test (SAT) scores. Or can the same goals be accomplished with a different curriculum? The initial reaction has been to offer remedial courses, hoping that they will catch up, or to offer "relevant" courses taught in traditional ways. If liberal education has true value, independent of its specific content, then it might have value for students at all levels of the intellectual spectrum.

Open admission advocates have suggested that this implies much more than an open door. It involves education of the public, recruitment, and ultimately curriculum and program revisions. The question has been asked, "Open admissions to what?" An open door policy without significant changes in curriculum offerings is a sham, at best. It is kinder to bar the door than to subject students to almost certain boredom, frustration, and failure. Indeed, some view admission acceptance as a contract between the student and the institution. The institution is then pledged to provide the appropriate learning experiences for the student.

In the past, higher education has spent time and money developing programs designed to change these students in such a way that they would succeed in the college system as it exists. Special counseling programs, remedial courses, and financial aid packages have been put together in an attempt to bring these students up to par with the rest of the students. There is little evidence suggesting that this tactic has been very successful. Differential admissions within and among institutions and two-year associate degree programs are necessary, if colleges remain otherwise unchanged. Such programs are workable but are not the real solution.

Student personnel workers in many institutions have taken some measure of responsibility for special programs for the new students and in many instances have been quite eager to do so. The programs are usually viewed as outside the curricula, certainly peripheral to the academic world, and student personnel workers often appear as the logical persons to staff a program that is intended to help students. By acquiescing to requests for staff remedial programs, student personnel workers have indeed helped a good number of students, but in turn they have delayed the need for institutions to examine the tougher questions related to curriculum change.

If this pattern is to be broken, student personnel workers will have to join forces with others who request that equal time and money be spent on revising course offerings and improving instructional techniques. Local research needs to be done at each institution on the subsequent fate of students with different entering skills. Faculty and administrators are going to have to encourage students to set and meet their own standards, which at times may be below or above those of the institution. These are possible new or expanded roles for student personnel staff.

Variety of College Options

The recent Carnegie Commission Report, *Less Time, More Options*, promises to have a significant impact on higher education. Both it and the Newman Report have suggested a reexamination of higher education in terms of the length of the program, the frequency of degrees, and the lock-step nature of current curriculums. The high school student of the future is certainly going to have many post-secondary options open to him. Indeed, ideally he will not be faced with a "go" or "no go" decision but also will have "go later" and "go now, stop, go later" options.

For the purposes of this discussion, a brief look will be given to several of the options receiving considerable national attention.

The Open University. These proposals and programs provide for the education and awarding of degrees to students who might never spend time on a college campus. Great Britain and Japan now have operational programs that are serving as models for U.S. planners. Television will be the primary medium, but tape cassettes, radio, films, and correspondence will also be employed. Students may have access to regional resource centers and libraries. The faculty is expected to include a variety of persons such as broadcasters, educators, and students. The curriculum will be "now" centered and courses will be more systematic treatments of topics, not unlike those now covered fleetingly by the Public Broadcasting Service. Dennis (1971) wonders whether such programs are the "other side of Sesame Street," and predicts that by 1976 there will be a University of North America offering external baccalaureate and graduate degrees for most tuition for those from 15 to 60.

Open universities face problems in the future that could jeopardize their credibility and existence. Faculty are certainly going to raise questions about the equivalency of TV courses to on-campus courses. The range of student characteristics within any single course may be even broader than within many entire colleges. This will certainly present problems for assessment of student performance and grading.

Such programs will require their share of financial support, and, more importantly, they will need the type of creative leadership that will prevent them from becoming second-class citizens in the higher education arena. Much research will be needed on this option, and evaluations will have to be made at the same time as programs and experiences are being planned. Little is known yet about the characteristics and needs of students who would pursue this option. How different will they be from other students? What combination of multimedia experiences will be most effective? How much personal contact with teachers and resource persons will make a difference? These questions will have to be answered as this option moves ahead in an attempt to democratize higher education fully.

University Without Walls. Among the innovative ventures are programs referred to as "universities without walls." These plans abandon a number of the traditional notions of what constitutes higher education. Rather than a circumscribed campus area, these proposals aim to provide education for students wherever they may be—at work, at home, in independent study, or in field work. The classroom lecture or discussion is no longer the sole instrument of instruction, and the faculty may include people within and without the educational world. Its students also do not fit the typical age mold (18 to 22) but may range from 16 to 60. Its goal is lifelong learners, and it hopes to accomplish this at the same time as it improves the educational experience, does a better job of accomplishing its goals, and does both more economically than current counterparts. Such a program is being planned in several locales including the consortium referred to as the "Union for Experimenting Colleges and Universities" (Zigerell, 1971).

These programs may overlap with the open university concept. One apparent distinction, however, is that the "university without walls" concept definitely implies the offering of unique educational experiences in off-campus settings for academic credit, whereas the open university could be limited solely to traditional courses shown on TV. some of the same uncertainties and unknowns about TV colleges hold true as well for universities without walls.

Again this venture is not new to the educational scene. Field courses have been offered before, as well as independent study programs. Community personnel have also been used as resource persons. What is new is the energy, the enthusiasm, and the concerted effort with which these programs are now being supported.

They might very well serve not only to extend the boundaries of the college but also to extend the notion of what constitutes an educational experience. Faculty may well become coordinators of learning-practicum experiences rather than lecturers and exam-givers. New educational experiences will also demand new evaluation techniques.

Community Colleges. Like other phenomenon in higher education, community colleges are not new, but their recent and predicted expansion and their potential role in the future merit considerable attention by anyone looking at the future of American higher education. By 1980 the number of community colleges is expected to increase by half to 1,200, while enrollment is expected to triple to over 3 million students (Cosand, 1968). Some predict, while other hope, that such institutions will truly become comprehensive and that many students of the future will take their first two years of college in such a setting.

Looking at the current junior college scene provides a brief glimpse as to what the future has in store for community colleges. Junior college students in the past have been below average on scholastic measures when compared to their counterparts at four-year colleges, and have been from lower sauce-economic backgrounds. But these gross indicators mask the diversity of patterns found between and within particular colleges. Currently about two-thirds of the entering students plan to go on to four-year colleges, while only about a third actually do.

Of particular significance is the general pattern of uncertainty about the future that has been found to be prevalent among junior college students. Should these institutions become truly community colleges, the uncertainty and reexamination of goals might very well be even more pervasive among the students, young and old. The chance for people of all ages to try a new course or area of study in a relatively low-risk situation in terms of both money and personal investment might be a stimulus for further exploration and growth. Success will undoubtedly lead many students to rethink their current level of aspirations.

In some ways the mission of these institutions is clearer than those of four-year schools. Teaching and community service are given special emphasis, while research and publication are underplayed. It remains to be seen, though, whether or not community colleges can maintain their distinctiveness without trying to emulate other institutions. Community colleges will not only have to resist the temptation to become like four-year institutions but will have to move progressively into new areas if they are to truly fulfill their mission. This may mean sponsoring storefront college centers, offering courses in bridge, dog obedience and yoga, and rewarding faculty members for good teaching rather than esoteric research. It may also mean finding new audiences for specific courses, as well as responding to community needs. Many community colleges have already launched successful ventures, such as these. Whether or not the entire establishment of higher education will reinforce these efforts or continue to snub its nose, remains to be seen.

As the job market remains tight, good faculty members should be readily available from the ranks of young, unemployed PhD's. However, special attention will have to be given to determine whether or not those available are truly committed to the community college mission.

There appears to be general agreement that community colleges, technical schools, and other nonfour-year, post-secondary schools will face the greatest influx of new students. Not everyone is optimistic that the challenge of maintaining a distinctive mission will be met. If it is, the manner in which it is may serve as an important model for all higher education. Many four-year institutions could profit by keeping an eye on the efforts of their no longer "junior" partners.

Less Time, Stop-Out, More Degrees. Among the predicted and suggested directions for higher education are changes in the length of degree programs, a breakdown of the lockstep pattern, and increased degree offerings, such as two-year associate degrees. These were among the major concerns of the Carnegie Commission Report (1971a). The general argument is that today's students know more when they enter college than did students in the past; therefore, some college programs are now stretched out too long. Some are asking why programs cannot be accelerated or pruned and result in three-year programs. They believe that at least such options should be available to students.

Implications. Among the projected changes in the higher education scene, probably no others represent a more difficult challenge for those supporting student development goals. These changes could involve the reshaping of what college life—the typical collegiate environment, in any case—will be like for many persons being exposed to a college education. This is a challenge that is going to require more than a restructuring of student personnel roles and techniques; it is going to necessitate a reconceptualization of how student development occurs and how it can be enhanced in different environments and through different experiences than those in a traditional on-campus setting.

The demands are clear. If regional or nationwide TV colleges become a reality, it is possible that there will be thousands of citizens obtaining college credit and degrees who will never move away from home, never live in a residence hall, or never participate in student activities. Separation from the parental roost will be less likely and the peer group contacts and the contexts in which they occur will be radically different from those which take place on the typical campus. In fact, the range of ages and interests among the students should prompt some thinking about the appropriateness of the expression, *student development.* Yet students will still have a good many of the same decisions to make. They will still have to choose their majors, their vocational goals, their marriage partners, and their sets of values. These developmental decisions remain whether the student is in a lecture hall, in his room watching a remote terminal, or at home with a videotape cassette.

The reduction of the length of time required for degrees and the provision or stop-in, stop-out options may be economically beneficial to institutions and even to students, but not necessarily educationally salutary. Certainly the educational benefits are not intrinsically apparent. Course content can be pruned or covered more rapidly, but questions remain as to whether or not developmental change will also accelerate and take place during a three-year period rather than a four-year period. There is little evidence at this point that limits significant developmental changes to four-year patterns, but the question needs asking, nevertheless.

The attention the recommendations for less time and more options are drawing now centers on the packaging of the product rather than the product itself. The process of streamlining education is appealing to the American mind but it could mask the need for more basic changes. It may also save money—which has even a stronger appeal. All are very viable arguments if one is thinking primarily in terms of course content or credit hours earned, but they are less critical if one is thinking in terms of student outcomes. In a sense these efforts are providing an answer to the wrong question. The question should not be how we can accomplish the same goals more efficiently and economically, but should be whether or not we are successful in achieving our goals in the first place, or even whether or not these goals are the most appropriate.

Educationally, a more fruitful direction would be to examine the relevancy of moving in the direction of criterion performance rather than simply repackaging. Assuming first of all that the course or experience leads to acquiring an important competency, the concern of future educators should be on achievement of those competencies. If one individual can acquire and demonstrate these in half a semester, then he or she should be given credit at that point. Movement toward individualizing instruction in this manner, which may mean some students will complete requirements (arrive at certain competency levels) in three years, others in four or even five years, would be an educationally sounder rationale for tackling the content and time question than simply changing the wrapper on the package or offering an economy model.

Despite this apparent bleak portrait, there are some very positive implications and potentialities to these suggestions and directions. The potential democratization of higher education is almost a utopian aspiration, which if fulfilled in any effective fashion portends a people's renaissance that may make the American cultural scene something to behold. The danger of mediocrity remains, but as a risk and not as an inevitability. The same could be said for the development of a climate in which lifelong education flourishes. A good deal of research on attitude and value change among students indicates that change occurs during the college years but that there is a good deal of stability after graduation. Is this, too, inevitable? Would not continual input during a lifelong period provide the opportunity to promote continual development? Are the stages of human development so rigid that changes in attitudes and even in life styles cannot occur at age 40, 50, or 60?

As old and young share classroom and other learning experiences, the relative influence of the peer group and adult modeling is going to have to be reexamined. The very definition of peer group is going to have to be expanded and redefined. Are two students, who are taking the same freshman courses, to be considered peers even if one is 18 and the other is 50?   ·

Students participating in these new educational options are going to have many of the same developmental concerns as students in more traditional settings. In fact, their need for some services may be greater. More options may lead to more anxiety and more uncertainty. This does not mean that student personnel functions and services as they exist now should simply be extended. Counselors at regional centers or available by phone or closed-circuit TV may be necessary and helpful for students participating in various kinds of off-campus college credit experience. This would be, however, a limited response to the challenge and not representative of a really true professional development.

New developmental models will have to be conceived that focus on human development in relatively normal noncollege living environments. Research from the field of adult education will have to be reviewed and new efforts extended to compile the characteristics and needs of this population. If student development is to have any relevance to human development in the context of lifelong learning experiences, then the customary focus on peer groups, residence hall life, and student activities is going to have to be complemented with attention being given to parent-student relationships, marriage relationships, home life, and personality change among different age groups.

Undergraduate Programs

In no other aspect of higher education has there been as much consensus about the need for change and as much talk about change itself than there has been about the undergraduate curriculum and how students learn and are taught. Comparisons of course descriptions in today's catalogs and those of 10 years ago would undoubtedly lead to finding some notable changes. But stepping into a classroom today and hearing a lecture would not be a dramatically different experience than it was years ago. The words are different, but the instruments are the same, and sometimes even the melody.

Some of the same issues that were being debated 20 years ago are still alive, though in new guises. The relative values of and the appropriate balance between general and professional education is still being debated, as are the merits of survey and introductory courses, and specialized and interdisciplinary studies. Students complain about the lack of relevance, and faculty are accused at best of conservatism and at worst indifference. Protest has seldom taken the form of public demonstrations, but student organized educational reform groups are active on many campuses. Discontent is evident in the parallel structures that have been established. The free universities, experimental colleges, and other innovative programs represent indirect attacks on the system. The disenchantment with the whole educational venture is also evident in the free school movements and voucher plans, with Illich's deschooling notions having as many implications for college education as for elementary schools (Illich, 1971).

Suggested changes and predictions can be examined in terms of their impact directly on the curriculum, teaching methods, and on the environmental setting.

Curriculum. Predictions and suggestions for the curriculum per se are not earthshaking and yet, if taken together, they could represent a major change from the collegiate experience as it exists today. Some of the major changes can be classified under the following categories:

1. *Changes in required courses.* These are numerous suggestions that the survey course be abandoned and that introductory courses and prerequisites be reduced, if not eliminated. Some interest remains in demanding exposure to selected areas of knowledge such as science, humanities, math, and language. However, there is a bit more faith in a cafeteria approach with the student selecting the specific course to fulfill requirements within some broad guidelines.

2. *Course content more contemporary and less sequential.* In the past a student was never allowed to take Contemporary History or Contemporary Literature until an entire sequence of other courses had been completed.

Now, it is not unique for a student to start out his freshmen year by being involved in the here-and-now. Interdisciplinary courses are receiving greater attention, though many are simply patch quilts of old content rather than problem-oriented new efforts.

3. *Variations in course experiences.* College education in the past had been identified with courses and credits to the point that it meant simply that a three-hour course met three times a week, a two-hour course met twice a week, and to take a two-hour course for three hours credit meant writing an extra paper. Suggestions for the future include more work-study courses, more time away from the campus, more foreign study, and simply a greater variety of ways of earning credit.

4. *Competency not credit.* The movement away from identifying college with just courses and credits also holds the potential to have an impact on the total structure of the collegiate experience. Four-one-four calendars have helped promote the value of minicourses, and it is possible that students will take fewer courses at one time in the future and the whole concept of prerequisites may be simplified. Concurrent with this movement is an increasing recognition of the value of nonresidential learning experiences. The idea that a person can gain college credit simply by taking an examination is gaining momentum and promises to open new doors and avenues for the older citizen as well as for the recent high school graduate.

5. *Teaching and Learning.* The renewed concern about the undergraduate program has prompted what some have called a new ethics of teaching. Different ways are being sought to reward good teachers, and there continues to be discussion of a doctorate of arts degree that would be intended for those pursuing college teaching as a career. However, one would have to search far to find dramatic differences in how most undergraduates are being taught today. Attending lectures, taking notes, and reading the book is still the learning pattern for most college students enrolled in regular course programs. The signs of change are present, however. They are not only being discussed but in some institutions implemented. Among the hopeful possibilities are:

1. *The increasing number of campus centers devoted to the improvement of teaching and learning.* Although perhaps just a beginning, they represent a testimony of faith and serve as a resource for faculty members sincerely interested in improving their teaching. The anticipated continuing scrutiny of the concept of tenure promises the possibility that accountability notions may affect the higher educational scene.

2. *There appears to be a growing recognition of the fact that learning can take place in many different modes.* The changes alluded to in the discussion of the curriculum apply here as well as though not frequently used yet, there appears

to be an increasing acceptance of credit by course examination or through such programs as the *College Level Examination Program* of the Educational Testing Service. The idea that students may gain valuable educational insights through work experiences with community resource persons and even from each other represent major changes from the traditional classroom-lecture-exam sequence.

3. *The marshalling of pro and con evidence about grading may promise a needed revolution in grading and evaluation.* Grades have been a source of irritation and a block to comfortable faculty-student relationships for years. Panned for unjustified as well as justified reasons, new efforts to implement Pass/Fail systems hold little promise unless they are accompanied by a clearer specification of criteria than has been true in the past. Movement from an A to F system to a High Pass to Fail system represents more tinkering with the system than a major change.

Still lurking in the background, but possibly gaining momentum, is an increasing interest in the criterion performance model with records indicating "complete" or "incomplete." This model clearly holds promise for skills courses, but still needs articulation for other areas. It is ironic that we have worried so much about assessing *what a student knows*, but so little about assessing *who he is becoming*.

4. *A rebirth of interest and appropriate use of TV, audio- and videotapes, and phone hookups is predicted.* The expected major impact is on the increased accessibility of college for those off-campus, but this renewed interest has implications for resident students as well. Individually paced instructional packages are being prepared for many college courses. As these gain some credibility it is possible that students will be able to start and stop independently of traditional academic calendars. The next step—for students to be able to pipe into their rooms or home their geography lectures, library resource materials, and progress report examinations—is not that far distant.

5. *The project method will increase in popularity as will independent study.* Spoon-feeding students soon forgotten facts is becoming a less and less popular art, even among the most rigid of the pedants. The fact explosion has prompted at least some professors to agree that how one learns and his resulting attitude and style of approaching new learning or problem-solving is as important as knowing names, dates, and places.

6. *Self-motivation will be relied upon almost exclusively for course assignments and accomplishments, rather than compulsory assignments.* If competency rather than time spent becomes the real criterion, then students will have to demonstrate their competencies independently of assignments done, and education becomes a potentially, truly self-developing process.

7. *Living-Learning Environments.* The impersonalism of the large universi-

ties, the coldness of high-rise cell block living units, and perhaps the awareness that much of the socialization benefits of college are a result of the total environment has prompted the development of coed living units, living-learning residential colleges, and cluster colleges. Several prognosticators see these movements continuing in the next decade. Yet, others see the trend as having peaked.

During the past decade, so-called experimental colleges have flourished, clearly demonstrating the importance of the living dimension of the living-learning symbiotic relationship. Most have been quite successful in establishing a new sense of community and a sense of "specialness" that nurtures growth among a good number of their students. Justifications given for such enterprises have been based on the fact that experimental colleges serve politically in an attempt to establish a parallel system to the regular university. Hopefully, these colleges can be a place where faculty members can test out new ideas and improve their teaching methods. Such hothouse endeavors can then serve as illustrative models for the rest of the university to emulate. In general, these ventures have resulted in a less intellectual climate than many of their planners had anticipated and a sizable number of students appear to be incapable of functioning in a free, nonstructured environment such as that fostered by experimental colleges. At this juncture these colleges have served as a place where faculty and students, who are already committed to trying something new, can gather with some sense of communality. They have not fallen on their faces as some faculty predicted, and they might claim that they have harmed no more students than the regular university curriculum. Yet, there is little evidence that their innovations have really taken, and the self-selective composition of both the faculty and students makes their results hardly generalizable.

Those who have been intimately involved with either cluster colleges or experimental colleges are strong advocates for extending the concepts to the total collegiate system. Indeed, it is doubtful that any enlightened college official will be able to justify construction of new residence halls that do not have adequate provisions for classroom and learning spaces that could make a living unit a potential living-learning environment.

Implications. The new emphasis on teaching, examining how students learn rather than only what they lean, cannot help but improve the undergraduate experience and foster student development. Many of the suggested and predicted changes are intended to individualize the learning experience and to promote greater bonds between the student's classroom experiences and his day-to-day life. The direction of these changes and their eventual reality cannot but have an impact on the student's self-concept and self-confidence.

Those concerned about total student development must, however, raise a number of questions and suggest some directions and alternatives. First of all, there must be concern about the extent and breadth of the suggested changes. Few of the revisions can be considered bold, and few have permeated the entire collegiate program even at any one large institution. Most of the changes are made cautiously and often are applicable for only a small and self-selective group of students.

Major changes are often initiated for special programs with special students, often with special funding. Innovators hope that their success, though seldom validated to other faculty members' satisfaction, will soon lead to major changes in the rest of the university or in other colleges. Yet, such experiments often lose their novelty and fail to gain refunding, while the traditional ventures march on and on. Innovations such as experimental colleges hold promise, but they hold no guarantee of ultimately changing the system.

Any one of the suggested changes in the undergraduate program could revolutionize higher education, if it was carried out to the fullest. The history of curricular reform in American higher education would not, however, be congruent with major or dramatic changes in the future. One group or the other of the triumvirate of students, faculty, and administrators has often been more conservative than the other, and change has been forestalled or slowed down. To bring about major change in the undergraduate program is going to necessitate commitment on the part of college academic departments that has not been evidenced in the past. Indeed, some suggest that major changes will not occur until the departmental structure as it now exists has been reconstituted.

On the surface this seems to be a radical solution, and, perhaps, an impossible one. The answer may life, however, in maintaining the departmental structure as a viable alternative for some students some of the time, but at the same time creating another framework such as a general college made up of faculty committed to undergraduates and to working with students on projects, interdisciplinary enterprises, and other combinations that do not fit into a departmental mold.

Critical to the success of any effort to revitalize undergraduate teaching efforts is a change in the reward system for faculty members. When faculty promotions and raises are based primarily on scholarly publications, only the rarest few can serve two masters: the students and the journal editors. Some graduate colleges are offering teaching doctorate called the doctor of arts degree. This is a fruitless effort unless the reward system is also changed. In this case a direct approach would seem more viable than creating an alternative degree. Improvement of the current graduate programs could be accomplished by including teaching experience and supervision as a major requirement for a Ph.D. who plans to teach. This may be too much to expect.

A neglected avenue of change is working directly with current faculty. Teaching-learning centers manned by staff who have some expertise in the psychology of instruction and learning offer that alternative. They might work with the interested faculty members first and hope that the good word will spread. Again, we clearly have a self-selective factor operating, but this time the participants are not isolated from their colleagues in some special venture nor are they working with a special clientele. Helping a math instructor figure out ways of reducing poor students' anxiety about math may well be something that he can share with his math colleagues and certainly something he can try out with typical students—those in his class. The instructor may even come back for more.

Such centers are probably less glamorous than experimental colleges and interdisciplinary courses, but the federal government and foundations should continue to fund such ventures. If institutions of higher learning are to give testimony to their renewed interest in the undergraduate, they must explore ways of rewarding good teaching and attempts to improve teachers. When promotion and tenure committees do look beyond research publications for criteria, they should consider participation in efforts to improve teaching as a rewardable behavior.

The suggestion and prediction that the curriculum of the future will deal more with the here-and-now is a step in the right direction in terms of student development, but it is not necessarily a full step. It is possible that a course in contemporary literature may be more interesting than reading *Beowulf* for many students, and it is also likely That an interdisciplinary approach to population problems may provide more opportunity for dealing with headline topics; however, being contemporary is not identical with being relevant. The key to relevancy is the individual student. Does it have meaning for him here and now, can he fit it into his past, does he see where it may lead him? These insights can be gained from Dostoevski as well as Tom Wolfe, or from studying the amoeba as well as population problems. The instructional process is as important in determining relevancy as is the content.

When professors seek help to improve their courses, they should be encouraged. Efforts to improve teaching and foster innovations should be applauded. However, it is noteworthy to examine the kinds of questions they ask.

Many professors, who are interested in change, are concerned about improving their teaching in order to accomplish the same goals they have always had without looking closely at those goals. They are concerned about technique rather than ends. They wonder how they can improve their examinations or whether or not using an overhead projector gets the idea across better. The goals and the criteria to assess them remain the same. The ethics professor wonders whether or not students know the rules of logic, not whether or not they make logical personal decisions. The psychology professor wants his students to have sufficient knowledge of terminology and an awareness of psychology as a behavioral science, but does not assess whether they have any better understanding of themselves or others. At the same time, a teacher of a skills course, who can more readily obtain objective evidence of his effectiveness than can some of his colleagues in other disciplines, frequently fails to determine whether or not his students have developed any new sense of competency or any new incentive to sharpen their skills or learn new ones. Teaching and curriculum innovators, whether they be audacious or faint-hearted, are doing an excellent job of asking if students are learning as well as they did under the old systems, but too few are asking whether or not that goal is sufficient.

It is disappointing to find so very few references among the suggestions for curriculum and program innovation that allude to the question of whether or not the affective life of students should be a formal concern. Curriculum planners tend to continue renovating rather than innovating. Switching from lectures to discussions or from textbooks to individualized packages represents major changes and needed ones; but, too often, they essentially represent ways of better achieving the academic goals of the university. To the extent that these efforts personalize and humanize the higher education experience for many undergraduates, they should in turn foster student development, but they still view student growth as one-dimensional.

The involvement of student personnel staff in the academic dimensions of campus life is limited in most college settings. When new programs develop or teaching innovations are explored, the academicians consult with those they respect and those they believe can help them. This is not generally a member of the student affairs staff. If a professor wants someone to help him decipher the dynamics of his classroom doldrums, he is most likely to seek out a colleague in his own department or someone else in another academic discipline. If he does seek out someone in student affairs, it will be because he has respect for that individual and because that person has demonstrated knowledge and skills that will be useful to him.

One of the major tenets of this monograph is that in the future the academic arena is going to become more important in promoting student development. If this is true, student personnel staff are going to have to become more involved with this dimension of a student's life. Their kind of input is needed when both goals and techniques are discussed. But the staff is going to have to possess the competencies and skills that command the respect of the academician. They may, in fact, have to become academicians themselves.

Kenneth E. Eble recently admitted to extreme pessimism regarding curricular innovation when he wrote: "The curriculum will always be an expedient to make the formal training of large aggregations of individuals manageable. If it can be kept from getting too much in the way of teaching and learning; that may be as much as can be hoped" (Eble, 1971). This attitude, while not entirely unrealistic, is hardly one to inspire change. To the extent that the curriculum is viewed as independent of teacher and learner, it is correct; but this fragmentation is impossible in the real world, if not in the abstract world.

Governance and Finance

It is extremely difficult to sort through the many guesses and recommendations regarding the future organizational structure of higher education and arrive at a true consensus. Some prognosticators have changed their minds from year to year and the resulting picture is contradictory. Some predict less leadership from university presidents while other expect a resurgence of visible presidential authority. A good number see faculties continuing to unionize, whereas others foresee a more shared governance as part of the future. These differences in opinion may be attributable to whether the forecaster is a realist or a dreamer. Never before have there been as many people and as diverse a group of people having a voice in university governance, yet at the same time there has probably never been a time when so many different people were so disgruntled or felt so powerless.

There is general consensus, however, that the future will see more state control of public institutions and more influence of the federal government on all institutions. State boards and state commissioners are an increasingly visible entity in many states, as the movement toward state planning and coordinating bodies continues.

Although students have been more involved lately in university governance than they have been in the recent past, it remains to be seen whether or not this will be a transitory phase or a lasting change. In a recent survey of student participation on university committees (Magrath, 1970), it was found that less than 3 percent of the colleges surveyed had students as voting members of a board of trustees and just over 3 percent had students voting on faculty selection, promotion, and tenure committees. Only a third had students as voting members of student life committees.

Accountability and cost efficiency promise to have major influences on the future of higher education. Student credit-hour-per-dollar will continue to be a critical index of a program's worth—at least in the minds of budget administrators. This means that very few innovative programs are going to be initiated unless they are financially self-sustaining or supported by outside funding. Kerr (1971) has recommended that one of the functions of a National Foundation of Higher Education would be to support innovative programs, and this may well be necessary if the tight budgeting continues.

Tuition increases can also be expected to continue, and students and their parents will be asked to share more and more of the educational costs, as will the federal government. As the job market demands fewer college graduates, the pendulum has swung from society at large bearing the major portion of the costs to it being a joint responsibility between society, students, and parents (Bowen, 1971).

Implications. Major restructuring of the organizational framework of higher education in the past has been rare and probably will continue to be so. For the most part there has been more concern about the structure and not enough concern about the process. Unfortunately that imbalance is likely to continue. Ideally, faculty, staff, and students should be equal members of a community, but the trend more recently has been for all parties to be adversaries. Unionization of faculties and collective bargaining could very likely result in the removal of the faculty as a powerful force in university decision-making. They would simply be employees. This could quite easily leave the major decisions up to the administrators and the students, who might become adversaries of the faculty.

A major student criticism of the 60's was directed at the impersonalization of the larger universities. The solution does not appear to be to tear down the buildings and disperse the students to countryside hamlets. Such decentralization is economically unsound and perhaps even educationally unwise. A more positive answer is one that would permit the student to be more involved in the decision-making that affects his personal life. Thus, if a student can personally work out how he meets certain degree requirements on his own or with the advice of someone else and not have to rely on a prescribed pattern of courses, his freedom is limited only by the number of courses offered. If the student can decorate his own room as he chooses or help determine the specific rules within his residence unit, the university is going to seem like a more personal place than it would be were all such decisions handed down from above.

Some type of financial and academic accountability cannot help but make the colleges and universities more responsive to the students and the public. Probably in no other financial transaction does a consumer have less opportunity to ask for his money back than a student does when he pays his tuition and obtains no benefits. The student is in effect not even buying knowledge, he is buying course credit and with no guarantee. Whether the student will benefit from more freedom, more accountability, and more consumer power, however, remains problematical. His interests will be met, but will his needs? The critical question is whether or not students will take personal risks if financial and academic risks are limited. Will he or she take courses that will necessitate an exploration of self, a challenge to cherished values, or a course that has no immediate payoff?

Major Trends and the Challenges

Several significant themes recur throughout the many reports making recommendations for higher education and among the predictions made by the seers. Each represents a challenge, and the responses made to these challenges will determine the shape of the future and could quite dramatically influence the extent to which colleges and universities will foster student development. Some of these have already been alluded to in the earlier discussion, but the major trends are important enough to sort out and look at independently.

1. *Continual and rapid change in society's values and mores.* Two conflicting movements have been characteristic of American society for some time—movement toward homogenization and movement toward pluralism. These concurrent trends almost define *American.* To survive in such a milieu, both the individual and society need a strong sense of identity. To grow, both require an openness that is rare. To survive and to grow, the individual student is going to have to be in an environment that is supportive and one that does not leave development up to chance.

Colleges and universities have hoped that students would be forced to confront their own value system by learning more about the values of others in different cultures. Relatively few systematic efforts are made, however, to guarantee that such self-examination takes place, and seldom are students asked to demonstrate an awareness of the origins or nature of their own value systems and what influences them. Students are more likely to be challenged by the values of their peer group than they are by their academic experience. If higher education is to provide the student of the future with the opportunity to gain insight into his own value formation, some definite focus will have to center on the student himself. He is going to have to become his own lab as he tests out his attitudes, reactions, and responses. A goal for higher education should be to provide the lab manual and guide.

This will necessitate, first of all, a commitment to the task, assignment of high priority in any reorganization, or rethinking about the curriculum and instructional methods. It also means making such experiences—reexamination of attitudes and values—a part of the formal curriculum, not simply part of the extracurricular.

2. *Universal higher education.* The trauma that secondary education went through with the movement toward universal high school education is now being faced anew by colleges and universities. Some type of post-secondary educational experience is now the rules rather than the exception for high school graduates, and some educators are advocating that all persons have two years of post-secondary education "in the bank."

The response of higher education thus far has been to provide a variety of options from which the student can choose. Community colleges, technical colleges, two-year programs, residential colleges, open universities, and regional universities all represent alternatives available to many high school graduates. These options are necessary, but they are insufficient in themselves and present new problems and risks. How, for example, are students to choose among the options available? It is one step toward democratization to open all the doors and permit entry, but how does the student decide what door is most appropriate for him? Ready access accompanied by easy exit encourages mobility, but it does not necessarily reduce wear and tear in the process.

In the past, secondary schools coped with universal education by using a track system based on abilities. In many instances this resulted in students of lower ability taking not only different level courses but taking courses with different content. Bright students took the college preparatory courses, while the less bright took vocational courses. Such differentiation has already taken place in higher education among and within institutions as distinct patterns (with some notable exceptions) of ability level, thereby distinguishing vocational-technical college students from community college students and both from four-year college students. Within universities there is very often a well-known "dumping ground" major or department and speedy exit for the unsuccessful.

Operationally, colleges have been saying that only certain kinds of students can be educated; the rest have to be trained. Meeting student needs has been translated into developing parallel systems with different content. The challenge of the future is not how to cope with large numbers of students, although that remains a formidable task. The real challenge lies in trying to accomplish the same kind of goals with different kinds of students. This may mean teaching the same content differently to different students in order to accomplish the same goals, or it may mean teaching different content in a way that accomplishes the same goals. This has seldom, if ever, been faced head-on by curriculum planners.

3. *The consumer revolution.* It remains to be seen yet whether or not the student role in university affairs will be more vocal or if there will be continuing interest on the part of students in actively participating in college governance. Whether interest wanes or not, the franchise has been given, and it is doubtful that it can ever again be ignored. The renewed interest in undergraduate education, curriculum revisions, examination of tenure policies, and the growing movement toward accountability have certainly been influenced if not actually brought about by student input. Gradual, but drastic reduction in parietal rules, which continues to occur, certainly serves to make the student an independent, free-choice consumer of the educational offerings. Even if this general movement abates, the variety of educational opportunities available will put the student in the position of effecting change with his pocketbook—if not his vote. During a time of restricted budgets, class registrations may have more of an impact on the curriculum than faculty vote. In some circles it is being predicted that the student and the federal government will be paying a greater share of the educational expenses in tuition, special funding, and loans. This too will serve to make students concerned consumers.

Colleges will be sorely pressed to resist trying to repackage their product in more attractive ways without changing the product. Instead, they should consider the challenge of revising the contract they now make with students. Instead of offering credits and degrees for time and money spent, they might offer skills and competencies. Suppose a standard tuition fee was charged that would bind the university to the student until the latter was able to exhibit skills and competencies to the satisfaction of the student, not the university? Such accountability would indeed support a consumer revolution.

4. *The changing locale and nature of the college experience..* There will probably always be students taking classes on campus, and "going away to college" will still be an annual fall event. It appears very likely, however, that eventually the resident student will be in the minority. If open universities, universities without walls, and regional colleges take hold as they are predicted to, many students will gain their college degree by commuting, working with local resource people, or studying in hometown libraries. It is not at all out of the realm of possibility that a student of the future may have access to the college degree without leaving his home.

Choices made at this juncture may well influence the course of these external degree programs and field experiences for some time to come. One very real possibility is that colleges and universities of the future will focus almost exclusively on skill development and the intellectual growth of students. Little or no attention will be given to providing an environment for social and personal development. Despite the efforts at establishing residential and cluster colleges and other living-learning environments, it is quite possible that because of fiscal considerations and political pressures, colleges and universities will wash their hands of other dimensions of student growth and attempt to become solely houses of intellect.

The challenge then is twofold. First, can and will the universities continue to attempt to integrate the living-learning experiences of on-campus students? Secondly, will some effort be made to accomplish student development goals in non campus environments?

5. *Lifelong education and full development of all citizens.* Neither of these trends are new to American education. Adult education has been a growing phenomenon for decades, and full development of all citizens is simply an extension of earlier democratic commitments. However, until now the will and technology to bring these to fruition have not existed concurrently. A few short years ago the story of a grandmother going to college was unique and intriguing enough to provide the theme for a movie comedy. Housewives who were awarded bachelors degrees after 10 year of night school had their picture in the paper alongside another picture of a married couple receiving their doctorates at the same time. Today, the creation of an Emeritus University for those between the ages of 55 and 69 (Camper, 1971) seems like a natural extension and development, as does the offering of college courses on Long Island commuter trains.

The appropriate response to these phenomena will have to consist of more than reshuffling the course requirements and admissions standards. It will mean more than just having a diversity of institutions such as comprehensive colleges, community colleges, and technical colleges. What will be needed is a new operational definition of what higher education is about. Education for professional development remains a major goal, as does education for skill development, and education for enrichment. All make up parts of education for full development; none can stand alone. Education for full development means the opportunity to discover new talents and interests, the chance to acquire new competencies and new skills, and the freedom to risk oneself in a new venture with minimal psychic cost. If these new trends are to lead to more than Wednesday evening chit-chats to pass the time, higher education and those concerned with human development will be challenged to conceptualize and program a higher education system that fosters continual growth and development, not just retooling or enrichment.

The Predicament and the Promise

Confucius says that "He who makes predictions and has no power to bring them into being will end his days eating abandoned birds' nests." No doubt the fate of one who tries to summarize the seers' words is even more distasteful. Certainly one who attempts this task for the higher education establishment takes on no less a challenge and may end up with no worse a fate than being a professor emeritus of higher education with a programmed response every five years of, "I was almost right." As has been pointed out repeatedly, the fate of higher education is integrally tied up with so many variable such as the nation's economy, the feelings towards technological progress, and the draft that is impossible to predict exactly how central higher education will be in the life of the nation in the future.

Given even the will of the nation, one must consider the bureaucracy that is higher education. A sizable number of the recommendations call for or demand significant changes on the part of faculty members. One needs to ask whether or not the faculty can really be expected to change. After all, it is their behavior that is central if higher education is to be different. All kinds of transformations may take place around them and in them; but if they do not behave differently, all else is in vain.

Given these provisos, one must still conclude that change is in the air and the wind is blowing in generally the right direction. The renewed interest in undergraduate education and the growing consumer(student) interest and power promise change in the system. The next decade holds the promise of being rich in thoughtful innovation. Even if such optimism regarding change on a large scale proves to be groundless, those involved in the higher education venture might do well to at least try to bring about change within their own sphere by starting with their own classes, departments, or staff. Robert F. Kennedy's words are appropriate and certainly present a viable motto: "Some look at what is, and ask why. I look at what could be and ask, why not."

Chapter 3
The Goal of Student Development: Is it a Myth?

The major focus of many of the recent and significant reports on higher education has been on numbers, years, degrees, access, options, organization, and finances. With the exception of the Hazen Foundation Report (Committee on the Student in Higher Education, 1968), little direct attention has been given the impact that the suggested changes will have on students, except for perhaps getting them in and out of college easier and more often. Some attention to new programs and procedures has been promised by both a new HEW Task Force and an upcoming Carnegie Commission Report. Hopefully, these efforts will give significant attention to students and less to logistics. Attention to numbers, procedures, and finances is important, but it should be preceded by a clear statement of goals and accompanied by an analysis of the relationship between projected changes and student outcomes. Concern for the pocketbook may ultimately lead to worthwhile program changes, but it would be nice if this occurred by design rather than by accident.

The preceding chapter attempted to illustrate some of the kinds of thinking that need to be done as the many recommendations and suggestions are considered for the future, but several important questions remain. Has student development ever been a real goal of higher education or is it a myth? Is it a viable goal for the future? If the starting place is the student, what does higher education want to achieve? Unless these questions are faced squarely, discussions about the future will continue to focus on budgetary concerns and innovations solely for the sake of innovation.

One other key question remains. What does the research and the conceptualization about student development have to say that might point to alternative directions for higher education? Much has been implied in earlier sections. In this chapter these will be given particular attention.

An Evolving History

A comprehensive review of the goals of higher education since the first days of the University of Paris and the Sorbonne would reveal that throughout history, almost without exception, the expressed or clearly implicit goals of colleges and universities have been to have an impact on students in ways more extensive than passing on facts, specific skills, or intellectual capacities. Universities have been characterized as seekers and preservers of truth, critics of society, havens for freedom, and nests for new ideas. When, however, their instructional role is examined closely and when one looks at what was intended to happen to the student, the goals almost universally include changing the student; in effect, making him a better person, a more humane being.

There have been some who look to the past for a philosophical or historical basis for diminishing the relative importance of individual personal development among students as a prime goal of college. They take historical solace in an appeal to the "knowledge for its own sake" argument. This is a losing argument, however, as the real debate was never between the intrinsic value of knowledge and personal growth; rather it was between the merits of practical, utilitarian, vocational training and those of a liberal education. Personal growth was explicit or implicit in all arguments. Cardinal Newman, for example, has often been quoted as supporting the pursuit of knowledge for its own sake as the proper stance for universities, but a closer reading finds him equally supportive of education for development:

. . . (university) education is the education which gives a man a clear conscious view of his own opinions and judgments, a truth in developing them, an eloquence in expressing them, and a force in urging them. It shows him how to accommodate himself to others, how to throw himself into their state of mind, how to bring before them his own, how to influence them, how to come to an understanding with them, how to bear with them (Newman, 1941, p. 196).

The debate regarding the value of a liberal education has lingered on but through the years personal development has remained a constant refrain in any series of goal statements. Those examining the aims of college during the current century of expansion have been equally constant in their support. Indeed, the student development movement might well regard Alfred North Whitehead as much a founding father as Nevitt Sanford. Whitehead spoke of an interrelationship between culture, intellect, and self-development:

Culture is activity of thought, and receptiveness to beauty and humane feeling. Scraps of information have nothing to do with it. What we should aim at producing is men who possess both culture and expert knowledge in some special direction. We have to remember that the value intellectual development is self development . . . [Whitehead, 1959, p.13].

In the past the threads of intellectual and personal development ran parallel, but in more recent years the theorists have suggested that they should be intertwined. Today there is much more of an inclination to see cognitive and affective growth as intimately related, and to view them as independent is inadequate and inaccurate. So when we look at the aims of higher education as expressed by Nevitt Sanford, we find a statement similar to those of Newman, Whitehead, and others, but one that moves a significant step beyond:

It is frequently said that the proper concern of higher education is with the intellect only. But the notion that the intellect is somehow disembodied or separated from the rest of the personality, is not only unintelligent, in that it favors no legitimate educational aim, it is actually perverse in its implications, in that it encourages the assumption that if one takes it upon himself to be a student he cannot at the same time be a human being [Sanford, 1970].

Is student development as a goal alive and well today? The final answer to this question must be "maybe," as the evidence is mixed depending on where you look and who you ask. Examination of college catalogs reveals personal growth, as expressed in terms of "increased self-awareness." Peterson (1971) reports that if you ask college administrators or students to rank or rate possible goals, humanistic goals remain quite high. The tie between the intellectual and personal dimensions has received no clearer support than a recent declaration by Paul Dressel:

The objectives in the cognitive and affective domains are not separable. Educated behavior always involves both affective and cognitive elements. Institutions of higher education involve, at every point in their operation, value commitments and value conflicts which have been largely unrecognized or ignored . . . Value-free intellectual change is an ideal unachievable by man, and probably undesirable in any case [Dressel, 1971, pp. 400–405].

With all this positive support, why the "maybe"? Primarily because very few discussions about the future of higher education consider the affective domain as they suggest changes and initiate new programs. Also because personal growth is expected to be a by-product of an educational venture or to be accomplished by extracurricular activities. Finally, there is very little effort to evaluate the personal growth of individual students during their college years. Transcripts may say something about how much content was learned, and administrators may be concerned about contentment among the student body, but no one assesses the personal growth of each student as he passes through the portals of academe.

Perhaps it would be more realistic to say that student development as a major educational goal now stands in jeopardy. In the past, it has often been relegated to out-of-class activities. In the future, it may be ignored. As we search for future directions, it is appropriate to glance at the results of research that has been done on student development.

Student Development Research—What Does It Say?

Serious psychological interest a research in the development processes of college students do not predate by many years Nevitt Sanford's *The American College* in 1962. About that same time Pace and Stern (1958) were developing environmental assessment measures designed specifically for the college scene, and people were still reacting to Jacob's (1957) conclusion that very few colleges were having an impact on the values and attitudes of college students. Prior to that time many were aware of the need for research, and some individual researchers were spinning out studies and weaving theories, but not in any fashion that would significantly influence the training or behavior of student personnel workers. Since that time, what can be called student development research has grown, and major compilations of research findings have been published (Feldman& Newcomb, 1969; Katz, 1968; Korn, 1970; Trent& Medsker, 1967). These efforts cannot be summarized in a few paragraphs, but it is appropriate to examine briefly (a) some general findings, and following Astin's (1970) model to look at, (b) student input characteristics, (c) the important environmental influences and their impact, and (d) the implications. Those interested in documentation of the summary can refer to the sources already listed or those given in the Suggested Reading List under "Student Development."

General Findings

A number of general conclusions can be drawn from the research conducted thus far on student development. It has been shown, for example, that colleges have a differential impact on student values and goals. Some are more potent than others and some college environments have a greater effect on some types of students than others.

As institutions vary, so do students; they have their own individual developmental rates and periods. Though all may enter with a high school diploma, similarities stop there in terms of their potential and readiness for change. The evidence suggests that personality changes are more likely to occur than changes in intellectual disposition. How the student views himself and others is more likely to be influenced during his college years than how he reasons and solves problems. Students most likely to exhibit greater changes in intellectual orientation are likely to be the bright and already intellectually inclined.

Generally, the changes are in directions consistent with the humanistic goals of education. Students become less authoritarian, dogmatic, and ethnocentric. The pattern of change tends to be in the direction of differentiation of self from others and integration of self into a whole—what is commonly referred to as developing a sense of identity.

Most freshmen start out the year with idealistic goals and are open and receptive to change. What changes do occur, especially those related to socialization, take place quite early—often during the first year of college. Many freshmen end the year unhappy and disenchanted. They are now committed to academic game-playing and grade-setting rather than scholarly learning.

Student Characteristics

The most predictive index of what students will be like when they finish college is what they were like when they entered. Eager and high-achieving graduates were more than likely bright, eager, and high-achieving freshmen. The shortcut to having good graduates is to have good freshmen. Some colleges and some programs appear to have more of an impact than others, but the effects are never completely independent of what the students were like initially. If one is going to fully understand student development during the college years, he must be aware of what students are like when they enter, and how this interrelates with the impact the college experience may or may not have on them.

The current generation of students is generally recognized as being more physically and psychologically mature than those students of 20 years ago. There is clear evidence that they are taller and on the average have reached pubescence at an earlier age. Although they may be less naive and more knowledgeable about the world around them, they are not any more sure of themselves or independent and, in fact, may be more anxious than students of a decade ago. A sizable number are concerned about larger issues than those surrounding their own personal lives. They react negatively to depersonalized treatment, to a lack of authenticity in interpersonal relationships, and to complacency. Further, they tend to be skeptical of tradition. Over half rate their college courses as irrelevant even before they start college.

Certain identifiable subcultures exist on most campuses. Though membership may overlap extensively, students within the subcultures can be predicted to behave in certain fashions and to be affected differentially by their college experience. Students in different curriculums, for example, have different personality characteristics, as well as interests. The pattern of research results suggests that initial differences are accentuated as students continue to pursue their majors, and within particular disciplines, they become more homogeneous.

Several other classifications of students, such as commuters, residence hall students, and protesters, yield distinct personality and need profiles. These input characteristics interact with the environment, resulting in a differential impact of the collegiate experience. Depending upon certain personality characteristics and socioeconomic backgrounds, for example, students vary systematically in their receptivity to change and their responsiveness to various teaching styles. Changes in authoritarianism are influenced by the student's receptivity. Student preferences for lectures and discussions, teacher-dominated, and student-centered teaching procedures will vary significantly with their need for order, variety, and structure.

Personality variables will also effect the extent to which they are influenced by their peer groups. Certainly a student who is quite open to revealing himself to others is apt to be changed more than one who is close-mouthed about himself.

Environmental Factors Influencing Change

During the past 15 years a major focus of research on student development has been on assessing the impact of various collegiate environments on students. Environmental pressures differ depending on whether or not the college is coed, public, private, a four-year or a two-year institution. Even within a particular college there may be many different environments, this being especially true for large universities. The amount of personal freedom present may well be a factor of the size and selectivity of the institution and even the socioeconomic background of students. Different professional groups on campus will perceive the same campus environment differently. The individual student's perception of the environment may well be influenced as much by who he is as by where he is. His own personal needs will affect how he interprets his surroundings and, in turn, the kind of impact they will have on him. His perceptions, of course, are open to change, e.g., seniors often see their college differently than freshmen.

One of the most potent environmental influences on student development in college is the peer group. While the faculty may play some role in the development of intellectual attitudes and perhaps in vocational choice, the dominant and single most important force remains the peer group. Its influence is most prominent in changing social attitudes and personality. Socialization, as much as information, is likely to have an impact on attitudes toward grades, future aspirations, and life goals. When entering freshmen are asked what they think will be the dominant influence on their future life, they suggest the academic side of campus life. When asked four years later, as seniors, what was the most significant event, they will describe a personality change that was influenced by an interpersonal relationship.

There is clearly an interaction between a student's characteristics and propensities when he enters college, the curriculum he chooses, and where he lives. Students start out with certain expectations about what a curriculum is like and what roles career professionals play. They are more likely to shift curricula than roles as they search for a best fit between their interests, their personalities, and the role of a person in a particular major or profession. Some curriculum and course experiences appear to have more of an impact than others. As might be expected, humanities and social sciences appear to have a greater impact on student development than do the sciences. Faculty influence on student attitudes and values is relatively limited when compared to the power of the peer group.

Challenge and sometimes even conflict appear to facilitate or accelerate change in students. Much is unknown about the particulars of this phenomenon, but some evidence suggests that congruence between environmental press and initial student characteristics leads to accentuation of any initial differences; whereas lack of congruence leads to changes in the student or the student's environment.

An undeniably important dimension of every student's environment is where he lives. The location and the physical makeup of the living environment are important as determiners of the amount and kind of interactions that take place with other students. Architectural designs, rules, and regulations certainly have an impact, mostly in providing an atmosphere that may reflect warmth and community or coldness and sterility.

Studies done specifically on residence hall life suggest again that the input variable is a factor. Different types of students chose residence halls than those who either chose apartment living or those who remain at home. Though socioeconomic background is a factor, it is not the sole determinant. Personality variables also play a role in choice of living environment. Students who chose to commute to college rather than live on campus have different interests and competencies than residents even before the school year begins. Available evidence suggests that they are also affected differently by their college experience. Their initial characteristics are different, their environment is different, and, as a result, the outcomes are also distinct. New ventures in residential college living-learning experiments also attract a particular clientele. Bright students with interests focusing on the humanities and from upper middle class backgrounds are the most likely applicants for such ventures.

Residence hall staff have seen their role expectation change from disciplinarian to counselor to educational programmer. At various times and in various institutions they serve all three capacities. Efforts to make residence halls living-learning environments have proved to be successful in terms of having a modest impact on the intellectual orientation of students and fostering modest attitudinal changes. They have been most successful in personalizing the educational experience and creating a sense of community. Success of such ventures in promoting academic growth, however, has not been fully documented or assessed.

More recent trends appear to favor giving students more voice in the design and regulation of their residence halls. Coed living units hold the potential for further development of clear conceptions of the sex roles and, at least, initial research findings are supportive; little, however, is being reported about any special programming being done.

However, cautious the researcher may wish to be, the weight of the evidence suggests that some colleges do have a significant effect on their students' values, attitudes, and eventual life styles. The self-confidence and self-concepts of students are enhanced resulting in a general decline in authoritarianism, dogmatism, and ethnocentrism. After four years they are more open, less conservative, somewhat less orthodox in their religious views, and more ready to express time pulses. Though the changes are seldom profound, seniors are occasionally found to be more interested in intellectual concerns.

Implications. A systematic review of the research literature related to student development cannot but leave at least two impressions. First, such research has come a long way. Sometimes the sophistication of the questions asked are not matched by a similarly sophisticated research design and instrumentation, and, at other times, an overly complex technique confuses an otherwise simple-minded question. On the whole, however, researchers are asking more complicated questions with more appropriate techniques than they did just a few short years ago. Secondly, one is more conscious of the long way research has to go to truly have an impact on college programs and curricula. Much more research needs to be done that examines the interaction of the environment, collegiate programs, and student characteristics. What combinations maximize change and growth? To answer the multitude of related questions will involve more program evaluation studies and more manipulation of program-student combinations than has been done to date.

Some have raised legitimate questions about the actual impact of the college experience itself as compared to that of original propensities and normal maturation. When these are sorted out the remaining changes attributable to the college experience may be disappointing, but still present. Some pessimists conclude that once initial student characteristics are controlled, however, few colleges have an impact that could not be ascribed chiefly to normal maturation. Even if this were to be entirely the case, the question remains as to whether or not colleges should persist in having student development as an objective. Lack of success should not necessarily deter renewed efforts. Failure should, in fact, lead to change, innovation, and continued evaluation. The eager receptivity of entering freshmen, often soon dampened, highlights the need for immediate changes in the freshman year. These changes must occur in both the curriculum and in living arrangements if they are to have a maximum impact. They must be designed to make use of the powerful influence of the peer group. It is extremely difficult to change student attitudes toward grades and professors once they have been through a year of college. Very little research or programming has been done yet to maximize the effect of the peer group, to foster student-faculty friendships, or to give credit for living-learning experiences that promote personal-social growth. Esthetic growth, for example, is often relegated to art and music appreciation courses that often seek academic respectability by requiring memorization.

One of the major goals of college in the minds of many—development of an intellectual orientation—receives very little support as actually occurring. As yet, this discouraging outcome has not caused many faculty to stand up, reply, or change. Efforts to improve undergraduate teaching, however, are being given increasing amounts of attention, and these attempts should be encouraged. Hopefully, the focus will be broader than just getting the content across, although more humanistic ways of accomplishing this limited goal deserve attention. Undoubtedly, like the evidence for attitude change in general, there are colleges and programs that are changing students' orientations to problem-solving, increasing rational thinking, and developing student interests in the arts; but, evidence suggesting that this is the general case is lacking.

More research is needed on the effect of differing degrees of congruence between initial student characteristics and the environment. Even from as little as we know about this, it would appear that collegiate course offerings, teaching styles, and living arrangements should present enough alternatives so appropriate matches can be made. A critical question remains as to whether or not students should be permitted to seek out their own match. The cafeteria style of programming—letting students pick out experiences for themselves—may lead them to choose experiences at which they will be quite successful, but it does not guarantee maximum growth or experimentation.

The significance of the importance of the peer group and the living unit cannot be underestimated and should not be ignored. Some of the findings do little more than validate common sense, but it still is amazing how often both college administrators and student personnel workers fail to make decisions or design appropriate programs. High-rise residence halls with cell-like rooms are a good case in point. One has to ask whether or not student development research really tells us that much more about how the living environment affects behavior than was known at least intuitively before some of the existing monstrosities were constructed. The only conclusion to draw is that such decisions were based mostly on physical and budgetary considerations. Research that is available now at least makes such decisions less justifiable and the decision-makers more culpable.

While the research findings have some definite implications for many collegiate settings, they do not have equal application and relevance for the variety of higher education institutions in this country. Close scrutiny of the findings reveals the narrowness of what we know about student development. Most of what we know is about the typical post-adolescent, white, middle class student enrolled in a four-year residential college. What about the older student enrolled in a two-year institution? We know, for example, that comparable developmental changes are less likely to occur among commuter students but also we know very little about what kinds of programs would enhance change for nonresidential students. We have attended quite closely to the academic progress of minority students, but we have paid less attention to their developmental status. We know that students with certain socioeconomic backgrounds are more receptive to new ideas than are other students, but we know little about making students more receptive in general. We know much about the modeling influence of the peer group, but very little about the potential similar influence of faculty models.

These limitations are significant. Unless those conducting research in student development expand their efforts to include new students in new settings and look at what kinds of environments facilitate growth among students, their efforts will make interesting journal publications, but will have little impact on what college education will be like in the future.

Sanford (1968) predicts that in the future student personnel staff will be doing more research on student development. If this is a legitimate goal, it has definite implications for the training of student personnel workers and how they spend their time. Certainly more research is needed but also consideration has to be given to how the research findings are translated into program changes.

The research results on the impact of the college experience on students leads to very few safe generalizations. Given the many possible permutations of institutional and individual characteristics, and being aware of the methodological limitations, one can be quite guarded in making conclusive comments, as were Feldman and Newcomb (1969), or fairly optimistic about the impact of colleges, as was Withey (1971) in a recent Carnegie Report.

Whether the findings are interpreted conservatively or liberally, one would still be remiss in not looking at some of the resulting key student development concepts and their implications.

Key Student Development Concepts

Implications. There are a few basic student development concepts that provide a framework within which it is possible to summarize what is known and to assess the needs of the future. Gradually, research evidence is adding cross supports to that frame. As yet, however, these concepts are seldom given due consideration as colleges and universities, individually and collectively, make plans for the future. It is important to note these concepts and to illustrate some of the alternative directions they suggest for higher education.

1. *Student characteristics when they enter college have a significant impact on how students are affected by their college experience.* Each student's personal history, his successes and failures, his interests and aptitudes, his family and peer group relationships, and his goals and aspirations add up to make a pattern of predispositions that effect how much he will be influenced by his courses, activities, and the people with whom he interacts. when and how are these assessed? What college takes these input characteristics into consideration when they help a student plan his program or when he wants to explore the appropriateness of various campus life styles? They are more likely to be the community colleges than four-year residential institutions.

The likelihood of change and growth among students is certainly related to the challenges residing in their new environment. If the student is thrust into a completely new environment in which peers and others adhere to drastically different views, the student might well become isolated or begin seeking a more compatible setting. If the environment is generally supportive with little challenge, his current views are likely to be extended. There appears to be a middle ground that is most conducive to change. Should the college leave the choice completely up to the student? Could the college outline the alternatives and relate them to student goals and expectations and, then, leave it up to them? Or should the college program the environment just as it does the registration process and require courses? What programming occurs now is more accidental than intentional. The rule, for example, that freshmen must live in residence halls is typically based on the assumption that this will make adjustment to college life easier, as well as fill up rooms.

Much more could be done to individualize college education based on the entry characteristics of students. Should students be encouraged to seek a best fit between where they are now and the collegiate program, or should they be encouraged to tackle new challenges that a less than best fit student environment might pose? Seldom are even these options presented to the student.

2. *The collegiate years are the period for many individual students when significant developmental changes occur.* This is a time in the life of many students when they are gaining independence from their parents, searching for some sense of autonomy, and forming concepts about themselves as separate individuals. At the same time, they are putting together a pattern

of interpersonal behavior, a career orientation, a value system, and a life style that may shape their future for some time.

From a developmental viewpoint the college years, especially the first year, represent critical stages in the developmental process. The move from home to the residence hall represents for most the first long stay away from home. Independence and autonomy are thrust upon them—sometimes reluctantly, sometimes with glee. They now have decisions to make—big and small. Whether it is deciding what to eat, when to sleep, or what courses to take, they are often on their own. The experience may be a long sought one, but not without its fears and queasy moments.

The independence gained is not just in superficial decision-making but the basic values of a student are now tested as he attempts to work through his ethical, religious, and moral values. At the same time that he separates himself from the ties of home and differentiates himself from the family as an independent decision-maker who controls his own existence, he must find some meaning in a new identity. The student tries to define who he is in terms of his major, his new associates, and his many aspirations.

3. *There are opportunities within the collegiate program for it to have a significant impact on student development.* On the whole, colleges and universities do little to see that these developmental processes occur when and how they should. It is true that persons not attending college go through the same developmental processes with little or no special attention, but individual growth in the dimensions mentioned are congruent with the goals of higher education and deserve attention. The need to provide for opportunities to explore and reassess values has already been discussed in another context, but a brief look at a few other developmental goals should be illustrative.

The choice of major and career is a good example. For many students this is essentially a trial and error process with the errors resulting in a sizable number of students being scarred. Many colleges provide vocational counseling and placement services, but for the most part these are remedial and terminal rather than developmental. Academic restrictions regarding withdrawing from courses in many institutions make it impossible for students to test out their interests and capabilities without fear of failure and loss of time, if not credits. The only career models available on most campuses are other students and college professors. These models provide the student with the chance to mach his current self with others, but do not enable him to find out how he can grow in new and realistic experiences. His exposure is almost entirely vicarious. Prestige and monetary expectations are key factors in the decision-making process for many students who seldom have the opportunity to test out the depth of their intrinsic interest.

Simulation games in some courses do provide students with opportunities to role play and learn about the decision-making process. Such efforts could be extended fruitfully to more courses and expanded to include other kinds of experiences. Most college students are vocationally concerned as they enter and leave college; this will be even more true for the new students. Provisions should be made for students to be able to explore more freely what various courses are like and the implications their reactions and capabilities have for career decisions.

Another area of personal development left even more to chance is social skill development. Somehow because students are bunched together in residence halls, because dances and movies are scheduled in the unions, and because spring comes once a year, social development is expected to occur as a mater of course. The flocking of students to campus gurus who sponsor sensitivity sessions, encounter groups, and the like is indicative of the profound need among students for closer interpersonal ties. Statistics on the dating patterns of college students suggest that many are lonely, lack confidence in their interpersonal relationships, and if fortunate, they grow more as a result of chance encounters than planned social activities. Like other patterns, students most active socially on campus were those who were most active during their high school years.

Sexual development is, of course, concurrent with other developmental processes occurring during the college years. Yet, this too is ignored as far as the formal college and university program is concerned. Some colleges offer marriage counseling and sex counseling, but for the most part these too are remedial efforts. Marriage and the family courses are most often taught as content courses. It is ironic that there is probably more formal sex education in fifth grade classes in America than in all the four-year offerings in the college curriculum. Development of interpersonal skills and concerns for sexual development are left to the extracurricular. This is a curriculum that is very real and very powerful, but its syllabus is not on file in the academic dean's office.

Creativity is seen by the current educational system as essentially a characteristic that makes itself evident and is basically an inherited trait rather than a developed one. In very few places in the curriculum, except perhaps in elementary schools, are provisions made to help the student develop the playfulness and the confidence necessary to tackle new forms. This is certainly true of the college environment. Clubs are available, sometimes even photography equipment is accessible. Although the opportunities are there, they are relegated to the extracurricular. Some colleges are too busy educating to think about making development of creativity among students a recognized part of the curriculum. Is enough known about creativity to offer a course in creativity? Probably not, but then it has not been tried much either.

4. *The environmental factors that hold the most promise for affecting student developmental patterns include the peer group, the living unit, the faculty, and the classroom experience.* These environmental presses interact with initial student characteristics.

As has been indicated before, the peer group is a potent force for change among student groups. Two questions need to be asked. How can the peer group power be utilized by colleges to maximize personal development among students? This is one question that student development research has focused on to the extent that it has looked at the impact of various living arrangements, roommate patterns, and other groupings. Seldom, however, is the second question asked—how is it possible to increase the potency of other environmental features? What about the faculty, for example?

There is evidence that students still need and, in fact, want adult influence. Yet, the models available on campus are limited. As *in loco parentis* diminishes, exposure to adult models, even in a paternalistic, disciplinarian role will be limited. The typical student spends some 15 to 20 hours a week in the presence of an adult faculty member, but much of this time is devoted to being talked *to* rather than *with*. Over the course of a semester the student may get to know something about the professor's personal life, but rarely does he get to know the professor. This is not to suggest that professors should bare their souls in the lecture hall or the seminar room. Self-revelation related to the subject mater could, however, serve to have a double-edged impact on students, affecting their personal and cognitive styles. What if, for example, a professor revealed how he confronted new problems by doing so in class? What if he revealed how he faced intellectual dilemmas, and what experiences shaped his value system—at least as it related to his discipline? For the most part, such revelations are accidental and anecdotal. The point is, that the professor does not have to have every student to his home for dinner nor does he even have to know every student by name in order to have this kind of impact; however, it may mean a considerable change in his classroom style and some sacrificing of content coverage.

Though the academic life seems to have little impact on student development and even how they think, it is not barren of potential. Typical faculty reactions to a call for educational reform is to respond with changes in course content. This may well be needed, but in view of the *fact explosion* (as contrasted to what has been labeled a *knowledge explosion*) it appears to be more important to concentrate on how students learn, what competencies they do develop, and their potential for learning in the future. In the past it was quite easy to dichotomize college life into the classroom and the curricular experiences that were intellectual and the out-of-class and extra-curricular experiences that were social. Research has clearly proved that in many instances this dichotomy is incorrect, though this is a hard pill for many to swallow. The academic, i.e., classroom activities, studying, grades, and exams is not necessarily intellectual at all, if by the latter is meant developing critical thinking and a rational approach to problem-solving. Much of the student's academic activity involves the aggressive ingesting of content material rather than reflective thought. If colleges really propose to have an impact on how students solve problems, then this means more attention is going to have to be given to cognitive development of students rather than content coverage.

Discussions about increasing the options available to those thinking about college should also focus on whether or not there are options within specific institutions. Evidence suggests, for example, that there is an interaction between teacher style and student characteristics that effect student out-comes. Some students thrive in a highly structured classroom setting while others suffer. Some do well when given the chance to move ahead without a professor on individualized programmed material, whereas others need per-sonal contact. Too often students have these options from across colleges or departments but not from within. If they are available, the proper matching of teacher and student styles are let to chance. As indicated earlier, the concern should be with student outcomes and adapting the teaching methods and procedures that provide the best means for arriving at these outcomes.

5. *Developmental changes in students are the result of the interaction of initial characteristics and the press of the environment.* Changes in students do not occur in a vacuum, nor do they necessarily occur automatically or in a positive direction. The concept of readiness has some relevance for those looking at student development, e.g., most students are very receptive at the beginning of their freshman year. Normal maturation may lead to developmental changes irrespective of the environment, but not independent of it. It is impotant to be cognizant that not only can growth be inhibited but that some changes can be regressive. For example, the self-concept of an 18-year-old can be drastically altered and his self-confidence dramatically diminished by academic failure.

The major weakness of higher education in the United States has been its unwillingness to establish programs and curriculum and to modify its instructional procedures in order to utilize its full potential for helping students develop. A significant case in point is the freshman year. Despite the accumulation of evidence that suggests the critical importance of the first year, the receptiveness of the new student, and its eventual shaping of his attitude throughout the rest of his college years, little has been done to change the current program. A change in the freshman year is so novel that whenever any university or college does make alterations, such as offering a freshman seminar, it is worthy of headlines or special mention in higher education journals. Major professors still teach graduate students and teaching assistants, who for the most part teach as they are taught. Some professors lecture to the large undergraduate sections.

Several educators have recently suggested that students teach students. Of course this already takes place, although the content is different from that of the classroom. Snyder (1971) has referred to this as the hidden curriculum. It is the process by which students learn what is actually expected, as compared to what is formally required. Through it they develop the stratagems and ploys necessary to learn the real syllabus and jump the real hurdles. Perhaps student to student teaching should be legitimatized. If the movement toward competency attainment vs. credit accumulation gains grounds, students may well seek out each other for help. This could help foster comradeship rather than competition.

These examples simply suggest that to promote positive developmental changes in students requires conscious manipulation of the environment even if that means a conscious decision not to change the environment.

The brief summary of research findings on student development and the outlining of the five basic concepts represents no new knowledge or even reformulation. Almost anyone who has been involved with college students and is at all enlightened would arrive at the same conclusions and assumptions without having had to survey the research literature or attended to the words of major theorists. It must be granted as well that many of the particulars of student development remain unknown. A whole new set of concepts might be needed for older students, commuters, or minority students. Nevertheless, a candid observer of the educational scene would have to admit that recognition of the few known concepts goes largely unnoticed as colleges plan programs and as major pronouncements about the future of higher education are being made.

The majority of suggestions for the future have looked at the means by which higher education can continue to accomplish the same ends. Questions have been asked as to how the traditional goals of higher education can be accomplished more quickly, more efficiently, and more creatively. These questions are undeniably important, but there is a real danger that one of the most important goals will be obscured in the process, perhaps even obliterated. Student development has historically been a major goal of higher education since its inception, and the research evidence suggests that college can and does have an impact on student development and that, indeed, cognitive and affective development are irrevocably interrelated.

These key concepts provide the foundation necessary for the processes needed to facilitate student development in a college setting. Grant and others (1971) while working with the Council of Student Personnel Associations, developed a series of 10 statements summarizing possible purposes and functions of "student development educators." This is a needed step if the behavior patterns and roles of student personnel staff are to change. Here, in abbreviated form, are the statements:

1. Assessing behaviors the student has already developed.

2. Formulating the student's behavioral objectives.

3. Selecting college programs that build on existing behaviors to accomplish the student's objectives.

4. Fostering student growth within the context of his own cultural background and encouraging his appreciation of the cultural backgrounds of the educational institution and of other students.

5. Developing physical environments, human groups, institutional organizations, and financial resources most conducive to the student's growth.

6. Integrating concurrent experiences outside the institution with the student's educational program as an aid in achieving the student's objectives.

7. Modifying existing behaviors that block further growth of the student.

8. Giving visibility to a value system that enables the student to judge the worth of behavior patterns.

9. Recording the student's progress as a means of facilitating his growth.

10. Identifying appropriate environments for continued development before and after the student leaves his present educational setting.

The student personnel profession has to guard carefully against three major dangers as it considers its future. First, it must not proceed as if these functions are the exclusive task of just the student personnel staff on a campus. Second, it must not fail to make these purposes and functions meaningful and operational in a variety of settings, with a variety of students, and to all students on a particular campus. And last, it must not miss the opportunity to integrate these purposes with those of the academic instructor. Student personnel staffs and academic staffs should no longer exist side-by-side as separate but (un)equal.

Chapter 4
Student Development and the Student Personnel Workers Tomorrow:
Some Alternative Roles

If the student personnel profession wishes to have significant input and influence on student development patterns of the future, its individual members are going to have to revise their own self-perceptions and the perceptions that others have of them. In the past, others have seen student personnel workers as essentially housekeepers, advisers of student activities, and counselors. While student personnel workers have professed themselves to be educators and to be interested in the whole student, they have served higher education essentially as housekeepers, activities advisers, counselors, and have even been viewed by many in the higher education arena as petty administrators. With the demise of the *in loco parentis* functions and reduction in parietal rules, the housekeeping role is a less viable one. Student activities advisers often work with the same small core of activist-leader type students who probably do mature and develop, at minimum, some leadership skills. Certainly the ultimate objective of staffs to improve the quality of life on campus is often achieved, but it is questionable that many students are affected in a developmental way. The future plight of organized student activities remains in doubt, as the appropriate and inappropriate use of student fees for campus newspapers, student conferences, and other such services is being questioned on many campuses.

Need for a New Role

This leaves the counselor role as the last touchstone and it, too, is being questioned in terms of its effectiveness with individual students and its impact on student life in terms of sheer numbers. Curricular offerings in counseling have traditionally served as the core of many student personnel professional programs. Counseling centers have often been the proving ground for many student personnel administrators, and the counseling role has been perceived by many as central to the definition of what a student personnel worker is. One has to ask whether this has been the case because of the particular skills that counselors have possessed or whether it is because counselors were the kinds of persons who were able to listen patiently and show sincere interest in students. Although they may well be interrelated, patience and sincerity have probably been more evident than technique.

Even the best staffed counseling centers see only a very limited percentage of students on campus and, in most instances, students go to counseling centers with academic problems and minor crises rather than personal-emotional problems. Undoubtedly the counseling, whether it occurs in the residence hall between a staff member and a resident or in a counseling center between a counseling psychologist and a student, does help some students during a developmental crisis. However, what about the more typical student who never sees a counselor, who never creates a disturbance in the residence hall, or who is never a campus leader? His contact with the student personnel staff is limited and his life style is affected very indirectly, if at all, by student personnel services or policies.

The most profound reason for the new emphasis on student development from student personnel workers is that they seek more fulfillment of their espoused goal of developing the whole student. With historical hindsight it is possible to say that higher education took the wrong fork in the road when it thrust personnel maintenance upon staff with specialized duties. Size also played a part, as our society has in the past held bigness in high esteem. But bigness necessitated specialization. Deans, rectors, and others were equally to blame when they accepted the responsibilities, although their culpability is limited because in many instances the tasks were accepted in good faith and/or by default. Since then student personnel workers have been on a constant ego trip of trying to professionals their responsibilities. The more successful these efforts have been, the further compartmentalized and specialized have become their own functions. Efforts to supposedly personalize the educational experience for students have sometimes even been counter-productive. Who turned the student into a number on an IBM card? It was not the classroom instructor, although he may have been guilty of other sins, principally those of omission.

To laud student personnel workers because they were interested in the whole student may have been necessary, as historically faculty members became less and less interested in the student's out-of-class activities. Some-one had to take up this responsibility. Didn't they? Monitoring residence hall life, handling discipline, dealing with vocational indecision, keeping track of academic records, and supervising activities became full-time positions and exclusive tasks. Implicit, though perhaps not intended, in a statement of philosophy espousing concern for the whole student is that no other university group is interested. Whether the traditional student personnel functions were pushed out of the academy, handed over innocently, or picked up by default makes little difference at this point in time. Operationally, student personnel workers have taken up the responsibilities, become specialists, and have been bitterly demanding equal recognition in the academic world ever since.

It is time for student personnel workers to recognize that they too have been dealing with only a part of the student, and it is no more valid for them to expect effectiveness in dealing with the student's development, independent of his academic life, than it is for the professor to think a student's personal self does not affect his academic growth. To have an impact on student development means being aware of and involved in the total environment of the student—not just where he lives or what organization he belongs to. A significant part of that environment is the classroom and the study desk, at least in terms of what that dimension of the environment is designed to accomplish. How can we as student personnel worker call ourselves educators when we do not know who is being affected by our educating. The truth is that we do not know whether or not true education is taking place as a result of our efforts. Further, the student has very little awareness that he is being educated, no idea of what he is to learn, and little or no feedback on whether he has learned anything?

In their present capacities student personnel workers are clearly providing services, needed ones perhaps, but whether or not they are educators or even student development specialists is another question. Such a broad use of the term might also encompass the book store salesman, the cafeteria waitress, and even the bicycle shop repairman. No, calling ourselves educators is perhaps satisfying to the ego and helps justify some mundane tasks to ourselves, but it is inaccurate.

If the student personnel worker needs a new role and if housekeeper, adviser, and good-guy models are no longer appropriate, what are some possible alternative roles?

Alternative Roles

Diagnostician. This is a role currently being filled in a limited manner for a limited number of students. There are several junctures during a student's college life when a bit of diagnostic work takes place. When his application is filed a determination is made as to whether or not he is potentially a successful student. This decision is made on the basis of high school rank and his admission test scores. Another diagnostic decision is sometimes made when the student chooses a particular major. A higher cutoff score or grade point average is the usual criteria for entrance into some of the tougher academic fields. Sometimes students with low test scores are required to take a remedial course. For the overwhelming majority of students this is the extent and level of the diagnostic effort. A very small percentage may seek vocational counseling during which some diagnostic work may occur. In almost all instances the focus of the efforts is on the academic or the aptitude dimensions. Can a student succeed in this college? Can he pass calculus? Can he draw a straight line? Rarely is an examination made of the student's total developmental history and potentialities. When is his receptivity to new ideas put to a test? When is he asked how he feels about the adequacy of his social skills? Does anyone suggest that he might think about developing a broader range of interests in the arts? Who helps him decide whether or not he is ready to benefit from living off-campus? The answer to these questions is "No" or "No one"—at least no one on the college scene outside of his peer group.

If higher education moves in the direction predicted and suggested, that is, more options, more students will have more decisions to make. Accessibility to the options may give future students more opportunity to explore by trial and error where he or she fits best, but floundering can be frustrating and self-defeating if it is entirely aimless. Older students, and students stopping out and stopping in, are going to be seeking counsel as to what options are best for them. If history repeats itself, the extension of student personnel services to these groups will be made, but only to their academic needs in terms of their competencies. Much more attention should be given to assessing the developmental status of the student on other dimensions and outlining, if not prescribing, alternative courses of action. This could very well be an ongoing role rather than one fulfilled only at entrance or terminal junctures. The diagnostician becomes next the prescriber and perhaps in turn the evaluator.

Consultant. Everyone on a college campus probably serves as a consultant at one time or another. Student personnel workers have been advisers more often than they have been consultants. The difference may at first appear to be fine and too subtle, but it can be significant. Thus, we have registration advisers, student activities advisers, fraternity advisers, and residence hall staff advisers. The adviser role, at least as it is operationally defined in many of these settings, is one that connotes being responsible and being a watchdog, as well as someone who may or may not have some expertise in the area. Student personnel workers have hoped to be friendly advisers—to keep the students out of trouble—at the same time as their input may actually promote positive changes and programming. Too often, although not always because of their own fault, advisers become too closely identified with the student or project on which they are advising. Success or failure of the enterprise reflects as much on the adviser as it does on the students— maybe even more so.

The consultant role presents on the surface only a slight shade of a difference from that of the adviser, but one that might well change the behavior of consultant and consultee, as well as their perceptions of the role. The consultant is first of all an expert; he has some wisdom, technology, or knowledge that makes his comments meaningful and worthwhile to the consultee. A major difference is that he is sought out by the consultee rather than being appointed, and, of course, he has no final say in the decision-making that may take place. He is a free agent, though he may be responsible to those who seek out his wisdom. He is more likely to be sought out in the initial stages of a venture than at the final step before action is taken, which is true in many adviser roles.

Many advisers ideally visualize themselves as consultants. However, seldom are all the ingredients present: being an expert, being sought out, not having final say in decision-making, and not being held responsible for the action taken.

An important consideration for this role is the administrative structure within which the role is fulfilled. In most instances, student personnel workers who do serve as true consultants do so in a subsidiary way, only indirectly related to their main function, or as one of their many responsibilities. Few are viewed to have consulting as their main responsibility. So it is that someone with some special knowledge about town resources is consulted about a related student activity, a residence hall staff member is asked what type of social function went well last year, or a dean is asked by a faculty group how he thinks students will react to a particular policy. Being consulted is not accidental or even peripheral, but it is more casual than systematic.

One possible role model for student personnel workers in the future is that of consultant. A consulting type agency might be established on campus that is staffed by experts in research, group behavior, student development, management, and counseling. They would be available to students, faculty, administration, or for work with groups and individuals. Some student development center and growth centers employ the consultant model. Certainly there would be nothing to inhibit the consultants from actively planning their own programs for change as well, but their main role would be as consultants to consumers.

Programmer. This role might be implemented in a number of ways and in both individual and group settings. It might be the natural follow-through of the diagnostician role with the programmer outlining various courses of action the student might take to accomplish certain objectives. If the student is mathematically proficient but has a weak vocabulary, courses, books, and skill programs could be outlined as alternative actions. If the student has had little exposure to the arts, he might be given a schedule of campus and community cultural events for the year. If the student lacks social skills, a sequential pattern of activities might be programmed for the student. All of this is based on the assumption that some type of assessment has taken place, that some feedback has been given to the student, and that the programmer and the student have mutually agreed on some realistic goals. Follow-up and evaluation would be critical.

The programmer might also be involved with groups in different settings. This role might entail helping a residence hall floor establish a floor government, assisting an experimental college plan its small group activities, or working with the student union committee to determine space needs. In this context the programmer is an expert in student environment programming. In some ways programming can also be viewed as a community-making function, at least in a residential setting.

Cross (1971b) has suggested that part of a new curriculum might be projects that involve students in making contacts with members of the community and in utilizing a variety of resources. She suggests that student personnel staff might very well serve as one member of a team that would help the student plan his project, find out about the available resources, and report and evaluate his experiences. The programmer in this capacity might have various subroles that could include supervising the student's off-campus experiences or being a process evaluator.

The programmer role is somewhat similar to the consultant role, but the relationships in the programmer role are more likely to be structured and to be somewhat more prescriptive than those of a consultant.

Technologist. As *in loco parentis* tasks diminish so will the adviser role. Somehow students will still have to make decisions about what courses to take and will need information about themselves and the available options in order to make decisions. One wonders whether or not much of this type of information and decision-making could be facilitated with computer assistance. Is it the lack of money or lack of will that inhibits implementation of programs already available? More instructors in the academic arena are giving closer attention to individualized instruction programs for their courses. Student personnel workers might serve a useful function as packagers of individualized advising units, which could be available in dorms and unions, on tape or in programmed text form.

College Professor. Some student personnel workers hold rank within academic departments. These are most likely to be members of the counseling center staff, or deans who often possess PhD's in psychology, education, or related fields. Joint appointments are generally more prestigious and although such a staff member has probably no more rights per se, it does permit him to participate in many faculty rituals. Whether a symptom, or part of the disease itself, faculty status does open doors sometimes not opened to other student personnel staff. Perhaps the teaching faculty see their practitioner colleagues only as lost sheep and not the black sheep they may view other administrators and staff to be.

Is it possible to accomplish some student development goals in an organized course-like fashion that could become courses for credit? Could practicum experiences in human relations or developing an awareness of self, participation in sensitivity sessions, involvement in leadership and decision-making programs be justifiably taken for credit? One of the major arguments of this monograph is that they can and should be. If that is so, then the logical step is to develop departments of human relations, development and growth, creative development, etc., which present theoretical concepts, but emphasize skill development and personal growth.

There are dangers in this alternative. Being accused of emphasizing the practical and the nonintellectual is one, but this effort would be no more practical than teaching rhetoric and, hopefully, more successful. Another danger is that of compartmentalizing the student, but no more than philosophy taught abstractly with no personal references. It would be difficult to grade, but no more than art appreciation; and it could be Mickey Mouse, but no more than many other required courses. If it tried to emulate other content courses, a human relations course would be no more successful than marriage and the family courses, art, and music appreciation courses. Certainly such a direction should not, however, be justified on the basis that it would be no worse than other college offerings. it would have to be much, much better, but the potential would certainly be there in terms of the subject matter, if not in terms of staff and methodology.

A somewhat less radical role would be one that involves a student development staff member as a team member in a course or program of courses. In such a capacity the philosophy or child development professor might present lectures and make some reading assignments, while the student development professor works with class groups in evolving personal meanings from the content and perhaps supervises practicum experiences. This model can be expanded to apply to entire program offerings as well as to individual courses.

Administrator. Responsibilities for student personnel functions have come close to reaching the pinnacle of the administrative ladder in many of our major institutions with vice-presidencies for student life, student affairs, or student services abounding. This is a difficult role for many student personnel workers. Just as they found the disciplinarian role difficult during the days when administrators were involved more in regulating student life, so they find the role of decision-maker arduous. As a professional group, student personnel workers are people-oriented, not generally aggressive or assertive. Many are uncomfortable in a role that often by its very nature means that they will not be liked by everyone. The "Peter Principle" also has some application for the student personnel workers, who are often promoted because of their visibility in being responsive to students and student interests. These are behaviors that are not necessarily rewarded in the administrative arena, where ability to work with peers may be the key to success.

The administrative role does hold some promise for the enhancement of student development concepts and programs. As students are involved more in university governance, and shared-authority principles remain as vestiges of participatory democracy in a university setting, ability to work with groups and some insight into student behavior may become more important administrative attributes than assertiveness.

As an administrator, the student personnel worker can also serve as a special spokesman for student development concepts and programs. In times of tight budgeting and restrictions on new programming someone, who sees student development programming as essential and not a frill, is needed to articulate the goals and purposes of such programming to legislators and budget administrators. Though unfortunately such positions do not guarantee access to the academic dimensions of collegiate life, there would be some interesting ramifications and possibilities if student development staff actually were in charge of academic programs, such as living-learning endeavors.

Behavioral Scientist. The behavioral scientist model for the student personnel worker is not new, but there is a growing interest in this as a viable role and by some as the role for the future. The advent of behavior modification techniques is just now sweeping counseling centers and it will probably not be long before more is heard about the use of contingency reinforcement and behavior engineering in residence halls and other aspects of campus life. Certainly modeling, feedback, and differential reinforcement have applications for classroom instruction.

Counselors' and deans' roles have gone through similar periods of metamorphosis with the former customarily a shot stride ahead. The role perceptions for these positions have gone through periods of being "nice guys," to being "understanding," and now to understanding not only the individual student, but the environmental context in which he lives. This role holds the potential of being one that systematically influences the environment and thus has an impact on students in broader ways than in a strictly one-to-one relationship. The dean has had the power to do this in the past without the conceptual or research base, but more and more new deans (often recruited from the ranks of counselors) have both the conceptual and the power base.

Unfortunately the use of the term behavioral scientist causes the stomachs of almost as many student personnel workers to churn as it does humanities professors. Management of the environment for some smacks of control and coldness, which those who enter the field primarily because of its helping relationship and people-oriented work sometimes have difficulty accepting. This dichotomy, between the scientist and the counselor (helper) is a false one that is more in the eyes of the beholder than it is in reality. To be scientific in one's thinking about students is not to be any less concerned with their freedom or their wholeness. There is no reason why a scientific attitude and approach to students and the use of related techniques cannot be employed to foster full student development and institutional change. Many deans, counselors, and other student personnel workers have been successful in the past, not because they ignored lessons from behavioral scientists, but because they wittingly or unwittingly applied them.

Adoption of this role has implications for training, and the focus of efforts to advance the science. It means that the student personnel worker is going to have to be aware of his techniques, sharpen them, be conscious of their use, and subject them to continuous evaluation.

Researcher. It is difficult to separate this role from a number of other ones already described, particularly the behavioral scientist and the consultant. In some ways it might be viewed as a function that would pervade a number of the other roles, rather than a separate role of its own. No satisfactory arguments can be raised that deny the value and the need for research about how students learn and what has an impact on their college experience, as well as results in change and growth.

This role, especially as it applies to student development, should not be independent of program-planning. When they have not been motivated by the need for publication and status, most research and evaluation efforts have been coincidental to program-planning, if not afterthoughts. The most valuable research will be that conducted by a team or someone who understands student behavior, the goals and purposes of higher education, and research methodology. More research is needed about student character-istics and college environments, but what is desperately needed is experimen-tal research—that which involves exposing students to different environ-ments and assessing the outcomes. Some available evaluation models can perhaps achieve this as well as the more sophisticated research designs.

When research, evaluation, and program-planning are tied together, they can be valuable assets in the effort to promote student development in college. Whether such a person or group of persons could hope to fulfill all the other needs of higher education and students in the future is doubtful, but most certainly every student personnel worker of the future should have a research mentality as he attempts to assess the impact of the environment on himself personally and his behavior on others.

Unemployment. This category is included with no intention to be funny and little motivation to be satirical. It is doubtful that the term *student personnel* or many of the functions served by such persons will disappear soon, despite economy and budget limitations. The question of whether or not these functions ever achieve professional status remains in doubt, however. Not every commentator viewing the student personnel movement sees professionalism as inevitable, the usual argument being that research and practice in the area lacks the theoretical base upon which most professions are founded. There is some evidence that recent efforts to conceptualize and theorize about student development may move us to the brink of having at least one cornerstone. However, even such a fortuitous occurrence would not guarantee growth of the profession. Lawyers are not needed in a totalitarian state, nor are waitresses in an automat. Student personnel—at least in the student development sense—may not be funded in programs that involve TV degrees, universities without walls, and a campus scene that retains little if any *in loco parentis* philosophy. Student services will still be needed, but not necessarily student development educators.

There is nothing magical about the roles that have been described. They may be combined in various fashions. Others who are concerned about the future of student personnel work suggest a similar variety of roles (Morrill& Hurst, 1971; O'Banion, 1971; Parker, 1971).

Essential Elements of an Ideal Role Model

It is not the intention of this monograph to outline in detail a new organizational chart for college student personnel functions or to specify the exact role that those concerned about student development in the future should fulfill. However, it would be unfair to the reader to have gone this far in suggesting the need for a new conception of student development and a new role for student personnel workers without at least suggesting some of the major ingredients that might make up this new role. Here are some of the key elements:

1. *Changes in attitude.* The new role will necessitate a change in at least two attitudinal stances that have been implicit if not explicit in role definitions in the past. First, there has to be a recognition that student personnel workers are not the only individuals on campus who are concerned about total student development. Unless the "student personnel point of view" permeates the campus, there is little chance that working with students exclusively in out-of-class activities is going to have more than a limited impact on a limited number of students. Secondly, student personnel workers are going to have to abandon any behavior patterns that border on paternalistic concern for students. If significant others on campus are also concerned about student development, then student personnel workers should align themselves with these groups and seek to have an impact on the total academic community. This new role should be one that does not

function primarily as an adversary of the faculty and administration nor as an ally of the students, but rather as an equal partner who seeks the attainment of the college's ultimate goals.

2. *Direct ties with the academic arena.* For years student personnel workers have identified themselves as educators who are concerned about the total student and whose role involves primarily the out-of-class activities. The particular province of the student personnel concern was the *extracurricular*. Extra in this instance meaning not only *outside of or beyond*, but to many *peripheral* and *unnecessary*. Use of the expression co-curricular instead of extracurricular represents a significant philosophical change but operationally represents little more than giving lip-service to an idea without program support. It is time now for student development functions to become curricular—with no prefix added. This means legitimatizing current out-of-class experiences by making them available more systematically to all students and by giving them some type of academic recognition. It also means that student development concepts, if not student personnel workers, should permeate the academic offerings and have an impact on not only what is taught but how it is taught. Until student development concepts and programs are fully integrated with the academic program, the total student notion remains a dream, not a reality.

These ties with the academic world can come about in several ways and probably true integration would include most all of them. A few of these might be having: (a) a significant portion of a student development staff reports directly to the school's academic dean; (b) an actual academic department with student development staff teaching classes in human relations, value assessment, personal and group decision-making processes, and human sexuality; (c) a consulting team that works with departments and individual professors to facilitate the structuring of curriculum and courses so that they might have the best chance for fostering student development; (d)a student development staff that serves as administrators or program developers for special academic programs, such as experimental colleges, community-action programs, and work-study-work programs; (e) a student development staff that works up out-of-class experiences into ones that with reading and supervision could become recognized for credit; (f) a team approach that relates to all curricular changes and innovations with members of the team representing expertise in course content, learning and teaching, and student development.

The purpose of these ties with the academic arena is not just to play at being academicians but to actually be academicians and ultimately to expand the typical concerns of the academician to include process as well as content, affective development as well as cognitive development, competency attainment as well as knowledge learned.

3. *Being professional behavioral scientists.* This role was discussed earlier as one of the possible future roles for student personnel staff. It deserves special mention as an essential element in any model for the future. In the past it was sufficient that student personnel workers knew student viewpoints and attitudes. Today, it is important that they not only know students but that they also understand them in a developmental context. In tomorrow's higher education it will be essential for student development staffs to be able to know, understand, and to program for changes in students that will be consistent with developmental growth. This means that the staffs will have to have some expertise in learning theory, growth and development, campus ecology, management theory, and evaluation. Given these competencies it is assumed that they are also effective themselves in implementing programs and bringing about change, which implies some measure of interpersonal skills.

This role—the applied behavioral scientist role—might serve as a unifying principle for the sometimes fractionalized student personnel profession.

4. *Some type of direct contact with every student.* One of the major weaknesses of current student development programs and student affairs functions is that they directly affect a small minority of students and even indirectly have almost no impact on the academic aspects of student life. Without inhibiting movements toward greater freedom of choice among students, it should be possible to inform students of the consequences of their choices and to offer alternative options. In the past this has been done traditionally with academic options. Typical questions include, "Am I ready to take advanced algebra?" or "What do I need to be able to get into law school?" No one on campus has dealt with assessment of the student's current status relative to developmental goals or providing him with options as to how these might be attained. The student's transcript and academic aptitudes are evaluated, but never his total developmental status.

These then are illustrative alternative roles and key elements of a model for student development educators in the future. Professional organizations within student personnel will have to examine these roles and models, search for additions and new combinations, determine how they might be integrated with the rest of higher education, and how they relate to training programs. "Tomorrow's Higher Education Project," sponsored by the American College Personnel Association, is potentially one such avenue for those within the profession to collaborate and join hands with their academic counterparts in developing new operational models for the promotion of student development.

Chapter 5
What Needs To Be Done

One of the major viewpoints expressed in this monograph is that if higher education is to continue to have an impact on student development, changes will have to be made in the academic arena that are consistent with this goal. This will mean more than reorganizing the student personnel staff or increasing the budget of the union program committee. What it will mean is changing what is taught and how it is taught. The few recommendations listed in this section are by no means new. Many similar recommendations were made by Katz (1968); more recently, some have been found in the Newman Report, though they are stated here in a different context. Hopefully, this rephrasing not only will add emphasis to their importance but also will provide a framework for a new dialogue to take place between the academicians and the student development staff. It is difficult to see how such a dialogue cannot help but lead to a reexamination of goals and means, which in turn will result in new cooperative efforts to promote student development in American colleges and universities. The following are some of the major recommendations of this monograph.

Recommendations

1. *Higher education must reaffirm its commitment to promoting student development throughout the variety of post-secondary school programs.* The value of vocational-technical programs and open universities for upgrading the skills of the citizenry, and for providing ready access to a college degree cannot be denied. Yet, the worth of this goal should not be assessed solely in terms of numbers of enrollees or even in terms of graduates. Manpower production alone is not appropriate evaluation criterion. Our society now recognizes that its future rests not on the expertise of its scientists, its technicians, or its electricians, but rather on the ethics, the will, and the humanity of its experts. At no other time in history have we been more aware of man's need for a sense of personal worth, his need to have an ability to interact with others, and his need to use his time creatively. If these are still worthy goals, they need reaffirmation at a time when cost efficiency has been getting more and more attention and career-oriented programs more prominence. It should not be a question of one or the other, career programs or development programs, but rather a question of balance and integration.

2. *A new curriculum is needed which is designed to have an impact on the affective life of students as well as their cognitive styles.* The major problems of

the individual center on his emotional life and his pattern of interpersonal relationships. Few current curriculums are designed to help students grow as persons, to add to their self-knowledge, to improve their effectiveness in interpersonal relationships, or to help them function better in groups. Development of creativity, sense of playful exploration in the arts, or a realistic awareness of sexuality are left almost entirely up to out-of-class experiences. The new curriculum should give academic credit for structured and unstructured experiences that foster this type of personal growth. Some of the goals of this new curriculum might be achieved within current offerings, but needed changes demand more than tinkering with current courses. A concern for the affective domain does not make a program any less intellectual. The goal would be to provide a confluent education, one which unites the affective and the cognitive.

3. *Colleges and universities should establish expectations for students and assess outcomes that cover the broad ranges of human behavior including the intellectual, personal-social, esthetic, cultural, and even the psychomotor dimensions.* Currently almost every post-secondary institution professes to be concerned about the whole student. But, for the most part, the real expectations, those which are evaluated, are those related to academic and skill accomplishments. The key is evaluation. Until efforts are made to assess individual student growth in a total fashion, the rest will not follow and these objectives will remain paper ones.

Not all institutions will want to give equal weight to all of the objectives nor should they try to accomplish them in the same fashion. A technical college, for example, would probably give proportionately more weight to knowledge and skill attainment than would a liberal arts college, which might give more attention to esthetic and cultural growth. Both, however, might want to see certain kinds of personal-social growth occur, though in different degrees or in different areas.

4. *Some significant portion of the undergraduate's program should include courses that are problem-centered.* At this juncture it is not necessary to scrap all the individual disciplines. But if some of the major objectives of a college education are to be achieved, in the future the student should be exposed to knowledge in a different format. He should be prepared to deal with change, to know how to tackle new problems, and to be aware of what facilitates decision-making. The most parsimonious way of accomplishing these ends is to tackle some of them head-on rather than indirectly. Or, for major portions of course experiences, another method may be to permit students to actually confront problems, to make individual and group decisions, and to have the opportunity to reflect on the processes that facilitate problem-solving and decision-making. Solving a problem or completing a project also serve to

provide students with a sense of accomplishment that is really not comparable to passing an exam. The product is often visible; the rewards derived more internally than competitively.

5. *Colleges and universities must work more aggressively to personalize and individualize the student's educational experience.* Barzun has declared that the term *multiversity* is a contradiction because no real university can be a center for learning without at the same time being somewhat like a community. Up to now too little attention has been given to humanizing the current scene. The problem can be approached from many different angles. One approach might be to decentralize as many functions as possible; another might be to remove as many specialists as possible who stand in the way of the student and his course of study. This might mean, for example, trusting the student and his adviser to arrive at a curricular program appropriate to the student's individual goals and needs. Another approach would be to expand the number of living-learning units and to structure them so that they will be more attractive to a broader range of students than now volunteer for experimental programs. Still another tactic might be to have both small and large groups of students study the same topic over a period of time, providing them with a common intellectual experience spiced with guest speakers. These and other approaches could be combined to personalize the student's living and learning experience on any size campus. Individualizing instruction is a viable goal, but it must not be accomplished solely by substituting a student-machine interface for a professor-student interface.

6. *Higher education must give high priority to improvement of undergraduate instruction.* This recommendation is not independent of the one suggesting emphasis on individualizing the educational experience. More options should be available for students to meet requirements within programs. For example, are there reasons, other than cost, why a student should not have available to him a number of ways of gaining credit for an introductory psychology course? Instead of offering the most efficient teaching procedure for the largest number of students, why not offer an assortment of approaches for the wide variety of students with individual goals? Options might include individualized programmed instruction, a discussion course, a lecture course, or a combination of these.

Every effort should be made to improve the freshman year. This should be the starting point of reestablishing the importance of the undergraduate program. Freshman seminars now being employed at some universities should be expanded.

Good teaching is the key. Any commitment to improvement of instruction is meaningless unless specific efforts to foster and reward good teaching are included. This may mean the revamping of tenure and promotion policies, which may well provoke further unionization of faculty. But it is a risk to be taken if the learning environment is to be improved. Foundations, the federal government, and individual institutions must continue to fund programs designed to improve instruction.

7. *Colleges and universities should continue to strive to devise ways of being accountable to their students and their publics.* Unfortunately, the word *accountable* itself often suggests a focus on monetary expenditures and budgets that is misleading. Educational accountability has a much broader definition. Colleges must learn to work toward creating learning environments and situations that foster the maximum possible student growth and accomplishment of all of the colleges' stated and implied objectives. For too long, evaluation of a college, both internally and externally, has consisted of focusing primarily on numbers: graduates, scholarship winners, books in the library, grade point averages, and faculty honors. The new focus has to be on kinds and qualities. How many graduates continue to read, think, and grow as persons is a long neglected criterion that needs to be resurrected if higher education is to serve more than a credential function.

Idealistic professors have been quoted as feeling that a failing student really represents a failure on their part. It is time for higher education in general to look closely at this attitude and to explore what acceptance of this tenet might mean for admissions policies, grading procedures, assignment of credit, and other institutional programs and policies. Of course, the failing student is let down no more than is the honors student who was not challenged or the average student who was spoon fed.

Though no easy task, higher education must strive to be responsive without catering to as well as being accountable to the right people and with the appropriate evidence.

8. *Colleges and universities should foster renewal through basic changes in existing programs in planned sequences rather than through establishment of parallel programs.* One of the traditional campus political stratagems has been to work around existing programs and personnel by establishing parallel structures and programs. The aim is to build up the new and phase out the old, much as new buildings are sometimes built on the sunny side of old ones. This may work with buildings and sometimes with programs and personnel. But too often the result is continued strife, double costs, and even the eventual fade out of the new program once it ceases to be a novelty. The head-on approach of renewal and innovation may be more painful and less glamorous. But, in actuality, perhaps it is no slower than the parallel system tactic.

9. *The administrators of colleges and universities should individually and collectively seek ways to involve professional student personnel staff in the academic*

life of higher education. This could be accomplished by appointing staff to academic committees, such as curriculum and goals committees. Suitably trained staff might also be asked to be involved in the planning and administration of new academic programs. Encouragement could be given to the formation of consulting groups composed of student personnel staff, social scientists, and educational psychologists who would be available to work with faculty and student groups in a consistently professional manner. The involvement of qualified student personnel staff in the academic dimension of college life might at first be quite informal. But eventually, and soon, these efforts should be legitimatized with formal appointments, and at larger institutions by the formation of a staff whose responsibilities are formally appointed and recognized to be in the academic sphere of college life.

For Student Development Educators

Our knowledge about student development both in terms of theoretical constructs and empirical findings is limited; it has in fact, just begun to take shape. There are signs that theory and research are beginning to converge and that in the future those involved in student development will not only be able to understand student development, but also will be able to specify the conditions necessary to promote positive student development. Even before this giant step is taken, there are new challenges. As the college experience undergoes major revisions with new students, new nonresidential learning experiences, and new emphasis on skill development, research and concern about the impact of college on attitudes, values, and personal development may prove to have been a passing fad. The very survival of the student development movement may depend on its ability to respond. The few recommendations presented here are reiterations of those implied throughout this monograph and specified in the sections exploring alternative role models for student development staff.

1. *The concern for student development needs to move from the extracurricular to the curricular.* This means that student personnel workers, counselors, deans, housing staff, and others who profess to be concerned about total student development must move into the academic world both to legitimatize experiences and programs now available and to humanize current curricular offerings. The mechanisms or models for accomplishing this move are not readily available. Current ties with academia are limited, at best, but again the commitment is the needed first step.

2. *Theories need to be constructed that attempt to conceptualize the potential impact of learning experiences throughout the entire human lifespan.* The growing

adult education movement in this country should have the beginnings of a literature that will serve as a starting point for some understanding of adult populations who return to school. So far most of student personnel efforts designed to work with this population have followed the remedial model used so often with special populations. Instead of examining the potentiality for offering unique educational experiences, the emphasis has been on trying to help these populations deal with adjustment problems.

Human development does not stop at marriage or age 21. Many development crises lie ahead, and answers are needed as to how learning experiences can help these become positive and growth-producing rather than just aging experiences. This would be only a half step unless processes are also sought by which these educational ventures can lead to further personal fulfillment, the acquisition of new ideas about self as well as new skills.

3. *Much more experimentation and innovation is needed to find ways to improve teaching-learning experiences and increase their potential impact on students.* Withey (1971) in a recent Carnegie Commission Report noted that much of the research on student ecology has been done by social psychologists who have found the peer group to be quite influential on student attitudes and values. His inference, though never explicit, is that these pairings are possibly hardly coincidental. If the classroom experiences do not now have a comparable impact, does this mean that they are inevitably so limited? There is a real question of economy here. Students spend 15 to 20 hours a week in a classroom in a generally controlled setting. If student development is an ultimate objective, why ignore this potential laden experience?

Current research efforts have been almost exclusively descriptive. The "know your students" motto has been well served by student personnel researchers. If we are ever to truly move from describing to prescribing alternatives, however, we are going to have to know more about the impact of different experiences on different students. This means more experimental research and more program evaluation. It is important that these efforts be carried on throughout all types of collegiate programs and not just four-year residential colleges.

4. *Some attempt must be made for the student development staff to have rather direct contact with most, if not all of the student body.* Recent professional statements (Grant, 1971) have agreed that the student personnel staff should be involved in the assessment of student goals and development status. This process needs to be formalized and some framework or structure provided that will bring it into being. Student personnel administrators would be unwise to move in this direction independent of the academicians. Indeed, this might be an avenue to seek and work out a joint program of assessment, prescription, and evaluation. Several in the profession have suggested the use

of a student profile that would include a record of the student's total development. With some creativity this notion could result in more than a report card, but in a really individual growth plan for all students.

5. *To effectively and efficiently be true agents for promoting student development, student affairs offices and functions must be dramatically reorganized.* Reorganization is not painless, and it is going to take some courage. First of all, it is going to necessitate sorting out the current student personnel functions that most directly have an impact on students in a developmental context. It is fine for maintenance and food service people to be imbued with the "student personnel point of view," but isn't what is expected in most instances common courtesy and an awareness of what the clientele is like?

Reorganization of student personnel staff might be initiated on the basis of distinguishing those who: (a)provide direct student services, (b)those who could be in a position to affect the living-learning environment, and (c)those who would be directly involved in the teaching-learning environment. In the past, student personnel has been service-oriented; only more recently has there been more than incidental consideration given to outreach activities aimed to shape the environment (Morrill, 1970). Any new organizational structure should provide for ties between student development staff and the academic arm of the university; and for residential colleges, between the total environment and the student development staff.

6. *Student personnel staffs are going to have to possess new sets of competencies.* They are going to be called on to understand students, to describe students, and to get along with students as they have in the past. But, in addition, they are going to be needed to design programs that will change the environment and provide a setting for optimal student growth. These competencies will need to have utility for classroom settings as well as residence hall settings, for academic programs as well as student activities, and for all students as well as the more visible. Actually, all other efforts will fail if student personnel staff who wish to function as student development educators do not have clearly demonstrated skills and competencies that have meaning for the academician.

7. *Student personnel staff involved in student development activities should align themselves more closely with other professional organizations concerned with higher education, such as the American Association for Higher Education.* Some have suggested that a number of subdivisions within the American Personnel and Guidance Association, whose major concern is with college students, might coalesce under a division that would focus on "human development" (Ivey, 1970; Hoyt, 1971). Such a move would be consistent with the thoughts expressed here. However, if the full spirit of this monograph were to be

implemented, some major alignment with professional groups who are also concerned about the academic side of the collegiate experience would be necessary.

Conclusion

The future holds challenges for higher education and student development that will have more profound consequences than those of enrollment fluctuations or financial limitations. The most important challenge of all is for higher education to face the need for a reaffirmation of student development as a primary goal. This means that educational institutions of all kinds and at all levels must ask themselves again whether they exist for the sake of *training* students or *educating* them. Are they satisfied, for example, if their students graduate with mathematical competencies, but are socially, culturally, and esthetically illiterate? Are they willing to establish developmental goals and plan programs that will promote the growth of every student, not just those with certain proclivities?

Acceptance of student development as a major goal means tackling the problems associated with bringing it into reality with new students in new settings. It means thinking through the implications for technical programs as well as liberal arts colleges, for commuters as well as for residential students, and for older students as well as for post-adolescents. First, there is the need to reaffirm and testify to the validity of the goal, then comes a commitment to create an environment for student development.

Student personnel workers have asserted their interest in student development for the better part of the last 25 years. Now, they must acknowledge that they are not the only laborers in the vineyard nor can they alone promote student development. In one sense this monograph is a model, itself, for one of the future roles for college student personnel staff. It has focused on the academic dimensions of collegiate life, aware that this is an unfamiliar arena for many student personnel workers, but sensing that the academic life cannot be ignored any longer as a potential avenue for promotion of student development. Indeed, it may soon be the only road left. In suggesting ways that academicians can accomplish their goals and at the same time foster student development, the emphasis has been on the interrelationship between these goals.

One of its major points has been that student development staffs must have input into and involvement with the academic dimensions of the collegiate experience. This could well be one of their most important functions in the future. However, it is not likely to be a function that is going to be handed them freely, nor is it a function they can usurp. It will be one that they will have to earn by possessing clearly defined skills and concepts.

I am not alone in asking student personnel workers to become behavioral scientists, but perhaps one of the few to suggest that they also be academicians. This suggestion has definite implications for the training of student personnel workers in the future and for organizational structures within which student development staffs operate. It remains problematic whether or not many of those persons attracted to student personnel work can or will want to become either behavioral scientists or in any sense of the word, academicians. Until a sizable proportion of them do, however, the fate of the profession and student development goals in higher education remains in jeopardy.

References

Astin, A. W. *The methodology of research on college impact.* Washington, D.C.: American Council on Education, 1970.

Bayer, A. E., & Astin, A. W. Campus unrest 1970–71: Was it really that quiet? *Educational Record*, 1971, 52, 301–313.

Berdie, R. F. Student personnel work: Definition and redefinition. *Journal of College Student Personnel*, 1966, 7, 131–136.

Bowen, H. R. Society, students and parents—a joint responsibility. In M. D. Orwig (Ed.), *Financing higher education: Alternatives for the federal government.* Iowa City: American College Testing, 1971.

Camper, D. *Daily Nebraskan.* November 12, 1971, p. 4.

Carnegie Commission on Higher Education. *Less time, more options.* New York: McGraw-Hill, 1971. (a)

Carnegie Commission on Higher Education. *New students and new places.* New York: McGraw-Hill, 1971. (b)

Committee on the Student in Higher Education. *The student in higher education.* New Haven: Hazen Foundation, 1968.

Cosand, J. P. The community college in 1980. In Alan C. Eurich (Ed.), *Campus, 1980.* New York: Delacorte Press, 1968.

Cross, P. K. *Beyond the open door.* San Francisco: Jossey-Bass, 1971. (a)

Cross, P. K. Student personnel administrators and the new students of the 1970's. Speech given at the Council of Student Personnel Associations in Higher Education, Washington, D.C., October 5, 1971. (b)

Dennis, L. The other side of Sesame Street. In G. Kerry Smith (Ed.), *New teaching, new learning: Current issues in higher education.* San Francisco: Jossey-Bass, 1971.

Dressel, P. L. Values, cognitive and affective. *Journal of Higher Education*, 1971, 42(5), 400–405.

Eble, K. E. Teaching: The curriculum will always be merely an expedient; don't let it interfere too much with teaching and learning. *The Chronicle of Higher Education.* November 8, 1971, 6.

Feldman, K. A., & Newcomb, T. M. *The impact of college on students.* San Francisco: Jossey-Bass, 1969.

Grant, W. H. A student development point of view of education. A proposal presented and accepted by the Council of Student Personnel Associations in Higher Education, October 1971.

Heath, R. *The reasonable adventurer.* Pittsburgh: University of Pittsburgh Press, 1964.

Hoyt, D. P. APGA: Cherish or perish? *Personnel and Guidance Journal.* 1971, 49, 431–438.

Illich, I. *Deschooling society.* New York: Harper & Row, 1971.

Ivey, A. E. The association for human development: A revitalized APGA. *Personnel and Guidance Journal.* 1970, 48, 528–532.

Jacob, P. E. *Changing values in college: An exploratory study of the impact of college teaching.* New York: Harper & Row, 1957.

Katz, J. *No time for youth.* San Francisco: Jossey-Bass, 1968.

Keniston, K. The agony of the counterculture. *Educational Record.* 1971, 52, 205–211.

Kerr, C. National Foundation for Higher Education. *Change,* 1971, 3, 8ff.

Korn, H. Higher education programs and student development. *Review of Educational Research.* Washington, D.C.: American Educational Research Association, 1969.

Lerner, M. Revolution, not death in nation's air. *Lincoln-Star Journal,* October 6, 1971.

Magrath, E. J. *Should students share the power?* Philadelphia: Temple University Press, 1970.

Maslow, A. *Toward a psychology of being.* New York: Van Nostrand, 1962.

Morrill, W. H., & Hurst, J. C. A preventive and developmental role for the college counselor. *The Counseling Psychologist,* 1971, 2, 90–94.

Newman, F. (Task Force Chairman) *Report on higher education.* Washington, D.C.: U.S. Department of Health, Education and Welfare, 1971.

Newman, J. C. The ideal of a university. New York: American Press, 1941.

O'Banion, T. *New directions in community student personnel programs.* Student Personnel Series, No. 15, Washington, D.C.: American College Personnel Association, 1971.

Pace, C. R., & Stern, G. G. An approach to the measurement of psychological characteristics of college environments. *Journal of Educational Psychology,* 1958, 49, 269–277.

Parker, C. A. Institutional self-renewal in higher education. *Journal of College Student Personnel,* 1971, 12, 405–409.

Penney, J. F. Student personnel work: A profession stillborn. *Personnel and Guidance Journal,* 1969, 47, 958–962.

Peterson, R. E. *The crisis of purpose; definition and uses of institutional goals.* Report No. 5, Washington, D.C.: ERIC Clearinghouse on Higher Education, 1970.

Reich, C. A. *The greening of America*. New York: Random House, 1970.

Revel, J. F. *Without Marx or Jesus: The new American Revolution has begun*. Garden City: Doubleday, 1971.

Rights for the Retarded. *Time*. October 25, 1971, p. 52.

Sanford, N. (Ed.). *The American College*. New York: Wiley, 1962.

Sanford, N. *Self and society: Social change and individual development*. New York: Atherton Press, 1966.

Sanford, N. The college student of 1980. In Alan C. Eurich (Ed.), *Campus, 1980*. New York: Delacorte Press, 1968.

Sanford, N. The goals of individual development. In C. Kerry Smith (Ed.), *1945–1970: Twenty-five years of higher education*, San Francisco: Jossey-Bass, 1970.

Snyder, B. *The hidden curriculum*. New York: Alfred A. Knopf, 1971.

Toffler, A. *Future Shock*. New York: Random House, 1970.

Trent, J. W., & Medsker, L. L. *Beyond high school: A study of 10,000 high school graduates*. Berkeley: Center for Research on Development in Higher Education, 1967.

Whitehead, A. N. The aims of education, New York: Mentor, 1959.

Williamson, E. G. *The student personnel point of view*. American Council on Education, Studies Series VI, Student Personnel Work, No. 13, Washington, D.C., 1949.

Withey, S. B. *A degree and what else?* New York: McGraw-Hill, 1971.

Zigerell, J. Universities without walls and without no illusions. *Educational Television*, October 1971, p. 17ff.

Suggested Reading List

While preparing this monograph nearly 1,000 articles, books, and papers were examined, reviewed, and read. Listed below are major articles and books, which some readers may find useful. They do not include sources already listed as references.

Higher Education

Aiken, H. D. *Predicament of the university*. Bloomington: Indiana University Press, 1971.

Ashby, E. *Any person, any study: An essay on higher education in the United States*, 1971.

Axelrod, J. An experimental college model: *Educational Record*, 1967, 48, 327–337.

Barzun, J. *The American university*. New York: Harper & Row, 1968.

Bell, D. *The reforming of general education*. New York: Columbia University Press, 1966.

Bell, D., & Kristol, I. (Eds.) *Confrontation: The student rebellion and the universities*. New York: Basic Books, 1968.

Bevan, W. Higher education in the 1970's: A once and future thing. *American Psychologist*, 1971, 26, 537–545.

Birenbaum, W. *Overlive: Power, poverty, and the university.* New York: Delacorte, 1969.

Caffrey, J. (Ed.). *The future academic community: Continuity and change.* Washington, D.C.: American Council on Education, 1969.

Carnegie Commission on Higher Education Series (New York: McGraw-Hill) which includes:

Cheit, E. F. *The new depression in higher education: A study of financial conditions at 41 colleges and universities,* 1971.

Dressel, P. L. The meaning of a college education. *The Journal of Higher Education,* 1968, 39, 481–489.

Dressel, P. L., & DeLisle, F. H. *Undergraduate curriculum trends.* Washington, D.C.: American Council on Education, 1969.

Dressel, P. L., Johnson, F. C., & Marcus, P. M. *The confidence crisis.* San Francisco: Jossey-Bass, 1970.

Folger, J. K., Astin, H. S.,& Bayer, A. E. *Human resources and higher education.* New York: Russell Foundation, 1970.

Frankel, C. *Education and the barricades.* New York: W. W. Norton, 1970.

Gaff, J. *The cluster college.* San Francisco: Jossey-Bass, 1969.

Goldberg, K., & Linstromber, R. C. The university as an anachronism. *The Journal of Higher Education,* 1969, 40, 193–204.

Gould, S. B. Higher education: In the eye of the hurricane. *The Journal of Higher Education,* 1969, 40, 169–180.

Gould, S. B. *Today's academic condition.* New York: McGraw-Hill, 1970.

Graubard, S. R., & Ballotti, G. A. (Ed.). *The embattled university.* New York: George Braziller, 1970.

Handlin, O., & M. F. *The American college and American culture.* New York: McGraw-Hill, 1970.

Harris, M. R. *Five counter revolutionists in higher education.* Corvallis: Oregon State University Press, 1970.

Henderson, A. D. *The Innovative spirit.* San Francisco: Jossey-Bass, 1970.

Hodkinson, H. Ideal governance structure would be larger and smaller simultaneously. *College and University Business,* April, 1970, 658–668.

Hodgkinson, H. L. *Institutions in transition,* 1970.

Idzerda, S. J. Higher education: Social adjustment or human liberation? *Motive,* 1967, 27,10–15.

Jencks, C. Social stratification and higher education. *Harvard Educational Review,* 1968, 38, 277–316.

Jencks, C., & Riesman, D. *The academic revolution.* Garden City: Doubleday, 1968.

Jennings, F. G. Junior colleges in America—The two year stretch. *Change,* March/ April 1970, 2, 15ff.

Jerome, J. *Culture out of anarchy: The reconstruction of American higher learning.* Chicago: Herder & Herder, 1971.

Johnson, E. L. Education: Cutting edge for social change. *Educational Record,* 1968, 49, 359–365.

Kauffman, J. F. The next decade. *National Association of Student Personnel Administrators Journals*, 1968, 6, 21–23.

Knowles, M. S. *Higher education in the United States: Current pictures, trends, and issues.* Washington, D.C.: American Council on Education, 1969.

Martin, W. B. The university as community. *Educational Record*, 1967, 48, 320–326.

Martin, W. B. The development of innovation: Making reality change. *National Association of Student Personnel Administrators Journal*, 1969, 6, 116–127.

Martin, W. B. Education as intervention. *Educational Record*, 1969, 50, 47–54.

Martin, W. B. *Conformity.* San Francisco: Jossey-Bass, 1969.

Mayhew, L. B. *Colleges today and tomorrow.* San Francisco: Jossey-Bass, 1965.

Mayhew, L. B. The future of American higher education. *Liberal Education*, 1967, 53, 453–462.

Mayhew, L. B. Toward an unknown station: Planning for the seventies. *Journal of the National Association of Women Deans and Counselors*, 1969, 32, 145–154.

Mayhew, L. B. *Arrogance on campus.* San Francisco: Jossey-Bass, 1970.

Mayhew, L. B. *The literature of higher education: 1971.* San Francisco: Jossey-Bass, 1971.

Maza, H. The proposed self-programming university. *Liberal Education*, 1967, 53, 463–465.

Medsker, L., & Tillery, D. *Breaking the access barriers: A profile of two-year colleges,* 1971.

Pearl, A. The more we change, the worse we get. *Change*, 1970, 2, 39–44.

Peterson, R. E. Reform in higher education—Demands of the left and right. *Liberal Education*, 1969, 55, 60–77.

Projections of Educational Statistics to 1979–1980. Washington, D.C.: U.S. Department of Health, Education and Welfare, 1970.

Regan, M. C. Student change: The new student and society. *National Association of Student Personnel Administrators Journal*, 1969, 6, 127–135.

Rever, P. R. *Open admissions and equal access.* Iowa City: American College Testing Program, 1971.

Riesman, D. The search for alternative models in education. *The American Scholar*, 1969, 38, 377–388.

Silberman, C. E. *Crisis in the classroom.* New York: Random House, 1970.

Smith, B. L. Education for serendipity. *Educational Record*, 1968, 49, 373–381.

Smith, B. L. Educational trends and the seventies. *American Association of University Professors Bulletin*, 1970, 56, 130–136.

Smith, G. K. (Ed.). *Stress and campus response.* San Francisco: Jossey-Bass, 1969.

Smith, G. K. (Ed.). *Twenty-five years: 1945–1970.* San Francisco: Jossey-Bass, 1970.

Spurr, S. H. *Academic degree structures: Innovative approaches,* 1970.

Taylor, H. *Students without teachers.* New York: McGraw-Hill, 1969.

Taylor, H. *How to change colleges.* New York: Holt, Rinehart & Winston, 1971.

The capitol and the campus: State responsibility for postsecondary education, Commission Reports, 1971.

The open door colleges: Policies for the community colleges. Commission Report, 1970.

Trow, M. Reflections on the transition from mass to universal higher education. Daedalus, Winter 1970.

Tyler, R. W. The changing structure of American institutions of higher education in the United States. Washington, D.C.: Government Printing Office, 1969.

Warren, J. R. Changing students and constant curricula. Education Record, 1970, 51, 182–187.

Wolff, R. P. The ideal of the university. Boston: Beacon Press, 1969.

Woodring, P. The higher learning in America: A reassessment. New York: McGraw-Hill, 1968.

Wrenn, C. G. Projections of change and their impact on college education. Liberal Education, 1968, 65, 601–609.

Yeo, R. D. Reading the higher education tea leaves. Educational Technolgoy, 1969, 9, 50–52.

Student Development

Astin, A. W. A program of research on student development. Journal of College Student Personnel, 1968, 9, 299–307.

Astin, A. W. The college environment. Washington, D.C.: American Council on Education, 1968.

Alfert, e. Developmental stage and choice of residence in college. Journal of College Student Personnel, 1968, 9, 90–93.

Apostal, R. A. Student subcultures and personal values. Journal of College Student Personnel, 1968, 9, 34–39.

Axelrod, J., & Freedman, M. Search for relevance. San Francisco: Jossey-Bass, 1969.

Baker, S. R. The relationship between student residence and perception of environmental press. Journal of College Student Personnel, 1966, 7, 222–224.

Baird, L. L. The effects of college residence groups on students' self-concepts, goals, and achievements. Personnel and Guidance Journal, 1969, 47,1015–1021.

Berdie, R. F. A university is a many-faceted thing. Personnel and Guidance Journal, 1967, 45, 768–775.

Bloom, B. S., & Webster, H. The outcomes of college. Review of Educational Research, 1960, 30,321–333.

Bloom, E., & Kennedy, C. E. The student and his parents. Journal of the National Association of Women Deans and Counselors, 1970, 33, 98–106.

Boyer, E. L., & Michael, W. B. Outcomes of college. Review of Educational Research, 1965, 35, 277–291.

Brown, D. R. Student stress and the institutional environment. Journal of Social Issues, 1967, 23, 92–107.

Brown, G. I. Confluent education: Exploring the affective domain. College Board Review, 1971,80, 5ff.

Brown, R. D. Manipulation of the environment press in a college residence hall. Personnel and Guidance Journal, 1968, 46, 555–560.

Chickering, A. W. College residence and student development. Educational Record, 1967, 48, 179–186.

Chickering, A. W. Institutional objectives and student development in college. *Journal of Applied Behavioral Science*, 1967, 3, 287–304.

Chickering, A. W. *Education and identity*. San Francisco: Jossey-Bass, 1969.

Chickering, A. W., & Kuper, E. Educational outcomes for commuters and residents. *Educational Record*, 1971, 52, 255–261.

Coons, F. W. The resolution of adolescence in college. *Personnel and Guidance Journal*, 1970, 48, 533–541.

Dressel, P. L. Values cognitive and affective. *Journal of Higher Education*, 1971, 42, 400–405.

Dreyfus, E. A. The search for intimacy. *Adolescence*, 1967, 2, 25–40.

Eddy, E. D., Jr. *the college influence on student character*. Washington, D.C.: American Council on Education, 1959.

Feldman, K. A. Studying the impacts of colleges on students. *Sociology of Education*, 1969, 42, 207–237.

Freedman, M. B. *The college experience*. San Francisco: Jossey-Bass, 1967.

Heath, D. H. *Growing up in college*. San Francisco: Jossey-Bass, 1968.

Ivey, A. E., Miller, C. D., & Goldstein, A. D. Differential perceptions of college environment: Student personnel staff and students. *Personnel and Guidance Journal*, 1968, 46, 17–21.

Ivey, A. E., & Morrill, W. H. Confrontation, communication, and encounter: A conceptual framework for student development. *National Association of Student Personnel Administrators Journal*, 1970, 7, 226–234.

Johnson, R. W., & Kurpius, D. J. A cross-sectional and longitudinal study of students' perceptions of their college environment. *Journal of College Student Personnel*, 1967, 8, 199–203.

Keniston, K. Youth, change, and violence. *The American Scholar*, 1968, 37, 227–245.

Keniston, K. What's bugging the students? *Educational Record*, 1970, 51, 116–129.

Heist, P. (Ed.). *The creative student: An unmet challenge*. San Francisco: Jossey-Bass, 1968.

McKeachie, W. J. Significant student and faculty characteristics relevant to personalizing higher education. In W. J. Minter (Ed.), *The individual and the system*. Boulder: Western Interstate Commission for Higher Education, 1967, 21–35.

McPeek, B. L. The university as perceived by its subcultures: An experimental study. *Journal of the National Association of Women Deans and Counselors*, 1967, 30, 129–132.

Matson, J. E. Student personnel services in junior colleges—A special challenge. *National Association of Student Personnel Administrators Journal*, 1967, 4, 161–164.

Newcomb, T. The contribution of the interpersonal environment to students' learning. *National Association of Student Personnel Administrators Journal*, 1967, 5, 175–178.

Newcomb, T. M., & Wilson, E. K. (Eds.). *College peer groups: Problems and prospects for research*. Chicago: Aldine, 1966.

Nichols, R. C. Personality change and the college. *American Educational Research Journal*, 1967, 4, 173–190.

Panos, R. J. Criteria of student development. *Journal of College Student Personnel*, 1968, 9, 308–311.

Pervin, L. A. The college as a social system. *The Journal of Higher Education*, 1967, 38, 317–322.

Plant, W. T., & Minium, E. W. Differential personality development in young adults of markedly different aptitude levels. *Journal of Educational Psychology*, 1967, 58, 141–152.

Richard, J. M., & Braskamp, L. A. Who goes where to junior college? *American College Testing Research Reports*, Iowa City: American College Testing Program, 1967.

Richards, J. M., Jr., Rand, L. M., & Rand, L. P. A description of junior colleges. *American College Testing Research Reports*, Iowa City: American College Testing Program, 1969.

Sanford, N. *Where colleges fail: A study of the student as a person*. San Francisco: Jossey-Bass, 1967.

Sanford, N. Education for individual development. *American Journal of Orthopsychiatry*, 1968, 38, 858–868.

Skager, R. W., & Braskamp, L. A. Changes in self-ratings and life goals as related to student accomplishment in college. *American College Testing Research Reports*, No. 16, Iowa City: American College Testing Program, 1966.

Trent, J. W., & Craise, J. L. Commitment and conformity in the American college. *The Journal of Social Issues*, 1967, 23, 34–51.

Tripp, P. A. Value making: A principle function of the college experience. *Journal of the National Association of Women Deans and Counselors*, 1966, 29,7–10.

Trow, M. The campus viewed as a culture. In H. T. Sprague (Ed.), *Research on college students*, Boulder: Western Interstate Commission for Higher Education, 1960, 105–123.

Wallace, W. Student culture research: Application and implications for structure and continuity in the liberal arts college. *National Association of Student Personnel Administrators Journal*, 1967, 5, 149–154.

Warren, J.R. Student perceptions of college subcultures. *American Educational Research Journal*, 1968, 5, 213–232.

Yonge, G. D. Students. *Review of Educational Research*, 1965, 35, 253–263.

Future of Student Personnel Work

Chickering, A. W. The young adult: A new and needed course for college personnel administrators. *Journal of the National Association of Women Deans and Counselors*, 1967, 30,98–107.

Fawcett, J. R. Before you jump. *Journal of College Student Personnel*, 11, 217.

Grant, H. Higher education and student personnel work in the yea 2000. *Journal of the National Association of Women Deans and Counselors*, 1968, 31, 140–141.

Greenleaf, E. A. How others see us. *Journal of College Student Personnel*, 1968, 9, 225–231.

Greenleaf, E. A. Who should educate the college student personnel worker and to what end? *National Association of Student Personnel Administrators Journals,* 1968, 6, 29–32.

Hoyt, D. P. The impact of student personnel work on student development. *National Association of Student Personnel Administrators Journal,* 1968, 5, 269–275.

Hoyt, D. P., & Rhatigan, J. J. Professional preparation of junior and senior college student personnel administrators. *Personnel and Guidance Journal,* 1968, 47, 263–270.

Hoyt, D. P. Student development philosophy and power. In *Campus-Community Mental Health Services,* Western Interstate Commission for Higher Education, October, 1971, p. 4.

Koile, E. A. Student affairs: Forever the bridesmaid. *National Association of Student Personnel Administrators Journal,* 1966, 4, 65–72.

Miller, T. K. College student personnel preparation—present perspective and future directions. *National Association of Student Personnel Administrators Journal,* 1967, 4, 171–176.

Moore, L. V. Some problems in the study of students' perception of personnel services. *Journal of the National Association of Women Deans and Counselors,* 1966, 30, 33–36.

Mueller, K. Educational issues and the training of student personnel workers. *National Association of Student Personnel Administrators Journal,* 1967, 4, 167–170.

Mueller, K. The future of the campus personnel workers. *Journal of the National Association of Women Deans and Counselors,* 1968, 31, 132–137.

O'Banion, T. The functions of college and university student personnel workers. *College and University,* 1970, 45, 296–304.

Osipow, S. H. Challenges to counseling psychology for the 1970's, 80's. *The Counseling Psychologist,* 1971, 2, 86–90.

Parker, C. a. Ashes, ashes . . . Paper presented at the American Personnel and Guidance Association Convention, St. Louis, Missouri, 1970.

Parker, C. A. Institutional self-renewal in higher education. *Journal of College Student Personnel,* 1971, 12, 405–409.

Pruitt, A. S. The differential rewards of student personnel work. *Journal of the National Association of Women Deans and Counselors,* 1966, 30, 40–45.

Raines, M. R. Student personnel development in junior colleges. *National Association of Student Personnel Administrators Journal,* 1967, 4, 153–161.

Rhatigan, J. J. Professional preparation of student personnel administrators as perceived by practitioners and faculty. *Journal of College Student Personnel,* 1968, 9, 17–23.

Rodgers, A. The new student dean: An innovator for student development. *National Association of Student Personnel Administrators Journal,* 1969, 6, 135–137.

Shaffer, R. H. Whither student personnel work from 1968 to 2018? *National Association of Student Personnel Administrators Journal,* 1968, 6, 9–14.

Shetlin, E. M. The Peter Principle and student personnel work. *Journal of College Student Personnel,* 1970, 11, 167–168.

Shoben, E. J., Jr. Psychology and student personnel work. *Journal of College Student Personnel,* 1967, 8, 239–245.

Shoben, E. J., Jr. The new student: implications for personnel work. *CAPS Capsule*, 1968, 2, 1–7.

Spolyar, L. J. Student power: Threat or challenge for student personnel? *National Association of Student Personnel Administrators Journal*, 1968, 6, 74–77.

Stark, M. Human relations as a student personnel service. *Journal of College Student Personnel*, 1966, 7, 275–278.

Stark, M. The student personnel administrator as an educator: The teaching of human relations. *National Association of Student Personnel Administrators Journal*, 1967, 5, 147–149.

Thoresen, C. E. The counselor as an applied behavioral scientist. *Personnel and Guidance Journal*, 1969, 48, 841–847.

Tripp, P. A. Student personnel workers: Student development experts of the future. *Journal of the National Association of Women Deans and Counselors*, 1968, 31, 142–144.

Williamson, E. G. Some unsolved problems in student personnel work. *National Association of Student Personnel Administrators Journal*, 1967, 5, 91–96.

Wrenn, C. G. The development of student personnel work in the United States and some guidelines for the future. In W. J. Minter (Ed.), *The individual and the system.* Boulder: Western Interstate Commission for Higher Education, 1967, 101–121.

Zaccaria, J. S. The behavioral sciences and the identity crisis of student personnel work. *Journal of the National Association of Women Deans and counselors*, 1968, 31, 103–105.

Student Affairs Administration in Transition

Everett M. Chandler

There is a transition stage in the organization of student affairs involving student personnel work as defined in the period following World War II and a newer concept of student development. An organizational model is proposed for the transition along with a proposed approach leading toward a student development goal.

Recently there have been articles indicating interest in overall administration, organization and what might be labeled the philosophical basis of student affairs work (Crookston 1972; Rickard 1972; Sandeen 1971). One can detect a state of doubt, sometimes confusion, and occasionally despair over the present condition of the profession and its place in higher education in such articles. Perhaps this state of feeling reflects a transitional period in the profession.

Since World War II, there appear to be two identifiable trends relating to the administration of student affairs. The first is exemplified by the writings of such authors as Wrenn (1951), Mueller (1961), and Williamson (1961) which set forth a framework for student personnel work based on the student personnel point of view. Three assumptions regarding students are the foundation for this viewpoint: (a) individual differences among students are anticipated: (b) the student is conceived of and treated as a functioning whole person; and (c) teaching, counseling, activities, and other organized educational efforts start from where the student is and not where the institution would prefer the student to be in development.

It is believed that few would take exception to these concepts. In translating these concepts to the job, it appears that these assumptions may not have been worked into the practice of student personnel as fully as originally conceived. During this same time period, administrators responsible for student personnel work identified a series of from 10 to 15 different functional services to students such as counseling, testing, placement, health, cocurricular activities, and financial aids. Skilled practitioners were

396

developed for these various areas of service. These services are frequently remedial or controlling in nature; these functional areas operate somewhat independently of one another. Neither students nor faculty were or are involved to any extent in planning, organizing, staffing, or evaluating them.

A second trend is of more recent origin and is frequently labeled student development. The entire campus is involved in facilitating the behavioral development of the student. The student is assessed as to where he is in terms of his goals. There is emphasis on the meaningful involvement of the student in the educational activities affecting him. The concepts are not so basically different than found in the student personnel point of view, but the emphasis on more intensive involvement of both student and faculty in cooperative efforts is. The emphasis requires new thinking and new attitudes about what is being done and how to do it.

Student personnel work often finds itself in a service station role with the staff waiting for customers and reacting to their declared needs; whereas student development is viewed as a preventive, proactive, collaborative role with the staff moving outward. The two approaches are not only separated by the nature of the duties performed but also by an attitude about why and how the work is done. The difference is not so much concept as it is practice.

Roles in Transition

It would appear that the student affairs profession may be in a state of transition. What are some of the indicators of transition and how do we operate in a transitional period? A few examples from recent literature indicate aspects of this transitional state. The NASPA research report on "Assumptions and Beliefs of Selected Members of the Academic Community" (Dutton and others 1970) shows differing role expectations for the Vice President for Student Affairs (VPSA) on the part of various members of the academic community. Students prefer an advocate role but are confronted often by an adversary relationship. The presidents feel that maintenance of control and order is the major responsibility of the VPSA and that this should not detract from other duties. The faculty appear to view student affairs as an academic civil service.

Sandeen (1971) declares that "college student personnel workers have not adequately defined their roles," adding that "too often there is a discrepancy between the educational goals of the institution and the goals that the dean and his staff may share [p. 223]." Thus, the role of the VPSA and his staff can be one of confusion. Rickard (1972) wisely warns the profession to be aware that the mere adoption of the title student development in a "frenetic search for relevance without examining and updating what the staff do is merely a semantic exercise [p. 222]." He states that the title *student development* without proper groundwork may cause both faculty and students to react unfavorably. There are faculty members who are unaware, uncaring, and sometimes unsympathetic to the work done by student affairs. The words student development imply only instructionally related development as viewed by some faculty members. A change in title to student development by student affairs may be seen by this type of faculty member as a real or implied threat to his real or assumed prerogatives and may draw a hostile reaction which may infect others not ordinarily involved in such matters.

It appears clear that the full scale implementation of a student development program requires a nearly complete acceptance of the concept by the vast majority of the entire academic community. It involves more than a reshuffling of departments in student affairs; attitudinal changes by the staff of student affairs, key administrators, and faculty leaders are necessary. It is not likely that all parts of the academic community will accept the concept at an equal pace. It appears that the student development concept will evolve on campuses in differing rates and by different means. There will be a transitional state of undetermined length and depth. This creates a situation in which the VPSA must consider organization in a transitional setting. If the goal of student development is desirable, both organization and attitudinal steps should be taken.

Implementation of Goals

First the attitudinal situation is of utmost importance. The VPSA needs to create an attitudinal environment favorable to the development of the program. To do this, he can begin by establishing objectives and strategies relating to student development. Among these can be a plan to use staff members to present ideas to the various parts of the academic community. Perhaps using a low profile, they can begin to gain understanding from those with whom they are in frequent contact. To accomplish this satisfactorily, the VPSA should establish a staff training program to provide his own staff with adequate insight into the student development goals and processes. The staff should collaborate in setting objectives related to student development in accordance with the degree of acceptance by the academic community of collaborative work by students, faculty, and student affairs at any given time. One facet of such training should be to teach patience in reaching the goals. As the program gains acceptance, other members of the academic community should be involved in the collaborative processes and the setting of objectives.

The effort expended by the staff to explain student development should not be so self-righteously done as to create a counterforce. There is a decided difference between defeating enemies and winning friends. After all, the student development concept does not seek to change the basic character of the institution, but it seeks to provide a more effective process to help students achieve within that institution.

Second, there are organizational responses that may be made within student affairs which would assist in heading toward the goal. Undoubtedly there are a number of organizational models that would work well. One model is suggested that would appear to work in institutions in the 7,500 to 20,000 enrollment range. Both smaller and larger institutions may have special needs and situations making the model less valid for them. Of course, individual institutions may have special characteristics, including particular types of presidents, deans, and others, and even curricular offerings that would invalidate this model.

It is also obvious that various institutions are in different places on any scale measuring the state of transition in student development. However, it is likely that there is a grouping together at some modal point indicating that a plan of organization will evolve that has similarities among the institutions.

Implementation of a Model

In considering this model the first premise is that student affairs is one of the major components of the university organization. As such it should report to the chief executive of the campus. This means that the VPSA should be an administrator. Occasionally, a desire can be detected among some colleagues not to identify fully with the administration. In fact, Hedlund (1971) in his article on the preparation for student personnel, foresaw a cleavage between administrative functions and student development functions. He forecasted a separation of the two, with administrative functions being assigned to an area consisting of persons who are professional administrators but not necessarily expert in the educational process. He indicated that an administrator needs managerial talent not required by an educator and that an educator needs human development talent not required by the administrator. The inference is made that these areas of expertise clash and cause problems for current administrators of student affairs. Sometime in the future the cleavage may occur, but it is believed that the presidents and the trustees who establish the administrative organization of the institutions will continue to expect the VPSA to perform both administrative and educational functions for some time to come. It is also believed that a good administrator can absorb both functions and perform them well. Presidents, academic vice presidents, and many corporate executives satisfactorily administer a number of varied activities.

As a major component of the institution, student affairs requires an administrator as its head. Such functions as planning, organization, communication, control, and evaluation are as essential to student affairs as to any other administrative organization. If the VPSA does not perform these functions, someone else in the institution will do it. It is suggested that the VPSA accept his role as administrator as the one best prepared to understand and support the desired objectives of the student affairs program as delineated by the president and as agreed on by student affairs staff, faculty, and students where collaborative efforts are employed.

Second, from the standpoint of organizational structure, it is believed that differing concepts of the student affairs program can be accommodated together in one organization. A portion of the work done in student affairs is strictly management. These services are needed and will continue to be located in the administrative structure. Another portion of the work can be closely related to the student development concept, and a third is the judicial-disciplinary control function.

The three areas named would be administered by professional staff members under the general direction of the VSPA. The first area should be directed by a person who has managerial skills. He might have business administration skills, education, and experience. His function would be to provide services such as admissions, records, placement, housing, and financial aids efficiently and well.

The second area should be administered by a human development consultant (Morrill, Ivey & Oetting 1968). Since the student development approach lends itself to the use of project, task force, and team approaches, the person taking the lead in this area may be rotated according to current needs and the collaborative interaction of students, faculty, and administration. Any given project agreed on through collaboration might call for the special skills of a specific staff member. This person would take the lead in administering this particular project. Another project might require a different project team with a different leader.

The third function of discipline-control would preferably be run by a person who is primarily educationally motivated but is able to perform the necessary control and discipline tasks as required by any given institution.

The three areas—managerial, student development, judicial control— would have subfunctions grouped under them. These subfunctions would vary from campus to campus according to the outlook and expectations of the functions in the eyes of the campus at large. Although it is recognized and hoped that each function would have a student development outlook, it is not realistic to expect everyone in the organization to have it in the same degree.

Managerial

There are many student personnel professionals who have performed their work ably and who hold tenured positions in their job. The tenure may be legal, or it may be a moral obligation to those who have served well for many years. Consequently, those whose outlook is more managerial than student development may be grouped together for this reason.

The general campus community, including students and faculty as well as administration, may expect certain functions to operate in relatively fixed ways. These ways may even be bound by statutory requirements. Such functions as records and placement may be located in the managerial section. Crookston (1972) pointed out that it should not be inferred from his strong advocacy of a newer student development approach that all student personnel methods should be abandoned, because some remedial and mental health functions as practiced under the student personnel point of view should continue. It is hoped that effort in leading these functions toward a proactive and collaborative approach would be ultimately successful and lead to less need for remediation. One organizational model suggested for the transitional stage is shown in Figure 1.

It is realized that the Figure standing alone reflects a hierarchical organization or a bureaucratic structure which is not intended. This form should be understood to portray location of functions: the assignment of functions in the chart is not meant to be arbitrary. For example, placement may not emphasize career development but may perform the essential managerial task of bringing employer and student together efficiently, providing an accurate available system of files and resumes. Most financial aid programs following detailed guidelines established by federal, state, and institutional agencies perform largely managerial operations. A large portion of the decision making in admissions work on many campuses involves application of state dictated entrance requirements. It is recognized that there is room for collaboration with faculty and students in some aspects of these services but not to the degree found in such functions as counseling or cocurricular activities. Obviously student and faculty collaboration is not barred in the managerial services, but the fact is that in practice it just has not occurred to

Figure 1
Student Affairs Division

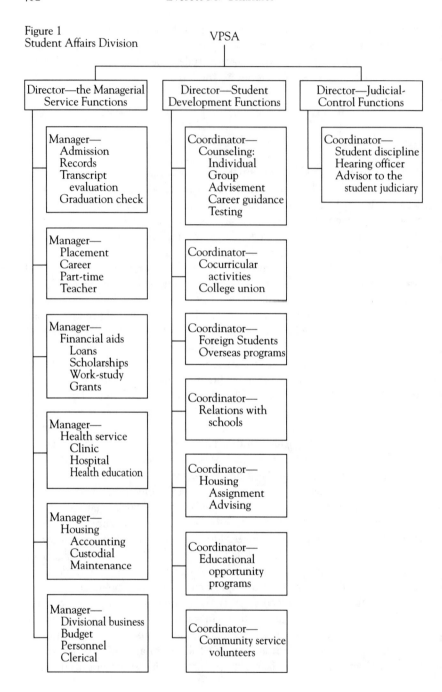

any great extent for the past twenty years or so. Certainly managerial services should not be performed in a cold punched-card manner calculated to cause student and faculty antipathy and even rejection. This is a matter of emphasis. It is believed that efficient service from this type of managerial function is the expectation of presidents, faculty, and students.

Student Development

In examining the functions listed under student development, it should not be thought that efficient service is to be forgotten—every office should strive for such a goal. However, the emphasis is not managerial. There is much more room for student and faculty input in the decisions which affect the student. The functions suggested for inclusion in this area are those which appear to be in a state where the initiation of a student development approach will be more readily understood and accepted, not only by the staff but also by the rest of the academic community.

An example of the team effort in student development might be the following hypothetical case. Residence hall students working with members of the counseling staff, health center, cocurricular activities staff, and the housing office might establish a team project for making the residence hall a more effective instrument for education through experiential learning in a living environment. Key faculty members in certain disciplines might also be involved. The group would establish behavioral objectives and an agreed-on means of achievement. The group would establish evaluative procedures and measures to ascertain progress toward the goal.

It is recognized that there are agreed-on objectives and, in addition, certain routines prescribed by law or by administrative direction that must be accomplished by various offices or positions in the student development area. Although some persons might assume that any managerial functions would compromise the proactive, collaborative approach necessary for student development, the fact that such work is done does not negate the student development approach and attitude, which is key to the success of student development. These assignments should be included in the administrative objectives. The procedure for accomplishing them should be done with a proactive collaborative approach, including staff of the department, students, and faculty where possible.

Judicial-Control

The judicial-control functions are not as extensive in terms of offices or personnel. Because of their influence (positive or negative) they have an importance beyond mere numbers. It is particularly important to separate out of counseling, housing, and cocurricular activities the functions relating to discipline and control. Such functions assigned to these other areas can impede a proactive collaborative student development effort because judicial-control functions are essentially an adversary relationship which creates a communication barriers.

The disciplinary and control functions can be combined in a small office. The advisorship of the student judiciary, performance of hearing officer tasks at lesser levels of discipline, gathering of evidence, arranging for judgmental hearings, and implementation of necessary due process procedures are tasks requiring professional leadership.

As a matter of fact, there are many student government leaders who prefer a legalistic role in dealing with the institution in regard to application of rules and regulations. The establishment of an office to carry out the function in an orderly, legalistic manner may meet a real need. In addition, the courts today are requiring a more legalistic approach in order to avoid having cases overruled.

Conclusion

The need for a transitional state comes about because there is an ongoing program of student personnel services on the majority of campuses. The present system is based on a traditional hierarchical administrative organization structure of authority and responsibility. In large part, student personnel work consists of a series of remedial services and the application of rules and regulations in control functions. The staff is usually passive, waiting to serve those who find their offices or apply corrective measures to those presumed to have erred.

Recently a strong trend is developing which is leading toward a student development approach. This approach requires both a change in attitude toward service to students and a change in the way of providing it. The staff is expected to move outward from their offices and to interact collaboratively with staff and students toward a common goal of aiding each student in his behavioral development. The emphasis on rules and controls is decidedly decreased.

On many, possibly a large majority of campuses, the total academic community is not ready to accept a full scale student development program emanating out of the student affairs area.

It is believed that the proposed transitional model is one way to enable student affairs administrators to initiate a student development program on campuses where the complete change to a student development concept would be difficult to achieve in the near future. Understanding of the program by an entire academic community may take time. Evidence of smooth working of the student development program in certain specific areas may hasten the day of full acceptance.

References

Crookston, B. B. An organizational model for student development. *Journal of the National Association of Student Personnel Administrators*, 1972, *10*, 3–13.

Dutton, T. et al. Assumptions and beliefs of selected members of the academic community. *A special report of the NASPA division of research and program development*. Bloomington, Indiana: National Association of Student Personnel Administrators, April 1970, 6.

Hedlund, D. E. Preparation for student personnel: Implications of humanistic education. *Journal of College Student Personnel*, 1971, *12*, 324–328.

Morrill, W. H.; Ivey, A. E.; & Oetting, E. R. The college counseling center: A center for student development. In J. C. Heston and W. B. Frick (Eds.), *Counseling for the liberal arts campus: The Albion symposium*. Yellow Springs, Ohio: Antioch Press, 1968, P. 141–157.

Mueller, K. H. *Student personnel work in higher education*. Cambridge, Mass.: Riverside Press, 1961.

Rickard, S. T. The role of the chief student personnel administrator revisited. *Journal of the National Association of Student Personnel Administrators*, 1972, *9*, 219–226.

Sandeen, A. Research: An essential for survival. *Journal of National Association of Student Personnel Administrators*, 1971, *4*, 222–227.

Williamson, E. G. *Student personnel services in college and universities*. New York: McGraw-Hill, 1961.

Wrenn, C. G. *Student personnel work in college*. New York: Ronald Press, 1951.

Student Development: What Does It Mean?

Clyde A. Parker

Three different uses of the term student development—humanism, complexity, and developmental stage theory—are reviewed. The latter is thought to be the most fruitful for the use of student personnel work. Two examples of the use of stage or hierarchal developmental theory for making changes in student personnel structures are described.

In recent years the field of student personnel work has been in search of new moorings. The field has never had a clear identity, and the student protest movement of the 60s intensified the feelings of identity diffusion amongst those on campus responsible for student welfare. One solution to the diffusion has been student development. To date, however, there have been very few attempts to translate the construct into operational structures or programs. Part of the difficulty has come from the rather vague, non-specific meanings attached to the term; another part has come from the inertia involved in changing organizations and institutions. In this article we will examine student development as a psychological construct and then illustrate the use of the construct in shaping the programs of two different institutions.

Student Development as a Psychological Construct

Development as the new humanism. Some writers equate student development with providing a rich environment productive of growth. There are no clear indications of what should result from such growth, but terms such as self-fulfillment, self-actualization and self-realization are used. The programmatic implications of such terms are unclear. An example of such a position is O'Bannion and Thurstone's (1972) recent book on student development in the community college. They did not define student development per se, but they did describe the student development worker on the one hand and a student development course on the other, as follows:

406

One way of describing the model that needs to be developed is to present an idealized prototype of the student personnel worker as a person. . . . [a] person who is needed has been described by Maslow as self-actualizing, by Horney as self-realizing, by Privette as transcendent-functioning and by Rogers as fully-functioning. Other humanistic psychologists . . . described such healthy personalities as open to experience, democratic, accepting, understanding, caring, supporting, approving, loving, and nonjudgmental. . . . They believe that every student is a gifted person, that every student has untapped potentialities, that every human being can live a much fuller life than he is currently experiencing. They are not only intersted in students with intense personal problems, they are interested in all students, in helping those who are unhealthy to become more healthy and in helping those who are already healthy to achieve yet even greater health [p. 204]. . . .

Such a course is a course in introspection: the experience of the student is the subject matter. The student is provided with an opportunity to examine his values, attitudes, beliefs, and abilities and an opportunity to examine how these and other factors affect the quality of his relationships with others. In addition, the student would examine the social milieu—the challenges and problems of society—as it relates to his development. Finally such a course would provide each student with an opportunity to broaden and deepen a developing philosophy of life. Such a course would be taught in basic encounter groups by well-prepared human development facilitators. In many cases sensitive instructors can work with student personnel staff to develop and teach such a course [p. 208].

Brown (1972) is another example of use of the student development construct in place of humanistic language. In his ACPA monograph he uses the term student development interchangeably to mean either holism, humanism, "affective" or "personal" development as opposed to intellectual development.

In general, student development theories of such "humanistic" or "affective" bent consist mostly of goals rather than propositional statements that tell us how such goals are reached by students. Although such end goals may be worthy, they are statements of final states rather than processes of development. The "developmental" is applicable only in the sense that growth occurs toward some goal.

Development as cognitive and behavioral complexity. Sanford (1966) has discussed developmental communities in a more general sense and higher education as a specific illustration of such a community. His construct of development can be more easily understood in the context of what it prescribes as characteristics of a development-promoting community. He said that there are three such characteristics. The first is the capacity to upend or disturb a person's equilibrium, so that new learning must take place before equilibrium can be restored. Although he felt that movement to complexity represents the desirable direction of change, even "regularity of change," he said that this movement had to be stimulated or provoked to counter the natural tendency toward equilibrium. This assumption directly contrasts the humanistic assumption of self-growth potential. He recognized that such upending experiences could have destructive as well as constructive effects.

Therefore, the second characteristic of such a community is the capacity to assess with high accuracy the capability of the individual to withstand stress and to make use of the upending experiences. Even in a fairly accurate assessment, there are bound to be mistakes. Therefore, it is necessary to have supportive resources available to sustain persons through precipitated crises. Examination of these characteristics revealed a construct based on a notion of development that occurs when the person is caused to analyze experience and discriminate between options; in effect he must take his previously organized self apart and reorganize it in a more complex way, which enables him to cope more effectively with new situations. Sanford says, for example:

. . . A high level of development in personality is characterized chiefly by complexity and wholeness. It is expressed in a high degree of *differentiation*, that is, a large number of different parts having different and specialized functions, and a high degree of *integration*, that is, a state of affairs in which communication among parts is great enough so that the different parts may, without losing their essential identity, become organized into larger wholes . . . [1962, p. 257].

Thus developments and growth for him are distinct processes, the latter having to do with enlargement, the former with differentiation and integration. The advantage of the complexity theory is that it does suggest a process for promoting development, but the content and end goals (intellectual competence, universal morality, affective freedom) are unspecified.

Development as stages. In contrast to the ambiguities of the humanistic theories, there is a group of developmental theories that are best described as stage or hierarchal theories. Such theories differ from those that have been described above in that stage theories postulate a regularity of change and form that is built into the organism, rather than simply change in form or feeling or complexity such as are involved in either the humanistic or complexity theories. Examples of such stage theories are presented by Erikson, Piaget, Kohlberg, and Perry. Some theorists would differentiate between the true stage theories such as those of Piaget (1970) and Kohlberg (1972) and hierarchal theories such as those of Erikson and Maslow in that the former have invariant structural properties in the person, while the latter refer to the sequence of developmental tasks which must be mastered if normal development is to occur. Kohlberg describes the essential characteristics of structural theories as a "series of stages from an *invariant developmental sequence*. The sequence is invariant because each stage stems from the previous and prepares the way for the subsequent stage [p. 4]." In somewhat greater detail Piaget (1960, pp. 13–14) outlined the criteria as follows:

1. Stages imply distinct or qualitative differences in . . . modes of thinking or of solving the same problem at different ages.
2. These different modes of thought form an invariant sequence, order, or succession in individual development. While cultural factors may speed up, slow down, or stop development, they do not change its sequence.
3. Each of these different and sequential modes of thought forms a "structured whole." A given stage-response on a task does not just represent a specific response determined by knowledge and familiarity with that task or tasks similar to it; rather it represents an underlying thought organization . . .
4. . . . stages are hierarchal integrations. Stages from an order of increasingly differentiated and integrated *structures* to fulfill a common function.

Although Piaget made specific reference to cognitive developmental stages, his formulation is applicable to other stage theories that might be applied to the development of the college student, such as Erikson's constructs of identity and intimacy or Super's constructs of vocational development. Since most research within the development frame has been done with children or young adolescents, we have little data available for appraising the usefulness of a stage developmental theory in the understanding of college students.

One exception to this is the work that Perry (1970) has done in the area of cognitive and ethical development. From his interviews with students, he was able to identify nine stages that seemed to fit the criteria cited above. They ranged from a basic duality of right and wrong, good and bad on the one end, to developing commitments, after a resolution of the available data is made, on the other. The exciting thing about Perry's scheme is that it is central to what the college experience is about and opens the way for relating other schemes of personality development to it.

We are not concerned here with the finer distinctions between stage and hierarchal models. The important consideration for our purposes is that stage theorists, because they deal with direction, level, and content of change, seem to offer greater possibilities for psychologists and others in higher education who are looking for ways to set directions for the processes of higher education. This makes it possible to prescribe what an educator should do.

In the case of the humanistic theorists we have some global virtues (Sprinthall 1972) that are to be attained, but little that is prescriptive of what a student personnel worker should do. In effect, they present slogans, some new some old, but few that suggest what programs should consist of. And we have had enough of that. The complexity theorists are more helpful in that they are able to show that by a series of upending and disquieting experiences an individual can be forced to reconsider his existing resolution of evidence, analyze his experiences, and reintegrate them into a more complex whole than existed before. However, what is lacking in that formulation is a consideration of the content of the experience.

In contrast, most stage theorists, by specifying the particular behaviors that are characteristic of particular stages, are able to specify what tasks must be mastered in order to make progress. In this way a curriculum can be devised that includes both the content and the necessary processes for mastery. We have not often thought along these lines about such matters in higher education and, particularly, in student personnel work.

Two examples have been selected to illustrate the usefulness of student development theory for student personnel work. In one case, the structure was not set, and a committee was given an institutional problem to solve. They applied developmental theory and evolved a program that has wide, institutional implications. In the second case, an organizational structure was imposed and a developmental theory was used to help define both organization and program. In this way the new organization would have unity of purpose, working relationship, and program.

Theory—Then Program

Augsburg College is a relatively small liberal arts college located in Minneapolis, Minnesota. It is church-related and has maintained an excellent reputation over the years. Like most private schools, it has been challenged by current changes in higher education to build a program that will attract a student body of sufficient size to make the institution viable. Recognizing that one of the crucial factors we have to cope with in our modern society is rapid change, particularly as it affects the relevance of the curriculum, steps were taken to evaluate and update the total program of the college as it relates to the employability of the graduates of the college. A committee was formed called The Committee on New Career Preparation (Augsburg College 1973) and given the following charge:

The Executive Committee of the Board of Regents requests the faculty of Augsburg College to strengthen the college's enrollment potential by identifying those new careers for which Augsburg College may appropriately prepare students to serve in society, and to design whatever curricular programs that will support such career preparations, at the same time indicating what programs, if any, are no longer essential to the growth and strengthening of this college and ought to be eliminated . . . [p. 1].

There was a liberal sprinkling of staff from the Center for Student Development on the committee. They had been giving serious thought to how the philosophy underlying that Center could be implemented. Rather than limiting the work of the committee to the specific charge from the Board of Regents, they began to ask some fundamental questions such as: What is a career; what is the relation between a career and one's life style; and how is all this related to the curriculum of the college? They came up with some answers that did not make the work of the committee easier and did not leave the college feeling very comfortable.

For example, they concluded that career preparation had to be approached as a much broader concept than vocational training. According to them, a career included much of what others might refer to as life style, involving vocation, avocation, leisure pursuits, aesthetic interests, and so on. In this way they saw a liberal arts college in interface with vocational preparation. They recognized that the demands of the limited job market required specialized preparations in at least one area of competency, but that the impact of the liberal curriculum was a necessity in preparing a person for a career in the larger sense.

More specific to our concerns here is the following statement from the committee:

Career preparation is a four-year process which begins with building realistic pre-college expectations with potential students and continues through regular advising and career development services in each year of the student's college education. [p. 4].

This is the nucleus from which their theory or career development began to take shape. The theory has not come from extensive empirical research or rigorous structural stage theory, but rather from close observation of students in that setting and from careful reasoning leading to logical conclusions about the sequence and kind of help students need. It is developmental in that it is sequential, in that the steps are qualitatively different, and in that the steps represent a hierarchal integration. Further, it has heuristic value in that it allows one to make deductions about potentially helpful interventions and curricular modifications. In addition, the committee has begun to hypothesize about how this development is normatively related to the four year liberal arts college experience.

The following statements explain the sequential steps shown in Figure 1 and are quoted from the Augsburg report (p. 35).

BUILDING EXPECTATIONS

The first step in career development starts during the admissions stage. Augsburg has a responsibility to promise only those things which can be delivered. We feel that the college must help the student preassess what experiences he can expect to have during his college days and the benefits a liberal arts degree may accrue.

SELF ASSESSMENT

The first task for the student at college is to assess himself. To be able to select appropriate career goals, a student must first know himself . . . his particular interest, abilities, values and background. Through the curriculum, personal and group counseling, vocational tests, life planning labs, and interaction with faculty and staff, the student can clarify values and explore tentative major areas.

HYPOTHESIS FORMATION

On the basis of his self assessment, he gathers information about the real world, forming career hypotheses, which are tentative ideas of where he can fit into the real world. Academic advising is crucial here as the student solidifies major plans.

REALITY TESTING

If self-assessments are valid, the student must confront the work world as a participant. Such encounters can be accomplished through field experiences, Metro Urban Studies Internship Program (MUSIP), Conservation of Human Resources (CHR) classes, and "Stop Out Career Day," which provides for one-to-one experiences for part of a day with resource people in the community.

SELLING SELF

When the student has made a career decision, the next step is to "sell himself" to an employer. He needs to know about appropriate job-seeking techniques and behaviors such as writing resumes, correspondence, and interviews. Seminars, job seeking groups, workshops, role playing and on-campus mock and real interviews with recruiters provide him with these learning experiences. This culminates in placement into graduate school, work, military or other alternatives.

HUMAN EFFECTIVENESS-ULTIMATE GOAL

The humanly effective or self-actualized person is always in the process of growing. He knows himself and is consciously competent, creative, flexible to change, sensitive to others and is characterized by dedication to something "bigger than himself" [p. 35].

Most of the interventions that are shown in Figure 1 are interventions that have been developed and tried in other settings or are part of the more

Figure 1
Augsburg College Career Development

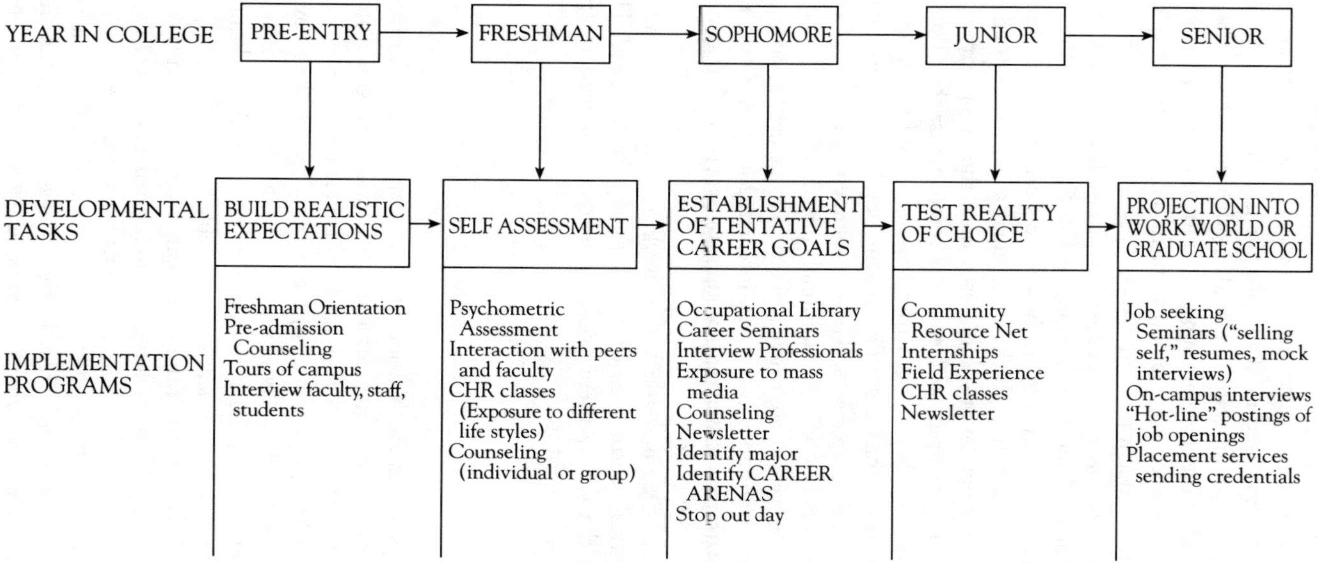

YEAR IN COLLEGE	PRE-ENTRY	FRESHMAN	SOPHOMORE	JUNIOR	SENIOR
DEVELOPMENTAL TASKS	BUILD REALISTIC EXPECTATIONS	SELF ASSESSMENT	ESTABLISHMENT OF TENTATIVE CAREER GOALS	TEST REALITY OF CHOICE	PROJECTION INTO WORK WORLD OR GRADUATE SCHOOL
IMPLEMENTATION PROGRAMS	Freshman Orientation Pre-admission Counseling Tours of campus Interview faculty, staff, students	Psychometric Assessment Interaction with peers and faculty CHR classes (Exposure to different life styles) Counseling (individual or group)	Occupational Library Career Seminars Interview Professionals Exposure to mass media Counseling Newsletter Identify major Identify CAREER ARENAS Stop out day	Community Resource Net Internships Field Experience CHR classes Newsletter	Job seeking Seminars ("selling self," resumes, mock interviews) On-campus interviews "Hot-line" postings of job openings Placement services sending credentials

traditional student personnel operation. The theory assists in putting a package together and in identifying the gaps in programming. It also shows how one type of program is related to other programs so that overlap can be eliminated or one program substituted for another. In other words, having a theory that guides program development helps to prevent a "grow like topsy" approach to student personnel work.

In this case, as mentioned earlier, the staff from the Center for Student Development through their work on the New Careers Committee was able to go even further by showing how the concern for career development could be implemented through the curriculum as well as assisted by the Center. These recommendations were based on a theory of learning that included didactic, experiential, and practical components; they thus suggested that the curriculum be arranged to reflect opportunities in all three modes of learning, using the Center for Student Development heavily for experiential and practical components. These recommendations bridged traditional student personnel work with traditional curriculum.

Thus, we have a case where a practical, expedient concern of the Board of Regents is translated into a well-integrated program fusing the work of the faculty with that of student development experts so that students might have the opportunity to progress systematically toward careers that allow self-expression. One may ask: Will it work, or is it operationally sound? These are empirical questions by which the theory may be tested. The point is that without the theory there would be neither a systematic program nor the opportunity to test it.

Program—Then Theory

Although it is much neater if an institution can take time to develop a rationale or a theoretical structure from which programs and organizations can emerge, it is not always possible. Frequently, decisions are made on an expedient basis; too often they are left that way, and we have to "just make the best of it." It is, however, possible to do more than that: If one is operating from a solid base of theory, he can always bring programs and organizational structures into a reasonable "best fit."

The University of Minnesota like most major institutions of higher education has been subjected to major reductions in its total operating budget. One of these budget revisions is reviewed here because it illustrates how theory can be applied to a set decision and how a program can be developed in line with that. In the College of Education there has existed for some time three separate units, each with its own special function, budget, and administration. The Student Personnel Office started as a counseling office with two counselors in 1946. Since then it has been given the responsibility for admissions, coordination of advising, scholastic progress administration, and institutional research-type information processing. More recently they have taken to the additional functions of conducting "growth groups" and doing some faculty consulting, particularly with student teaching supervisors.

The Bureau of Recommendations has had the responsibility for the placement of pre-service teachers and graduate students, and has maintained a placement file for all former graduates who chose to file with them. The Office of Clinical Experiences has coordinated and administered the student teaching experiences of the college, providing direct supervision of students and supervising teachers.

As part of the retrenchment and reallocation program, the Dean of the College announced that the Student Personnel Office and the Bureau of Recommendations would merge into a single office. In doing so he provided a general explanation as follows (University of Minnesota 1972):

. . . I had seen things moving in from several different directions that indicated maybe that we had come too far in thinking about our students as being the responsibility of some of us part of the time. One of the reasons had to do with finances . . . We were running into deficits in some of these operations which were being made up from various sources. Those sources are drying up. I think also, there was a serious need for information. As I saw it, some of the operations being conducted by one office were needed in the other office. [p. 1].

With that general rationale, representatives of the two offices began in early fall of 1972 to make plans for the merger that would take place the following summer. In early spring, after a considerable amount of planning had occurred, the dean announced two further decisions. One was that the Department of Clinical Experience would also be merged into the new unit and that the entire unit would be moved into a separate building, becoming the sole occupant of the former University YMCA. As might be expected, this shift in organizational components and location upset previous plans. A decision was then made to invite an outside consultant (the present author) to assist the group in what was thought might be some difficult decisions regarding both staff allocation and programming. This consultant was interested in employing student development theory to such problems and took that opportunity to see what could be done in a situation where the limiting structures, staff, and general functions had been prescribed.

The realitites of the limitations imposed by the merger were imemdiately apparent. There was the physical constraint of a new building, the space of which had to be allocated so that it would be possible to carry out whatever functions the new unit ascribed to itself. There was the constraint of three existing staffs experienced in carrying our responsibilities of their former units. And there was the constraint of the existing functions themselves. All of these had to be unified within a finite period of time, while at the same time keeping the units functioning so that their clientele were not abused. Since this required the intricate coalescing of many factors, it was recommended that a flow chart be created showing how all of the separate tasks had to flow together in order that the overall task be accomplished on time. These functions in planning were then overlaid with a timeline so that each function had a deadline and those staff members assigned to that planning function would know when their work was due.

A central concern of all staff members was to find out what were the common goals of all three units. The following is a partial answer given by the task force assigned to answering that question (University of Minnesota 1973, p. 1):

1). "Student development," "career development," and "student services" are three concepts which have been mentioned as potentially fruitful for organizing the efforts of our merged units.
   A. Responsibilities of the Bureau of Recommendations go beyond student development. (The population served by the Bureau is much larger and more varied than that served by student personnel and clinical experiences.)
   B. While service to students is a primary function of each of our units, "student services" appears to be too limiting and unfruitful as a unifying concept.
   C. Career development does have potential for housing the functions of our merged units.
2). Career development can be viewed from several perspectives:
   A. Career development may have as an object of central concern each or all of the following.
      1) Students in the College
      2) Staff in the College
      3) Teachers in the Profession

It was agreed that the construct of career development was something that all units had in common, and that a useful unit of the College could be built around it. There was less understanding along programmatic lines of exactly which functions would be involved and how they would be carried out. A preliminary formulation is shown in Figure 2 where one can see that the sequence of steps required in the career development theory is derived from

Figure 2
Education Career Development "Stages" and Supportive Functions

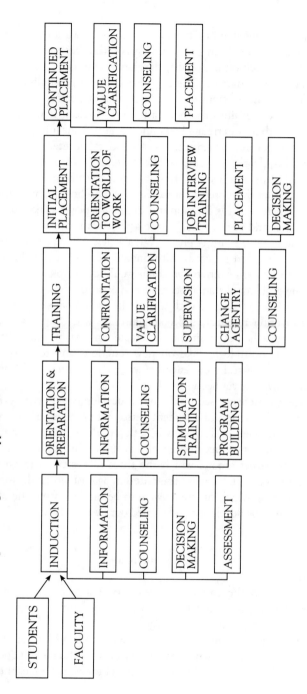

the logical progression one makes through an educational institution. They are assumed more from the structure of the institution than from any empirical research on personality development or from any careful consideration of the alternatives. There is also a strong possibility that they were derived from the existence of the particular structures and personnel that were being formed into the new unit. Nevertheless, it was possible for the staff to see their interrelatedness and to give a meaning to the new unit which went beyond the expediency of a budget squeeze.

It is also clear that some of the programs necessary to carry out the sequential steps of induction, training, and placement might be relevant in several or all of those steps. For example, counseling might be useful in each of those steps, whereas decision making might play a major role at the time of induction and at the time of initial placement. Supervision seemed most crucial during the training phase. What is less obvious is that the staff that had been identified primarily with one agency might now be appropriately used in a number of functions which would cut across old unit lines. This raised the problem of staff allocations and organizations.

One reality to be coped with was the fact of the administrators of the old units expecting responsibility commensurate with that asked for in their former units. It was desirable to create an organization with as much flexibility as possible to take on new functions and to carry out the old functions in new and more effective ways. At the time of this writing these problems have not yet been solved.

In this example we see again that a developmental view can shape the structure and function of a student personnel program, even when many of the limits are present. This view is both a philosophy (a set of values) and a psychology (a set of operations) of education. In this case, it formed the unifying construct around which the three offices could merge. Once that direction was set, it served as the criterion against which decisions could be made regarding which functions were to be retained from the old units and which were to be developed and carried out by the new one.

Conclusions

The trend in the past several years to change the language of student personnel work into what may be a more respectable language of student development may only be a mirage and a subterfuge if, in the process of changing titles, we only opt for what Sprinthall (1972) has called a "new bag of virtues" rather than a new theory of what should and does happen to students in the collegiate environment. The position taken here is that a developmental stage theory has greater potential than other developmental theories for assisting in the resolution of curricular decisions and for structuring those services and learning experiences which have traditionally been called student personnel work. In the examples cited, the stage theories used were weak when compared with more solidly based psychological theories, yet they were instrumental in shaping programs and organizational structures, and they had some relevance for curricular decisions. Future work in the student personnel field should concentrate on the creation and testing of sociopsychological theories that can be applied to higher education for the furtherance of student development.

References

Augsburg College. The Report of the Committee on New Career Preparation, Minneapolis, Minn., Augsburg College, Spring 1973. (Mimeograph)

Brown, R. D. Student development in tomorrow's higher education: A return to the academy. Washington, D.C.: American College Personnel Association, 1972. (Monograph)

Erikson, E. H. *Identity, youth, and crises.* New York: W. W. Norton, 1968.

Grant, W. H. A student development point of view of education. A proposal presented and accepted by the Council of Student Personnel Associations in Higher Education, Ithaca, N.Y., October 1971.

Maslow, A. H. *Motivation and personality.* (2nd ed.) New York: Harper & Row, 1969.

O'Bannion, T., & Thurstone, A. *Student development programs in the community junior college.* Englewood Cliffs, New Jersey: Prentice Hall, 1972.

Perry, W. *Intellectual and ethical development in the college years.* New York: Holt, Rinehart, & Winston, 1970.

Piaget, J. The general problem of the psychobiological development of the child. In J. M. Tanner and B. Inhelder (Eds.) *Discussions on child development.* Vol. 4. New York: International Universities Press, 1960. Cited by L. Kohlberg. The concepts of developmental psychology as the central guide to education: Examples from cognitive, moral and psychological education. In M. C. Reynolds, (Ed.) *Psychology and the process of schooling in the next decade.* Minneapolis, Minnesota: University of Minnesota, 1972.

Sanford, N. Developmental status of the entering freshman. In N. Stanford (Ed.) *The American college.* New York: Wiley, 1962.

Sanford, N. *Self and society.* New York: Atherton Press, 1966.

Sprinthall, N. S. Humanism: A new bag of virtues for guidance? *Personnel and Guidance Journal,* 1972, 50, Pp. 349–356.

University of Minnesota. Minutes of Student Personnel Office and Bureau of Recommendation Merger, College of Education, University of Minnesota, November 1972.

University of Minnesota. Report of Committee on Unifying Concepts for Student Personnel Office, Bureau of Recommendations and Clinical Experiences Office Merger, College of Education, University of Minnesota, April 1973.

Some Future Directions for Student Personnel Administration

Thomas R. Harvey

This author sees the field of student personnel administration taking on significant changes over the next 25 years: It will begin to merge with educational administration; it will have to help higher education in general to accept the concept of avuncularity in place of "in loco parentis"; and it will have to conceive of functions and paradigms—particularly counseling, curriculum, ombudsman, bureaucracy, and environment—instead of offices.

The field of student personnel administration is currently deluged by volume after volume describing the current crisis: Is student personnel dead? Has it ever been alive? What is its future role? Where is it going from here? These are all frequent and important questions that are being raised about the future role of student personnel administration. The last five years have seen a major identity crisis descend upon the field of student personnel administration. This crisis, however, has been a healthy one, for out of it are emerging new visions of appropriate personnel functions.

These new visions do not evolve out of a vacuum, however. Student personnel administration has been and will continue to be a function of societal and institutional redefinitions. Many additional factors and imperatives will reshape and redirect the field.

In the first place the role of undergraduate education in preparing students for vocational roles in society is being questioned. Well over 50 percent of all students graduating from college enter professions for which they received no professional preparation (Mayhew 1969). Furthermore, achievement in college, as measured by grades, bears little significant relationship to achievement in postacademic situations. Factors such as motivation, socio-economic background, and self-concept bear much stronger relationships to success (Hoyt 1968; Spaeth & Greeley 1970). And college graduates are finding that the knowledge they acquired as undergraduates quickly becomes obsolete (Berg 1970; Carnegie Commission 1973b).

421

Related to these points is the current crunch in the labor market and the increasing disregard by many youth for material accumulation (Carnegie Commission 1973a). Finally, it is becoming increasingly clear that in the future leisure and quasi-volunteer services will become more time consuming than employment. Along these lines, the National Association of Business Economists (NABE) projects some interesting statistics. Hypothetically, let us assume that you all work a 40-hour week and began employment at age 21. According to the NABE you will retire at age 38, after essentially 17 years of vocational life. This does not mean that there will be less societal work, only less employment needs. People will become more fully involved in leisure and quasivolunteer social services. All of these factors combine to suggest that undergraduate education may need to get out of the business of professional or vocational preparation and back into the business of human development.

The second major factor contributing to the redirection of student personnel administration is that the concept of "in loco parentis" is now obviously dying. Increased student independence and expectations have made this quite clear. The problem, however, as to what should appropriately replace it still exists. The university still needs to establish some sort of explicit relationship with students.

The third important factor is that the faculty boom is now over. Faculty will be afforded much less autonomy as their mobility becomes more limited. One of the effects of the past boom has been that individual faculty members could become highly specialized and parochialized. They have been able to ignore a number of institutional functions by turning them over to other specialists instead (Honey 1972). One set of these functions has concerned the extracurricular and personal development of the students. With the PhD labor crunch at hand, faculty members may be much more interested in reassuming some previously specialized student personnel functions.

These fundamental reconsiderations within higher education will cause major shifts in the role and nature of student personnel administration. Obviously, it is impossible to foresee what these consequences might be; but it is possible to make some predictions. For example, over the next 20 years there will be less of a distinction between educational administration and student personnel administration, with the two concepts probably merging; this has already happened in many places. In the past, a functional necessity has been personnel specialization and separation, but in the future such specialization will be neither functional nor possible. As the purposes of higher education begin to shift back to student development and as faculty members reassume personnel functions, student personnel administration will have to merge into educational administration within the university.

This does not suggest that the field will disappear. On the contrary, it will become increasingly important for future institutions to have articulate administrators whose primary concern is for students, those who use students as the keyhole through which they view the rest of the imperatives of the institution. It is just that these administrators will no longer be separated or isolated from the mainstream of educational administration.

Another consequence of the changing nature of student personnel administration might be that the concept of "avuncularity," borrowed from Hefferlin (1969), who uses it in a somewhat different context and meaning, will emerge in place of in loco parentis. "Avuncular" is drawn from the Latin word *avunculus* meaning "uncle." The uncle figure serves a distinctly different familial role from the parent. The uncle is available for advice, guidance, even protection, when the individual needs it. However, he does not exercise control or constraint upon the student. In essence, he gives the student large measures of freedom, while defining the student's heavy burden of responsibility. This is perhaps the ideal role for institutions of higher education to take at present. They would be available to render to students a large measure of freedom for trying out new ideas and conceiving new life styles. At the same time they are there to initiate the student slowly but surely into a concern for responsibility.

This concept does not argue that responsibility is an unimportant element, but rather that it is an element that when too fully introduced to human beings in an adolescent period may limit their ability to experiment and use freedom most fruitfully. Responsibility must be defined for the individual so that he can take full advantage of it. He grows into responsibility; he is not thrown into it. The avuncular institution gives him a maximum amount of freedom with limited but increasing degrees of responsibility.

In avuncular institutions, faculty and administrators alike must be prepared to give up their paternalism and custodial care. They must accept the dilemmas and inconveniences that student freedom brings and share the burden of educating human beings for taking on responsibility. Faculty and administrators must learn to become uncles or aunts instead of parents.

A third direction that seems to be emerging is that personnel services are becoming defined less by offices and more by functions. Undoubtedly there will always be some need for office designations but probably to a far smaller degree than currently assumed. At this point some suggestion of possible alternative paradigms of personnel functions might be appropriate. These paradigms are not necessarily mutually exclusive, and none of these is more appropriate than any other for any individual student personnel administrator. The match must include the personnel administrator, the institution, institutional purposes, and the individual whom he is serving. Five possible paradigms can be suggested.

The counseling paradigm. In this model most of the administrator's concern is for a dyadic relationship with students, that is, the relationship between himself and one student. In this context some administrators may be more concerned with the hygenics of counseling, others with the pathology. Some may be more concerned with strengthening the essential health of individuals, whereas others may be much more concerned with finding the essential illness of individuals and then curing them. Both are legitimate functions in a counseling mode, but each has different kinds of orientations and concerns.

This administrator's essential belief is that the institution needs to be humanized and that the most effective way to humanize it is by dealing with students as individuals. He also believes that the institution currently is not functioning as a humanitarian institution and that his role is to serve that function. He sees paper work as a necessary evil and committees as terribly time consuming and wasteful. The creditability of the administrator's role rests on his personal creditability with his students on a one-to-one relationship and his ability to personalize the institution. Most programs of student personnel administration put heavy emphasis on this paradigm.

The curriculum paradigm. This student personnel administrator directs most of his attention to affecting curriculum development in favor of the student. He attempts to determine student needs and then interacts with faculty and administrators to design curriculums that reflect those needs. A great deal of his time is spent dealing with the faculty. He sits on curriculum committees; he submits proposals and suggests ways of integrating the curriculum with the cocurriculum. He recognizes curriculum as a central thrust within the institution and sees his role as one which creates an effective curriculum that reflects the needs of the students. In essence he is the student advocate in curriculum development. His creditability is essentially based on his ability to create student-centered curriculums. Many newer programs of higher education and instructional development prepare such personnel administrators.

The ombudsman paradigm. Most of this administrator's concern is for dealing with student problems. He is the arbiter and mediator between the institution and the individual. This paradigm does not suggest that he directly serve the role of the ombudsman, but rather that he fulfill the type of function that the ombudsman would serve in an institution. In fact, an effective student personnel administrator in this paradigm obviates a need for ombudsmen on many campuses. This administrator does not solicit student problems, but he gladly accepts them and acts to facilitate their resolution. He knows the institution extremely well and is well respected as a problem solver by all the constituencies. He is seen as not aligned to any constituency but as a free agent and problem solver within the institution. His creditability rests on his ability to solve problems.

The bureaucratic paradigm. This administrator recognizes the importance of an efficently operating university. His concern is for balancing the budget and maintaining facilities. He realizes that if he fails to do this the institution may no longer remain solvent and therefore might not exist. The majority of his time is spent dealing with administrators. He usually is socially mobile within the institution and has a high degree of loyalty to it. He understands concepts of administration, management, and decision making, and to him bureaucracy is not a bad word but the reality of the formal organizational pattern by which the purposes of the university are achieved. He delegates all necessary student contact to subordinates because his time is limited and he prefers to spend it dealing with bureaucratic needs. Most programs of higher education currently focus on this paradigm.

The environmental paradigm. The concern of this administrator is with his relationship to groups. Rather than working in a one-to-one relationship, he works on the one-to-groups relationship. He recognizes that he does not have enough time to deal with all students on a one-to-one basis, so he concentrates on helping individual student development by establishing an effective and potent educational environment within the institution. He considers curriculum too confining a concept for institutional concern and focuses instead on a variety of functions that exist within and beyond the curriculum. He must by necessity have a strong knowledge of the research done on college students and an understanding of its implication for his college or university.

This paradigm is probably the most demanding and all inclusive of the paradigms and calls for the most skilled administrator—he must have concern for counseling relationships, for the imperatives of the institution, for individuals' problems, and for the nature of the curriculum in higher education. His essential concern is with creating an educational environment that no longer needs him. He attempts to work himself out of a job by having the other major constituencies within the university assume major responsibilities for an effective educational environment. Although in all probability he will never fully reach his goal, he strives to bring all other major constituencies into a concern for the student.

No one of these five paradigms is correct; and no one of them is incorrect. Each one of us is probably best represented by a combination of these. Higher education, however, is most in need of the environmental administrator, the one who can orchestrate institutional resources for the total benefit of students. This paradigm is far more synoptic than the others; yet it is not in itself sufficient. An institution that does not have some individuals distinctly concerned with counseling, curriculum, student problems, or institutional maintenance can not be entirely beneficial to its students.

The choice of model depends fundamentally on the kind of talents and predispositions of the person who is the administrator. In choosing his model, however, the administrator must also take into account the needs of his institution and the needs of the individuals whom he seeks to serve. In addition, he must be sure that when he chooses one model, the other paradigms and paradigmatic needs are in some way dealt with and incorporated into the current institutional structure. He shares a responsibility for seeing that all five functions are fulfilled within the institution.

In summary, this author feels that the field of student personnel administration will take on significant changes over the next 25 years: It will being to merge with educational administration; it will have to help higher education in general to accept the concept of avuncularity in place of in loco parentis; and it will have to conceive of functions and paradigms— particularly the five paradigmatic functions of counseling, curriculum, ombudsman, bureaucracy, and environment—instead of offices.

If such a regeneration of the field is to be successful, three things must occur. First of all, those who are established practicing professionals in the field must be open to redefining the role of student personnel administration in higher education. Second, those who are accepted and valued counselors, supporters, and scholars of college student personnel administration must share with all a responsibility for both maintaining that valued link with the heritage of the field and helping to create desirable alternative futures. Third, programs of higher education must attempt to anticipate future needs of higher education and create scholarly practitioners who can use insights of knowledge to inform their actions. In concert, the practitioners, scholars, and students of higher education can create a very exciting and significant system for the year 2000.

References

Berg, I. Education and jobs: The great training robbery. New York: Praeger, 1970.

Carnegie Commission. Graduates and jobs. Hightstown, N.J.: McGraw-Hill, 1973. (a)

Carnegie Commission. Purposes and performance of higher education in the United States. Hightstown, N.J.: McGraw-Hill, 1973. (b)

Hefferlin, J. B. L. Dynamics of academic reform. San Francisco: Jossey-Bass, 1969.

Honey, J. C. Will faculty survive? Change Magazine, 1972, 4(5), 24–31.

Hoyt, D. P. Criterion problems in higher education. In O. Milton and E. J. Shoben, Jr. (Eds.), *Learning and the professors*. Athens: Ohio University Press, 1968. Pp. 125–135.

Mayhew, L. B. *Contemporary college students and curriculum*. Atlanta, Ga.: Southern Regional Examination Board, Monograph #14, 1969.

Spaeth, J. L., & Greeley, A. *Recent alumni and higher education*. Hightstown, N.J.: McGraw-Hill, 1970.

Student Development Services in Post-Secondary Education

Preface

This document decribes the ideal roles for the student development specialist. While the committee acknowledge a gap between theory and practice, they are very conscious of practitioners whose behavior now models some of the basic concepts. The philosophy in this document is operational in a significant number of institutions. It now becomes appropriate to set forth lofty though obtainable goals for staffs to move toward with varing speeds and degrees of success.

It should be further noted that the Phase II document, "A Student Development Model for Student Affairs in Tomorrow's Higher Education" (JCSP, July 1975), makes assumptions about roles and urges competency development in terms similar to those of this document. This instance of mutual reinforcement should be a matter of satisfaction and encouragement to the committees responsible for each statement.

Gerald L. Saddlemire

Introduction

The Commission on Professional Development of the Council of Student Personnel Associations in Higher Education (COSPA) was given the task of revising "A Proposal for Professional Preparation in College Student Personnel Work." However, after reading the statement, the commission members saw that the basic formulation of an operational philosophy (*The Student Personnel Point of View*) would have to be reviewed before any attempt could be made at a statement on professional preparation.

The commission, after reviewing the *Student Personnel Point of View* documents of 1937 and 1949, began a free-floating brainstorming discussion from which concenus began to emerge.

Certain points of view emerged as keystones of the commission's thinking:

1. The orientation to student personnel is developmental.

428

2. Self-direction of the student is the goal of the student and is facilitated by the student development specialist.
3. Students are viewed as collaborators with the faculty and administration in the process of learning and growing.
4. It is recognized that many theoretical approaches to human development have credence, and a thorough understanding of such approaches is important to the student development specialist.
5. The student development specialist prefers a proactive position in policy formulation and decision-making so that a positive impact is made on the change process.

The commission then prepared a working paper on the philosophy and subsequently one on professional preparation. This was submitted to the COSPA Council and distributed to its constituent groups for reactions. It was also presented at a program session of the American College Personnel Association Convention in Chicago in spring 1972 and published in the January 1974 issue of the *Journal of College Student Personnel.*

This paper reflects reactions, criticisms, and suggestions received. The title, "Student Development Services in Post-Secondary Education," should be viewed as an inclusive term for the areas usually included in student personnel programs. Harold Grant (ACPA), George Jones (ACURA), and Gerald Saddlemire (ACPA) drafted statements that became the basis for this document. King Bradow ACURA), Alva Cooper (CPC), Virginia Kirkbride (NAWDAC), Jack Nelson (ACUHO), Robert Page (ACUHO, former chairman of the commission), and Harold Riker (ACUHO) contributed to the development of the paper from its inception to its final form.

The commission hopes that this document will be used for the professions as a point of departure for assessment, innovation, and development.

Alva C. Cooper, *Chairman*
Commission on Professional Development
Council of Student Personnel Associations
in Higher Education
July 14, 1972

Student Development Services in Post-Secondary Education

The purpose of student development services in post-secondary education is to provide both affective and cognitive expertise in the processes involved in education. The specialists providing these services function in a cooperative-integrative role with the student who seeks development toward self-direction and interact with the faculty members who are concerned with the academic content to be acquired in this development. The student development specialist bears a responsibility toward the broad spectrum of persons who can profit from post-secondary education.

Collectively, we use an educational institution to structure behavioral development so that it occurs in the most effective and efficient manner. Education includes the content of behavior (what is to be developed by a person) and the process of development (how and when it is to be acquired). Educators include experts in content and process. In general, faculty tend to emphasize content, and student development specialists tend to emphasize process.

Assumptions of Student Development Specialists

Human beings express their life goal as becoming free, liberated, self-directed, and they seek it through a process variously called self-actualization, individuation, ego integration, full functioning, and behavioral development.

The student development specialist believes that the potential for development and self-direction is possessed by everyone. Education is a way of assisting in developing these potentials.

The student development specialist believes that acceptance and understanding of persons as they are is essential. Since human potential cannot adequately be measured, a person's possession of unlimited potential may be assumed.

Clientele

The student development specialist deals with human relationships among individuals, groups, and organizations. To do so, the specialist should be familiar with the dynamics of social structure and should be able to utilize this knowledge in facilitating student growth.

The individual. The student development specialist will draw from various conceptual models available from philosophy, psychology, theology, physiology, and other disciplines in dealing with individuals. It is further recognized that an individual's behavior is affected by involvement with other people. The expression of behavior by an individual, however, may be public or private.

The group. Groups may provide a powerful learning environment to promote individual development. Involvement or participation in a group contributes to individual growth. Groups also provide a structural unit for facilitating and promoting collective experience and normative behavior.

The organization. Organizations comprise varied components of groups and individuals. As social systems of differing sizes and relationships, they enable individuals to strengthen and/or learn additional coping behaviors such as cross-cultural understanding, methods of conflict management, skills in problem-solving, decision-making, and other leadership approaches.

The educational institution is composed of individuals, groups, and organizations that may provide a complete and balanced environment for human development.

Competencies

The student development specialist provides expertise in the following:

1. Assistance in establishing goals for development based upon an appreciation of the unlimited potential of human beings. The goals are not only ultimate, but also intermediate, leading sequentially toward completeness.

2. Assistance in the assessment procedures necessary for any individual, group, or organization to progress toward defined goals.

3. Use of various methods of change such as organizational development, systems theory, intervention theory, futures intervention to facilitate behaviorial development within the individual, the group, the organization, and the institution.

The competencies of each student development specialist are used in functions categorized as administrative, instructive, and consultative. These functions are integrated according to the particular responsibilities that are assumed. One may be primarily an administrator in the morning, use instructor competencies later in the day, and then participate in an evening event requiring consultant competencies. The likelihood of having a role exclusively as administrator, instructor, or consultant is minimal.

Administrative function. Titles applicable to this function are vice-president, dean, and director, along with staff members such as associates or assistants.

Instructor responsibility. When this responsibility is emphasized, the student development specialist usually carries the title of dean or professor, with staff members having the rank of associate or assistant. The staff is organized into schools or departments emphasizing staff relationships rather than the line relationships of the administrator role. As a result, evaluations and participation in decision-making among colleagues are more highly valued.

Consultant responsibility. Major titles are counselor and consultant, with the staff associated with the counseling center serving the entire institution.

Functions

Administrative function. The function is based on the premise that a systematic approach to human relationships helps to achieve continuous growth. This is gained through organization emphasizing coordination, communication, supportive services, rules, and regulations established and maintained through the personal competency of the leader, whose commitment is primarily to the educational goals of the institution. Typical administrative concerns are for clear definition of rights and responsibilities, for means of accountability, and for program development.

In this function, achieving goals efficiently and effectively and the concept of doing are valued as the bases for movement toward continuous growth.

Instruction function. This function emphasizes exploration of knowledge and integration of experience as the primary means by which the student moves toward full development. Knowledge is gained through investigation, research, and experience and is disseminated through various forms of teaching. Academic competencies, including the ability to teach and to do research, are elements of the instructor function both inside and outside the traditional classroom. The interdisciplinary and applied field of student development is paramount.

In this function, knowing oneself and one's environment is valued as the basis for movement toward continuous growth.

Consultant function. This function is based on the premise that the student has personal responsibility for individual development. The consultant helps the individual focus on relationships that foster self-achievement and that encourage personal initiative, involvement, and responsibility for further progress. Professional competence to counsel, consult, intervene, and collaborate with individuals and groups is basic to the consultant function. The consultant works with other educators to help provide the necessary physical, social, financial, and intellectual resources for student development.

In this function, the concept of becoming is an essential source of personal satisfaction and fulfillment.

Table 1 summarizes the major elements of the three functions. A change in any of the items affects and changes each of the other aspects because of the interrelatedness of functions and the various elements of functions.

The elements of the three functions are listed in separate columns, but the functions must come together in various combinations for each

Table 1
Major Elements of the Three Functions

	Administering	Instructing	Consulting
Approach	Structure Objectives	Knowledge	Personal responsibility
Process	Organization	Teaching & Research	Counseling & collaboration
Staff qualifications	Leadership/ Management Objectives	Scholarship Leadership Research	Facilitation
Context	Primary commitment to the institution	Primary commitment to the discipline	Primary commitment to students
Titles	Vice-President of Director	Dean Professor	Counselor, advisor, or consultant
Structure	Division	Dept. or School	Counseling center
Modes	Doing	Knowing	Becoming

practitioner. For example, the vice-president for student affairs will spend a substantial amount of time administering but will also be instructing and consulting to the extent appropriate to the particular task to be performed.

The ultimate goal of all three functions is to contribute to continuous, positive self-development. Major attention is thus given to relationships that respect existing self-direction and encourage initiative, involvement, and responsibility for further development.

In all three functions research plays an integral part.

Implementation

The organization of Student Development Services may vary, depending on the unique purposes, functions, and changing aspects of a particular institution. It may also be influenced by the performance and integration of respective functions. The staff may be organized around functions with relationship to clientele and use of competencies contained in each area, around competencies, or around clientele. At present, no single structure seems superior.

Professional Preparation

Strong grounding in and commitment to student development purposes and assumptions, development of the competencies required, practicing and performing the respective functions, and consideration of various approaches to organization should be included in any preparation program. The emphases, sequences, and methods of instruction can vary from program to program; yet each can prepare professionals of excellence.

Program of studies. Curricular innovation is necessary in graduate programs preparing persons for student development services during the last third of the twentieth century. A critical need exists for professionals who give assertive leadership regardless of changing job title, excised organizations, declining budgets, diversifying student bodies, and often hostile public opinion. At the same time these professionals must be open, warm, optimistic human beings. Comfortable conformity to guidelines based on traditional patterns of graduate education will not suffice. The following recommendations are general approaches to professional preparation consistent with the purposes and practices recommended in preceding sections.

Since students development is seen to be the process by which individuals gain increasing mastery of their own self-direction and fulfillment, this process should be the basic means of professional education for the student development specialist. The goal of a professional program should be the preparation of persons who, in addition to having a high level of self-development, have skills to collaborate with others in their self-development. They must be able to use their competencies in assessment, goal-setting, and change processes as appropriate in implementing the roles of consultant, administrator, and instuctor in relationships with individuals, groups, and organizations.

General goals should be translated into the specific competencies needed for functioning in the professional role of the student development specialist in the processes involved in education. These objectives should be stated in measurable terms in order that performance criteria can be developed for evaluation. The following is an example of a listing of program objectives.

Objectives are categorized according to three competencies: (1) helping students move toward goals; (2) assessing status, abilities, and progress; (3) using strategies of change to facilitate human development. Within each category of competency, objectives are listed that illustrate the three possible functions of the student development specialist; administering, instructing, and consulting.

The essential features of these functions are as follows: (1) Administrative—organize, coordinate, communicate, support, write and enforce rules and regulations, be accountable, assume and protect rights and responsibilities, and emphasize staff relationships in departments. (2) Instructional—know individuals, groups, and organizations through investigational research in order to teach. (3) Consultative—be available for student and faculty member collaboration for policy determination and problem-solving that relates to improvement of student learning and environment modification.

The student development specialist is expected to master the following behavioral objectives:

I. Helping clientele move toward goals.

(These behaviors are necessary professional competencies to help students with their goals.)

A. Be able to apply various aspects of personnel management.
1. Write job descriptions.
2. Administer salary schedule.
3. Recruit professional staff.
4. Evaluate staff.
5. Administer inservice training.

B. Draw up and justify a budget showing fiscal management that follows planning, programming, and budgeting principles.

C. Be able to apply legal decisions and legal processes to the collegiate institution and to all of its constituents—faculty, students, administration, and nonprofessional staff.

D. Identify and assist undergraduate students who are underprepared for higher education learning experiences.
1. Describe elements of an academic-assistance program.

E. Identify the characteristics of critical thinking and problem-solving so they may be applied to improved self-understanding.

F. Demonstrate how to assist students in developing comprehensive career planning and implementation.

G. Demonstrate the ability to establish a productive counseling relationship with individuals and with groups.

II. Assessing status, abilities, and progress

A. Write a report describing the emerging style of governance on the campus and describe the political and social matrix: student, faculty, and administration.

B. List and describe the opportunities for learning in the external community so that student development may take advantage of the complete resources of a region.

C. Construct and apply a model for measurement of the effectiveness of the student development program.
1. Identify quantifiable outcomes of such functions as counseling, financial aids, residence halls, academic assistance, student activities.

D. Be able to state the purposes, values, competencies, and roles of a student development specialist.

    E. Assess behavior of the college population using clinical and objective methods.
      1. Write a comparison of life styles and cultural differences of student subgroups.
      2. State the principles of growth and development patterns of the student.
    F. List the general characteristics of American institutions of higher education and compare them with the specific characteristics of the local institution.

III. Using principles and techniques for change to facilitate human development
    A. Act in accordance with the list of values (based on professional assumptions) in dealing with students from diverse backgrounds.
    B. List strategies of conflict resolution on campus.
      1. Demonstrate conflict strategies of management in the power models and the collaborative models of administration.
    C. Conduct personal growth seminars and discussion groups for improvement of self-understanding.
    D. Write our a program of requirements for use by architects.
      1. Describe student needs to the designer of specific educational facilties.
    E. Seek solutions to student-related problems, using fact-finding and analysis, given an attitude of serving as defender and interpreter of student concerns.
    F. Critique research studies in human behavior in order to describe the application of the findings to the campus population.
    G. Complete a research project that tests a hypothesis related to student behavior or institutional characteristics.

The general final objective for a preparation program is this: Given a real or simulated situation where the student development specialist will emphasize one of the three roles—administrative, instructional, or consultative—the specialist will demonstrate specific competencies in three areas: goal-setting, assessment, and the process of change applied to the individual, group, and organization.

The criteria for the list of objectives are derived from the concept that the student development specialist performs so that clientele are able to (a) achieve goals, (b) manage conflict, and (c) become more self-directed and self-fulfilled.

The student development specialist should be able to be perceived as a resource of personal satisfaction and fulfillment. Students should be involved in an ongoing process of self-assessment, goal-setting, use of resources, and behavioral change. Professors of student development, student development specialists, and graduate students should continually relate as full collaborators. Internships and other supervised practice should be available as needed in pursuance of particular objectives. Graduate students should be adequately compensated for the professional services they provide during their program of professional preparation.

The administrative organization of the program should clearly identify the student development program as a graduate program in its own right. Representatives of related departments should be consulted regularly to insure an adequate multidisciplinary base for the curriculum. To continually improve the program, feedback should be obtained from the field on the performance of graduates.

A master's degree program should be directed toward the preparation of the beginning professional who holds basic humanistic values and evidences potential for facilitating student development. Specialist or sixth-year programs should provide resources for acquiring more sophisticated levels of competence and functions in specific settings of student development. Programs at the doctoral level should give particular attention to values, compentencies, and functions needed for leadership in higher education. Programs at this level require a commitment to scholarship and human development.

Admission, Evaluation and Professional Endorsement

Students seeking admission to programs of professional preparation should be assessed on the bases of values, competencies, and functions. They will be required to perform as student development specialists.

Continuing evaluation during the professional preparation program should be based on the same criteria. Those endorsed by the graduate program for admission to professional practice will thus exhibit behavior most consistent with the professional purposes, values, competencies, and functions stated in this document.

Student Services vs. Student Development: Is There a Difference?

James J. Rhatigan

The topic assigned to me underscores the latest of an historical series in the profession's search for identity. My first reaction to Dorothy Truex's request to offer this presentation was similar to that of Mark Twain, who was asked to outline his views of heaven and hell. "I'd rather not," he said, "I have friends in both places." But the discussion of our appropriate role continues, and it seems unlikely that it ever will be finally resolved. I do not find that disturbing.

Groping, floundering, and self-criticism may spur any human being or organization to necessary change, but the self-denigration that has crept into the debate in our field has been nonproductive. One of the few times I feel badly about my work occurs at our national meetings, where every crisis looms larger than life and selected persons who have so little faith in what we do resume their predictable collective brooding.

If you came to this session expecting to hear a negative rendition of our work, you will be disappointed. My thesis, such as it is, is one of evolution rather than a portrayal of reconceptualization. Henry Borow (1959), I believe, rightly observed that ". . . the attractiveness of theory among those who write about students is unmatched by those who serve students." We represent diverse activities and programs rather than doctrinal positions, and there are good reasons why this will likely continue. I do not make any special claim of being correct in my assessment. One of the pleasures of working in this field, if one ignores the anxieties also engendered, is that we are not locked into a guild, bound by masters of the craft, nor crusty with the limitations of doctrine. But much of what I see as health, others interpret as confusion—even deterioration.

The agenda of many critics, of course, is to focus on the best rationale for our role in higher education. I find this heartening because it suggests legitimate introspection, a concern for doing the best within us, and a readiness to change according to the needs of an unknown future. I am discouraged by it only because it implies that there may be a "correct" posture. It has also led some to the view that much of what we do now is not worthwhile. "Housekeeping functions," "policemen," "handholders" are a few of the friendlier criticisms made as often by those in our own ranks as by outsiders. It is not always clear where these critics get their information; if citations are given at all, they are typically references from limited research or observation by a few persons who from time to time felt it important to put down their impressions about how the field was progressing. I have indicated elsewhere that we are paying a price for our neglect of history; much has been lost because it was never recorded (Rhatigan, 1974). We have gleaned something about our origins from the proceedings of our three principal associations, but other traces of the past are slim. The hard facts are that our predecessors never thought to record their roles in any thorough or systematic way, producing a legacy of indifference that I fear may also be our bequest unless we recognize the importance of history in developing professional identity. Many practitioners today, as well as some of their teacher-scholars have, without adequate evidence, written off the early deans as mere disciplinarians, ignoring the basic humanism which permeates the content of the early proceedings.

One or two illustrations may be helpful. The authors of a recent book note: "One of the historical models for the student personnel worker is that of regulator or repressor. . . . He tends to behave in ways that regulate, repress, reject, reprove, reprimand, rebuff, reserve, reduce, and even remove human potential" (O'Banion and Thurston, 1972). This rather strained attempt at alliteration was offensive to me, and no citation was offered to support this damaging conclusion. Despite the *in loco parentis* philosophy which characterized an earlier period in American history, is this really an accurate characterization? Is it unreasonable to expect that loving, caring, and sharing would have been at least potential behaviors of those acting in lieu of parents?

Samuel Eliot Morison, an eminent historian, had this to say about LeBarron Briggs, appointed as a dean for student relations at Harvard in 1890. "He performed the miracle of exercising a personal influence on a large and increasing student body. The humanity, perception, and kindly humor, which enliven his printed reports, were so evident to the undergraduates that it is said that men used deliberately to 'get into trouble with the office' in order to talk with the dean" (Morison, 1930). Other examples could be offered from the proceedings of the early deans. But such source material is scarce.

I worry about future workers and writers in our field. What if they stumble onto O'Banion and Thurston and miss Morison? If this happens, one can expect additional negative interpretations of the past with O'Banion and Thurston used as a citation, which is how bad scholarship and ill-got reputations are perpetuated. We don't need new myths, but some existing ones aren't serving us very well. I hasten to add that the criticism of O'Banion and Thurston is in no way intended to generalize to their book in its entirety, which I feel will benefit us in other ways.

One piece by James Penney (1969) that I found both humorous and irritating provides an additional illustration of the concern of our detractors. In an article entitled "Student Personnel Work: A Profession Stillborn," Penney bemoans our failure to develop a true profession. From his citations, Penney appears to be unaware of earlier writing on this subject including a definitive, well written, but sympathetic statement on the same subject twenty years earlier (Wrenn and Darley, 1949). He derides our scholarship, which I found humorous since his own article borders on sniping. He fails to define "profession," for example, and neglects to point out that we meet some criteria but not others. Lest you feel I am unduly harsh, let me quote his concluding sentence: "The long sought 'profession' of student personnel work has not been, is not, and *will not be* (emphasis added) recognized or accepted as a vital aspect of the academic world." Such a conclusion is not scholarship; in my view it's a wish, and one wonders about the motives underlying it.

Are we above criticism, then? Few would take such a position, but there are critics who are sympathetic to our ambitions but dissatisfied with our practices and who have constructive suggestions that deserve our attention.

I turn now to the question, "Is there a difference between the concepts of student services and student development?" If there is, there need not be. There does appear to be an unfavorable attitude toward the concept of student services growing among some writers and practitioners and an attraction toward student development as a shorthand way of describing our work. I feel this debate, if developed properly, can only be helpful as we collect, distill, and attempt to practice the best of the concepts embodied therein. The two nomenclatures carry very little consistent meaning, however, as one soon discovers in looking at these issues. One is inclined to answer the question by accepting the COSPA (1972) suggestion that we begin thinking in terms of "Student Development Services." That should make everyone (or no one) happy! While the COSPA report contains more jargonese than some would prefer, I found it worthy of attention and recommend it to anyone who might not have reviewed it to date.

I believe the developmentalists would argue that it is time to move student affairs from the carnival grounds to the main tent, developing integral ties with the total processes of teaching and learning that occur on the campus. The concept of service, while it may have served a useful role, is now dated; and if we are to survive, a clearer conceptualization of a central mission than presently exists, including specific behavioral techniques, will be required. Except for some emerging suggested models, there appears to be little strategy in the surprise we plan to spring on our academic colleagues. Burns Crookston, Earl Koile, Bob Brown, Hal Grant, and Clyde Parker are some voices that have given this thoughtful attention. I will not deal with them specifically, with the exception of Crookston, in this paper.

If I have any quarrel at all with the devotees of student development, it is that they have stolen all the good words, as Crookston (1972) aptly illustrates. Consider these descriptions: Student personnel is seen as authoritarian, student development as egalitarian; student personnel is reactive, student development is proactive; student personnel is passive and remedial, student development is encountering and developmental; the former is corrective and controlling, the latter is preventive and confrontive; student personnel is cooperative, student development is collaborative; and finally student personnel is status oriented, student development is competency oriented. You'll have to admit that it would be easy to take sides in a controversy spelled out this way.

Perhaps the easiest way to look at this issue is merely to ask: What things are we doing now that should be maintained or further developed? What should be abandoned? What new efforts should be undertaken at this point in our history? And how should these judgments be made?

I am apprehensive that our efforts to establish a definable territory will unintentionally lead us away from humanistic efforts and toward technocratic expertise, much of which doesn't yet exist. This is not a new apprehension; Williamson (1961) attempted to dismiss it as baseless, but such a disclaimer is open to challenge. I identify with some of the emerging concepts of student development, but I don't want to be cast as a "developer" working (as Flip Wilson would put it) with the "developee." I can't really see how that would do much to foster symbiotic relationships. We need to be working toward programs and ideas that will be useful to students while not writing off as "ancillary" that which is already effective in a personal, human sense. Unless the concepts surrounding student development receive more careful articulation, they run the risk of simply reflecting an inferiority complex seeking relief. I would cast my lot with "substitute parents" before I would enter the chambers of a "developer"; fortunately, there are other alternatives.

A regrettable flaw in the thinking of student development apostles is the assumption that much more will become possible if we move, organizationally, directly into the academic hierarchy. Crookston (1973), for example, argues that the "human development component should be given special status within the institution, perhaps as an academic subdivision." This is tantamount to saying that what we could not accomplish on our own can be done under the protective wing of an academic vice president, an officer already burdened with multiple responsibilities. Perhaps it reflects a hope that what could not be accomplished working with a fellow colleague will become possible in working for him or her. I am not convinced that this would be helpful or necessary. Some programs of this type already exist, and have for many years, and I don't find much in those institutions that would produce a stampede to that model. But if it happens, it won't be fatal to our work, though it may indeed take care of some illusions.

Can the concept of personal development be accommodated within a service structure? A final answer does not exist, of course, but Prior (1973) suggests adding a human development component to our traditional offices. This may satisfy those who want to explore new terrain but feel locked in by old purposes, structures, and functions. I am attracted to this arrangement because it represents an evolutionary development which does not reject the practices that still are serving students well. I'm skeptical, however, about the need for it and the assumption that it makes possible significant improvements in effectiveness.

I find it useful to look to my own campus, which has a Division of Student Services. We perform the functions typically associated with such an operation. Happily, the fine people in the division have never given any indication of feeling that they are wasting their working lives. Neither have I heard any gnashing of teeth about our role vis-a-vis the faculty. We aren't keeping score as to who is doing the most for and with students. Sometimes we work in collaboration with faculty—some things we do according to our agendas and they theirs—and we find it simple to respect each other.

Without having the palace revolution some are advocating, there are things we need to do to further our work. Merely stating that we have cornered the market on student development, or intend to, is not one of my recommendations. I have no grandiose blueprint for the future. I do feel compelled, however, to offer a few suggestions as we continue to search for effective ways to proceed.

1. First, I think it would be healthy if we would disabuse ourselves of the quasi-paranoid view that there exists a conspiracy to keep the student affairs staff out of the academic arena. It implies that we need special permission to enter it. I have seen no evidence that good ideas have been rejected just because they came from the student personnel staff. Wanting to participate is not enough. Those who wait to be asked will be retired before the request comes, as everyone on the campus has his own territorial imperatives. We

will need to earn our forum since it is not inherent in our positions. But there is both beauty and opportunity in this. If we are interested in teaching and learning, it seems to me that this will be evident in our activities. Among other things, we will read and distill the literature of higher education and convey our views regularly to our academic colleagues. Then should ad hoc or regular university or college assignments develop, or should problems emerge or plans be needed, our own names will as likely be considered as other administrators and faculty as these positions are filled, or problems are considered, or plans and programs are formulated. Access is of course an indispensable ingredient in all of these, but competency is the bottom line of the issue, for us and all others.

On my campus, Student Services personnel vote in the Deans' Council and the Administrative Council, have both *ex officio* and elected representatives in the University Senate, chair the University Senate Committees on Faculty Welfare, Admissions and Exceptions, and Faculty Promotion and Tenure Appeal, have members on the Academic Standards and Practices Committee, the Student-Faculty Relations Committee, the Steering Committee on Academic Planning, Land Use Design and Planning Committee, the Committee on Teaching, and a number of other University Committees, if one is interested in tangible signs. (But these tangible signs are not guarantors of campus effectiveness, nor is the absence of such signs necessarily indicative of ineffectiveness.) Most of the staff teach regularly. Well, "Hooray for us," you say? Hardly. No one on our campus has raised questions about our participation in the academic arena. Why? Because no one thinks of it as unusual.

I doubt that my campus is unique in this regard. I suspect that those playing similar roles have not written articles extolling their campus significance for fear of appearing ridiculous and self-serving; but by not stating somewhere what we are doing, there are those who will conclude that our critics must be right—we are doing nothing or are wasting our time out there in "ancillary land."

2. I believe that we should increase our use of the classroom vehicle as a tool in our own work. Some immediate gains can be made here, and tremendous potential exists. It is regrettable that "relevance" has become such a garbage-can word, for it conveys an important message. Students today, while studying economics, may learn nothing about the economics of their own lives—e.g., the difference between no-load and front-load mutual funds, personal finance, and related issues. They might sit through an introductory course in psychology without learning anything about the nature of interpersonal communication and relationships. Through their veneer of sophistication, there is ample evidence that they know little of

human sexuality. In view of changing man and woman relationships, a course of "Marriage and the Family" might take on a different meaning than that offered by the Sociology Department. While studying European or American history, minority students and women might wonder if they were around at all or if their ancestors did anything of note. What kinds of liability, life, property, health, theft, and auto insurance should one consider upon graduation (or presently for that matter)? Academic courses concerned with "Insurance" may consider these questions too mundane. How do we assist students who are grappling with personal value issues? Is career development a legitimate area of study for credit? Death and dying is a subject of increasing interest on the part of students; how should it be dealt with?

We could help correct these deficiencies, and staff members are doing so on some campuses. How many of us offer such courses? What is preventing us from doing so? We need not offer all these ourselves, but we can encourage and influence on-campus or off-campus experts to join us in building classroom experiences that are responsive to bona fide student needs.

3. We should strive to broaden our concept of service. The word need not be linked to "service station" as our detractors are fond of doing. It may include some routine activities that must be done; not all of life's circumstances hang on a dramatic edge. But it may include any event in the life or environment of any one of our students. Working with people is our heritage. Whether this is in remedial, preventive, or developmental circumstances seems wholly incidental to me, as is whether our help is direct or indirect. It also seems appropriate to note that doing things for people is not necessarily inhibitive of growth, nor is it necessarily evidence of a controlling administrative mind, nor does it necessarily convey subtle and insidious motives, nor is it paternalistic (except perhaps in the sense of caring for the well-being of others), nor is it evidence of a status orientation. I grew up in an environment where doing things for people did not have a negative connotation, and nothing in my experience has caused me to change this view.

Does this make us simple-minded "goodie two shoes" running around helping people? That's how we have been cast by some. Brown (1972) deridingly calls us the "good boys." I look again to my own campus for some illustrations: Three years ago one of the Associate Deans in our division started a day care center for the children of students, proceeding literally on a hairpin and a shoestring. Today we have about a hundred youngsters in the program and are painfully aware of the potential that still exists. Is this a student development program? Will we be held in greater esteem by the academic community because of this program? Could somebody else on the campus have done this better? I don't know, and fortunately the Associate Dean didn't give a damn; she recognized a need and met it.

An Associate Director in a program that has a large number of minority and low-income students associated with it is of similar disposition. She has shaken loose support from the County Health people who were reluctant contributors, found free dental care for people with decaying teeth, arranged for free physicals for these young adults, found mechanics to fix broken-down cars, arranged transportation for those who had none, and performed countless other services. Her message to students is, "You're going to make it even if I have to jerk you by the lapels." They believe her. And the retention statistics indicate the power of belief. Do our faculty accord us greater esteem because of this effort? I doubt that such a question would even enter her mind. It's irrelevant and should be. Are these "developmental" notions? I doubt that they enjoy such exalted status, but I believe that some students would not be on our campus "to be developed" without the presence of this woman.

In 1968, sensing that academic due process was more myth than reality on our campus, I asked the President if we could examine the issue. Shortly thereafter a committee was formed with the Vice President for Student Affairs as a member. A court system was developed that was ratified by our University Senate and adopted by the general faculty. The court has three faculty and two students as members, and if they feel a student has been unfairly treated, they can overturn a classroom grade—and have. Was I motivated by a "service" or a "developmental" impulse? We'll never know.

As a result of a recent tragedy, two of our staff are conducting a month-long family crisis intervention workshop this month for the 429 police officers in our city. Should a Student Services operation be involved in such activities? After all, this activity does not relate to services for students.

Student personnel staff members on our campus are currently represented in the city on the Boards of Big Brothers and Big Sisters, the Red Cross Board of Directors, the Wichita Drug Council, the Board of the County Mental Health Association, the Council on Alcoholism, a half-way house, the YWCA, the Wichita Council of Churches, and the Metropolitan Area Planning Commission. Does this give us "community clout?" Have we made points with the faculty and administration? Maybe so. But our involvement is intended to reflect a concern for the community of which our students are a part. It's a simple idea of "service."

The foregoing illustrations of concerns and emphases on our campus probably don't differ materially from those on other campuses that claim to serve students. Hopefully you are not spending much time considering whether they are developmental or service programs, or whether they are "vital" to the academic community. "Vital" (Penney's word) is nearly useless as a descriptive term; I prefer to think of these simply as activities worth doing.

4. We should develop a tolerance for ambiguity and uncertainty as they will be with all of us in our working lifetimes. In his *Adventures of Ideas*, Alfred North Whitehead (1933) comments that "insistence on clarity . . . is based on sheer superstition as to the mode in which human intelligence functions." I believe this should serve as a useful reminder to all of us as we thread our way through an individual campus, a city, a state, a nation, and a world that bear on our futures. We will have to accommodate to outside influences beyond our control and to seek the potential contributions that we can make, as they occur or as best we can anticipate. The "new" student—whether rural poor, ghetto black, blue-collar white, returning homemaker, veteran, older, or part-time (in differing combinations) will require different responses from us. These will be human responses, and we need not be apologetic if we have to borrow from other disciplines in learning how to make them. The consumer movement is spreading to the campus; the legal needs of students are growing; the purpose of liberal learning must be better articulated or we will all be impoverished. How will we accommodate to nontraditional study and to students to learn through newspaper or television sets and rarely come to the campus? The questions and opportunities are numerous. I would frame around them the contention that there is no messiah coming that will bring meaning to our work. We were born, found our strength, and have flourished from the campus up, not from theory down. The only shame of this rests with those who are ashamed of it. They will continue to view our survival as a complete mystery.

If we engage in a close look at our work, it might result in the view that we are limited largely by our energy, our ideas, and our view of ourselves. These are significant factors, but factors for which we must accept responsibility. Again, we are not unique in this regard. If the student affairs program fails at Wichita State University, it will not be the fault of faculty or other administrators. The responsibility is ours. I am proceeding on the assumption that a career of service is a worthy way to spend a lifetime. I wish for each of you the freedom to work with and in behalf of students, to meet your human needs and theirs.

References

Borow, H. Modern perspectives in personnel research. In *Personnel services in education: The fifty-eighth yearbook of the National Society for the Study of Education.* Chicago: University of Chicago Press, 1959.

Brown, R. D. *Student development in tomorrow's higher education: A return to the academy* (Monograph). Washington, D.C.: American College Personnel Association, 1972.

Council of Student Personnel Associations in Higher Education (COSPA). Student development services in higher education, (mimeographed) July 14, 1972.

Crookston, B. B. An organizational model for student development, *NASPA Journal,* 1972. 10, 4.

Crookston, B. B. Education for human development. In Charles F. Warnath and Associates, *New directions for college counselors.* San Francisco: Jossey-Bass, Inc., 1973, 63–64.

Morison, S. E. (Ed.) *The development of Harvard University.* Cambridge: Harvard University Press, 1930, XXXV.

O'Banion, T. and Thurston, A. (Eds.) *Student development programs in the community junior college.* Englewood Cliffs, New Jersey: Prentice-Hall, Inc., 1972, 201.

Penney, J. F. Student personnel work: A profession stillborn. *Personnel and Guidance Journal,* 1969, 47, 968–972.

Prior, J. J. The reorganization of student personnel services: Facing reality. *Journal of College Student Personnel,* 1973, 14, 202–205.

Rhatigan, J. J. History as a potential ally. *NASPA Journal,* 1974, 11, 11–15.

Whitehead, A. N. *Adventures of ideas.* New York: MacMillan and Company, 1933, 91.

Williamson, E. G. *Student personnel work in colleges and universities.* New York: McGraw-Hill, 1961, 119.

Wrenn, C. G. and Darley, J. G. An appraisal of the professional status of personnel work. In E. G. Williamson (Ed.), *Trends in student personnel work.* Minneapolis: University of Minnesota Press, 1949, 264–287.

Milieu Management

Burns B. Crookston

Presentation of an emerging key role of the principal student affairs officer

This paper is in large measure an outgrowth of a week-long conference on student development sponsored by the American College Personnel Association in June, 1974 in which a small group, including this writer and John Blackburn, chairman of this program, were invited to conceptualize a model building phase of ACPA's Student Development in Tomorrow's Higher Education project. The result was the publication of a conceptual and operational draft model (Miller and others, 1974) that is now under active consideration by that association. The statement included an articulation of theoretical and methodological foundations for student development in higher education. Among the conclusions reached by the drafting group was that in order to achieve the goals of student development certain basic competencies should be developed by all members of the academic community, but, depending on the nature of the division of labor, each person should develop at least one of these competencies to a higher degree, as suggested by the following chart:

CHART I
BASIC COMPETENCIES NEEDED TO FOSTER STUDENT
DEVELOPMENT IN THE ACADEMIC COMMUNITY

Academic	*Student Development*	*Administrative*
INSTRUCTION	Instruction	Instruction
Consultation	CONSULTATION	Consultation
Milieu Management	Milieu Management	MILIEU MANAGEMENT

The academic community is subdivided into three basic functions: academic, student development, and administration. The drafting group agreed that in order to maximize the achievement of the goals of student development and of the college, which ideally should be one and the same, individuals should

448

possess the same basic *competencies* in instruction, consultation, and milieu management, but with expertise in one or more of them. Thus, those whose functions are primarily academic should be experts in *instruction* (teaching and research), but they also should know how to *consult* with students, staff, and colleagues and others, and be familiar with the concept, scope, problems and functions of *milieu management*. Those whose functions are primarily student developmental should be experts in *consultation*, but with competencies in instruction and milieu management. Finally those whose functions are primarily administrative should be experts in *milieu management* with competencies in instruction and consultation that are also utilized at appropriate times. This commonality of competencies possessed by all facilitates collaborative efforts within the community toward human development goals. At the same time it reduces the likelihood of conflict and misunderstandings that often take place under the usual sharp distinctions drawn among traditional functions in the academic, student affairs, and administrative sectors.

Milieu Management

Our focus here is on milieu management both as a concept integral to student development and as an emerging key role of the principal student affairs officer (PSAO), whom we believe is the most logical person in the central administration to whom the primary responsibility for milieu management (MM) should be designated.

Definitions

What is our milieu? For our purposes it is more than the physical environment in which the institution is located; it includes the intellectual, social, esthetic, creative, cultural, philosophical, emotional, and moral environments as a totality; it includes the interactions among the individuals in all such groups. Milieu involves the interface between and among all those groups that comprise the institution and the interface of these groups with outside groups and environments. And it involves the impact of outside or inside forces on the milieu, whether enhancing or retarding, whether interaction or oppressive, whether collaborative or competitive.

What is milieu management? It is the systematic coordination and integration of the total campus environment—the organizations, the structures, the space, the functions, the people and the relationships of each to all the others and to the whole—toward growth and development as a democratic community. In furtherance of human development theory the relationship of the whole milieu with all its parts, and vice versa, must be symbiotic, or mutually enhancing or growth producing.

Implicit in this definition is goal directionality, the uses of power, influence, skill, and technology toward the creation of a milieu in which optimum conditions for human development prevail; a power that ideally must be derived from the community served and is, as a consequence, an expression of the common will.

Why should MM be the responsibility of the principal student affairs officer? In a recent study of 627 colleges and universities (Crookston and Atkyns, 1974) the principal student affairs officer has in the past decade clearly emerged as a major administrative office on the same level as academic affairs and business affairs at 86 percent of the institutions. Five functional areas are now identified for student affairs: (1) all teaching, counseling, consulting, evaluation, and research functions related to, or labelled as student development that are either institutionally assigned to student affairs, or which function in collaboration with the academic sector; (2) all administrative or para-academic functions assigned to student affairs, such as discipline, scholastic standards, admissions, registration, orientation, records, and student leaves of absence; (3) all other programs and services provided for students by professional or paraprofessional staff that fit into the conventional historic definition of the functions of student personnel work; (4) all activities, programs, and functions generated by, run by and/or controlled by students, or run by students under the control of the institution (even when there is no direct administrative control there is an implicit coordinate or consultative responsibility in student affairs); and (5) all management functions assigned, including housing, college unions, food services, bookstore, and other auxiliary services as the case may be (Crookston, 1975). Thus, the PSAO is the one officer who not only has direct concerns with the students on a 24-hour basis, but has many functions and connections that are academic or feed into the academic sector, business management functions, and functions that lead off campus into the larger community. All this places the PSAO in a strategic position to effectuate milieu management.

Thus, next to the president, who, of course, has to be concerned with the total milieu, the principal student affairs officer is the most logical choice, in terms of preparation (training and experience), span of administrative and program responsibility, and philosophical perspective and who by definition must look upon the campus in its total environmental and ecological perspective. Ideally the entire leadership of the college should be possessed of such perspective, but as a practical matter the burdens of instruction and research and fiscal management and accountability are likely to fall too heavily on the principal academic and business officers respectively for them to give priority to MM.

The Need for a Conceptual Framework

If we think of milieu management as directional (that is, in the direction of student development) rather than merely accepting the status quo and doing the best we then can with it, we need to operate within some type of conceptual framework for student development. A number of such theories have emerged to prominence in recent years. Erik Erickson's and Jean Piaget's theories are examples of life stage or chronological models. Kohlberg's moral development and Maslow's needs toward self-actualization are examples of the hierarchical theories of human development. Blocker (1974) has devised an ecological model of student development by means of superimposing Maslow's hierarchy of needs on Erikson's framework. Using an elementary school example Blocker took Erikson's state "where the child starts to develop understanding and avoid inferiority" and observed that at the same time the child is dealing with Maslow's safety and security needs in preparation for dealing with love and esteem needs. In the light of this dual framework Blocker conceptualized an ecological system represented by the elementary school classroom that could include three ecological subsystems: (1) *the opportunity structure,* the problems the child can learn to master mixed with an optimum environmental stimulation—neither too demanding nor threatening on the one hand, not too boring on the other; (2) *the support structure,* the cognitive and affective resources in the environment for coping with stress, and (3) *the reward structure,* environmental supports such that effort expended will have a payoff toward higher self-esteem. Thus, Blocker combines two theories of human development, places them into an ecological context and comes out with a conceptual framework for utilizing the total environment in support of student development.

The critical point for us here is to emphasize the importance of college in general, and the student affairs organization in particular, in establishing a conceptual framework which forms the basis for the development of a program of milieu management as a vital supporting framework for student development (whether it be Erikson, Maslow, Chickering, or your own conceptual framework tailored to fit the goals of your college and the needs of the members of your campus community).

An example

It is in this spirit that the following conceptual framework is offered as one example of attempting to develop milieu management strategies in the college setting. With apologies to Maslow, here is one way to conceptualize the problem. Let us return to one of our basic premises, that the goals of human development are twofold, the actualization of the individual and of society, and that neither is possible without the other; thus, the relationship between the two must be symbiotic, that is, mutually growth producing.

In order to understand the nature of the symbiotic relationship between individual and group or community, it is useful to compare it with two other modal relationships that are descriptive of the way an educational institution, or an organic component of it, relates to the student. These are the homeostatic mode and the egoistic mode.

Homeostatic mode. Homeostatis is the tendency of an organism to maintain itself in a state of dynamic balance or *equilibrium* of component parts that is optimum to the maintenance of life. Thus, if a person is short of water, a state of thirst ensues until a drink of water restores the balance and satisfies the thirst. In a human society such needs are often satisfied through the dependability of others, as in the case of safety needs.

Social needs such as those for affection, acceptance, love, or security are entirely dependent on a proper response from others, who are also preoccupied with meeting those same needs for themselves. Satisfaction of these needs can lead to feelings of *acceptance* of self and others and the capacity to love and be loved. Failure to meet these needs leads to defensive responses of *rejection* of self and others, feelings of inadequacy, and the triggering of various *compensation* mechanisms.

CHART II
MODAL RELATIONSHIPS OF INDIVIDUAL TO GROUP OR COMMUNITY

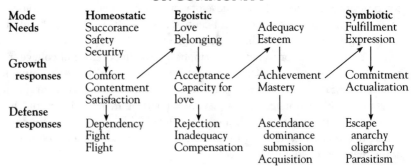

Mode	Homeostatic	Egoistic		Symbiotic
Needs	Succorance	Love	Adequacy	Fulfillment
	Safety	Belonging	Esteem	Expression
	Security			
Growth responses	Comfort	Acceptance	Achievement	Commitment
	Contentment	Capacity for	Mastery	Actualization
	Satisfaction	love		
Defense responses	Dependency	Rejection	Ascendance	Escape
	Fight	Inadequacy	dominance	anarchy
	Flight	Compensation	submission	oligarchy
			Acquisition	Parasitism

Egoistic, or Power mode. In the egoistic mode the needs expressed are for *adequacy* and *esteem.* If fulfilled one has a sense of value and worth through *achievement* and *mastery.* Thwarting of these needs can lead to drives toward *ascendancy,* to do better than others, or to have power over others, perhaps to gain respect through coercion; or toward *acquisition* to acquire goods and wealth as a display of achievement, or to buy respect, status or prestige. The egoistic drive toward power is also the expression of unresolved homeostatic needs. For example, if one is hungry and food is scarce, one way to get it is by using power to intimidate, coerce, or manipulate others. Or if one feels insecure or afraid, these feelings can be overcome either by increasing one's power (*dominance*) or by becoming dependent upon one who is more powerful (*submission*).

Symbiotic mode. In a symbiotic relationship, like Carl Rogers' "basic striving," the needs expressed are for *expression* and *fulfillment.* The growth response is commitment to the larger whole, the extension of the self into the group; the self thus becomes actualized. Such terms as Maslow's "actualization" are used to describe the symbiotic goals of human development because they imply a process of expanding, growing, becoming rather than an end-point as expressed by such terms as "fulfillment," "goal attain-ment," "adjustment," or "maturation." Thus the symbiotic goals of human development may be conceptualized as multi-dimensional, in an expanding, unending sphere or universe, rather than as linear, where there must be a beginning and an end point, or end state. That is why the *output* of the symbiotic mode is defined as a *process. Thus, in human development theory, the ends are also the means.*

Modal Instrumentalities in the College Milieu

Chart III depicts the instrumentalities that might be found in varying degrees on a given campus that purports to be a vehicle through which students are "educated." Despite the legal closing of the *in loco parentis* era in American higher education (when the institution was viewed as a *family* and the president and other authority figures in the administrative and faculty served as *parents* to the students who were regarded as *children*), paternalism is still reflected in the attitudes and behaviors of many of those in student affairs, and certainly persists among many faculty and administrators. This parent-child relationship has two faces; that of the benevolent caring, nurturing parent, and that of the authoritarian, control-ling punishing parent. The student development movement emerged in large measure as an effort to change the relationship with students from one of control to one of collaboration; from a status-based authority figure to a competency-based expert and thus, hopefully to reduce the likelihood of negative responses which are largely based on reactions to parental authority.

Increasingly the college, and particularly the large university, is being thought of as an *enterprise,* run by *entrepreneurs* in which the learner is viewed as an output or *product.* More recently, as a reflection of the rise of consumerism in the wider society, the student is becoming viewed as the *consumer,* the product becoming the act of certification at the end of the production line—graduation.

Power. The only instrumentality shown (Chart III) in which the power and control are not vested in those individuals who are at the top of a hierarchy is the *community.* Here control rests in the *membership,* who can use it to invent *processes* by which all can move toward their individual and collective goals. The leadership, and any other instrumentalities created, are responsible to a constituency who hold the ultimate power.

CHART III
MODAL EDUCATIONAL INSTRUMENTALITIES

Mode	Family	Agency	Guild	Enterprise	Community
Control	Parent	Professional	Master	Entrepreneur	Membership
Relationship	Child	Client	Apprentice	Consumer	Constituent
Output	Nurturance	Service	Credentials	Product	Process
Response	Growth	Adjustment	Skill	Skill	Symbiosis
Goal	Maturity	Well-being	Competence	Competence	Democracy
End	Independence	Independence	Independence	?	Interdependence
Negative responses	Dependence Rebellion Flight	Dependence Avoidance Apathy	Dependence Rebellion Flight Apathy	Dependence Rebellion Slavery	Flight to anarchy oligarchy Parasitism
Milieu Management strategies	Consultation Training Primary groups Temporary systems	Consultation Training Proaction Outreach Client participation Organizational development	Consultation Training Consumer advocacy Consumer participation Organizational development	Consultation Training Community development Organizational development	

The consumer in a managed society. From what I have said thus far it should be clear that I am troubled by what seems to be an increasing drift toward a society of consumers whose lives are managed by enterprises. Consider for a moment the way we live—in condominiums which provide all the comforts, including managed diversions, entertainment, and social activities. But the consumer *has* become increasingly effective in influencing the enterpreneural power structure *in order to get what they want.* Thus the rise of consumer groups of all kinds for many purposes. These consumer needs are primarily homeostatic and egoistic—for better, safer products, more conveniences, a more pleasant environment, better services. The consumer is concerned with power only to the extent that those who have it give them what they want. The consumer lives in the here and now. The consumer values goods, gadgets, and experiences that can provide instant gratification.

Big Brother? Aside from the Big Brother issue is the broader question of the ethics of MM. Is milieu management in reality nothing more than manipulation? Is it in a sense directed toward bringing about behavior change through the manipulation of the environment?

Let us first define manipulation as a deliberate attempt to change behavior of others *without their knowledge and consent* regardless of whether such behavior change is good or ill. In a symbiotic academic community, which by definition must be committed to a democratic philosophy, whatever power the milieu manager possesses is not an expression of coercion or manipulation, but is an expression of the common will through the exercise of power derived from the community. There can be no manipulation unless there is an abuse of power in which the milieu manager acts contrary to the wishes of the community. Thus, the *child,* the *apprentice,* the *client,* or the *consumer* revolts, flees, protests, or counter manipulates, because unlike the constituent, they do not have the built-in power to reverse the situation.

This is not to suggest that the PSAO as milieu manager should not use legitimate administrative power to help create an actualizing environment. It means ethical use of power with the full knowledge, urging, or consent of those in the milieu.

MM Strategies

A number of milieu management strategies become obvious when viewing Charts II and III. If the direction of MM, congruent with the goals of student development, is to create an environment in which the general movement of the milieu is in the direction of a symbiotic community, then the employment of such strategies as consultation skills, organization development methodologies, and various kinds of training become appropriate for most areas, with other specific concerns, such as helping the masters move more in the direction of student-centered teaching and a learning partnership or shared journey, being applied as needed. However, first things first. The following steps are suggested.

1. *Data Collection.* What information is available from within and outside the milieu? What additional data do we need to gather? Banning (1974) has reminded us there is a wealth of rarely used and often readily available data all over the campus that need only be gathered in one place and systematically organized and interpreted. Examples are the storehouse of information on students in admissions and records offices, office of institutional research, various administrative offices, from academic deans, the campus engineer, architect, planner, police, the environmental health and safety officer, from faculty research studies, from the library, and so on.

Hundreds of institutions provided the data base for the ACE studies of entering college freshmen over a period of several years. Each institution was given the national norms on dozens of demographic, personal, and attitudinal variables along with a print-out of data for the local school. Only a handful of institutions utilized this gold mine of data. There are other well known instruments such as the CCI and the institutional Goals Inventory that can provide the milieu management team with a picture of what the campus is like along certain variables selected.

2. *Interested people.* Included in the data collection process is the identification to people from the faculty, students, staff, administration, interested citizens, families, government, and other areas who are concerned with aspects of the physical, social, cultural, psychological, and personal environments—from just plain interested persons who want to help, to experts in environmental psychology, community psychology, human development, ecology, organization and community development, and various related areas of research and technology. Such a group should be gathered and their resources brought to bear on various strategies for changing the milieu into a place in which actualization might be more possible.

3. *A base of operations.* A place on campus should be identified in which data can be stored and processed and from which the people can organize to function in the milieu. If there is a center for student or human development, that would be a logical base. Or it could be an expansion of an officer of institutional research and development, or of environmental health and safety. It is easier to expand an existing operation than to start a new one.

4. *Improving Community Governance.* In an incisive analysis of the present state of governance in higher education, Millett (1974) has observed that there are signs the new community governance model—the move toward more egalitarian representation of faculty, students, and administration in the affairs of the institution—appears to be weakening. The students, having gained new personal and social freedoms, seem less interested in the broader

issues of governance. All involved are discovering that the deliberations of legislation take vast amounts of time, and many are questioning whether the cost in time and energy is worth the effort. Millet thinks the faculty, having enjoyed formulating institutional policies, are now reluctant to join with the rest of the university to legislate on academic matters where heretofore they had enjoyed considerable autonomy. The prior system of governance, often referred to as an organized anarchy, failed during the past decade on the institutional policy front, but has worked well to serve the vested interests of departmental fiefdoms.

Although one may agree on the surface with the logic of Millet's analysis, the problem appears to have deeper roots—the pervasive influence of the *consumer syndrome* on the attitudes and values of members of the academic community. It is acceptance of the attitude that the work should be done by someone else, that the final responsibility rests with someone else, that the commitment of the participant in governance does not go beyond the decision making stage, and that commitment to action, of carrying out the will of the majority is up to someone else. It is the idea that governance is somehow directed to affect the other guy, not me. Hence the faculty are glad to get involved in matters other than instruction and research, but are highly reluctant to have others involved with their own vested interests.

The problem for the milieu manager then is first one of education and training, and second, building interlocking relationships between and among governance units within the milieu.

John Blackburn has observed that in development of a community there must be a transcendent value upon which commitment can be based. This is a value that is over-arching, held in common by everyone in the community even though values on other issues may differ widely. Such a value is not likely to be found at a large complex institution. The MM should focus instead on the smaller, discrete communities that do exist within the institution, concentrate community building efforts on them, and then try to build a system of interrelated communities as a means to move toward a community of the larger whole.

One of the critical ingredients for the development of commitment to a democratic community is the capacity of the system of governance to find room for the participation of all members of the community in one way or another. We know that participation in the processes helps solidify commitment to the goals. It is amazing how narrow and simplistic is the concept of governance in the minds of many persons who think of governance as legislation—as parliamentary procedures, voting and making laws. In a democratic society governance includes all those processes within an organization that move it toward its goals. These processes can be categorized into three types: those having to do with the establishment of *goals*, with *policies*, and with *procedures*. Goals are contained in the basic documents of the community—the social contract, the constitution, the charter. Policies are the moral, philosophical, conceptual framework that express the lines of action to be taken toward the achievement of the goals. Procedures are the ways and means, the methods to be used.

There are four levels of participation in community governance: 1. *Conceptualization*, the generating of ideas, development of goals, rationale, philosophy; 2. *Authorization*, the decision making processes, the formal acts of the policy making or law making body that spell out what is to be done and who is authorized to do it on behalf of the community; 3. *Implementation*, the execution or carrying out of what is authorized by the community; and 4. *Evaluation*, the collection and analysis of data that tells the community whether its objective has been achieved, whether effectively or ineffectively, and whether it was accomplished within the established policy framework. Members of the community should be afforded the opportunity to participate in any of these levels of governance. The interests of the symbiotic community are furthered by the efforts of the MM to facilitate this process through programs of training to help members function more effectively at any level of participation, through systems linkage between self-governing groups within the larger community, and through organizational development consultation with governing units as organizations.

5. *Who is involved?* Everyone in the campus community should be involved in the creation and development of a symbiotic community—faculty, students, staff, administrators, librarians, maintenance workers, cooks, janitors, craftsmen. It is time to think of the community as a whole, not merely a place that is for students to develop and faculty to teach and do research. This means thinking of a health service for all, not just for students, a library for all, counseling for all, life planning programs for all, organization development, and human development training for all. The MM must have the authority to impact all components of the campus, to have a significant role in the staff and human development of *all* employees.

6. *The physical environment.* By this is meant 1) places to interact, work, talk or play; 2) places to watch, listen, sense, or emote; places to be alone for privacy, peace, solitude, study, or meditation. Environmental psychologists and engineers have learned much about the uses and interrelationships of space, the effects of light, humidity, noise, and temperature. Planning, reconstruction, and management of the physical environment, including traffic flow and walk patterns, movement, and esthetics should be a concern of the milieu manager.

Finally, we are now coming to a stage in our own development as professionals concerned with helping other human beings live out their lives toward actualization, when we must realize that it takes more than focus on the individual, the group, or even the community to create optimal conditions for human development; it requires the marshalling of all forces in the environment.

References

Banning, J. H., Kaiser, L. An Ecological Perspective and Model for Campus Design. *Personnel and Guidance Journal*, 52, 1974, 370–375.

Blocher, D. H. Toward an Ecology of Student Development. *Personnel and Guidance Journal*, 52, 1974, 360–369.

Crookston, B. B. An Organizational Model for Student Development. NASPA Journal, 10, 1972, 3–13.

Crookston, B. B. Education for Human Development. In Warnath, C. F. and Associates, *New Directions for College Counselors.* San Fransciso: Jossey-Bass, 1973, Ch. 2, 47–65.

Crookston, B. B. and G. C. Atkyns. *A Study of Student Affairs: The Principal Student Affairs Officer, the Functions, the Organization at American Colleges and Universities.* The University of Connecticut Research Foundation, 1974, pp. 58.

Crookston, B. B. Student Personnel—All Hail and Farewell! 1975, Unpublished manuscript.

Miller, T. K. and others. *A Student Development Model for Student Affairs in Tomorrow's Higher Education.* The American College Personnel Association, 1974.

Millett, John. Governance and Leadership in Higher Education. *Management Forum*, 3, December, 1974.

A Humanistic Direction for Student Personnel—Student Development Educators

Robert J. Nash, Kenneth P. Saurman and George M. Sousa

An enlarged role for student personnel professionals is presented, including a major instructional emphasis to make them co-equal with teaching faculty. The focus is on a humanistic redefinition of teaching and learning as operationally applied to the student development educator both in and outside conventional classrooms. Specific examples of this partnership at selected institutions are included.

At this time student personnel is showing signs that it finally has the potential to make an outstanding contribution to higher education. Since 1969, when Penny (1969) sounded the premature death knell that student personnel workers could never be recognized as "vital contributors to the academic world," student personnel administrators have worked feverishly to produce a large body of literature attempting to define an acceptable role for the professional. In the past, enthusiasts have exhorted student personnel workers to become counselors, managers, advisers, quality control engineers, and even something ominously called "multi-specialists." Recently a crescendo of voices has urged retrenchment and a concentration of efforts on mastering a series of micromanagerial tasks including budget reform, specification of management goals and objectives, identification of legal responsibilities, and defining affirmative action guidelines (Prior 1973; Rhatigan 1975).

What is most upsetting about these proposals is a tendency to trivialize or totally ignore the most pressing and controversial concerns of higher education today. Many young people are questioning the value of higher education, either by staying away from the university in droves or by enrolling in vocational training programs. The general public is urging massive financial cutbacks to higher education as an expression of a waning faith in the occupational usefulness of higher learning. Many faculty are suffering from the most acute kinds of identity crises due to the sudden downswing in the prestige of publication and an upswing in instruction. Yet, student personnel professionals are content merely to maintain a precarious position in higher education by becoming narrowly proficient in the neutral techniques of mid-level management (Saurman& Nash 1975).

However, what is needed at the present time is not retrenchment but an enlargement of the professional function of student personnel administrators to include instructional reform. Instructional reform (both in and out of the classroom) is the centripetal point where all the problems of higher education coalesce, because it is at this point where the systematic transmission of knowledge, skills, and values occurs and where students feel most tangibly the quality (or lack of it) in higher education. Because of the increasing pressure from a variety of accountability-minded constituencies, faculty are desperate for instructional assistance.

Student personnel workers must seize the opportunity to render faculty this instructional assistance. In order to do this, though, student personnel professionals must become student development educators who have the training, knowledge, and responsibility to become co-equal partners with faculty in the instructional process. Even though initially some faculty will reject student development educators as being well-intentioned but academically unqualified, there must still be a persistent effort to advocate and implement reform in all areas of instruction at the university level.

Although some student affairs professionals are now active in teaching, at best these efforts are sporadic and remote; few such teachers actually draw on a background in student development theory, the social sciences, learning theory, group process, and organizational analysis to systematically improve the quality of instruction throughout institutions. These instructors fail to capitalize on a generalistic view of higher education and knowledge—a view not circumscribed by the academician's tendency to see the discipline as a narrow knowledge shaft.

In reaction to the narrow subdivisions of the disciplines, Cross (1974) suggests an approach to curriculum building that draws on a repertoire of learning involving ideas, people, and things. She reasons that most learners have specific talents either to comprehend abstract issues, foster interpersonal relationships, or to undertake mechanical manipulations. Rather than as-sume that all learners learn in the same way, she recommends that students be encouraged to pursue excellence in one special competency while achiev-ing at least minimal competency in the other two areas.

This insight has considerable implications for the "new learners" who in the future will bombard the halls of academe in increasing numbers. Older men and women, housewives, veterans, Black and other non-white learners, and students from lower socioeconomic backgrounds will all be seeking help from faculty to realize their personal and professional aspirations. What is especially awesome about this new group of students, however, is that their prior learning styles will have been refined, not in the college-tract curricula of elite, suburban high schools, but in the streets, at home with families, in the military, by exposure to the media, and by a series of gut-level survival incidents in all types of informal learning settings.

In order to respond to these unconventional learning styles, student personnel professionals must become student development educators. These educators are talented teachers who have a thorough mastery of humanistic psychology, learning theory, a variety of instructional methods, and a sophisticated grasp of human development concepts. They also possess such operational skills as empathy development, resource allocation, organizational development, and communications enhancement. Furthermore, they are philosopher-activists who prod faculty and administrators to examine instructional and curricular goals and the underlying educational assumptions, values, and teaching methods in terms of their influence on the total development of students.

What follows below is a brief overview of humanistic psychology and its educational and instructional implications for student personnel professionals. Also described are some current institutional experiments that concretely embody many of these concepts.

Humanistic Learning Theory

There are signs that an interest in pedagogy is resurfacing in higher education. The surge of new learners to campuses highlights the need for a new conception of teaching and learning which incorporates the developmental-instructional principles of humanistic psychology, the human potential movement, existentialism and phenomenology, ethical-moral-cognitive stag theory, and perceptual psychology. Because the new learners do not fit the monolithic liberal arts model of the "typical" college student (i.e., all students are able to write and articulate ideas cogently and clearly and prefer to intellectualize an insight in favor of acting on it), some faculty in the arts and sciences are beginning to reach for help from the same educationists they earlier dismissed so contemptuously (Gaff & Wilson 1971).

Bombarded daily by students who may learn more easily through physical activity, concrete problem solving, visual sources, meaningful labor, and an introspective grappling with the archetypal existential questions, faculty are now turning to centers for instructional improvement for a conceptual understanding of student learning needs and for technical help in developing flexible repertoires of teaching skills.

Conceptually, there is a growing body of evidence that students of all ages and backgrounds learn best when they invest themselves in personal ways in their learning (Maslow 1968; Nyberg 1971; Soderquist 1964). Briefly, humanistic education is premised on the belief that total learning embraces three stages, not necessarily in an invariable sequence or hierarchy: the acquisition of information, ideas, and knowledge; the discovery of the personal meaning which the information, ideas, and knowledge hold for the learner; and the translation of personal meaning into thoughtful and consistent public behavior of some kind. Unfortunately, instructors pay the price for ignoring the validity of these simple learning principles.

The major assumptions of humanistic learning theory are summarized as follows:

1. Learners are unique in how each one learns conceptual and concrete material. In contrast to the behavioral view, learning styles are often idiosyncratic, at times unpredictable, and always a function of needs, perceptions, world views, and goals at the time when learning occurs. Teaching modes successful with some students are often unsuccessful with others.

2. Learners have an unremitting drive to realize personal potentialities, to strive continually to grow in intellectual and emotional capacities not yet fully developed. There are no hopeless or untalented learners; there are only learners who have not been encouraged by teachers to realize potentialities.

3. Learners have feelings that powerfully influence thinking. Often a learner's thoughts about subject matter are filtered through feelings about the value of the material to be learned. A learner's feelings about the self, others, the educational experience in general, and the content to be studied in particular are always the decisive determinants of whether anything ever really gets learned in educational settings.

4. Learners constantly act and think on the basis of what is of value at the moment. Values are basic sources of meaning which influence actions and thoughts in subtle and persistent ways. Learners are always establishing priorities concerning educational activities, and these priorities are rooted in values.

5. In order to make deliberate and informed choices, learners need a variety of extra classroom opportunities to process impersonal classroom information and ideas through intense self-disclosures with significant others. Learners also need numerous opportunities to elicit clarifying responses from experienced teachers.

Implications of Humanistic Learning Theory for Teachers

What follows from these fundamental principles of humanistic learning theory is a need for teachers:

• Who are constantly aware of each learner's unique style of learning and able to construct curricula and use a variety of teaching methods that correlate with these unique learning styles. This will require teachers to employ a variety of teaching methods perfected by the human potential movement; role playing, Gestalt activities, communications labs, values clarification and other simulation games, independent learning modules, and psycho-and sociodrama activities. New approaches to evaluation will also be necessary based on "multiple indices" models.

• Who perceive students not simply as superior or inferior information receptacles to be evaluated on the basis of an ability to absorb and reproduce the teacher's ideas, but as people who are capable of unlimited personal growth and an enormous capacity for intellectual and emotional development.

• Who know how to involve students in the personal discovery of the meaning of ideas. Educators must be adroit at knowing how to elicit students' genuine feelings about the concepts and data being analyzed in the classroom without having the discussion degenerate into an aimless probing of emotional sensitivities totally devoid of intellectual insight.

• Who are effective at helping students clarify personal and academic beliefs and values and skilled at aiding learners to choose wisely by helping them expand their options. Educators must help students to understand that the richest learner is potentially the one who has the greatest number of options for decision making by virtue of an expanded awareness of alternatives.

• Who know how to enable students to share conceptual ideas and insights openly and nondefensively with others in discussion groups. This will mean that teachers must be sensitive to the tremendous educational value of group processes and skilled at provoking meaningful "whole-person" dialogue at appropriate times and places.

• Who can listen with discrimination and empathy to a learner's unexpressed meanings. Teachers must be able to reach out beyond a student's written and verbal expressions in classrooms and faculty offices in order to grasp the unintended but significant deeper meanings behind the words.

Student Development Educators as Humanistic Teachers

There is mounting evidence everywhere that faculty are actively beginning to pursue instructional assistance through faculty development programs, on-campus instructional alternative centers, teaching improvement grants, and even through informal gatherings of colleagues to share the latest, most successful teaching coups (Semas 1975). Even though some faculty still stubbornly refuse to admit the importance of pedagogy, preferring instead to take refuge in the shibboleth that subject matter is valuable for its own sake, there is less tenacious clinging to the belief that the lecture method is the best way to penetrate the intellectual defenses of ignorant students (Axelrod 1973). Even intransigent faculty realize that the forcible penetration of students' minds is, at best, a form of intellectual rape, calculated only to build stronger student resistance to learning.

By value inclination, professional training, and educational skills, the student development educator is uniquely qualified to help faculty revitalize teaching, construct more realistic and imaginative curricula, and assist students of all ages and backgrounds to grow and excel. Student personnel professionals have traditionally nourished perceptions of themselves as transitional or "phantom" figures in higher education, neither strictly administrators, academicians, or students. Actually, this ephemeral role designation has been an advantage: Over the years student personnel have had to cultivate profound interest in, and knowledge about, a variety of university constituencies. This intimate interaction with students in all sorts of out-of-classroom places has resulted in the adoption and mastery of a variety of professional roles, such as counselors, advocates, adversaries, advisers, clarifiers, friends, confidantes, and morale boosters.

In all of these transactions, both in and out of classrooms, student personnel professionals have functioned as teachers. In order for students to learn the requisite skills, understandings, and values to improve their living situations and to fulfill their maximum personal and social potentialities, a theory of learning and human development and certain kinds of interpersonal and technical teaching skills must be used. And what student personnel workers have mastered, mostly as a consequence of on-the-job, trial-and-error training, has been such basic teaching skills as listening, empathy, group leadership, values clarification, intervention techniques, and attending-responding-understanding-acting behaviors. Also they have learned to appreciate the necessity of presenting ideas and information clearly and cogently.

This authentic concern for, and profound knowledge about, students and developmental needs can be highly useful to teaching faculty. Combined with an extraordinary problem-solving ability and an inexorable enthusiasm for creative instructional procedures, a development educator's comprehension of students' needs can be of immense help to faculty in the conversion of didactic classroom teaching styles to humanistic procedures. In a general sense, student development educators can be most beneficial by helping faculty to:

• Move from a "remedial" to a "developmental" concept in teaching the new learner. This necessitates the total development of a student's attitudes, values, and skills which may not be obviously related to the subject matter of the course. The instructional task thus becomes not merely the remediation of reading and writing skills, but the development of a student's personal awareness, including the cultivation of vital living skills. No longer can a student's classroom learning rate be mistaken for his or her learning potential, which results in a continuing misreading of a student's real educational needs.

• Understand and try to change the existing structural and philosophical constraints of educational organizations on improved faculty teaching and student development, i.e., the interlocking press of curricular, bureaucratic, credit, administrative, and instructional subsystems on classroom learnings.

• Understand the plurality of student value systems and a multiplicity of ways individual students perceive and experience the processes of higher education.

• Realize that there is a demonstrable universe of alternatives in the way students learn and teachers teach.

• Translate subject matter expertise into nontechnical language and devise a variety of experiential delivery systems which connect academic material more directly to students' genuine needs and interests.

• Develop a consistent and applicable philosophy of education and a psychology of teaching premised on the insights of humanistic learning theory.

In a specific sense, the development educator can assist faculty to become more humanistic teachers in at least three ways:

1. Show faculty how to cultivate helping skills. Effective helping begins with the assumption that the total teaching-learning process is rooted in the human interaction between the teacher and the learner. The central insight of humanistic psychology is that each person brings perceptions, assumptions, attitudes, feelings, and skills to the learning situation, and the learning situation is shaped by these elements in turn. Useful skills might include how to involve students affectively in the classroom, how to be more skillful questioners and clarifiers, how to listen more empathically, and how to respond more supportively.

2. Help faculty develop an awareness of the group dynamics of the classroom. Faculty who understand the basic principles of group dynamics can use this awareness to develop the class as a group. The student development educator can assist on two levels. First, workshops and seminars

highlighting the interpersonal dynamics of all learning groups can be offered which give an understanding of such technical group constructs as membership characteristics, communication patterns, norms, dominance-submission patterns, discussion ploys, and climate (Gorman 1969). A second possibility might be actually working with faculty in classrooms as observers and group facilitators (Katz 1962). Faculty can also be helped to devise effective evaluation systems by learning how to develop clear and achievable teaching goals consistent with philosophical purposes.

3. Sensitize faculty to the needs, deficits, and strengths of the new learners. Some of the educational deficits of this group, influenced in part by prior schooling, include low self-concepts, easy discouragement, initial mistrust of counselors and teachers, difficulty in formulating realistic or long-germ goals. Faculty must begin to use instructional approaches that build upon the strengths of students rather than accentuate weaknesses.

Faculty attitudes toward the learner will have a direct impact on the amount of learning that actually takes place. Research shows that negative faculty attitudes contribute to the high dropout rate in some open admissions programs. Many community college faculty hold unfavorable attitudes toward students, thereby unwittingly conditioning students for failure (Hagen 1973). However, faculty attitudes are not immutable. Skeptical attitudes are often influenced by bad experiences with previous students who showed little enthusiasm for a course. In order to protect their fragile self-image, some faculty defensively conclude that students' failures are primarily the result of a lack of intellectual ability. If faculty can learn some new instructional approaches to assure successful academic achievement for the new learner, there is a strong possibility that faculty stereotypic and negative attitudes will improve and, in some cases, change drastically.

Two provisos must be noted regarding generalizations about the needs of new learners. First, the new learners' needs are human needs, present in one form or another in all college students. Second, too easily extrapolating from generalized needs to some composite type called a "new learner" must be avoided. Tolson (1972) contends that the subtle paternalism and feeling of superiority rampant in higher education today often makes counselors and teachers (who usually do not come from the ranks of the new learners) prone to deal with intellectualized roles rather than with real people.

Pitfalls in the Co-Equal Relationship

Primary among the dangers that could threaten any possible merger between personnel professionals and teaching faculty is an evangelical over commitment to humanistic psychology. The student development educator must be wary of conveying to skeptical faculty an obsession with a student's deeper levels of feelings and attitudes to the total denigration of the intellect as a valuable way of knowing. The educator must also guard against a naive rejection of the power of environmental, historical, and genetic processes in shaping the new students' behaviors. Nothing will alienate faculty more quickly than a blithe disregard for the influence of social and historical realities on student values and academic performance. Another danger is the tendency of some humanists to freeze analysis at the phenomenological level of navel-gazing and self-probing, thus denying the need for the social action necessary to create a world where introspection can occur in the first place. Finally, when humanists ignore the importance of basic intellectual skills, they forget the Maslovian insight that intellectual competence is a basic human need, necessary for self-esteem and fundamental to further growth toward self-actualization (Maslow 1962).

Operationally, the humanist educator must be conscious of the temptation to use excessive jargon in dealings with faculty. Professionals need to monitor their language constantly, by being sensitive at all times to the reactions of clients. Unfortunately, some professionals are tempted to snow faculty with specialized terminology. This frequently happens because student personnel workers perceive college faculty as being critical of their academic backgrounds. Thus, arcane language is used as a defense. If advice is worthwhile, it should be given in simple and direct language.

Another anger is the tendency of many experts to be insensitive to the developmental needs of *professional* clients. If it is true that every person has a need to feel competent, then this is especially true of the teacher whose principal occupational reward is psychic meaning and satisfaction. An awareness of these needs involves avoiding a "this is what is being done wrong" approach and starts with the strengths of the teacher.

Another pitfall involves subscribing to what Maslow (1962) calls the "psychoanalytic myth"—the belief that insight is all that is needed to produce behavioral change. Too many consultants feel that a task is completed once the diagnosis of a situation is given. This diagnosis is then held to be so complete that all that remains is for the client to change self-defeating behaviors and beliefs.

In contrast, research in behavior change demonstrates that such change is unlikely to occur before a lengthy and agonizing period of reappraisal. The change process is difficult and long because it necessitates the personal modification of long-entrenched patterns of thinking and behaving which belong to the client, not the expert (Wheelis 1973). The consultant must be ever sensitive to a teacher's need for dignity and professional competency.

Support and understanding are never conveyed by haughtiness. Some instructional experts approach their clients with a smugness born of possessing the holy grail of methodology. The antidote to a know-it-all professionalism is for development educators to present compassionate observations of a teacher's performance. These observations must always be grounded in rational, clear, and convincing criteria of what constitutes instructional effectiveness. In addition, the educators must avoid unnecessary defensiveness about questions and criticisms, even when these smack of vindictiveness or sour grapes. The approach should always be gentle, helpful, and authentic.

These potential problems speak to the need for student development educators to exemplify the spirit of humanism. These are also reminders to transfer the interpersonal and counseling skills honed in student personnel training to consulting roles. The sine qua non for a co-equal partnership must be mutual respect, and because few faculty are likely to give trust gratuitously to an outsider, the personnel professional as educator must always be more tentatively helpful than certain, more patient and plodding than aggressive.

At the outset, the development educator must characterize the relationship by persistently trying to see the teaching-learning situation as faculty see it. Initially, this may require avoiding larger philosophical debates in response to a remark like the following: "John is not college material!" Subsequent discussion must start with the fact that John is indeed in the teacher's classroom, and both John and his teacher have vested interests in the learning experience. With tact, the student's case is furthered without directly estranging the faculty member. There is also a possibility that even a modicum of success by the student could change the teacher's negative attitude.

Selected Programs as Examples of the Partnership

Currently, student development educators around the country are engaged in the instructional process in three ways: teaching, curricula development, and counseling. While it is true that some of these experiments are still in the early stages, each is dramatic testimony that the student development educator (SDE) can successfully augment the efforts of teaching faculty both in and out of conventional classrooms.

Teaching Experiments

In at least two institutions, SDEs are teaching courses predicated on the humanistic principle that a student's personal choices should illuminate career decisions, future life-style goals, and personal values development.

Tollefson (1975) describes a program at Fulton-Montgomery Community College in Johnstown, New York, where SDEs teach seminars on: (a) "College Life Advisement"—personal growth microlabs designed to strengthen the student's self-concept through increased self-awareness; (b) "Achievement-Motivation"—designed to give students the opportunity to develop personal and professional aspirations and achieve a more self-directed style of living; (c)"Human Relations and Group Dynamics"—uses both affective and cognitive approaches to develop skills and knowledge in areas of social communications; (d)"Studies of the Person"—designed to offer students a chance to study personal development from a variety of perspectives in a group experience.

At Oakton Community College in Morton Grove, Illinois, SDEs offer the following (Donohue 1973): (a) "Human Potential Seminars"—psychology courses for two credits that focus on human development by using student's strengths, values, successes, and goals as subject matter; (b)"Communication 101"—a speaking and writing skills course; (c)"Women's Potential Seminars"—designed for older women unsure of decisions to return to school and insecure as students; (d)"Success Seminar Projects"—conducted in cooperation with the developmental reading program; (e)"Human Sexuality Seminars"—content includes morals, ethics, values, and behavior vis a vis human sexuality.

At Boston University, the mission of the Student Academic Support Services Division, formerly Student Affairs, has been broadened to include active involvement in the various schools and colleges of the University. "Life-Planning Seminars" are offered in the Schools of Nursing, Public Communication, and the College of Basic Studies. These seminars, facilitated by members of the counseling staff and graduate students in the School of Education, focus on the implementation of life plans based on each student's values, skills, interests, and needs.

Around the country, there are a variety of alternatives to standard curricula for the new learner where students define educational goals through contract learning, independent study, and experiential as well as classroom learning. At the University of Vermont, undergraduate students construct pre-student development majors through an individually designed program. SDEs, working in such programs as the University Year for Action, teach these students subject matter in addition to serving as advisers and mentors.

In another experiment at Vermont—"Directed Instruction"—student personnel students are encouraged to team teach with undergraduate and graduate faculty, acting as teaching assistants and team teachers in courses as varied as "Introduction to Education as a Profession" and "Learning and

Human Development." SDEs function as co-equal teachers in many of these courses and also act as instructional consultants for faculty.

The satellite or house plan is another version of the cluster concept, where students, professors, counselors, administrators, and SDEs function as co-equal educational members of the instructional unit. At Oakton Community College, the house plan divides the 2,400 students into four houses of 600 apiece, served by 30 faculty per house. Included on each faculty team are two SDEs who, in addition to offering developmental seminars, critically observe teaching and learning transactions and assist faculty teams to develop helping relationship skills in the classroom (Jordan 1971).

Curricular Experiments

SDEs are beginning to influence curricular revision around the country. In addition to introducing such developmental studies as communications seminars, human sexuality, life-style planning, women's and men's potential projects, achievement motivation, and studies of the person. SDEs are functioning as curricular consultants in such external-degree programs as that at Empire State in New York and the University of Mid-America. At Evergreen State College and New College in Florida curricula are oriented around interdisciplinary projects and themes (usually sociopolitical in nature) and SDEs and faculty work closely together to cultivate intimate learning communities (Bradley 1975; Evergreen State 1973; Heiss 1973).

In the future, it is conceivable that SDEs will assist faculty on a variety of student-development issues as they relate to curricular revision. Further, as unconventional alternatives to standard curricula multiply in the next few years and students fulfill learning requirements through such means as independent studies and directed instruction, SDEs will be needed to perform such coextensive curricular functions as advising, researching, consulting, training, planning, supporting, coordinating, and evaluating.

At Johnson State College in Vermont, SDEs comprise the core instructional staff for the PROVE program. These instructor serve in all of the above capacities in this special program for disadvantaged students. All the seminars and workshops receive full credit in the more conventional college programs.

Counseling-Teaching Experiments

In the institutions described, SDEs are functioning simultaneously as counselors and teachers. The unique needs of the new learners demand that teachers first be persons who can relate to students as persons. The new learner requires humanistic educators who are egalitarian and who are able to stimulate richer personal insights in classrooms.

At such institutions as Mount Royal College in Calgary, Alberta, and Fulton-Montgomery Community College, SDEs are doing outreach counseling whose objectives are to anticipate possible student problems, design preventive programs, and reach students in their own habitats. Also, there is life-style planning with students at these colleges. Student development educators are deprofessionalizing the counseling process in some colleges by training students to become peer counselors, and by encouraging self-help seminars whenever appropriate. At Colorado State College at Fort Collins, SDEs are educating faculty on the uses of counseling techniques in the classroom and on the value of listening skills and clarifying questions from small and large group discussions (Tollefson 1975).

Summary

It has been argued that student personnel professionals must be ready to serve with faculty in the instructional process as co-equal educators by drawing on the personnel professionals' traditional strengths and abilities. The framework for achieving this goal is a humanistic philosophy of teaching and learning which recognizes that all learners, regardless of unorthodox personal background of unconventional academic experience, are intelligent and productive persons who are capable of developing both intellectually and personally. By a humanistic rationale for effective teaching and learning and through a variety of teaching methodologies it has been shown that student development educators have a major role to play in meeting the needs of students, especially the new learners, in the last quarter of this century.

References

Axelrod, J. *The university teacher as artist*. San Francisco: Jossey-Bass, 1973.

Bradley, A. P., Jr. *A role for faculty in contract learning: Toward a theory of nontraditional faculty development*. Paper presented at the National Conference on Higher Education, American Association for Higher Education, Saratoga Springs, New York, March 1975.

Cross, K. P. New forms for new functions. In D. W. Vermilye (Ed.), *Lifelong learners—A new clientele for higher education*. San Francisco: Jossey-Bass, 1974. Pp. 86–92.

Donohue, J. P. *Report on the student development program to the Board of Trustees.* Unpublished report. Morton Grove, Ill.: Oakton Community College, 1973.

Evergreen State College. *The Once-Over-Lightly.* (admissions brochure) Olympia, Wash.: Evergreen State College, Office of Admissions, 1973.

Gaff, J. G,. & Wilson, R. C. Faculty values and improving teaching. In G. K. Smith (Ed.), *New teaching, new learning.* San Francisco: Jossey-Bass, 1971. Pp. 39–46.

Gorman, A. *Teachers and learners: The interaction process in education.* Boston: Allyn & Bacon, 1969.

Hagen, D. L. The basis for community college faculty attitudes toward academically disadvantaged students. *Phi Delta Kappan,* 1873, 54, 414.

Heiss, A. *An inventory of academic information and reform.* Berkeley, Calif.: Carnegie Foundation for the Advancement of Teaching, 1973.

Jordan, R. L. *The college group concept at Oakton Community College: Ends and means.* Unpublished report. Morton Grove, Ill.: Oakton Community College, 1971.

Katz, J. Personality and interpersonal relations in the classroom. In N. Sanford (Ed.), *The American college.* New York: Wiley, 1962. Pp. 396–417.

Maslow, A. H. *Toward a psychology of being.* New York: Van Nostrand, 1962.

Maslow, A. H. Some educational implications of the humanistic psychologies. *Harvard Educational Review,* 1968, 38, 685–696.

Nyerg, D. *Tough and tender learning.* Palo Alto, Calif.: National Press Books, 1971.

Penny, J. F. Student personnel work: A profession stillborn. *Personnel and Guidance Journal,* 1969, 47, 958–961.

Prior, J. J. The reorganization of student personnel services: Facing reality. *Journal of College Student Personnel,* 1973, 14, 202–205.

Rhatigan, J. J. Student services vs. student development: Is there a difference? *Journal of NAWDAC,* 38, 1975, 51–59.

Saurman, K. P., & Nash, R. J. M. B. O. student development and accountability, A critical look. *NASPA Journal,* 1975, 12, 179–189.

Semas, P. W. The search for skilled teachers. *Chronicle of Higher Education,* 29 September 1975, 11, 3.

Soderquist, H. O. *The person and education.* Columbus, Ohio: Charles E. Merrill, 1964.

Tollefson, A. L. *New approaches to college student development.* New York: Behavioral Publications, 1975.

Tolson, H. Counseling the disadvantaged. *Personnel and Guidance Journal,* 50, 739.

Wheelis, A. *How people change.* New York: Harper Torchbooks, 1973.

Student Personnel—All Hail and Fairwell!

Burns B. Crookston

In the recent literature the following terms have been used concurrently and at times interchangeably: student personnel, student affairs, personnel work, student development, and human development. The assumption that these terms refer to the same thing is symptomatic of the confusion that has been rampant in our field for many years, particularly the past decade. An examination of the literature and convention programs over the past several years suggests three schools of thought on the subject of terminology: (a) those who cling to the old student personnel point of view will argue that all the above terms are descriptive of student personnel work, the more glamorous terms of student development and human development being at best merely stylish window dressing and at worst a passing fad; (b) those who insist there are important differences, that the terms have distinct, if not separate meanings, and that to continue glossing over them will only compound the confusion that exists not only among the professionals in the field but also within the public they serve; and (c) those who insist what we call ourselves is irrelevant, that there is a need for what we do and the proof of the pudding is how well we do our job, regardless of what it is called.

My position supports the second view: There are important distinctions that must be made, not only for our own peace of mind but also for the benefit of faculty, administrators, parents, students, and public. The major premises to be developed here are (a) that *student personnel work* as historically defined is no longer a viable concept; (b) that *student affairs* should be used to describe an area, sector, or administrative subdivision; (c) that *student development* should be used to describe the underlying philosophy of the field and the operating concepts therein, and (d) that the nomenclature of the campus has already made the above a reality; therefore, the professional literature and professional associations should adjust in usage and nomenclature respectively.

474

Student Personnel Work

For more than a half century we have lived with the term *student personnel work*, a descriptive anomaly that has seldom been clearly understood by faculty, administrators, alumni, parents, or even students. The word *personnel*, a military term borrowed from the French which refers to manpower, as distinguished from *material*, which refers to equipment, was first used at Northwestern in 1919 by a former World War I army officer, Clarence S. Yoakum, to describe a newly organized placement bureau (Cowley 1936). The rapid expansion of vocational guidance, testing, and placement activities in colleges and universities that took place in the decade of the twenties was accompanied by the parallel establishment of *personnel offices* or *personnel bureaus* to describe not only the place on campus in which these functions were exercised but also the functions themselves. By the end of a decade the term *student personnel work* had been expanded to describe a new "extra class domain" (Cowley 1936; Lloyd-Jones 1929, 1934) that included virtually all noninstructional activities of the college. Thus we had taken a bureaucratic term quite properly used initially to describe placement, testing, and vocational guidance functions and made it a generic term for all activities, programs and services outside the classroom, laboratory, and library that were in any way connected with developing the student. We then added to this conglomeration an educational philosophy undergirding what we called the "student personnel point of view" and said we were "educating" the students. There is little evidence that very many people outside the field have become believers.

An Educational Philosophy? During a time when existentialism had yet to make its impact on higher education, Taylor (1952) had delineated three generally accepted philosophies: rationalism, neo-humanism, and instrumentalism. To the rationalist the sole aim of education is the *development* of intellect and reason. Neo-humanism, while recognizing the primacy of cultivating the mind, assumes a dualism of mind and body, reason and emotion, thought and action, instrumentalism emphasizes the full and creative development of the whole person.

In relating educational philosophies to student personnel work, Lloyd-Jones (1952) observed that under rationalism there was little use for student personnel work save discipline and remedial services. It was at the neo-humanist institutions where student personnel work showed its greatest growth. Even Cowley, who has been given credit for coining the term *holism* to describe education for the *whole* person, while espousing instrumentalism, actually practiced neo-humanism. He was careful to define student personnel work as *extracurricular*. The faculty, assured that student personnel workers had no intention of invading the sacred groves of academe, allowed or encouraged student personnel people to proceed with the development of often elaborate programs, services, and activities to develop the student outside the classroom. It appears no mere coincidence, therefore, that the philosophical statements of student personnel work during that growth period, the most notable being the *Student Personnel Point of View* (Report of a Conference on the Philosophy and Development of Student Personnel Work (1937), were clearly neo-humanist, thus giving free rein to the establishment of a separate administrative subdivision with a line to the president of a separate administrative subdivision with a line to the president often coordinate to the academic sector advocated by Lloyd-Jones (1934) and Cowley (1936).

Under instrumentalism, espoused by Clothier and others as early as 1931, student personnel work would serve as an integral component of the total education effort of the institution. And here we come to the crux of the matter. Although writers in the student personnel field during the late forties, fifties, and early sixties extolled the virtues of instrumentalism as a concept, like Cowley twenty years earlier, they were, with few exceptions, content to develop the student *outside* the classroom. Not only was the practice of neo-humanism less threatening to the student personnel worker, in reality there was little choice. Rationalism prevailed at most institutions. Those who were concerned with the matters of the mind held the power, which they were reluctant to share with student personnel workers. From the standpoint of the student personnel worker, implementation of instrumentalism might also signify the end of a laboriously gained separate administrative domain.

Attempts at Bridge Building. As the separatist student personnel programs and services grew, sometimes into large, complex bureaucracies, serious communication problems developed within, as well as with other sectors in the college. The thrust of the movement that had gained strength outside the instructional program now sought stronger ties with the academy. Attempts to build bridges between student personnel and the academy, particularly around strengthening general education (Blaesser 1949; Brouwer 1949; Hardee 1955), led to a broader definition in the literature of that period. Student personnel work now included those processes and functions that helped build curricula, improve methods of instruction, and develop leadership programs (Arbuckle 1953; Barry & Wolf 1957; Blaesser & Crookston 1960; Wrenn, 1951). Student personnel work no longer merely *supplemented* the academic program, it was *complementary* to it. The student personnel worker had become an "educator" collaborating with the classroom teacher toward the development of the student as a whole person (Lloyd-

Jones 1953; Williamson 1961), holistic in ideal, yet still dualistic in practice. Williamson (1961, 1963), having endured three decades of frustration with faculty rejection of student personnel work, during which the latter had moved from "ancillary" to "supplementary" to "complementary" but never central to the educational enterprise, insisted his holistic out-of-the-classroom student personnel worker was now an "educator" concerned with matters intellectual as well as social, civic, and emotional. The emergence of the concept of student development in the sixties came out of the recognition that such out-of-class education would never be fully effective until it became incorporated into the total philosophical and educational fabric of the institution.

Student Affairs

For a half century we have tried to convince both ourselves and our public, within and without education, that personnel work meant what we wanted it to mean, rather than what the dictionary said and the public understood. Unfortunately, it has never found its way into any language save our own private jargon. And now there has even been a decrease in the use of the term *personnel* in the nomenclature of our own sector of the campus. There is evidence that such titles as *student affairs, student relations, student life,* and *student services* emerged as expressions of a need to find more descriptive terms (Crookston 1974). In a recent study (Crookston & Atkyns 1974) of a stratified, representative national sample of 627 four-year colleges and universities, only 12.1 percent used *student personnel* in the generic title of the area and only 2.8 percent of the principal officers used *personnel* in their own title. Conversely, the legitimation of the term *student affairs* to describe a major administrative subdivision or sector had become clearly predominant. In the same study 52.3 percent of the institutions called the sector the division, department, or office of student affairs. The most commonly used title for the principal officer was vice president, dean, director, or coordinator of student, college, or university affairs.

The Crookston-Atkyns study also confirms the establishment of *student affairs* as a major administrative subdivision on the same level, in relation to the president, as academic affairs, business affairs, and other principal areas such as development or public affairs at 86 percent of the institutions. Not only has the student affairs sector as a major subdivision increased nationally when compared with a study conducted in 1962 (Ayers, Tripp & Russel 1966) but its scope has been greatly expanded. Out of a list of 81 functions known to exist in the student affairs sector at one place or another, the present study showed there are 37 functions that are the responsibility of student affairs at over half the institutions. These include management functions an d academically related programs and services as well as all those programs, functions, and services usually included in the old student personnel list.

An Operating Definition. Regardless of its merit as a descriptive term, student affairs is now firmly established as a major administrative subdivision in American higher education. But let us not lead ourselves into another nomenclature dilemma. Student affairs is not a philosophy, theory, or concept; it is an area, sector, or administrative subdivision within which there are people, programs, functions, and services, many, if not all, of which contribute to the development of students as whole persons. Within this definition of student affairs, the following functions are identified: (a) all teaching, counseling, consulting, evaluation, and research functions related to or labeled as student development that are either institutionally assigned to student affairs or that function in collaboration with the academic sector; (b) all administrative or para-academic functions assigned to student affairs, such as discipline, scholastic standards, admissions, registration, orientation, records, and student leaves of absence; (c) all other programs and services provided for students by professional or paraprofessional staff that fit into the conventional historic definition of the functions of student personnel work; (d) all activities, programs, and functions generated by, run by, or controlled by students, or run by students under the control of the institution (even when there is no direct administrative control, there is an implicit coordinate or consultative responsibility in student affairs); and (e) all management functions assigned, including housing, college unions, food services, bookstore, and other auxiliary services. Also emerging is *milieu management*, the marshalling of all forces in the educational environment toward the creation of conditions most propitious for student development (Miller et al. 1974).

Student Development

Space does not permit a delineation of the dramatic parade of interlocking and interacting events and circumstances of the past decade that gave rise to the insurgence of *student development* in the terminology of the field. As already intimated, student development is not a new concept; it is a return to holism reinforced with the unerring vision of hindsight. Freed at last from the necessity of exercising the benevolent control of the parent and from adherence to the remedial model of counseling, professionals in our field, within a time-frame of only a few years, have found themselves free to relate to students not on the basis of status, but competency; not reactively, but proactively.

Behind the clamor of demonstrations and disruptions, along with changes in student affairs, some rather dramatic were also taking place within many classrooms. Existentialism, the focusing inward on the self, the belief that existence precedes one's essence, and that the individual must take responsibility for one's life, has had great impact. As the examining of one's life becomes academically legitimate, the pedagogical focus must necessarily turn from the subject to the student.

As the new legally defined adult students assume increased initiatve and responsibility for their learning, the teacher must acquire more versatility on role responses. The result has been new developmentally oriented courses using teaching approaches that focus on the student's application of knowledge to their own growth and development as persons able to cope in a world of accelerating change. This means classroom teachers, like the student development professionals, must be capable of working effectively within a developmental frame; facilitating, collaborating, consulting (Crookston 1973). Thus, the chasm that has so long separated "teaching" in the classroom and "educating" outside appears to have narrowed to bridgeable proportions on a number of campuses. Such teachers and staff members are both talking the language and using the methodology of student development. Could this mean the dawn of a new era of holism in practice as well as in theory? Certainly the increased viability of student affairs as coordinate to academic affairs in the policy-making arena of the college can strengthen the odds. But time alone can tell.

Definitions. Student development has been defined as the application of the philosophy and principles of human development in the educational setting (Crookston 1972a; Miller and others 1974). Human development refers to the knowledge, conditions, and processes that contribute both to the growth, development, and fulfillment of the individual throughout life as a realized person and effective, productive citizen, and to the growth and development of society. Education for human development is the creation of a humane learning environment within which learners, teachers, and social systems interact and utilize develomental tasks for personal growth and societal betterment. The teaching of human development includes any experience in which a teacher interacts with learners as individuals or in groups that contributes to individual, group, or community growth and development and that can be evaluated (Crookston 1972a, 1962b, 1973).

While the above definitions argue that human development is the generic descriptive term for the field, for our purpose there is the difficulty that human development is too encompassing. It includes those processes that affect the development of persons in the whole of life—in any setting, be it school, work, family, group, community, or society at large, and at any age in any circumstance. On the other hand, student development by definition must imply a developmental process limited to an educational setting; it is, therefore, the more preferable term to describe our particular field. While student development suggests that only students are to be developed, this difficulty can be surmounted by the suggestion that all those in the educational setting by definition are "students" at one time or another, depending on the nature of the task and the type and quality of the interaction or transaction involved.

Proposed Nomenclature

Our analysis leads to the following conclusions and proposals: (a) *Student personnel work* should be given its due and retired into history. Efforts should be made in the professional literature and in other communications not to use the term to describe contemporary programs, services, or concepts. Although it is legitimate to use the term in its proper definition to refer to specific functions such as placement, it is recommended that a ten-year moratorium be placed on any such public use of the term, after which presumably there should be no mistake as to its proper meaning and usage, (b) *Student affairs* should be used to describe the sector or administrative subdivision on campus within which there are people, programs, functions, and services, many, if not all, of which contribute to student development, (c) *Student development* should be used to describe the concept, philosophy, underlying theories, and methodologies utilized in the many settings in which student development occurs. (d) Professional associations should change their names accordingly. The following are recommended: (a) Change American Personnel and Guidance Association to Association of Human Development Professions. This adds one word (professions) to a proposal already made by Ivey (1970). The recent addition of the Public Offender Counselor Association highlights the character of the present APGA that reflects the wide spectrum of concern that extends beyond the educational institution into the whole of life. An association of professions concerned with many aspects of human development is both apt and appealing. (b) Changing American College Personnel Association to the Association for College Student Development is under current consideration and should be supported. Most other organizations within APGA now appear functionally descriptive. The long controversy around the use of the term *guidance* is recognized but cannot be dealt with here. (c) Change the names of Personnel and Guidance Journal, Journal of College Student Personnel, and NASPA *Journal* to eliminate *personnel* and make appropriate rewording. The latter two come easy: *Journal of College Student Development* and *Journal of Student Affairs Administration.* The former requires additional consideration. Of equal importance is editorial consistency in the use of terminology. (d) Change National Association of Student Personnel Administrators to National Association of Student Affairs Administrators. There are those within NASPA who would like to change the name to National Association of Student Development Administrators. This would be a mistake because it would confuse a concept with a territory, the same confusion that now exists in their present title with the term *personnel.* Despite the double entendre, student affairs, like academic affairs, has become the accepted term for our sector. Calling the sector *student development* is bound to raise unnecessarily the territorial hackles of academicians who can rightfully claim that student development is also their proper business, a claim with which we should all most heartily agree.

Finally, perhaps all of the above might persuade those in our academic colleges who are responsible for the training of professionals in our field to do something about changing their archaic course titles and degrees, many of which suggest we are still training student personnel workers to function in the 1950s.

"Student Personnel—All Hail and Farewell!" was edited by Carolyn Palmer, *administrative assistant for staff development in the Housing Division of the University of Illinois.*

References

Arbuckle, D. S. *Student personnel services in higher education.* New York: McGraw-Hill, 1953.

Ayers, A. R.; Tripp, P. A.; & Russel, J. H. *Student services administration in higher education.* Washington, D.C.: U.S. Department of Health, Education & Welfare, 1966.

Barry, R., & Wolf, B. *Modern issues in guidance-personnel work.* New York: Teachers College Press, 1957.

Blaesser, W. W. The future of student personnel work in higher education. In J. G. Fowlkes (Ed.), *Higher education for American society.* Madison: University of Wisconsin Press, 1949.

Blaesser, W. W., & Crookston, B. B. Student personnel work—College and university. *Encyclopedia of Educational Research* (Third Edition), 1960, 1414–1427.

Brouwer, P. J. *Student personnel services in general education.* Washington, D.C.: American Council on Education, 1949.

Clothier, R. C., et al. College personnel principles and functions. *Personnel Journal,* 1931, *10,* 11

Cowley, W. H. The nature of student personnel work. *Educational Record,* April 1936. 3–27.

Crookston, B. B. A developmental view of academic advising as teaching. *Journal of College Student Personnel,* 1972, 13, 12–17. (a)

Crookston, B. B. An organizational model for student development. *NASPA Journal,* 1972, 10, 3–13. (b)

Crookston, B. B. Education for human development. In C. F. Warnath (Ed.), *New directions for college counselors.* San Francisco: Jossey-Bass, 1973. Pp. 47–64.

Crookston, B. B., & Atkyns, G. C. *A Study of student affairs: The principal student affairs officer, the functions, the organization at American colleges and universities, 1967–1972. A preliminary summary report.* Storrs, Conn.: University of Connecticut Research Foundation, 1974.

Hardee, M. E. (Ed.) *Counseling and guidance in general education.* Yonkers-on-Hudson, N.Y.: World, 1955.

Ivey, A. E. The association for human development. A revitalized APGA. *Personnel and Guidance Journal,* 1970, 48, 527–532.

Lloyd-Jones, E. *Student Personnel Work at Northwestern University.* New York: Harper & Brothers, 1929.

Lloyd-Jones, E. Personnel administration. *Journal of Higher Education,* March 1934, 5, 141–147.

Lloyd-Jones, E. Personnel work and general education. In N. B. Henry (Ed.), *General education* (Fifty-First Yearbook, Part I). Chicago: University of Chicago, National Society for the Study of Education, 1952. Pp. 214–229.

Lloyd-Jones, E. Changing concepts of student personnel work. In E. Lloyd-Jones & M. R. Smith (Eds.), *Student personnel work as deeper teaching.* New York: Harper, 1954. Pp. 1–14.

Miller, T. K. et al. *A student development model for student affairs in tomorrow's higher education.* Washington, D.C.: American College Personnel Association, 1974.

Report of a Conference on the Philosophy and Development of Student Personnel Work in College and University. *The Student personnel point of view* (American Council on Education Studies). Washington, D.C.: ACE, 1937.

Taylor, H. The philosophical foundation of general education. In N. B. Henry (Ed.), *General education* (Fifty-First Yearbook, Part I). Chicago: University of Chicago, National Society for the Study of Education, 1952. Pp. 20–45.

Williamson, E. G. *Student personnel services in colleges and universities.* New York: McGraw-Hill, 1961.

Williamson, E. G. Commentary. In E. Lloyd-Jones & E. M. Westervelt (Eds.), *Behavioral science and guidance: Proposals and perspectives.* New York: Columbia University, Teachers College, Bureau of Publications, 1963. Pp. 54–59.

Wrenn, C. G. *Student personnel work in college,* New York: Ronald Press, 1951.

Institutional and Personal Tort Liability

Edward H. Hammond

Student affairs administrators in post-secondary educational institutions share a common fear regarding personal and institutional liability for acts and decisions committed while carrying out their official duties. This fear, generated by the unknown, has caused increasing concern in the last decade.

This concern has been documented in the recent federal court decision of *Bradshaw v. Rawlings* (1979). In this landmark decision, now under review at the request of Delaware Valley College, the Pennsylvania Association of Colleges and Universities, and the American Council of Education, the court ruled that the institution was subject to liability based upon negligent supervision of a student activity, when it participated in the planning of an activity involving consumption of alcoholic beverages by persons foreseeably under the legal drinking age. The court accepted the premise that a college administrator does not, in all instances, have a duty to supervise student activities. However, the court noted that, in this case, the staff member of the college had participated with the students in planning the function at which beer was to be served and assisted in the disbursement of funds to purchase the beer. The institution was permitted to argue to the jury that it was not negligent because it was powerless to control the beer drinking habits of college sophomores. Subsequently, the jury rejected the college's defense that it had acted in a reasonable manner under the circumstances.

Before analyzing this case and others that involve tort liability, one must look carefully at any legal difference that may exist between public and private institutions. The key to this discussion is the student-institutional relationship. This relationship currently is being interpreted by the courts to be contractual. This definition was first offered in *Booker v. Grand Rapids Medical College* in 1909. From that point until the sixties, the courts were reluctant to apply contractual theory, largely because of the "Minor status" of most of the students, *Ryan v. Hofstra University* (1971). Since the change in the age of majority and the age to enter into contracts, this judicial reluctance has disappeared, *Zumbrunv. University of Southern California*

(1972). Therefore, in the final analysis, the legal implications of tort liability are shared equally by administrators and staff of both public and private institutions because of the now universal application of contract theory to the student-institutional relationship.

Tort liability is an area of civil liability and is the greatest risk for the student personnel profession. A tort is an improper interference with another individual in such a manner as to cause injury to that party. Such interference may be intentional, as in the case of assault and battery; or unintentional, as in the case of negligence. Regardless of whether there is intent to do harm, tort liability exists.

There are many reported cases in which an injured party has attempted to hold college or university officials personally liable for the torts they committed while acting in their official capacities. For staff members to be held personally liable, they must have committed the tortious act, directed or supervised it, or otherwise participated in its commission. Staff members may not be personally liable for torts of other institutional agents merely because they are connected with the institution. An individual staff member sued in a personal capacity may not be shielded by sovereign immunity or charitable immunity defenses which sometimes protect the institution itself.

If a staff member commits a tort while acting on behalf of the institution and within the scope of authority delegated to him or her, both the staff member and the institution may be liable for the harm caused by the tort. The institution's potential liability does not relieve the individual of any measure of personal liability if the judgment is severable; the injured party could choose to collect a judgment solely from the individual and the individual would have to claim against the institution for any part of the judgment which he was required to pay. However, where the individual staff member and the institution are both potentially liable and the judgment is joint; the individual may receive practical relief from the liability if the injured party receives the entire judgment from the institution. But, it is important to note that there is no guarantee that the court will permit that nor that the institution will choose to pay the entire amount.

In one such case, *Gambet v. Vanderbilt University* (1918), a student, who was injured in the fall of an elevator in the building of the university, attempted to hold staff members at the institution personally liable for the injury suffered. Staff members were charged with the responsibility for supervising the building. The court held that the injuries were caused by the staff's negligence to perform its duties with respect to the upkeep of the building. It also appeared from the evidence that the staff knew that the elevator was unsafe, but permitted its use despite that knowledge. On this basis, the court held the staff personally responsible and liable for damages suffered by the injured student.

One finds an interesting parallel and an important distinction in the case of *Scott v. Burton* (1938). In this case, the trustees and staff of the institution were not held to be personally liable for a student's injury sustained in falling from an alleged negligently constructed and maintained dormitory fire escape. The institution was held to be solely liable in this case because the staff had nothing to do with the construction of the building and there was no evidence that they knew of the dangerous condition prior to the injury. The courts have been willing to forego personal liability where the staff had no prior knowledge of the conditions that caused the injury. In the final analysis, it is very clear that student affairs staff members must take affirmative action to remove any dangerous condition from the public. Failure to take adequate steps to remove the dangerous condition places the staff member in a position of being held personally liable for any damages that may occur.

If student affairs staff members commit torts while acting outside the scope of their delegated authority, they would be personally liable but the institution would not be held liable. Thus, an injured party could obtain a judgment only against the individual and only the individual staff member would be responsible for satisfying the judgment. In some cases, the institution may affirm the individual's unauthorized action in which case the individual may be deemed to have acted within the scope of delegated authority and both the institution and the individual would be potentially liable.

The theory of "respondeat superior" also comes into play in cases involving staff members charged with the responsibility of supervising other employees. The theory here simply means that the supervisor is liable, in certain cases, for the wrongful acts of subordinates (*Southern Paramount Pictures Company v. Gaulding* (1919); *State of Delaware v. Pittinger* (1919). The theory applies only when the employees operate within the scope of authority that has been appropriately delegated. However, if the behavior which causes damage is outside the scope of authority and can be legally classified as a frolic, the supervisor can successfully claim "a detour in frolic" defense.

In the case of personal tort liability linked to a staff member by the concept of "respondeat superior", actual knowledge of the damage is important in claims involving civil rights. In *Walker v. University of Pittsburgh* (1978), the court held that a staff member cannot be held vicariously liable on grounds of "respondeat superior" for torts of subordinates, since there was no prior knowledge of the claim. In this case, the complainant was unable to prove any personal knowledge or actual participation on the part of the staff member and the denial of the constitutionally protected rights of the defendant.

Officers and staff members of public institutions can sometimes escape tort liability by providing the defense of "official immunity". For this defense to apply, the individual must have acted within the scope of officially delegated authority and just have been involved in a discretionary judgment connected directly to an institutional policy. Because it involves the elements of discretion and policy judgment, official immunity is more likely to apply the higher in the authority hierarchy a particular individual may be.

One consistent thread that winds its way through all the cases cited above is the responsibility of an administrator to take affirmative action to protect others when a dangerous condition exists. In *Perkins v. The State Board of Education* (1978), the court observed that the "standard of care" owed students was that of reasonable supervision commensurate with the age of the student. But, a greater degree of care was required if the student was being exposed to inherently dangerous activity or objects. In this particular court case, the staff member was not found negligent in providing adequate supervision; and the court held that the staff member's conduct was consistent with the reasonable standard of care delineated by the appropriate professional organization. Almost every activity that we are involved in has some standard of care that has been developed and promulgated by an appropriate agent. In the supervision of intramural activities, for example, the use of mountain climbing equipment, scuba equipment or swimming pool, reasonable standards of care have been developed and promulgated by the appropriate national organizations. As long as we fulfill those standards of care, neither the institution nor the personal staff will, in all likelihood, be held liable.

In addition to exercising reasonable standards of care, the institution also has the responsibility or duty to warn individuals of hazards. In *Rice v. Florida Power and Light Company* (1978), the duty of the University, or landowner, to maintain the premises in a reasonably safe condition for use in a manner consistent with the purposes of the premises and to warn any user of the premises of "latent perils" has been affirmed. The court has held that the responsibility of the institution to warn students of "latent perils" exists in cases where the institution has known of the perils or should have known of the perils, but in cases where the student, by exercise of due care, does not know the danger.

This legal doctrine has been applied to a whole variety of circumstances. In the last year, ski resorts have been required to provide appropriate warning of the latent hazards of skiing to anyone using their slopes. This requirement of "due warning" also applies to a wide variety of student activities and programs where a latent danger exists. The responsibility of the institution is clear; to warn the student or the user of the premises or equipment of the danger. The warning places the individual student in the position of being knowledgeable and also responsible.

In *Shannon v. Washington University* (1978), the court stated that the duty of an institution to care for its premises and equipment is more strict than that of a municipality. Ergo, the size of one's property does not absolve from its duty to its users. Institutions must maintain, in a reasonably safe fashion, those areas intended for use by students; failure to do so is negligent. It is also important to note that a student's contributory negligence exists when the condition is so clearly obvious that the reasonably prudent person would be bound to see and avoid the danger. Failure to avoid danger can lead to significant risks.

In the landmark case of *Bradshaw v. Rawlings* (1979), the student received an award of over $1,000,000. This award was made because the court held that the evidence was sufficient to establish that the driver of the car was intoxicated and that intoxication was a substantial factor in causing the accident. The defendant college could be held liable for negligence in its supervision of an extra-curricular picnic at which the beer was consumed.

In the final analysis, the court held that the college owes a duty to use due care under the circumstances to prevent the unreasonable risk of harm to students attending institutional functions. Negligence is the institution's conduct which fell below the standard established by law for the protection of others against unreasonable risk or harm. The jury, therefore, rejected the college's defense that it acted in a reasonable manner under the circumstances, and the institution's liability is predicated on the concept of wont of due care which a reasonable man would exercise under these circumstances.

Regardless of the outcomes of the appeals in this case, it is now clear that both institutions and staff members can and will be held liable for actions or inactions that harm students unless reasonable standards of care and due warning of hazards are provided. The use of these and other risk management techniques are going to have to become a more important part of student affairs operations. Without the use of such techniques, the individual staff member and the educational process is in danger. The historical defenses of sovereign immunity and educational immunity are no longer accepted by the courts. The only real defense is the use of reason in our approach to the co-curricular educational opportunities we provide.

References

Booker V. Grand Rapids Medical College 120 N.W. 589 (1909).
Bradshaw v. Rawlings 464 F Supp. 175 (E.D. Penn. 1979).

Gambet v. Vanderbilt University 138 Tenn. 616, 200 S.W. 510 (1918).

Pennsylvania Association of Colleges and Universities and American Council on Education, Amici Curiae Brief in Support of Defendant Delaware Valley College (1979).

Perkins v. The State Board of Education 364 So. 2d 183, Ct. of Appeals La., 1978.

Rice v. Florida Power and Light Co. 363 So 2d 834 (D.C. App. Fla. 1978).

Ryan v. Hofstra University 324 N.Y.S. 2d 964 (1971).

Scott v. Burton 137 Tenn. 147, 114 S.W. 2d 956 (1938).

Shannon v. Washington University 575 S.W. 2d 235 (Mo. ct. App. 1978).

Southern Paramount Pictures Co. v. Gaulding 24 Ga. App. 478, 101 S.E. 311 (1919).

State of Delaware v. Pittinger 293 F. 853, 855 (1923).

Walker v. University of Pittsburgh 457 F. Supp. 1000 U.S.D.C. (W.D. Penn. 1978).

Zumbrun v. University of Southern California 25 Cal. App. 3d 101 Cal. Rptr. 499 (1972).

Student Personnel Training for the Chief Student Affairs Officer: Essential or Unnecessary?

Paul A. Bloland

A former football coach is appointed as a dean of students. A popular history professor becomes vice-provost of student affairs. A business executive is named vice-president for student affairs. An attorney, a public relations executive, a college chaplain, an assistant dean of academic affairs receive the chief student affairs officer mantle at college after college. In some instances we can identify the apparent reasoning behind the appointment. An unpopular dean is replaced by a popular professor. A series of bitter legal skirmishes with students leads to the installation of an attorney in the student affairs role. A coach is appointed with instructions to bring a rowdy residence hall under control. In other instances the reasoning is not as clear.

For years student personnel administrators have attempted through professional associations, national meetings, publications, and graduate training to build a professional identity. More recently we have begun to speak of ourselves as student development educators who possess unique understandings and insights into the ways students grow and learn (a claim which may cause some consternation among our faculty colleagues who sometimes see themselves in that same business). Because appointment to the position of chief student affairs officer is regarded by many as the top rung of the student affairs career ladder, the nature of the experience and training of those appointed is important to the self-concept or identity of the field. If there were an indispensable specialized content in the field, the executive leadership of the student affairs component would need to possess expertise in it in order to perform satisfactorily. Apparently, this is not the case.

Facets of this question have been addressed by Penney (1969,1972), McConnell (1970), Patzer (1972), and Bloland (1974) among others and it was Penney (1972) who pointed out that "there has been no evidence produced to show that . . . non-professionally trained workers have performed

489

less effectively than have workers with full professional backgrounds" (pp.8–9). A 1974 study of Crookston and Atkyns indicated that 38%, over a third, of those chief student affairs officers responding reported that the field of study for their highest degree was in other than professional education while, of those who held faculty appointments as well, about 66% held rank in academic fields other than professional education. Admittedly these ratios mask the precise nature of the prior preparation but one can reasonably assume that professional education as a field of study, most often the home of student development/student personnel graduate education, is not viewed as critical preparation for high-level student affairs positions.

Why not? Why isn't seemingly pertinent training and experience seen as prerequisite to appointment as a chief student affairs officer? After all, the chief fiscal officer is expected to have training and successful experience in money management and the academic dean must have come from the disciplinary ranks of the teaching faculty. My contention is that a student affairs background provides no particular advantage because it is not congruent with the role expectations actually held for the position. I have advanced my argument in the form of four propositions, each controversial if not outrageous.

Four Propositions

The personal qualities of the student personnel worker are inversely related to the requirements for success as a chief student affairs officer. The personal needs and qualities which motivate individuals to prepare for a career in a helping profession such as counseling, student personnel work, or group work are not always the same qualities which are esteemed in high-level management positions (Tilley, 1973). Beginning student personnel workers are most often influenced by a personal value system which is humanistically oriented and which seeks fulfillment in service to others. The entry jobs throw them into direct contact with students who voluntarily seek their services. They are or become very student oriented and see their role as facilitating student goals whether vocational, personal, educational, or extracurricular. The graduate program of preparation reinforces these values and teaches skills for facilitating student growth and development.

Conversely, the chief student affairs officer, particularly in large and complex institutions, is a manager and a supervisor dealing with budgets, staff development, policy questions, extra-institutional publics, and problem solving. Members of the president's staff and management team are oriented toward promoting institutional welfare and achieving institutional goals, which may not always coincide with student goals. The qualities, personal and professional, which make for success in management terms are not necessarily those which typify a good counselor or student personnel worker. In fact staff persons who are particularly empathic and effective as counselors may have developed an orientation which is antithetic to management efficiency, organization, and a managerial perspective (Pietrofesa & Vriend, 1971; Brown, 1972). They may see the student's point of view to the exclusion of the overall institutional view or fail to see the implications of student concerns in the wider institutional perspective. The chief student affairs officer who remains a student advocate while ascending to top management is viewed with suspicion and concern by fellow administrators who find this behavior threatening and who proceed to isolate him or her from the real decisions (McConnell, 1970). "Which ballpark do they play in—the kids' or the adults?" (Hodgkinson, 1970, p.50).

Student personnel workers, when they begin to report directly to the president as chief student affairs officers, have changed career fields from student personnel to professional administration. The demands of high level administration are such that professional student personnel workers, once elevated to membership on the president's administrative team, must develop a whole new set of management skills and a new orientation if they are to survive and be effective. Through goal-setting, organization, and the allocation of financial resources, they may establish the conditions under which student development can be facilitated but they no longer personally practice the skills and expertise which characterize the student personnel field. They become administrators who happen to be specializing in student affairs.

The new relationship is somewhat analogous to the role played by the hospital administrator who is not a physician. While physicians manage the medical programs of the hospital because only they have the professional expertise and status to direct the highly skilled staffs in their specialities, hospital administrators provide the conditions under which physicians can perform their tasks with a minimum of distracting responsibility. To the extent that hospital administration *requires* administrative skills not readily acquired through the practice of medicine, professional administrators are to be preferred to the physician. However, physicians who have developed administrative skills along the way and enjoy using them would be preferable choices as hospital administrators. They would still be physicians but would be practicing management, not medicine.

In the same way, the administration of a complex student affairs program may require administrative skills for which trained student personnel professionals are ill-prepared. If they have acquired such skills while rising through middle management positions or by training it would be better to have them manage a student affairs program than professional administrators with no experience in student affairs. But, having accepted this assignment, I would argue that they are no longer practicing professional student personnel workers but are not, in effect, professional administrators assigned to student affairs. Having become professional administrators, it seems reasonable to assume that they in turn can be replaced by other professional administrators.

The relationship between chief student affairs officers and their presidents is more important than their professional expertise in student personnel work. This proposition follows from the preceding one; namely, that if chief student affairs officers are no longer student personnel professionals, their expertise in that field becomes secondary to their ability to respond to the needs of the president as a member of the management group. Certainly it would be useful in terms of providing knowledgeable staff leadership if the chief student affairs officer possessed training in both student development and the management of student affairs programs. However, such training is not usually a prior condition for appointment. It is more important to have the confidence of the president as one whose judgment is proven and reliable, whose decisions hold up under scrutiny, who is sensitive to potential problems, and one who can be relied upon to handle these problems with a high degree of political sophistication when they do occur. Not to be minimized is the president's need to be surrounded by staff people whose loyalty is to the president, not to a special constituency or professional ideology, and who are capable of handling high policy as the president's agent or surrogate (McConnell, 1970).

Pending education reform, the expertise of the student personnel/student development specialist seemingly is irrelevant to the academic programs of most colleges and universities. This proposition is a deliberate exaggeration but it derives from the nature of most academic programs in higher education today. The typical university, four-year college, and community college is predicated on a model of education which is content-bound and cognitively-based, an education founded upon the cultivation of intellectual skills and understandings. An emphasis upon the mind is central, with classroom teaching and research the preferred means by which the intellect is trained and strengthened.

In contrast, the student personnel point of view (American Council on Education Studies, 1938, 1949) emphasizes the educational potential of the institutional environment for the development of the whole person in emotional and physical as well as intellectual terms. The more recent statements of the student personnel point of view (ACPA, 1975; Miller & Prince, 1977) build upon this orientation and go on to say that the "development of the whole student is the mission and task of the whole college" (Miller & Prince, p.5). The developmental approach calls for an understanding of and a commitment to both a philosophy and a theory-based model of education as well as competencies and strategies for its implementation. For the developmental approach to be effective, traditional cognitively oriented institutional programs would have to yield to a broadened emphasis upon meeting the developmental needs of students in both cognitive and affective terms. For implementation, staff with special training in the principles and procedures of developmental education would be required. Presumably, the administrative leadership for the educational reform of the college would then need to be derived from those who possess this specialized training and philosophical commitment.

However, most of the press for reform has been generated by the student personnel/student development field itself and the response of the academic community has been decidedly restrained. In fact, according to Terenzini (1973), who studied the relative views of college and university presidents and chief student affairs officers on the goals of student affairs programs, presidents agreed least with those goals which involved student personnel programs in the academic and intellectual development of students. If student affairs division involvement in academic programming is seen as inappropriate and student development, our unique educational contribution, is viewed as peripheral to the actual curricular thrust of most institutions, it follows that expertise in its implementation is also peripheral. Consequently, there is no particular advantage to appointing chief student affairs officers from the ranks of those who possess it.

Implications

To the extent that these propositions and observations possess at least face validity, I would like to examine some of the implications. First and foremost, the stated problem, whether or not trained professionals get the top jobs, is not the real problem. The concern lies instead in the possibility that the student personnel/student development field is suggesting models and preparing graduate students for a world of higher education which does not yet exist. Since it does not exist, our experts are not in demand as teachers and administrators in that world.

Plato (1978) points out in a thoughtful and disturbing analysis of the student development reform movement that, facing a threat to its vested interests, the student personnel field has made an effort to expand the role of expert by seizing on the concept of student development. I would ask if, in our effort to find a campus role for ourselves as experts, we have in effect painted ourselves into a corner? We may become experts in an area which has no perceived relevancy to what has been the "proper and appropriate" business of higher education; namely, the creation and dissemination of knowledge.

Traditional student personnel work at least found a measure of acceptance as a needed support system for the academic program. For student development to win similar acceptance it must create a demand for widespread educational reform. As Miller and Price put it, ". . . the whole institution must be committed to the goal of student development" (1977, p.148). But until and unless colleges and universities begin to conceive of their task in this broadened perspective, they have no great need for educational leadership uniquely schooled in the techniques and strategies of student development.

Second, since reform is still pending and student personnel/development programs are not built into the academic equation, they do not share proportionately in institutional resources and may indeed become expendable when expenses must be pared. Services which are clearly supportive such as financial aids, admissions and records, and residence halls suffer the least but those which offer presumed (at least by the student development educator) educational purpose and program are exceedingly vulnerable at budget time. Indeed, one has the impression that as long as the college is financially viable and as long as we continue to perform those traditional tasks we have successfully sold to the academic community, we will be permitted to amuse ourselves with teaching non-credit developmental courses, occasional consultation, and outreach counseling. But when the financial crunch comes, we are back to the basics with the student personnel program stripped to its conventional essentials. Since a student development model of education is not one of those essentials, it follows that managers trained in that model are not essential either. Only when a student development model is the academic program can this contingency be avoided.

Finally, those of us who are involved in the professional preparation of student personnel workers need to re-examine the realities of the world of higher education as we design our training programs. If, as I have suggested, student personnel/student development and administration are essentially two different career fields, the differences should be reflected in the content of the graduate training offered for each.

For example, a program for administrators would enroll mature students with some demonstrated talent for management. Conducted at the doctoral level, it would be highly eclectic, borrowing from many relevant disciplines and, as suggested in Appleton, Briggs, and Rhatigan (1978), would not be "a program in student personnel administration but rather the administration of higher education" (p.176). The student affairs element would not be neglected. Hopefully, it would have comprised the content of a master's degree program for those aspirants intent upon moving up the administrative ladder in student affairs. The advanced program, while it might include student affairs applications and field work, would recognize the professional administration of higher education as a career field separate and distinct from a specialty called student development.

A student personnel/student development preparation program, on the other hand, would focus on the graduate schooling of prospective faculty and staff who would be prepared to plan curricula and execute college and university educational programs founded upon developmental theory and research and, incidentally, to do some of the needed research themselves. They would also be ready to act as missionaries to the academic community, spreading the gospel of educational reform. Administrative skills should, of course, be taught because they are useful at most levels of responsibility in the field. But we should concentrate our training efforts on the teacher/practitioner who will be performing the specialized tasks of student development and not attempt to produce chief student affairs officers in a master's degree program. The aim at the doctoral level should be to prepare student development educators to enter administration, if that is their goal, as academic leaders, not as general all-purpose administrators.

In summary, I have answered my initial question by arguing that the requirements of top-level student affairs administration are such that prior training in student personnel/student development may be desirable but is unnecessary, that the growing professional specialization called student development education is a field distinct from the administration of higher education, and that differences between the two should be reflected in the training programs designed for each. Underlying these differences is the forty-year effort on the part of the student personnel movement, of which student development is the latest manifestation, to effect a transformation of the goals of higher education from a focus in the intellect only to a concern for the whole student—"physically, socially, emotionally and spiritually, as well as intellectually" (American Council on Education Studies, 1949, p.1). While this effort has been narrowly influential, it has not been broadly accepted. Its experts and adherents have not been and are not now invited to plan, teach in, or administer the campus-wide academic program and, as has been pointed out, are not even viewed as essential to the management of their own programs.

Although the kind of academic environment in which the student development movement could make its optimal educational contribution appears to be far from attainment, change is possible. Student development educators today are in much the same position as other educational reformers of the past. The general education movement, the establishment of experimental colleges, the drive for academic acceptance launched by non-traditional professions, all required significant changes in the then-current definition of higher education. The student personnel movement itself led the attempt to reintegrate the curriculum and extracurriculum into a more holistic college life (Brubacher & Rudy, 1976). If the aim is to reform the nature of higher education by involving the entire academic community in intentional student development, then that community must be sold on this concept as a viable goal of education and sold by none other than its practitioners and adherents. Currently, there is no discernible institution-wide demand for student development specialists or administrators; it will have to be created.

References

American College Personnel Association. A student development model for student affairs in tomorrow's higher education. *Journal of College Student Personnel*, 1975, 16, 334–341.

American Council on Education Studies. *The student personnel point of view.* Washington, D.C.: Author, 1937.

American Council on Education Studies. *The student personnel point of view.* Washington, D.C.: Author, 1949.

Appleton, J. R., Briggs, C. M., & Rhatigan, J. J. *Pieces of eight.* Portland, Oregon: NASPA Institute of Research and Development, National Association of Student Personnel Administrators, 1978.

Bloland, P. A. Professionalism and the professional organization. In Harrington, T. F. *Student personnel work in urban colleges.* New York: Intext Educational Publishers, 1974.

Brown, R. D. *Student development in tomorrow's higher education.* Washington, D.C.: American College Personnel Association, 1972.

Brubacher, J. S., & Rudy, W. *Higher Education in transition.* (Rev.) New York: Harper & Row, 1976.

Crookston, B. B., & Atkyns, G. C. A study of student affairs: The principal student affairs officer, the functions, the organization at American colleges and universities 1967–1972. A preliminary summary report. Storrs, Conn.: University of Connecticut Research Foundation, 1974.

Hodgkinson, H. L. How deans of students are seen by others—And why. *NASPA Journal*, 1970, 8, 49–54.

McConnell, T. R. Student personnel services—Central or pheripheral? *NASPA Journal*, 1970, 8, 55–63.

Miller, T. K., & Prince, J. S. *The future of student affairs.* San Francisco: Jossey-Bass Publishers, 1976.

Patzer, R. D. The student personnel administrator: Pusillanimous pussycat or tempestuous tiger? *NASPA Journal*, 1972, 9, 235–242.

Penney, J. F. Student personnel work: A profession stillborn. *Personnel and Guidance Journal*, 1969, 47, 958–962.

Penney, J. F. *Perspective and challenge in college personnel work.* Springfield, IL.: Charles C. Thomas, Publisher, 1972.

Pietrofesa, J. J., & Vriend, J. The school counselor as a professional. Itasca, Ill.: F. E. Peacock, 1971.

Plato, K. The shift to student development: An analysis of the patterns of change. *NASPA Journal*, 1978, 15, 32–36.

Terenzini, P. T. The goals of student personnel work: Views from the top. *NASPA Journal*, 1973, 11, 31–35.

Tilley, D. C. Student services and the politics of survival. In Katz, J. (Ed.). *Services for students.* San Francisco: New Directions for Education, Jossey-Bass, Inc., 1973, 113–125.

V

Diversity, Values and Professionalism

During the decade of the 1980's, issues associated with the increasing diversity among higher education's student population, multiple court decisions, retrenchment, values education, and student conduct help and the status of the field dominate the professional literature. Students, plugged into themselves with walkman cassette players and video games are seemingly less aware and less interested in their peers and neighbors with whom they share their environment, whether in the classroom or on a residence hall floor. These students, the sons and daughters of the college generation of the 1960's, are characterized by Levine (1980) as ". . . going first class on the Titanic". Their attitudes and values lead many to label them members of the "Me generation" (Levine, 1980). The concepts of personal commitment and integrity come under scrutiny. Campus issues confronting student affairs professionals increasingly focus on student misconduct involving: academic dishonesty, falsification of records, abuse of alcohol and drugs, misuse of property and general campus crime. Certain voices in student affairs and higher education, propose that practitioners assume a position of values neutrality. Seeking to remind us of the traditional responsibility of higher education and student affairs for the intellectual and moral development of students, several authors speak out in support of the role of values development and education.

As this period unfolds, the publication of Gilligan's *In a Different Voice* (1982) alerts professionals to new research findings suggesting that differing patterns of moral and ethical development exist for men and women. Value judgments and moral decisions are now examined and understood in terms that emphasize either an ethic or care or justice. Value judgments and moral decisions are examined now with a new understanding and the relationship between one's values and behavior is underscored.

Student affairs, the term describing not only the administrative unit on a

499

college or university campus but the field of practitioners itself, has replaced student personnel as recommended by Crookston (1975). Student development is the accepted label for a philosophy and/or an operational model that guides daily practice. In this decade also the Journal of College Student Personnel becomes the Journal of College Student Development.

An additional role for the chief student affairs officer, that of mentor, is recommended by Schmidt and Wolfe (1980) in their article, "The Mentor Partnership: Discovering Professionalism." The authors suggest that experienced practitioners share their knowledge and insights with proteges by serving in one or more of the following roles: consultant/advisor, role model, or sponsor. Each of these roles fosters the socialization and professional advancement of New Professionals.

Carpenter, Miller and Winston (1981) substantiate the existence of a unique theory base and a set of criteria for preparation for entry-level positions in student affairs and conclude that the field is "an emergent profession" (p. 16). These two factors are components of Wilensky's developing profession against which student affairs can be measured.

The progress of student affairs in its efforts to gain professional status is explored by Stamatakos as he reapplies the traditional eight criteria that define a profession applied earlier by Wrenn and Darley (1949). In a two part article, Stamatakos evaluates and measures the field against each criterion and offers recommendations to assist us in achieving those criteria which remain unmet. His conclusion is that as a field, we remain, as before, ". . . en route to professional status" (Wrenn & Darley, 1949, p. 178).

The continued influence of legal concerns on practice is represented by Hammond's (1981) discussion of the implications of viewing students as consumers and the implementation of contract theory. Citing significant court cases from the 1960's and 70's, he addresses the concept of community and the effects of a new student-institutional relationship, precipitated by the lowering of the age of majority, have on student affairs practice.

Sandeen (1982) identifies current attitudes, thinking and issues of importance to student affairs professionals and casts a prophetic eye toward the years ahead. While students' rights, financial aid, accreditation and preparation remain key issues, our most important task will continue to be not only our own professional development, but the development of the field as well.

One of the early voices challenging us to return to our traditional commitment to moral and ethical development is McBee's (1982). She perceives a general deterioration in students' moral conduct on many campuses. The need to teach ethics and to model ethical behavior has never been greater. McBee understands that students must learn to develop their own set of internal controls in view of the lessening influence of contemporary family and church structures.

Reflecting the changing nature of the student population, Hughes (1983) draws our attention to a group of older students, non-traditional adult learners. In these pages he synthesizes 71 pieces of literature, including the new body of adult development theory, and proposes appropriate responses for student affairs professionals. Hughes suggests that practitioners assume the role of advocate for their campus, underscores the need for programming and services and challenges higher education to respond ". . . quickly and effectively to an ever-changing student population" (p. 61).

Ways of dealing with issues of student conduct are the subject of the research reported by Dalton and Healy (1984). Chief student affairs officers were queried about their use of values education activities to address a range of student conduct issues. Among the techniques reported, developing self-awareness and independence, tolerance and respect are viewed as deterrents and corrective behaviors to student misbehavior.

Within the covers of the Silver Anniversary issues of the *Journal of College Student Personnel* in 1984, Delworth and Seeman translate the research findings of Gilligan (1977, 1982) to student affairs practice. Ethics of caring and fairness are discussed and professionals are cautioned against applying male models of development to all students. "The 'ethics of care' belong . . . (the) vocabulary and . . . work of all student services professionals" (p. 492).

Attempting to discover what is known about Black students' experiences on the campuses of predominantly White institutions (PWI's). Sedlacek (1987) presents a twenty year (1960 to 1980) review of higher education and student affairs literature. Continuing problems with self-concept, racism, developing community, and a general lack of support persons are identified as persistent problems. A set of recommendations is offered to improve the experience of Black students on PWI's.

In commemoration of the 50th anniversary of the publication of the Student Personnel Point of View, a joint ACE/NASPA committee accepts a charge to prepare a statement describing contemporary student affairs. A description of core values and a statement of purpose are presented within a context that stresses the implementation of student development theories and stratefies. This document becomes a catalyst for considerable discussion and is the focus of several journal articles, one of which is presented in this chapter.

Gibbs and Szablewicz (1988) address the implications of several recent court cases on the relationship between the student and the institution including the application of contract law, landowner liability, and guest and host negligence. For these authors, the field may be experiencing a new form of *in loco parentis* under which institutions need to ". . . protect students from physical harm but are not empowered to police and control students' morals" (p. 104).

Delworth (1989) addresses the issue of identity formation with an emphasis on gender and ethnicity. In one of a series of articles that underscores the need for professionals to consider the differences of the students with whom they interact, the need to be sensitive to the application of monocultural theories is highlighted. In addition, she reminds us of the changing demographics of our colleagues and the need for the field to reflect the changing society outside academia's walls.

The influence of four philosophical perspectives (rationalism, neohumanism, pragmatism and existentialism) on student affairs practice and preparation is addressed by Knock, Rentz and Penn (1988). From a focus on intellectual development and empiricism to a recognition of the value of out-of-classroom learning, ". . . the pedagogical focus must necessarily turn from the subject to the student" (p. 120). By espousing student development theories and strategies of intentionality, student affairs is gradually becoming a partner within the academy.

Hughes (1989) suggests a metaphor that "asserts that a significant role for student affairs is to provide a balanced learning climate for students by acknowledging and fostering those values that develop attributes traditionally considered 'feminine'. . . ." (p. 19). She connects the core values of the field and the feminization ethic within student affairs to a new role associated with sex role development and to transformative leadership models. When student affairs views "masculine and feminine behaviors and values as integrative and equally viable for men and women," (p. 25) a new dimension of the whole person philosophy will be achieved.

Ebbers and Henry (1990) recognize that appreciating and celebrating the increasing diversity on college and university campuses suggests a new role for student affairs professionals: facilitators of cultural competence. To fulfill this role, the cultural competence of staff members must not only be assessed, but addressed. To facilitate learning they suggest that professional development activities might include microcultural simulations, case studies and cross-campus networks and exchange programs.

The Mentor Partnership: Discovery of Professionalism

Janet A. Schmidt and Janice Sutera Wolfe

The mentoring relationship provides mutual enrichment and benefit.

While current student personnel issues such as restricted budgets, personal accountability and increased government regulations necessarily have been the focal concerns of chief student personnel officers, the growth and development of the new professional staff who work with them on these priorities have not been given much attention. New student personnel professionals need suitable mentors who will provide guidance, support and opportunities for them.

Student personnel literature to date fails to emphasize and define the functions and significance of the mentor-protégé relationship. Our purposes are: to describe the functions of a mentor; to suggest guidelines for choosing a mentor; to delineate the rewards of the relationship for the mentor and the protégé; and lastly, to highlight research pertaining to aspiring women professionals.

This article is addressed to two audiences: the potential mentor, who may be a chief personnel administrator, a faculty member, or a counselor, and to the new professional in student personnel. We hope to persuade both the mentor and the protégé that developing mentor relationships is a vital activity and one that should be encouraged as a conscious professional practice.

Functions of a Mentor

As noted in the introduction, mentors are by definition, colleagues and supervisors who actively provide guidance, support and opportunities for the protégé. The functions of a mentor consist of acting as a role model, a consultant/advisor and a sponsor. These functions are delineated as follows:

Role Model: "If You Can, I Can."

One of the primary and most easily recognized functions of a mentor is to act as a role model for the protégé. Briefly, a role model is a person who demonstrates a highly skilled level of performance that is considered worthy of imitation. Role models may or may not be aware that newcomers regard them in this fashion. New professionals often look to senior members of the administrative staff for role model possibilities, although the faculty too may be a source for such figures.

The role model provides the new professional with standards of behavior and professional activity. For example, the manner and style that the role model uses to deal with conflict, interact with colleagues, supervise subordinates, and balance personal life with professional demands are significant. Further, role models furnish the new professional with career advancement patterns and histories of professional achievement. Role models, then, can illustrate how a professional behaves as well as what a professional does.

Contrary to common assumption, research suggests that the role modeling process is not one of complete imitation of the model by the protégé. White (1952) notes that identification with the role model does not generally occur on a global basis and instead maintains that protégés are highly selecting in adopting role model characteristics which meet their immediate needs. More recently, Bucher and Selling (1977) support White's suggestion of selective role model incorporation and identified three types of incomplete modeling processes: partial, stage and option.

In the partial role modeling process, the most common of the three types, individuals select desired attributes from several different role models. Typically, protégés choose attributes which they regard as compatible with their sense of self and projected professional image. In this way, protégés are able to construct their "ideal" professional self from the various models available.

In the stage modeling process, newcomers seek out more advanced colleagues as information sources concerning future periods of personal and career development. Because such models are in a more advanced stage of professional experience they can provide newcomers with tested advice on how to avoid certain difficulties or to achieve similar successes.

In the option modeling process, the newcomer seeks out a model with an unusual or deviant career pattern. Career histories which are different from the standard are useful because they give newcomers evidence that alternatives and variations are possible despite the prevalence of the status quo.

In short, no matter which role modeling process is adopted, a role model is vital to the newcomer in student personnel for patterning a professional image compatible with self perception and professional expectation.

Consultant/Advisor:
"I've Traveled This Route Before."

In addition to the role model function, a mentor may act as a consultant or trusted advisor to the newcomer. Acting as a consultant/advisor, the mentor provides information from a variety of professional experiences that can benefit the protégé facing a situation for the first time. In this capacity, the mentor can be seen as a teacher, basing the instruction on personal experience and knowledge.

Some of the most relevant information shared with the new professional includes: how to deal appropriately with the political system in which the protégé functions; how to set and meet professional standards; and how to maintain one's personal sense of self in relation to the work self.

Experienced professionals have usually learned the significance of politics in the course of their own career development. Politics, as used here, refers to the dynamics of making policy in contrast to implementing policy or policy administration. The focus may range from intra-office to university-wide affairs. A necessary prerequisite for astute political decision making is an awareness of the system's norms and standards. While norms may be overt, explicitly stated rules, policies and procedures, they may also be covert, relying on tacit understanding and adherence by system members. In most instances, new professionals are initiated to the overt or formalized norms of their job setting. However, the covert or informal system is by definition obscure and thus more likely to be problematic for newcomers. Having little experience or sensitivity in identifying these subtle, covert norms, the new professional can benefit greatly from the mentor's guidance.

Mentors can heighten the protégés' understanding of the overt and covert political dynamics by directly discussing questions such as the following: who has the ultimate power to make important decisions, who is affected by the decisions made, what is the basis of the reward system, what is the history of today's situation, and so on. Discussions focusing on questions such as these should especially point out that competence in handling job responsibilities is not enough to guarantee professional success and/or to qualify for rewards. Newcomers must become aware of how the total system operates. Having done so, new professionals can better determine their own role as well as the consequences of violations or adherence to the system's norms. Thus by stressing to the newcomer the importance of political factors, the mentor may be considered a translator of the political arena.

The process of setting and meeting professional standards of performance may be compared to the traditional advising process. An advisor helps each advisee identify goals and implement a plan to meet them. A new professional needs both the challenge and the support of an advisor who interprets, praises, and offers constructive criticism. Specifically, mentors should help their protégés learn a method of objective evaluation which can be applied to personal activities as well as professional and institutional decision-making. Also the mentor can offer an alternative frame of reference for interpreting the protégé's experience in meeting goals and can offer personally tested, specific suggestions for self and program reform. Ultimately, the mentor's goal is to establish optimal conditions through which a protégé can learn to recognize the characteristics that produce quality in professional performance.

Assisting protégés gain an awareness of the political ropes of an institution and helping them to set and meet professional standards are two ways that mentors actualize the consultant/advisor function. Mentor support and encouragement is also needed by the protégé in learning to maintain a personal sense of self in relation to a professional self image. Young men and women may fall victim to certain psychological inhibitors which undermine their professional achievement. DiSabatino (1976) in an article about women specifies four of the most common inhibitors: fear of failure, low self esteem, ambivalence toward success and role conflict.

Fear of failure often results in dependence upon others and consequently discourages a sense of competence and independence on the part of the new professional. Low self esteem can lead to demeaning one's own accomplishments and having others do so as well. In the case of the third inhibitor, any possible ambivalence that new professionals may have about the shift they must make in their personal lives to accommodate their professional role may also result in diminished professional accomplishment. In other words, the rewards of professional activity may not seem to be worth the sacrifices. The last inhibitor, role conflict, is often exemplified as a conflict resulting from participation by women in "masculine" sex-typed occupations. This conflict may occur between the roles the newcomer adopts, such as the roles of spouse and professional, or between the self and any particular role, for example, ambivalent feelings toward the professional role.

In either case, the conflict between societal expectations and sexual identity may also be an issue for men particularly in the field of education. The result of such role conflict may be a lower quality of professional output. The mentor's role in these situations is to serve as an example of a well-integrated professional, supporting and challenging the protégé to find a balance between personal and work responsibilities.

Sponsor: "I'd Be Happy to Recommend."

The third major function of the mentor is to act as a sponsor or "door opener" using connections with others in field to promote the professional development of the protégé. Job leads, availability of grant monies, personal recommendations all may be exchanged by senior professionals to benefit protégés. Furthermore, mentors can encourage protégés to develop their own contacts with other professionals by attending national conventions, participating in regional activities and collaborating on projects.

In addition, the mentor should recognize that much of the profession's knowledge base exists only within the minds of established professionals. Mentors therefore should be "mental door openers" by exposing newcomers to their own thinking and work as well as that of associates.

In brief then, as sponsors, mentors act as their protégés' advocates, helping them make connection with the profession's informal network of influence and ideas.

Considerations in Choosing a Mentor

Based on the functions of a mentor delineated above, the following factors are important when selecting a mentor. The mentor should provide: an interest in the protégé's professional development; exposure to knowledge and learning; and a similar or shared value system.

Without the mentor's interest in the protégé's life and career, a mentor relationship can hardly be said to exist. To be most helpful, the mentor should be familiar with the protégé's personal goals and talents, and should try to identify aspects of the protégé's development where change should be encouraged. These activities should produce a personal relationship that enhances the protégé's performance and professional development.

A mentor of superior professional achievement with a diverse range of interests and activities offers the greatest potential for learning and development of the protégé. The mentor's publications, involvement in professional organizations on a local or national level and focused career history reflect a high standard of professional competence and attest to skill in handling political dynamics.

The protégé may also want to consider at what cost the potential mentor achieved professional success. In this context, the new professional should examine the mentor's value system and the resulting priorities. If a well-rounded outlook on life and an appreciation of experiences outside the job sphere are important considerations to the newcomer, then perhaps a similar viewpoint should be sought in the mentor as well.

In contrast to the mentor attributes outlined above, Bucher and Stelling (1977) identified two poor mentor candidates. The first, a "charismatic" model, is a globally idealized person who inspires awe and adulation. While new professionals may seek to emulate the charismatic model's traits, the model is perceived as perfect and, as a result, out of reach. The second type, "negative" models, are persons viewed as possessing attributes and behaviors that should be actively avoided. Ironically for the protégé, having a mentor who is too outstanding can be as limiting as an inferior figure. Protégés benefit most from interacting with genuine professionals who admit failure as well as triumph.

While considerations such as personal interest, professional achievement, value orientation and the desirability of a reachable role model are clearly important when selecting a mentor, the significance of the mentor's sex is an issue that arouses some debate. There is no doubt that having a personally committed mentor is an asset. However, problems may arise when a mentor relationship and a romantic component are combined. Such an interest in the protégé may provoke gossip damaging to both the mentor and protégé alike. The protégé must also consider whether a break in the affectional tie would signal the end of professional sponsorship. Furthermore, the protégé may be courting long term dependence on the mentor. Instead of learning, maturing and advancing professionally with a greater sense of self-confidence, the protégé may find progress slowed by maintaining the relationship status quo.

The complexities of male/female dynamics may be minimized or avoided if the newcomer chooses a mentor of the same sex. However, for women, historically and continuing today, suitable female mentors in most profes-sions simply have not been available. This is not to say that newcomers should never choose mentors of the opposite sex. Indeed, one potential contribution of a different gender mentor would be to demonstrate how a strong relationship can be developed and maintained without a romantic, sexual component. Likewise, such a relationship; with an opposite sex mentor may expose the newcomer to the "masculine" or "feminine" point of view pertaining to professional issues and concerns. Thus, in addition to performing the functions of a mentor outlined in the previous sections, an opposite sex mentor may provide the newcomer with a broader understanding of the human perspective.

In the final analysis, perhaps the most important factor to consider in choosing a mentor is a willingness to give personal time and attention. In order for the new professional to benefit from the mentor's knowledge, personal interest and value orientation, the mentor must recognize the relationship by devoting personal energy.

The mentor's efforts on behalf of the protégé may be motivated by a desire to expose the newcomer to the history of the profession as well as to future trends. Or the mentor may want to repay a debt—perhaps to a former mentor—and choose to be active in the education of newcomers. Alternatively, established professionals may wish to alleviate some of the "hard knocks" they had to endure. Whatever the mentor's motivation, the newcomer should look for a mentor who is willing to contribute time and energy to the personal transmission of professional knowledge and expertise.

From the Mentor's Standpoint: Rewards

While obviously benefitting the protégé, the mentor/protégé relationship fulfills personal and professional needs of the mentor.

Personally, the mentor may derive satisfaction in witnessing the protégé advance within the profession. By identifying with the newcomer, the mentor may feel a vicarious sense of pleasure and accomplishment. If the newcomer works directly with the mentor, the relationship may ease the mentor's transition to retirement or reassure the mentor that someone will continue to advance contributions made (Epstein, 1977).

From a professional standpoint, having a protégé or two underscores the mentor's own status and power. The emphasis placed by academic faculty on selecting and advising superior graduate students underscores this advantage. Faculty have long realized the immediate benefits of working with good graduate students as well as the later prestige of being connected with the successful rising young stars. For the woman mentor, having protégés may help to secure her own position as well as increase the possibility that other women are ready to advance into new positions.

Becoming a mentor benefits not only the mentor and the protégé, but serves the profession as well. Erikson's (1959) stage of "generativity vs. stagnation" is significant in this context. In choosing generativity over stagnation, the mentor takes responsibility by caring for other adults and attempting to foster their growth and development. While the mentor relationship may be crucial in triggering and working through this stage, successful resolution in generativity may also increase the probability of a positive outcome in Erikson's last stage: integrity versus despair. As society becomes increasingly older, the fulfillment and satisfaction of the older generation are correspondingly greater concerns. Mentorship is one way in which older workers may realize the significance of their lives and professional contributions.

Summary

Mentors accomplish the mentorship process by functioning as role models, sponsors, and advisors to their protégés. As suggested throughout this article, the young professional reaps substantial benefits from the mentor relationship. Perry (1971) maintains that young people build their conception of themselves from the perceptions that significant others have about them and therefore stresses the importance of collegial behaviors and attitudes.

Mentors serve a particularly important function for aspiring women professionals. Tidball (1973) delineated the positive relationship between sponsorship or role model attention to newcomer achievement. From a different perspective, Epstein (1970) pointed out that in the upper echelons of a profession, evaluation and advancement of aspiring workers can only be accomplished by those already in top positions. Because all too often women are not a part of this elite group, female newcomers are hindered. Mentors also may be helpful in counteracting the effects of "internal inhibitors" or personal ambiguities (DiSabatino, 1976) which may slow a new professional's progress.

The lack of suitable mentors for up-and-coming young professionals, particularly women, can be seen as a dangerously limiting condition for the profession as well as the individuals. Levinson (1976) calls mentorship the "essence of adulthood" and suggests it may be impossible to become a mentor without first having had a mentor. We hope this article will encourage senior student affairs professionals to recognize the personal and professional importance of the mentor relationship and to choose to become actively involved in the process.

While newcomers often come to the attention of their future mentors by virtue of personal recommendations or competent performance, they need not be passive. Using the guidelines suggested here, new professionals may take the initiative to identify and approach potential mentors themselves.

Whether the senior professional or the newcomer makes the first invitation, a conscious commitment to the mentor relationship has enormous potential for mutual environment and benefit. In the long run, the profession, too, is enhanced because the result of the mentorship process, a competent new professional, is the mentor material of the future.

References

Bucher, R. & Steeling, J. G. *Becoming professional*. Beverly Hills: Library of Social Research, Sage Publications, 1977.

DiSabatino, J. Psychological factors inhibiting women's occupational aspirations and vocational choices: Implications for counseling. *Vocational Guidance Quarterly*, September 1976, 43.

Epstein, C. F. Encountering the male establishment: Sex-status limits on women's careers in the professionals. *American Journal of Sociology*, 1970, 75, 965–982.

Erikson, E. H. Identity and the life cycle. *Psychological Issues*, 1959, 1.

Levinson, D. J., Darrow, C., Klein, E., Levinson, M., & McKee, B. Periods in the adult development of men: Ages 18–45. *The Counseling Psychologist*, 1976, 6.

Perry, W. *Intellectual and ethical development in the college years*. New York: Holt, Rinehart, & Winston, Inc., 1970.

Tidball, M. E. Perspective on academic women and affirmative action. *Educational Record*, 1973, 54, 130–135.

White, R. W. *Lives in progress: A study of the natural growth of personality*. Holt, Rinehart, & Winston, 1952.

Toward the Professionalization of Student Affairs

D. Stanley Carpenter, Theodore K. Miller and Roger B. Winston, Jr.

An assessment with recommendations for continued professional growth.

The many various roles played by higher education over the years have included that of socializer for the aristocracy, trainer of the technical expert, educator of the future leader, continuing instructor to the masses, transmitter of the culture, and even parent. Most of these functions as well as many others, are still being performed and have received varying degrees of acceptance over the years. One important area of concern, the intentional development of the total student, has not been systematically emphasized until relatively recently.

Appleton, Briggs, and Rhatigan (1978) suggest that certain faculty and officers of institutions have always had the values and morals of students as a concern, and that this concern is the basis for the practice of student affairs work. Students, administrators, faculty members and the public at large, on the other hand, hold disparate views of the responsibilities inherent in the field of student affairs which promotes somewhat of an identity crisis for many practitioners. In spite of such factors, the growth and development of college students can be influenced most effectively when both the total student and the full institutional and community environment are deliberately considered. Successful student affairs work demands highly skilled, well-trained individuals who are able to conceptualize and apply theory to practice and who seek to communicate and collaborate with all higher education constituencies. There is a pressing need for a well-qualified group of professionals to mediate the various perceived roles of student affairs workers and to take responsibility for defining appropriate methods for systematically facilitating the development of students.

The purpose of this article is to show that the field of student affairs is, more than ever before, an emergent profession with its own distinct theory base and preparation criteria. This will be accomplished through analyzing pertinent literature and using a sociological model of professionalism.

Student Affairs Work as a Profession

The terminology pertinent to student affairs work as a field is a subject of controversy in itself. This paper uses Crookston's (1976) nomenclature, which denotes student affairs as the name of the field, student development as the theory base, and student personnel as an archaic concept entirely. However, many of the sources examined use the term "student personnel work" interchangeably with "student affairs work."

Before broaching the question of professionalism, a discussion concerning definition is appropriate. Berdie (1966, p. 132) stated:

student personnel work is the application in higher education of knowledge and principles derived . . . particularly from psychology, educational psychology, and sociology. . . . The student personnel worker is the behavioral scientist whose subject matter is the student and whose sociopsychological sphere is the college.

Cowley (1964) rejected this scientific concept when he called for recognition of the fact that the one common tie for student affairs workers was that they "served students in various non-curricular ways. In short you [student personnel workers] are student services officers" (p. 67).

Differing from a strict interpretation of either of these points of view, Shaffer (1967, p. 181) notes that institutional actions speak louder than words and that

a major responsibility of student personnel administrators, therefore, is to lead in the initiation and development of programs by which all educational forces in the college community are mobilized to contribute to student growth and development in a unified and coherent way.

More recently, Miller and Prince (1976, p. 3) defined student development practice as "the application of human development concepts in postsecondary settings so that everyone involved can master increasingly complex developmental tasks, achieve self direction and become interdependent." From such alternative views, the divergence and convergence of student-affairs-work theory have emerged. The behavioral scientist and the service technician diverge from traditional academe; the environmental generalist and the student development educator converge with academe in new and creative ways.

The formentioned dissonance in role definition is echoed in the question of professionalism. Dewey (1972) points out that the student affairs field is in trouble and always has been because of a lack of attention to professional preparation, selection for preparation, and a lack of realistic examination of the role of student affairs. Wrenn (1949) applied fairly stringent sociological criteria and found student personnel lacking as a profession. Shoben (1967) attributed this to the fact that the field began as a "point of view." Because of this orientation, the field has been overly concerned with housekeeping details and has remained essentially contentless. Koile (1966) essentially agreed with Shoben that the promise of the Student Personnel Point of View (American Council on Education, 1949) had never been realized, that student affairs had no clear body of knowledge, skills or ethics, and that student affairs as a field was on the fringe of education. In this same vein, Parker (1977) more recently commented on the difficulty of using human development as a theory base because of its breadth.

Perhaps the toughest critic of student affairs professionalism was Penney (1969), who pointed out that the field was over 50 years old which is time enough, in his view, to prove itself. Penney could find no basic literature in the field and pointed to the preoccupation of practitioners, including their literature, with "housekeeping" details and to the lack of exclusivity of student affairs work.

Fortunately, not all related literature is so depressing. A great many writers have offered suggestions to solve the field's problems, or delineated trends which indicate that the difficulties are either subsiding or manageable. As early as 1958, Williamson noted that professional preparation for student affairs work was very complex. He indicated that successful practitioners must not only be good at a specialty area, but should also be conversant with higher education theory and the liberal arts. Williamson insisted that student affairs workers were united in their focus upon the developmental processes of a clear-cut clientele (i.e., the college student) and left little doubt that he considered student personnel work to be an identifiable activity with its own characteristics.

Miller (1967) pointed out the emerging role of the student affairs worker as educator rather than administrator or counselor. The role of this educator lies in the creation of a total learning environment. This role

implies the professionalization of the field. It implies as theoretical framework from which to operate. It further implies that the individuals who carry out the required functions will have experienced a formal and effective academic preparation program which has helped them to assimilate and integrate appropriate knowledge, skills, attitudes, and patterns of behavior necessary for them to successfully implement their educational goals (Miller, 1967, p.124).

Penn (1974) assumed that student affairs was an emergent profession when he called for professional organizations to give shape to preparation programs through concrete criteria. While noting that student affairs work seems not to be a profession (and perhaps should not be), Bloland (1974) made several important points about the field. First, he noted that just as the promotion of human development seemed a rallying point for the American Personnel and Guidance Association's divisions, so perhaps could student development be a basis for student affairs work. Bloland noted that for the field to survive, the professional organizations were going to have to define a content base, become more active on a national and regional basis, and work for public rec- ognition.

Earlier, Trueblood (1966) took a much different position when he attacked three myths about the preparation of student affairs practitioners. First, student affairs workers do not have to be grounded in the liberal arts. Second, the need for specialized knowledge confuses degree preparation with inservice training and properly written job descriptions. And, third, the idea that a liberally-educated person could "pick up" enough to be a good student affairs worker was only true at the bottom or paraprofessional levels of the field. Trueblood called for thorough, professional preparation for student affairs work distinct from that of other disciplines.

Nygreen (1968) commented that student affairs work had aspects of an office, a profession, and a calling.

We can distinguish trends toward increasing professionalization in the emphasis upon a high degree of generalized an dsystematic knowledge, in a primary orientation toward community interest rather than individual self-interest, and in the attempts through voluntary associations and work socialization to develop a higher degree of self-control of behavior. We recognize some of the needs of the institutional setting to provide more of a bureaucratic pattern of coordination of services. We are able to distinguish some of the useful effects of the ideology of service to clients in controlling the bureaucratic effects of an office, a profession, and a calling. The ensuing conflicts cannot be avoided, but recognizing them should help us to encompass them more effectively (p. 287).

This statement constituted a fairly significant endorsement of the profes- sionalism of student affairs work when considered in light of two further facts. First, Pavalko (1972) has since delineated some of the problems of professionals in bureaucracies, and they are remarkably similar to Nygreen's concerns for student affairs workers (i.e., institution vs. client needs). Second, most "profession" theorists identify commitment in the sense of a "calling" as an attribute of professionalism. Hence, Nygreen's (1968) statement about student affairs work can be interpreted as supporting the contention that student affairs work has many of the characteristics of a profession.

The most telling arguments against the professionalism of student affairs work have been the lack of consensus on theory base, training standards, the role of student affairs, and, most importantly, the apparent unwillingness of the field to deal with these problems in substantive ways. Our contention is that the critics were (and are) incorrect. One has only to read Miller and Prince (1976), Crookston (1976) and Rogers (1980) for three examples of fundamental literature concerning the field's emerging developmental theory base. Professional preparation has been discussed at length in monographs (Knock, 1977) and in the journals, as a trend toward the establishment of professional standards and guidelines gains strength (Knock, 1976; Miller, 1980; Penn, 1974). In short, student affairs work is moving ever closer to the profession end of the profession-occupation continuum (Pavalko, 1971), and deserves to be called an emerging profession.

A Sociological Perspective of Student Affairs Work

In view of the differences of opinion concerning student affairs as a profession, it is instructive to analyze the field in a systematic way. The study of professionalism has become the province primarily of the field of sociology, especially occupational sociology. One of the most noted scholars in this field, Wilensky (1964) put forth a model describing the professionalization process of any given field as including five basic steps.

First, Wilensky said, a group of people begin doing a necessary job full time. The history of student affairs work has been well documented and indicates that there has existed a need for non-teaching faculty and staff members in higher education. The roots of the field include counseling, administration, activities coordination, discipline, housing, financial aid, health, and other functions related to the educational and developmental needs of students. The need for such work continues and, in fact, has become more pressing in view of the growing emphasis upon the total student. Another factor indicating the need for individuals concerned with students' development is the growing complexity of higher education. Institutions of all types are being asked to do more things for more and different types of people. Fitzgerald (1978) noted that there would continue to be a place in higher education for human service workers despite decreasing enrollments and resulting retrenchment.

The second step in the Wilensky model is the emergency of training programs with the result that a cadre of professionally educated practitioners become teachers rather than service technicians. A recent review cited 72 such programs and noted that professional preparation in student affairs appears well-established in many graduate schools (Miller & Carpenter, 1980). Additionally, if position vacancy announcements which indicate professional training as an employment criterion are any indication, the efficacy of hiring professionally educated people for positions in the field is becoming increasingly accepted.

The formation of professional associations is a third step in professionalization. The emergence of the American College Personnel Association (ACPA), the National Association of Student Personnel Administrators (NASPA), and the National Association for Women Deans, Administrators, and Counselors (NAWDAC), as well a a multitude of more specialized associations, is clear evidence that this is occurring in the field of student affairs. These professional associations help identify the core functions of a profession and delegate appropriate tasks to others. Examples of these are the concern with defining the proper role of paraprofessionals and activity related to establishing professional standards and guidelines for the field. Professional associations also preside over internal conflicts such as that between old-line practitioners who learned their trade on the job and the formally educated "young Turks." In student affairs, this conflict is exemplified by the differences between those who proclaim student development as a new theoretical foundation for practice and those who profess that the field has been involved in student development for years under other names.

Professional associations also work to establish their "turf" through competition with "neighboring" associations. This leads to the fourth step, that of political maneuvering to gain legal or practical sanctions against unauthorized practitioners (outsiders). In student affairs, the current trend toward the development of professional standards for practice and preparation falls into this category. Miller (1980) reporting to the ACPA membership, outlined a plan for developing such standards through the Council for the Advancement of Standards for Student Services/Development Programs (CASSS/DP). The CASSS/DP is composed of representatives of the major student affairs generalist associations (ACPA, NASPA, and NAWDAC) as well as a host of more specialty-oriented organizations. The standards produced by interassociation task forces and endorsed by CASSS/DP are intended for widespread use by higher education institutions and their accrediting agencies, thus further defining student affairs work as a profession.

Finally, the fifth step is the development and adoption of an enforceable and enforced code of ethics. Real progress in this area has been slow but there exists an awakening interest. Winston (1980) as chairperson of one association's task force has created a "working draft" of a "Statement of Ethical and professional Standards." It seems likely that a comprehensive statement of standards will be adopted by ACPA by 1981. Presumably, the Council for the Advancement of Standards for Student Services/Development Programs (CASSS/DP) will consider general ethical standards as a part of its work as well.

Using Wilensky's (1964) criteria, the field of student affairs has made great progress in the first three areas, a beginning in the fourth, while the fifth seems still to be in a very elementary stage. More cohesiveness appears, essential among the various professional associations if the field is to meaningfully accomplish steps four and five.

Significant obstacles to the comprehensive professionalization of student affairs remain. Many questions and issues need to be answered and resolved in the near future. Three important questions are:

1. Where do practitioner's loyalties and commitments really lie? In other words, are student affairs workers most concerned with self-interest, with institutional/bureaucratic expectations, or with their college student clientele?

2. Can someone else do the job just as well as professionally trained student affairs practitioners? This involves a threat to exclusive jurisdiction. It also reflects upon the solidarity of practitioners as to the essential skills and competencies required for practitioners.

3. Is the theory base so broad as to be indefinable and/or part of another profession(s), or is it so narrow and precise that it can be easily and quickly learned by nearly anyone?

Answers to questions such as these will come only from the united and collaborative efforts of concerned professionals. Until these and other issues are systemically examined and analyzed, questions will continue to be raised regarding the extent to which student affairs reflects a consistent, coherent field of endeavor.

Conclusions and Recommendations

Certain professional activities seem indicated by the literature and analysis herein.

1. The three major generalist professional associations (NASPA, NAW-DAC, and ACPA) need to increase their efforts to collaborate on study and action concerning professional issues. The formation of the Council for the Advancement of Standards for Student Services/Development Programs (CASSS/DP) is an important new beginning.

2. Efforts toward a workable Code of Ethics must be intensified. This is crucial if student affairs work is to take its place among the pantheon of respected professions. To accept and incorporate ethical codes from other professions is not acceptable.

3. More emphasis must be placed upon evaluation and research in order to more precisely ascertain the impact upon the development of students brought about by the activities of student affairs practitioners and programs.

4. Student affairs practitioners must continually strive to conduct themselves in a competent, professional manner. Only thus will they gain acknowledgement as integral and essential components of the higher education community.

Greenwood (1957), one of the pioneers identifying the attributes of professions, once analyzed social work and concluded that as practiced that field coincided with professional criteria so closely that it was in fact a profession. It is argued here that student affairs is a profession also "at least in practice. . . if not in theory . . ." (Trueblood, 1966, p. 80). Student affairs work, then, deserves recognition as an emerging profession. The field must strive to maintain and continue its progress. Those of us employed therein must reflect the essence of professional dignity in all that we do. We must never forget that others judge the field of student affairs by observing the behavior of each of us as individuals.

References

American Council on Education. The student personnel point of view. Washington: The Council, 1949.

Appleton, J. R., Briggs, C. M., and Rhatigan, J. J. *Pieces of eight*. Portland, Oregon: NASPA Institute of Research and Development, 1978.

Berdie, R. Student personnel work: Definition and redefinition. *Journal of College Student Personnel*, 1966, 7, 405–409.

Bloland, P. A. Professionalism and the professional organization. In T. F. Harrington (Ed.), *Student personnel work in urban colleges*. New York: Intext Educational Publishing, 1974.

Cowley, W. H. Reflections of a troublesome but hopeful Rip Van Winkle. *Journal of College Student Personnel*, 1964, 6, 66–73.

Crookston, B. B. Student personnel—All hail and farewell. *Personnel and Guidance Journal*, 1976, 55, 20–29.

Dewey, M. D. The student personnel worker of 1980. *Journal of the National Association of Women Deans, Administrators, and Counselors*, 1972, 35, 29–64.

Fitzgerald, L. E. Dedication. In J. Eddy (Ed.), *College student personnel, development, administration and counseling*. Washington: University Press of America, 1978.

Greenwood, E. Attributes of a profession. *Social Work*, 1957, 2, 45–55.

Knock, G. H. (Ed.). *Perspectives on the preparation of student affairs professionals*. Student Personnel Series No. 22. Washington, D.C.: American College Personnel Association, 1977.

Koile, E. A. Student affairs: Forever the bridesmaid. *NASPA Journal*, 1966, 4, 65–72.

Miller, T. K. College student personnel preparation: Present perspective and future directions. *NASPA Journal*, 1967, 4, 171–178.

Miller, T. K., and Carpenter, S. D. Professional preparation for today and tomorrow. In D. G. Creamer (Ed.), *Student development in higher education: Theories, practices & future directions*. Washington, D.C. American College Personnel Association, 1980.

Miller, T. K. and Prince, J. S. *The future of student affairs: A guide to student development for tomorrow's higher education*. San Francisco: Jossey-Bass Publishers, 1976.

Nygreen, G. T. Professional status for student personnel administrators. *NASPA Journal*, 1968, 5, 283–291.

Parker, C. A. On modeling reality. *Journal of College Student Personnel*, 1977, 18, 420–425.

Pavalko, R. M. (Ed.). *Sociological perspectives on occupations*. Itasca, Illinois: F. E Peacock Publishers, Inc., 1972.

Penn, J. R. Professional accreditation: A key to excellence. *Journal of College Student Personnel*, 1974, 15, 257–259.

Penney, J. F. Student personnel work: A professional stillborn. *Personnel and Guidance Journal*, 1969, 47, 958–962.

Rodgers, R. F. Theories underlying student development. In D. G. Creamer (Ed.), *Student development in higher education: Theories, practices, and future directions*. Washington, D.C.: American College Personnel Association, 1980.

Shaffer, R. H. Meeting the challenge of today's students. *NASPA Journal*, 1967, 4, 4–6.

Shoben, E. J. Psychology and student personnel work. *Journal of College Student Personnel*, 1867, 8, 129–244.

Trueblood, D. L. The educational preparation of the college student personnel leader of the future. In G. J. Klopf (Ed.), *College student personnel in the years ahead*, Washington, D.C.: American Personnel and Guidance Association, 1966.

Wilensky, H. L. The professionalization of everyone. *American Journal of Sociology*, 1964, 70, 137–158.

Williamson, E. G. Professional preparation of student personnel workers. *School and Society*, 1958, 86, 21–23.

Wrenn, G. G. An appraisal of the professional status of student personnel workers, Part I. In E. G. Williamson (Ed.), *Trends in student personnel work*. Minneapolis: University of Minneapolis Press, 1949, 264–280.

Reference notes

Miller, T. K. Agenda for the eighties: Professionalism challenges and opportunities for the American College personnel Association. (Report to the ACPA Business Meeting). Mimeograph. 1980.

Winston, R. B., Jr. Statement of ethical and professional standards (Third Draft). Mimeograph, 1980.

Student Affairs Progress Toward Professionalism: Recommendations for Action Part 1

Louis C. Stamatakos

Using the same basic approach and traditional criteria as Wrenn and Darley in their analysis of 1949, the author explores in this article the progress of student affairs work during the ensuing years in fulfilling the criteria for professionalism and concludes that college student affairs is still "enroute to professional status." Recommendations for assertive and cooperative action by the major professional organizations are presented.

Underlying our daily endeavors within the broad field of student affairs work is a basic assumption critically important to how we perceive ourselves and our colleagues, carry out our responsibilities, and determine the quality of our programs. The assumption is: As individuals and as groups, we believe ourselves to be "professionals," and we believe our calling and colleagues with whom we work and with whom we have established formal organizations to be "professional."

As manifested throughout much of our literature, association programming, and development of our graduate professional preparation programs, the assumption of accepted or arrived-at-professionalism is not only implied but also boldly asserted. During recent years we have witnessed a number of direct and indirect references about our "professionalism" in our literature (Greenleaf, 1968; Hanson, 1976; Humphries, 1977; Knock, 1977; Koller, 1978; Mestenhauser, 1976; Penn, 1974; Sherburne, 1970: Stamatakos & Oliaro, 1972; Truitt & Gross, 1970). In our literature and in convention and workshop speeches throughout the nation, references to professional behavior, standards, competencies, performance, and achievement are abundant. With rare exception, writers and speakers exhort student affairs professionals to master and practice those behaviors that help us professionally achieve our common goals.

Occasionally, we have witnessed an iconoclast among us who dared challenge this assumption. Penny (1969), in his near infamous "College Student Personnel: A Professional Stillborn," developed a strong case against our presumption of professionalism by soundly criticizing our literature as well as our point of view. Thirty years ago, Wrenn and Darley (1949), in a systematic analysis using eight traditional criteria, found that student affairs had made little progress toward (a) the application of standards of selection and training, (b) the definition of job titles and functions, (c) the self-imposition of standards of admission and performance, and (d) the legal recognition of the vocation. The profession did get fairly good marks on (e) the development of a professional consciousness and of professional groups, (f) the performance of a socially needed function, (g) the possession of a body of specialized knowledge and skills, and (h) high moral and personal integrity in lieu of the development of a code of ethics.

Another review three decades later, and using the same review criteria of professionalism (Wrenn & Darley, 1949), seems to be in order to determine if, during these ensuing years, student affairs has taken the steps necessary to achieve the status of profession. I believe that when we face ourselves objectively, we may be forced to conclude that speeches and journal articles notwithstanding, we still do not truly "qualify" as a profession. If it is found that we do not "formally" qualify as a profession but are of the belief that achieving professional status is desirable and attainable, it would seem to be appropriate to recognize our shortcomings and deal with them forthrightly. I have chosen to follow the basic approach and methodology used by Wrenn and Darley (1949)—that of examining the more recent and available literature in student affairs pertinent to the subject, reflecting on the knowledge and experiences of student affairs colleagues as well as that of my own as a former practitioner presently teaching in a professional preparation program.

The Self-Imposition of Standards of Admission and Performance[1]

Darley (Wrenn & Darley, 1949) chose to discuss "selection into the field" under the criterion heading, "The Self-Imposition of Standards of Admission and Performance" (p. 28). Wrenn also included a discussion on the topic of "Standards of Admission" when he analyzed the criterion, "The Application of Standards of Selection and Training" (p. 268). For the purpose of my analysis, "standards of admission" shall deal with the skills and competencies student affairs professionals are expected to and actually possess at the time they enter the practice of the profession.

Hanson's report to the American College Personnel Association's Executive Council revealed that among his survey of ACPA's leaders, 70% judged 18 basic skills and competencies to be very important, and a total of 43 skills and competencies were judged to be very important by more than 53% of the leaders (Hanson, 1976). Minetti agreed on as being very important to the professional preparation of student personnel workers. In a recently completed doctoral dissertation study, Ostroth (1979) revealed that 36 basic competencies (derived from Minetti, 1977) were perceived to be at least "moderately important" by respondents responsible for hiring entry-level staff.

Although there are indications that employers are seeking more professionally prepared staff, as evidenced in job descriptions circulated nationally each year, knowledge of the actual qualifications (possession of agreed on skills and/or competencies) of the applicants who are hired puts into serious question the fulfillment of this criterion of professionalism.

In certain highly specialized areas (e.g., health services and counseling), staff hired will most likely have met the preparation standards of their specialties. Insofar as I am able to determine, there is no published research evidence to support the notions that, generally, (a) employers consciously attempt to determine if applicants for positions in areas other than health and counseling actually possess the general skills and competencies advocated and expected by the profession, (b) those hired for student affairs positions, do, in fact, possess the general skills and competencies that characterize positions sought or filled, or (3) professional preparation programs educate specifically and adequately for the development of agreed upon skills and competencies (Brown, 1972; Council of Student Personnel Associations, 1975; Newton & Hellenga, 1974; Newton & Richardson, 1976: Parker, 1971; Rentz, 1976).

Excluding the 95 formal preparation programs that affect more than 1,000 people planning entry into the field each year (Greer, Blaesser, Herron, & Horley, 1978), I, in consultation with colleagues, estimate that concurrently another 1,200 or so "paraprofessionals" assume a wide variety of student affairs positions—making their entry into the field as crossovers from faculty and staff positions in higher, elementary and secondary education, business, industry, the military, clergy, and so forth. Although many of these paraprofessionals (possibly composing half of all practitioners) may have had previous training and experiences in areas somewhat similar or related to college student affairs, my experience and observation over 30 years reveals that once on the job, most of these staff members will not undergo substantive in-service training and will not undertake formalized and specialized professional preparation in student affairs graduate programs. Given a quality range from excellent to inadequate formal graduate preparation for the remaining half, one can understand the tremendous eclecticism, inconsistency, and wide variance of philosophies and practices that characterize the profession of student affairs. (Interestingly, our profession has been so characterized from its beginnings [Mueller, 1961].)

Many articles have been written on the topic of accountability in and evaluation guidelines for the administration of student affairs (Bishop, 1974; Boylan, 1973; Carranza, 1978; Casse, Gillis & Mueller, 1974; Chamberlain, 1978; Casse, Gillis & Mueller, 1974; Chamberlain, 1978; Freeman, Nudd & O'Donnel, 1972, Harpel, 1975; Levy & Schreck, 1975; Nordvall, 1977; Peterson, 1975; Wallenfeldt, 1976.) To my knowledge only one article, however, has been published in recent years in a major student affairs journal on the specific topic of a unit's actual exercise of accountability for maintaining standards of performance (Fisher & Howell, 1972). No article in recent memory has dealt with actual research on the profession's mainte-nance of standards performance. It might be safely assumed that in the absence of such evidence, standards maintenance may exist and have been alluded to (Knott, 1977), but its exercise, intensity, and quality probably varies widely from institution to institution.

Examination of this first criterion leads to the conclusion that it is not, in any great measure, satisfied.

Recommendations

Practitioners and preparation program faculty, through the direct and long-term co-sponsorship of the profession's major and specialty associations, need to conduct joint research to determine needed and desired skills and competencies for positions at all levels in the profession (Domeier, 1977). Once agreed on through the medium of association-sponsored conferences, a vigorous and sustained dissemination and promulgation campaign should be undertaken to effect their acceptance and exercise in hiring practicing performance evaluation and as instructional objectives professional prepara-tion programs (Knock, 1979).

Through similar interassociation cosponsorship, in-service, staff develop-ment training models should be created specific to skills-building and compe-tency development relative to specialty areas within typical student affairs divisions (Beeler & Penn, 1978; Stamatakos & Oliaro, 1972; Truitt & Gross, 1966). Executive and supervisory staff will need to be prepared for their training roles and aided in their efforts in providing incentives for participa-tion in staff development activities and in pursuing professional graduate studies. Such aid could include various forms of certification, recognition, fellowships, and cost-sharing. (Not to be overlooked is the interest shown in these areas by various philanthropic foundations during recent years.)

There is every reason to believe that as we continue to insist on the rigorous application of specific standards of admission, more qualified applicants will be prepared by our professional preparation programs, and as we insist on and support continued staff development, staff will respond to our expectations of improved performance, especially as such activities lead to recognition forms of certification, job enrichment, and increased responsibility. Business management literature of recent years reveals the value and desired outcomes result from creating and maintaining performance standards and review procedures (Blackburn & Clark, 1975; McGregor, 1966; Miner, 1969; Reider, 1973). It behooves student affairs administrators and staff at all levels to develop and impose standards of performance on themselves, if for no other reason than to know what they are supposed to be doing and how well they are performing. Not exempt from such reasonable professional expectations are directors and faculty of professional preparation programs. Maintaining standards of performance is not a matter of choice; it is mandatory for improving the quality of our work as well as for purposes of achieving professional status.

Defining Jobs and Titles

Wrenn (Wrenn & Darley, 1949) believed that job functions and titles were in need of greater definition and standardization "to make clear that specific knowledges and skills are involved in the job and to what extent such jobs can be performed by a person with general academic qualifications as opposed to specially qualified and trained individuals" (p. 274). At the time of his observations, the profession "sported 216 different job titles" (p. 724).

Though somewhat restricted and dated, most published literature on this topic provides some direction for discussion and conjecture. Hershenson (1970), Rhatigan & Hoyt (1970), and Libby (1974) focused their attention on chief student personnel officer's "functions," "functional responsibilities," and "functional arrangements." On the other hand, Sheldin (1965), Ayers, Tripp, and Russel (1966), Dutton (1969), O'Banion (1970), and Cochran (1977) examined "roles" of chief student personnel officers (CPOs) and deans of women. For the most part, these investigators and writers described patterns of roles and functions manifested or assumed by CPOs representing a cross-section of institutions. In the absence of any professional association's effort to define jobs, agree on titles, and promulgate those agreements nationwide, it seems that by accident rather than design that job functions are becoming more similar among CPOs of like institutions (Crookston, 1974).

On closer examination, however, one finds a troublesome disparity between titles and actual functions between CPOs at large as compared with small institutions. One will find vice-chancellors, vice-presidents, deans, and directors of students, student life, student affairs, student development, student services, and student personnel (Crookston, 1974), whose responsibilities will range from total responsibility for most all traditional student affairs functions to only a select few, or extend to include intercollegiate athletics, alumni affairs, institutional budget, vehicular traffic, campus safety, and physical plant management. Although Rhatigan and Hoyt (1970) found that on large campuses (1,000 or more) there was a fairly high degree of standardization of CPOs functions, their study did not include the hundreds of small institutions where one will often find the CPO also coaching, teaching, recruiting, testing, and directing placement services.

A search of the published journal literature revealed no study of recent years on "middle management positions in student affairs. The last major study that included such positions was conducted by Ayers, Tripp, and Russell (1966) whose findings are too limited for this analysis. One recently completed nationwide study that investigated procedures and criteria used in selecting "entry-level" student affairs professionals, revealed considerable standardization of titles and descriptions at that level (Ostroth, 1979).

In view of the preceding discussion, it can be reasonably concluded that although there has not been an actual nationwide, professionally sponsored activity directed toward defining jobs and titles, there has been more than incremental movement toward consistency of titles and job definition. It is quite clear, however, that as long as the profession does not directly confront and deal with the matter of title and job definition, and as long as a wide variance exists among type, size, administrative structures, and styles of collegiate institutions, this criterion may never be totally satisfied.

Recommendations

Definition and standardization of jobs and titles has been left to chance and evolution in student affairs. If jobs and titles are to ever possess the validity and credibility that professionalism requires, our professional associates will first have to initiate systematic studies that will determine and describe "that which is" at all levels of professional practice and across all types of institutions. Once such knowledge becomes available, the second step, developing standardization of titles and job functions (agreeing on what ought to be), could be easily accomplished through jointly sponsored conferences specific to this purpose. Subsequently, well-orchestrated programs of dissemination and promulgation of agreed on job definitions and title specifications will have to be initiated and sustained until such time that a high degree of consistency becomes evident in actual practice.

The studies suggested here need not be long-term or complex because scientific sampling methods are available and appropriate. An abundance of research talent is readily available within dozens of doctoral-level preparation programs throughout the country. The sponsorship, coordination and financial support for such studies should be the mutually shared responsibility of our associations.

The Possession of Specialized Knowledge and Skills[2]

In 1949, Wrenn asserted, "The kind or amount of specialized knowledge or skill possessed by members of a profession is actually less significant than the combination in which these knowledges and skill are possessed. This combination is what enables a professional worker to apply his knowledges and skills to a given problem" (p. 275). Wrenn described a wide range of specialized knowledges and skills (nearly all counselor skill related) as being appropriate and needed in student affairs work, and noted that "many well-trained personnel workers at the Ph.D. level have this combination of knowledges and skills" and that our "vocation does have a specialized body of knowledges and skills" (p. 276).

At the time of the Wrenn-Darley analysis, student affairs work was in its "life adjustment" stage of evolution and the recommended and most available preparation program for job entry was "counseling and guidance educator" at the master's and doctoral levels. During the ensuing 30 years, a dramatic evolution from "life adjustment" (counseling emphasis) to "student development" has taken place. Student development along with the contemporary specializations of financial aids, career development and placement, developmental education services, residence hall programming, minority, women's and handicapped services, intramural administration, commuter services, and older student programs has prompted serious questioning of the appropriateness and validity of the centrality of a counseling emphasis in the majority of preparation programs. Faculty of a number of preparation programs have determined that graduate students must have knowledge and skills in areas of organizational and human development and administration more so than in counseling. In addition, both counseling-oriented and administration-oriented programs are also available (Rodgers, 1977). Thus, the commonality of possessed skills and knowledge in the profession seems doubtful.

With due respect to Wrenn, I contend that suggesting what knowledge and skills need to be manifested by the "compleate" student affairs professional, and the actual existence and effective combination of these skills and knowledge within the general population of the profession, are two different things. The number of student affairs workers possessing the doctoral degree is at question as is the proportion of this number possessing the "right" combination of understanding and knowledge and able to effectively apply such to given situations. These are important distinctions when one considers the variance in preparation program emphasis and the fact that the most typical degree in our field is the master's, even among chief student affairs officers. To my knowledge, no evidence exists to support the notion that among master's degree holders across all position levels in student affairs, the great majority are in counseling, student affairs or, for that matter, in a related behavioral science area.

The literature advanced by student affairs professionals and professional associations and used in instructional contexts is expected to reflect specialized knowledge and to aid both future and current student affairs workers in developing the unique skills needed for professional practice. Penney (1969) has maintained that such a body of literature has not been developed to any great extent. The writer's exposure to and use of the literature over the past 30 years had led him to acknowledge the validity of Penny's assertion. Most of our basic literature is an interesting mixture of borrowed educational philosophy, psychology, sociology, anthropology, and organizational and administrative theory. Because student affairs is admittedly an applied field, this "borrowed mixture" is not totally undesirable.

What is most compunctious, however, is that most of the literature written specifically for the student affairs profession over the past two decades is "descriptive" of what have been and currently are the functions and practices of the profession . . . with the exception of Mueller's (1961) philosophically sound text, *Student Personnel Work in Higher Education*; Brown's (1972) monograph, *Tomorrow's Higher Education*; the recent book by Miller and Prince, *The Future of Student Affairs* (1976); Parker's *Encouraging the Development of College Students* (1978); portions of Eddy's *College Student Personnel Development, Administration, and Counseling* (1977); and Packwood's *College Student Personnel Services* (1977). Descriptive literature does little other than to orient a reader to what is. It does not teach skills and foster depth of understanding, nor does it, in most instances, direct the reader toward what should be exemplary performance and practice in the field.

For depth of understanding, philosophical direction, and basic knowledge, we have had to turn to the literature of other professions and near-professions such as those mentioned earlier. Acknowledging Arbuckle (1953), Lloyd-Jones and smith (1954), Wrenn (1951), Williamson (1961), and Mueller (1961), whose writings dealt substantively with philosophy, rationales, objectives, and controversy, and taking into consideration the optimism of Reilley and Cauthen (1976), we are still far from having achieved a decent modicum of specialized knowledge and skill. It is reasonable to conclude that given the schism that continues to exist between those who favor administration, or counseling, or developmentalism as the basis of student affairs practice, existing literature as well as current knowledge and skills will continue to remain relatively superficial, eclectic, inconsistent, and lacking in professional distinction.

Implications

Approaches to responding to our professional weaknesses in these two areas have been many and varied. Some investigators have studied practitioners to determine what they do and what knowledge and skills they need to do their jobs well. Subsequently, courses are structured and literature is developed or borrowed for teaching purposes and for sponsoring workshop and conference programs that show-and-tell people how to do it. This approach has been somewhat characteristic of student affairs work for more than a half century, and the net result has been found wanting.

Another approach has been to describe certain desired outcomes that characterize the profession's practice in certain areas, such as residence hall life, student activities, counseling, and then develop specialized literature, courses, practica, and association-sponsored programs particular to the areas. This approach has been dependent on the quantity and quality of leadership within the areas and, all too often, such specialization has led to fragmentation of professional perceptions and practice.

Others have sought to write comprehensive pieces (e.g., monographs, books) intending to focus the profession's attention upon basic constructs that need to be known and practiced in the profession. These efforts too have fallen short, not so much because of their quality but, generally, because of the practitioner's refusal to read, accept, learn, and incorporate their contents in practice.

On the whole, only a miniscule amount of the profession's literature has been a result of a deliberate and systematic research-based attempt to respond to the need for basic constructs, specific knowledge and its application in the work setting. With the exception of Brown's monograph, (Brown, 1972)

Miller and Prince's *The Future of Student Affairs* (Miller & Prince, 1976), our professional associations have not deliberately, individually, or collectively sponsored or commissioned (in a well-thought-through, comprehensive, and systematic manner) compendia of literature directly applicable to fulfilling the profession's need for basic specialized knowledge and skills.

A task force of the most respected thinkers of our profession should be commissioned by a consortium of our professional associations to determine with a high degree of specificity the basic as well as specialized knowledge needed by the profession. Upon receipt of the commission's report, the association consortium should create and finance the mechanisms and human resources necessary for the intentional development, publication, and dissemination of that knowledge. Much of the basic literature has been in published forms for many years but not readily available (out of print or scattered in books, pamphlets, brochures, journals), and needs only to be consolidated in convenient and relatively inexpensive forms.

As a case in point, the Student Personnel Point of View (SPPV) (American Council on Education, 1949) is the basic philosophical foundation upon which our activities and programs are predicated. Yet, most professionals with whom I have spoken during the past two decades have never seen the entire statement, have only a vague recollection of its basic assumptions and objectives, and, for all practical purposes do not consider its basic tenents in structuring their activities and programs. And, most importantly, the SPPV has not appeared in its entirety in the basic published literature of the profession in 30 years.

Skills-building workshops have revealed serious deficiencies among professionally prepared and paraprofessionals. The approach advocated above could serve well in the development of compendia of general and specialized skills, and including examples of instructional and experiential activities appropriate to skills development (e.g., *Preparation of Guidance Associates and Professional Counselors within the Framework of a Competency-Based Program* (1973). This effort should also include formats and instructional modes appropriate to professional preparation programs, in-service staff development, workshops, conferences, and conventions.

References

American Council on Education. *The student personnel point of view.* Washington, D.C.: Author, 1949.

Arbuckle, D. S. *Student personnel services in higher education.* New York: McGraw-Hill, 1953.

Ayers, A. R.; Tripp, P.A.; & Russell, J.S. *Student services administration in higher education.* Washington, D.C.: U.S. Department of Health, Education and Welfare, 1966. (Superintendent of Documents Catalog No.FS5.253:53026).

Beeler, K. D., & Penn, J. R. A *handbook on staff development in student affairs.* Corvallis: Oregon State University Book Stores, Inc., 1978.

Bishop, J. B. Some guidelines for the development of accountability systems. *NASPA Journal,* 1975, *12,* 190–194.

Blackburn, R. T., & Clark, M. J. Assessment of faculty performance: Some correlates between administrator, colleague student and self-ratings. *Sociology of Education,* 1975, *48,* 242–56.

Boylan, H. R. Approaching accountability: Some steps along the way. *NASPA Journal,* 1973, 10, 322–327.

Brown, R. D. *Student development in tomorrow's higher education: A return to the academy* (Student Personnel Series No.16). Washington, D.C.: American College Personnel Association, 1972.

Carranza, E. Guidelines for client evaluation of student services programs. *NASPA Journal,* 1978, *15,* 25–30.

Casse, R. M., Jr.; Gillis, A. L.; & Muller, J. Student services accountability utilizing a data information system. *NASPA Journal,* 1974, *12,* 36–43.

Chamberlain, P. C. The new management tools: Problems and potential. NASPA Journal, 1975, *12,* 171–178.

Cochran, J. Redefining a traditional personnel position. *NASPA Journal,* 1977, *15,* 58–60.

Council of Student Personnel Associations in Higher Education. Student development services in post secondary education. The Council, 1975. (Available from Chairperson, College Student Personnel Department, School of Education, Bowling Green State University, Bowling Green, Ohio).

Counselor Education Division, North Texas State University. *Preparation of guidance associates and professional counselors within the framework of a competency-based program.* Washington, D.C.: American Personnel and Guidance Association, 1973.

Crookston, B. B. The nomenclature dilemma: Titles of principal student affairs officers at NASPA institutions. *NASPA Journal,* 1974, 11, 3–6.

Domeier, P. E. A study to examine the training of student affairs administrators for specified competency tasks. (Doctoral dissertation, Michigan State University, 1977), *Dissertation Abstracts International,* 1977, 38. (University Microfilms No. 777–25–234).

Dutton, T. B. *Research needs and priorities in student personnel work: A position paper.* Portland, Oregon. National Association of Student Personnel Administrators, 1968, 5pp. (Mimeograph)

Eddy, J. *College student personnel development, administration and counseling.* Washington, D.C.: University of America Press, 1977.

Fisher, M. B. & Howell, J. H. Evaluation and accountability? *NASPA Journal,* 1972, 10, 118–23.

Freeman, J.: Nudd, T. R.: O'Donnell, T. A quality control program for student personnel services, *NASPA Journal*, 1972, 9, 279–82.

Greenleaf, E. A. How others see us. *Journal of College Student Personnel*, 1968, 9, 225–231.

Greer, R. M.: Blaesett, W. S.: Herron, R. D.: & Horle, R. F. College student personnel graduate placement. *Journal of College Student Personnel*, 1978, 19, 342–48.

Hanson, G. R. *Identifying student development staff competencies and skills* (ACPA professional skills and competencies identification progress report). Report to the American College Personnel Association Executive Committee. Midyear meeting. Chicago, Illinois, 1975. (Mimeograph)

Harpel, R. L. Accountability: Current demands on student personnel program. *NASPA Journal*, 1975, 12, 144–57.

Hershenson, D. B. A functional organization of college student personnel services. *NASPA Journal*, 1970, 8, 35–38.

Humphries, J. W. Student personnel professionals: Is there a future? *Educational Record*, 1977. 58, 59–65.

Knock, G. H . The importance of a continuing dialogue between "those who do" and "those that teach." *NASPA Zephyr* (NASPA Region IV-East). 1979, 4, 1–2.

Knott, E. J. Some perspectives on carts and horses in student development. *Journal of College Student Personnel*, 1977, 18. 434–44.

Koller, S. J. *A descriptive analysis of the professional and research orientations of the college student personnel graduate students, graduates and faculty/administrators at the University of Wisconsin-LaCrosse*, 1978. Master's thesis, College of Education, University of Wisconsin, La Cross, 1978.

Levy, S. R. & Schreck, T. C. Management effectiveness: An introduction. *NASPA Journal*. 1975. 12, 142–43.

Libby, G. W., Jr. Functions of chief student personnel officers in selected colleges. *NASPA Journal*, 1975, 11, 7–10.

Lloyd-Jones, E. & Smith, M. R. (Eds.). *Student personnel work as deeper teaching*. New York: Harper Bros., 1954.

McGregor, D. *Leadership and motivation*. Cambridge, Mass.: MIT Press, 1966.

Miller, T. K. & Prince, J. S *The future of student affairs*. San Francisco: Jossey-Bass, 1976.

Miner, J. B. *Personnel and industrial relations:* New York: Macmillan, 1968.

Minetti, R. H. An analytical description of the relationship between the academic training and assistantship experiences of master's degree programs in student personnel administration (Doctoral dissertation, Michigan State University, 1978). *Dissertation Abstracts International*, 1977, 38, 64–66. (University Microfilms No. 780, 3534).

Mestenhauser, J. A. Are we researching for identity as professionals, semi-professionals or dedicated good guys? *National Association for Foreign Student Affairs Newsletter*. 1976, 27, 9–10.

Mueller, K. H. *Student personnel work in higher education*. Boston: Houghton Mifflin, 1964.

Newton, F. B. & Hellengon, G. Assessment of learning and process objectives in a student personnel training program. *Journal of College Student Personnel,* 1976, 15, 426–30.

Newton, F. B. & Richardson, R. L. Expected entry level competencies of student personnel workers. *Journal of College Student Personnel,* 1976, 17, 426–30.

Nordeal, R. C. Evaluation of college administrators. Where are we now? *NASPA Journal,* 1977, 17, 53–60.

O'Banion, T. Functions of college and university student personnel work. *College and University Bulletin.* 1970, 45, 296–304.

Ostroth, D. D. *Procedures and criteria used in selecting entry-level college student personnel professionals.* Doctoral dissertation. Michigan State University, 1979.

Packwood, W. T. *College Student Personnel Services.* Springfield, Ill.: Charles C. Thomas, 1977.

Parker, C. A. Institutional self-renewal in higher education. *Journal of College Student Personnel.* 1971, 12, 405–409.

Parker, C. A. (Ed.), *Encouraging development in college students.* Minneapolis: University of Minnesota Press, 1978.

Penn, J. R. Professional accreditation: A key to excellence. *Journal of College Student Personnel.* 1974. 15, 257–59.

Penney, J. F. College student personnel: A profession stillborn. *Personnel and Guidance Journal.* 1969, 47, 958–62.

Peterson, J. Implications of the new management technology. *NASPA Journal.* 1975. 12. 158–70.

Rhatigan, J. G., & Hoyt, D. P. Student personnel administration: Faculty-trainer perceptions and the reality of practice. *NASPA Journal.* 1970, 7. 156–63.

Reider, G. A. Performance reviews—A mixed bag. *Harvard Business Review,* 1973. 51. 61–67.

Reilley, R. R. & Cauther, I. A. The literature of college student personnel—A sample. *Journal of College Student Personnel.* 1976. 17, 363–67.

Rentz, A. L. A triadic model master's program in student development. *Journal of College Student Development.* 1976, 17, 453–58.

Rodgers, R. F. Student personnel work as social intervention. In G. H. Knock (Ed.). *Perspectives on the preparation of student affairs professionals* (Student Personnel Series No. 22). Washington, D.C.: American College Personnel Association, 1977.

Sheldin, M. A. The role of the women dean—1965. *Journal of the National Association of Women Deans and Counselors.* 1965, 29. 3–9.

Sherburne, P. R. Rates and patterns of professional mobility in student personnel work. *NASPA Journal.* 1970. 8. 119–23.

Stamatakos, L. C. & Oliaro, P. M. In-service staff development: A function of student personnel. *NASPA Journal,* 1972. 9, 269–73.

Trembley, E. L. & Sharf, R. S. Accountability strategies for student affairs. *NASPA Journal.* 1975. 12. 249–256.

Truitt, J. W. & Gross, R. A. *In-service education for college student personnel* (NASPA Bulletin, No. 1). University of Illinois, Champaign, Ill: National Association of Student Personnel Administrators. June, 1966.

Wallenfeldt, E. C. Evaluation of the chief administrator. *NASPA Journal*, 1976. 13, 5–11.

Williamson, E. G. *Student personnel services in colleges and universities*. New York: McGraw-Hill, 1961.

Wrehn, C. G. & Darley, J. G. An appraisal of the professional status of personnel work (Parts I and II). In E. G. Williamson (Ed.). *Trends in student personnel work*. pp. 264–287. Minneapolis: University of Minnesota Press. 1949.

Wrenn, C. *Student personnel work in college*. New York: Ronald Press, 1951.

Student Affairs Progress Toward Professionalism: Recommendations for Action Part 2

Louis C. Stamatakos

In Part 1 of this two-part treatise, I examined three of eight traditional criteria used by Wrenn and Darley (1949) to determine student affairs' progress toward becoming a profession: (a) the self-imposition of standards of admission and performance, (b) the definition of jobs and titles, and (c) the possession of specialized knowledge and skills. It was found that student affairs had not made sufficient enough progress to satisfy these three criteria. Recommendations were made for leadership and concerted action on the part of our professional associations to ameliorate serious deficiencies.

Part 2 is a continuation of the analysis of the remaining criteria: (d) the securement of legal recognition of the vocation, (e) the development of a professional consciousness and professional groups, (f) the performance of socially needed functions, (g) the development of a code of ethics, and (h) the application of standards of selection and training. Recommendations will follow each analysis.

The Securement of Legal Recognition of the Vocation

In the student affairs profession, only counselors meeting specific certification and licensure standards have received legal recognition, and this development has taken place in only two of the 50 states (American Personnel and Guidance Association, 1979). Higher education student affairs staff members who are engaged in counseling on a full-time basis represent but a very small percentage of the total profession; and of those who do counsel, few are actually required by state law to be certified as having met formal training standards.

Proponents of licensure might argue that licensure would ensure minimum

536

standards of education, supervised practica, internships (field experiences), technical training, and some reasonable guarantee of competency. Those opposed to licensure would contend, however, that it is (a) not needed at this stage of the profession's development, (b) inappropriate and does not lend itself to the varied and ill-defined specialties contained in the profession, and (c) a poor substitute for implementing standards and procedures for accrediting professional preparation programs and maintaining standards of admission and performance in the field.

The near-total absence of discussion of this topic in college student affairs literature reveals no expressed need or attempts toward securing legal recognition of our profession. As a group, student affairs workers seem to be content to view themselves as professional educators (student development facilitators) or administrators of educational/service programs who tend to seek only one kind of recognition—recognition from faculty colleagues—of being titled professors, or at least being viewed and respected as co-equal "educators."

Recommendations

Social rather than legal recognition seems to be more appropriate to the profession and its educational purposes. And, given the environment in which student affairs functions, education and educator seem to be more generic and more appropriate umbrella term(s) through which we define our distinctive purposes, roles, activities, and outcomes. However, if we are truly educators in the complete sense of the word, then the concept of "educator" needs to become an integral and predominate self-perception of every student affairs professional and the intrinsic operational theme (the sine qua non) of most of our functions.

Unfortunately, this self-perception is not very apparent in the profession. most members of our profession rarely, if ever, use the term educator in the description of their work, even when pressed to do so. Coordinating, administering, managing, developing, and serving are more often than not the descriptive words used. Despite frequent attacks on educators by critics of colleges of education, to be truly an educator is to follow one of life's highest and most humanistic callings. If student affairs is every to return to the academy (Brown, 1972) and become an integral part of the community of scholars, student affairs professionals must first be "educators." And, to be an educator one must first perceive and believe oneself to be an educator. One need only to turn to the writings of Lloyd-Jones and Smith (1954), and Mueller (1961), to be reminded of our profession's basic mission.

It is in this context that I suggest that as a general policy and as found appropriate and fitting, in all the profession's descriptive and sponsored literature, programs, committees, commissions, task force designations (titles), and professional preparation programs, educator, educational roles, educational responsibilities, educational outcomes, and so forth should become paramount concerns. And, in a matter of time, such an overall indoctrination should become manifest in our practices, performance, literature, and professional preparation, and ultimately in the manner in which we will be perceived by the educational communities in which we practice (Brown, 1972).

It is also recommended that our association consider sponsorship of annual Outstanding Student Affairs Educator awards whose recipients will have manifested those educator behaviors that are deemed appropriate, fitting, and truly exemplary in the recipient's area of responsibility. Such association recognition will serve to acknowledge and support the fundamental educational role that is preeminent in our profession, viewed in the broader context of the profession (i.e., administrating, coordinating, directing, advising, consulting, or teaching).

The Development of a Professional Consciousness and Professional Groups

It is quite apparent that student affairs, with its three major national organizations, American College Personnel Association (ACPA), National Association for Student Personnel Association (NASPA), and National Association for Women Dean and Counselors (NAWDAC), coupled with two dozen or more national associations of a specialty nature (Michigan College Personnel Association, 1977) and hundreds of regional, state, and local associations (most with specified membership qualifications), has established professional groups as well as a national consciousness.

This professional consciousness is very much in evidence as manifested by and through the development of support of approximately 100 graduate professional preparation programs, the publication of dozens of journals and hundreds of newsletters, the sponsorship of hundreds of professional conferences, meetings, and workshops each year, and the innumerable references to the need for practitioners to become more professional—as cited earlier in this discussion.

Professional consciousness has also become manifest in faculty, staff, student, and alumni recognition of student affairs importance to the well-being and totality of the collegiate experience. The phenomenal increase in the hiring of professionally prepared staff in all areas of student affairs stands in testimony of such awareness and consciousness.

Recommendations

Although I concluded that student affairs has, generally speaking, satisfied this criterion, I do not believe that the profession is manifesting the maturity of its years in its current forms of consciousness.

Student affairs professional associations exist for a number of good reasons, among which is the responsibility for providing creative, courageous, and assertive leadership that constantly challenges accepted assumptions, sets professional standards and goals, ventures into uncharted waters, elevates the thinking and operational levels of preparation and professional practice, and demands outstanding performance of its members. Unfortunately, our association's' leadership, although well-intentioned, has not performed admirably in these areas. In fact, one could suggest that with the exception of ACPA's Tomorrow's Higher Education Project (THE, 1975), our leadership has been rather timid, conforming, and choosing to react to and follow national movements and trends rather than to lead.

Examples of such lack of mature self-assurance is amply evident in national convention programs that are conspicuous in their absence of debates, intellectually stimulating and challenging symposia, and presidential speeches that agitate members to action. And, our literature has tended to parallel convention programming—focusing on descriptions and how-to-do-it, and avoiding intellectual discourse.

I am not advocating intellectual pomposity and superficiality. I am, however, recommending that our chosen leaders provide us with leadership and the literary and public forums for debate and controversy (intellectual feasts, or so to speak), the necessary ingredients for learning, growth, and purposeful action that manifest the essence of professionalism.

The Performance of Socially Needed Functions

Darley (Wrenn & Darley, 1949) raised some interesting problems regarding the kind of justification to be applied to the question of performance of a socially needed function. Do we judge the need for student affairs efforts upon proven ability to serve, educate, or develop students, or upon the basis of competence to solve or cure student problems, or both? I admit facing the same difficulty, one increasingly difficult to cope with because today's

programs and services are more varied in purpose and outcomes than those
of the 1940s.

A few simple illustrations, without citations, may serve to make the point.
Those wishing to evaluate the profession's usefulness from a purely "services"
orientation will disregard the profession's educational and developmental
commitments and rely on numbers of students "served" by a specific function
(e.g., financial aids directors can examine the number of dollars allocated,
work-study positions filled, and number of students receiving aid). This
services approach, however, is simplistic and disregards the developmental
and educational activities to which financial aids administrators have sub-
scribed. The same can be said for other service-oriented students affairs
functions, such as placement and records.

Those who believe that residence halls work involves education as well as
socialization can turn to proving the efficacy of affective, cognitive, and
physical development programming. Assuming that residence hall staffs
could reasonably prove positive cause-and-effect relationships for their programming efforts, such an approach would omit certain basic "service"
functions (e.g., food and maintenance services, security). Analogously,
others, such as counselors, who may believe their activities result in improved
student insights and adjustment, need to prove these outcomes through
sophisticated research studies that tend to ignore referral activities and other
vital services provided to other academic and student affairs units. Those
choosing service and educational/developmental outcomes as justification
criteria are faced with the problem of determining and justifying the importance of both. This course of action, however, creates a dilemma when one
of the two chosen approaches proves to be more "measurable" but is not
deemed the more important.

It is quite apparent that no single, or for that matter, multiple approach
to any or all programs and services related to student affairs will be sufficiently
responsible in justifying their necessity, outcomes, existence, or continuance.
The most obvious response to this criterion may lie in the phenomenal
growth and simple acceptance of student affairs as the catalyst for collegiality
and as a "given" in American higher education, faculty detractors notwithstanding.

During periods of economic strain and realignment of priorities, if one
were to ask the faculty if student affairs is performing socially needed
functions, they might say "no." And, even during periods of relative stability,
faculty tend to view students affairs as peripheral (Astman, 1975). But, the
record speaks for itself. when the faculty find themselves having to accept
responsibility for carrying out the myriad of student affairs functions for any
extended period of time, they plead for professionally educated staff to help

them or to assume those responsibilities for which the faculty are not prepared and in which they show little sustained interest. Student use of the many services provided and their involvement in the social and developmental programs sponsored, more than adequately support the fulfillment of this criterion. In fact, many student affairs administrators complain that their budgets and staffs cannot handle the current pressure on the traditional, let alone newer programs demanded by students.

Recommendations

Performing a socially needed function and justifying a student affairs division and its component parts for budgetary purposes are two different matters, even though they are generally grouped together when student affairs workers talk about accountability, performance, funding, and so forth. Given the pecuniary pinch and realignment of priorities that confront all educational institutions, student affairs, however, must be assertive and creative in determining its rightful place in higher education during the decades ahead. It cannot afford to wait for "outsiders" to develop and force upon it unacceptable models for evaluation and assessment. It is the task and responsibility of its collective associations to assure the profession that it will be assessed or evaluated on its own, not upon others' philosophies or terms.

A number of systems or accountability models have been suggested in some of our contemporary published literature that attempt to account for student development outcomes and costs. Critics in our profession have, however, for a number of reasons, found fault with all of them, leaving the typical student affairs officer at a loss to choose one over another, or none.

It is this context and with a sense of urgency that I recommend that student affairs' major organizations provide leadership in developing philosophically sound models for evaluating or assessing the entire range of student affairs functions. Such models could include many already in use and judged acceptable as well as models developed through the efforts of combined, coordinated, and commissioned task forces.

The Development of a Code of Ethics

It has been generally believed that a universal code of ethics cannot be developed for a profession as broad and varied such as student affairs. During the past 20 years, we have accepted the American Personnel and Guidance Association's code of ethics (APGA, 1971), which is primarily directed toward counselor/client relationships, but which has yet to receive endorsement of procedures for its enforcement (APGA, 1979). The National Association of Student Personnel Administrators (NASPA, 1960) developed a Statement of Principles and Ethical Practices of Student Personnel Administrators that lacked the breadth, sophistication, and specificity necessary for broad application in student affairs.

In recent years, the American College Personnel Association (ACPA, 1976) developed and approved a code of ethics for student affairs staff involved in group work. The National Association for Foreign Student Affairs (NAFSA, 1971) revised its Statement of Responsibilities and Standards in Work with Foreign Students in 1971. And, as of this writing ACPA is in the process of drafting a code of ethics presumably sufficiently broad enough to cover the entire spectrum of student affairs work (Winston, 1979). Concurrently, NASPA is drafting a Statement on Professional Ethics (Dalton, 1980).

Overall, one can conclude that we have a number of codes of ethics and statements of responsibility under which to work, but to date none so broad as to be applicable to the variety of responsibilities assumed under the general rubric of student affairs. The challenge of creating and adopting a useful and professionally "universal" code of ethics has been accepted by ACPA. In the meantime, student affairs professionals need to remain aware of the conflicting loyalties each specialty creates and of the "ethical issues involved in our daily work" (Wrenn & Darley, 1949).

Recommendations

Although it may be a few years before a final set of professional and ethical standards is approved by ACPA and other student affairs societies, it is not too early to begin planning the development of processes and procedures through which standards are to be promulgated and enforced. To the best of my recollection, it has taken APGA nearly two decades or more to create a mechanism for enforcement and, to date, the mechanism is not yet "established." To delay this specific consideration may be to invite and reinforce the justified criticism of laypersons and the general public who charge that professional associations are much more concerned about the welfare of their membership than the protection of those whom the profession is to serve.

The Application of Standards of Selection and Training

As it manifests itself, this criterion virtually transcends and affects nearly all of the criteria mentioned and requires greater explication.

The 1977 Directory of Preparation Programs in College Student Personnel (ACPA, 1977) lists 91 educational institutions that claim to be preparing 2,741 graduate students for professional responsibilities in college student affairs work.

Admissions requirements to these programs ranged from none stated to any one or more of the following: interest in the field; graduation from an accredited college; earned grade point average of 2.00, 2.24, 3.00, 3.25 or better in the last two years of undergraduate school; no undergraduate major specified; undergraduate major preferred in behavioral sciences, extensive involvement in co-curricular activities and residence halls during undergraduate years; letters of recommendation; required Graduate Record Examination, Miller Analogies, and/or psychological inventory scores; no required test scores; no interview; required on-site interviews; highly selective admission; accepting any applicant. It is apparent that despite Wrenn's suggestion that students be selected on the basis of intelligence and proven academic prowess as well as emotional and socially-based qualities (Wrenn & Darley, 1949), the quality of admitted students to professional preparation programs is inconceivably broad, loose, inconsistent, and, for all practical purposes, lacking in reasonable standards.

Most preparation programs reveal a traditional emphasis in counseling or administration, with some programs emphasizing student and organizational development (Rodgers, 1977). Closer examination reveals that similarities between programs is random at best, although in many programs there are common cores of counseling and/or administration courses and some consistency in required coursework in testing and measurement and basic research methodology.

Many are one-year programs containing a single survey course in student affairs administration, a course in student activities and leadership development, and a practicum, while others are very comprehensive, containing a full complement of courses in student development and student affairs administration, counseling, three or more required practica, core courses in research, testing, evaluation, history of higher education, philosophy of education, the college student, a minor in behavioral science or other related areas, and requiring two years to complete.

Preparation standards, journal articles, association papers, and adopted statements notwithstanding (Association for Counselor Education and Supervision, 1973; Brunett, 1954; Caple, 1972; COSPA, 1964; COSPA, 1975; Hedlund, 1971; Ostroth, 1975; Rentz, 1976), a careful review of a random sample of the descriptive information and course syllabi of preparation programs will reveal a glaring lack of specificity regarding the knowledge to be learned and the skills students are expected to develop during the duration of their graduate program of studies. In plentiful supply are statements and inferences about "acquainting," "orienting," and "familiarizing" students to areas of emphasis. Rarely will one find a direct cause-and-effect statement about the processes through which a student will learn desired skills. Entering students and future employers are expected to accept on good faith the mission statements of preparation programs.

Gary Knock's Perspectives on the *Preparation of Student Affairs Professionals* (Knock, 1977) contained six different models, ranging from emphasis on student development to administration and organizational theory, and highly specialized preparation for community college student affairs work. Interestingly, none provided for differentiation between MA and PH.D. level preparation. It is quite clear that within and between actual and proposed professional preparation programs, there is little if any consistency in nature, content emphasis, or duration. This absence of standards has been lauded, aided, and abetted by some members of our profession who firmly believe that variety is necessary for assuring flexibility and diversity of process and outcome to supply the profession with diverse talent to match its equally diverse practices. This is an interesting, circular dialectic that fails to recognize or ignores the recommendations of the profession's chosen leaders, writers, and commissioned position papers on the topic of professional preparation standards (ACPA, 1967; ACPA, 1975; Anderson, 1948; APGA, 1969; Blaesser & Froelich, 1950; Brown, 1972; COSPA, 1975; Houston, 1949; Miller & Prince, 1976; Robinson, 1966; Wrenn, 1948; Wrenn & Darley, 1949).

Further compounding preparation problems, until very recently no ACPA, NASPA, OR NAWDAC committee, commission, or task force was "vigorously" investigating and dealing substantively with the development of professional preparation standards. The Association for Counselor Education and Supervision (ACES), however, did submit to the American Personnel and Guidance Association (APGA) a set of standards (ACES, 1973) that does include student affairs preparation and that, in the opinions of many student affairs preparation faculty, is not totally appropriate for application to student affairs work (Pruitt, 1979). It was not until 1978 (APGA, 1978) that ACES initiated the use of this document as a basis for accrediting programs in counseling and student affairs, and in 1979 began conducting workshops for the training of accreditation teams. In view of this assertive move by ACES, ACPA quickly established a committee on the topic in November of 1978 with the expectation that the committee would write into the ACES document standards appropriate to student affairs preparation (where such was an integral part of the counselor training program) for association review and acceptance at the Los Angeles Convention of ACPA in March 1979. ACPA did provide leadership in this area and is now working cooperatively in a consortium of major student affairs organizations to be called the Council for the Advancement of Standards for Student Services Development Programs (Interassociation Conference, 1979). One of the its major tasks will be to develop specific accreditation standards applicable to student personnel preparation not directly a part of counselor education programs.

A dissertation study of doctoral level preparation programs in college student affairs administration by Rockey (1972) revealed that the most outstanding programs (and there were few of these) were those that shared the following characteristics: high standards of admission, quality faculty, quality graduates, and visible leadership in the field by faculty and graduates. These same programs had the largest number of full-time faculty, strong supporting academic departments, and graduate student support systems (assistantships, specialized library resources, etc.), well-conceived curricula, depth and breadth of course requirements (with sufficient elaboration), required and sufficient internships, and substantive coursework outside the field of education. Assuming that one could reasonably expect similar program characteristics at the MA level, one would have to conclude that not many of the 95 listed programs (ACPA, 1977) would currently qualify.

In considering but one important variable, the number of faculty devoted exclusively to instruction in student affairs, one can readily conclude that, at the time of this writing, this expectation faces some serious confrontations in the immediate future, which can render it near-futile. Many preparation programs of considerable size rely totally on administrators to instruct in student affairs courses. In addition, programs that heretofore have been staffed with full-time faculty are now confronted with faculty retirements and with little or no prospect of their replacement as Colleges of Education continue to experience declining enrollments and faculty positions are eliminated in an effort to reduce costs.

The object of this discussion has been to alert the reader that the professional preparation in student affairs is inconceivably inconsistent in entry, nature, quality, scope, skill development, support systems, expectations, and outcomes. Furthermore, it can be concluded that, in general, after students have successfully completed a program of studies in a typical program, the profession cannot be assured that they will be adequately or reasonably well-prepared to carry out the variety of responsibilities particular to job-entry positions or that they have the leadership potential and depth of understandings necessary for upward mobility.

If factual, this finding is somewhat disconcerting when one considers that the MA is the most typical degree held by student affairs professionals and that eight percent of the 1977 MA graduates of reporting institutions were hired as "chief student affairs officers" (Greer, Blaesser, Herron, & Horle, 1978). In view of the preceding and the immediate discussion, it is also reasonable to conclude that the practice of the profession is probably as much at variance as the learning outcomes of its preparation programs, and that such manifestations of practice and preparation are characteristics hardly expected or desired of an established profession.

Recommendations

Assuming ACPA does carry through with the work already done on creation of accrediting standards for professional preparation, some of the problem areas discussed will, eventually, be ameliorated. Others, however, will be left untouched, and it is in this regard that I recommend our professional associations begin to address themselves to these issues as soon as possible.

If it is determined that some preparation programs are not, in any real sense, truly preparing student affairs professionals but are bootlegging them through counselor, pupil personnel, or educational psychology programs, should such institutions be listed in association-sponsored directories of professional preparation programs? Such listings do provide programs with a sense of undeserved legitimacy.

Ph.D., Ed.D., and Ed.S. curricula in student affairs have, for the most part, been totally neglected in the development of core programs at the MA level. Given the number of institutions "claiming" post-MA degree plans in student affairs administration, are they going to develop like Topsy (as in the case of MA programs), with little or no guidance and direction from our associations? It is quite apparent that core curricula and accrediting standards need to be developed for this level of preparation as well.

Few full-time teaching positions exist in professional preparation programs. Their establishment can result from the development and enforcement of accrediting standards. Our professional associations should be active in creating and maintaining incentives for attracting and keeping quality faculty in its preparation programs.

Many of our existing faculty are in need of retooling—upgrading understandings, knowledge, and skills so that they, in turn, can teach these to their students. Possibly up to 80 percent of full-time as well as part-time instructional staff are badly in need of updating themselves, especially in the area of student development. Our associations need to consider co-sponsorship of workshops, institutes, travel, and study grants for this purpose.

Conclusion

In concluding this review of student affairs' proximity to meeting professional criteria, one must accept that although the field aspires and at the same time perceives itself as professional, developments during the 30 years since the Wrenn and Darley study do not justify a claim of professional status.

Student affairs has been in a state of becoming for over a century and has become accepted as a traditional educational/service function of American higher education. It has managed to attract bright, vigorous, educator-leaders who share and perform educational and service activities that are essential components of a rich and meaningful collegiate experience. The objects of its activities (students), as well as the faculty and staff, alumni, parents, and others who support higher education, have come to expect, indeed, demand of student affairs diligence, care, skill, competence, ethical behavior, leadership, and educationally sound service programs. Stated in another way, the expectation is: professional preparation, professional behavior, professional performance, and continual professional development. Whether the field formally "qualifies" as a profession at the present time or will qualify by the year 2000 should have little bearing on the quality of service provided and the quality of individual or collective performance and outcomes. Student affairs is obligated by tradition, by past and present service, by a commitment to a philosophy or point of view (ACES, 1949), and by a professional conscience to be as professional as humanly possible.

As a field, student affairs has witnessed some rather unsystematic, accidental, but positive evolutionary changes in the movement toward professionalism during the past three decades. Regretfully, these movements have not been as directional and significant as they could or should have been. In view of the increasing pressures of accountability throughout all of higher education and in consideration of rising expectations of professional practice and outcomes, it seems reasonable and appropriate to acknowledge that student affairs is still "en route to professional status" (Wrenn & Darley, 1949, p. 178). The task before us is to accept and respond cooperatively, systematically, and vigorously to the constant challenge of becoming a profession.

References

American College Personnel Association. Task Force on Group Procedures. The use of group procedures in higher education: A position statement by ACPA. *Journal of College Student Personnel*, 1976, 17, 161–168.

American College Personnel Association. *Directory of preparation programs in college student personnel.* Washington, D.C.: American College Personnel Association, 1977.

American College Personnel Association. Professional Preparation and Standards Committee. The role and preparation of student personnel workers in institutions of higher learning. *Journal of College Student Personnel,* 1967, 8, 62–65.

American College Personnel Association. A student development model for student affairs in tomorrow's higher education. *Journal of College Student Personnel,* 1975, 16, 334–341.

American Council on Education. *The student personnel point of view.* Washington, D.C.: Author, 1949.

American Personnel and Guidance Association. Ethical Standards. *Personnel and Guidance Journal,* 1971, 50, 327–330.

American Personnel and Guidance Association. Ethics to be enforced. James Terrell, Chairperson, APGA Ethics Committee. *Guidepost* (Letters to the editor), March 1, 1979, p. 2.

American Personnel and Guidance Association. Guidelines for graduate programs in the preparation of student personnel workers in higher education. *Personnel and Guidance Journal,* 1969, 5, 493–498.

Anderson, G. V. Professional standards and training for college personnel workers. *Educational and Psychological Measurement,* 1948, 8, 451–459.

Association for Counselor Education and Supervision. *Standards for the preparation of counselors and other personnel services specialists.* Washington, D.C.: Association for Counselor Education & Supervision, 1973. (Mimeo)

Astman, S. K. Faculty perception of the student personnel staff: Implications for survival. *Journal of the National Association for Women Deans, Administrators, and Counselors,* 1975, 38, 65–70.

Blaesser, W. W., & Froelich, C. P. Major issues and trends in the graduate training of college personnel workers. *Educational and Psychological Measurement,* 1950, 10, 588–595.

Brown, R. D. *Student development in tomorrow's higher education: A return to the academy* (Student Personnel Series No. 16). Washington, D.C.: American College Personnel Association, 1972.

Brunett, C. W. Selection and training of school and college personnel workers. *Review of Educational Research,* 1954, 24, 121–133.

Buback, K. A. (Ed.). *Directory of professional organizations for student personnel administrators in higher education.* Michigan: The Committee on New Professionals, Michigan College Personnel Association, May, 1977.

Caple, R. B. A molar model for the training of student personnel workers. *Counselor Education and Supervision,* 1972, 12, 31–41.

Council of Student Personnel Associations in Higher Education. *A proposal for professional preparation in college student personnel work.* Ohio: Bowling Green State University, 1964.

Council of Student Personnel Associations in Higher Education. *Student development services in post secondary education.* Ohio: Bowling Green State University, 1975.

Dalton, J. Proposed statement on professional ethics (draft). *NASPA Region IV-East Newsletter*, 1980, 5, 2–3.

Greer, R. M.; Blaesser, W. S.; Herron, R. D.; & Horle, R. F. College student personnel graduate placement. *Journal of College Student Personnel*, 1978, 19, 342–348.

Hedlund, D. E. Preparation for student personnel: Implications for humanistic education. *Journal of College Student Personnel*, 1971, 12, 324–328.

Houston, C. G. Limited survey of professional standards and training of college personnel workers. *Educational and Psychological Measurement*, 1949, 9, 445–446.

Interassociation Conference on Student Development and Services Accreditation Issues. Minutes of the conference held at Alexandria, Virginia, October 25–26, 1979; Theodore K. Miller, Acting Chairperson. (Mimeo)

Knock, G. H. (Ed.). *Perspectives on the preparation of student affairs professionals* (Student Personnel Series No. 22). Washington, D.C.: American College Personnel Association, 1977.

Lloyd-Jones, E., & Smith, M. R. (Eds.). *Student personnel work as deeper teaching.* New York: Harper Bros., 1954.

McGregor, D. *Leadership and motivation.* Cambridge, Mass.: MIT Press, 1966.

Miller, T. K., & Prince, J. S. *The future of student affairs.* San Francisco: Jossey-Bass Publishing Company, 1976.

Mueller, K. H. *Student personnel work in higher education.* Boston: Houghton Mifflin, 1961.

National Association of Student Personnel Administrators. Statement of desirable conditions and standards for maximum effectiveness of the college administrator. *NASPA Journal*, 1971, 9, 3–6.

National Association for Foreign Student Affairs Committee on Professional Development. *Statement or responsibilities of and standards in work with foreign students* (Rev.). Washington, D.C.: Author, 1971.

Ostroth, D. D. Master's level preparation for student personnel work. *Journal of College Student Personnel*, 1975, 16, 319–322.

Pruitt, A. S. Preparation of student development specialists during the 1980's. *Counselor Education and Supervision*, 1979, 18, 190–198.

Rentz, A. L. A triadic model master's program in student development. *Journal of College Student Personnel*, 1976, 17, 453–458.

Robinson, D. W. Analysis of three statements relative to the preparation of college student personnel workers. *Journal of College Student Personnel*, 1966, 7, 254–256.

Rockey, M. C. Doctoral preparation programs in college student personnel in selected universities in the United States (Doctoral dissertation, Michigan State University, 1972). *Dissertation Abstracts International*, 1972, 33. (University microfilms No. 73–12, 809)

Rodgers, R. F. Student personnel work as social intervention. In G. H. Knock (Ed.), *Perspectives on the preparation of student affairs professionals* (Student Personnel Series No. 22). Washington, D.C.: American College Personnel Association, 1977.

THE (Tomorrow's Higher Education Project). A student development model for student affairs in tomorrow's higher education. *Journal of College Student Personnel*, 1975, 16, 334–341.

Wrenn, C. G. The greatest tragedy in college personnel work. *Educational and Psychological Measurement*, 1948, 8, 412–429.

Wrenn, C. G., & Darley, J. G. An appraisal of the professional status of personnel work. In E. G. Williamson (Ed.), *Trends in student personnel work* (Parts I and II). Minneapolis: University of Minnesota Press, 1949, pp. 264–287.

Selected Readings

American Personnel and Guidance Association. Guidepost. Washington, D.C.: author, December 1978, p. 1.

Arbuckle, D. S. *Student personnel services in higher education*. New York: McGraw-Hill, 1953.

Ayers, A. R.; Tripp, P. A.; & Russell, J. S. *Student services administration in higher education*. Washington, D.C.: U.S. Department of Health, Education, and Welfare, 1966. (Superintendent of Documents Catalog No. FS5.253:53026)

Beeler, K. D., & Penn, J. R. *A handbook on staff development in student affairs*. Corvallis: Oregon State University Book Stores, 1978.

Bishop, J. B. Some guidelines for the development of accountability systems. *NASPA Journal*, 1975, 12, 190–194.

Blackburn, R. T., & Clark, M. J. Assessment of faculty performance: Some correlates between administrator, colleague, student and self-ratings. *Sociology of Education*, 1975, 48, 242–256.

The New Student-Institutional Relationship: Its Impact on Student Affairs Administration

Edward H. Hammond

College students are now regarded as legal adults in almost every phase of community life.

"Students who, by reason of the 26th Amendment, become eligible to vote when 18 years of age—are adults who are members of the college or university community. Their interests and concerns are often quite different from those of the faculty. They often have values, views, and ideologies that are at war with the ones which the colleges traditionally espoused . . ." *Healy v. James* (1972).

The impact of this statement did not become clear to many college administrators until the age of majority was lowered in all of the states in the early 1970's. With this social movement aimed at lowering the age to vote, the right to enter into contracts was also affected. The resulting action complicated the legal interrelationship between the individual student, his or her common and separate needs, and the institution which existed to serve them. The change in the age of majority illuminated these relationships in a manner which should allow people to identify more accurately and respond more appropriate to the problems which are presented. Such insights are directly traceable to the recent tendency to turn to the community and consumer models in explaining the legal structure and functions of institutions of postsecondary education (Hammond & Shaffer, 1978).

The question of the status of the students and their relationship to the institution is basic to any discussion of thestudent-consumer relationship and its obligations. The determination of status contains the rationale and foundation for the basic student/institution relationship. During recent years, a vast reappraisal by the courts of the importance of postsecondary education has occurred. The question of whether or not this education is a right or a privilege is the basis for determining the student's status. The court initially observed in *Brown v. The Board of Education* (1954) that "it is doubtful that any student may reasonably be expected to succeed in life if he is denied the opportunities of an education."

Later, in 1961, the court continued its investigation by considering the nature of the interest involved and stated in *Dixon v. The Alabama State Board of Education* (1961) that, "the precise nature of the private interests involved in this case is the right to remain at an institution of higher education." Later in that same year, the court went on to say in *Knight v. Tennessee State Board of Education* (1961) that "whether the interest involved be described as a right or a privilege, the fact remain that it is an interest of almost incalculable value . . . the private interests are to be evaluated under the due process clause of the Fourteenth Amendment, not in terms of labels or fictions but in terms of their true significance and worth." The court in *Crane v. Crane* (1964) concluded that "it is a truism that in this country the luxuries of yesterday are the necessities of today, and it would seem that the matter of higher education, more than almost any other subject, equates itself completely and appropriately with Justice Holmes' 'felt necessities of the time'." (Hammond, 1975)

If the institution claims, as it must if given the above legal decisions, that the student status is one of privilege before admission and of right after matriculation, then it must assert some principle of obligation. Ever since *Carr v. St. John's University* (1962), the application of contract theory to the student/institution relationship has become an increasing fact of life for postsecondary education. For example, the court in the case of *Anderson v. The Regents of the University of California* (1972) stated, "By the act of matriculation, together with the payment of required fees, a contract between the student and the university is created." In *Goldberg v. The Regents of the University of California* (1967) the court stated, "A contract is created with the State which by its very nature incorporates constitutional principles of fairness." While the function of an institution of postsecondary education is generally to impart learning and advance the boundaries of knowledge, this function carries with it the administrative responsibility for the welfare, control, and regulation of the academic environment including the responsibility to provide the education promised by the contract.

Since the contractual relationship between the student and a college arises out of both oral and written elements, as defined by *Zumbrum v. University of Southern California* (1968), the specifics of articulation and registration clearly are the keys to the development of the agreement. This theory assumes that the student and the university are parties to a contract, each given certain benefits and obligations. The institution in advertising, seeks students, and in extending admission makes an offer to the student, and the student by registration accepts. The student agrees to pay tuition and fees and the college agrees to provide instruction as described and the appropriate earned degree if the student remains in good standing academically and abides by the institution's reasonable rules and regulations. This definition of the student/institution relationship extends to both public and private institutions and was first offered in *Booker v. Grand Rapids Medical College* (1909). But, from that point until the 60's, the courts were reluctant to apply the contract rule regularly because of the "minor status" of the students (*Kaufman v. American Youth Hostel, Inc.*, 1958; and *Ryan v. Hofstra University*, 1971). With the change in age of majority and the age of entering into contracts discussed earlier, this judicial reluctance has totally disappeared (Hammond & Shaffer, 1978).

Important new clarification of the student/institution relationship was found in the now famous case of *Bradshaw v. Rawlings* (1979). In this case the plaintiffs brought a negligence action arising out of an automobile accident which occurred following a sophomore class picnic at which the driver had become intoxicated. In this appellate decision, which has greatly affected institutional and staff liability, the court reaffirmed that the student/institution relationship and its competing interests are much different today than they were in the past. "At the risk of oversimplification, the change has occurred because society considers the modern college student an adult, not a child of tender years." The judges went on to conclude that "because the circumstances show that the students have reached the age of majority and are capable of protecting their own self interests, we believe that the rule should be different. We conclude, therefore, that in order to ascertain whether a specific duty of care can be extended from Delaware Valley College to its injured student, we must first identify and assess the competing individual and social interests associated with the parties" *Bradshaw v. Rawlings* (1979).

Because of this appellate decision, it would appear that there is no duty to control the conduct of the student as to prevent him or her from causing physical harm to another based upon the special relationship existing between the student consumer and the institution. Bradshaw's primary argument was that the college acknowledged that 1) its students did drink beer at the picnic, 2) that this conduct violated a school regulation and state law, 3) that the institution created a known probability of harm to a third person, and 4) that knowledge by the college of this probablye harm imposed a duty on the college either to control Rawlings' conduct or to protect Bradshaw from possible harm.

The court was aware that a private host in Pennsylvania who supplies intoxicants to a visibly intoxicated guest may not be held civilly liable for injuries to third parties caused by the intoxicated guest's negligence, *Manning v. Andy* (1973). Only licensed persons engaged in the sale of intoxicants have been held civilly liable to injured parties, and the source of this liability derives from common law and the State's Dram Shop Statute. The court ruled, "Because the Pennsylvania Supreme Court has been unwilling to find a special relationship on which to predict a duty between a private host and his visibly intoxicated guest, we predict that it would be even less willing to find such a relationship between a college and its student under the circumstances of this case" (*Bradshaw v. Rawlings* (1979).

What then is the college's responsibility to its student consumer? As Prosser (1964) has emphasized, the concern that there is or is not a duty begs the essential question—whether the student consumer's interest is entitled to legal protection against the institution's conduct. The court in Bradshaw ruled that duty is not sacrosanct in itself, but only in expression of the sum total of those considerations of policy which lead the law to say that a particular student consumer is entitled to protection. Thus, under the enrollment contract, we must perceive duty simply as an obligation to which the law will give recognition in order to require one person to conform to a particular standard of conduct with respect to another person.

These abstract descriptions of duty cannot be helpful unless they are directly related to the competing individual public and social interests implicated in the student/institution relationship. That interest is a social fact, a phenomena existing independently of the law, which is reflected by a claim, demand or desire that people seek to satisfy, and it has been recognized as socially valid by authoritative decision makers in society (Towns, 1943). Certainly, the plaintiff in the Bradshaw case possesses an important interest in remaining free from bodily injury and thus the law protects his right to recover compensation from those who negligently caused him injury. The institution, on the other hand, has an interest in the nature of its relationship with its adult students, as well as an interest in avoiding responsibility that it is incapable of performing.

The court concluded in Bradshaw that the "modern American college is not an insurer of the safety of its students. Whatever may have been its responsibility in an earlier era, the authoritarian role of today's college administrators has been diluted in recent decades. Trustees, administrators and faculties have been required to yield to the expanding rights and privileges of their students." By constitutional amendment (United States Constitution Twenty-sixth Amendment); by written and unwritten law, *Goss v. Lopez* (1975), *Papish v. Board of Curators* (1973), and *Healy v. James* (1972); and through the evolution of new customs, rights formerly possessed by college administrators and faculty have been transferred to student con-sumers.

The college students today are no longer minors; they are now regarded as legal adults in almost every phase of community life. A time existed when college administrators and faculty assumed a role "in loco parentis." Students were committed to their charge because the students were considered minors. A special relationship was created between the college and the student that imposed a duty on the college to exercise control over student conduct and, reciprocally, gave the students certain rights and protection by the college. In the 1960's "in loco parentis" died and people embarked on a constitutional relationship with their students which lasted until the movement to reduce the age of majority began. This movement, taking place almost simultane-ously with key legislation and case law lowering the age of majority, produced fundamental changes in society. "A dramatic reproportionment of responsibility in social interests of general security took place. Regulation by the college on student life on and off the campus has become limited. Adult students now demand and receive expanded rights of privacy in their college life. College administrators no longer control the broad areas of general morals. Today students vigorously claim the right to defend and regulate their own lives. Especially, have they demanded and received satisfaction of their interest in self assertion in both physical and mental activities, and have indicated what may be called the interest in freedom of the individual will" *Bradshaw v. Rawlings* (1979).

Cases

Anderson v. Regents of the University of California, 22 Cal. App. 3d 763 (1972).

Booker v. Grand Rapids Medical College, 156 Mich. 95, 130 N.W. 586 (1909).

Bradshaw v. Rawlings, 464 F. Supp. 175, aff in part, rev in part, 612 F 2d 135 (1979).

Brown v. Board of Education of Topeka, 347 U.S. 483, 74 S. Ct. 686 (1954).

Crane v. Crane, 45 Ill. App. 2d 316, 327, 196 N.E. 2d 27, 33 (1964).

Carr v. St. John's University, 17 App. Div. 2d 632, 231 N.Y.S. 2d 410, aff'd 12 N.Y.S. 2d 802, 187 N.E. 2d 28 (1962).

Dixon v. Alabama State Board of Education, 186 F. Supp. 945 (D.C. M.D. ala. 1960) aff'd F. 2d (8th Cir. 1969).

Goldberg v. Regents of the University of California, 57 Cal. Rptr. 463 (Ct. App. 1967).

Goss v. Lopez 419 U.S. 565 (1975).

Healy v. James, 408 U.S. 169 (1972).

Kaufman v. American Youth Hostel, Inc., 13 Misc. 2d 8 (1957), 174 N.Y.S. 2d 580 (1957), 177 N.Y.S. 2d 587 (1958).

Knight v. Tennessee State Board of Education, 200 F. Supp. 174 (M.D. Tenn. 1969).

Manning v. Andy, Pa., 310 A. 2d 25 Int. Liq. 299 (1973).

Papish v. Board of Curators of the University of Missouri, 410 U.S. 667 (1973).

Ryan v. Hofstra University, 67 Misc 2d 651, 324 N.Y.S. 2d (1971).

Zumbrum v. University of Southern California, 25 Cal. App. 3d 1, 101 Cal. Rptr. 499 (1972).

References

Hammond, E. H. *Justice on Campus: Individual Rights v. Institutional Needs.* Paper presented to the American College Personnel Association Workshop, Cleveland, Ohio, April 3, 1973, and published in Viewpoint, Georgia Student Press, January, 1973.

Hammond, E. H. & Shaffer, R. H. (Eds.). *The legal foundations of student personnel services in higher education.* Washington, D.C.: American College Student Personnel Association, 1978.

Prosser, W. *Law of torts.* 333 (ed ed. 1964).

Towns, H. R. *Social process.* Glencoe, Indiana: Free Press, 1943.

Student Services in the '80's: A Decade of Decisions

Arthur Sandeen

It is time to focus on our own development as professionals and as a profession.

To have been asked to talk about the future is both tantalizing and hazardous. It gives one the opportunity to make statements which do not have to be supported by data, but it also subjects one to a future accountability that is quite unnerving. With that caveat, here is what I propose to discuss in the time we have together this evening.

1. First, I will make some comments on our current attitudes, with references to the past;
2. Second, some comments on what "student affairs" is today, and
3. Finally, some comments about issues that I see and hear, and some possible projects and problems to address in the next few years.

So, first, some comments about our current attitudes. In Greek legend, Sisyphus, the King of Corinth, was accused of being disrespectful to Zeus, and was sentenced to hades where, for all eternity, his task was to push a heavy rock up a hill, only to have it roll backwards time and time again. For some, Sisyphus stands as a symbol of eternal frustration and fruitless drudgery; whereas, for others, his determined struggle represents life itself and provides meaning and inspiration. This symbolic legend illustrates for me some of the difficulties I believe our profession is facing today.

For reasons that have always remained a mystery to me, the student affairs profession has engaged in a good deal of self-defeating behavior. Since the day I read my first Journal article as an eager graduate student in 1961, I have had to listen to and occasionally read the doomsday predictions of several self-proclaimed prophets who spelled the immediate demise of the profession. Where these soothsayers are now is anyone's guess, but somehow the profession remains. Our own members have accused us of being irrelevant,

557

parental, reactionary, weak, arrogant, and unscholarly. We are also guilty of being crises oriented, mouthpieces of the president, unneeded advocates of the students, the self-appointed conscience of the campus, and an appendage of the faculty. We are said to possess no body of knowledge, and finally, are now engaged in a futile effort to cling to in loco parentis as the last possible justification of our existence.

Whatever the purpose of such self-flagellation might be, the facts of our present condition and history of our profession clearly contradict such pessimism. While student affairs has not yet fully matured as a profession, it is clearly in its most healthy state since our beginnings in the late 19th century. There are now more institutions with more professionally trained student affairs staff, conducting more diverse tasks than ever before. Our several professional associations are active and strongly oriented to improving campus educational programs and the professional development of their members. Our literature is growing, and gaining in both diversity of point of view and quality. On countless campuses around the country, student affairs staff at all levels, from orientation and admissions, financial aid and student housing, to student health and college unions, career planning and student activities are successfully and actively engaged in planning and implementing educational programs for students. Student affairs, especially in the past 25 years, has expanded dramatically and become a vital part of the educational program of many institutions.

Of additional irritation to me is the ignorance of some of these doomsday prophets concerning the history of our profession. For example, some have characterized the men and women deans of the 1920's, 1930's, and 1940's as authoritarian and prudish regulators of student behavior. Anyone who has taken the time to read and study the history of our profession as well as institutional histories cannot help but be impressed by the contributions of such pioneers as Scott Goodnight at Wisconsin, William Aldermann at Beloit, Thomas Arkle Clark at Illinois, or Bill Tate at Georgia. They were men of vision and courage who, by sheer force of personality, inspired generations of students and helped to humanize the nature of higher education.

Perhaps the most unfairly maligned and misunderstood, however, have been the Deans of Women during the period 1910–1950. In virtually every institution, they served as the sole voice of women's educational needs and rights, and their courage and professionalism have been among the most outstanding of any in higher education. A careful reading of the proceedings of the annual conferences of the National Association for Women's Deans, Administrators, and Counselors will impress one with the deep educational concern and compassion of these professionals. Such Deans as Marion Talbot of Chicago, Helen Schleman of Purdue, Kathryn Towle of Berkeley, and Etter Turner of Stetson are not well-known, unfortunately, by members of our profession today; but they made great contributions to the education of women many years before Title IX, Affirmative Action, and the ERA.

Consider, for example, the pioneering work of Lois Kimball Mathews, Dean of Women at Wisconsin, who wrote in her 1915 book (one of the best ever written in our field): "The Dean of Women had her own way to make and her position to form in the midst of all sorts of difficulties. There was real antipathy to the appointment of women on faculties composed almost exclusively of men . . . Appointed under such circumstances, the new Dean had to make good against tremendous odds in which personality and charm weighed out of all proportion to their real importance." Or listen to her views of women students at Wisconsin in 1915: "The danger is that coeducational institutions will continue to be in the future as the vast majority have been in the past—institutions for men, with requirements set at a man's pace and to meet his needs, where women are admitted, rather than institutions which provide equal readiness, ingenuity, and enthusiasm in courses for both sexes. Men administrators in coeducational institutions have attempted almost single-handed to work out women's problems." . . . On the needed qualities of the Dean of Women . . ." No glorified chaperone will be able to grasp the situation and cope with it: No woman who merely 'loves girls' in a vague, emotional fashion will be able to convince a faculty of men or a body of hard-headed trustees of the necessity under which they labor of meeting the present economic, social, intellectual, and spiritual needs of women. More than charm and natural social gifts are required of a leader in women's education: The times call for intellectual, spiritual, and social equipment of the highest order on the part of those who are to contribute a sane, clear-cut and large minded point of view."

It is clear to me that our profession has been graced by some giants-some great educational pioneers. The needs of the students, many times ones not in vogue with the faculty or the public, have always been the basis of our priorities and actions. At many points in our history, it was the student affairs staff that served as the buffer, bringing new students to campus and initiating services for them into the institution. On scores of campuses since 1900, it has often been student affairs staff who have made it possible for institutions to adapt to necessary changes—for example, coeducation, testing, academic advising, housing, racial integration, and student rights.

So, yes, we do have inflation, and flattened enrollments, and less mobility and a public which has notified us that higher education's short-lived honeymoon of the middle 1960's is over. And yes, job burnout in all fields is a reality to face squarely. But it is also true that in the short 75–year history of our profession, we have never been as strong as we are now. There is no monolithic structure in our field. Our diversity is a great strength. We have a large number of highly competent people with good ideas, courage, and a willingness to work hard. Let's remember our history as we move ahead in our efforts to improve the education of students. I am proud to be a member of this profession. The fate of Sisyphus does not represent frustration and drudgery, but determination and dedication in striving for high ideals. And that is the very essence of our profession.

Now that I have that off my chest, I want to make a few comments about what "student affairs" is today. It is not uncommon in 1981 for a student affairs division to encompass everything from admissions and intercollegiate athletics to bookstores and student health, registration and religious services, to academic advising and international programs. What do most of us think of when we talk about "student affairs"? I suggest that with our current scope of responsibilities on many campuses, it is no longer accurate to think only in traditional terms such as counseling, student activities, residential programs, and student conduct. To be sure, these activities are still very important, but they alone do not reflect what we are all about. On some campuses, this has caused some confusion among presidents, students, faculty, and student affairs staff. If we have viewed ourselves in a limited manner for years, it is often difficult for us to see ourselves in new leadership roles on the campus. Our very success at some institutions today is often a function of our ability and willingness to move into areas of responsibility that have not been traditionally ours. If the chief student affairs office conceives of student personnel work as being exclusively concerned with traditional services, then it is unlikely that that division will be as vital a part of the total campus educational program as it could be. I recognize that there are hazards to diversity, and I do not advocate the petty building of empires. This is a much debated topic in our field now, and I look forward to discussing it further with you.

I submit, however, that the expansion in the way we think about our roles as student affairs professionals has been a major factor in the development of such programs in recent years as child care, alcohol abuse prevention, community service liaison, wellness clinics, career development and cooperative education programs, student consumer protections, and benefits, and services to special students. One of our strengths in this field has always been our ability to identify real needs, and then to take the leadership in developing and implementing services and programs to meet these needs. In my view, we should be the most perceptive observers of campus needs, and we should be aggressive initiators of proposals, new programs and services. If we claim that high attrition rates for athletes, lack of parking for commuters, inadequate numbers of computer terminals, or poor campus lighting are not in the traditional purview of what we call "student affairs" then we are writing ourselves out of a significant role on the campus. Whether we work in financial aid, the student life office, intramurals, student health, the registrar's office, or the counseling center, we need to think beyond our proscribed duties, to the campus as a whole. I believe we are at a very important time in our profession on many campuses; we can choose to be passive and assume merely a complementary role on the sidelines of higher education, or we can join the fray in the middle of the field, roughing it up with the first team. What direction we choose, I submit, may be largely a function of how we perceive of the term "student affairs."

Any listing of current issues in our field reveals both the biases and the limitations of the person doing the listing. This one of mine is no exception. Nevertheless, here are major issues I see us facing at this time in the profession, together with some suggestions as to what we might do about them.

1. *How we conceive of the field.* I have already alluded to this matter with my previous comments, of course, but I want to elaborate further here. When E. G. Williamson chaired the ACE committee on student affairs in the 1930's, the Student Personnel Point of View was produced, and later revised in 1949. Since then there has been a very rapid expansion of higher education, and of services and programs in this field. Since 1950, I think of Williamson's book, Kate Mueller's books, the Miller and Prince volume, the ACPA project on tomorrow's higher education, and Delworth and Hanson's book as the major works in our field. While each of these had had an impact, I believe we need a major effort, similar to the 1937 ACE committee, to review the nature of our profession, and to define what now constitutes "student affairs." The Student Personnel Point of View is a beautiful piece of work and it deserves a careful reading again by all of us. However, the world of higher education has changed dramatically since it was last revised 32 years ago, and our profession could be significantly revitalized by a wide-ranging debate as to the essential nature of our business. A national drafting group should be appointed to accomplish this task, composed of leaders from the major professional associations. Yes, we are tremendously diverse and this is a great strength for us, but we are strongly in need of intellectual and conceptual leadership. Unfortunately, it has been quite absent since the passing of E. G. Williamson.

2. *The accreditation process.* Many of you in this room have participated in the accreditation process as members of visitation teams. Others of you have been on the "other end": that is, you have been at institutions where an evaluation took place. The accreditation process, whatever our personal

views about it, can have a significant impact upon our programs. The problem is that student affairs campus programs may be evaluated in the accrediting process, according to standards we do not accept, by persons who had very little, if any, experience in the field. To a very large extent I suggest that this is our own fault—1) for not being more aggressive in our insistence on being involved in the accreditation process and 2) for our own negligence for not developing professional standards of good practice within our profession. I recognize clearly the difficulties in defining good standards of practice in a field as diverse as ours. However, if we do not take the initiative and do this, it will be done de facto for us by others. When I assumed my current position in 1973, a 10-year study had just been completed by the Southern Association of Colleges and Schools. There were several volumes of reports done on the institution and its programs and on the visitation team of some 25 persons. There was not a student affairs person represented. The report clearly reflected this, and the recommendations made by the visiting team were not only not helpful to the student affairs campus program, they also served to reinforce some inaccurate stereotypes about the services and programs among faculty and administration on the campus. I suggest that it is the responsibility of the major professional associations in our field, despite our historical differences, to join forces and draft a set of standards of good practice that will be acceptable to most institutions for the accreditation process. My experience with the regional accrediting associations is that they are open to our suggestions and participation, and would welcome such input. However, in the absence of it, we will continue to have our campus programs subject to the arbitrary whims of whomever might be a member of a visitation team.

3. *Professional preparation programs.* What academic preparation individuals should undergo before entry into this profession has always been a matter of great debate. A 1934 Journal article by Eugenie Leonard, Dean of Women at Syracuse, described the most respected training program in the country at that time at Syracuse. In the 1940's and 1950's, Minnesota, Columbia, and Syracuse provided the major leadership in our field regarding professional preparation, and the impact of their graduates continues to this day. In the 1960's and 1970's Indiana and Michigan State seemed to gain the most visibility. Now it appears that Ohio State and UCLA may provide the major leadership during the 1980's. We have all benefited from the leadership that has emerged from these fine training programs. However, the evidence still suggests that the gap between the practitioners and the trainers is too wide: communications are too infrequent, and considerable dissatisfaction with training programs continues. In a survey completed several years ago, it was clear that there was great proliferation of graduate training programs in our

field, especially at the Master's level, at institutions with inadequately trained faculty. For our national associations to continue to ignore this harmful development is, in my view, an admission that we either do not have acceptable standards or that we apparently don't think it makes much difference what one studies or where. I am currently conducting a study of my own on this topic, and have asked a large sample of chief student affairs administrators for their views about the academic preparation programs. The preliminary results indicate some clear directions—this group, which has responsibility for hiring staff, has generally a low opinion of the quality of current academic training programs and of the qualifications of faculty members conducting them. There are notable institutional exceptions, and the chief student affairs administrators strongly urge that the professional associations themselves accept responsibility for cleaning up our act. Around the turn of this century, the Flexner report resulted in a complete overhaul of medical education in this country, and helped to eliminate the majority of medical preparation programs, too many of which had proliferated at that time. I believe a major responsibility we have in our profession now is to do the same thing, and this should be initiated by the professional groups themselves. This is not at all to suggest that there should be one curriculum or one way to prepare students for our field. As a person responsible for hiring people for several years myself, I perceive very significant differences in the quality of various professional preparation programs and I believe we have a responsibility to our students to protect them from some of the very weak programs that currently exist.

4. *The rights of students.* During the 1960's there was a great deal of turmoil in the country and, of course, on the campuses as well. One of the best documents ever produced in our field emerged in 1966 in the form of the joint Statement on Rights and Freedoms of Students, an effort of 10 professional associations, including NASPA, NAWDAC, The National Student Association, and AAUP. This document set forth the essential requirements for student freedom to learn and served as an important guideline for hundreds of campuses for the next several years. It is a landmark in our profession, and one of the most important documents in our history. There are clear indications that the pendulum has now swung back toward conservative views, and the repercussions for student academic freedom on the campus may be considerable. Some of us here in the room are old enough to remember the McCarthy era and its impact upon campus life, and there are some fairly scary correlates to that movement with the moral majority. If some student organizations are subjected to political scrutiny because of their current unpopularity with societal groups, the atmosphere for student academic freedom on our campus could become chilling. The educational

impact, of course, would be devastating. While I am not one to over-emphasize a problem, it seems to me to be an appropriate time to reconvene that 1966 group for the purpose of updating and revising the Joint Statement on Rights and Freedoms of Students. There have been significant changes on the campus since 1966, and we should take the leadership as a profession in insuring the rights of our students for freedom to learn. We need a new statement, and we should take the lead.

5. *Relationships with other associations.* One of the greatest dangers for our field, in my view, is to construct our own language, our own jargon, our own associations, and our own little world. It is very comforting, and it is downright intoxicating at times as we almost convince ourselves that we are doing something so esoteric that no one else can understand it, appreciate it, or be effective participants in it. But there is no secure corner in the world of higher education in the 1980's, and I believe the most fatal mistake we could make during this decade is to try to carve out our own such corner. Our strength lies not in isolation but in cooperation. The best student affairs programs I know on various campuses are those that are integrated with academic affairs, administrative affairs, and development. The chief student affairs officer on the campus in the 1980's must be a full member of the management team that runs that campus. Student learning problems and educational issues do not conform neatly to organizational charts—they must be considered as a whole, and we must conceive of new organizational arrangements, programmatic ties, and staff liaison with our colleagues throughout the campus. This must also be true in our professional associations. Our student affairs groups can maintain their own identity, but we will gain greater strength for our members and for our students if we join with the American Council on Education, the National Association of Land Grant Colleges and Universities, The National Association of Independent Colleges and Universities, and other such generalist organizations in joint projects and efforts to serve the campuses.

6. *Student financial aid.* Why do I identify this specific service? Because in my view it is currently the most important student service that affects all of our campuses. Some of our institutions now are dependent upon federal financial aid programs for their actual survival. Financial aid is by far the most debated and most controversial matter regarding higher education in the congress year after year. The diversity of our student bodies and the access principle are largely dependent upon the provision of financial aid. On my own campus, 65% of our students will receive more than 50 million dollars in various forms of aid during the coming year. But what have we done with student financial aid as a student service within our profession in the past 10 years? What we have done, I suggest, is we have turned it over to

the computer people and the technical experts. We have allowed it to become something other than a student personnel function. It is clear that students view financial aid in the same manner that citizens view public assistance programs. Is the financial aid office really part of the educational program of the campus? Is it administering funds and programs in a humane manner with concern for individuals? The Student Financial Aid Association is very effective politically, has survived, and has grown significantly. But what have the rest of us in student affairs done to accommodate their needs? The next logical step in federal financial aid is to remove it completely from the college campus and have it administered by state or federal bureaus, similar to food stamps, welfare, or aid to dependent children. If we do not want this to happen, we ought to get involved in the process.

7. *Research on students*. Theodore Newcomb with his Bennington studies, Nevitt Sanford with the Vassar studies, Philip Jacob in the 1950's, Kauffman's Hazen Foundation study, Joseph Katz in his Stanford-Berkeley studies of the 1960's, Alexander Astin with his work on retention, attrition, and financial aid, Arthur Chickering in his work with commuters and residents, and Arthur Levine's recent work for the Carnegie Policy study group, all stand out as landmarks that have helped us understand the nature of students more effectively. While these studies have been extremely valuable to us, they have largely been initiated from outside the profession. We are still too heavily dependent upon work carried on by others to form the basis for decisions that we make in our own field. I would like to suggest that our professional associations create some substantial projects in the next few years, conducting major studies of college students. We have plenty of competent people to carry on such work in critical areas as student consumerism, academic rights, student advising needs, commuter student needs, older student problems, minority student follow-up, and the like. We have been too dependent upon others and it is time for us to reflect our maturity as a profession and assume responsibility for some of this work ourselves.

8. *Professional development*. I have neighbors who are pharmacists, attorneys, physicians, and nurses. Each year these professionals are required to attend various educational programs designed to keep them up-to-date in their fields. If they do not participate in these programs, they are no longer permitted to practice. They attend these required educational programs in addition to their regular professional conferences of their associations, and they pay for them. I have been curious since I've been in this business why we do not have any such requirements. Once I received my Ph.D. degree from Michigan State in 1965, I have never been required to attend any kind of educational program to keep me up-to-date with my own profession. My institution did not require it, my own professional association had no such

requirement, and neither did any state organization. While there are, of course, hazards to such regulations, it is difficult for us to claim that we are, in fact, a profession when we do not assume more actual responsibility for our own ongoing professional learning. We certainly have at least the same kinds of needs as my neighbors do. In my own state I have suggested the creation of a state-wide student affairs professional development institute, to be staffed by a full-time person, supported by dues from participating professionals in student affairs. This institute, under the leadership of a full-time director, would conduct workshops and learning programs for practicing student affairs people. There is currently a task force in our state studying the feasibility of this, and I am pleased that the reaction to it so far is favorable. I believe that there is a strong need for such continuing education for all of us. It is high time that our professional associations assume leadership in creating such opportunities and requirements.

So what are the critical decisions for the decade of the 1980's? As you can tell from my comments, I have a great deal of confidence in our own profession and our ability to adapt to changing needs and problems. It is my feeling that we have matured sufficiently as a profession now; and that our most important task in the next 10 years, besides doing our jobs on the campuses with students, is to focus on our own development as professionals and as a profession. And the responsibility for this is ours. Let's get on with it.

References

Mathew, S. L. K. *The dean of women.* Boston, MA: Houghton-Mifflin Co., 1915.

Moral Development: From Direction to Dialogue

Mary Louise McBee

Moral and ethical behavior dialogue is essential

Moral* Development: From Direction to Dialogue

Within the past year, news media across the United States covered the following events on college and university campuses:

. . . A university's homecoming parade is disrupted by its students on the parade route throwing rotten eggs and yelling obscenities at fellow students riding on the floats.

. . . City police close a fraternity party and the fraternity president is jailed on charges of operating a disorderly house. Fraternity members imported a strip show from a neighboring town for a pledge party. Later fraternity members engaged in sexual intercourse with the women while fraternity brothers watched.

. . . Eighteen students are charged in connection with cutting down 30-foot cedar trees valued at $750 from a university's forestry school property. The tree was later found decorated as a Christmas tree at a fraternity house.

. . . A Rhodes scholar applicant is disqualified when it is learned that his application to the institution was falsified by denying enrollment in a previous institution where he made less than satisfactory grades.

. . . A sophomore liberal arts student believes he has developed foolproof cheating methods. On tests requiring knowledge of formulas, he crams as many as possible on the back page of his blue book prior to

---

*Terminology in this paper varies but "morals", "ethics", "values", and "character" all refer in one way or another to right conduct.

the examination and then rips out the page before he turns in
the booklet.

These isolated incidents, but similar and equally serious incidents occur
daily on campuses across the country. Accounts of student pranks are, of
course, part of the lore of colleges and universities. Education and discipline
have always gone hand in hand (Bracewell, 1972, p.1). The positions of
dean of men and dean of women were established to control undesirable
activity and to oversee the morals of the young men and women enrolled at
the institution. There are at least two differences, however, that may
distinguish the current scene from earlier year: (1) the incidence of unacceptable conduct has increased and (2) colleges and universities now seem
unwilling to do much about this unacceptable conduct. Herein lies the
problem. Higher education's reluctance in recent years to take action
against unacceptable behavior gives the appearance of tacitly condoning the
misconduct. This reluctance began in the 1960's and represented a dramatic
departure from higher education's historical position. After two decades of a
laissez-faire approach in student conduct, it appears that higher education
has worshipped a false and impossible notion of value neutrality (Hill, 1980).

This paper will explore how this change on the part of colleges and
universities developed and suggest a new approach for solving a growing
concern about the ethical development of students. This proposed approach
involves actively creating opportunities to talk with students about values
issues. Four assumptions are made:

(1) That behavior is a reflection of the values one holds.
(2) That higher education is responsible for transmitting moral and
     ethical values to the youth with whom it works.
(3) That higher education is failing to provide moral and ethical educa-
     tion and this failure has been paralleled by a decline in individual be-
     havior.
(4) Higher education needs to return to a concern for individual ethics.

Unethical Conduct: The Problem We Face

The Carnegie Council on Policy Studies in Higher Education's Report,
Fair Practices in Higher Education (1979) decried "a general decline in
integrity of conduct on campus" and "signs of deterioration of important
parts of academic life." The council cited higher default rate on student
loans, nonpayment of veterans' loans, and mounting theft and destruction of
valuable property, especially library books and journals.

In regards to deterioration of ethical standards, cheating gets the most attention. Again, the Carnegie Council (1979) cited a "significant and apparently increasing amount of cheating" at the nation's colleges. In another survey (Seib, 1980) 88% of medical students questioned said they had cheated sometime in college; 58% said they had cheated while in medical school. Wynne (1979) reports that in two surveys of national samples of students in American research universities, the proportion of students who admitted to cheating rose 87% from 1969 to 1976.

Alcohol abuse is also an increasing problem on most campuses. Nearly 90% of the campus population drinks alcohol, about a third of those student drinkers are "problem drinkers" with the number rising all the time, according to a study completed by Dr.GeraldoGonzalez, Director of the Campus Alcohol Information Center at the University of Florida and President of the Nationwide BACCHUS (Boost Alcohol Consciousness Concerning the Health of University Students). Gonzalez reported that nearly 80% of all campus vandalism is related to alcohol consumption (Fite, 1982, b).

In short, there is much evidence of increasing misconduct including the abuse and misuse of property, cheating, defiance of authority, and irresponsibility in the use of alcohol and other drugs for higher education to continue to ignore the situation.

Young people themselves are concerned about values and about the moral ambiguity of the times in which they live. Levine (1980) speaks of the mood of despair among young people and their pessimism about the future of the country. Students describe life as "going first class on the Titanic." This perhaps explains, said Levine, why suicide had become the second leading cause of death among students in the 1970's.

Changes Resulting from Court Decisions

Historically, colleges and universities, along with the home and the church, are viewed as primary transmitters of moral standards. Colleges have viewed guiding conduct and forming student character as central to their mission. All of this changed in the political turbulent 1960's. A great many events contributed to this change. The 1969 *Dixon v. Alabama State Board of Education* decision, probably more than any other single event, brought about a dramatic shift. Essentially, Dixon and subsequent related court cases, struck down the concept of in loco parentis. This caused colleges and universities to rethink their philosophy and approach in working with students. From that point until the present, more by default than design, colleges and universities have given the impression that in student conduct "anything goes." This was the beginning of a gradual erosion of student behavior and ethical conduct.

Prior to Dixon, education was viewed as a privilege, not a right. Colleges and universities, with the courts blessing, said in effect that the privilege of an education carries certain student responsibilities which the college could specify. This privilege could be taken away in the same manner that a parent could deny privileges to an erring child. Until Dixon the courts held that a college knows what is best for its students and that anything the college does in its own best interest is also in the students' best interest (Fischer, 1972). Thus a college or university could invoke penalties, apply curfews, restrict students to campus, and even deny the privilege of attending the institution, temporarily or permanently. This was the essence of in loco parentis. This student/institutional relationship changed abruptly with Dixon. The court affirmed in Dixon that a college education is not only a privilege but a right, and "rights" and "privileges" receive quite different treatment under the law (Fischer, 1972). Education, as a right, is a constitutionally protected interest an cannot be denied without due process.

Following Dixon, colleges often lost a proper balance between student rights and responsibilities. The courts, in turn, tended to define too narrowly what the institution could and should be concerned about. Many of the standards of conduct on which the institution had always stood firm, and which had been viewed as desirable and worth protecting, were set aside. Honor codes disappeared. Institutional safeguards against cheating were relaxed. Regulations governing overnight visits in residence halls or apartments of the opposite sex were dropped as were restrictions on the use of alcohol. The abuse of addictive drugs became a problem. In short, virtually overnight colleges and universities dropped many if not most of their regulations governing student life. In this narrower definition of its role, higher education lost much of what had been valued in the academic environment. Students, and some student personnel administrators, viewed the institutional retreat from values concerns as a victory for freedom. But the victory came at a price. A great deal of what was important for the students, the institution, and society was sacrificed. Higher education's new posture on student conduct was soon perceived by parents, students, and the community as "we no longer care or are concerned about how you behave?"

Not only were major changes occurring on college campuses during the decade of the 1960's but equally dramatic changes were occurring in the larger society. Colleges and universities do not operate in a vacuum. Rather, as instruments of society, they are an expression of the prevailing forces and values of that society. As such, there has been a slow but persistent shift in society's external social controls. The shift has been occurring since the Victorian era. The major benchmarks were: post World War I, post World War II, and prior to and during the Vietnam War.

There is now a growing national concern about the decline in ethical standards. There is a widespread uneasiness that higher education has allowed questions of values and ethics to be pushed to one side. The time has come for a reassessment—a reassessment of our individual and collective standards of conduct and education's role in setting these standards.

Concern for Ethical Development: A New Approach

Perhaps in the past we have relied too much on external controls. The in loco parentis posture of colleges prior to the 1960's was extreme and needed to be changed. Now that the external controls are gone students must be guided to develop internal controls. This is an opportunity for professional educators to put energies into equipping students to think more critically and carefully about moral problems and to assist them in developing a sound basis for making their own moral decisions.

Education has two great goals—developing intellect and developing character. Students should not only be educated; they should also be people with integrity (Lickona, 1980). Fite argues cogently, "the standards, principles and behavior on a college campus should be better than in the general society. Why? Because we claim to be educated" (1982, p.9). The challenge then is to move students and the campus community not back to the superimposed responsibility and dedication. How can we raise student awareness of social and ethical issues to new levels? How can we foster commitment to fundamental values so that our vast knowledge will be used in a more just, decent, humane, and civilized way? Fite (1982) sees this renewed attention to values as higher education's unfinished agenda.

Higher education could fulfill its responsibility for moral development in two ways: the teaching of ethics as content and the demonstration of ethics, that is, by the faculty and administration serving as models and the institution serving as a laboratory for the practice of values taught (McBee, 1980). To make the college and university campus a better laboratory, an effort should be made to sensitize the entire college community to values issues. Bennett has said "There is no curriculum, no program, no course that has the moral power of example" (1980, p.27). We cannot expect right conduct from the students unless the institution itself is an example of noble behavior. This means that the policies and practices of the institution must be honest, open, and fair. It means that administrators and faculty must be

men and women of character "who know the difference between right and
wrong, good and evil, who make some effort to live the difference, and who
have an interest in instilling that difference in others" (Bennett, 1980,
p.27). Efforts to build character in any other campus environment will be
doomed to failure.

Following are some proposed steps to involve students, faculty, and
administrators in a dialogue on value issues and the complexity and ambiguity
of moral decisions:

(1) Create a faculty/student/administrator committee and charge it with
developing a statement on academic honesty, or code of campus
interpersonal ethics, or a code of campus conduct. Such a committee
at the University of Georgia developed a brochure on Academic
Honesty. The committee appointed by the Vice President for Student
Affairs, worked for over a year on the document which became an
official statement of University policy on academic integrity. The
frank and clearly stated code is distributed to all new students and
their parents when they come to the campus for orientation sessions.

One public school system developed a statement of moral principles
to be communicated to students, as well as a code of ethics for its
faculty. Among its faculty provisions are: As a professional person
I will:

. . . be an exemplar to our students . . .
. . . respect the integrity and personality of the individual person . . .
. . . encourage respect for learning and dedication to quality work . . .
. . . exhibit fairness, modesty, and graciousness toward others
(Thomas and Lewy, 1980, p.6).

(2) Have department heads, deans, and the academic vice president
encourage or require faculty to use a portion of class time at the
beginning of a new quarter or semester in a discussion of academic
honesty. In addition to a review of the institution's academic regulations the instructor could use the opportunity to discuss the importance of academic honesty and of students' responsibilities to themselves, to other students, and to the academic community. Students
reported for cheating violations can no longer argue, "I didn't know
the professor felt so strongly about it. He never mentioned it!" A
discussion as suggested above should clear up any questions about the
professor's views.

(3) Use an already constituted campus committee, or create one, for
the discussion of campus value-laden problems. Many colleges and
universities have student union or student government committees, or
special advisory committees to the President or Vice President of the

institution which could be used for this purpose. For example, the University of Georgia recently used a student advisory committee to the Vice President for Academic Affairs for such a discussion. Following a winter storm in Athens, university students gathered to enjoy the snow on a public street paralleling the campus. The behavior deteriorated to a near riot situation. Property was damaged and stolen, car doors were opened and hard-packed snow balls were thrown at passengers. Several persons were injured and hospitalized. The students knew the issues firsthand because many of them were there when the problem developed. They had an opportunity to discuss with administrators and each other the ethical issues involved. How better to foster growth than for young people to consider, deliberate, and work together on common problems and develop reasonable standards and expectations for themselves and their peers.

(4) Sponsor speakers and/or panels that address ethical issues. Residence hall councils, interfraternity and panhellenic councils and student union program committees are good avenues for such programs. Speakers or panels might consider campus issues or ones that plague society in general, such as the prevention of and/or intervention efforts aimed at adolescent pregnancy, drug and alcohol abuse, family violence, poverty, and discrimination. For example, a student union Ideas and Issues Committee at the University of Georgia recently sponsored a speaker on pornography. Over two hundred students and twenty-five faculty took part in a two-hour heated discussion.

Students need help in examining the society in which they live. In an informal give-and-take setting, students can consider the nature of a just society; circumstances under which laws should be disobeyed; protecting personal freedom and well-being while considering human society as a whole.

Summary

Colleges and universities can and must recapture their credibility as standard bearers of moral and ethical behavior. They can and must help students protect and internalize ethical values and conditions. The university can and must encourage students to be honest, responsible, fair, dependable, considerate, courteous, diligent, and self-disciplined. "A higher education that does not foster, support, and implement an examination of the moral life will fail its own purposes, the needs of its students, and the welfare of society." (Seib, 1980, b, p.80). One way higher education can renew its efforts in this area is by establishing opportunities for dialogue with students about moral obligations.

References

Bennett, W. J. The teacher, the curriculum, and values education development. In *Rethinking college responsibilities for values*. M.L.McBee (Ed.), San Francisco: Jossey-Bass, Inc., 1980.

Bracewell, W. R. Balancing students' rights and institutional needs. In *Proceedings Substantial justice on campus: Individual rights v. institutional needs*. W. R. Bracewell (Ed., The University of Georgia Center for Continuing Education, November 19–21, 1972.

Carnegie Council on Policy Studies in Higher Education. *Fair practices in higher education: Rights and responsibilities of students and their colleges in a period of intensified competition for enrollment*. San Francisco: Jossey-Bass, 1979.

Dixon v. Alabama State Board of Education 294 F 2d 150 (5th Cir. 161), Cert. denied, 286 U.S. 930 (1961).

Fischer, T. C. Challenging from the courts. In *Proceedings Substantial justice on campus: Individual rights v. institutional needs*, W. R. Bracewell (Ed.) The University of Georgia Center for Continuing Education, November 19–21, 1972, 5–24.

Fite, G. C. *The unfinished agenda*. An unpublished address to The Founders Day Banquet, University of Georgia, Athens, January 26, 1982.

Fite, G. C. Florida study announces a rise in campus drinking. *The Red and Black* (student newspaper, University of Georgia, Athens) January 8, 1982, p. 2.

Hill, I. *Common sense and everyday ethics*. American Viewpoint, Inc., 1720 Rhode Island Ave., N.W., Washington, D.C., 1980, p.4.

Levine, A. When dreams and heroes died: A portrait of today's college student. San Francisco: Jossey-Bass Publishers, 1980.

Lickona, T. Preparing teachers to be moral educators: A neglected duty. In *Rethinking college responsibilities for values*. M. L. McBee (Ed.), San Francisco: Jossey-Bass, Inc., 1980, 51–64.

McBee, M. L. The values development dilemma. In *Rethinking college responsibilities for values*. M. L. McBee (Ed.), San Francisco: Jossey-Bass, Inc., 1980, 1–7.

Seib, G. F. Why are they cheating? *Wall Street Journal*, June 10, 1980, p.24.

Seib, G. F. *The teaching of ethics in higher education*. A report by the Hastings Center. Hastings-on-Hudson, N.Y.: Institute of Society, Ethics and The Life Sciences, 1980.

Thomas, M. D., & Lewy, R. Education and moral conduct. *Character*, 1980, 1(3), 2–7.

Wynne, E. A. Facts about the character of young Americans. *Character*, 1979 1(1), 1–7.

The Non-Traditional Student in Higher Education: A Synthesis of the Literature

Rees Hughes

Resources and interesting data are presented.

Colleges and universities throughout the United States are experiencing a dramatic shift in the composition of their student populations. No longer is the typical student the full-time resident student between the ages of 18 and 22. So dramatic are these changes that the growth and survival of institutions of higher education are dependent upon the ability of these institutions to attract and retain older students. Currently, over one-third of all college students are over the age of 25 and by the year 2000 there will be in excess of 20 million adult students (Betters-Reed, 1980). The importance of these students is heightened by the nationwide diminution of secondary school enrollments. Brodzinski (1981) claims that by 1995, "there will be a 20 percent drop in the number of 18–24 year olds from the 1980 levels" (p. 1).

Three critical questions guide this synthesis of the diverse literature on non-traditional students, the answers to which student personnel administrators must thoroughly understand and effectively integrate in order to be a part of this transformation in higher education. Who is the non-traditional student? What do they want from higher education? How can student personnel professionals respond?

None of these queries are easily answered. Even defining the non-traditional student has been a source of ever-increasing ambiguity. Returning students, stop-outs, re-entry students, older students, and adult learners have been variously used in the literature. Although disabled, minority, and economically disadvantaged students have often been labelled non-traditional, they constitute distinct populations with needs and characteristics quite different than the older or returning non-traditional student. Age has generally been used to identify this older or returning non-traditional student. However, the cut-off has ranged from 22 years (Leckie, 1978;

Weathersby and Tarule, 1980) to 30 years of age (Rawlins, 1979; Rawlins and Davies, 1981). Other factors have also served as critical variables, such as married/unmarried, commuter/resident, and part-time/full-time (Staman, 1980). This lack of a consistent definition in the literature has made it difficult to extract a clear picture of who the non-traditional student is.

A second difficulty in responding to the three questions is the inadequacy of the available research. As has often plagued our profession, the studies on non-traditional students reviewed in this article, on the whole, have a number of serious weaknesses that could potentially undermine their conclusions and limit their generalizability. They are frequently institution specific. They rely heavily upon descriptive or survey data and self-report. Experimental and longitudinal designs, which could potentially be illuminating, are virtually non-existent. The existing research frequently does not adequately control for systematic variation from extraneous sources. Bias could occur because many samples are predominantly composed of respondents who are accessible and cooperative. The return rates are often exceedingly low. Bias could occur because many survey instruments are not rigorously developed so as to avoid building in, for example, a tendency to agree with positive statements. As future research is undertaken on the non-traditional student, this caveat warrants consideration. Hence, the paucity of rigorous research on the non-traditional student and the absence of a consistent definition of the non-traditional student have made it very difficult to discuss this group of students.

The Non-Traditional Student—Characteristics

Not only do the variety of existing definitions inhibit the creation of a meaningful composite of the non-traditional student, but so does the fact that non-traditional students are not a single population. They cannot be effectively considered and treated en masse. They defy generalization. Adult development theorists go so far as to posit a whole range of age-linked life stages that suggest the existence of a different set of needs, goals, and foci for each stage (Chickering, 1976; Knox, 1977; Levinson, et.al., 1978).

The multiplicity of attitudes, interests, values, expectations, and motivations highlighted in the literature is aptly exemplified by the myriad of reasons older students have given for re-entering school. They have returned for career advancement and intellectual stimulation (Malin, Dougherty, and Skinner, 1979), self-fulfillment (Rawlins, 1979), and personal satisfaction (Billingham and Travaglini, 1981). Morstain and Smart (1977) went so far as to identify five types of adult learners: non-directed, social, stimulation-seeking, career-oriented, and life change learners. The life-changers are, for example, very different from those with a primary goal of career advancement. This serves to underscore the difficulty of making any meaningful generalizations by examining solely non-traditional student characteristics.

However, a number of authors have worked to clarify a useful traditional/non-traditional student dichotomy. Three characteristics consistently appear in the literature and seem to accurately differentiate between non-traditional and traditional students.

A number of authors focus on the issues of *multiple commitment* and *off-campus 'directedness'*. White (1981) notes that the non-traditional student is:

1. responsible for him or herself, and frequently directly responsible for the well-being of others;

2. perceived by others as generally fulfilling several roles typical of mature adults in our society (e.g., worker, taxpayer, voter, concerned community citizen, spouse, parent); and

3. one who perceives formal educational activity as only one of several competing or conflicting priorities, and often as incidental activity, though one of increasing importance. (p. 2).

This is reinforced by Baillie (1976) who characterizes the older student as usually currently employed or has been employed, married or has been married, has a family and is a tax paying citizen. The family or work environment often take precedence over the educational environment. Holtzclaw (1980) identified the lack of time due to these family and work commitments as a barrier preventing non-traditional students from centering on-campus.

The third key variable, a preference for informal learning, is amplified in the literature. Hameister and Hickey (1977), in contrasting traditional and non-traditional students, found that non-traditional students are influenced by informal education, often do not understand formal education, lack study and communication skills but have relevant work experience, base their frame of reference on life experiences, and often cannot be judged accurately on their academic potential. White (1981) explains the contrast in educational needs and expectations further,

Youth traditionally engaged in formal learning with the notion that the experience would be stored up for later use; living begins after learning is completed. More mature adults insist on putting their learning to work relatively soon. They are less subject-matter and more problem-solving centered, even when learning has no more immediate application than a better understanding or appreciation of some remote aspect of life. Adults want and expect their learning to help them understand and deal with those situations faced in their every-day lives (pp. 2–3).

The need non-traditional students have for practical and tangible learning experiences was supported by Ward and Korz (1969), Jurand-Salter (1980), and Holtzclaw (1980). In summary, these three characteristics—diversely committed, not campus-focused, and preference for informal learning—which contrast traditional and non-traditional students, provide a useful foundation upon which to build a greater understanding of the older student. These are represented in Table 1.

Table 1
Key Differences Between
Traditional and Non-Traditional Students

NON-TRADITIONAL STUDENTS	TRADITIONAL STUDENTS
multiple commitments	limited commitments
not campus focused	campus focused
informal learning	formal learning

Additional Characteristics

A number of studies have produced additional characteristics of the non-traditional student. However, these differences seem to either emanate from the three critical attributes, be specific to a very limited population, or appear inconsistently in the literature. Nonetheless, they do serve to help rough in the basic outline of the non-traditional student.

In a study of students over the age of 21 entering 600 two and four-year colleges and universities between 1966 and 1978, Solmon and Gordon (1981) found that older students thought they needed more remedial work, especially in mathematics, than did traditional students, and had lower high school grade-point averages than did younger students. Business was the most popular field of study among adult students. This reinforces the conclusion expressed by McCrea's (1979) study of 1,067 women over the age of 24 at a large urban university. A definite trend was revealed at that time away from education and liberal arts toward business, accounting, and urban studies.

The low self-confidence about the ability to succeed in academe reappears in a number of studies. Lance, Lourie, and Mayo (1979a) found, in an examination of 583 returning students (over the age of 24 who had been out of school two years or more), that the fear of not being smart enough, fear of failing, concern over ability to study and learn, and fear of a dulled memory were mentioned as some of the greatest hurdles. Roehl (1980) recommends acceptance of re-entering students as they are, stressing their independence, avoiding destructive criticism, and recognizing their progress in order to facilitate development of self-confidence. However, re-entering students with shorter interruptions in schooling were less concerned about academically-related issues.

One of the most comprehensive needs assessments of returning adult students was done through the Two-Year College Development Center at the State University of New York at Albany (Mangano, Corrado, and Frank, 1979). Returning students rated twelve items significantly more important than the traditional-aged students rated them. These included: preregistration as well as speedy registration procedures; evening and weekend classes and evening and weekend registration; credit for out-of-college experiences; and independent study courses. Traditionally-aged students indicated a greater need for extracurricular activities and for personal development. Both returning adult and traditionally-aged students evidence a marked preference for concentration, study-skill, and memory improvement; for a broad educational background with a number of courses providing specific job skills; and for relaxed, informal, encouraging instructors who have a realistic view of a student's responsibilities outside class, and who use many examples in their lectures. Older students expressed a preference for faculty who base final grades on several activities, who provide alternative assignments and retests, and who modify course outlines to satisfy student interests. Older students underscored the difficulty of registration, the limited hours of the financial and office, the cafeteria, placement, tutoring, orientation, and the childcare services as sources of dissatisfaction. Interestingly, full-time older students were found to respond in a similar fashion to traditional students.

A great volume of research exists on a sub-group of the total wave of non-traditional students—the re-entering woman. Research indicates that women older students have a greater need for services than do men (Lance, Lourie, and Mayo, 1979b; Mangano and Corrado, 1979). There are the female single parents who have outside responsibilities, limited time for study, inadequate study skills and educational motives that are almost exclusively oriented toward employment (Hooper and March, 1980). There are married women students who Berkove (1979) found more than likely have continued to take full responsibility for preparing meals, doing laundry, and shopping for food. There are women who Ryan (1979) characterizes as experiencing the fear of isolation, the guilt of spending time, money and effort in education, the belief that they are not worth the trouble they may cause their family, and spousal disapproval. Hall and Gleaves (1981) also mention the frequent lack of home and community support and the fear of isolation and discomfort. In conclusion, non-traditional women students face unique difficulties not dealt with by non-traditional men students because of differing goals and differing family responsibilities (Tittle and Kenker, 1977). The support for the special challenge facing women returning to college is quite evident throughout the literature.

In summary, it can be said that, perhaps for no other reason than sheer quantity of evidence and its relative unanimity, higher education today is dealing with two major populations known as traditional students and non-traditional students. This evidence tends to indicate that these two groups have quite different expectations and needs of higher education. Yet, non-traditional students cannot be perceived as one uniform group.

Non-Traditional Students—Needs and Responses

The diversity of non-traditional students combined with their multiple commitments and off-campus focus has made this a difficult group to service. In fact, by 1974 Glass and Harshberger (1974) had found that only one half of all institutions of higher education had designed any kind of specific response to older students. This may, in part, be an outcome of the low rate at which non-traditional students utilize campus services (Alford, 1981). The literature recommends a four-pronged effort to address the needs of non-traditional students: services, programs, advocacy, and the academic delivery system.

Ideally, institutional responses to non-traditional students both practically and logically follow from non-traditional student needs. Because of that relationship, they are being treated together in this article. Unfortunately, in reality the response can be characterized quite differently. Responses have generally been fragmented attempts to deal with immediate problems instead of a comprehensive, total response. Nonetheless, colleges and universities are committing energy and resources to modifying and creating programs to meet the needs of the rising numbers of non-traditional students. This is occurring in terms of services, programs, advocacy, and the academic delivery system.

Services range from those which are insignificant in cost and readily available to services and facilities which are high in cost and require lengthy start-up times. Institutions may, as suggested by Jurand-Salter (1980) and Alford (1981), need to make existing services more available by changing or increasing hours or locations. Conveniences and accessibility of services should be a high priority (Hall, 1980; Scott, 1980). This is exemplified by services such as registration (Kegel, 1977), cafeteria hours, library and bookstore hours (Mangano, and Corrado, 1979). These and other key points extracted from the literature regarding the needs of non-traditional students are summarized in Table 2.

Table 2
Service and Support Needs

1. *Need convenient and accessible services* (Hall, 1980; Scott, 1980).
2. *Need to be thoroughly oriented* (Roach, 1976; Kegel, 1977; Rawlins, 1979; Lance, Lourie, and Mayo, 1979b; Rawlins and Davies, 1981).
3. *Need to receive accurate information through regular communication* (Cross, 1978, Kegel, 1977; Jurand-Salter, 1980; Nayman and Patton, 1980; Heinlein and Byers, 1981) to counter lack of awareness (Fauquet, 1978; Rawlins, 1979; Reehling, 1980; Rawlins and Davies, 1981).
4. *Need financial support* (Kegel, 1977; Rawlins, 1979; Jurand-Salter, 1980; Hooper and March, 1980; Holtzclaw, 1980). *This is especially true for divorced women re-entering college* (Smallwood, 1980).
5. *Need child care* (Ryan, 1979; Tittle and Kenker, 1980; Hooper and March, 1980; Creange, 1980; Hall and Gleaves, 1981).
6. *Need career counseling services* (Hiltunen, 1978; Ryan, 1979; Lance, Lourie, and Mayo, 1979b; Scott, 1980; Malin, et.al., 1980) *with specific information* (Center for Educational Development, 1980) *and a career counseling curriculum* (Muskat, 1978).
7. *Need appropriate person counseling* (Simpkins, 1980).

Orientation programs designed specifically for the non-traditional student are frequently mentioned in the literature (Kegel, 1977; ACPA, 1980). The 583 responses to a questionnaire distributed by Lance, Lourie, and Mayo (1979b) indicated highest demand for an appropriate campus orientation and a specifically designed re-entry admissions counselor. Cohen (1980) states that, "Ideally orientation for the adult learner should be a twice-weekly program throughout most, if not all, of the initial semester" (p.26). Once comfortable with the non-academic resources, the non-traditional student needs a "first hand familiarity with academic programs and require-ments" (p.26). Authors like Roach (1976) and Ryan (1979) underscore the desirability of a special orientation program for returning women students. Several institutions report highly successful orientations where the student's spouse and/or family were included in the orientation process.

Jurand-Salter (1980), Kegel (1977), and Hooper and March (1980), among others, urge institutions to alter the foundation upon which they base financial aid packages. They recommend a need-based system that does not penalize student families with one wage earner and students attending on a part-time basis.

The importance of child care services is widely affirmed (Mangano and Corrado, 1979; Hooper and March, 1980). This is particularly so for single parents, who are generally women. Creange (1980) even warns that lack of child care may be considered a violation of Title IX of the Educational Amendments of 1972 because of its disproportionately heavy impact on women.

Career and personal counseling and peer group support and counseling have also received considerable professional attention (Ryan, 1979; Simpkins, 1980). These services have played an integral role in the education of non-traditional women. Scott (1980), in a review of the research on returning women, concludes that group counseling, support groups, and career decision-making workshops can be helpful. Richmond (1981), in a survey of 767 non-traditional women students found that only one third had ever received counseling. Similarly, Alford (1981), concluded after surveying 343 older students at the University of Houston, "more can be done with both curriculum and advisement and counseling to accommodate the job-related goals that were rated as so important by adult students, to help them clarify career goals and acquire job skills" (p. 129).

Other relevant services range from overnight on-campus accommodation (Rawlins and Davies, 1981) to special meal plans and from Adult Student Resource Centers (Shuster and Berner, 1980) to small study lounges. The promotion of these services and the effective communication of information regarding academic requirements and programmatic opportunities is, perhaps, the most essential service. For example, in a study of 700 full and part-time undergraduate students over the age of 25 at the University of New Brunswick (Heinlein and Byers, 1981) forty per cent were not aware that they had an academic adviser and more than half were not aware of available student services. Jurand-Salter (1980) suggests an informational brochure aimed at older learners; Kegel (1977) recommends a newsletter directed toward older students; Nayman and Patton (1980), in examining successful media campaigns, suggest that pull out supplements to the school newspaper describing services, programs, and curriculums, special sections in the college catalogue, and computer-prepared mailings to the non-traditional student population have been quite effective.

Access to existing services is a key element of the response to non-traditional students. This necessitates bridging the information gap and ensuring the relevance of these services to the older student. Child care, peer support and counseling also appeared frequently in the literature as have a number of innovative and often unique services.

The programmatic response that has specifically been aimed at non-traditional students has often emanated from the campus women's center and been directed toward the returning women (Mawson, 1979; Lordi, 1980). The adult Student Resource Center (Shuster and Berner, 1980), although desirable, has not proliferated resulting in a somewhat fragmented institutional response. Programs have ranged from brown bag lunches to family-oriented movies and from weekend intramurals to a seminar on note-taking or interviewing skills or tenant rights. Yet, developing programs for non-traditional students is a special challenge because of the diversity of the needs this group represents (Pitman, 1977).

Adult development literature (Weathersby and Tarule, 1980) suggests that programming, to be effective, needs to be designed in a way that supports or promotes development. Diagnostic programs that help adult students to formulate and clarify educational goals and to understand their own developmental needs in the context of life planning were recommended. Knox (1980) continues,

As adults better understand the orderly and sequential changes in characteristics and attitudes that have happened to them and to others in the past, they will become more able to predict and understand their subsequent behavior. A developmental perspective can enable adults to grasp essential current and unfolding features of their own lives . . . (p.19).

In practice, however, the implications of adult development research have rarely been applied. Programs have evolved in a much more haphazard manner often based upon the findings of an institutional needs assessment.

There are many examples of needs assessments in the literature that have sought to clarify the programmatic needs of non-traditional students. Kelman and Staley (1974–75), for example, sampled 301 non-traditional out-reach programs. Two-thirds of the women favored workshops on job applications and resume writing skills, nearly 55 percent favored workshops on reading, note-taking, and paper-writing skills, and about half, a workshop on mathematics-science study skills and a tutoring-learning laboratory. About 75 per cent were interested in social get-togethers with other returning women. Nearly 60 percent favored the availability of a life-planning workshop. Lance, Lourie, and May (1979b) found speed reading to be the most requested educational counseling service and career development the most demanded program among their 583 participants. Fauquet (1978) found that most of the married students in his sample of 440 non-traditional students wanted social programming. The most consistent themes in the literature are:

1) programs directed toward improvement of academic "survival" skills such as study skills and test-taking skills;

2) programs designed to improve skills of a more personal nature such as time management or assertion training;

3) programs related to career exploration or development such as resume writing; and,

4) programs of a social nature.

Although social programming is mentioned in the literature (Mangano, Corrado, and Frank, 1979; Jurand-Salter, 1980), the non-traditional students' participation in out of class activities is often limited to those directly related to their academic progress (Pitman, 1979). The specifics of the programmatic response have been detailed in Table 3 and Table 4.

A necessary complement to services and programming has been advocacy. In order to develop a consistent and comprehensive response to non-traditional students, the non-traditional student perspective must be represented at all levels of institutional planning (Kegel, 1977). The needs of the returning adult must be considered in new construction, in scheduling classes, in evaluating available academic, lounge, and recreational space, and in decisions impacting parking, among others. "Advocacy can be as complex as involvement on campus-wide planning boards, active lobbying with individual service agencies, or as simple as a phone call" (Jacoby and Girrell, 1981, p.39). Nationwide, exemplary institutions have established returning student associations (Payette, 1980) or professionally-staffed offices charged with being the voice of the adult student population (Shuster and Berner, 1980). Certainly one of their primary functions is to enhance campus awareness of non-traditional student issues. Kegel (1977) talks about the importance of making faculty and counselors aware of and responsible to the presence and needs of adult students. Hooper and March (1980) reinforce the importance of intra-university publicity to increase understanding of the plight of single women parents. In general, outside the impetus generated from the women's movements, minimal effort has been made to ensure representation for this diverse and often diffuse group, the non-traditional student.

Table 3
Personal/Social Developmental Needs

1. *Need to counter self-doubts* (especially non-traditional women students) (Lance, Lourie, and Mayo, 1979a; Holtzclaw, 1979; Roehl, 1980; Jurand-Salter, 1980; Lam, 1981).
2. *Need communication skills improvement* (Kelman and Staley, 1974–75; Hameister and Hickey, 1977).
3. *Need to learn to manage time and set goals* (Mangano, Corrado, and Frank, 1979; Scott, 1980).
4. *Need a place to study at home* (Lance, Lourie, and Mayo, 1979a).
5. *Need encouragement from family* (Mangano, Corrado, and Frank, 1979). *This is especially true for non-traditional women students* (Roach, 1976; Ryan, 1979; Berkove, 1979; Scott, 1980; DeGroot, 1980; Hooper and March, 1980; Hall and Gleaves, 1981).
6. *Need peer support* (especially non-traditional women students) Rawlins, 1979; Scott, 1980.
7. *Need assertion skills improvement (non-traditional women students)* (Scott, 1980).
8. *Need for social activities* (Kelman and Staley, 1974–75).

Table 4
Academic Preparation Needs

1. *Need study-skill improvement* (Hameister and Hickey, 1977; Rawlins, 1970; Mangano, Corrado, and Frank, 1979; Smallwood, 1980; Hooper and March, 1980; Reehling, 1980).
2. *Need remedial work especially in mathematics* (Kelman and Staley, 1974–75; Solmon and Gordon, 1981).
3. *Need improvement of test-taking skills* (Mangano, Corrado, and Frank, 1979; Simpkins, 1980).
4. *Need to improve concentration and memory* (Lance, Lourie, and Mayo, 1979; Mangano, Corrado, and Frank, 1979; Simpkins, 1980).
5. *Prefer academic counseling to be readily available* (Fauquet, 1978; Mangano, Corrado, and Frank, 1979) and to be comprehensive (Olski, 1980).

The fourth and final arena of response is through the academic delivery system. "If colleges take adult students seriously," Weathersby and Tarule (1980) posit, "They will design more flexibility into course structures and teaching methods, as well as into meeting times and places and support services" (p. 45). The literature recommends a myriad of possible responses. A paucity of research exists on the effectiveness of these responses.

Many of these responses are detailed in Table 5 and Table 6. Other suggestions include the expansion of the external degree programs (Hooper and March, 1980), a continued emphasis on part-time programs (Flaherty, 1978), and the addition of short courses and one-unit modules focusing on different areas of problem-solving and life skills (Holt, 1979). Leckie (1978) poses a redefinition of education as a lifelong process of inquiry rather than a given number of classroom hours or books read. Within this rubric, there would be little questioning of the practice of giving credit for life-experience recommended strongly by Mangano, Corrado, and Frank (1979), Fisher-Thompson (1980), and Jurand-Salter (1980). Fisher-Thompson (1980) also notes that college transfer policies, graduation requirements, and residency requirements become difficult problems for non-traditional students the longer one has been out of school. Problems with credit transfer lead to repeated or extra course-work. These problems may be alleviated by giving elective credit for older courses, providing for credit-by-examination, or by allowing credit for selected life experiences. Residency requirements are often an effective barrier to re-entering women who may have been required to move with their family or are unable to attend full-time.

Table 5
Academic Administrative Preferences

1. *Prefer a minimum of red tape* (Jurand-Salter, 1980).
2. *Prefer evening classes* (Kegel, 1977; Mangano, Corrado, and Frank, 1979).

3. *Prefer flexibility in curriculum and scheduling* (Center for Educational Development, 1980).
4. *Prefer quick and simplified registration* (Kegel, 1977; Mangano, Corrado, and Frank, 1979).
5. *Prefer evening and weekend registration* (Mangano, Corrado, and Frank, 1979).
6. *Prefer flexibility in receiving credit (e.g., for out-of-college experiences, by exam, etc.)* (Mangano, Corrado, and Frank, 1979; Fisher-Thompson, 1980).

Table 6
Academic Instructional Preferences

1. *Prefer problem-solving focus* (Cross, 1978; Holtzclaw, 1980; White, 1981).
2. *Prefer actual learning experiences* (Ward and Korz, 1969; Holt, 1979; Jurand-Salter, 1980; Robinson, 1980; Holtzclaw, 1980; Hall and Gleaves, 1981).
3. *Prefer learning that is incorporated into an existing framework of learning and experience* (Cross, 1978).
4. *Prefer individual approach to instruction* (Hameister and Hickey, 1977).
5. *Prefer a teaching approach other than lecture* (Cross and Zusman, 1977).
6. *Prefer that grades not only be based on tests* (Mangano, Corrado, and Frank, 1979).
7. *Prefer that more than one way to meet course requirements be provided* (Mangano, Corrado, and Frank, 1979).
8. *Prefer instructors who are interested in progress, who are relaxed and informal in the class, who use many examples, and have a realistic view of students' outside duties* (Mangano, Corrado, and Frank, 1979).

Kegel (1977), Mangano, Corrado, and Frank (1979), Ryan (1979), and Holtzclaw (1980), among others, urge maximum range and flexibility in the scheduling of courses. Evening classes are imperative for any institution that aspires to retain adult students. Similar access, as mentioned earlier in this article, must be made available to academic support services, to faculty advising, and to registration.

The most subtle responses to non-traditional students from within the academic delivery system is the adaptation of teaching methods by the individual faculty member. Table 6 outlines this arena in detail. It reiterates the importance of practical learning experiences, of flexibility, and of a problem solving focus. The real challenge for the faculty lies in effectively instructing a classroom of students of many ages and maintaining a respect for the needs of those that do not fit a 'lockstep' curriculum (Greenberg, Bergquist, and O'Donnell, 1980).

Non-Traditional Students—Conclusions

Non-traditional students, variously defined, have become a major constituency within the system of post-secondary education in the United States.

The increase of older students coupled with the concurrent dimunition of traditionally-aged students has made understanding who this student population is and what it is they want from higher education a matter of institutional survival. Three key differences emerge from the literature that most effectively establish a useful traditional/non-traditional student dichotomy. Non-traditional students generally have multiple commitments, are not campus-focused, and prefer informal learning. Traditional students, by contrast, can be characterized as having limited commitments, as being campus-focused, and as preferring formal learning. However, future research could greatly enhance the understanding of the implications of these differences. Why do non-traditional students leave school? What attracts non-traditional students to a specific institution? What factors contribute to non-traditional student satisfaction? How do different sub-groups within the non-traditional student population vary on these factors?

The expectations and needs of non-traditional students tend to emanate from the foundation provided by these three critical factors and are also reflected by the institutional responses. The constellation of institutional responses fall into four primary categories: services, programs, advocacy, and the academic delivery system.

Although adult development theory provides an appropriate theoretical framework, it has rarely been used to establish a comprehensive institutional response. With few exceptions, institutional response to non-traditional students appears to e a series of efforts each designed to resolve an immediate problem. It is, admittedly, difficult to do otherwise. However, a fragmented response has the potential to erode both an institution's ability to attract and to retain non-traditional students. Whereas, a more comprehensive response may provide an important recruiting advantage in a highly competitive market place. A more comprehensive response may increase non-traditional student satisfaction and in turn improve retention rates. The tradeoff warrants careful consideration.

In designing an institutional response, one final implication of the literature applies. Because each institution is a unique composite of students, curriculum, faculty, staff, resources, history, physical plant, and environment, each institution has an equally unique ideal response. There is no package solution. The literature provides but an array of possibilities from which, after thorough planning, the most appropriate mix should be chosen.

In conclusion, the challenge facing student personnel is greater than purely responding effectively to non-traditional students. The challenge is to integrate into higher education an ability to respond quickly and effectively to an ever-changing student population. This wave of non-traditional students is not a new phenomenon. Post-secondary education, following World

War II, was inundated with veterans who were "beginning their college careers, on the average, at the comparatively ripe age of 23" (Weber, 1947, p. 47). By 1947, nearly two-thirds of the student body was composed of veterans of World War II. They, too, faced problems in "guidance, study and adjustment, housing, finance, budgeting, social life, and getting a job" (Hoover, 1947, p. 37).

So it is that the cycles of history have again brought this question to the fore in the 70's and 80's. And, for certain, it will happen again.

References

ACPA. Orientation for the nontraditional commuting student. Unpublished Document. American College Personnel Association, 1980.

Alford, J. L. An assessment of the student support services needs of selected adult college students. *Dissertation abstracts*, January, 1981, 41 (7), 2880A.

Baillie, O. The non-traditional student needs assessment project: Counseling assistance for older students. Unpublished Document. University of Massachusetts, 1976.

Berkove, G. F. Perceptions of husband support by returning women students. *Family Coordinator*, 1979, 28, 451–457.

Betters-Reed, B. Orientation for the non-traditional commuting student. Unpublished Document. American College Personnel Association, 1980.

Billingham, C. J., & Travaglini, J. Predicting adult academic success in an undergraduate program. *Alternative Higher Education*, 1981, 5, 169–182.

Brodzinski, F. R. Adult learners—the new majority: A demographic reality. In Arthur Shribert (Ed.) *New directions for student services: Providing student services for the adult learner*. San Francisco: Jossey-Bass, 1980.

Center for Educational Development. Returning students increase in number, bring change to U and its classrooms. Comment No. 45. University of Minnesota, May 1980.

Cross, K. P. The adult learner. *Current issues in higher education: National conference series*. Washington: American Association for Higher Education, 1978.

Cross, K. P., & Zusman, A. *The needs of non-traditional learners and the responses of non-traditional programs*. Berkeley: Center for Research and Development in Higher Education, University of California, 1977.

Chickering, A. W. Development as a major outcome. In Morris T. Keeton & Associates (Eds.) *Experimental Learning: Rationale, Characteristics, and Assessment*. San Francisco: Jossey-Bass, 1976.

Cohen, R. D. Assisting the adult learner in 'settling-in'. In Arthur Shriberg (Ed.) *New Directions for Student Services: Providing Student Services for the Adult Learner*. San Francisco: Jossey-Bass, 1980.

Creange, Campus child care; a challenge for the 80's. Field Evaluation Draft,

Women's Re-entry Project, Project on the Status and Education of Women, Association of American Colleges, May 1980.

DeGroot, S. C. Female and male returnees: Glimpses of two distinct populations. *Psychology of Women Quarterly*, 1980, 5, 358–361.

Fauquet, T. W. A survey of non-traditional students at the University of Florida. Paper presented at American Personnel and Guidance Association, Washington, March 1978.

Fisher-Thompson, J. Barriers to re-entry women: College transfer policies, residency and graduation requirements. *Field Evaluation Draft, Women's Re-entry Project, Project on the Status and Education of Women*, Association of American Colleges, May 1980.

Flaherty, E. G. Higher education responds to the needs of the adult part-time student. *College Student Journal*, 1978, 12, 375–378.

Greenberg, E., Bergquist, W., & O'Donnell, K. (Eds.) *Educating learners of all ages: New Directions in Higher Education No. 29*. San Francisco: Jossey-Bass, 1980.

Hall, R. M. Re-entry women: Part-time commitment. *Field evaluation Draft, Women's Re-entry Project, Project on the Status and Education of Women*, Association of American Colleges, October 1980.

Hall, R. M., & Gleaves, F. D. Re-entry women: Special programs for special populations. *Field evaluation Draft, Women's Re-entry Project, Project on the Status and Education of Women*, Association of American Colleges, April 1981.

Hameister, D. R., & Hickey, T. Traditional and adult students: A dichotomy. *Lifelong learning: The adult years*, 1977, 1, 6.

Heinlein, R. L., & Byers, E. S. Assessment of support service: Needs of adult students. *Canadian Journal of University Continuing Education*, 1981, 7, 35–40.

Hiltunen, W. The occupational objective of the thirty year old and over woman student at Orange Coast College. *College Student Personnel Abstracts*, 1978, 14, 138.

Holt, D. Preparing for tomorrow's students. *Community College Review*, 1979, 7, 22–25

Holtzclaw, L. R. Learning problems of adults in higher education. *North Central Association Quarterly*, 1980, 54, 355–364.

Hooper, J. O., & March, G. B. The female single parent in the university. *Journal of College Student Personnel*, 1980, 21, 141–146.

Hoover, E. B. The problems of the married veteran at college. *Educational Outlook*, 1947, 22, 36–40.

Jacoby, B., & Girrell, K. W. A model for improving services and programs for commuter students. *NASPA Journal*, 1981, 18, 36–41.

Jurand-Salter, L. Re-entering academe: The older student on campus. *Teaching Learning Issues*, 1980, 46, 14. (Learning Research Center, University of Tennessee).

Kegel, P. L. How well do we serve the adult student? *Lifelong Learning: The Adult Y ears*, 1977, 1, 10.

Kelman, E., & Staley, B. The returning woman student: Needs of an important minority group on college campuses. *Student Development Report*, 1974–75, 12, 2, Colorado State University.

Knox, A. B. *Adult development and learning: A handbook on individual growth and competence in the adult years for education and the helping professions.* San Francisco: Jossey-Bass, 1977.

Knox, A. B. Understanding the adult learner. In Arthur Shriberg (Ed.) *New directions for student services: Providing student services for the adult learner.* San Francisco: Jossey-Bass, 1980.

Lam, Y. L. J. Relationship between anxiety and classroom behaviors of adult learners. *British Journal of Educational Psychology,* 1981, 51, 90–96.

Lance, L., Lourie, J., & Mayo, C. Difficulties of re-entry students by sex and length of school interruption. *Journal of National Association for Women Deans, Administrators, and Counselors,* 1979a, 41, 39–42.

Lance, L., Lourie, J., & Mayo, C. Needs of re-entry university students. *Journal of College Student Personnel,* 1978b, 20, 479–485.

Leckie, S. The new student on campus. *Educational Horizons,* 1978, 56, 196–199.

Levinson, D. J., Darrow, C., Klein, E. B., Levinson, M., & McKee, B. *The seasons of a man's life.* New York: Alfred A. Knopf, 1978.

Lordi, V. S. Women's centers work for returning adults. In Arthur Shribert (Ed.) *New directions for student services: Providing student services for the adult learner.* San Francisco: Jossey-Bass, 1980.

Malin, J. T., Dougherty, T., & Skinner, W. K. *Adult attending colleges: Goals and change.* Paper presented at American Psychological Association, New York, September 1979.

Malin, J. T., Bray, J. H., Dougherty, T. W., & Skinner, W. K. Factors affecting the performance and satisfaction of adult men and women attending college. *Research in Higher Education,* 1980, 13(2), 115–129.

Mangano, J. A., & Corrado, T. J. Responding to the needs of re-entry adults in two-year colleges. Research report, State University of New York, Albany, September 1979.

Mangano, J. A., Corrado, T. J., & Frank. J. *Re-entry adult student project: Dissemination packet.* Albany: Two-Year College Development Center, 1979.

Mawson, C. D. Women's centers: A critical appraisal and case study. *Personnel and Guidance Journal,* 1979, 58(1), 61–65.

McCrea, J. M. The new student body: Women returning to college. *Journal of the National Association for Women Deans, Administrators, and Counselors,* 1979, 43, 13–19.

Morstain, B. R., & Smart, J. C. A motivational typology of adult learners. *Journal of Higher Education,* 1977, 48, 655–679.

Muskat, H. S. Women re-entering college: Some basic ingredients for curriculum development. *Personnel and Guidance Journal,* 1978, 57, 153–156.

Nayman, R. L., & Patton, D. G. Offering effective student development programs for the adult learner. In Arthur Shriberg (Ed.) *New directions for student services: Providing student services for the adult learner.* San Francisco: Jossey-Bass, 1980.

Olski, K. Problems and issues raised by returning adults. *Alternative higher education,* 1980, 5, 100–105.

Payette, D. L. The adult learner and student programming. In Arthur Shriberg (Ed.) *New Directions for student services: Providing student services for the adult learner*. San Francisco: Jossey-Bass, 1980.

Pitman, R. Evening commuters, priorities of student services. *The Commuter*. University of South Florida, 1979, 4.

Rawlins, M. E. Life made easier for the over-thirty undergrads. *Personnel and Guidance Journal*, 1979, 58, 139–143.

Rawlins, M. E., & Davies, K. Today's challenge: Adults in college. *Lifelong Learning*, 1981, 4, 12.

Reehling, J. E. They are returning: But, are they staying? *Journal of College Student Personnel*, 1980, 21, 491–497.

Richmond, L. J. Statewide assessment of career aspiration and job attainment among women returning to college in Maryland. *College Student Personnel Abstracts*, 1981, 16, 420.

Roach, R. M. Honey, won't you please stay home. *Personnel and Guidance Journal*, 1976, 55, 86–89.

Robinson, J. Oldies but goodies. *Journal of the National Association of Women Deans, Administrators, and Counselors*, 1980, 43, 27–32.

Roehl, J. E. Self-concept and the re-entry woman. *Lifelong Learning*, 1980, 3, 12.

Ryan, M. The mature woman in higher education: What's a nice old girl like you doing in a place like this? Unpublished Report. Kent State University. August 1979.

Scott, N. A. *Returning women students: A review of research and descriptive studies*. Special monograph, National Association for Women Deans, Administrators, and Counselors, 1980.

Shuster, D. T., & Berner, A. J. The role of the adult student resource center. In Arthur Shriberg (Ed.) *New directions for student services: Providing student services for the adult learner*. San Francisco: Jossey-Bass, 1980.

Simpkins, T. C. College at middle age. *College Student Journal*, 1980, 14, 2–4.

Smallwood, K. B. What do adult women college students really need? *Journal of College Student Personnel*, 1980, 21, 65–73.

Solmon, L. C., & Gordon, J. J. *The characteristics and needs of adults in post-secondary education*. Lexington, Massachusetts: Lexington Books, 1981.

Staman, E. M. *Factors affecting traditional versus non-traditional student subscription to higher education*. Paper presented at Association for Institutional Research, Atlanta, April, 1980.

Tittle, C. K., & Kenker, E. R. Re-entry women: A selective review of the education process, career choice, and interest measurement. *Review of Educational Research*, 1977, 47, 531–584.

Tittle, C. K., & Kenker, E. R. *Returning women students in higher education: Defining policy issues*. New York: Praeger, 1980.

Ward, R. F., & Korz, T. E. *The commuting student: A study of facilities at Wayne State University*. Detroit: Michigan State University, 1969.

Weathersby, R. P., & Tarule, J. M. *Adult development: Implications for higher education.* Washington: American Association for Higher Education, 1980.

Weber, C. A. Veterans question college program. *The School Executive,* 1947, 66, 47.

White, R. K. *Working with the adult student.* Paper presented at National Association of Student Personnel Administrators, New York, April, 1981.

Using Values Education Activities to Confront Student Conduct Issues

Jon C. Dalton and Margaret A. Healy

Student affairs personnel were queried on how they are applying values education to promote personal and social development while handling student conduct problems.

Introduction

Student conduct problems are on the increase at most colleges and universities and require more time and attention by university officials. Recent reports on student behavior problems on campus indicate that the incident rate for offenses such as academic dishonesty, theft, and vandalism have greatly increased (Hill, 1980). Of particular concern has been an increase in assault and rape at many colleges and universities (Williams, 1982).

College officials have responded to this increase in student conduct problems in a variety of ways. Many schools have increased their campus security operations in order to combat the most serious forms of crime and misconduct (Jacobs & O'Mera, 1980). More use has been made of students to assist with security patrols and to monitor campus buildings. Many schools have initiated information programs to increase awareness of and responsibility for personal safety and security on campus. But one of the more important and least noticed impacts of increased student conduct problems has been to prompt renewed interest in the ethical conduct of students and a search for ways to promote more responsibility in student behavior.

Changing Role of Student Discipline

During the late 1960s there was a rather abrupt abandonment of in loco parentis as a defining principle for student discipline in much of higher education. One of the results of this important shift was a decline in the student discipline function in colleges and universities. That trend may now be changing as a result of the significant increase in student behavior problems and a renewed public interest in a more active role by higher education officials in confronting college student conduct and discipline. Moreover, research over the past decade has provided new understanding about the process of moral development and ways to promote such development in college students through educational interventions.

With the demise of in loco parentis many student affairs professionals adopted a laissez-faire position of noninvolvement in the student discipline role. Since the courts declared students to be legal adults, student conduct problems came to be viewed by many student affairs staff as matters to be addressed by law enforcement officials or, secondarily, as matters for personal counseling. Other student affairs professionals assumed what Gary Pavela describes as a procedural approach to college student discipline (Pavela, 1983). This approach focused almost exclusively upon providing formal procedures for processing student conduct violations but paid relatively little attention to the implications of such conduct for student development. Both the laissez-faire and the procedural approaches avoided the appearance of in loco parentis, but they presented serious problems for student affairs staff concerned about the social and ethical development of college students. Both approaches failed to help students understand why some forms of conduct are morally inferior and how they may learn to cope more responsibly with serious ethical problems.

One of the ways in which student affairs staff have attempted to address ethical issues in student conduct is through values education activities. Values education activities are specific educational interventions designed to teach about values and the valuing process. The present study is an effort to determine how student affairs staff address value issues that relate to student conduct problems, what student conduct problems concern them most, and what values they believe should be promoted in student conduct.

Design of Study

In an effort to learn more about the means used by student affairs staff to influence values related to student conduct issues, a questionnaire sponsored by the NASPA Division of Research and Program Development was mailed to the chief student personnel officers of all NASPA member institutions. The questionnaire had five parts: (a) a section on activity objectives in which respondents described the activities they utilized to promote values development in students, (b) a section on activity organization in which the amounts of time and participants in these activities were reported, (c) a section in which the background of the activity participants was reported, (d) a section on activity resources which requested information on funding and education resources, and (e) a section on activity evaluation. Three copies of an 18–item questionnaire were mailed to 1102 chief student personnel officers holding membership in NASPA in June, 1982. Of the 1102 institutions surveyed, 623 responses were received from 232 colleges and universities. Of the 623 responses, 372 came from public institutions, 131 from private religious colleges, and 110 from private secular colleges. No follow-up mailing was conducted. Subjects were asked to identify student conduct issues as well as the values education approaches and activities sponsored by student affairs at their institutions that address these conduct issues. Frequency data were collected and cross-tabulations were compiled using institutional type, student conduct issues, values education activities, and ethical values as variables.

Analysis of Results

When asked what student conduct issues were addressed by values education activities, respondents identified the following ten issues as most important:

Table 1
Student Conduct Issues for 623 Responses

Issues	n	%
1. Irresponsible behavior	336	54
2. Interpersonal conflicts	318	51
3. Disrespect of others	249	40
4. Alcohol/drug abuse	202	32
5. Prejudice	182	29
6. H ealth/wellness	168	27
7. Academic dishonesty	141	23
8. Sexism	140	22
9. Racism	136	22
10. Sexual behavior	129	21

Four of the issues (disrespect of others, prejudice, sexism, racism) reflected concern on the part of the respondents with students, social attitudes, and treatment of others. Over half the respondents identified interpersonal conflicts and irresponsible behavior as their most serious student conduct issues.

When asked to identify the values education activities utilized in helping students confront ethical issues in conduct problems, respondents reported the following activities most frequently:

Table 2
*Activities Used for Values
Education Interventions*

Activity	Total		Public		Re ligious		Private	
	n	%	n	%	n	%	n	%
1 Alcohol Education	72	12	45	12	14	11	13	12
2. Values Clarification	68	11	39	10	15	11	14	13
3. Judicial Boards	56	9	33	9	12	9	11	10
4. Leadership Training	52	8	41	11	4	3	7	6
5. Faith Development	50	8	16	4	24	18	10	9
6. Human Relations	39	6	22	6	9	7	8	7
7. Orientation	34	5	20	5	8	6	6	5
8. Volunteer Projects	26	4	16	4	6	5	4	4
9. Career Development	27	5	17	5	5	4	5	5
10. Sexuality Programs	25	4	18	5	4	3	3	3
11. Contemporary Issues	23	4	12	3	6	5	5	5
12. Other Activities	151	24	97	26	24	18	24	22
Total	623	100	372	100	131	100	110	101

The survey responses reveal that a wide variety of activities are used as a means to help students think and act ethically. Alcohol education and values clarification activities were the most frequently mentioned but over 20 types of educational activities were reported by respondents. In order to ascertain if particular values education activities were used to address specific issues, subjects were asked to identify activity interventions by student conduct issue. This information is reported in Table 3:

Table 3
*Values Education Activities Used Most
Frequently to Address Conduct Issues*

Issues	%*	Issues	%*
Irresponsible Behavior		*Interpersonal Conflicts*	
1. Judicial Boards	17	1. Values Clarification	14
2. Alcohol Education	14	2. Leadership Training	11
3. Leadership Training	11	3. Judicial Boards	10
4. Values Clarification	10		
Disrespect of Orders		*Alcohol/Drug Abuse*	
1. Judicial Boards	15	1. Alcohol Education	35
2. Faith Development	11	2. Judicial Boards	12
3. Values Clarification	11	*Health/Wellness*	
Prejudice		1. Alcohol Education	21
1. Human Relations	18	2. Values Clarification	13
2. Values Clarification	13	*Sexism*	
3. Faith Development	11	1. Values Clarification	13
Academic Dishonesty		2. Sexuality Programs	12
1. Judicial Boards	31	3. Faith Development	11
2. Faith Development	12	4. Human Relations	11
3. Values Clarification	10	*Sexual Behavior*	
Racism		1. Sexuality Programs	
1. Human Relations	20	1. Sexuality Programs	16
2. Values Clarification	13	2. Values Clarification	16
3. Faith Development	11	3. Faith Development	13

*Percent of Total Responses

The results indicate that many different educational activities are used to address conduct issues. No activity was used by more than 35% of the respondents to address any specific conduct issue. However, the data show that values clarification, faith development, and judicial board activities are highly popular and used to address most of the conduct issues.

In order to ascertain the most important values promoted through different values education activities, subjects were asked to rank the most important value objectives of each type of activity. A summary of this information is provided in Table 4:

Table 4
Values Promoted in Educational Activities

Issues	%*	Issues	%*
Alcohol Education		*Values Clarification*	
1. Responsibility for self	86	1. Self awareness	69

2. Self awareness 67
3. Self discipline 56
4. Respect for others 43
5. Helping others 24

Leadership Training
1. Cooperation 72
2. Understanding others 43
3. Self awareness 36
4. Assertiveness 26
5. Helping others 25

Faith Development
1. Religious belief 86
2. Respect for others 34
3. Helping others 26
4. Self awareness 26
5. Responsibility for self 26

Orientation
1. Responsibility for self 75
2. Self awareness 44
3. Cooperation 37
4. Respect for others 28
5. Understanding others 28

Career Development
1. Self awareness 78
2. Responsibility for self 74
3. Independence 30
4. Individual effort 30
5. Assertiveness 26

2. Responsibility for self 50
3. Understanding others 46
4. Respect for others 32
5. Individual effort 13

Judicial Board Training
1. Fairness 65
2. Honesty 49
3. Respect for others 47
4. Responsibility for self 47
5. Self discipline 33

Human Relations
1. Respect for others 77
2. Understanding others 67
3. Self awareness 51
4. Tolerance 49
5. Cooperation 13

Volunteer Projects
1. Helping others 89
2. Understanding others 70
3. Respect for others 41
4. Self awareness 36
5. Cooperation 30

Sexuality
1. Self awareness 73
2. Responsibility for self 68
3. Respect for others 48
4. Assertiveness 36
5. Understanding others 32

*Percent of activity responses

Discussion

The most serious conduct issues identified by respondents involved problems of social offense or injury such as interpersonal conflicts, disrespect of others, prejudice, academic dishonesty, sexism, and racism. These issues parallel to a great extent the student conduct problems reported in the literature. Such conduct no doubt concerns student personnel staff because it violates central values in the academic community such as tolerance, fairness, and respect for differences. Moreover, such conduct creates social disruption and reflects significant problems in ethical development. The reported conduct issues suggest that student affairs staff are especially concerned with student behavior problems that disrupt community life and that offend or injure others. The survey results indicate that a variety of educational interventions are used by student affairs staff as means to confront ethical issues in student behavior. A majority of those responding indicated that they sponsored one or more educational activities designed to influence student values related to a campus conduct issue. This finding suggests that student affairs staff regard student conduct issues as significant matters for educational intervention and that they use values education activities as a means to promote ethical awareness and value development in students.

Some activities such as judicial boards, leadership training, faith development, and human relations training are often used individually or in combination to address several of the conduct issues identified.

Staff in religious institutions utilize faith development activities much more frequently than do staff in public or private secular institutions and this no doubt reflects their special orientation to religious development in students. Staff in public institutions utilize leadership training more frequently than their counterparts in other institutions, perhaps because this activity provides a secular approach to value issues that avoids the appearance of promoting specific values or beliefs.

The wide variety of activities used for values education interventions indicates that student personnel staff use many types of values activities when confronting student conduct issues. No single activity was used by a majority of respondents. However, over half of the respondents reported that they sponsored six popular activities to address values issues. These activities (alcohol education, values clarification, judicial boards, leadership training, faith development, and human relations) are used in varying combinations to address almost all the student conduct issues identified.

The values promoted by student affairs staff in educational activities reflect special concern for developing self-awareness and independence as well as tolerance, respect, and fairness toward other individuals. These values are perhaps regarded as both deterrents and correctives to student behavior problems as well as important student development outcomes. The popularity of these values among student personnel staff suggests that they may constitute a set of core values that are regarded as essential in the educational development of college students.

If present trends continue, student conduct issues may increasingly represent one of the most strategic areas for student development intervention particularly in the area of values education. It is clear that student affairs staff are doing considerably more than merely administering student conduct procedures. They are actively engaged in activities designed to influence student values in order to promote personal and social development and to ameliorate student conduct problems. Values education activities may represent one of the best strategies for confronting student conduct issues in a manner that avoids in loco parentis problems of meddling and moralizing on one extreme and a laissez-faire avoidance on the other.

References

Hill, F. W. (1980, October). Taming campus vandals. *American School and University Journal*, 53, pp.44–48.

Jacobs, J. B., & O'Mera, V. A. (1980, spring). Security forces and the transformation of the American university. *College and University Journal*, 55(3), 283.

Pavela, G. (1983, January 26). Sanctions for student misbehavior: let the punishment fit the crime. *Chronicle of Higher Education*, p.52.

Williams, D. A. (1982, January 25). Crime on campus. *Newsweek*, p.82.

Applying a Model of Planned Change to Program Innovation in Student Affairs

Don G. Creamer
and
E. G. Creamer

A discussion is presented concerning the results of a survey of chief student affairs officers to determine the nature of program innovations using student development goals.

Practitioners in student affairs constantly strive to enhance the effects of their efforts through program improvement. Yet, because change requires control or management of many institutional conditions beyond the immediate influence of student affairs professionals, these efforts often fall short of expectations, or worse, they simply fail. Studies of organizational development and of planned change are not abundant in student affairs, yet insight into the interaction of institutional factors is imperative to ensure successful program implementation. In this study we explored selected issues in organizational development, specifically the application of a model of planned change in higher education to current programming efforts reported by chief student affairs officers (CSAOs).

The application of organizational development principles in higher education is not common but is increasing steadily, as indicated by an increase in reports in the literature (Blaesser, 1978; Borland, 1980; Glaser, Abelson, & Garrison, 1983; Hammons, 1982; Hipps, 1982; Martorana & Kuhns, 1975). This literature is devoted almost totally to research and reports of practitioners, based on models of change largely unsupported by theories of organizational change. Without such a theoretical basis the contributions of the research to general knowledge and to actions of scholars and practitioners are weak (Huse, 1980) because they cannot supply a guide for actions across multiple settings and problems.

This study was designed to enhance the understanding of planned change in higher education, especially as it relates to implementing efforts to infuse student development goals and principles into formal programming for students. Although programming for students in all kinds of colleges and universities increasingly may include developmental goals, little is known about the strategies used to implement program changes successfully. This study was developed from an analysis of survey data about efforts toward planned change in higher education and an emerging model of planned change. Responses from institutions reporting successful projects were compared to those from institutions reporting less successful projects. The study focused specifically on descriptive and comparative discussions of projects reported to be under way in student affairs, and it was based on early phases of a research project designed to yield substantive theory of planned change in higher education.

Method

Glaser et al. (1983) presented a summary of several models of planned change in higher education, giving major attention to the AVICTORY model attributed to the work of Davis and Salasin (1979). The model is based on a synthesis of 1,200 publications and is an acronym for the eight determinants of change: ability, values, ideas, circumstances, timing, obligation, resistance, and yield. Each of these factors is an element associated with the successful adoption of change.

The AVICTORY model was used as a preliminary guide for our study. The model was revised, however, after several inadequacies were discovered during testing of its explanatory power in an actual case, which involved an attempt to implement an institution-wide project for planned change. Data collected during this initial, indepth case study suggested that the AVICTORY model did not allow sufficient emphasis on the separate role of leadership and advocacy and that resistance seemed to be allowed more significance than was supported by early findings. The revised model was renamed the Probability of Adoption of Change (PAC) model.

The PAC model was composed of eight key variables: circumstances, value compatability, idea comprehensibility, practicality, leadership, championship, advantage probability, and strategies (see Table 1). Each key variable was composed of specific, discernible elements of an organization that define and shape the nature and strength of the variables.

After pretesting of the survey, a 35-item survey designed to collect responses about change efforts under way in student affairs was mailed in October 1984 to 740 voting delegates of the National Association of Student

Table 1
Differences Between Change Projects Rated as Successful and Unsuccessful

Model variables	Survey item	Chi-square
Circumstances	Source or impetus of change (Internal or external)	6.96*
Value compatibility	Source or impetus of change (Internal or external)	6.96*
Idea comprehensibility	Documented goals	0.10
	Reason for opposition	4.29
Practicality	Use of available or additional resources	0.01
	Reorganization necessity	0.64
Leadership	Leader during planning	13.71*
	Leader during implementation	3.06
Championship	Advocated during planning	27.61*
	Participants involved in implementation	1.06
	Opponents during planning	23.64*
	Opponents during implementation	21.93*
Advantage probability	Reason for opposition	4.29
Strategies	Time spent planning	1.71
	Time anticipated for implementation	8.51*
	Percentage of student affairs involved	1.17
	Opposition strength	3.56
	Use of feedback	3.00
	Plans for evaluation	0.06

*p<.05.

Personnel Administrators (NASPA). This population was selected because of its national distribution across institutional types and because we assumed that its members would be leaders in the profession and among the most likely to be involved in change projects. *Planned change* was defined in the survey as a long-term, systematic, and purposeful effort to change existing policies and practices to incorporate (a) new behaviors, values, or goals, (b) new technological innovations, or (c) structural changes in the communication or authority systems of an organization.

Respondents were asked (a) to identify any project under way at their institution that conformed to the definition; (b) to answer forced-choice questions about the origin of the idea for the project, its goals, scope, and sources of opposition; and (c) to identify the major leaders, advocates, and opponents during planning and implementation. Respondents were asked to indicate whether student development goals were explicit, implicit, or not a part of the change project. They also were asked whether the project was implemented through existing or new resources and to evaluate the success of the implementation of the project goals. The survey items were designed to represent a series of discreet inquiries and, therefore, could not be examined for reliability by conventional methods.

Responses were received from 280 (38%) of those surveyed, with 163 (58%) of the respondents reporting purposeful change efforts under way and 117 (42%) responding that no such efforts were under way. Tests of significance on each variable contained in the PAC model were conducted using chi-square analyses by comparing successful and less successful efforts. Institutional characteristics of schools represented by persons reporting change projects and of those represented by persons reporting no projects also were compared by this method.

Results

The value of these findings should be judged with two caveats in mind. First, the modest percentage of overall returns from the survey, despite the use of a follow-up procedure 1 month after the initial mailing, raises questions about the accuracy of data indicating the numbers of planned change efforts under way. The suspicion that those persons not responding represented colleges with no projects for change under way seems justified. The finding that 42% of institutions had no projects probably understates the condition when looking at the entire population surveyed. Second, the meaning of the standard of success should be examined carefully. *Success* referred to the likelihood that the goals of the planned change project would be adopted or institutionalized, and success was reported in nearly 80% of the cases. The respondents often were identified as the champions or leaders of the effort, and it seems possible that their judgments may not have necessarily mirrored the perceptions of all constituents involved.

Distribution of Change Institutions

Respondents reporting projects under way were more likely than were those reporting no programs to be from relatively small, private institutions that did not offer degrees beyond the master's level. This finding was particularly pronounced for institutions reporting change efforts with explicit student development goals. Respondents from public institutions were significantly less likely than were those from private institutions to report change projects with either implicit or explicit student development goals [x^2 (2, n = 163) = 8.25, $p < .01$].

Areas of Change

We categorized into major areas all responses to an open-ended question asking for the name and description of the project and any explanatory documentation. The most frequently listed areas are summarized in Table 2. Areas in which explicit student development goals were reported by a majority of the respondents are indicated. Although no differences were statistically significant at less than a .05 level of probability, notable differences appeared in the types of projects reported by 2-year and 4-year colleges, colleges offering programs toward a master's degree, and colleges granting doctoral degrees. Residence hall programming and reorganization without

Table 2
Focus of Change Projects Cited

Area	Percent (n = 163)	Explicit SD goals[*]
Reorganization with student development goals	12	+
Reorganization without explicit student development goals	11	
Automation projects	10	
Student development curriculum	9	+
Residence hall programming	7	
Long range planning	6	
Orientation to student life programs	6	+
Career planning and placement	5	+
Alcohol and substance abuse education programs	4	
Academic advising programs	4	+
Retention programs	4	
Academic enrichment (including remedial programs)	3	
Staff development programs	3	
All others	18	

[*]These explicit student development goals were cited by a majority of the respondents.

explicit, underlying student development goals were most frequently cited in the larger, doctoral granting institutions, whereas reorganization efforts with explicitly formulated student development goals and the implementation of student development curricula were most frequently cited by 4-year institutions. Only a few community colleges reported change projects that fit our definition.

As might be expected, reorganization or modification of the authority and reporting structure was the most frequently cited focus of change projects. Programs with explicit student development goals, however, were reported by over 45% of the respondents, and an additional 46% indicated projects with implicit student development goals. The cover letter accompanying the survey, however, expressed particular interest in programs with explicit student development goals.

Model Variables

Differences between the responses from projects rated as largely or somewhat successful and those rated as largely or somewhat unsuccessful are summarized in Table 3, which includes a list of the model's components, the major survey items designed to measure them, and the statistics resulting from a comparison of percentages of successful and less successful projects. Only results from 19 of the 35 survey items are presented in Table 3. Other items on the survey were not used to measure the model's variables but were designed to elicit clarification of the nature of the project, such as a list of explicit goals for student development.

Projects considered successful or less successful varied significantly on 6 of the 19 variables summarized in Table 3. These variables included (a) the source or impetus of change, (b) the leader during the planning of the project, (c) the advocates during the planning of the project, (d) the opponents during the planning of the project, (e) the opponents during the implementation of the project, and (f) the time anticipated for implementation. Projects rated as more successful and those rated as less successful were not found to differ significantly on such variables as the reason, source, or strength of opposition, the leader during implementation of the project, use of new or available resources, or the percentage of the total student affairs staff involved in the change project. A discussion of each of the key variables of the PAC model, which includes and explanation of the applicable survey questions and the findings when successful and less successful programs were compared for each variable, is below.

Circumstances. The majority of respondents reporting change projects

Table 3
Elements of the PAC Model

Key variables	Variable elements
Circumstances	Refers to the source of impetus for change; may be either internal or external and may either include or exclude an integrative or supportive environment for change. The presence or absence of felt need is included.
Value compatibility	Refers to the degree to which the proposed change seems compatible with existing values, norms, procedures, or facilities.
Idea comprehensibility	Refers to the degree of clarity, simplicity, and timing of the idea.
Practicality	Refers to the availability of appropriate staff skills, knowledge, attitudes, and resources.
Leadership	Refers to actions of "prime movers" or "changemasters" who focus energy and resources within the organization toward the implementation or adoption of the idea on a continuing basis, including the processing of and action on new information gained through feedback and monitoring systems.
Championship	Refers to persevering advocacy by influential persons, other than the leader(s), who are assigned or who assume responsibility for implementing the change.
Advantage probability	Refers to the perception of demonstrable gains, the likelihood of achievement of stated goals, and the probability of solving vexing problems felt by many people.
Strategies	Refers to the interventions or actions taken to implement the idea. Includes intensity and forms of communication used to inform constituents of the idea, plans proposed and undertaken, progress achieved, and evaluation of effects. Also includes actions to ensure integration of efforts toward common purposes.

indicated that the major impetus for change originated within the institution, with nearly 50% reporting that an institutional leader provided the major impetus. Nearly 87% of the reported projects were motivated by internal forces, with only a small number indicating that an outside consultant, evaluation team, or management consultant provided primary impetus. Persons reporting projects rated as successful were significantly more likely than were those reporting projects rated as less successful to identify the impetus for the change project to originate from the institution rather than from external sources, such as from regulatory requirements or from the actions of consultants or evaluation teams.

Value compatability. This variable was not addressed directly by questions in the survey; however, it can be assumed that projects promoted by persons or organizations within the institution are more likely to be compatible with the institution's values than are those promoted by external forces.

Idea comprehensibility. Survey recipients were asked to respond to several questions about idea comprehensibility, including the frequency of communicating the idea and the medium used. Over 80% of the respondents indicated that the goals of the project had been documented, with college memos and policy statements listed most frequently as means of documentation and college catalogs listed least frequently. No significant differences were found between successful and less successful projects on the criteria of whether the project goals were documented or the number of places they were documented. Few respondents recognized serious opposition to their change projects and fewer than 10% identified confusion about the goals and purposes of the project as the main source of opposition to the project. No significant differences between successful and less successful projects were found regarding the main reason identified for opposition.

Practicality. Findings from the survey indirectly suggest the association between practicality and success. Perhaps as an indication of the economic realities facing higher education, the majority of respondents (67%) reported that change was implemented largely through available resources and personnel. This was the case even though nearly 46% of the respondents reported that either major or minor changes to the organizational structure were necessary. No significant differences between successful and less successful projects were found regarding the use of new or existing resources or whether reorganization was required to implement the project goals.

Leadership. Survey respondents identified the CSAO most frequently as the leader of the change effort during both the planning and the implementation stages. The CSAO was less likely to be the leader during implementation (48%) than during planning (60%), whereas a unit or department head within student affairs was the next most frequently cited leader during both planning (18%) and implementation (25%).

Significant differences were found between the projects evaluated as successful and those evaluated as less successful regarding leadership during the planning of the project. Less successful projects were significantly less likely to identify the CSAO as the main leader during planning. The president was much more frequently listed as the leader during planning in the less successful projects. Similar differences were not found, however, regarding the leader during implementation.

Championship. The majority of respondents (64%) identified the CSAO as the main advocate for the change, with the president and other student affairs professionals listed as main advocates by nearly 15% of the respondents. Respondents indicated most frequently (46%) that a group, including student affairs staff persons and others, was primarily involved in the implementation of the change.

As with the variable of leadership, significant differences were found between the projects rated as successful and those rated less successful on some variables related to championship. Less successful projects were significantly less likely than were successful projects to have had the CSAO or the president as the main advocate during planning. Student affairs professionals other than department heads were more likely to have been identified as the main advocate during planning of the projects evaluated as less successful than during those rated successful. No significant differences were found, however, between successful and less successful projects regarding those persons assigned major responsibility for implementing the change.

Opponents during both planning and implementation of the projects also varied between successful and less successful projects. Projects rated as less successful were more likely to have experienced opposition, with opposition among the student affairs staff cited as frequently as opposition from other sources. The major sources of opposition from other sources. The major sources of opposition identified most frequently by respondents did not vary between the planning and implementation of the project.

Advantage probability. Of the respondents, 9% noted a lack of awareness of tangible benefits of the project as a major reason for opposition to the change.

Strategies. The authors assumed several strategies to be associated with the adoption of change including the amount of time spent in planning, opportunities to include feedback and evaluation from constituent groups, and the extent of involvement from student affairs staff persons. Other strategies, such as commitment of new resources, clarity of the articulation of goals, and sustained leadership, were addressed above.

Most respondents reporting change projects noted that (a) less than 1 year was spent in planning, (b) the original plan was altered slightly after feedback from faculty members, students, student affairs professionals, or administrators, and (c) most projects involved less than 25% of the student affairs professional staff. Successful and less successful projects only differed significantly on the time anticipated for implementation. Persons reporting less successful projects anticipated a longer period of time for implementation of the project goals than did those reporting successful projects.

Discussion

Data from this survey were gathered primarily to identify institutions with efforts for planned change that incorporated student development goals. The data, however, provided additional perspectives on the continuing evolution of the PAC model. Analyses of survey results underscored the importance of two of the variables—leadership and championship—in the PAC model but gave little statistical support for the significance or role of other variables identified in the model.

Although there is some debate over the relative importance of external versus internal change agents, the literature about planned change and organizational development emphasizes the role of influential leaders and champions in adopting planned change efforts (Blaesser, 1978; Glaser et al., 1983; Moss-Kanter, 1983). Survey responses suggest that CSAOs are the dominant leaders of change in students affairs.

The findings suggest that the position of institutional leaders and champions who plan and support an idea and the position of the opposition's leader may be more influential to the eventual adoption of the idea than the characteristics of the idea, its sources, or the nature of the opposition. Baldridge and Deal (1975) similarly suggested that the individual characteristics of these leaders have much less to do with the adoption of the effort than does their position in the organization and their ability to control sanctions.

Survey findings did not emphasize the role of either leaders or participants during implementation of the change projects. This finding suggests that respondents believed that leadership during planning was far more crucial than leadership during the actual implementation. This finding may indicate bias on the part of respondents, who were most likely to be CSAOs and leaders during early stages of the project, or the finding may be interpreted to mean that implementation of the project goals was largely considered a fait accompli after top-level support had been solidified.

Analyses of preliminary findings of variables in the PAC model seem to support the omission of at least two variables frequently included in other models of planned change. The lack of significance between successful and less successful programs regarding the strength of the opposition as well as the finding that only a minority of the respondents reported serious opposition to their efforts suggests that recognizing and combating opposition may not be a vital, discrete element associated with successful projects in the areas explored. Similarly, analysis of data from both the survey and the preliminary case study support the omission of resources as a key variable in the successful adoption of the goals of change projects in student affairs. The issue of availability of resources may be influential in the very early decision to evaluate the feasibility of undertaking a change project but may become a minor factor in projects that are in advanced stages of planning and implementation.

Analyses of the findings from the survey consistently point to the role of people in student affairs who create the impetus for the change and provide professionals to serve as both leaders and champions for the project. This finding seems to contradict the literature about organizational development with its customary emphasis on the role of change agents or consultants from outside the institution (Huse, 1980).

Change projects currently initiated in student affairs in higher education settings, particularly those motivated by student development goals, may differ from change projects without this emphasis. Similarly, such projects may flourish more readily inenvironments, such as those of small, liberal arts colleges, that are more congruent with student development goals than in environments of larger, generally public institutions, which endorse and serve more comprehensive goals. Although the likely setting for the implementation of projects with student development goals may differ from that of other change projects in higher education, nothing in the survey findings suggests that major components of the model are not equally as valid in explaining the probability of the adoption of change in other settings.

Data collected through the survey did not provide insight into the relative weight of each of the components in the model, nor did the data provide perspectives other than those provided by the single respondent completing the survey. Intensive case study analysis, planned as the next step in data collection, could supplement existing data by (a) affirming or refuting the role of each key variable and its elements, (b) determining whether the sequence of occurrence of key variable indicators is a crucial aspect of the model, (c) illuminating relationships or interactions among the key variables as a significant determinant of the likelihood of adoption of projects, (d) expanding perspectives of actual institutionalization of projects by including observations from a broad range of participants, and (e) offering at least tentative explanations for the success or failure of projects.

References

Baldridge, V., & Deal, T. (1975). *Managing change in educational organizations*. New York: Wiley.

Blaesser, W. W. (1978). Organization change and student development. *Journal of College Student Personnel, 19,* 109–118.

Borland, D. T. (1980). Organization development: A professional imperative. In D. G. Creamer (Ed.), *Student development in higher education* (pp. 205–228). Carbondale, IL.: American College Personnel Association.

Davis, H. R., & Salasin, S. E. (1979). Change: Decisions and their implementation. In S. Feldman (Ed.), *The administration of mental health services* (2nd ed.) (pp. 383–433). Springfield, IL.: Charles C. Thomas.

Glaser, E. M., Abelson, H. H., & Garrison, K. H. (1983). *Putting knowledge to use.* San Francisco: Jossey-Bass.

Hammons, J. (Ed.). (1982). *Organization development: Change strategies* (New Directions for Student Services, No. 37). San Francisco: Jossey-Bass.

Hipps, G. M. (Ed.). (1982). *Effective planned change strategies* (New Directions for Institutional Research, No. 33). San Francisco: Jossey-Bass.

Huse, E. (1980). *Organization development and change* (2nd ed.). St. Paul, MN: West.

Martorana, S. V., & Kihns, E. (1975). *Managing academic change*. San Francisco: Jossey-Bass.

Moss-Kanter, R. (1983). *The changemasters: Innovations for productivity in the American corporation*. New York: Simon & Schuster.

Black Students on White Campuses: 20 Years of Research

William E. Sedlacek

Literature is discussed in terms of eight noncognitive variables affecting Black student life. The author recommends actions for student affairs professionals.

From the 1960s to 1980s people in the United States have witnessed a broad sweep of social change in the country. With issues pertaining to Blacks, people have seen a complex mixture of overt repression, social consciousness, legal changes, backlash, assassinations, political interest, disinterest, and neglect. Higher education has gone about its business during this turbulence.

There are many ways in which student affairs professionals might try to understand what Black students have experienced during the last 20 years. The purpose of this article is to examine this period through student affairs research on Black undergraduate students at White institutions. Such an article accomplishes several purposes. First, it allows for a focus on an area in which Black students have had to deal directly with a system largely run by Whites for Whites (Sedlacek & Brooks, 1976). Second, it allows one to step back and get a perspective on where student affairs has been and where it to be going. Third, it puts an emphasis on empirical research rather than commentary, wishful thinking, or frustration.

An index of the maturity of the student personnel profession may be found in its success in providing systematic knowledge on which to base its development. The May 1986 issue of the Journal of College Student Personnel, with articles by Brown, Cheatham, and Taylor, provided a lively discussion of how student affairs professionals can learn about Black students on White campuses. Should student affairs professionals go to the literature and see what the research says (Brown, 1986; Cheatham, 1986) or offer broad generalizations about Blacks based on a nonempirical synthesis (C.A.Taylor, 1986)? This article is in support of the former position.

The literature was organized using a model based on noncognitive variables

613

that have been shown to be related to Black student success in higher education (Sedlacek & Brooks, 1976; Tracey & Sedlacek, 1984, 1985, 1987; White & Sedlacek, 1986). Arbona, Sedlacek, and Carstens (1987) found that the noncognitive variables were related to whether Blacks sought services from a university counseling center.

There are limitations to using the noncognitive model. These include limiting the articles included, not using conventional categories (e.g., admissions, student activities) that may be easier to understand than the noncognitive model, and forcing a structure in areas where it does not belong. The two major questions addressed in this article are: (a)What have we in student affairs learned in 20 years of research? and (b)How can we use what we have learned?

Description of the Model

Sedlacek and Brooks (1976) hypothesized that there were seven noncognitive variables that were critical in the lives of minority students. How students adjusted to these dimensions and how faculty and staff encouraged this adjustment would determine the success or failure of the minority student. Tracey and Sedlacek (1984, 1985, 1987) demonstrated the validity of the seven variables plus an eighth, nontraditional knowledge acquired, by showing the usefulness of a brief questionnaire (the Noncognitive Questionnaire [NCQ]) in predicting grades, retention, and graduation for Black students for up to 6 years after initial matriculation. White and Sedlacek (1986) demonstrated the validity of the NCQ for Blacks in special programs. The noncognitive variables of the NCQ are:

1. *Positive self-concept or confidence.* Possesses strong self-feeling, strength of character, determination, independence.

2. *Realistic self-appraisal.* Recognizes and accepts any deficiencies and works hard at self-development. Recognizes need to broaden his or her individuality; especially important in academic areas.

3. *Understands and deals with racism.* Is realistic based on personal experience of racism. Not submissive to existing wrongs, nor hostile to society, nor a "cop-out." Able to handle racist system. Asserts school role to fight racism.

4. *Demonstrated community service.* Is involved in his or her cultural community.

5. *Prefers long-range goals to short-term or immediate needs.* Able to respond to deferred gratification.

6. *Availability of strong support person.* Individual has someone to whom to turn in crises.

7. *Successful leadership experience.* Has experience in any area pertinent to his or her background (e.g., gang leader, sports, noneducational groups).

8. *Knowledge acquired in a field.* Has unusual or culturally related ways of obtaining information and demonstrating knowledge. The field itself may be nontraditional.

Self-Concept

Many studies demonstrate that the way Black students feel about themselves is related to their adjustment and success at White institutions (Bayer, 1972; Bohn, 1973; Deslonde, 1971; Dixon-Altenor & Altenor, 1977; Gruber, 1980; Kester, 1970; Stikes, 1975). An early study of Bradley (1967) of "Negro" undergraduate students in predominantly White colleges in Tennessee showed that they had not achieved a feeling of belonging. This aspect of self-concept, that of seeing oneself as part of a school, or identified with it, is a common thread running through the literature on Black students' self-concept for several decades. For instance, Sedlacek and Brooks (1976), Astin (1975, 1982), and Tracey and Sedlacek (1984, 1985, 1987) provided evidence that identification with an institution is a more important correlate of retention for Blacks than for other students.

In addition to the usual school pressures, a Black student must typically handle cultural biases and learn how to bridge his or her Black culture with the prevailing one at the White university. DiCesare, Sedlacek, and Brooks (1972) found that Blacks who made this transition were more likely to stay in school than were Blacks who did not. Burbach and Thompson (1971) and Gibbs (1974) found that cultural adaptation had an influence on the self-concept of Black students; Sedlacek and Brooks (1972a) and White and Sedlacek (1986) found that this was also true for Blacks in special programs.

Pfeifer and Sedlacek (1974) noted that successful Black students may receive considerably different profiles on standardized personality measures than their White counterparts. The successful Black student is likely not only to seem "atypical" but is also inclined toward and experienced in taking less common paths to goals than the successful White student. Thus, there is evidence that important cultural differences between Blacks and Whites affect the manner in which self-concept is put into practice.

An important area of literature that has been developing concerns racial identity. Cross (1971) presented the model and Hall, Freedle, and Cross (1972) studied four stages of Black identity: (a) pre-encounter, when a person thinks of the world as the opposite of Black; (b) encounter, when experience disturbs this view; (c) immersion, when everything of value must be Black; and (d) internalization, when it is possible to focus on things other than one's racial group. Hall et al. (1972) demonstrated that it is possible for lay observers to identify these stages.

Parham and Helms (1985a) found that Black self-esteem is low in the pre-encounter stage, becomes more positive as one reaches the encounter stage but drops as one enters immersion, and is unchanged during internalization. Parham and Helms (1985b) found that Black male students were more likely to endorse the pre-encounter stage and less likely to endorse internalization than were Black female students. Ponterotto, Anderson, and Greiger (1985) found that Black female students in the internalization stage had more positive attitudes toward counseling than did Black men in the same stage. Carter and Helms (1987) found that these stages were related to value orientations of Black students. Using other instruments, Kapel (1971); Olsen (1972); Polite, Cochrane, and Silverman (1974); Smith (1980); and Semmes (1985) provided further evidence that cultural and racial identity are related to self-concept.

Realistic Self-Appraisal

An important variable that exists in combination with self-concept is how well Black students at White schools are able to assess how they are doing. This self-assessment pertains to both academic issues and student life. Success for any student involves the ability to "take readings" and make adjustments before the grades are in or before fully developing a lifestyle that is not conducive to success. Because faculty members, students, and staff often view Black students differently than they do White students, it is harder for Blacks to get straightforward information on which to base their evaluations of how they are faring.

White faculty members may give less consistent reinforcement to Black students than they give to White students (Sedlacek & Brooks, 1976). For Blacks who are trying to make realistic self-appraisals, faculty reinforcements that are too negative cause as many problems as those that are solicitous. For example, Christensen and Sedlacek (1974) demonstrated that faculty stereotypes of Blacks can be overly positive.

Some researchers have identified poor communication with faculty, particularly White faculty members, as a problem for Black students (Allen, Bobo, & Fleuranges, 1984; Jones, Harris, & Hauck, 1973; Van Arsdale, Sedlacek, & Brooks, 1971; Willie, 1971; Willie & McCord, 1972). Thompson and Michel (1972) found that what they called grade deflecting, or the difference between the grade expected and the grade received, by Black students correlated positively with students' perceived prejudice of the instructor. Switkin and Gynther (1974) and Terrell and Barrett (1979) found that Black students were generally less trusting than were White students.

Blacks may find it especially difficult to get close enough to faculty, staff, and other students to become a central part of the informal communication system that is critical in making self-assessments. Nettles, Thoeny, and Gosman (1986) found faculty contact outside the classroom to be a significant predictor of grade point average (GPA) for Black students. Braddock (1981) found such faculty contact more important to Black student retention at predominantly White schools than at predominantly Black schools. Fleming (1984) found that Blacks in predominantly Black colleges were better able to make self-assessments than were Blacks at predominantly White schools, presumably in part because Blacks were more involved in the communication and feedback system in Black schools.

Understanding and Dealing with Racism

There are two components in this variable. First, does the Black student understand how racism works? Can the student recognize it when it is occurring? Does the student have an effective way of handling racism, a way that allows Black students to pursue their goals with minimum interference? It is a curvilinear variable in that a Black student can have difficulty with racism because of naivete about it or preoccupation with it. An optimal strategy is one in which Black students have differential response patterns to racism. They take action when it is in their best interests and do not take action when it might cause them more trouble than it is worth to them. Each student must make those decisions individually. A Black who "chooses" to confront all examples of racism may be effective in many ways, but he or she is unlikely to remain in school or get high grades.

Handling racism is further complicated by the distinction made between individual and institutional racism (Barbarin, 1981; Racism/Sexism Resources Center for Educators, 1983; Sedlacek & Brooks, 1976). Institutional racism involves policies and procedures, either formal or informal, that result in negative outcomes for Blacks. Institutional racism is often more of a problem for Blacks than is individual racism. Tracey and Sedlacek (1987) pointed out the uniqueness of this problem for Black students. How well White students are able to negotiate the campus system predicts their success in school. The same is true for Blacks, except that their treatment by the system will, in many ways, be because they are Black (Deslonde, 1971; Garcia & Levenson, 1975; Webster, Sedlacek,& Miyares, 1979). The following are some of the more common forms of racism faced by Black students at predominantly White institutions.

Admissions

There is considerable evidence that traditional measures such as standardized tests and high school grades are not as valid for Blacks as they are for Whites (Baggaley, 1974; Borgen, 1972; Pfeifer & Sedlacek, 1971, 1974; Sedlacek, 1974, 1986; Tracey & Sedlacek, 1984, 1985, 1987). Most institutions, however, have continued to employ traditional measures for Black students from the 1960s to the 1980s (Breland, 1985; Sedlacek & Brooks, 1970a; Sedlacek, Brooks, & Horowitz, 1972; Sedlacek, Brooks, & Mindus, 1973; Sedlacek, Lewis,& Brooks, 1974; Sedlacek, Merritt,& Brooks, 1975; Sedlacek & Pelham, 1976; Sedlacek & Webster, 1978).

The negative outcomes in admissions for Blacks include being rejected for admission because of invalid measures or being accepted on the basis of "lower standards" that may result in the reduced self-esteem of Black students and the increased probability that White students and faculty will stereotype Blacks as less able than Whites. This stereotype, in turn, leads to more negative treatment of Black students.

There are also many forms of institutional racism in the methods employed to study admissions of Black students, including predicting 1st-year performance before Black students have fully adjusted to the White campus (Farver, Sedlacek, & Brooks, 1975; Kallingal, 1971; Tracey & Sedlacek, 1984, 1985, 1987) and using statistical and research procedures that are biased against Blacks (Sedlacek, 1986). These procedures result in invalid bases for admission decisions made about Blacks. Sedlacek and Brooks (1973) presented an example of using research information to work against racism in admissions.

Relationships with Faculty

The difficulties Black students have with White faculty are discussed above under "Realistic Self-Appraisal." Black students have consistently reported believing that White faculty are prejudiced toward them (e.g., Allen et al., 1984; Babbit, Burbach, & Thompson, 1975; Boyd, 1973; Butler, 1977; Dinka, Mazzella, & Pilant, 1980; Egerton, 1969; Jones et al., 1973; Semmes, 1985; Smith, 1980; Thompson & Michel, 1972; Westbrook, Miyares, & Roberts, 1977). This prejudice can take such forms as lower expectations of Black students than are warranted, overly positive reactions to work quality, reducing the quality of communications, and reducing the probability that faculty know students well enough to write reference letters.

Black students have expressed concerns about the lack of Black faculty and staff in a number of studies (Boyd, 1979; Matthews & Ross, 1975; Southern Regional Education Board, 1971; Willie, 1971). Absence of powerful Black figures as role models has strong effects on the feelings of loneliness and isolation of Blacks. The lack of a variety of viewpoints or cultural perspectives relevant to Black students can also affect their learning, development, and identification with the institution. Sedlacek and Brooks (1973) discussed an example of racism in academic coursework and how to reduce it.

Campus Life

Problems for Black students have been documented in residence halls (Piedmont, 1967) and fraternities (Tillar, 1974), with campus police (Eliot, 1969; Heussenstamm, 1971; Leitner & Sedlacek, 1976), and in interracial dating (Day, 1972; Korolewicz & Korolewicz, 1985; Merritt, Sedlacek, & Brooks, 1977; Patterson, Sedlacek, & Perry, 1984; Petroni, 1973; Schulman, 1974; Tillar, 1974; Willie & McCord, 1972), athletics (Green, McMillan, & Gunnings, 1972; McGehee & Paul, 1984), and campus life in general (Babbitt et al., 1975; Dinka et al., 1980; Fenton & Gelason, 1969; Fleming, 1984; Heyward, 1985; Lunneborg & Lunneborg, 1985; Minatoya & Sedlacek, 1980; Reichard & Hengstler, 1981; Trow, 1977; Westbrook et al., 1977; Willie & McCord, 1972).

Burbach and Thompson (1971) reported that contradictory norms on campus cause problems for Black students. Martinez and Sedlacek (1982) found that when Whites entered a predominantly white university in the early 1980s they expected the social norms to be conservative on social and political issues (e.g., government policies, abortion rights) but liberal on personal freedoms (e.g., drug use, sexual behavior). Black students tended to expect the norms to be exactly the opposite. Martinez and Sedlacek (1983) also found that students in general were more tolerant of people with racist or bigoted attitudes in 1981 than in 1970 on a predominantly White campus. That the campus environment could be seen as confusing and hostile to Black students should not be hard to understand.

Attitudes of White Students

The discomfort of White students around Blacks and the negative stereo-types of Blacks held by White students have been well documented during the period studied (Peterson et al., 1978). These underlying attitudes do not seem to have changed throughout the years. For example, a series of studies at the University of Maryland employing the same instrument, the Situational Attitude Scale (Sedlacek & Brooks, 1972b), and the same methodology, has shown consistently negative attitudes of White students toward Blacks in a wide variety of situations (e.g., Carter, White, & Sedlacek, 1985; Minatoya & Sedlacek, 1984; Miyares & Sedlacek, 1976; Sedlacek & Brooks, 1970b; White & Sedlacek, 1987). Studies at other institutions have supported this finding (e.g., Gaertner & McLaughlin, 1983; Greenberg & Rosenfield, 1979). Sedlacek, Troy, and Chapman (1976) have demonstrated, however, that it is possible to alter racial attitudes in an orientation program using an experimental-control group approach.

Community Service

As part of a viable support system, Blacks need to have identification with and be active in a community. The community may be on or off campus, large or small, but it will commonly be based on race or culture. Because of racism, Blacks have been excluded historically from being full participants in many of the White-oriented communities that have developed in the United States and in the educational system. Thus, Blacks need a supportive group that can given them the advice, counsel, and orientation to sustain them as they confront the larger, often hostile systems they must negotiate. Many researchers have documented that Blacks seem to be more community oriented than are Whites (Bayer, 1972; Centra, 1970; Davis, 1970; Greene & Winter, 1972; Lyons, 1973; Reichard & Hengstler, 1981; Southern Regional Education Board, 1972). Additionally, Bohn (1973) and Pfeifer and Sedlacek (1974) found that a high score on the California Psychological Inventory (CPI) (Megargee, 1972) Communality scale, which measures a community orientation, was associated with Black student success (i.e., retention and grades).

Other researchers have shown that Blacks often believe that they do not belong on predominantly White campuses (Bradley, 1967; Kleinbaum & Kleinbaum, 1976; Lunneborg & Lunneborg, 1985; Madrazo-Peterson & Rodruguez, 1978). The idea that there needs to be a "critical mass" or sufficient number of Blacks on a campus to develop a community or communities has been discussed by Astin and Bayer (1971), Willie and McCord (1972), and Fleming (1981, 1984). Thus, a relevant community is probably harder for Blacks to develop on a White campus than on a Black campus.

Bennett (1974) reported that Blacks preferred to separate residence hall floor. Davis (1970), in an experimental study, found that Blacks who lived on an all-Black floor in a residence hall were more positive toward their institution than were those who lived on a mixed-race floor.

Athletics may be an important way for Blacks to develop a community on campus (Mallinckrodt & Sedlacek, 1987; Reichard & Hengstler, 1981). Mallinckrodt and Sedlacek found that Blacks who made use of campus gymnasiums were more likely to stay in school than were those who did not.

Mallinckrodt and Sedlacek (1987) also found that Blacks who were interested in activities sponsored by the student union had better retention than did those who were not interested. Webster and Sedlacek (1982) found the student union to be a central part of Black students' community development.

Long-range Goals

The extent to which Black students are able to defer gratification is correlated with their retention and grades in school (Tracey & Sedlacek, 1984, 1985, 1987). The reason this is an issue is yet another form of racism. Blacks have had a more capricious experience in setting goals and receiving reinforcement for their accomplishments than have Whites. Sometimes things work out for Blacks; sometimes they do not. Whites are more likely to understand that if they accomplish A they can go to B. For Blacks, this is less clear. A key assumption in the higher education system is that students work currently for rewards received later.

Astin (1975) found that those Blacks with lower aspirations and vaguer goals than other Blacks were more likely to leave school,. Nolle (1973) supported Astin's conclusion by noting that Black high school students with specific plans for college were much more likely to attend college than were those with less clear goals. Bohn (1973) found that black college students who made plans were more successful than were those who did not. Greene and Winter (1971) found that Black leaders in campus organizations were more apt to have long-range goals than were other Black students. Other studies that provide general support for the importance of this variable include Baer (1982) and Stikes (1975). Berman and Haug (1975) and Wechsler, Rohman, and Solomon (1981) provided evidence that developing long-range goals may be a bigger problem for Black women than for Black men.

Strong Support Person

Because Black students are dealing with racism and face difficult adjustments to a White university, they are particularly in need of a person they can turn to for advice and guidance. As discussed above, however, Black students often find difficulty forming relationships with White faculty and staff (e.g., Boyd, 1973; Dinka et al., 1980; Simon, McCall, & Rosenthal, 1967). Additionally, Black faculty and staff are often not available, and Black students have expressed a need for more Black faculty and staff in general (Burrell, 1980; Willie, 1971; Willie & McCord, 1972) and more Black counselors in particular (Abbott, Tollefson, & McDermott, 1982; Wolkon, Moriwaki, & Williams, 1972). Genshaft (1982) found that therapists believed that Blacks were less attractive clients and had a poorer prognosis than did other clients. Parham and Helms (1981) presented evidence that client race was not a predictor of counselor race preference, but racial identity was. Blacks in the encounter and immersion stages wanted Black counselors, whereas those in the internalization stage had no preference (see previous discussion). Brooks, Sedlacek, and Mindus (1973), R. L.Taylor (1977), and Webster and Fretz (1977) have found that Blacks often turn to friends and family for support, which is further evidence of the importance of the variable.

Leadership

Successful Black students have had successful leadership experiences. They have shown the ability to organize and influence others, often within their cultural-racial context. As with acquiring knowledge or in doing community work, Blacks often do not show leadership in traditional ways. Black students are more likely to exhibit leadership off campus, in the community, or in their church than are White students. When Blacks show leadership on campus it is often through informal or Black-oriented channels, which are less likely to be validated by White faculty, students, or personnel workers.

Bayer (1972) found that Black students were oriented toward being community leaders. Greene and Winter (1971) showed evidence that leadership was important to Black students. Beasley and Sease (1974) demonstrated that scores of Blacks on the leadership portion of the American College Testing Program's student profile section correlated positively with GPAs.

Heyward (1985) concluded that Blacks do not look to White faculty and staff as role models for their leadership. They look to other Blacks or develop their own styles and forms of leadership.

Nontraditional Knowledge

Because Blacks have not always been welcomed in the formal educational system, they have developed ways of learning outside the system. These ways are often creative and culturally relevant. Astin (1975) found that Blacks who were able to demonstrate knowledge they gained in nontraditional ways through credit by examination were more likely to stay in school than those who could not. The increase in student retention associated with demonstrating knowledge in this way was more than twice as great for Blacks as for Whites.

Hayes and Franks (1975) reported that Blacks saw more opportunities than did Whites for public discussions and debates, which could translate into learning opportunities. Black (1971), in a study at historically Black colleges, found that Blacks who developed an independent learning year fared better than did a group of Blacks in a control group who pursued the regular curriculum.

Discussion

There has been considerable research on Black students in the last 20 years. What has been learned from this research? Although it is difficult to determine whether the problems of Blacks on White campuses have changed during this period, it is clear that it is possible to better measure, define, and articulate those problems than at any time previously. Blacks seem to have continued to have difficulties with self-concept, racism, developing a community, and the other noncognitive variables discussed. There is a model available, however, to organize thinking about Black student problems and ways to measure those problems, to work with Black students or others on campus, and to improve student life for Blacks. Perhaps most important, the variables identified correlate with Black student academic success. There is less need to guess or hope that what is being done is helpful. AppendixA contains some recommendations for improving Black student life on White campuses in terms of each noncognitive variables.

Some of the noncognitive variables discussed and conclusions reached may seem applicable to all students. Although this may be true to some degree, the evidence presented is intended to show that the points raised are unique to Blacks, in intensity if not in form. For instance, many White students may have self-concept problems, but these do not include the alienating effects of racism. Whites may lack a support person, but the process of developing such a relationship is not the same as for Blacks because of racial and cultural variables. The researchers have demonstrated the many unique aspects of being Black on a White campus.

Another area of research that seems illuminating but did not exist until recently is the work on racial identity of Blacks, discussed under self-concept. One can measure change and development in an area that has been shown to be important to Blacks. There are many other specific results of the studies discussed above that should be interesting and useful to practitioners.

Why cannot one be more sure that life has changed for Blacks on White campuses? First, there has been very little evaluation research. Most of it has been descriptive. Descriptive research is helpful, but it does not focus on change. For instance, Black students have reported being concerned with racism from the 1960s through the 1980s. But is it the same racism? Do past and present Black students mean the same thing when they refer to racism? Longitudinal studies over time or even cross-sectional studies done the same way in the same place are not common. Perhaps the way the literature was organized does not lend itself to the analysis of trends. The noncognitive variables are assumed to be underlying dimensions, which could take different forms at different times. For instance, institutional racism may be more likely to take the form of dropping a Black studies program or providing inadequate funding for a Black fraternity in the 1980s than involving police brutality or allowing Blacks into White fraternities in the 1960s. Some forms of racism (e.g., admissions, attitudes or White students), however, seem to have changed little over the years. In any case, it is still racism and it seems that Blacks are obligated to deal with it if they are to succeed in school.

As the research on Black students was examined one thought seemed to stand out. How ironic that educators so often think of Black students as less capable than other students. Black students need to have the same abilities and skills as any other student to succeed in school, and they are dealing with the same problems as any other student. They also, however, are confronting all the other issues discussed in this article. One could make the case that the best students in U.S. colleges and universities are Black students. The typical Black graduate from a predominantly White school may possess a wider range of skills and be able to handle more complex problems (e.g., racism) than most other students.

How can student affairs professionals use what has been presented here? Generally, one should be able to be much more sophisticated in student services work for Blacks using the information in this article. There exists much information demonstrating that Blacks are not a monolithic group and indicating how one might approach them individually or collectively. There is also more information about the many ways the educational system works against the best interests of Blacks. One can use this information to work with non-Black students, faculty, and staff to improve Black student life. Below are a number of specific things that can be done based on a review of this literature.

1. Organize programs and services for Black students around some specific variables that have been shown to be important. Whether it is one of the noncognitive variables presented here or some other scheme, use it. There is little excuse for vague, general programs or "seat-of-the-pants" needs analyses given the state of knowledge available.

2. Evaluate all programs. This should be done with an experimental-control group model if possible. If one has specific goals, and can measure concepts better, it should be possible to dramatically increase this type of research, and repot it in student affairs journals.

3. Work at refining the variables and concepts presentd here, either through programs or further research. The student services profession is on the brink of being able to work with more useful, higher order concepts than those currently employed on behalf of Black students; help the process along.

4. Share the information from this review and the results of individual work in Black student services with others outside studen affairs. Much of what has been done in the profession would be of use to such people as faculty and academic administrators.

5. The last bit of advice is more personal. Be confident. Many researchers over many years have developed a literature that can be used. Whatever a person's role, he or she should be able to fulfill it better withthis information.

References

Abbott, K., Tollefson, N., & McDermott, D. (1982). Counselor race as a factor incounselor preference. *Journal of College Student Personnel, 23*, 36–40.

Allen, W. R., Bobo, L., & Fleuranges, P. (1984). *Preliminary Repot: 1982 undergraduate students attending predominantly white state-suppoted universities.* Ann Arbor, MI: Center for Afro-American and African Studies.

Arbona, C., Sedlacek, W. E., & Carstens, S. P. (1987). *Noncognitive variables in predicting counseling center use by race* (Counseling Center Research Report No. 3–87). College Park: University of Maryland.

Astin, A. W. (1975). *Preventing students from dropping out.* San Francisco: Jossey-Bass.

Astin, A. W. (1982). *Minorities in American higher education: Recent trends, current prospects and recommendations.* San Francisco: Jossey-Bass.

Astin, A. W., & Bayer, A. E. (1971). Antecedents and consequents of disruptive campus protests. *Measurement and Evaluation in Guidance, 4*, 18–30.

Babbit, C. E., Burbach, J. J., & Thompson, M. A. III. (1975). Organizational alienation among Black college students: A comparison of three educational settings. *Journal of College Student Personnel, 16*, 53–56.

Baggaley, A. R. (1974). Academic prediction of an Ivy League college; moderatd by demographic variables. *Measurement and Evaluation in Guidance*, 5, 232–235.

Barbarin, O. A. (Ed.). (1981). *Institutional racism and community competence.* Bethesda, MD: National Institute of Mental Health.

Bayer, A. E. (1972). *The Black college freshman: Characteristics and recent trends* (Research Repot No. 3). Washington, DC: American Council on Education.

Beasley, S. R., Jr., & Sease, W. A. (1974). Using biographical data as a predictor of academic success for Black university students. *Journal of College Student Personnel*, 15, 201–206.

Bennett, D. C. (1974). Interracial ratios and proximity in dormitories: Attitudes of university students. *Environment and Behavior*, 6, 212–232.

Berman, G. S., & Haug, M. R. (1975). Occupational and educational goals and expectations: The effects of race and sex. *Social Problems*, 23, 166–181.

Blake, E., Jr. (1971). A case study in producing equal educational results: The thirteen college curriculum program. In F. F. Harcleroad & J. H. Cornell (Eds.), *Assessment of colleges and universities* (Monograph 6, pp. 55–61). Iowa City, IA: American College Testing Program.

Bohn, M. J., Jr. (1973). Personality variables in successful work-study performance. *Journal of College Student Personnel*, 14, 135–140.

Borgen, F. H. (1972). Differential expectations? Predicting grades for Black students in five types of colleges. *Measurement and Evaluation in Guidance*, 4, 206–212.

Boyd, W. M. II. (1973, Winter). Black student, White college. *College Board Review*, 90, 18–25.

Boyd, W. M. II. (1979). *Today's Black students: A success story* (Reseach Repot No. 21). Washington, DC: Association of Governing Boards.

Braddock, J. H. II. (1981). Desegregatio and Black student attrition. *Urban Education*. 15, 403–418.

Bradley, N. E. (1967). The Negro undergraduate student: Factors relative to performance in predominantly White state colleges and universities in Tennessee. *Journal of Negro Education*, 36, 15–23.

Breland, H. M. (1985). *an examination of state university and college admissions policies* (Research Repot No. 85–3). Princeton, NJ: Educational Testing Service.

Brooks, G. C., Jr., Sedlacek, W. E., & Mindus, L. A. (1973). Interracial contact and attitudes among university students. *Journal of Non-White Concerns in Personnel and Guidance*, 1, 102–110.

Brown,R. D. (1986). Research: A frill or an obligation (Editorial)? *Journal of College Student Personnel*, 27, 195.

Burbach, H. J., & Thompson, M. A. III. (1971). Alienation among college freshmen: A comparison of Peurto Rican, Black, and White students. *Journal of College Student Personnel*, 12, 248–252.

Burrell, L. F. (1980). Is there a future for Black students on predominantly White campuses? *Integrateducation*, 18(4), 23–27.

Butler, M. L. (1977). *Students needs survey report.* Fayetteville: University of Arkansas, Office of Student Services.

Carter, R. T., & Helms, J. E. (1987). The relationship of Black value-orientations to racial identity attitudes. Measurement and Evaluation in Counseling and Development, 19, 185–195.

Carter, R. T., White, T. J., & Sedlacek, W. E. (1985). White students' attitudes toward Blacks: Implications for recruitment and retention (Counseling Center Research Report No. 12–85). College Park: University of Maryland.

Centra, J. A. (1970). Black students at predominately White colleges: A research description. Sociology of Education, 43, 325–339.

Cheatham, H. E. (1986). Equal access: Progress or retrogression. Journal of College Student Personnel, 27, 202–204.

Christensen, K. C., & Sedlacek, W. E. (1974). Differential faculty attitudes toward Blacks, females and students in general. Journal of the National Association for Women Deans, Administrators, and Counselors, 37, 78–84.

Cross, W. E., Jr. (1971, July). The Negro to Black conversion experience. Black World, pp. 13–27.

Davis, J. S. (1970). A study of attitudes held by Black students living in residence halls. Columbia: University of Missouri.

Day, B. (1972). Sexual life between Blacks and Whites: The roots of racism. New York: World.

Deslonde, J. L. (1971, February). Internal-external control beliefs and racial militancy of urban community college students: The "problem of militancy." Paper presented at the meeting of American Educational Research Association, New York.

DiCesare, A., Sedlacek, W. E., & Brooks, G. C., Jr. (1972). Nonintellectual correlates of Black student attrition. Journal of College Student Personnel, 13, 319–324.

Dinka, F., Mazella, F., & Pilant, D. E. (1980). Reconciliation and confirmation: Blacks and Whites at a predominantly White university. Journal of Black Studies, 11, 55–76.

Dixon-Altenor, C., & Altenor, A. (1977). The role of occupational status in the career aspirations of Black women. Vocational Guidance Quarterly, 25, 211–215.

Egerton, J. (1969). State universities and Black Americans: An inquiry into desegregation and equity for Negroes in 100 public universities. Atlanta: Southern Education Foundation.

Eliot, T. H. (1969). Administrative response to campus turmoil. Washington, DC: American Council on Education.

Farver, A. S., Sedlacek, W. E., & Brooks, G. C., Jr. (1975). Longitudinal predictions of university grades for Blacks and Whites. Measurement and Evaluation in Guidance., 7, 243–250.

Fenton, J. H., & Gleason, G. (1969). Student power at the University of Massachusetts: A case study. Amherst: University of Massachusetts, Bureau of Government Research.

Fleming, J. (1981). Stress and satisfaction in college years of Black students. Journal of Negro Education, 50, 307–318.

Fleming, J. (1984). Blacks in college. San Francisco: Jossey-Bass.

Gaertner, S. L., & McLaughlin, J. P. (1983). Racial stereotypes: Associations and ascriptions of positive and negative characteristics. *Social Psychological Quarterly*, 46, 23–30.

Garcia, C., & Levenson, H. (1975). Differences between Blacks' and Whites' expectations of control by chance and powerful others. *Psychological Repots*, 37, 563–566.

Genshaft, J. L. (1982). The effects of race and role preparation on therapeutic interaction. *Journal of College Student Personnel*, 23, 33–35.

Gibbs, J. T. (1974, april). *Patterns of adaptation among Black students at a predominantly White university: Selected case studies.* Paper presented at the meeting of the American Orthopsychiatry Association, San Francisco.

Green, R. L., McMillan, J. R., & Gunnings, T. S. (1972). Blacks in the Big Ten. *Integrateducation*, 102(2), 32–39.

Greenberg, J., & Rosenfield, D. (1979). Whites' ethnocentrism and their attributions for the behaviors of Blacks: A motivational bias. *Journal of Personality*, 47, 643–657.

Greene, D. L., & Winter, D. G. (1971). Motives, involvements and leaderships among Black college students. *Journal of Personality*, 39, 319–332.

Gruber, J. E. (1980). Sources of satisfaction among students in postsecondary education. *American Journal of Education*, 88, 320–344.

Hall, W. S., Freedle, R., & Cross, W. E., Jr. 1972). *Stages in the development of Black identity* (Research Repot No. 50). Iowa City, IA: American College Testing Program.

Hayes, E. J., & Franks, J. (1975). College environment: Differential perceptions of Black minority students. *Journal of Non-White Concerns in Personnel and Guidance*, 4, 31–36.

Helms, J. E. (1984). Toward a theoretical explanation of the effects of race on counseling: A Black and White model. *Counseling Psychologist*, 12, 153–164.

Heussenstamm, F. K. (1971, February). Bumper stickers and the cops. *Transaction*, 8, 32–33.

Heyward, S. L. (1985, Fall). Facilitating the educational development of Black students at predominantly White institutions. *Carolina View*, 1, 14–18.

Jones, J. C., Harris, L. J., & Hauck, W. E. (1973, February). *Differences in perceived sources of academic difficulties: Black students in predominantly White collegess.* Paper presented at the meeting of the American Educational Research Association, New Orleans.

Kallingal, a. (1971). The prediction of grades for Black and White students at Michigan State University. *Journal of Educational Measurement*, 8, 265–265.

Kapel, D. E. (1972, April). *Attitudes toward selected stimuli: Communality and differences within and between two dissimilar high risk Black college groups.* Paper presented at the meeting of the American Educational Research Association, Chicago.

Kester, D. L. (1970, March). *NOR CAL—An impressive achievement: A review.* Paper presented at the meeting of the California Junior College Association, San Diego.

Kleinbaum, D. G., & Kleinbaum, A. (1976). The minority experience at a predominantly White university—A repot of a 1972 survey at the University of North Carolina at Chapel Hill. *Journal of Negro Education*, 45, 312–328.

Kochman, T. (1981). *Blacks and White styles in conflict.* Chicago: University of Chicago.

Korolewicz, M., & Korolewicz, A. (1985). Effects of sex and race on interracial dating preferences. *Psychological Reports, 57,* 291–296.

Leitner, D. W., & Sedlacek, W. E. (1976). Characteristics of successful campus police officers. *Journal of College Student Personnel, 17,* 304–308.

Lunneborg, P. W., & Lunneborg, C. E. (1985, August). *The challenge to counselors of minority achievement in higher education.* Paper presented at the meeting of the American Psychological Association, Los Angeles.

Lyons, J. E. (1973). The adjustment of Black students to predominantly White campuses. *Journal of Negro Education, 42,* 452–466.

Madrazo-Peterson, R., & Rodriquez, M. (1978). Minority students' perception of a university environment. *Journal of College Student Personnel, 19,* 259–263.

Mallinckrodt, B., & Sedlacek, W. E. (1987). Student retention and the use of campus facilities by race. *NASPA Journal, 24*(3), 2832.

Martinez, a. C., & Sedlacek, W. E. (1982). *Race and sex differences in college student perceptios of the social climate* (Counseling Center Research Repot No 8–82). College Park: University of Maryland.

Martinez, A. C., & Sedlacek, W. E. (1983). Changes in the social climate of a campus over a decade. *College and University, 58,* 254–257.

Matthews, D. E., & Ross, E. (1975). Observations from the placement front: Insensitivity and racism are not dead. *Journal of Non-White Concerns in Personnel and Guidance, 3,* 100–103.

McGehee, R. V., & Paul, M. J. (1984, March). *Racial makeup of central, stacking, and other playing positions in Southeastern Conference football teams, 1967–83.* Paper presented at Conference on Sport and Society, Clemson, South Carolina.

Megargee, E. I. 91972). *California Psychological Inventory handbook.* San Francisco: Jossey-Bass.

Merritt, M. S., Sedlacek, W. E., & Brooks, G. C., Jr. (1977). Quality of interracial interaction among university students. *Integrateducation, 15*(3), 37–38.

Minatoya, L. Y., & Sedlacek, W. E. (1980). Background and attitude toward interracial contact: A profile of Black and White university students. *Integrateducation, 18*(4), 43–45.

Minatoya, L. Y., & Sedlacek, W. E. (1984). Assessing attitudes of White university students toward Blacks in a changing context. *Journal of Non-White Concerns in Personnel and Guidance, 12,* 69–79.

Miyares, J., & Sedlacek, W. E. (1976). *Trends in racial attitudes of White university students* (Cultural Study Center Research Repot No. 5–76). College Park: University of Maryland.

Nettles, M. T., Thoeny, A. R., & Gosman, E. J. (1986). Comparative and predictive analyses of Black and White students' college achievement and experiences. *Journal of Higher Education, 57,* 289–318.

Nolle, D. B. (1973, April). *Black adolescents educational expectations: Reflections of fantasies or indicators of realities?* Paper presented at the meeting of the Southern Sociological Society, Atlanta.

Olsen, H.D. (1972). Effects of changes in academic roles on self-concept of academic ability of Black and White compensatory education students. *Journal of Negro Education*, 41, 365–369.

Parham, T. A., & Helms, J. E. (1981). The influence of Black students' racial identity attitudes on preferences for counselor's race. *Journal of College Student Personnel*, 28, 250–257.

Parham, T. A., & Helms, J. E. (1985a). Attitudes of racial identity and self-esteem of Black students: An exploratory investigation. *Journal of College Student Personnel*, 26, 143–147.

Parham, T. A., & Helms, J. E. (1985b) Relation of racial identity attitudes to self-actualization and affective states of Black students. *Journal of Counseling Psychology*, 32, 431–440.

Patterson, A. M., Jr., Sedlacek, W. E., & Perry, F. W. (1984). Perceptions of Blacks and Hispanics of two campus environments. *Journal of College Student Personnel*, 25, 513–518.

Peterson, M. W., Blackburn, R. T., Gamson, Z. F., Arce, C. H., Davenpot, R. W., & Mingle, J. R. (1978). *Black students on White campuses: The impacts of increased Black enrollments*. Ann Arbor, MI: Institute for Social Research.

Petroni,F., (19783). *Interracial dating: The price is high*. New York: Grossman.

Pfeifer, C. M., Jr., & Sedlacek, W. E. (1971). The validity of academic predictors for Black and White students at a predominantly White university. *Journal of Educational Measurement*, 43, 67–76.

Pfeifer, C. M., Jr., & Sedlacek, W. E. (1974). Predicting Black student grades with nonintellectual measures. *Journal of Negro Education*, 43, 67–76.

Piedmont, E. B. (1967). Changing racial attitudes at a southern university: 1947–1964. *Journal of Negro Education*, 36, 32–41.

Polite, C. K., Cochrane, R., & Silverman, B. I. (1974). Ethnic group identification and differentiation. *Journal of Social Psychology*, 92, 149–150.

Ponterotto, J. G., Anderson, W. H., Jr., & Greiger, I. (1985, May). *Black students' attitudes toward counseling as a function of racial identity*. Paper presented at the meeting of the Western Psychological Association, San Diego.

Racism/Sexism Resource Center for Educators. (1983). *Definitions of racism*. New York: Author.

Reichard, D. J., & Hengstler, D. D. (1981, May). *A comparison of Black and White student backgrounds and perceptions of a predominantly White campus environment: Implications for institutional research and program development*. Paper presented at the meeting of the Association for Institutional Research, Minneapolis.

Schulman, G. I. (1974). Race, sex and violence: A laboratory test of the sexual threat of the Black male hypothesis. *American Journal of Sociology*, 79, 1260–1277.

Sedlacek, W. E. (1977). Should higher education students be admitted differentially by race and sex? The evidence. *Journal of the National Association of College Admissions Counselors*, 22(1), 22–24.

Sedlacek, W. E. (1986). Sources of method bias in test bias research. In *Measures in the College Admissiosn Process* (pp. 86–92). New York: College Entrance Examination Board.

Sedlacek, W. E. (in press). Institutional racism and how to handle it. *Health Pathways.*

Sedlacek, W. E., & Brooks, G. C., Jr. (1970a). Black freshmen in large colleges: A survey. *Personnel and Guidance Journal,* 49, 307–312.

Sedlacek, W. E., & Brooks, G. C., Jr. (1970b). Measuring racial attitudes in a situational context. *Psychological Reports,* 27, 971–980.

Sedlacek, W. E., & Brooks, G. C., Jr. (1972a). *Predictors of academic success for university students in special programs* (Cultural Study Center Research Repot No. 4–72). College Park: University of Maryland.

Sedlacek, W. E., & Brooks, G. C., Jr. (1982b). *Situational Attitude Scale (SAS) manual.* Chicago: Natresources.

Sedlacek, W. E., & Brooks, G. C., Jr. (1973). Racism and research: Using data to initiate change. *Personnel and Guidance Journal,* 52, 184–188.

Sedlacek, W. E., & Brooks, G. C., Jr. (1976). *Racism in American education: A model for change.* Chicago: Nelson-Hall.

Sedlacek, W. E., Brooks, G. C., Jr., & Horowitz, J. L. (1972). Black admissions to large universities: Are things changing? *Journal of College Student Personnel,* 13, 305–310.

Sedlacek, W. E., Brooks, G. C., Jr., & Mindus, L. A. (1973). Black and other minority admissions to large universities: Three year national trends. *Journal of College Student Personnel,* 14, 16–21.

Sedlacek, W. E., Lewis, J. A., & Brooks, G. C., Jr. (1974). Black and other minority admissions to large universities: A four year survey of policies and outcomes. *Research in Higher Education,* 2, 221–230.

Sedlacek, W. E., Merritt, M. S., & Brooks, G. C., Jr. (1975). A national comparison of universities successful and unsuccessful in enrolling Blacks over a fiveyear period. *Journal of College Student Personnel,* 15, 57–63.

Sedlacek, W. E., & Pelham, J. C. (1976). Minority admissions to lage universities: A national survey. *Journal of Non-White Concerns in Personnel and Guidance,* 4, 53–63.

Sedlacek, W. E., Troy, W. G., & Chapman, T. H. (1976). An evaluation of three methods of racism, sexism training. *Personnel and Guidance Journal,* 196–198.

Sedlacek, W. E., & Webster, D. W. (1978). Admission and retention of minority students in large universities. *Journal of College Student Personnel,* 19, 242–248.

Semmes, C. E. (1985). Minority status and the problem of legitimacy. *Journal of Black Studies,* 15, 259–275.

Simon, R. J., McCall, G., & Rosenthal, E. (1967, April). *A selective evaluation of their university by Negro and White undergraduates.* Paper presented at the meeting of the Midwest Sociological Society, Des Moines.

Smith, D. H. (1980). *Admission and retention problems of Black students of seven predominantly White universities.* New York: National Advisory Committee onBlack Higher Education and Black Colleges and Universities.

Southern Regional Education Board. (1972). *Impact: A project report on compensatory instruction in community colleges.* Atlanta:Author.

Stikes, C. S. (1975). A coneptual map of Black student development problems. *Journal of Non-White Concerns in Personnel and guidance,* 4, 24–30.

Switkin, L. R., & Gynther, M. D. (1974). Trust, activism, and interpersonal perception in Black and White college students. *Journal of Social Psychology*, 94, 153–154.

Taylor, C. A. (1986). Black students on prdominantly White college campuses in the 1980s. *Journal of College Student Personnel*, 27, 196–202.

Taylor, R. L. (1977). The orientational others and value preferences of Black college youth. *Social Science Quarterly*, 57, 797–810.

Terrell, F., & Barrett, R. K. (1979). Interpersonal trust among college students as a functionof race, sex and socioeconomic class. *Perceptual and Motor Skills*, 48, 1194.

Thompson, M. S., & Michel, J. B. (1972, August). *Black students' perceptions of prejudice and grade deflection*. Paper presented at the meeting of the american sociological Association, New Orleans.

Tillar, T. C., Jr. (1974). A study of racial integration in southeastern social fraternities. *Journal of College Student Personnel*, 15, 207–212.

Tracey, T. J., & Sedlacek, W. E. (1984). Noncognitive variables in predicting academic success by race. *Measurement and Evaluation in Guidance*, 16, 172–178.

Tracey, T. J., & Sedlacek, W. E. (1985). The relationship of noncognitive variables to academic success: A longitudinal comparison by race. *Journal of College Student Personnel*, 26, 405–410.

Tracey, T. J., & Sedlacek, W. E. (1987). Prediction of college graduation using noncognitive variables by race. *Measurement and Evaluation in Counseling and Development*, 19, 177–184.

Trow, M. (1977). *Aspects of American higher education*. New York: Carnegie Council on Policy Studies in Higher Education.

Van Arsdale, P. W., Sedlacek, W. E., & Brooks, G. C., Jr. (1971). Trends in Black student attitudes at a predominantly White university. *Negro Educational Review*, 22, 133–145.

Webster, D. W., & Fretz, B. R. (1977). *Asian-American Black, and White college students' preferences for help souces* (Counseling Center Research Report No. 10–77). College Park: University of Maryland.

Webster, D. W., & Sedlacek, W. E. (1982). The differential impact of a university student union on campus subgroups. *NASPA Journal*, 19(2), 48–51.

Webster, D. W., Sedlacek, W. E., & Miyares, J. (1979). A comparison of problems perceived by minority and White students. *Journal of College Student Personnel*, 20, 165–170.

Wechsler, H., Rohman, M., & Solomon, L. (1981). Emotional problems and concerns of New England college students. *American Journal of Orthopsychiary*, 51, 719–723.

Westbrook, F. D., Miyares, J., & Roberts, J. (1977). *Perceived problem areas by Black and White students and hints about comparative counseling needs* (Counseling Center Research Report No. 11–77). College Park: University of Maryland.

Westbrook, F. W., & Sedlacek, W. E. (in press). Workshop on using noncognitive variables with minority students in higher education. *Journal for specialists in Group Work*.

White, T. J., & Sedlacek, W. E. (1986). Noncognitive predictors of grades and retention for specially admitted students. *Journal of College Admissions, 3,* 20–23.

White, T. J., & Sedlacek, W. E. (1987). White student attitudes toward Blacks and Hispanics: Programming implications. *Journal ofMulticultural Counseling and Development,* 15, 171–183.

Willie, C. V. (1971, September). *The student-teacher relationship experienced by Black students at White colleges.* Paper presented at the meeting of the American Sociological Association, Denver.

Willie, C. V., & McCord, A. S. (1972). *Black students at White colleges.* New York: Praeger.

Wolkon, G. H., Moriwaki, S., & Williams, K. J. (1972). Race and social class as factors in the orientation toward psychotherapy. In *American Psychological Association Proceedings* (pp. 373–374). Washinton, DC: American Psychological Association.

Appendix A
Recommendations for Improving Black Student Life on White Campuses by Noncognitive Variable

Self-concept: Measure self-concept (see Hall et al., 1972; Tracey & Sedlacek, 1984). Develop counseling programs or workshops employing racial identity (Helms, 1984) or noncognitive variables (Westbrook & Sedlacek, in press).

Realistic self-appraisal: Work with faculty and academic administrators on communication with Black students. Faculty should initiate contact more than they usually do and employ feedback in varied and frequent ways. Help Black students interpret feedback from system. Examine Kochman (1981) for differences in Black and White communication styles.

Understanding and dealing with racism: Become familiar with racism and what can be done about it (Racism/Sexism Resouces Center for Eucators, 1983; Sedlacek, in press; Sedlacek & Brooks, 1976). Specific forms of racism can be addressed by (a) employing nontraditional admission predictors that are more valid for Blacks than those currently employed (Sedlacek, 1986; Tracey & Sedlacek, 1987), (b) increasing the numbers of Black faculty and staff (Peterson et al., 1978), and (c) working to change attitudes of White students, faculty, and staff (Sedlacek, Troy, & Chapman, 1976).

Demonstrated community service: Help Whites understand the need for Black communities on and off campus. Use student union programming (Webster & Sedlacek, 1982) and facilities management (Mallinckrodt & Sedlacek, 1987) as methods of developing Black communities on campus.

Long-range goals: Financial aid dispersed as a lump sum may hurt Black student development in this area. Consider a program that gives Black students funds for accomplishing individually set goals. Goals can be set at longer and longer intervals. A midwestern university employs this system successfully. In the short run, use the concept that Black students may be motivated to use available student services by promoting a more immediate reward system than commonly employed (Arbona & Sedlacek, 1987).

Strong support person: Develop relationships with Black students early, ideally before matriculation through recruiting and orientation programs. Develop a pool of faculty, staff, peers or off-campus mentors and link Black students with others individually or in groups.

Leadership: Foster and identify nontraditional and racially based forms of student leadership on and off campus. Formally encourage schools and specific departments to offer leadership awards for such achievements as eliminating racism, Black journalism, and race-related community projects. Make faculty aware of nontraditional student leaders in their departments. Help students to recognize their nontraditional leadership and include such leadership roles in resumes and applications for jobs and further education.

Nontraditional knowledge acquired: Encourage Blacks to demonstrate knowledge gained outside the classroom through credit by examination or listings on resumes and applications. Encourage faculty to identify extramural learners and work with them.

A Perspective on Student Affairs:
A Statement Issued on the 50th Anniversary of
The Student Personnel Point of View

Foreword

Nineteen eighty-seven marked the 50th anniversary of *The Student Personnel Point of View* statement published by the American Council on Education. The statement, revised in 1949, has served as a foundation document for the student affairs profession.

In January 1986, the NASPA Board of Directors unanimously endorsed a proposal to establish a blue ribbon committee to reexamine *The Student Personnel Point of View* and prepare a statement that sets forth the essential assumptions and purposes that underlie our work in student affairs. In February 1986, ACE agreed to participate in this initiative with NASPA.

President Chambers appointed a Plan for a New Century Committee, chaired by Dr. Arthur Sandeen, Vice President of Student Affairs, University of Florida. The committee formally convened five times during 1986–87. In addition, 18 different public forums were held to solicit ideas. Committee members also corresponded with dozens of leaders of higher education, student affairs professionals, faculty, and others to solicit ideas and reactions about current perspectives on student affairs. In June 1987, the committee completed its consultations and deliberations and prepared its report, *A Perspective on Student Affairs: A Statement Issued on the 50th Anniversary of the Student Personnel Point of View.*

The report was unanimously endorsed by the NASPA Board of Directors at its July 1987 meeting. The ACE Board of Directors received the report at its October 1987 meeting.

This statement reveals what the higher education community can expect from student affairs. It is issued in commemoration of the 50th anniversary of the 1937 Student Personnel Point of View, but is in no way intended to be a revision of either the 1937 of 1949 statements. It is a perspective written

635

in 1987 to stimulate greater understanding of student affairs among leaders in higher education.

Student affairs is a main component of a college or university and must not become isolated as an entity unto itself. This statement is intentionally addressed to presidents and chief academic, financial, and student affairs officers and other leaders in higher education.

NASPA believes that A *Perspective on Student Affairs* will play an important role in the contemporary scene and in the history of higher education and the student affairs profession. The statement enumerates the major assumptions and beliefs which guide student affairs practice. It describes what institutions and individual students can expect from student affairs professionals. A *Perspective on Student Affairs* will serve as a stimulus for discussion and debate within the higher education and student affairs profession. This discussion and debate should foster a renewed understanding and appreciation of the contributions student affairs professionals make to institutions of higher education and the students they serve.

NASPA is pleased to present A *Perspective on Student Affairs* which was made possible by generous grants from Marriott Education Services and American College Testing.

Judith M. Chambers
NASPA President 1986–87

A *Plan for A New Century* Committee Members

Dr. Rober L. Albright, President, Johnson C. Smith University, Charlotte, North Carolina

Dr. Margaret J. Barr, Vice Chancellor for Student Affairs, Texas Christian University, Fort Worth, Texas

Dr. Anne E. Golseth, Dean of Students, Ohlone College, Fremont, California

Dr. George D. Kuh, Associate Dean, Academic Affairs, Indiana University, Bloomington, Indiana

Dr. James W. Lyons, Dean of Student Affairs, Stanford University, Stanford, California

Dr. James J. Rhatigan, Vice President for Student Affairs, Wichita State University, Wichita, Kansas

Dr. Arthur Sandeen, Vice President for Student Affairs, University of Florida, Gainesville, Florida, and Committee Chairman

Staff support was provided by Ms. Sarah Resnick, Administrative Assistant in the Office of Student Affairs at the University of Florida.

Acknowledgements

The Plan for a New Century Committee wishes to express its appreciation to NASPA for its sponsorship of this report. The committee is grateful to Marriott Education Services, which provided a generous grant supporting the committee's work. A grant from American College Testing made it possible to print and distribute the report.

Finally, the committee expresses its thanks to our many colleagues in student affairs who made helpful suggestions to us during the year.

Introduction

In 1937, the American Council on Education (ACE) sponsored an invitational conference for educational leaders whose interest in students extended beyond the classroom. The conference resulted in a report, The Student Personnel Point of View, which became a foundation document in the field of professional practice known as student affairs. A revision of the report was published by ACE in 1949. Both documents helped create an understanding of the role of student affairs in higher education.

On the 50th anniversary of the 1936 statement, the American Council on Education applauds the National Association of Student Personnel Administrators for offering this statement. Its purpose is to present a perspective on what the higher education community can expect from student affairs.

The following commentary provides a review of the development of student affairs as an integral part of American higher education. A perspective on higher education is presented which emphasizes the changes in students and institutions which are influencing the educational environment.

Student affairs professionals hold a set of assumptions and beliefs which shape their work. These points of view are discussed and provide the foundation for the role of student affairs in an institution. Finally, specific expectations for student affairs professionals are presented.

Historical Overview

In the colonial college, faculty were concerned in equal measure with the intellectual, religious, and moral development of students. White male students, entering institutions as early as age 13, were exposed to religious teaching, and this pattern existed in most colleges throughout the 18th century and for at least half the 19th century. Higher education continued to serve a homogeneous clientele within a religious framework.

Changes in higher education after the Civil War contributed significantly to the emergence of student affairs work. These changes were in part a reflection of a rapidly growing population, unprecedented industrial growth, and federal legislation which dramatically altered the nature and purpose of public higher education.

As a result, the purposes of higher education were broadened to include education for responsible, enlightened citizenship as well as vocational training. Programs of study became more specialized and options available to students increased as some institutions began to emphasize graduate study and research, technical training, and teacher preparation. With an expanded curriculum came a more diverse student population. Students came from a broader economic spectrum and had different expectations for their collegiate experience. The number of coeducational institutions increased rapidly, and women's colleges prospered. Institutions for Black Americans were founded because Black students were excluded from most colleges and universities.

Changes in the American professoriate also occurred. A growing number of faculty pursued graduate study at German institutions where they were introduced to scholarly research grounded in the scientific method. In the German system, faculty showed little interest in students' activities beyond the classroom, an attitude often reflected by American faculty returning from study in Europe. Although American institutions were influenced by varying degrees by these changes, the prestigious, complex institutions were affected most. It was at these institutions where the student affairs field emerged.

Some university presidents responded to changes in faculty interests and values by appointing persons to be responsible for student matters. Frequently, they were called Dean of Men or Dean of Women, and their initial charge was to resolve student problems and to administer campus discipline. No formal body of knowledge or preparation specific to student affairs work was available. These pioneers compensated by maintaining a flexible approach to work, and by sharing information with each other. The first formal program of study in student affairs was a program in vocational guidance offered at Teacher's College, Columbia University, in 1916.

Within the next two decades, the expansion of student affairs prompted the American Council on Education to assess the growing field. The result of that study was the publication of The Student Personnel Point of View, in 1937. The document described a number of functions for this field, noted the need for coordinating student affairs programs and services with other units in the institution, and emphasized the importance of educating the whole student.

The tenets of the original statement were reaffirmed in a revision published in 1949. However, the experience of World War II underscored the need for additional goals for higher education, including:

- education for democracy
- education for international understanding
- education to solve problems.

The authors of the revised document described the contributions student affairs could make in helping institutions and students attain these goals.

During the 1950s and 1960s, enrollments at many institutions more than doubled, faculty were in short supply, and the federal government invested unprecedented resorces for facilities, research, and student aid. Explosive growth in the number of public community colleges provided higher education opportunities to nearly every high school graduate and to older citizens. The scope of student affairs responsibilities also expanded as students became more varied in their abilities, age, aspirations, and racial and ethnic backgrounds. "Great Society" policies and civil rights legislation, judicial intervention, the Vietnam War, and a change in the age of majority fueled student activism on many campuses and forced a reassessment of the relationship between student and college.

Many significant changes have occurred within colleges and universities since 1937. The practitioners and scholars who contributed to The Student Personnel Point of View wrote from their time and place. Yet the themes and issues addressed in their work are important in understanding why student affairs is a major component of an institution of higher education.

The Current Context of Higher Education

Institutional diversity is one of the greatest strengths of American higher education. Together, over 3,000 colleges and universities serve about 13 million students. Some institutions emphasize baccalaureate education grounded in the liberal arts tradition. Others have multiple purposes and include undergraduate, graduate, professional, and technical education and serve thousands of students from around the world. Still others are community oriented, and their offerings reflect local or regional educational needs. The role of student affairs is largely determined by the mission and goals of the institution.

The traditional purposes of higher education are to preserve, transmit, and create knowledge; to encourage personal development; and to serve society. In addition, college and university programs help individuals cope with significant life transitions—from adolescence to adulthood, from dependence to personal autonomy, from one occupation to another. Technological advances and escalating rates of change add to the complexity and challenge associated with these transitions.

Once perceived as isolated "ivory towers" institutions of higher education now frequently collaborate with government and industry. At the same time, the nation's investment in education subjects colleges and universities to scrutiny and control by federal and state agencies, accrediting bodies, and professional associations. Alumni, parents and family members, legislators, unions, corporate and philanthropic sponsors, and other special interest groups all believe they have a stake in the enterprise and compete for the attention of faculty and administrators. The offices and administrative structures created to respond to these outside pressures have increased institutional complexity.

Differentiation and specialization in academic disciplines, and expanding responsibilities in research, teaching and community service have contributed to stress within the professoriate. Institutions are sometimes confronted with financial problems, often triggered by enrollment shortfalls. At many institutions, class size has increased, particularly in the first two years of undergraduate study. Informal interaction with faculty enhances students' academic success and satisfaction, yet the frequency and quality of contact between professor and student often is unacceptably low. These factors have placed additional demands on students, faculty, and administrators.

While colleges and universities have changed in recent decades, so have students. More than half of all high school graduates enroll in colleges or universities, compared with only 20 percent in 1950. Women now outnumber men. Older citizens are returning to college. Fewer than half of undergraduates are 18–22 years old or are enrolled for full-time study on a residential campus. Many students are inadequately prepared for college level work, and are uncertain about their educational and career aspirations. Although many students attend college for traditional reasons, others enroll to acquire specific skills or information rather than to pursue a degree. Enrollment patterns vary. Some students take one or two classes a term while others are enrolled full time. Many work full time while taking classes. Others leave college but later return and resume their studies. Most take five or more years to obtain the baccalaureate degree.

On some campuses, students reflect the cultural, ethnic, and racial diversity of the United States. International students comprise a significant proportion of some student bodies. Students from low-income remain underrepresented. By the year 2000, more than half of the students on many campuses are expected to be people of color, and the average age will be over 25. There will be more students for whom English is a second language. Students with physical and other disabilities will attend in increased numbers.

Substantial changes have occurred in student characteristics and the nature and organization of colleges and universities. Student affairs assists institutions in responding to changing conditions by providing services and programs consistent with students' needs and the institutional mission.

Assumptions and Beliefs

Student affairs professionals share some assumptions and beliefs that shape their work. These assumptions and beliefs guide their responses to new issues, changing times and circumstances, and recurring events. The following list is not exhaustive, nor will all student affairs staff agree that each guides their work to the same degree; the higher education community is too diverse for that to be the case. Yet, these ideas have remained remarkably unchanged over time and have been successfully applied to different collegiate settings.

No one of these assumptions and beliefs is unique to student affairs. Indeed, they are held by many others in higher education. It is the combination of these assumptions and beliefs that is distinctive. Together, they define the special contributions made by student affairs.

• The Academic Mission of the Institution is Preeminent

Colleges and universities organize their primary activities around the academic experience: the curriculum, the library, the classroom, and the laboratory. The work of student affairs should not compete with and cannot substitute for that academic experience. As a partner in the educational enterprise, student affairs enhances and supports the academic mission.

• Each Student is Unique

Students are individuals. No two come to college with the same expectations, abilities, life experiences, or motives. Therefore, students will not approach college with equal skill and sophistication, nor will they make equally good choices about the opportunities encountered there.

• Each Person Has Worth and Dignity

It is imperative that students learn to recognize, understand, and celebrate human differences. Colleges can, and indeed, must, help their students become open to the differences that surround them: race, religion, age, gender, culture, physical ability, language, nationality, sexual preference, and life style. These matters are learned best in collegiate settings that are rich with diversity, and they must be learned if the ideals of human worth and dignity are to be advanced.

• Bigotry Cannot Be Tolerated

Any expression of hatred or prejudice is inconsistent with the purposes of higher education in a free society. So long as bigotry in any form exists in the larger society, it will be an issue on the college campus. There must be a committment by the institution to create conditions where bigotry is forthrightly confronted.

• Feelings Affect Thinking and Learning

Although students are in college to acquire knowledge through the use of their intellect, they feel as well as think. Students are whole persons. How they feel affects how well they think. While students are maturing intellectually, they are also developing physically, psychologically, socially, aesthetically, ethically, sexually, and spiritually. This is true regardless of age. Helping students understand and attend to those aspects of their lives can enhance their academic experiences.

• Student Involvement Enhances Learning

Learning is not a passive process. Students learn most effectively when they are actively engaged with their work in the classroom and in student life.

• Personal Circumstances Affect Learning

Physical disability, financial hardship, family circumstances, medical and psychological problems, and inadequate academic skills are examples of situations which often affect learning. Whenever possible, colleges and universities should assist students when such circumstances interfere with learning.

• Out-of-Class Environments Affect Learning

Out-of-class social and physical environments are rarely neutral; they help or detract from students' social and intellectual development. Interactions between students and their environments shape attitudes, readiness to learn, and the quality of the college experience.

Colleges' New Liabilities: An Emerging New *In Loco Parentis*

Annette Gibbs

and

James J. Szablewicz

The authors describe and document the changing legal theories about the college-student relationship currently used by the courts. These most recent legal actions focus on contract law, landowner liability, guest and host, and negligence.

Until the 1960's, the relationship between a college and its students was much like that between a parent and child. Indeed, for all practical purposes, the college stood in *loco parentis* and was the de facto and de jure guardian of students' health, welfare, safety, and morals. But with the cultural revolution of the late 1960's, this relationship changed. In the wake of student protests against the Vietnam war and racial inequality, a new student independence emerged. Society eventually perceived the college student as an adult rather than a child. An arm's length relationship developed between colleges and students, which respected students' individual, academic, and political freedoms.

During the 1980's, however, the college-student relationship began to show signs of change yet again. Students began to expect their colleges to get them jobs, provide them with tuition assistance, and establish their careers. They likewise demanded protections—protections against criminal attach, against harm inflicted by others, and against injuries often sustained because of their own carelessness.

Courts and commentators have struggled to define this new student-college relationship, using theories of contract, landowner liability, guest and host,

Annette Gibbs can be contacted at the Center for the Study of Higher Education, Curry School of Education, University of Virginia, Charlottesville, VA 22903. James J. Szablewicz can be contacted at the law firm of Williams, Mullen, Christian, and Dobbins, Richmond, VA.

and consumerism. To date, no single doctrine or label has been developed that explains this new relationship. There is a clear trend emerging, however, toward use of tort (i.e., negligence) theory and analysis by the courts that, in large measure, is supplanting other notions of contract, consumerism, and student rights. Exploitation of this trend by plaintiff students has resulted in colleges being held liable in often extreme circumstances.

The New Liability of the 1980s

In the early 1980s, courts began to hold colleges liable for personal injuries to students arising in widely varying factual contexts. This has not been a uniform development because many courts have refused plaintiff students' claims. The fact remains, however, that state appellate and supreme courts in such divergent jurisdictions as Massachusetts, Colorado, and California have held colleges responsible for injuries to students, often in extreme and extraordinary circumstances. In addition, and perhaps just as significant, students have increasingly brought such negligence suits.

Liability for Sexual Attacks on Students

In *Relyea v. State* (1980), the plaintiff student sought damages from her state college after she was sexually attacked on the college grounds. In her suit the student claimed that the defendant college had a mandatory, nondiscriminatory duty to provide reasonable security for all persons lawfully on campus, particularly for students enrolled in classes at the college. Rather than viewing this case as a unique student-college situation, however, the Florida Court of Appeals used a more standard tort analysis of landowner liability and withheld liability. The court held that a landowner may have a duty to protect those on his or her property from criminal attack if such attack is foreseeable, but that generally a landowner is not the ensurer of the safety of his or her invitees (*Relyea*, 1980). Because the attack was not foreseeable, the college was not liable, and the Florida court thus ignored the plaintiff's argument that the college owed her a special duty of safety and protection solely because she was a student.

A similar case 3 years later made its way through the Massachusetts courts, but with different results. In *Mullins v. Pine Manor College* (1983), the plaintiff student was sexually attacked on the college grounds by a nonstudent assailant and brought a negligence claim against the college for her injuries.

The Massachusetts Supreme Court, though refusing to reinstate an *in loco parentis* doctrine, held the college liable:

Of course, changes in college life, reflected in the general decline of the theory that a college stands in loco parentis to its students, arguably cut against this view (plaintiff's claim that the school owed her duty of protection). The fact that a college need not police the morals of its resident students, however, does not entitle it to abandon any effort to ensure their physical safety. Parents, students, and the general community still have a reasonable expectation, fostered in part by colleges themselves, that reasonable care will be exercised to protect resident students from foreseeable harm. (*Mullins*, 1983, p. 335)

The *Mullins* ruling was not based on strict liability as such, but rested on more traditional tort analysis. To be successful, a plaintiff must show that the harm suffered was foreseeable by the defendant, and that the harm was caused by an act or an omission of the defendant. In this case, the plaintiff had to show either that the college's failure to exercise due care increased the risk of harm or that the harm was suffered because of this student's reliance on the college's undertaking to provide students in general with protection (*Mullins*, 1983). The plaintiff in this case successfully demonstrated the latter.

The real importance of the *Mullins* case lies not in the tort formula used, but the court's recognizing the plaintiff student's right rely on the college's duty, or voluntary undertaking, to provide protection for her safety. This is a right that will be enforced by the court against the college when breached. The *Mullins* court thus took the one step that the *Relyea* court did not—using the college-student relationship to augment and extend the standard landowner-premises liability analysis. Though factually the same, the *Mullins* and *Relyea* cases turned out differently precisely because the *Mullins* court held the college to a somewhat higher standard of care with respect to its students than the typical premises owner has to his or her invitees.

The California courts have used an analysis similar to *Mullins* to extend liability. In *Petersen v. San Francisco Community College* (1984), the court held the defendant college liable for a sexual attack on a student that took place in the college parking lot. Liability here was based on the college's duty to provide safe premises through the exercise of due care. The court initially imposed liability using the same standards on which general landowner-premises liability is based, and the language of the ruling clearly holds colleges to a somewhat higher standard than the typical landowner, stating that the defendant college was "responsible for *overseeing* its campus" (*Peterson*, 1984, p. 1202).

The *Peterson* court's analysis hinged on the existence of a special relation-ship between the parties that gives rise to a duty of care. The special relationship explicitly pointed to by the court is "that between a possessor of land and members of the public who enter in response to the landowner's invitation" (*Peterson*, 1984, p. 1196). This is the same point at which the *Relyea* court's analysis stopped. But like the Supreme Court of Massachusetts in the *Mullins* case, the California court here takes that extra step that, implicitly at least, caused liability to attach.

Indeed, it is clear from language in the *Peterson* ruling that there is something even more special about the student-college relationship that is the basis for liability:

In the enclosed environment of a school campus where students pay tuition and other fees in exchange for using the facilities, where they spend a significant portion of their time and may in fact live, they can reasonably expect that the premises will be free from physical defect and that school authorities will also exercise reasonable care to keep the campus free from conditions which increase the risk of crime. (*Peterson*, 1984, p. 1201)

Thus, it was the plaintiff's status as a student in the circumstances of this case that was "relevant . . . to the question of liability" (*Peterson*, 1984, p. 1198). It seems to be this special college-student relationship that gave rise to a duty of care in this case.

Liability for Alcohol-Related Accidents

with their refusal to hold colleges liable for injuries to students arising from a misuse of alcohol, state courts in a variety of jurisdictions seemingly have drawn the line on the liability of colleges, generally. There has been little unity in the courts' analyses in these cases, and, accordingly, the court rulings do little to provide guidelines for when liability in general will or will not attach. Even so, some of the legal parameters of liability are implicit in these court decisions.

In *Bradshaw v. Rawlings* (1979), the plaintiff students brought a negligence suit against Delaware Valley College following an automobile accident the occurred after a college-sponsored sophomore class picnic where the student driver had become intoxicated. In rejecting the plaintiff students' claim that the college had a duty to protect their safety, the court explained that "the modern American College is not an insurer of the safety of its students" (Bradshaw, 1979, p. 138), and thus did not owe them a duty of care.

The *Bradshaw* ruling must be limited to its specific facts. Colleges may not owe students a duty of care when it comes to their own reckless use of alcohol, but they surely owe students a duty of care in the area of keeping the campuses safe from the acts of criminal assailants, as the *Mullins* and *Peterson* cases have shown. Subsequent case law has in effect reduced the meaning of *Bradshaw* to be simply that colleges will not be held liable in negligence suits based solely on alcohol-related injuries.

More recent alcohol-related cases have explicitly limited their rulings to the case facts. For example, in *Campbell v. Board of Trustees of Wabash College* (1986), the court refused to hold the defendant college liable for injuries to a nonstudent who became intoxicated at a college fraternity party, stating: "Colleges and fraternities are not expected to assume a role anything akin to *in loco parentis* or a general insurer" (*Campbell*, 1986, p. 232). The court distinguished its ruling from cases such as *Peterson* and *Mullins* because they do not involve the use of alcohol (Campbell, 1986, p.232).

Although not explicit in the *Campbell* ruling, it seems obvious that another reason the court denied liability was because the plaintiff was not a student, but a third party not officially connected to the college in any way. Because there was no college-student relationship, the court had no basis upon which to find any duty of care.

Linking the student alcohol consumption facts with the college-student relationship notion, the Utah Supreme Court denied liability in another 1986 case, *Beach v. University of Utah*. The court ruled that, despite the existence of a college-student relationship, there was no basis for "imposing an affirmative duty upon the University to protect Beach from her own intoxication" (*Beach*, 1986, p.416). The *Beach* ruling accordingly supports the proposition that alcohol consumption falls outside the scope of the college-student relationship.

Thus, although the alcohol liability cases do not say much about when colleges owe their students a duty of care, they do say when such a duty does not exist—when students' injuries stem from their own alcohol abuse. A recent California case imposing liability for an alcohol-related injury, *Zavala v. Regents of University of California* (1981), is an anomaly in that the plaintiff was a nonstudent and that liability attached because the university actually served the alcohol and was thus liable under a dram-shop type theory. Accordingly, it seems that where the students can protect themselves better than the colleges, where students' own negligence caused their injuries, there will be no liability. Yet, the *Whitlock* case discussed below suggests that contributory negligence in general does not bar liability. Thus, the line may well be simply that there is no liability where the contributory negligence is in the form of alcohol abuse.

Whitlock v. University of Denver

In what is perhaps the most extreme liability case of recent vintage, *Whitlock v. University of Denver* (1985), the Colorado Court of Appeals held the defendant university liable for injuries sustained by a student during a trampoline accident at a school fraternity house. Using an ordinary negligence analysis, the court stated that "a legal duty to use reasonable care arises in response to a foreseeable risk of injury to others" (*Whitlock*, 1985, p.1074). The court listed three factors that placed a legal duty on the university: (a)the university exercised a degree of control over the fraternity, (b)it leased the house and property to the fraternity, and (c)it was aware of the presence and inherent danger of the trampoline (*Whitlock*, 1985, p.1075). The court ruled that these factors were "abundant and sufficient evidence upon which a duty could be based and upon which a jury could . . . find the defendant's negligence to be greater than that of the parties" (*Whitlock*, 1985, p.1076).

The *Whitlock* case is significant because it imposed liability where it would not heretofore be expected. The factors that imposed a duty of care upon the University of Denver were circumstances common to most colleges with on-campus fraternities. Further, the University of Denver acted much like any other college would regarding the fraternity and trampoline—with deference to student discretion and autonomy. Finally, the plaintiff student's contributory negligence did not absolve the university of liability. Whitlock had been drinking beer, vodka, and Scotch until 2:00 a.m. the day of the accident, jumped on the trampoline all that afternoon, and was finally injured when he jumped on the trampoline that evening in the dark while at a party at the fraternity house (*Whitlock*, 1985).

The Whitlock decision clearly has extraordinary implications for higher education law. In the dissenting opinion, Judge Sternberg concluded that "the result reached by the (court's) majority is to make the university an insurer against every accident involving the trampoline that might occur" (*Whitlock*, 1985, p.1078). The practical effect of the *Whitlock* opinion may extend even further. As Richard A. Fass analyzed the ruling: "The court has suggested that a college or university might be obligated to warn or protect students from all identifiable risks associated with college life!" (Fass, 1986, p. 37). If this is true, the college owes its students an absolute duty of protection, the breach of which constitutes legal culpability.

Whitlock currently is being heard by the Colorado Supreme Court, with a decision still pending. An affirmation would, of course, emphasize the scope of the college's duty to protect students. A reversal would not lessen the importance of the case, however. Even if ultimately struck down the fact is that a jury and an appellate court have imposed this extraordinary liability on the university, the sole rationale seemingly being that Whitlock was a student and thus was owed a duty of protection.

The *Whitlock* case is an extreme extension of the sexual assault cases such as *Mullins*. It clearly stands for the proposition that colleges owe their students a duty of protective care in virtually all circumstances of on-campus life except blatant intoxication. Yet, the ruling in *Whitlock* only hints at the basis for this extreme extension of liability—the essence of the college-student relationship itself.

The College-Student Relationship

In all of the recent negligence-personal injury cases brought by students against their colleges, including those that reject liability, the courts used a common thread of analysis. In each case, the court has held that a special relationship between the plaintiff student and the defendant college must be demonstrated to create a duty, the breach of which causes liability to attach. For example, the *Peterson* case discussed above, the court stated:

A duty may arise, however, where (a) a *special relation* exists between the actor and the third person which imposes a duty upon the actor to control the third person's conduct, or (b) *a special relation exists* between the actor and the other which gives the other a right to protection. (*Peterson*, 1984, p.1196, citing the Restatement 2d of Torts, Section 315).

In each case, the court has struggled with traditional legal theories to define the relationship between the student and college. It is clear, however, that none of these theories fit with the courts' final rulings.

For example, in *Bradshaw v. Rawlings*, discussed above, the court refused to hold the defendant college liable because the plaintiff student failed to establish that the college owed him a duty of custodial care arising from a special relationship (*Bradshaw*, 1979). The court analyzed the case using a guest-host relationship rather than a college-student relationship, and concluded that applicable law did not impose liability upon a private host who supplies intoxicants to a visibly intoxicated guest (*Bradshaw*, 1979). Further, and more important, such a guest-host relationship did not apply to the student-college context (*Bradshaw*, 1979). Yet, the court stopped short of explaining hat exactly constitutes this student-college relationship.

Often the college-student relationship is described as contractual. For example, *American Jurisprudence* states that "the relation of a private college or university to its students is based on contract" (15A *American Jurisprudence* 2nd, Colleges and Universities, Section18, 1976). This view suggests that students are consumers in a marketplace where they contract for their fair share of various rights and duties. This consumerism view also suggests that students stand at least on equal footing with colleges as far as bargaining power in the contracting process is concerned.

Victoria Dodd (1985) emphasized in her article, "The Non-Contractual Nature of the Student-University Contractual Relationships," that the college-student relationship is neither contractual nor consumer oriented. Dodd argued that there are no elements of contract law in such a one-sided contractual arrangement as that found here, where the student has no control over the contractual elements and where all the elements favor the school: "In effect the student agrees upon matriculation to abide by and tolerate every action of the school, except those of an arbitrary and capricious nature, while the school promises almost nothing in return" (Dodd, 1985, p.726). Furthermore, students cannot be classified as consumers in a marketplace because they usually are not free to choose the college they will attend. So, unlike the variety of choices available in traditional markets, "the competition for educational admission can create a situation in which students can shop at only one store" (Dodd, 1985, p.718).

Dodd (1985) concluded that:

Laws of contract are not in fact being applied in student-university cases. Nor should they be. Instead, theories of tort law should be applied more frequently to issues concerning the student-university relationship, as the basic conceptual premises of contract law are not truly reflective of that relationship and thus are not appropriate analytical tools in the education law area. (p.702).

Thus, she suggested that there is something unique about the student-college relationship that gives rise to legal duties enforceable under tort law analysis. The case law clearly supports Dodd's analysis because there are virtually no cases that protect students under the banner of contract, or "consumerism," despite the popularity of the latter term in the administrative literature. Rather it is tort law—negligence—upon which the courts are hanging their hats. And it is the college-student relationship that activates this tort law—a relationship that the courts are increasingly viewing as special.

Conclusion

Courts in several jurisdictions have found the student-college relationship to be a special one that, either explicitly or implicitly, gives rise to a college's duty to protect students from physical harm. In some extraordinary circumstances, such as those in the *Whitlock* case, the college has even become the ensurer of students' safety in the eyes of the court. It is this duty that is the key element, not the court's judicial label for it. Also, as the cases have shown, this duty arises only when there is a true college-student relationship. Thus, despite various courts' analyses using tort theories such as landowner liability, such theories clearly do not adequately explain the differences between cases that impose liability and those that reject it. Indeed, only when the courts have taken that extra step—pinpointing the relationship as in the *Mullins* case—has liability been imposed upon the college defendants.

To some observers, this trend in the courts has resembled a return to, or a new form of, in *loco parentis* under which colleges must protect students from physical harm but are not empowered to police and control students' morals. For example, in commentary in *West's Education Law Reporter*, Barbara Jones analyzed the *Whitlock* ruling and concluded that it "may be the beginning of a return to in *loco parentis*" (Jones, 1986, p.999).

What is clear is that litigious students are using tort theories to take advantage of the legal system for their own benefit, as are many other parties in today's litigation-crazed society. But the students are doing so precisely because contract-consumerism theories have gotten them nowhere in the courts. It is important to keep in mind that it is not the courts that give plaintiffs their arguments, but rather the plaintiffs' arguments that give the courts theories upon which to base their decisions.

Perhaps this extension of liability is the courts' solution to Dodd's one-sided college-student contractual relationship. When the students put forth legal arguments hinging upon the colleges' duty to provide them with protective care, the courts have responded, imposing liability upon the colleges. Thus, although students are relatively powerless contractually, they may be able to shape the college-student relationship courtesy of the judicial system and its willingness to apply tort law concepts.

References

American Jurisprudence 2nd, Colleges and Universities, Sec. 18, 1976.

Beach v. University of Utah, 716 P. 2d 413 (Utah, 1986).

Bradshaw v. Rawlings, 612 F. 2d135 (3d Cir. 1979), cert. denied, 446 U.S.909 (1980).

Campbell v. Board of Trustees of Wabash College, 495 N.E. 2d227 (Ind. App. 1 Dist. 1986).

Dodd, V. (1985). The non-contractual nature of the student-university contractual relationship. *University of Kansas Law Review*, 33, 701.

Fass, R. A. (1986, January/February). In loco parentis revisited? (PartII) *Change*, 18(1), p. 34.

Jones, B. (1986, Nov.27). In loco parentis reborn: Whitlockv. University of Denver. *West's Education Law Reporter*, p. 995.

Mullins v. Pine Manor College, 389 Mass. 47, 449, N.E.2d 331 (1983).

Peterson v. San Francisco Community College District, 685 P.2d 1193 (Cal. 1984).

Relyea v. State, 385 So. 2d 1378 (Fla. App., 4th Dist. 1980).

Whitlock v. University of Denver, 712 P. 2d 1072 (Colo. App. 1985).

Zavala v. Regents of University of California, 125 Cal. App. 3d 646, 178 Cal. Rptr 185 (1981).

Identity in the College Years: Issues of Gender and Ethnicity

Ursula Delworth

The author explores gender and ethnicity in relation to one theory of development, and raises concerns regarding all such theories.

Scholars and practitioners have given increased attention to issues of gender and ethnicity in recent years, and to the implications these issues present for college student development (e.g., Fleming, 1984; Gilligan, 1982; Josselson, 1987). The vast amount work in these areas, however, has proceeded on parallel but quite separate tracks. That is, one study or one program will attend to women, and another to an ethnic group, most often blacks. Rarely will the two intersect. Yet it is in this intersection, this convergence of gender and ethnicity, that the most helpful and accurate answers to develop problems lie. Only by considering both factors will we be able to adequately attend to the developmental concerns of all students, and thus promote student success in our institutions.

There are, of course, variables of impact beyond gender and ethnicity. Some concerned with student development point to differences in *timing*— the point in the life cycle at which students enroll in our colleges and universities. Our sociologist colleagues, as well as others in our field, point out the significance of factors such as socio-economic status and the nature of a specific institution. All of these matter in the development of students, but we have to start somewhere in making sense of any number of complex variables. The factors of gender and ethnicity are crucial ones, in that they profoundly influence the development of every individual. This article explores some dimensions of gender and ethnicity in relation to one theory of development, and raises concerns regarding all such theories.

Let us begin with female development. We have learned from Gilligan (1982), Belenky, Clinchy, Goldberger, and Tarule (1986), Miller (1976), and others, that women conceptualize and experience the world "in a different voice," a voice that centers on relationship and connectedness, and is less abstract than the male voice. Women's dominant fear is being stranded, of being isolated from others, versus men's fear that others will get too close, and they will then be somehow diminished. As a result, experiences such as achievement and affiliation are different for men and women. For women, to *know* is to *connect*, rather than to *master*.

Current theories and constructs of human development, including those that focus on students in the college years, do not attend adequately to these very fundamental differences in male vs. female perceptions an "ways of knowing." In particular, the pervasive focus on increasing autonomy in late adolescence ignores the female developmental need to remain connected in meaningful ways. Any theory of identity development which can be used to understand both women and men must somehow deal appropriately with this issue of *separationindividuation*—how we both loosen connections and liberate ourselves to move in new directions, yet at the same time strengthen our capacity for intimacy and relatedness to others.

Currently, no one theory really attends adequately to these deep differences between male and female perceptions. Most theories work much better for the more linear, hierarchical progression of male development than for the somewhat tangled, complex web that women weave in an attempt to make sense of the world.

But there are some clues, some models to which we should attend. Of particular importance may be the work both originally and more recently done with Marcia's (1980) model of identity development. Marcia took Erikson's (1950) theory of identity formation and developed a model that focused on two key elements—*crisis* and *commitment*. He reasoned that to form an adult identity, each individual must experience some crisis in ideas derived from the ascribed identity of childhood. The young person must consider possibilities, experiment with different choices, and eventually take commitments regarding what to believe and what to become. The person who is able to do this successfully is considered, in this model, to be . But three other possibilities remain for the college student. He or she may avoid the whole process, neither experiencing crisis nor forming commitments, thus remaining in a state of identity diffusion. Or, a student may bypass the crisis and simply carry forward previously incorporated ideas and goals, thus having a foreclosed identity. Conversely, a student may be in a moratorium position, still experiencing crisis and unable as yet to forge commitments.

As Marcia (1980) views this, the position names are meant to be descriptive, with both positive and negative aspects potentially associated with each style. He views adolescents as beginning with either a foreclosed or diffused style or position, and through the crisis of moratorium hopefully moving toward identity achievement. This achievement, in Marcia's view, is one of the key tasks of the college years (at least for traditional-age students).

Marcia (1980) and his colleagues have divided college students into these four statuses with great reliability. In terms of psychological variables, students in the two positions that involve crisis—identity achievement and moratorium—were consistently found to be healthier and more developmentally mature. At least those were the results for males. Consistent findings for women were not obtained at all until Schenkel (Schenkel & Marcia, 1972) expanded the category of commitments to include sexual values and standards, in addition to occupation and religious and political ideology originally postulated by Marcia. With this addition, women could be consistently assessed in terms of their identity status—but with different results. Among female subjects, commitment, not crisis, was the predictor of psychological well-being. Both committed groups—the identity achieved and the foreclosed—consistently scored highest on psychologically-valued dimensions such as self-esteem and law anxiety.

As is usual when such differences are found, there was great concern expressed by scholars in the 1970s that women were, perhaps, not being helped to explore their identities through crisis, and dire predictions were voiced for the future of these women. Josselson (1987) has provided some answers regarding what these differences really mean. She first studied and classified a group of college women, using the Marcia (1980) model, in1971. Ten to twelve years later, she re-interviewed a number of these women. Some of the moratorium and diffused women had moved into a committed position, as would be expected. The identity achievers were doing well in their lives, as would also be expected. Less expected, perhaps, was the finding that the foreclosed women remained in that status, and were, for the most part, leading healthy, happy, and productive lives. Josselson found, on other words, that for women, the continued adherence to ascribed beliefs and patterns of childhood did not lead to pathology or great problems in living; that the so-called normative identity crisis of the college years can be avoided without dire consequences.

What does all this mean for us? This research both assures and challenges us in our work with female and male students and in our efforts to help them succeed in higher education. It also raises more questions than we can answer definitively, and gives us some room to explore and speculate.

First, it seems clear that for white males, the crisis of moratorium, though painful, is productive and probably necessary for achievement of a secure adult identity. Avoiding this crisis by maintaining old beliefs carried through family and culture is associated with lower self-esteem and lack of mature development. Thus, using Sanford's (1962) notion of "challenge," our programs and services that aid Anglo males by introducing alternate systems of thinking and behaving are ultimately productive. In Perry's (1970) closely related system, this is the "treatment of choice" for dualistic thinkers.

An appeal to the crisis of moratorium may also be a productive route for some women. However, given women's greater centering on relationships, adherence to old and familiar patterns (what some would call "traditional" ways of thinking and behaving) is not necessarily antithetical to achievement of a mature identity and psychological well-being. For white women, the role of carrying on the culture, of focus on family and clan, can be the basis of a fulfilling and solid identity. this may be difficult for us to hear, in that it reminds us of old messages that consign women to hearth and home and speak of biology as destiny. Yet it also fits with what Gilligan (1982) and others have been telling us regarding the "ethics of care" and the centrality of relationships for women.

Josselson (1987) brings the ethics of care and the centrality of relationships together with the concept of "anchoring." She defines anchoring as "the communion aspect of the separation-individuation process after late adolescence. That is, if something is separated from, something else must be found to replace it. That which is individuated must be reworked into something new" (p.174). Women, she states, require these anchors. Women who have anchored in their primary families choose to become "purveyors of the heritage," the essence of foreclosure status. Identity achievers tend to anchor in husband and children, friends, and career. Moratorium and diffused women are, then, anchorless, and thus outside the relational web so necessary for mature female development.

So far, this discussion has focused on implications for females and males of one major ethnic group—Anglos. How does the research apply to those of differing ethnicity? We don't know, so here we have to extrapolate and raise questions. In such a risky venture, it is useful to discuss how the research on Marcia's (1980) model might relate to Fleming's (1984) study of Black students in both White and Black colleges. Fleming paints a rather grim picture of Black males in White colleges: "The distressing feature of this profile is that [these] men, initially competitive and career-oriented, undergo excessively frustrating experiences that thwart virtually every evidence of academic drive. To be sure, there are gains in educational aspirations, but these gains occur in the context of falling grades in the critical major subject, diminishing feelings of intellectual ability, declining social adjustment, and losses in perceived energy level suggestive of emotional strain" (pp.168–169).

This profile suggests that the *normative* crisis of white male development becomes a *monumental* crisis for Black, and perhaps other ethnic minority, males. Many minority, males at white institutions may thus become psychological (if not actual) dropouts and fall into the diffused category. Unable to deal with an overwhelming crisis, unsure of commitments, they withdraw from the struggle and make no movement toward the resolution that would signify an adult identity. An immediate answer to this problem, of course, is for us to devise ways to make the crisis moremanageable, so that these students can move on and through it toward identity achievement.

But identity achievement is a tricky issue where ethnicity is concerned. What part does achievement of a solid ethnic identity have in the overall picture? Research (Sedlacek, 1987) suggests hat it is of utmost importance for both achievement and satisfaction. Thus, do models developed and tested first for white males and then for white females, have any relevance? an the Marcia (1980) model be expanded further, to include ethnic values for blacks and other minorities, as it was expanded to include sexual values for females? Perhaps it can. If it were expanded, it would make sense to hypothesize that ethnic identification would be a strong determinant for placing minorities in phases, as sexual and religious values are for females. It would also be hypothesized that at least for black males, placement in the foreclosure category would be consistent with some of the positive values that accrue to white women in this category. That is, black males who come to a white institution with a strong sense of ethnic and cultural identity and who remain relatively unchallenged by new perspectives, may achieve well both academically and in terms of personal development. Such men might be protected and strengthened by ties to family. In other words, foreclosure may work for some men too!

For black, and perhaps other minority, women, the picture is even more complex than for black men, a fact reflected in the differing outcomes found in some studies for these women in black vs. white colleges. According to Fleming (1984), while black males do better overall at black colleges, black females exhibit strong improvement in academic functioning but show losses in social assertiveness in such environments. In white institutions, black females tend to cope, but are often socially isolated. Thus, neither environment provides ground for optimal development (Fleming, 1984; Hughes, 1987). It seems that identity achievement for these women would necessarily involve the development of their own views on sexual and religious matters, as it does for white women, but also a solid sense of ethnic and cultural identity, as hypothesized to be important for minority men. Foreclosure may be a positive status for many of these women, but it may also interfere with achievement strivings, if support for such strivings is not available in the closed system that defines foreclosure status. Some minority women may opt for a type of identity achievement that closely parallels that of white males, an identity achievement that focuses on occupation and ideological commitment. Issues of intimacy and relatedness, central to the women's model, may be deferred or ignored. Hughes (1987) reports findings from both black women and black men that they must defer social, personal, emotional, and cultural development until they have left the predominantly white campus environment. To the extent this is true, the impact of such deferral on the development of black women may be especially harmful.

The message in all this is that some of what we have discovered about female development and ways of knowing, especially the centrality of relationship, may be helpful in understanding ethnic minorities of both genders, and especially males. Connectedness to culture may well operate for these minority students in the same way connectedness to family and other close persons may operate for females—as a secure home base from which to challenge and explore the larger world. Josselson (1987) notes that women on the road to identity achievement often connect closely with males in romantic relationships as a secure base while they individuate from their families of origin. In much the same way, rituals and traditions inherent in the culture of origin may serve as a base for minority students. In the case of foreclosed students, the retained closeness to families of origin serves many females well. It may well do the same for minorities, both male and female.

These thoughts are just a few aspects of the multitude of theories, constructs, and practices we need to re-explore with the dual ideas of gender and ethnicity in mind. Doing so will aid us in enhancing the effectiveness of our services and in the retention of students—of both genders and a diversity of ethnic backgrounds.

References

Belenky, M. F., Clinchy, B. M., Goldberger, N. R., & Tarule, J. M. (1986). *Women's ways of knowing.* New York: Basic Books.

Erikson, E. H. 91950). *Childhood and society.* New York: Norton.

Fleming, J. (1984). *Blacks in college.* San Francisco: Jossey-Bass.

Gilligan, C. (1982). *In a different voice.* Cambridge, MA: Harvard University Press.

Josselson, R. (1987). *Finding herself.* San Francisco: Jossey-Bass.

Hughes, M. S. (1987). Black students' participation in higher education. *Journal of College Student Personnel, 28*(6), 532–545.

Marcia, J. E. (1980). *Identity in adolescence.* In J. Adelson (Ed.), Handbook of adolescent psychology (pp.159–187). New York: Wiley.

Miller, J. B. (1976). *Towards a new psychology of women.* Boston: Beacon Press.

Perry, W., Jr. (1970). *Forms of intellectual and ethnical development in the college years: A scheme.* New York: Holt, Rinehart, & Winston.

Sanford, N. (1962). *The American college.* New York: Wiley.

Schenkel, S., & Marcia, J. E. (1972). Attitudes toward premarital intercourse in determining ego identity status in college women. *Journal of Personality*, 40, 472–482.

Sedlack, W. E. (1987). Black students on white campuses: 20 years of research. *Journal of College Student Personnel*, 28(6), 484–495.

Feminization and Student Affairs

Marvalene Styles Hughes

This article examines the evolving feminization of the student affairs profession.

Introduction

Student affairs has espoused values of educating the whole person for several decades, assuming that both male and female students will develop thier cognitive and noncognitive dimensions to become broadly educated. Apart from the efforts of student affairs, however, the academic community has offered little to include balance in sex role development for men and women in their social, emotional, spiritual, and psychological spheres. Education does not identify sex role development for male and female students as one of its fundamental principles. This void exists with respect to the training and practice of student affairs professionals, as well. In reviewing student affairs practice to ensure breadth of objectives and approaches, a number of questions pertaining to sex role development might be raised: Does the profession of student affairs reflect the philosophy, values, and characteristics typically assigned to the "masculine" or the "feminine"? Have women's historical contributions to the profession influenced the values which undegrid our theory and practice? Do these values suggest a relationship of student affairs to feminist epistemology? Is the profession entering another era of feminization? Is the evolving feminization viewed positively or negatively? What are the implications for leadership development in student affairs?

Purposes

This article offers a metaphoric view of the academic community as one typically designed to promote and reward "masculine" development by focusing mainly on cognitive learning experiences and rewarding "masculine" principles, such as competition, aggression, ambition, independence, and analytical behaviors. (French's [1985] suggestion to enclose "masculine" and "feminine" in quotations, to remind us of the falseness of those separations, will be followed.) This metaphor further asserts that a significant role for student affairs is to provide a balanced learning climate for students by acknowledging and fostering those values that develop attributes traditionally considered "feminine," such as expressive/communal (Cook, 1987), supportive/nurturing (Cann & Siegfried, 1987), and affiliative traits (Gilligan, 1982).

The principles set forth in this article are: (a) that the functions and values of student affairs are congruent with perceived principles typically associated with the "feminine" ethic, (b) that these principles are essential to the development of male and female students who seek *whole-person* education, and (c) that student affairs leaders must be trained to honor and promulgate sex role balance in all students' development.

An Historical Reflection

The current status of student affairs is best understood when placed in an historical context of higher education in the United States. In earlier years, the assumption was that colleges not only prepared students for "civic, professional, and business careers, but also somehow made them 'better,' more moral, more humane people" (Fenske, 1980, p. 4). Administrators and faculty were intimately involved in students' developmental process, with "the development of character and values" seen as "a central part of the faculty member's role" (Fenske, 1980, p. 13).

When special interest, cocurricular, and social groups, such as Greek letter societies, intercollegiate athletics, drama, student publications, forensics, and literary societies evolved, the academy's response was to hire student services personnel. As the role of the college faculty gravitated increasingly to research and information dissemination, faculties' responsibilities decreased in the area of character development (Fenske, 1989). A gradual return, however, of the developmental function ascribed to faculty in earlier years is witnessed in various current practices, such as the resurgence of mentoring programs and networking.

When character development was viewed as essential to higher education, it remained largely the responsibility of administrators and professors (Fenske, 1989). As intellectual development, research, and instruction replaced character development as a primary role of the administrator and professor,

character development became increasingly the purview of student personnel. With current trends in higher education stressing assessment, retention,
and student development, student affairs is gaining renewed prominence in
the academy.

Women's Influence on the Student Affairs Profession

Women's presence has been prominent, since the earliest conceptualizations of student affairs, in designing training programs and in forming
professional organizations. Gilroy (1987) conducted an historical study of
selected women pioneers who were among the first graduates of the preparation program in student personnel at Teachers College, Columbia University.
Gilroy's data reveal that Teachers College became the center of activity fro
training, and between 1913 and 1932, 375 women were offered the diploma
Adviser of Women or Adviser of Girls. In 1928, the first doctorate for deans
of women was offered, and in 1932 training for men began, at which time
women advocated changing the name of the specialization to Student
Personnel Administration. Indeed, Gilroy documented that women were the
profession's pioneers, convincing college administrators to offer a major
course, between 1916 and 1917, entitled *Problems for Advisers of Women
and Girls.*

It is significant that women began to envision a national organization for
women deans as early as 1903 (Gilroy, 1987). Deans of Women met in small
groups regionally and locally until a group received approval to meet officially
with the National Education Association (NEA) on July 6, 1916. The
National Association of Deans of Women (NADW), currently the National
Association of Women Deans, Administrators and Counselors (NAWDAC),
became a department of NEA in 1918 and was preceded only by two
other student personnel related organizations, the American Association
of Collegiate Registrars (1910) and the National Vocational Guidance
Association (1913).

Gilroy's (1987) study reminds us of women's unsung contribution to our
professional foundations. Women were the first to suggest a gender-free name
for the profession by changing it to Student Personnel Administration. In
1949, Esther Lloyd-Jones (one of Gilroy's research clients), suggested the
gender-free title of Dean of Students for men and women. It was also Lloyd-
Jones who argued early on the centrality of student affairs to the mission of
education as opposed to a peripheral service-provider status.

Strengths in the "Feminine" Ethic for Student Affairs

A major strength of student affairs lies in those traits, characteristics, and values that are closely aligned with the "feminine" ethic. It is vital for the profession to claim these values, identify their strengths, and underscore the vitality of those values we promulgate through student development.

Society's values are shifting, and with those shifts there is greater understanding and acceptance of behaviors perceived as "Feminine." Furthermore, the challenges confronting corporations and institutions to sensitize their employee cultures to a diverse work force require relational and affiliative skills. As the paradigm shift in leadership development is introduced in society and in corporate institutions, student affairs functions could gain centrality in the educational mission.

Student Affairs Values as "Feminine" Values

Hogg (1988) presents a personal perspective delineating three values in student affairs: tolerance, compassion, and human empowerment. Hogg views tolerance as an attribute that prevents dualistic thinking and dogmatic beliefs. One concludes from this scheme that one mission of student affairs practitioners is to strive to promote tolerance and to challenge students who are dualistic thinkers.

The second value, compassion, Hogg (1988) explains as one's sense of responsibility to the greater human community and to the security of the planet. Compassion in Hogg's model promotes generativity or commitment to the development of others. Hogg's paradigm of human empowerment teaches responsible exericse of power, be it personal, social, or political, and implies that values within the student affairs profession may be used as a basis to understand our mission in education.

Upon examination, the values of tolerance, compassion, and human empowerment bear more than a casual similarity to principles perceived as "feminine." Other student affairs values closely aligned to the "feminine" include: supporting, nurturing, providing service, promoting advocacy, ensuring justice and equity, and encouraging affiliative behaviors.

Jung (1968) informs us that women and men are endowed with the capacity to develop their "masculine" and "feminine" archetypes. Jung's portrayal of the "anima" and "animus" suggests that these latent archetypes may be unevenly developed in some men and women as a result of their socialization. Nonetheless, Jung suggests that all humans have access to these inherent "masculine" and "feminine" qualities.

Similarly, the right brain/left brain theories offer a paradigm from which to conclude the existence of "masculine" and "feminine" qualities in all individuals (Ornstein & Thompson, 1984). Both theories can be used in an applied sense, to assist student affairs to understand, emb race, and promulgate a major strength it brings to the academy—the ability to develop students' noncognitive areas, traditionally associated with the "feminine" principle.

Student Affairs and the Feminization Ethic

Student affairs practitioners challenge and support students (Sanford summarized by Widick, Knefelkamp & Parker, 1980); they guide students in their development of identity, intimacy, and generativity (Erickson, summarized by Widick, Knefelkamp & Parker, 1980). These developmental challenges enlist from student affairs practitioners sensitivity to and skills in those areas traditionally seen as "feminine" in nature, that is, traits that are supportive (Cann & Siegfried 1987), relationship-oriented, affiliative, and social in nature (Gilligan, 1982, O'Neil, 1981). Cook (1987) describes "feminine" characteristics as those that are "expressive/communal, focusing upon emotionality, selflessness, sensitivity and interpersonal relationships" (p. 472). In general, these functions and values are believed to lie "within the private sphere of home and family rather than within the public sphere" (Kaplan & Sedney, 1980, p. 40). The paradox for student affairs may be that its practitioners and educators demand a place for the "feminine" ethic in the public educational sphere.

"Feminist" values are associated primarily with women and their nurturing role in the home rather than with men and the external world to work (Kaplan & Sedney, 1980; Olds, 1981). Women, and the affective values ascribed to them, have historically been undervalued or negatively valued in our society (Dusek 1987; Kaplan & Sedney, 1980; Olds, 1981; Richardson, 1981; Skovholt, 1978). Strachan & Strachan (1985) have reiterated the inferior nature attributed to "feminine" qualities by societies. The "feminine" was believed, accordingly, to have little to do with serious world matters.

Sex Role Development and Transformative Leadership Models

Cann & Siegfried (1987) note that, in our Western society, "maleness equates with effective leadership" while "femaleness" does not (p. 401). Directive, structuring roles are seen as "more consistent with the male sterotype," while supportive styles are "associated with females" (p. 402). For males, perceived qualities listed include dominance, analytical ability, forcefulness, aggressiveness competitiveness, sternness, toughness, ambition, assertiveness, independence, autocratic behavior, and confidence. For females, compassion, excitability, sentimentality, sensitivity, gentleness, understanding, mildness, emotionality, affection, appreciation, dependence, and submission are perceived as dominant traits (p. 405).

Despite the rise of feminism, research documents that "masculine" rather than "feminine" qualities are the ones valued in our leaders (Cann & Siegfried, 1987). We are approaching transformation, however, in leadership development. Maccol (1981) has identified attributes of transformative leaders; leaders are caring, respectful, responsible, and flexible people. The new age leader is not limited by organizational structure, is willing to share power, is introspective and conscious of weaknesses and strengths, is concerned with developing the self and others, is not afraid of "feminine" nurturing attributes, is conscious of the needs of people to live balanced lives, and is unafraid of emotions and disciplined subjectivity. Maccoby's attribtes are analogous to the values of student affairs and feminist philosophy; thus, the new age leaders' values are becoming more congruent with the values of students affairs and feminist philosophy.

"Feminine" Behaviors in the Workplace and Academy

In a study of traits viewed as important in managers, Cann & Siegfried (1987) found that perceived "masculine" traits were most valued by a manager's superiors, while subordinates most valued perceived "feminine" traits in their managers. Cann & Siegfried conclude that the manager's role would seem to require an androgynous style. "Masculine" directive behaviors will likely appeal to superiors, and may influence superiors' impressions of managers' effectiveness. Alternately, the manager's subordinates are likely to appreciate sterotypically "feminine" behaviors, to create a supportive work climate (p. 406). In other words, while society subscribes to the idea that "masculine" traits and values are more appropriate to the workplace, Cann & Siegfried found that people prefer to work for and with those who demonstrate "feminine" traits and values.

The valuing of "masculine" qualities is prevalent in the academy as well. Student affairs practitioners are expected to "prove" their competence and worth on the basis of "masculine" leadership qualities. However, the very nature of the student affairs profession demands that student affairs personnel provide for the "feminine" or nurturing, affiliative, and supportive needs of students.

This paradox places the student affairs profession in a unique bind. As Pfeffer & Davis-Blake (1987) note, "Feminization of any profession in a society that values masculine principles has resulted in the past in labeling the work done as 'women's and can be paid less than work doen by men. Where womenare in the majority, the work is seen as . . . less valuable, critical, or economically important" than work done by men (p. 7).

Economic Impact of Feminization on Professions

Historically, professions dominated by women have been accorded less status than those dominated by men (Acker, 1980; Berger & Wright, 1978; Bose & Rossi, 1983; Buttner & Rosen, 1987; Stevens & Hoisington, 1987). It has been found that, "the proportion of women in an occupation is negatively related to the prestige of the occupation" (Pfeffer & Davis-Blake, 1987, p. 7). Tuchey (1974) has recognized that male and female college students rate feminized professions as having less prestige and as being less desirable as personal career choices than professions dominated by males. Similar views have been found among male high school students (Heilman, 1979).

The clearest evidence of the status accorded "women's work" is the fact that comparable jobs for women pay less, even after two decades of affirmative action designed to correct inequities. In 1986, for example, women averaged 69 cents for every dollar earn ed by men in the same professional role, up from 60 cents per dollar in 1963 (Buttner & Rosen, 1987; Green & Epstein, 1986).

The labor market is segmented by gender, with males preferred for employment over women (Blau, 1977, Pfeffer & Davis-Blake, 1987; Strober & Tyack, 1980). When men are unavailable for work, women are seen as acceptable substitutes. The fields of teaching and medicine, for example, were once exclusively male. Then the doors were opened to women primarily in service capacities; that is, women handled more rudimentary, less skilled tasks, becoming nurses and elementary and secondary school teachers. Essentially, this circumscription of opportunity was an extension of the jobs women traditionally did in the home, "such as teaching small children, nursing, and house cleaning" (Borker, 1987, p. 185).

As more and more women entered the fields of nursing and education, a clear dichotomy appeared, separating men's and women's roles. The presence of women freed men to perform the "important" work of doctors, university professors in technological and scientific areas, and academic administrators. Similarly, when male professor sand administrators abandoned student development functions or the "feminine" side of the academy, student affairs personnel moved in to pick up the slack.

"Masculine" Traits in the Workplace and Academy

The academy is organized under the rubric described by Kantor (1977) in the corporate world, that is, the "masculine" ethic. Kantor notes that men dominate management and positions of power, while women are caretakers, as secretaries or wives, of the corporate structure. The world of higher education is, by and large, a "masculine" world. Moore (1982) describes higher education as 80% male and 91.8% white. One can hypothesize that the predominant values in the academy are "organizations, and institutions, the "masculine" principle has been overused while the "feminine" principle has atrophied.

Skovholt (1978) describes "toughness, rationality, objectivity, dominance, aggression, self-reliance and anger" as traditionally male traits valued in Western society (p. 7). O'Neil (1981) describes a "masculine mystique and value system" (p. 67) that includes the concepts of male superiority, power and dominance, logic, and competition. Central to the "masculine" mystique, O'Neil says, is the belief that

vulnerabilities, feelings and emotions in men are signs of femininity and to be avoided. . . . Men seeking help and support from others show signs of weakness, vulnerability, and potential incompetence. . . . Interpersonal communications that emphasize human emotions, feelings, intuitions, and physical contact are considered feminine and to be avoided. . . . Self-definition, self-respect, and personal worth are primarily established through achievement, success, and competence on the job. . . . Male power, control, and competition are the primary means to becoming successful and insuring personal respect, economic security, and happiness. (p. 67)

The cost of "masculine" behavior to the exclusion of "feminine" behavior is high, physically and psychologically. Males experience "higher mortality, more suicides, greater incidence of fatal diseases (cardiovascular, cirrhosis of the liver, pneumonia, tuberculosis, etc.), more migrants, ulcers, hypertension, alocholism, less tolerance for stress, and more pervasive interpersonal isolation than women" (Crites & Fitzgerald, 1978, p. 11). As women gain prominence in the "masculine" world, there is reason to believe similar qualities will be attributed to them. Masculine socialization encourages manifestation of control, power, and competition, resulting in sex-role strain and conflict, particularly in a society such as ours, which is moving toward a new definition of sex-appropriate behaviors (O'Neil, 1981).

Still in its embryonic stage, student affairs is viewed as a service-providing profession rather than a central educational dimension in the academy. Seldom are service-providing roles viewed as agentive, of high status, and of primary importance. Thus, it is critical to develop strong leaders in student affairs who can strengthen the profession's image as student development educators. In the unequal and subsequently uneasy "marriage" between student affairs and academic affairs, student affairs has emerged as a dynamic partner.

Gender Statistics in Student Affairs

Not only are the roles and values of student affairs aligned with the "feminine" ethic, but the profession is increasingly attracting women (Fenske & Hughes, 1989). Of the member of the American College Personnel Association, 58% are female (American Association of Counseling and Development, 1988). More than six years ago, Moden, and Wilson (1982) found student affairs professionals in Region IV-East of NASPA to be 51% female. Today, the NASPA (1989) statistics reveal that 55% of its members are male and 45% female.

These are only numerical data of organizational affiliation by sex. The most salient issue of feminization is discerned not from gender count, but from values of professionals in student affairs. It would be instructive to examine other national student affairs organizations to determine statistics and values, and to study the implications these statistics and values have for leadership training and the future of student affairs. With the growing trends, the profession faces the possibility of reversing sterotypes that accompany feminization and demonstrating the positive contributions feminization has offered to enhance the quality of life in the academy.

Changing Sex Roles

Skovholt (1978) stated more than a decade ago, "There seems to be little doubt that roles we think of as traditional for men and women are undergoing an evolution that verges on revolution" (p. 3). Gender roles are being reappraised in light of the successes of the women's movement and in terms of the negative consequences of traditional male socialization (Berger &

Wright, 1978; Cann & Siegfried, 1987; Carter, 1987, Cook, 1987; Crites & Fitzgerald, 1978; Kaplan & Sedney, 1980; O'Neil, 1981; Richardson, 1981; Skovholt, 1978).

The women's movement, writes Olds (1981), "has done much to widen the range of acceptable behavior for women . . . by allowing women more access to the world of masculine-dominated behavior and institutions" (p. 9). With the push for affirmative action in the 1970s, "a generation of women saw themselves as empowered individuals who could exercise options to be partners, wives, mothers and professional women" (Hughes, 1988, p. 63).

Men's and women's roles are changing. Gender role alignment in "American society is currently experiencing a sex-role reevaluation," with new definitions emerging for male and female sex roles (O'Neil, 1981, p. 61).

Integration of "Masculine" and "Feminine" Principles

In the past, masculinity and femininity have been seen as polar opposites, with masculinity valued over feminiity (Bem, 1975; Dusek, 1987; Kaplan & Sedney, 1980; Olds, 1981; Richardson, 1981; Skovholt, 1978; Strachan & Strachan, 1985). Men and women whose behavior did not follow the socially ascribed "masculine" and "feminine" roles were seen as deviant (Bem, 1975; Carter, 1987; Kaplan & Sedney, 1980; Richardson, 1981). With the development of the psychological constructs of sex role balance, this was no longer the case (Richardson, 1981). Balanced sex role development suggests that the healthy, competent adult in contemporary society—regardless of sex—is that individual capable of expressing a broad range of traits and characteristics in situationally-appropriate circumstances (Bem, 1975; Carter, 1987; Dusek, 1987; Olds, 1981; Richardson, 1981).

In our society it is easier for a woman to adopt "male" behavior and escalate her status than it is for a man to adopt "female" patterns. When a woman moves in the direction of "masculinity" she is, in a sense, "moving up" and is rewarded to the point where here competence and capabilities might threaten her male competitors. When a man moves toward "femininity," he is, unfortunately, seen as surrendering something of greater value, as "stepping down." Research has warned of the physical, psychological, and social problems resulting from traditional male socialization; when males join in the chorus, society must learn to reinforce their willingness to step aside from the pinnacle of power and refrain from demanding that they "act like men."

Acceptance of feminist epistemology as a philosophical foundation would, in effect, free men and women in student affairs to express the full range of human values and emotions. They could thereby accept their "masculine" and "feminine" behaviors. Women and men would be equally free to be assertive or dependent, supportive or confrontational, stern or gentle, and sentimental or forceful. Males and females would be empowered, and become, as Olds (1981) suggests, fully human. As a model of well-being, feminist epistemology offers a broad behavioral repertoire, "flexibility in response to situational demands," and "effectiveness," defined as "greater success in encounters with the world" (Kaplan & Sedney, 1980, p. 9)

Implications and Recommendations

With beliefs transforming rapidly in our culture, those values heretofore perceived as "feminine" and devalued are gaining acceptance in the academy and in the workplace in general. The profession of student affairs must claim its alignment with transformative leadership values, such as feminist values, which offer nonhierarchical principles. In promulgating values of mutual care, respect, and support, the profession can promote an integrative, balance sex role perspective within the academy. When we view "masculine" and "feminine" behaviors and values as integraative and equally viable and necessary for men and women, student affairs will offer a deeper dimension to its *whole person* philosophy. When "masculine" and "feminine" principles are equally valued within our society, the human race will advance. Student affairs can play a vital role in this transformation.

Leadership education in student affairs will be strengthened as our trainers and practitioners understand our history and claim the richness of women's ealier involvement in shaping the profession. Women were and are central shapers in student affairs and, thus, in the humanization of higher education. Men and women in the profession are encouraged to gain confidence and competence in the power of the "feminine" ethic that undergirds student affairs, and to integrate these concepts into program planning for today's college students. Male and female professionals who subscribe to a rounded sex role perspective have the opportunity to model those behaviors to college students.

Student affairs professionals are partners in higher education who offer a unique and necessary balance to the goals of education. We can assure that the "feminine" ethic is introduced in the academy through cocurricular experiences an thereby prepare male and female students for the increasing feminization of our global society. Lenz & Myerhoff (1985) inform us that we live amidst two cultures in transition. The "feminine-inspired process of social and psychological change has been so subtle, even subliminal, that its absorption into our thoughts, actions, and interactions has been as inconspicuous as the absorption of nutrients from the soil by plants in the forest" (p. 12). Similarly, America is becoming subtly feminized as women move increasingly into the public arena and the corporate world (Lenz & Myerhoff, 1985).

As "feminine" values are interwoven into the mainstream cultural and societal fabrics, students in higher education will need the skills and tools student affairs can provide. When this process occurs, the academy will integrate the "feminine" teachings of the profession with a rounded perspective toward the education of our present and future generations. The time is here for sex role fluidity in men and women to be endorsed.

Men and women in student affairs can help the academic community to become more compassionate, nurturing, and tolerant; such attributes are vital to the growing diversity and heterogeneity of the student population. Student affairs can no longer remain merely the opposite polarity on a gender-related dialectic; it should prescribe inegration to educational institutions.

With the growing trend of feminization, more males in student affairs are needed as role models for students and faculty. Student affairs training programs are encouraged to escalate recruitment of males and members of diverse population groups. The student population is moving toward increasing diversity, domestically and internationally. Clearly, the educational model in the academy is inadequate to respond to diversity and to the transformative leadership which must accompany it.

References

Acker, J. R. (1980). Women and stratification: A review of recent literature. *Contemporary Sociology, 9* (January), 25–39.

American Association of Counseling and Development. (1988). *Monthly report* (March). Alexandria, VA: Author.

Bem, S. L. (1975). Sex role adaptability: One consequence of psychological androgyny. *Journey of Personality and Social Psychology, 31*(4), 643–643.

Berger, M., & Wright, L. (1978). Divided allegiance: Man, work and family life. *Counseling Psychologist, 7*(4), 50–52.

Blau, F. D. (1977). *Equal pay in the office.* Lexington, MA: D.C. Heath.

Borker, S. R. (1987). Sex roles and labor force participation. In D. B. Carter (Ed.), *Current conceptions of sex roles and sex typing: Theory and research* (pp. 181–191). New York: Praeger.

Bose, C. E., & Rossi, P. H. (1983). Gender and jobs: Prestige standings of occupations as affected by gender. *American Sociological Review, 43,* 316–330.

Buttner, F. H., & Rosen, B. (1987). The effects of labor shortages on starting salaries for sex-typed jobs. Sex Roles, 17(1/2), 59–71.

Cann, A., & Siegfried, W. D., Jr. (1987). Sex stereotypes and the leadership role. Sex Roles. 17(7/8), 401–408.

Carter, D. B. (Ed.) (1987). Current conceptions of sex roles and sex typing: Theory and research. New York: Praeger.

Cook, E. P. (1987). Psychological androgyny: A review of the research. Counseling Psychologist, 15(3), 471-513.

Crites, J. O., & Fitzgerald, L. F. (1978). The competent male. Counseliing Psychologist, 7(4), 10-14.

Dusek, J. B. (1987), Sex roles and adjustment. In D. B. Carter (Ed.), Current conceptions of sex roles and sex typing: Theory and research (pp. 211–222). New York: Praeger.

Fenske, R. H. (1980). Historical foundations. In U. Delworth, G. R. Hanson, & Associates (Eds.), Student services: A handbook for the profession (pp. 3-24). San Francisco: Jossey-Bass.

Fenske, R. H. (1989). Evolution of the student services profession. In U. Delworth & G. R. Hanson (Eds.), Student services: A handbook for the profession (2nd ed., pp. 25–56). San Francisco: Jossey-Bass.

Fenske, R. H., & Hughes, M. S. (1989). Current challenges: Maintaining quality amid increasing student diversity. In U. Delworth & G. R. Hanson (Eds.), Student services: A handbook for the profession (2nd ed., pp. 555–583). San Francisco: Jossey-Bass.

French, M. (1985). Beyond power: On women, men, and morals. New York: Ballantine Books.

Gilligan, C. (1982). In a different voice: Psychological theory and women's development. Boston: Harvard University Press.

Gilroy, M. (1987). The contributions of selected Teachers College women to the field of student personnel. Unpublished doctoral dissertation, Teachers College, Columbia University, New York.

Green, G., & Epstein, R. (Eds.). (1986). Employment and earnings. Washington, DC: Bureau of Labor Statistics, U.S. Department of Labor.

Harter, C., Moden, G., & Wilson, P. (1982). Women and minority professional staff in student personnel: A census and analysis. NASPA Journal, 20(2), 42–50.

Heilman, M. E. (1979). High school students' occupational interest as a function of projected sex ratios in male-dominated occupations. Journal of Applied Psychology, 64, 275–279.

Hogg, A. (1988). An architecture of values in student development: A personal perspective. Journal of the Arizona College Personnel Association, Spring, 53–56.

Hughes, M. S. (1988). Developing leadership potential for minority women. In M. Sagaria (Ed.), Empowering women: Leadership development strategies on campus (New Directions for Student Services, No. 44, pp. 63–75). San Francisco: Jossey-Bass.

Jung, C. G. (1968). Aion: Researches into the phenomenology of th self. In R.F.C. Hull (Trans.), Collected works of C. G. Jung (Vol. 9, Part 2, 2nd ed.). Princeton, NJ: Princeton University Press (Bollingen Series XX).

Kantor, R. (1977). *Men and women of the corporation.* New York: Basic Books.

Kaplan, A. G., & Sedney, M. (1980). *Psychology and sex roles: An androgynous perspective.* Boston: Little, Brown.

Lenz, E., & Meyerho9ff, B. (1985). *The feminization of America: How women's values are changing our public and private lives.* Los Angeles: Jeremy P. Tarcher.

Maccoby, M. (1981). *The leader: A new face for American management.* New York: Simon and Schuster.

Moore, K. (1982). *Leaders in transition: A national study of higher education administrators.* University Park: Pennsylvania State University. (ERIC Document Reproduction Service No. 225 459)

National Association of Student Personnel Administrators (NASPA). (1989). *Membership report* (May). Washington, DC: Author.

Olds, L. E. (1981). *Fully human: How everyone can integrate the benefits of masculine and feminine sex roles.* Englewood Cliffs, NJ Prentice-Hall.

O'Neil, J. M. (1981). Male sex role conflicts sexism, and masculinity: Psychological implications for men, women, and the counseling psychologist. *Counseling Psychologist* 9(2), 61–80.

Ornstein, R., & Thompson, R. F. (1984). *The amazing brain.* Boston: Houghton Mifflin

Pfeffer, J., & Davis-Blake, A. (1987). The effect of the proportion of women on salaries: The case of college administrators, *Administrative Science Quarterly, 32*, 1–24.

Richardson, L. W. (1981). *The dynamics of sex and gender: A sociological perspective* (2nd ed.). Boston: Houghton Mifflin.

Skovholt, T. M. (1978). Feminism and me n's lives, *Counseling Psychologist, 7*(4), 3–14.

Stevens, G., & Hoisington E. (1987). Occupational prestige and the 1980 U.S. labor force *Social Science Research, 16*, 74–105.

Strachan, E., & Strachan, G. (1985). *Freeing the feminine.* Dunbar, Scotland: Labarum Publications Ltd.

Strober, M. H., & Tyack, D. (1980). Why do women teach and men manage? A report on research on schools. *Signs, 5*(3), 494–503.

Touhey, J. C. (1974). Effects of additional women professionals on rating of occupations prestige and desirability. *Journal of Personality and Social Psychology, 29*, 86–89.

Widick, C., Knefelkamp, L., & Parker, C. A. (1980). Student development. In U. Delworth, G. R. Hanson, & Associate (Eds.), *Student services: A handbook for the profession* (pp. 75–116). San Frnacisco: Jossey-Bass.

Our Philosophical Heritage: Significant Influences on Professional Practice and Preparation

Gary H. Knock, Audrey L. Rentz, and J. Roger Penn

The authors examine the influence on student affairs of four philosophical perspectives: rationalism, neohumanism, pragmatism, and existentialism.

Introduction

Professional practice and preparation in college student affairs have been shaped by the *Student Personnel Point of View* (American Council on Education, 1937, 1949). But while the *Student Personnel Point of View* has provided the foundation for professional activity during the past 51 years, direct examination of the influence of certain philosophical positions allows appreciation of the richness of the profession's philosophical heritage.

The goals, functions, and activities of an institution's student affairs division are created and sustained by two conditions: administrative requirements and educational philosophy. There is no doubt that administrative requirements are immediate and influential. Philosophy, however, is not absent from the decision-making that shapes and gives direction to the student affairs mission. Professional practice and preparation have been influenced directly by convictions about the nature of human beings and the purposes of higher education. Four philosophical perspectives—rationalism, neohumanism, pragmatism, and existentialism—have had particular impact.

Rationalism

Rationalism is one of the oldest philosophies of Western civilization. It deals more with the nature of humans and the nature of knowledge than with the nature of reality itself. A fundamental assertion of rationalism is that the essence of human nature is its rational character. A human being's intellect and reasoning power create a separation between the human organism and other living creatures. Rationalism holds that the aim of education is intellectual development (Taylor, 1952). At the college level, this aim is achieved through a liberal arts curriculum based on classical writings (Adler, 1951; Hutchins, 1936).

Rationalism had considerable influence on purposes and practices in higher education during the final decade of the 19th century. The goal of developing the intellect of students and the assumption that truth can and must be verified empirically were then becoming more widely accepted in America. In those institutions that embraced rationalism, the individuality and personal development of students were not matters of concern, nor was the welfare of students outside the classroom and laboratory.

Rationalism: Professional Practice and Preparation

Rationalism has provided limited but definable philosophical support for student affairs by shaping practices primarily concerned with creating and controlling a campus environment in order that students will develop intellectually. The policies and practices of a student affairs division are intended to support and enhance such an environment. For example, rationalism supports an authoritarian approach to student discipline: student conduct regulations are viewed as universal and based on absolute concepts of right and wrong. The legal concept of in loco parentis fits naturally and logically with rationalism. Residence hall programming is geared only to academic matters supportive of intellectual development. Student activities may be available but are not regarded as contributing to the students' education. Counseling and career development services are viewed as nonessential, since they do not contribute directly to intellectual development.

There were no programs to prepare individuals for student affairs positions during the late 19th century when rationalism was widely accepted. Graduate education, however, which was influenced significantly by rationalism, would become the accepted model of professional preparation. The model of graduate education transported to the United States from Germany in the 19th century, was based on an understanding and appreciation of rational approaches to knowledge and a commitment to research (Farmer, 1950). It was adapted to the needs of professional education in the 20th century. The adaptation has not always been smooth, since the purposes of professional education do not always coincide with the traditions of graduate education (Passmore, 1980).

Neohumanism

During the 20th century, the emergence of the psychology of individual differences influenced conceptions of the processes of teaching and learning, and the science of psychometrics gave rise to a view that the individual is and functions as a total entity with various parts contributing to development (Thorndike & Hagen, 1969). A philosophy of neohumanism was expressed at this time and represented a new perspective on the human being as a learner, recognizing the primacy of cultivating the intellect but assuming a dualism of mind and body, thought and action, and reason and emotion (Crookston, 1976). Neohumanism views higher education as embracing more than intellectual development, including intentional efforts to develop many dimensions of human personality.

Neohumanism: Professional Practice and Preparation

Neohumanism philosophically supports the notion that providing services to and for students is a responsibility of a collegiate institution. Concern for more than just the intellectual development of college students, and attempts to meet a variety of human needs within the campus environment, led to the broadening of the in loco parentis concept in the mid-20th century. In loco parentis was reconceptualized by some practitioners to mean that the desired relationship between students and their institution is an educational one (Callis, 1967). While neohumanism embraces a view of student growth and development that emphasizes more than a cognitive learning, it supports a concept of student affairs work as extracurricular in nature (Crookston, 1976). Cultivation of the intellect is primary and the mission of the curriculum. Development of other forms of the human personality is second-ary and thus the focus of the extracurriculum. Student affairs is considered part of the extracurriculum, and policies and practices are to be supportive of the academic mission. Counseling, for example, should focus exclusively on academic goal-setting, improvement of study skills, and decision-making about academic majors and career plans. Organized student activities should be regarded as valuable but tangential to the central mission of intellectual development. Residence life programs should be planned to complement the content of academic courses. Student involvement in organizations and service projects should be encouraged but managed by student affairs so that students have sufficient time for study and academic pursuits.

If programs of professional preparation for student affairs had developed in concert with professional practice in the early 20th century, it would be possible to comment on the specific influence of neohumanism on preparation curricula. This was not the case. Rationalism and neohumanism did, however, influence the thinking and motivation of persons who accepted student affairs positions in the early and mid-20th century. Cowley (1957) describes the three kinds of people then engaged in student affairs work— humanitarians, administrators, and scientists. The humanitarians arrived first and tended to be sentimentalists in that "they often advocate[d] building Utopias without knowing much about architecture and construction engineering" (p. 21). The second wave of student affairs professionals were appointed "primarily because of their administrative ability rather than because of any compelling interest in students" (p. 21). The psychologists, the scientists in Cowley's depiction, arrived on the scene just after World War I and brought a rigor and commitment to counseling and research that contributed to increased status for student affairs as a profession. In reality, these three groups had relatively little in common. Cowley has observed that the student personnel movement of the post-World War I period was not a movement at all, but "a collection of independent wheels turning at different rates and often in different directions" (p. 20).

Pragmatism

Pragmatism gained popularity as a philosophy of education in the United States through the writings of William James (1907) and John Dewey (1916). To the pragmatist, knowing involves an interrelationship between the object to be known and the knower. There is no separation of fact from value, body from mind, or the world to be known from the knower. Theories of knowledge and of values emphasize the continuity of knower and unknown and the relationship of object and observer. Pragmatism begins with the specific and particular experience rather than with universal truths. It assumes that all things are known within the context of their utility. While the rationalist seeks to answer the question, "Is it true?", the pragmatist asks, "Does it work?" Truth is viewed as dynamic rather than static, and subject to constant change in a world subject to change. Values assume importance in all areas of knowledge and living. Pragmatists perceive values as particular and unique to the individual observer and the result of human choices based on the interrelationship of person and environment. Education is geared toward harmony of the rational and emotional states of human beings. Students are encouraged to learn by doing and to apply knowledge to seek solutions to problems.

Pragmatism: Professional Practice and Preparation

Pragmatism emphasizes the full and creative development of the whole student. Programs and services that intentionally provide opportunities for students to experience the utilitarian value of various forms of knowledge are evidence of institutional policies based on pragmatism. Student affairs efforts such as career development, counseling, student activities, living-learning environments, student government, and leadership training demonstrate a philosophy of pragmatism. Pragmatism is also reflected in student organizations intended to provide opportunities for applying knowledge to real situations such as defining and pursuing common goals, preparing for and meeting financial obligations, participating in democratic decision-making, and contributing to conflict resolution. Educational pragmatists do not seek to merge the efforts of the curriculum and extracurriculum, and the historical division between academic and student affairs is regarded as appropriate despite the espoused goal of educating the whole student (Crookston, 1976).

Graduate-level courses and programs of preparation for student affairs were fairly well-defined by the mid-20th century. (The first graduate course was offered in 1916 at Columbia University.) The preparation programs of this period were modeled on graduate education in psychology. Rationalism was giving way to pragmatism in American higher education, and psychology, which was well on its way to being a science by 1900, did not escape the effects of this philosophical shift (Thorndike & Hagen, 1969). The assertion by Williamson (1939) that counseling is the basic type of personnel work gained acceptance, and educating the counselor who would work in various settings became the central mission of the preparation programs of the time. These programs emphasized the understanding of psychometrics, trait-and-factor counseling, and vocational choice theory. Concepts of human behavior and performance were related to personal adjustment and decision-making.

Pragmatism helped expand educational goals beyond intellectual development by providing underpinning theories about how to help people make decisions about study, work, self-development, and personal adjustment. It should be noted, however, that the graduate student of this period who studied psychology with the goal of a career in student affairs, expected to deal with college students within the extracurriculum and outside the classroom (Williamson, 1961).

Existentialism

A philosophy of existentialism emanates from the writings of such 19th century European thinkers as Kierkegaard (Arbaugh & Arbaugh, 1967) and Nietzsche (Mencken, 1913). Existentialism places existence prior to essence. *Essence* refers to the substance of things that is permanent and unchangeable. In contrast, *existence* is neither created by human beings, nor can it be analyzed by rational thinking. The existentialist asserts that a person exists first and subsequently thinks, speculates, and contemplates this existence. Existentialism rejects a dichotomy between subject and object. A human being is not a subject who perceives an object, but rather a part of every object encountered.

The individual's existence is the central force in the analysis of things because each individual creates a personal world and gives meaning to phenomena in that world. Sartre (1957) asserts that "Man is nothing else but what he makes of himself" (p. 15). Existentialism views the human being as moving toward personal essence, as bridging the gap between the finite and the infinite. People are and must be responsible for what they are and for what they become. If essence (what a person consists of) precedes existence (the fact that a person is), then human beings would be determined. Since, however, people do not have a previously given essence, each person is both free and responsible.

Within the context of higher education, existentialism places responsibility for learning and development on the student. The existentialist believes each student creates his or her own curriculum within the context of a course, an academic program, or a social learning situation. What one has learned in the past does not determine what one will or should learn in the future. The student is the ultimate chooser; the subject matter focuses on finding self; and the teacher is the facilitator.

Existentialism: Professional Practice and Preparation

Crookston (1976) has observed that the emergence of the concept of student development in the late 1960s came out of the recognition that out-of-class education of college students would never be fully effective until it became incorporated into the philosophy and educational fabric of the institution. Existentialism, with its focus on the self, its belief that existence precedes one's essence, and its conviction that each individual must take responsibility for his or her own life, supports the concept of student development. In recent years, both student affairs practice and professional preparation have been significantly influenced by the student development concept (Parker, 1974) and the philosophy of existentialism (Crookston, 1976). In particular, this concept and philosophy influenced the refocusing of professional practice to both the in-class and out-of-class life of college students. Crookston notes, "As the examining of one's life becomes academically legitimate, the pedagogical focus must necessarily turn from the subject to the student" (p. 28).

Programs and policies developed by student affairs professionals that emphasize the importance and value of membership in an academic community reflect the influence of existentialism, as do personal wellness programs, open admissions, educational programming for nontraditional students, alcohol awareness efforts, learning assistance, and support services for special student subcultures. The goals and policies of such traditional areas as counseling, residence living, campus judicial programs, student government, and leadership training have also been altered by existentialist thought. The influence is most obvious in policy changes that place responsibility for personal conduct with each student and remove it from both parents and institutions.

By the 1980s the student affairs profession became interested in facilitating student development in intentional ways (Brown, 1972; Crookston, 1975; Miller & Prince, 1976; T.H.E. Phase II Model Building Conference, 1975). No longer was there concern only with the out-of-class life of students. By this time, approximately 95 graduate-level preparation programs were in existence, and many of them were attempting to equip their students with the knowledge and skills needed to operationalize the concept of student development in meaningful ways (Parker, 1974; Rocky Keim, 1984). The *Preparation Standards and Guidelines at the Master's Degree Level for Student Service/Development Professionals in Post Secondary Education* (Council for the Advancement of Standards, 1985) provides specifications for three preparation program emphases: administration, counseling, and student development. Existentialism has influenced the nature of professional preparation by causing consideration and reconsideration of the ways in which student affairs professionals interact with students and also by causing faculty members of preparation programs to consider how to facilitate the development of future professionals. In discussing professional preparation for the 1980s, Shaffer (1984) remarks, "Preparation must include attention to an individual's own life goals, self-image, personal aspirations, standards, and motivations in addition to the usually expected thorough grounding in professional theory and competencies" (p. 15).

Summary and Implications

As an applied field, student affairs has been appropriately concerned with administrative requirements and the immediate needs of students. Philosophical matters, or what Tripp (1968) calls "philosophical anxieties," are often considered less directly. Nevertheless, educational philosophy, both institutional and personal, contributes to policy-making and program development. It is necessary to reflect regularly on the *Why* and the *How* of the student affairs mission. This applies equally to those who practice and those who prepare practitioners. As Thomas Carlyle noted, "Nothing is more terrible than activity without insight."

References

Adler, M. J. (1951). Labor, leisure, and liberal education. *Journal of General Education, 6*, 175–184.

American Council on Education, Committee on Student Personnel Work. (1937). *The student personnel point of view.* Washington, DC: American Council on Education.

American Council on Education, Committee on Student Personnel Work. (1949). *The student personnel point of view* (rev. ed.). Washington, DC: American Council on Education.

Arbaugh, G.E., & Arbaugh, G.B. (1967). *Kierkegaard's authorship: A guide to the writings of Kierkegaard.* Rock Island, IL: Augustana College Library.

Brown, R. D. (1972). *Student development in tomorrow's higher eduation: A return to the academy.* Washington, DC: American College Personnel Association.

Callis, R. (1967). Educational aspects of in loco parentis. *Journal of College Student Personnel, 8*(4), 231–233.

Council for the Advancement of Standards for Student Services/Development Programs. (1985). *Preparation standards and guidelines at the master's degree level for student service/development professionals in post secondary education.* Washington, DC: Author.

Cowley, W. H. (1957, January). Student personnel services in retrospect and prospect. *School and Society,* pp. 19–22.

Crookston, B. B. (1975). Milieu management. *NASPA Journal 13*(1), 45–55.

Crookston, B. B. (1976). Student personnel—all hail and farewell. *Personnel and Guidance Journal, 55*, 26–29.

Dewey, J. (1916). *Democracy and education.* New York: Macmillan.

Farmer, P. (1950). Nineteenth century ideas of the university: Continental Europe. In M. Clapp (Ed.), *The modern university* (pp. 3–24). Ithaca, NY: Cornell University Press.

Hutchins, R. M. (1936). *The higher learning in America.* New Haven, CT: Yale University Press.

James, W. (1907). *Pragmatism.* New York: Longmans, Green.

Mencken, H. L. (Ed.). (1913). *The philosophy of Friedrich Nietzsche.* Port Washington, NY: Kennikat Press.

Miller, T. K., & Prince, J. S. (1976). *The future of student affairs.* San Francisco: Jossey-Bass.

Parker, C. (1974). Student development: What does it mean? *Journal of College Student Personnel, 15*(4), 248–256.

Passmore, J. (1980). The philosophy of graduate education. In W. K. Frankena (Ed.), *The philosophy and future of graduate education* (pp. 40–63). Ann Arbor, MI: University of Michigan Press.

Rocky Keim, M. C. (Ed.). (1984). *Directory of graduate preparation programs in college student personnel.* Alexandria, VA: American College Personnel Association.

Sartre, J. P. (1957). *Existentialism and human emotions.* New York: Philosophical Library.

Shaffer, R. H. (1984). Preparing for student personnel in the 1980's. In A. F. Kirby & D. Woodward (Eds.), *Career perspectives in student affairs* (pp. 11–21). Columbus, OH: National Association of Student Personnel Administrators.

Taylor, H. (1952). The philosophical foundation of general education. In N. B. Henry (Ed.), *General education: 51st yearbook, part I* (pp. 20–45). Chicago: University of Chicago Press, National Society for the Study of Education.

T. H. E. Phase II Model Building Conference. (1975). A student development model for student affairs in tomorrow's higher education. *Journal of College Student Personnel 16*(4), 334–341.

Thorndike, E. L., & Hagen, E. (1969). *Measurement and evaluation in psychology and education* (3rd. ed.). New York: John Wiley.

Tripp, P. A. (1968). Student personnel workers: Student development experts of the future. *Journal of the National Association of Women Deans, Administrators, and Counselors,* Spring, 142–144.

Williamson, E. G. (1939). *How to counsel students.* New York: McGraw-Hill.

Williamson, E. G. (1961). *Student personnel services in colleges and universities.* New York: McGraw-Hill.

Believing is Seeing: Alternative Perspectives on a Statement of Professional Philosophy for Student Affairs

Elizabeth J. Whitt, Jill Ellen Carnaghi, Jack Matkin, Patrick Scalese-Love, and David Nestor

The authors examine the search for a professional philosophy in student affairs and the appropriateness of the Student Personnel Point of View *in light of alternative world views.*

Introduction

The golden anniversary (1937–1987) of the *Student Personnel Point of View (SPPV)* revived debate about the role of a statement of professional philosophy in student affairs work. Is a statement of professional philosophy necessary? Is it desirable? Is it achievable? If student affairs work had a philosophy statement, what would it "look like"? Do we already have a unifying statement in the 1937 and 1949 versions of the *Student Personnel Point of View* (American Council on Education, 1937, 1949)?

In this article, we consider some possible answers to these questions. First, we briefly discuss the history of the search for professional philosophy in student affairs work. Second, we describe two alternative ways of viewing the world that may influence the necessity, desirability, and possibility of arriving at a unifying philosophy for student affairs. Finally, we examine the appropriateness of the SPPV (American Council on Education, 1939, 1949) as a philosophy statement, in light of these different world views.

The Search for a Professional Philosophy

A profession's philosophy is the articulation of its basic premises and values about people and institutions and the reasons for the profession's

683

existence. Implicit in this definition is consensus; the members of a profession share basic premises, values, and purposes—they share a world view. A professional philosophy can provide a foundation for identity and practice and a framework for interpretation and understanding (Penney, 1972; Stamatakos & Rogers, 1984).

The call for development of a unifying statement of philosophy in student affairs is nothing new. For nearly fifty years, student affairs staff and faculty have attempted to identify the premises and values underlying their work (Appleton, Briggs, & Rhatigan, 1978; Cowley, 1983; Greenleaf, 1983; Mueller, 1961; Stamatakos & Rogers, 1984; Wrenn, 1983). The profession has, at the same time, been characterized by a lack of consensus concerning the purposes and roles of student affairs (Appleton, Briggs, & Rhatigan, 1978; Penney, 1972). Stamatakos and Rogers (1984) claim the basis of confusion is the absence of an agreed-upon professional philosophy.

In response to such concerns, student affairs leaders have met on several occasions to develop coherent philosophical statements. In 1937, a committee sponsored by the American Council on Education wrote the *Student Personnel Point of View*; it was revised in 1949. Both iterations of the *SPPV* identify the basic purposes of American higher education as the creation and dissemination of knowledge, the preservation and enrichment of culture, the development of the whole student, and the education of students for responsible citizenship in a democracy (American Council on Education, 1937, 1949). The documents also describe the roles and functions of student affairs within the framework of the purposes of higher education. Stamatakos cites the SPPV as "the basic philosophical foundation upon which our activities and programs are predicated" (p.111).

More recently, the Council of Student Affairs Associations (COSPA) (1975) codified the beliefs, assumptions, and purposes of student development and the roles and functions of student affairs workers in *Student Development Services in Post-Secondary Education*. Additionally, the *Student Development Model for Student Affairs in Tomorrow's Higher Education (T.H.E.)* American College Personnel Association, 1975) asserted the importance of human development concepts for student affairs and identified student affairs roles and purposes. In 1987, a committee sponsored by the National Association of Student Personnel Administrators (NASPA) wrote *A Perspective on Student Affairs*, which included statements of student affairs assumptions, beliefs, and roles.

Nevertheless, the debate about what constitutes student affairs work and what student affairs staff value and believe continues:

The profession of college student affairs is in a state of confusion, discordance, and doubt about its appropriate role in a changing college environment. . . . The profession not only lacks a coherent and consistent philosophy but also lacks understanding and agreement regarding the individual components that constitute such a philosophy. . . . Without knowing what it believes, its values have no grounding other than rerooting themselves in the expediency of what the profession does. (Stamatakos & Rogers, 1984, pp.400, 410)

Whether the student affairs profession can or should have a "coherent and consistent" philosophy will be discussed later in this article. First, however, we provide a context for that discussion by examining world views, the basis from which one develops assumptions about the usefulness of statements of professional philosophy.

Of Paradigms and World Views

At the broadest level, a paradigm is a set of beliefs and assumptions that affects the creation and interpretation of knowledge and that comprises implicit and explicit views of reality (Morgan, 1980). Paradigms or world views define and order life, describing for individuals and societies "what is and how it is" (Newton & Caple, 1985, p. 163).

The Western World View

The current Western world view was developed during the 18th century and is based on faith in objective neutral science as a means to discover truth; in the rational, mechanical assumptions of Newtonian physics; and in the Cartesian split between mind and body, the knower and the known (Lucas, 1985). In this conventional world view, a single truth or reality exists separate from the context in which it is viewed and from the person or organization doing the viewing (Schwartz & Ogilvy, 1979). This reality, or truth, can be discovered if one looks hard enough with the proper tools, for example, random sampling and quantitative data analysis (Lincoln & Guba, 1985). Future states follow from past and present actions in rational and predictable ways and effects are traceable to identifiable causes (Schwartz & Ogilvy, 1979).

An example of the influence exerted by the conventional world view is the pervasiveness of the bureaucratic model of organizing. Weber's ideals of efficiency, rationality, impersonality, predictability, and technical competence form the basis for many of our past and current assumptions about organizations and organizational and personal effectiveness, including the

need for hierarchical staff arrangements and communication and the importance of planning and goal-setting (Clark, 1985). The efforts of the Western
Interstate Commission for Higher Education (WICHE) to provide guidelines
and structures for systematic program development (e.g., Moore & Delworth,
1976) are an example of the application of conventional beliefs to institutions of higher education.

A Conventional Perspective on Student Affairs Philosophy

Within the conventional paradigm, consensus about reality, or truth, can
be achieved by rational analysis and communication, and such consensus is
necessary for organizational effectiveness. This is reflected in the assertion by
Stamatakos and Rogers (1984) that the student affairs profession will be in a
state of confusion until consensus is reached on a statement of philosophy.
Until that time, important professional issues will be determined on the basis
of current and individualistic inclinations, which can be expected to lead to
actions that are not consistent, congruent, or integrated.

Stamatakos and Rogers (1984) have also stated that a meaningful statement of professional philosophy should identify four critical and interrelated
components: the profession's basic premises, values, roles and functions, and
identity. By explicating what the profession believes, what it values, what it
does, and what it is, a statement of philosophy offers members a perspective
from which to view their context, their decisions, and their practices. It
provides a firm foundation for the profession to determine its direction,
clarify its contributions, evaluate its effectiveness, and rise above immediate
needs and pressing necessities to identify what is truly important and
appropriate. Looking at student affairs from the conventional paradigm, one
can see that achieving a common identity through articulation of basic
beliefs, values, and tenets is not only possible, it is critical to claiming the
profession's place in higher education.

An Alternative World View

During the past decade, a number of theorists have asserted that conventional organizational theory has reached its limits in accommodating and
explaining the complexities of modern organizations (Clark, 1985; Schwartz
& Ogilvy, 1979). These limitations in dealing with complexity and ambiguity have led some scholars to speculate that the conventional paradigm is

crumbling (Schwartz & Ogilvy, 1979; Weick, 1979) and that we are now in the midst of

a shift from a world view characterized by a mechanistic paradigm heavily influenced by causal scientism—in which objectivity, control, and linear causality are superordinate—to a world view characterized by a much more complex, relational, and context-bound paradigm. (Kuh, Whitt, & Shedd, 1987, p. 2)

In the remainder of this article, we refer to this new world view as the *emergent paradigm*, a phrase that captures its evolutionary nature. A shift in paradigms implies a fundamental change in basic beliefs and assumptions about the nature of reality.

Those who study organizations from the emergent perspective have questioned the basic assumptions of the bureaucratic model, including goal-directed behavior, linear relationships between plans and outcomes, hierarchical authority structures, and linear communication patterns (Clark, 1985). These theorists focus instead on the importance of subjectivity and phenomenology for understanding behavior in organizations: "There is no 'real world' (i.e., a single reality or truth) to be discovered—only varied multiple realities to be individually and collectively constructed and understood" (Kuh, Whitt, & Shedd, 1987, p. 10).

An Alternative Perspective on Student Affairs Philosophy

The assumption that student affairs staff share a common view of the profession's basic premises, values, roles, and functions, which can be captured in a single philosophy statement is congruent with the conventional world view that one reality or truth can be found for the entire student affairs field. But does this world view reflect or accommodate what we see when we look at student affairs work and its broader context, higher education? Colleges and universities have been variously described as loosely coupled systems (Weick, 1982), organized anarchies (Cohen & March, 1974), and arenas of political conflict (Baldridge, Curtis, Ecker, & Riley, 1977). Underlying these descriptions is the recognition that institutions of higher education are characterized by ambiguity, uncertainty, and fragmentation, not rationality, predictability, and consensus.

Evidence of ambiguity and uncertainty in student affairs is plentiful. Our work settings and job responsibilities involve multiple goals, unclear means and ends, disagreement about priorities, and competing values and preferences (Kuh, 1983). For example, although Chickering's (1969) seven vectors are used as a theoretical basis by many student affairs staff, one soon learns when working with students that supposedly discrete, rationally developed tasks such as developing interdependence and freeing interpersonal relatioships are actually indistinct and overlapping.

We can look at ambiguity in student affairs from the conventional world view and see disorder in need of "fixing" by means of tighter organization or more uniform guiding principles. Or we can look at the situation from the emergent paradigm and recognize that, because the future is indeterminate and beliefs and actions context-bound, intentional strategies (e.g., creating philosophy statements or long-range plans) cannot eliminate uncertainty or ambiguity.

If our "alternative" view is a useful description of student affairs, any shared picture of the field will be so general that a resulting philosophy statement will be ineffective in guiding or providing a sense of identity. Even if we could, for example, agree that fostering student growth is a basic value, at any given institution agreement among all involved about what *growth* means, what *to foster* implies, or even who *students* are is unlikely. The meaning we take for these words is shaped by our individual and institutional contexts; such diversity and variety cannot be captured in a single philosophical statement.

Conventional and alternative perspectives on a statement of student affairs philosophy are summarized below. According to the conventional view, a professional philosophy is objective, simple, determinate, and based on belief in linear causality. The emergent view sees professional philosophy as perspectival and context-bound, indeterminate, and a product of mutually shaping events and activities.

Conventional Perspective

A professional philosophy is . . .

Objective. Activities, job tasks, and professional identity and values can be studied from the "outside" with value-neutral instruments and mental processes. Example: A single "reality" can be discovered for student affairs; a single unifying philosophy can be identified for student affairs work.

Simple and Reductionistic. Activities, job tasks, professional identity, beliefs, purposes, and values can be reduced to their simplest components and, thereby, be predicted, explained, and monitored; complxity requires simplification. Example: A consensus of basic premises, beliefs, values, purposes, roles, and functions can be achieved and is, in fact, essential.

Determinate. Future states follow from present in rational, predictable ways. Example: Past and present activities can form the basis for a philosophy statement that informs activities for the future.

Causal. Activities, job tasks, professional identity, beliefs, purposes, and values have identifiable causes and rationales. Example: A professional philosophy statement provides a foundation for identity and practice and a framework for interpretation and understanding of student affairs work.

Emergent Perspective

A professional philosophy is . . .

Perspectival and Context-bound. Activities, job tasks, and professional identity and values can bedescribed and understood only in terms of each individual's experiences, values, and expectations, and the institutional context in which they occur—*believing is seeing.* Example: The diverse needs, experiences, values, and beliefs of student affairs staff and their institutional contxts cannot be captured in, or unified by, a statement of professional philosophy.

Complex and Diverse. Understanding student affairs job tasks and activities requires increasingly complex views of professional identities, values, and contexts, the whole transcends the parts. Example: Discussions among student affairs staff of similarities and differences in needs, values, beliefs, and experiences can be worthwhile for developing complex understandings; ambiguous preferences, unclear means and ends, competing values, and multiple goals are to be exploited for the innovative and complicated views they provide.

Indeterminate. Future states of the profession are unknowable; ambiguity and disorder are to be expected and valued. Example: The future identity, values, needs, or character of student affairs cannot be predicted from the past or present or dictated by statements of current philosophy.

Mutually Shaping. Activities, job responsibilities, and profession a lidentity and values are generatd by complex and interactive factors that blur distinctions between cause and effect. Example: Discussions about professional philosophy among student affairs workers at a specific institution can provide those workers with a basis for identity and practice at that institution.

(Adapted from: Kuh, Whitt, & Shedd, 1987)

Conclusion

The intent of this article is to highlight key issues in the debate about the need for a unifying philosophy statment for student affairs. Readers' world views will influence their conclusions about the usefulnes and desirability of such a statement. Our world views lead us to conclude that a single statement of professional philosophy cannot adequately represent the range of needs, experiences, values, and beliefs present among student affairs professionals. We also believe, however, that the process of discussing needs, experiences, and beliefs is extremely impotant. Sharing values and philosophies about student affairs work and affirming professional commitments can be a very healthy process. In this way, each professional can develop her or his own understanding of student affairs.

The *SPPV* (American Council on Education, 1937, 1949) and all other documents critical to the evolution of student affairs can aid us in discovering an identity at the context-specific level. The COSPA (1975) and T.H.E. (ACPA, 1975) models and the NASPA statement of perspective provide different ways to describe roles, tasks, and purposes for student affairs staff. They may help staff members at a given institution discover and affirm shared assumptions and values, which may in turn contribute to greater understanding and sense of community among those involved.

Finally, we hope the general debate about our philosophy and identity will continue. As Kathleen Plato stated in 1978,

The profession must go beyond total acceptance of a single approach as the legitimate rationale for the profession . . . . There should be a realization of the limitedness of a single position and a continual scrutinization of the dominant approach. What is needed is a continuous debate of the merits of this particular approach. . . . If this does not take place, student personnel will be unprepared for the next inevitable "crisis of purpose." (p. 36)

References

American College Personnel Association (ACPA). (1975). A student development model for student affairs in tomorrow's higher education. *Journal of College Student Personnel*, 16(4), 334–341.

American Council on Education. (1937). *The student personnel point of view* (American Council on Education Studies, Series 1, Vol.1, No.3). Washington, DC: Author.

American Council on Education. (1949). *The student personnel point of view* (American Council on Education Studies, Series 6, Vol.13, No.13). Washington, DC: Author.

Appleton, J. R., Briggs, C. M., & Rhatigan, J. J. (1978). *Pieces of eight: The rites, roles, and styles of the dean by eight who have been there.* Portland, OR: NASPA Institute of Research and Development.

Baldridge, J. V., Curtis, D. B., Ecker, G. P., & Riley, G. L. (1977). Alternative models of governance in higher education. In J. V. Baldridge & T. Deal (Eds.), *Governing academic organizations* (pp.2–25). Berkeley, CA: McCutchan.

Chickering, A. W. (1969). *Education and identity.* San Francisco: Jossey-Bass.

Clark, D. L. (1985). Emeging paradigms in organizatioal theory and research. In Y. S. Lincoln (Ed.), *Organizational theory and inquiry: The paradigm revolution* (pp. 43–78). Beverly Hills, CA: Sage.

Cohen, M. D., & March, J. D. (1974). *Leadership and ambiguity: The American college president.* New York: McGraw-Hill.

Council of Student Personnel Associations (COSPA). (1975). Student development services in post-secondary education. *Journal of College Student Personnel,* 16(6), 524–528.

Cowley, W. (1983). The nature of student personnel work. In G. L. Saddlemire & A. L. Rentz (Eds.), *Student Affairs: A profession's heritage* (pp. 47–73). Alexandria, VA: ACPA Media. (Original work published 1936).

Greenleaf, E. A. (1983). How others see us. In G. L. Saddlemire & A. L. Rentz (Eds.), *Student affairs: A profession's heritage* (pp. 268–279). Alexandria, VA: ACPA Media. (Original work published 1968).

Kuh, G. D. (1983). Guiding assumptions about student affairs organizatios. In G. D. Kuh (Ed.), *Understanding student affairs organizations (New Directions for Student Services,* No. 23, pp. 15–26). San Francisco: Jossey-Bass.

Kuh, G. D., Whitt, E. J., & Shedd, J. D. (1987). *Student affairs, 2001: A paradigmatic odyssey.* Alexandria, VA: ACPA Media.

Lincoln, Y. S., & Guba, E. G. (1985). *Naturalistic inquiry.* Beverly Hills, CA: Sage.

Lucas, C. (1985). Out at the edge:Notes on a paradigm shift. *Journal of Counseling and Developmetn,* 64, 165–172.

Moore, M., & Delworth, U. (1976). *Training manual for student services program development.* Boulder, CO: Western Interstate Commission for Higher Education (WICHE).

Morgan, G. (1980). Paradigms, metaphors, and puzzle-solving in organization theory. *Administrative Science Quarterly,* 25, 605–622.

Mueller, K. H. (1961). *Student personnel work in higher education.* Boston: Houghton Mifflin.

National Association of Student Personnel Administrators (NASPA). (1987). *A perspective on student affairs.* Washington, DC: Author.

Newton, F. B., & Caple, R. B. (1985). Once the world was flat: Introduction and overview. *Journal of Counseling and Development,* 64, 163–164.

Penney, J. (1972). *Perspective and challenge in college student personnel work.* Springfield, IL: Charles C. Thomas.

692   Elizabeth J. Whitt et al.

Plato, K. (1978). The shit to student development: An analysis of the patterns of change. *NASPA Journal*, 15(4), 32–36.

Schwartz, P., & Ogilvy, J. (1979). *The emergent paradigm: Changing patterns of thought and belief* (Analytical Report, No. 7). Menlo Park, CA: SRI International.

Stamatakos, L. C. (1981). Student affairs progress toward professionalism: Recommendations for action, part I. *Journal of College Student Personnel*, 22(2), 105–113.

Stamatakos, L. C., & Rogers, R. (1984). Student affairs: A profession in need of a philosophy. *Journal of College Student Personnel*, 25(5), 400–411.

Weick, K. E. (1979). *The social psychology of organizing* (2nd ed.). Reading, MA: Addison-Wesley.

Weick, K. E. (1982, June). Administering education in loosely coupled schools. *Phi Delta Kappan*, pp. 673–676.

Wrenn, C. G. (1983). The fault dear Brutus . . . . In G. L. Saddlemire & A. L. Rentz (Eds.), *Student affairs: A profession's heritage* (pp. 171–178). Alexandria, VA: ACPA Media. (Original work published 1949).

Cultural Competence: A New Challenge to Student Affairs Professionals

Larry H. Ebbers and Shirley L. Henry

The authors argue for a prominent student affairs role in increasing the cultural competence *of staff.*

The greatest challenge for America's colleges and universities in the 1990s may be to create a climate in which the student body not only accepts and appreciates diversity but learns to celebrate it as well. Historically, societal changes have heralded the advent of new expectations and responsibilities for the student affairs professional. The current movement to more actively recruit minority students is no exception to this historical model.

Wright (1987) cautions that the continued growth of predominantly white higher education institutions will depend on their ability to respond to the "developmental, academic, and social needs of minority students" (p. 97). Wright believes the future reputation of student affairs professionals as innovative leaders will be judged by the quality of programs and services provided to these students. With the advent of the nationwide emphasis on minority recruitment, it seems that a role for student affairs is to increase the cultural competence of staff.

The term *cultural competence* is familiar to persons in the field of social work and is defined by Cross, Friesen, Mason, and Rider (1988) as "the effectiveness of a helper's work with someone of a different ethnicity, culture, or race." The authors further suggest that cultural competence not only applies to individual professionals but that "it is an agency, local, state, federal, and ultimately global issue" (p. 5).

According to Cross (1988), a culturally competent system of care acknowledges and incorporates—at all levels—the importance of culture, the assessment of cross-cultural relations, vigilance toward the dynamics that result from cultural differences, the expansion of cultural knowledge, and the adaptation of services to meet culturally unique needs" (p. 1).

Culturally competent professionals do not attempt to conduct themselves as though they were members of a culture different from their own. They do, however, reflect an internalized awareness of specific cultures and an ability to carry out professional activities consistent with that awareness" (Green, 982, p. 52).

Pounds (1987) attributes the success of programs developed for Black students of well-defined program goals and regular evaluation. She cautions that "whether services are separate or mainstreamed, intra-instructional cooperation is necessary" (p. 37). It is time that student affairs administrators, their staff, and representatives from academic departments become involved jointly with evaluating the cultural competence of campus programs and personnel.

What are the necessary components of services for minority students and how should personnel be trained to become more competent in dealing with cultural diversity? An evaluation of current knowledge, values, and program purposes can aid in determining the answers to these questions (Northern, cited in Lum, 1986).

Fleming (1984) found that Black students on predominantly White campuses face the problem of faculty expectations of assimilation without the benefit of program changes to assist that assimilation. This problem of adjustment may be common to other minority groups as well.

The knowledge base for this issue has grown in the past decade under such terms as multicultural nonsexist education, human relations training, and cross-cultural awareness. Literature from the mental health profession is more abundant in the area of understanding the role of cultural difference (McManus, 1988). Mental health models such as "ethnic competence" (Green, 1982) and "ethnic minority practice" (Lum, 1986) may serve as guides to professionals in other fields.

In addressing the issue of cultural competence, it is important to consider specific training needs for the profession. Answers to the following questions must be found.

What is cultural competence?
What level is desirable?
How is it attained?
How is it measured?
Should this training become an integral part of the preservice program experience?
Should it be included as an intensive segment of on-the-job inservice?

Cross (1988) suggests a continuum that might be used by student affairs administrators to understand and evaluate the current level of staff and institutional cultural competence. The continuum moves from the most negative—which destroys a culture, toward the most positive, advanced level of competence—an agency actively involved in adding to the knowledge base by research, publishing, program development, and dissemination. By assessing the current status of cultural competence, administrators can determine institution and staff competence, identify deficit areas, and develop program goals and objectives for improvement.

Most college and university student affairs programs promote cultural awareness and acceptance. Training efforts that include experiential simulation activities such as Bafa-Bafa and programs to promote acceptance such as Programming for Diversity (University of California at Davis, 1987) help increase awareness. Although these traditional approaches are important program components, they do not address the deeper understanding involved in cultural competence as defined here. An intensive study of attitudes, policies, and program practices must be undertaken if cultural competence is to be achieved (Cross, Friesen, Mason, & Rider, 1988).

The need to increase minority representation in our profession must be addressed. Merely adding more minority professionals may not, however, sufficiently address the problem of cultural competence for staff. Adding minority representation to our ranks is an imperative first step. To assume that this automatically leads to better understanding of all minority groups and develops cultural competence may be erroneous. In order to extend the cultural competence of student affairs staff, it may first be necessary to identify areas in which individuals are bound within their own cultures. It is important to extend this individualized search of personal cultural binding to all staff members, including those who represent minority cultures.

McManus (1988) suggests that it is necessary for professionals to be cognizant of the influence their own culture has had in determining how they think and act: "A purposeful self-examination of cultural influences can lead to a better understanding of the impact of culture on one's own life. Only then can the complexities of cross-cultural interactions be fully appreciated" (p. 2). Green (1982) supports McManus' position by suggesting that "the first step in ethnic competence is to become aware of the limitations of one's own culture" (p. 54). This understanding of personal culture leads to an appreciation of how cultural differences shape thinking and behavior.

Typically, student affairs programs target expanding awareness and acceptance of minority cultures on the part of the majority culture members. It is important, however, to expand the cultural awareness and acceptance of all staff and students. How individual mannerisms, speech, values, and behaviors are bound by culture is important learning for minority personnel as well as those from the majority culture. A culturally diverse staff, although a vital element, does not facilitate this learning or guarantee cultural competence.

A fallacy is inherent in the expectation that minority professionals automatically relate with understanding to other minority cultures; it is unreasonable to expect exposure to and an understanding of all minority cultures. Minority and majority culture professionals are products of their cultural experiences. In developing staff cultural competence, all staff members should be given the benefit of training to increase their skills.

King (1986) suggests that the promotion of cultural diversity should emphasize the meaning and nature of groups, development of images, differing perspectives of reality, and the value of cross-cultural communication. This range of understanding seems an appropriate beginning for the development of cultural competence and essential to both majority and minority staff persons.

If cultural competence is to be achieved it will be necessary for involved professionals to assume postures of mutual help and learning, and establish an environment that facilitates this exchange. Through such "helping-seeking behavior" an individual of a different cultural background is identified as someone with much to contribute to mutual learning and is not perceived as merely dependent in the relationship. Probable outcomes of such an environment are an increased climate of trust, mutual effort, and staff cultural competence. (Green, 1982, p. 28).

Certainly, it is unreasonable to assume that complete understanding of all cultures is possible. However, to maximize staff competence, microculture simulation activities might be included with acceptance/awareness training. These preservice and/or inservice training models would include the development of microcultures in which persons are placed in the planned environment to experience a diverse culture. This segment of training could emcompass a day or several days and would be planned to involve the norms, values, and behavior patterns unique to the culture being studied.

A study of the Peace Corps model of culturalization by immersion might assist in the development of microculture simulation training efforts. Community leaders representative of the local minority group can be recruited to assist in the development of each cultural experience.

The work currently being done by Northern Illinois University and the University of Florida are exemplary of cultural awareness activities. Northern Illinois hosted the Region IV-E Drive-in Conference on Racial Discrimination on Campus. The intent of this one-day workshop for campus teams and advisors was to plan ways to combat discrimination and promote appreciation of racial and cultural diversity. The University of Florida sponsors a weekend retreat involving faculty, students, and student affairs personnel; its purpose is to explore issues of common concern, especially racial understanding and cultural awareness.

These models can be expanded to include a microcultural simulation experience in which participants are not only involved in discussions about diversity or "told" about cultural differences, but are given the opportunity to "live" the difference. A national cross-campus network of student affairs professionals could emerge to exchange campus presentations of culture simulation experiences. Sharing training events will facilitate broader understanding and increase staff cultural competence, at minimum cost.

The promotion of regional and national cultural simulation experiences, similar to a case-study approach to learning, could become an important activity for professional organizations. The nationwide involvement of university and college personnel in such programming is limitless and exciting.

In summary, further research needs to be conducted by student affairs professionals to analyze staff development and preservice programs in order to determine the development of cultural competence. The expansion of programs to address identified deficit areas should include personal culture assessment and microculture simulation training events. Program plans should also encompass cultural enrichment for all staff members regardless of their ethnic/racial background.

References

Cross, T. L. (1988). Cultural competence continuum. *Focal Point*, 3(1), 1.

Cross, T., Friesen, B., Mason, J., & Rider, M. E. (1988). Developing cultural competence for agencies. *Focal Point*, 2(4), 5–7.

Fleming, J. (1984). *Blacks in college.* San Francisco: Jossey-Bass.

Green, J. W (1982). *Cultural awareness in the human services.* Englewood Cliffs, NJ: Prentice-Hall.

King, L. R. (1986, February). *Cultural diversity: New directions for education.* Paper presented at the Western Meeting of the National Social Science Association, Seattle, WA.

Lum, D. (1986). *Social work practice and people of color: A process-stage approach.* Monterey, CA: Brooks/Cole.

McManus, J. D. (1988). Services to minority populations: What does it mean to be a culturally competent professional? *Focal Point*, 2(4), 1–5.

Pounds, A. W. (1987). Black students' needs on predominantly white campuses. In D. J. Wright (Ed.), *Responding to the needs of today's minority students (New directions for student services,* No. 38, pp. 23–38). San Francisco: Jossey-Bass.

University of California at Davis. (1987). *Programming for diversity.* Unpublished manuscript, University of California at Davis, Department of Student Affairs.

Wright, D. J. (Ed.). (1987). Summary and annotated references. In D. J. Wright (Ed.), *Responding to the needs of today's minority students (New directions for student services,* No. 38, pp. 95–102). San Francisco: Jossey-Bass.